THE LITTLE BOOK

A Spirit-Filled Daily Devotional

By: Samuel N. Greene, Ph.D.

Revelation 10:8
"Go and take the little book which is open in the hand of the angel"

Glory Publishing, Inc.

𝔊𝔩𝔬𝔯𝔶 𝔓𝔲𝔟𝔩𝔦𝔰𝔥𝔦𝔫𝔤, 𝔍𝔫𝔠.
www.GloryPublishingInc.com

About the Author:
www.Brother-Sam.org

All Scriptures used in this book were taken from the King James Version.
Also, we have decided not to capitalize any names of the devil and his kingdom.

ISBN 978-1-937199-62-3

Printed & Bound in the United States Of America
Produced at Narrow Way Ministries, *NWmin.org, Brother-Sam.org*

Copyright © 2013   All Rights Reserved

This book may not be reproduced, in whole or in part, in any form (beyond that permitted by copyright laws) without the original publisher's permission. This applies particularly to reproductions, translations, microfilms, and storage and processing in electronic systems.

THE LITTLE BOOK
Foreword

The inspiration for this devotional came from the Lord Jesus Himself. It was all prompted by the Spirit of God. All the glory and honor goes to Jesus alone for everything that has been written and created to complete this unique devotional. I don't believe any man could write three hundred and sixty five messages, or people could type, bind and assemble a book as quickly as we have done it without the Holy Spirit guiding, directing and leading. I really cannot take credit for any of this.

Please, know in the depths of your heart this was written for you. May this be a blessing to you to help you in your daily walk with God. May it help you understand the Scriptures more and give you more revelation and insight into the workings and ways of God. It is truly my heart that you would become a true disciple and that you know the Lord intimately. My love for you is boundless.

The title for this book came out of Revelation 10 when John, who had been boiled alive and yet survived, had been sent to the isle of Patmos. The Scriptures say twice he was the disciple whom Jesus loved. John also was the disciple who laid his head upon the breast of Jesus. "*Patmos*" literally means my killing. It was there he would receive the revelation of Jesus Christ. While there, he was visited by a messenger from God. God Himself spoke to John from heaven, telling him to go to the messenger that had a little book in his hand that was open. I believe this little open book is the Word of God opened with revelation and understanding streaming through it. Even though John was the greatest apostle and was well known in the Kingdom of God and on earth, he was instructed to take the book. God said, "*Go and take the little book that is in the hand of the angel*" (Revelation 10:8). John humbled himself, obeyed, and kneeled to the messenger saying, "*Give me the little book*" (Revelation 10:9). That is what this devotional is all about.

The "little book" is not really so little, but profound and deep. The Bible defines it elsewhere as the unsearchable riches of Christ (Ephesians 3:8). His ways are as profound as the sea, past finding out (Romans 11:33). But yet, we are called to know the mysteries of the Kingdom (Mark 4:11). So, this devotional has been written to provide some answers to those that ask you of the hope within you (I Peter 3:15), to provide a place for you to be instructed, encouraged, inspired, blessed, assured, and to be an avenue for you to meet powerfully with the Lord Jesus every day of your life through His Word.

I dedicate this book to the body of Christ, and particularly to the remnant all over the world, who daily give themselves to the Word of God, to studying it and walking it out, to worshipping Him with passion, and have a great desire to become true living disciples.

To that end, this devotional has been written. I pray years from now, when I'm long gone, it will be said of this book "that he, being dead, yet speaketh," that the words God gave me will live on and continue to minister to the entire remnant everywhere. God bless you, and may the Lord greet you every day as you open this book; may it inspire you, encourage you and strengthen you, as it gives you understanding. It was written with great love and affection for you, and with absolute devotion to God the Father, my Savior and Lord Jesus, and the precious Comforter the Holy Spirit. I now surrender this book into your hands and heart. May God bless you as you read it. Take it and eat it up.

Jesus is Precious!

Brother Sam Greene

The Little Book
Acknowledgements

Thank you to my assistant and son in the faith, as well as friend, Andrew Jensen. Without you this devotional could never have happened. Your diligence, faithfulness, and loyalty are a joy to my heart. I love you. Thank you for everything.

Thank you to all who typed, edited, transcribed, did artwork, etc. Jesus, nor I, will ever forget your faithfulness and loyalty.

Thank you to all the Narrow Way churches and Bible Schools all over the world for your dedication to Jesus and me.

Thank you to my wonderful family, for allowing me to do God's will, time and time again. I love you more than life.

Thank you to my precious wife, Katie. You truly are a virtuous woman, as well as my "True Companion." I can't imagine life without you. Thank you for giving me to the Lord and allowing Him to use me. You will forever be "My Dolly." I love you!

Thank you to Narrow Way Ministries in Jacksonville, FL. No pastor could have a better group of people to pastor. I love you with all my heart. Thank you for all of your support.

Thank you to my Master. Oh, how I love You. You are the pearl of great price. Without You, I am nothing. Thank You for the gift of revelation. "I am my beloved's and my beloved is mine." You wrote this devotional, so to You belongs all the glory, honor, and praise.

"Israel Doth Not Know, My People Doth Not Consider"
Isaiah 1:3

DAY 1

We see in this passage that God's people do not know Him, and even worse, they don't even consider Him. Isaiah 1:3 says, *"The ox knoweth his owner, and the ass his master's crib: but Israel doth not know, my people doth not consider."* Even an animal knows where he gets his food and provision, and from where his blessing comes. But Israel didn't know, nor did they even consider! This is shameful, but I think it's true of many in the body of Christ.

Far too many times, the Lord has visited us and He was not even acknowledged. Consider the story of Samuel and how the Lord called him many times. It says in I Samuel 3:10 that the Lord *"called as at other times"* insinuating that Samuel didn't respond earlier to the Lord. In I Samuel 3:7 it says, *"Samuel did not know the Lord, neither was the word of the Lord yet revealed unto him."*

How many times has the Lord called us and we didn't answer? For example, in Song of Solomon 5:2, the Bridegroom shows up at the bride's house knocking, trying to get in and He says, *"My head is filled with dew, and my locks with the drops of the night."* This is a type and shadow of the anointing and the presence of God drawing us. She answers Him in Song of Solomon 5:3 by saying, *"I have put off my coat; how shall I put it on? I have washed my feet; how shall I defile them?"* What an excuse! The Bible is very clear that when the Lord reaches for us and comes to us, dripping with anointing, wanting to speak to us and have communion with us, that we, as His bride and people, should respond to Him.

Shoes in the Scriptures represent our walk in God. The fact that the bride had taken off her shoes lets us know that she had stopped walking with Him in an intimate way. The bride had lay down and gone to sleep. There are two kinds of sleeping in the Bible: one is a resting in the Lord and waiting for Him; whereas, the other one is slothfulness and laziness. In this case it was laziness, as she had laid down and stopped walking with the Lord and didn't respond when His anointing and presence called her.

In Jeremiah 2:32 it says, *"Can a maid forget her ornaments, or a bride her attire? yet my people have forgotten me days without number."* How sad it is to think that our precious husband Jesus desires to be with us more than anything, to come and visit us and yet we don't receive Him. How grieved must this make His heart! I don't know about you, but I don't ever want to forget Him days without number.

Today, I know from where my provision comes. I know who loves me and takes care of me, and it's Him and only Him. We must have a great desire within us to respond to Him when He calls and to answer Him. How sad it is that this won't be the case for many Christians as Matthew brings out:

> "*²¹Not every one that saith unto me, Lord, Lord, shall enter into the kingdom of heaven; but he that doeth the will of my Father which is in heaven. ²²Many will say to me in that day, Lord, Lord, have we not prophesied in thy name? and in thy name have cast out devils? and in thy name done many wonderful works? ²³And then will I profess unto them, I never knew you: depart from me, ye that work iniquity*" (Matthew 7:21-23).

How can it be that we move in the gifts of the Spirit, prophesy in His name, cast out devils in His name, do many wonderful works, perhaps even miracles, and yet still do not know the Lord?

There are two types of knowing: knowing someone mentally and casually, and then the kind of intimate knowing like Genesis 4:1 says, "*And Adam knew Eve his wife; and she conceived.*" Our God wants us to know Him! As a matter of fact, Psalms 46:10 reads very clearly, "*Be still, and know that I am God.*" God wants His people to come to a great relationship with Him. Jesus said in John 17:3, "*And this is life eternal, that they might know thee the only true God, and Jesus Christ, whom thou hast sent.*" I John 5:20 says, "*And we know that the Son of God is come, and hath given us an understanding, that we may know him that is true, and we are in him that is true, even in his Son Jesus Christ. This is the true God, and eternal life.*"

Knowing God is eternal life. Knowing Him intimately is what the Lord is after. Never let days without number go by without you spending time with the Lord. Today make a decision that you will come before the Lord once every day, and open your heart to Him. Invite Him to come and have communion with Him.

Never let it be said of us that we did not know or did not consider. We want to stand before the Lord on that great day and be welcomed from a knowing smile, one that says, "I know you and I love you. Come and enter into My presence."

Oh, my friend, knowing Him intimately is what God is after. Most people don't know this and don't even consider what God is after. This is it! This is what He wants! Know Him today; spend time with Him today. Open your heart to Him. Have communion with Him. Look up now, face to face into the eyes of Jesus, and embrace Him. You will surely bless His heart, and by doing so, be blessed yourself.

"He Brought Me Up"
Psalms 40:2

Here in Psalms 40 we read:

> "I waited patiently for the Lord; and he inclined unto me, and heard my cry. He brought me up also out of a horrible pit, out of the miry clay, and set my feet upon a rock, and established my goings. And he hath put a new song in my mouth, even praise unto our God: many shall see it, and fear, and shall trust in the Lord." (Psalms 40:1-4)

Oh, what a glorious truth this is for us today! If we would just incline our hearts toward Him, cry from the depth of our being, and patiently wait for Him, know that He will bring us up; He will bring all of us up. David was in a horrible pit and in miry clay. In my own life God has faithfully brought me up and out of many horrible pits? We have a promise in Psalms 34:19 that says, *"Many are the afflictions of the righteous; but the Lord delivereth them out of them all."*

In Acts 16: 25-29 we learn that Paul and Silas had their feet bound in stocks inside the inner prison. As they prayed and sang praises to God, all of the prisoners heard them; but God also heard them. God sent an earthquake just inside the prison, and it set everyone free from their shackles and bonds. What do people hear us say when we are in a horrible pit and the miry clay? They should hear us crying out and inclining our hearts to the Lord, confessing, "He will bring us out."

Today, God will bring you up from that horrible pit and out of the miry clay. He does not want you there. John 10:10 tells us He came that you might have life and have it more abundantly. God wants to set your feet upon a rock; that rock is Christ Jesus and His Word. He wants to establish your goings and to help you down the narrow way (Matthew 7:14). The Lord wants to help you to find the path of the just which is the shining light which shines more and more upon your situation (Proverbs 4:18). He wants you to find the highway of holiness (Isaiah 35:8). Let Him!

He will bring you up. Far too many individuals are trying to bring themselves up. In our flesh we can do nothing. John 6:63 tells us, *"It is the spirit that quickeneth; the flesh profiteth nothing: the words that I speak unto you, they are spirit, and they are life"*. Also in Matthew 26:41 we hear the Word of the Lord when He says, *"Watch and pray, that ye enter not into temptation: the spirit indeed is willing, but the flesh is weak."* We need a Savior; we need a Redeemer; and we simply need Jesus. He will raise you up, just like Jesus raised up Lazarus. In John 11:44, *"Jesus saith unto them, Loose him, and let him go."* You can be loosed and let go today. Not only that, but as he brings you up and brings you out, He is going to put a new song in your mouth, even praise to God. I tell you the true worshippers and praisers are those who have known great sin, great sorrow, and great trouble. God's great grace, mercy, and His forgiveness has surrounded them and brought them out of their horrible circumstances.

Let Jesus bring you up out of that horrible pit today. Coming out of that clay is a process. Sometimes, it seems for every step you take, you take two steps back. But God will establish your goings, and a new song will be heard in your mouth, as you give your praise to God. And because of you, just like those prisoners with Paul and Silas, many people shall see the hand of God in your life. It will cause them to fear, but they shall turn and trust in the Lord. He brought me up. Let Him bring you up today. Praise God!

"Take No Thought"
Matthew 6:31

Here in Matthew 6, we find Jesus giving us an example of how we're to believe and know that God has provided everything that we'll ever need to live in this life. He begins by saying:

DAY 3

"²⁷Which of you by taking thought can add one cubit unto his stature? ²⁸And why take ye thought for raiment? Consider the lilies of the field, how they grow; they toil not, neither do they spin: ²⁹And yet I say unto you, That even Solomon in all his glory was not arrayed like one of these. ³⁰Wherefore, if God so clothe the grass of the field, which to day is, and to morrow is cast into the oven, shall he not much more clothe you, O ye of little faith?" (Mat. 6:27-30)

We don't need to worry about clothing. Psalms 19:1 says, *"The heavens declare the glory of God; and the firmament sheweth his handywork."* How beautiful is our creation, and if God can so clothe this universe with such beauty, He will certainly clothe you and me with what we need.

He then goes on to say, *"Therefore take no thought"* (Matthew 6:31). What an interesting statement. That's what we're constantly doing it seems: thinking. We have to really try and believe God to not take thought. We have to try to do as it says in II Corinthians 10:5, *"Casting down imaginations, and every high thing that exalteth itself against the knowledge of God, and bringing into captivity every thought to the obedience of Christ,"* because our thinking is usually contrary to the Word of God. Romans tells us, *"The carnal mind is enmity against God"* (Romans 8:7). Paul said in Philippians 4:8, *"Finally, brethren, whatsoever things are true, whatsoever things are honest, whatsoever things are just, whatsoever things are pure, whatsoever things are lovely, whatsoever things are of good report; if there be any virtue, and if there be any praise, think on these things."* Our minds have to be renewed and cleansed by the Word of God. God doesn't want us reasoning. Jesus said in Mark 2:8, *"Why reason ye these things in your hearts?"*

So, *"Therefore take no thought,"* He says, *"saying, What shall we eat? or, What shall we drink? or, Wherewithal shall we be clothed?"* He's speaking of our daily provision in every aspect of life. Remember Peter tells us that *"all things that pertain unto life and godliness"* He's already provided for us. Philippians 4:19 says, *"But my God shall supply all your need according to his riches in glory by Christ Jesus."* David said in Psalms 37:25, *"I have been young, and now am old; yet have I not seen the righteous forsaken, nor his seed begging bread."* It is not the will of God that you and I suffer in need for clothing, food, drink, etc. The things we need to live this life have already been provided.

Matthew 6 continues, *"³²(For after all these things do the Gentiles seek:) for your heavenly Father knoweth that ye have need of all these things. ³³But seek ye first the kingdom of God, and his righteousness; and all these things shall be added unto you."* May God give us the grace and revelation to know that as we seek Him first, then all these things have been added to us and we need to take no thought. May God help you to do that today!

"For His Name's Sake They Went Forth"
III John 7

In this day of great television ministries and the overemphasis on prosperity and blessing upon the believer, very little is heard about preaching the gospel to the poor. And too much is heard about ministers being blessed and receiving monetary goods. Here in III John, it says, "*7Because that for his name's sake they went forth, taking nothing of the Gentiles. 8We therefore ought to receive such, that we might be fellowhelpers to the truth*" (III John 7-8).

It was for His name's sake that they went forth. The Bible says in Zechariah 2:8, "*After the glory hath he sent me unto the nations.*" The ministry is not a business or a job, but a calling. We do it for Jesus' name sake. Remember that a name always reveals character. We go forth, because His character is impeccable, merciful, and loving.

For that reason, we go forth and we take "*nothing of the Gentiles,*" or the nations. I have been rebuked many times for not charging people in the nations of the world for my plane tickets and accommodations. It is hard for me to charge when freely I have received, and am called to freely give (Matthew 10:8). I understand that we need to take care of ourselves and that ministers live off the gospel. However, at the same time, I do believe there is quite an emphasis on men being blessed. Notice what Jesus said in Luke 9 when He gave the twelve disciples "*power and authority over all devils, and to cure diseases*" and "*sent them to preach the kingdom of God, and to heal the sick.*" He said to them, "*Take nothing for your journey, neither staves nor scrip, neither bread, neither money; neither have two coats apiece*" (Luke 9:1-3). Take nothing for your journey; what an interesting principle. Paul says in I Corinthians:

> "*16For though I preach the gospel, I have nothing to glory of: for necessity is laid upon me; yea, woe is unto me, if I preach not the gospel! 17For if I do this thing willingly, I have a reward: but if against my will, a dispensation of the gospel is committed unto me. 18What is my reward then*" (I Corinthians 9:16-18)?

What is the reward for those of us who preach the gospel? He continues to say, "*Verily that, when I preach the gospel, I may make the gospel of Christ without charge, that I abuse not my power in the gospel*" (I Corinthians 9:18). Isn't that something? Remember that John said, "*We therefore ought to receive such.*" We need to receive men and women of God like this, "*that we might be fellowhelpers to the truth*" (III John 8).

We go forth for His name's sake. We are not interested in the praise of men (John 12:43) or making money or becoming famous. We simply go forth, taking nothing of the Gentiles simply because we love the Lord and we're obeying His command to make disciples of all nations (Matthew 28:19).

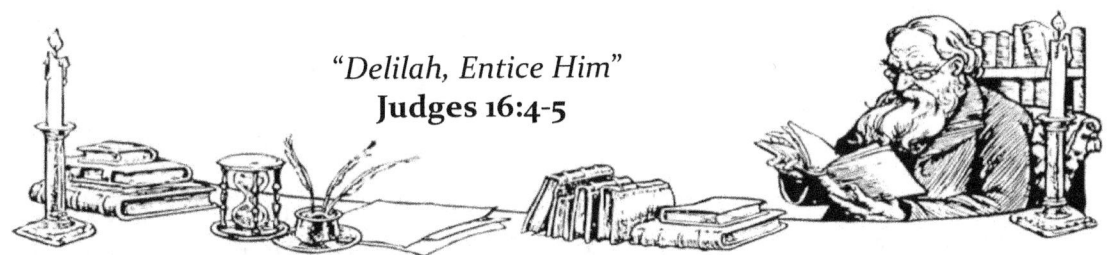

"Delilah, Entice Him"
Judges 16:4-5

DAY 5

Here in Judges 16, we find a story of great seduction and deception. Samson, the great judge of Israel and mighty man of God, who did wonderful things for the Lord and His people, had personal problems in his life. He had things that he never addressed particularly lust and perversion. Eventually, lust and perversion grew up and caused the anointing of God to lift off his life for a season. He was captured and brought bound to the Philistines with his eyes put out, only to walk in circles grinding, meal all day long. The enemy is out to seduce every one of us. Let's look more closely at Samson's story:

> "⁴And it came to pass afterward, that he loved a woman in the valley of Sorek, whose name was Delilah. ⁵And the lords of the Philistines came up unto her, and said unto her, Entice him, and see wherein his great strength lieth, and by what means we may prevail against him, that we may bind him to afflict him: and we will give thee every one of us eleven hundred pieces of silver" (Judges 16:4-5).

Delilah is a type of the strange woman in Scripture. She is a type of Babylon or the harlot church. She is also a type of the adulterous woman. The lords of the Philistines are a type of demon powers. Delilah was supposed to entice Samson and see from where his great strength came, so that the demons could prevail against him. This is the enemy's calling card.

The word *"Delilah"* literally means in the Hebrew "to be brought down, lustful, pining with desire, longing, dainty one, delicate." The Greek word for *"seduce"* means "to lead astray; to stray from the truth; to roam from safety, truth, or virtue." In other words, the strange woman is constantly out there trying to lead us astray from the truth. We have to be careful. Proverbs 7:25 warns us, *"Let not thine heart decline to her ways, go not astray in her paths."* She can also be a type of false doctrine; since in Proverbs 7:5, it describes her as one who *"flattereth with her word."* Therefore, Delilah can represent so many things at different levels. She represents false doctrine, the harlot church, and those things that try to seduce us and lead us astray from our purity and simplicity in Christ Jesus.

Jesus warned about the Delilahs of our day when He said in Mark 13:22, *"For false Christs and false prophets shall rise, and shall shew signs and wonders, to seduce, if it were possible, even the elect."* The Bible also says in Hebrews 5:2 that our great high priest Jesus *"can have compassion on the ignorant, and on them that are out of the way."* Paul warns us in I Timothy 4:1 that, *"the Spirit speaketh expressly, that in the latter times some shall depart from the faith, giving heed to seducing spirits, and doctrines of devils."* He also said in Colossians 2:8, *"Beware lest any man spoil you through philosophy and vain deceit, after the tradition of men, after the rudiments of the world, and not after Christ."*

Delilah represents anything that mocks and saps the spiritual strength of the believer. Judges 16 explains, *"¹⁶And it came to pass, when she pressed him daily with her words, and urged him, so that his soul was vexed unto death. ¹⁷That he told her all his heart..."* (Judges 16:16-17). Note it says *"daily"* here. The enemy is daily after us. Psalms 56:2 says, *"Mine enemies would daily swallow me up."* The enemy comes at us all the time, seducing and bringing temptation, so that our soul is vexed and, if we are not careful and strong enough, we will eventually break and give our enemy all our heart. When Samson finally gave in to her, it says in that he *"wist not that the Lord was departed from him"* (Judges 16:20).

Today, let's not allow Satan to get an advantage over us. Let's not be *"ignorant of his devices"* (II Corinthians 2:11). And for any Delilahs that come to entice us or lead us astray, we simply won't go to the way of her house (Proverbs 7:8). As James 4:7 exhorts us, we will *"resist the devil, and he will flee."*

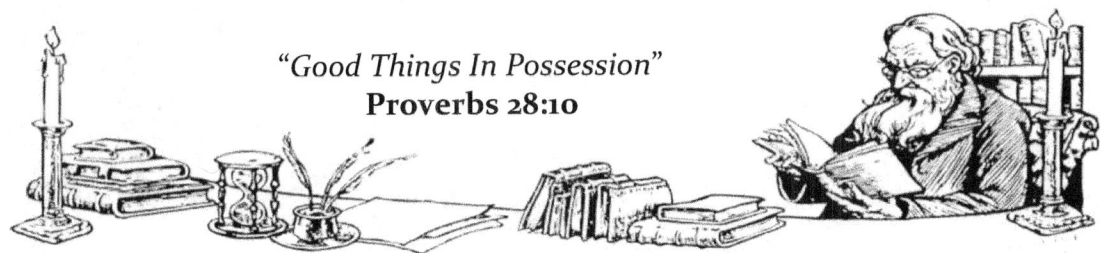

"Good Things In Possession"
Proverbs 28:10

DAY 6

One of the great things about walking with Jesus is that one of his covenant names to us is Jehovah-Jireh, which means "God, our provider" or "The Lord who sees." Proverbs 28:10 says, *"The upright shall have good things in possession."* Then in Proverbs 15:6, *"In the house of the righteous is much treasure."* In Proverbs 28:20, *"A faithful man shall abound with blessings."* This is what God wants for our life. Jesus came *"that they might have life, and that they might have it more abundantly"* (John 10:10).

I taught prosperity for years and I struggled with this principle; then I began to see in the Scriptures the principle of suffering, and I began to teach only suffering. God eventually brought a balance to me. I used to despise the overabundant teachings on prosperity because I felt they were shallow and that the teaching of riches was not born of the Spirit of God. Then one day I read the Scripture in II Corinthians 8:9, *"Yet for your sakes he became poor, that ye through his poverty might be rich."* The Lord would not let me leave that passage; I kept coming back to it. I asked him what He was trying to say to me, and He told me to look up the Greek word for *"rich"*. I did and was surprised to see that it meant "natural, material wealth." I could no longer deny that God actually wants us to have good things in our lives. He wants us to have natural treasure.

The Bible says in Luke 6:38, *"Give and it shall be given unto you; good measure, pressed down, and shaken together, and running over, shall men give unto your bosom."* This is the word of God for our lives. It says in Proverbs 11:25, *"The liberal soul shall be made fat* (or "prosperous" in the Hebrew): *and he that watereth shall be watered also himself."* If we are liberal, we water, and we give, then we will be made fat with the blessing of God, even as treasures. Psalms 115:14 says, *"The Lord shall increase you more and more, you and your children."* So, it's not just me that gets blessed, but my seed, my children.

We all know the passage in Proverbs 3:9-10, "*Honour the Lord with thy substance, and with the firstfruits of all thine increase* (you're tithing and giving offerings more than your tithe)*: So shall thy barns be filled with plenty* (natural provision)*, and thy presses* (spiritual provision) *shall burst out with new wine* (Holy Ghost)." Zechariah 8:12 says, *"For the seed shall be prosperous; the vine shall give her fruit, and the ground shall give her increase, and the heavens shall give their dew; and I will cause the remnant of this people to possess all these things."* What a God we serve! Psalms 16:11 reads, *"In thy presence is fulness of joy; at thy right hand there are pleasures for evermore."* Our God so abundantly provides for us and blesses us. We are to be blessed abundantly. Let this be your confession and your testimony today. Remember today that it says in Ephesians 3:19, *"And to know the love of Christ, which passeth all knowledge, that ye might be filled with all the fullness of God."*

"A Chosen Vessel"
Acts 9:15

DAY 7

There is a glorious truth here, speaking about the Apostle Paul, when God called him on the road to Damascus. The Lord spoke to Ananias later because of Ananias' concern of Paul's past of persecuting Christians. It says in Acts 9, *"But the Lord said unto him, Go thy way: for he is a chosen vessel unto me, to bear my name before the Gentiles, and kings, and the children of Israel"* (Acts 9:15).

I want you to know today that you are a chosen vessel. The Bible says in I Peter 2:9, *"But ye are a chosen generation, a royal priesthood."* You are a chosen generation. Jesus said in John 15:16, *"Ye have not chosen me, but I have chosen you."* He continues in verse 19, *"I have chosen you out of the world."* What a wonderful thing to know that we've been chosen by the Lord. It may be that we've been chosen in the furnace of affliction (Isaiah 48:10), but nonetheless, we're the chosen of the Lord. Psalms 132:13 says, *"The Lord hath chosen Zion."*

Many times we find that God's chosen are not the ones we would choose or what the world would choose, as Paul said in I Corinthians:

> *"But God hath chosen the foolish things of the world to confound the wise; and God hath chosen the weak things of the world to confound the things which are mighty; ^{28}And base things of the world, and things which are despised, hath God chosen"* (I Corinthians 1:27-28).

II Thessalonians 2:13 says, *"God hath from the beginning chosen you to salvation through sanctification of the Spirit and belief of the truth."* II Timothy 2:4 says God has chosen us *"to be a soldier."* James 2:5 says God has *"chosen the poor of this world rich in faith."* I Peter 2:4 calls us *"chosen of God, and precious."* In Revelation 17:14 it says, *"They that are with him are called, and chosen, and faithful."* You and I are the chosen of the Lord. And being the chosen in the Lord is something to rejoice about.

Remember when Samuel went to Jesse's house to anoint one of Jesse's sons? All seven of Jesse's other sons passed before him, and the Lord did not choose any of them for the Lord said to Samuel, *"Look not on his countenance, or on the height of his stature; because I have refused him: for the Lord seeth not as man seeth; for man looketh on the outward appearance, but the Lord looketh on the heart"* (I Samuel 16:7). Seven is the number here for perfection, or human perfection. God passed them by to find David, a man after God's own heart, and said to Samuel, *"Arise, anoint him: for this is he."*

God has chosen Zion. Like David, He's chosen us, the foolish, the weak, and the despised. It doesn't matter about these things. He's still chosen us. We are the chosen generation that is called to be with Him. So let's rise up today and recognize we are the chosen of the Lord!

"Love Not The World"
I John 2:15-17

In this passage of Scripture, the great apostle John leaves for us an amazing admonition to which all of us should take heed, for it deals with our walk with God on a daily basis. I John 2 tells us:

DAY 8

> *"Love not the world, neither the things that are in the world. If any man love the world, the love of the Father is not in him. For all that is in the world, the lust of the flesh, and the lust of the eyes, and the pride of life, is not of the Father, but is of the world. And the world passeth away, and the lust thereof: but he that doeth the will of God abideth for ever"* (I John 2:15-17).

If we have this revelation operating and working in our lives, I believe we can grow that much stronger in grace and become the people God wants us to be.

As Christians, we are to be daily conformed into His image, as II Corinthians 3:18 says, *"But we all, with open face beholding as in a glass the glory of the Lord, are changed into the same image from glory to glory, even as by the Spirit of the Lord."* Romans tells us that we are *"to be conformed to the image of his Son"* (Romans 8:29). So the image of Christ is what we're after. This means to have God's character and nature worked out in our hearts and lives. But we were born in iniquity and conceived in sin (Psalms 51:4-5). We have an Adamic nature that still haunts, torments, and tempts us. All of us, no matter who we are, have the remaining motions of sin in our lives.

Therefore we must constantly be vigilant to have before us these words *"love not the world."* *"The world"* is not speaking of the cosmos or the stars, moon, and universe; it is speaking of all that is in the world. Certainly, we don't need to love the world, because if we do, the love of the Father is not in us. This does not mean that the Father doesn't love us; it means our love for the Father wanes as our love for the things of the world increases.

Instead of loving the world, John exhorts us to do the will of God. You and I need to practice the will of God. We need to recognize what the world is, those things that we must fight and put to death every day in our soulish man. The word *"lust"* here simply means "desire." *"The lust of the flesh"* constitutes all manner of things, any evil desires that would not be pleasing to the Lord Jesus or the things that are shameful. It is anything that we couldn't do with Jesus watching us.

John then says, *"The lust of the eyes."* Ecclesiastes tells us, *"The eye is not satisfied with seeing"* (Ecclesiastes 1:8). We can never see enough. As some have said, you can never get enough of a good thing. But many times, that good thing is a bad thing. *"The lust of the eyes"* means that you're coveting something other than what is godly. We need to make a covenant with our eyes, as Job says, and not look upon a maid (Job 31:1).

We need to just simply make a covenant with our eyes to not look upon anything that would take us from the Spirit of the Lord.

He continues to say, *"The pride of life, is not of the Father, but is of the world."* The pride of life is the original sin. The pride of life is the thing with which most of us struggle. We must fight it. We must resist it. We must humble ourselves in the sight of the Lord (James 4:10). We must walk in humility and *"be clothed with humility: for God resisteth the proud, and giveth grace to the humble"* (I Peter 5:5).

James 4:4 says, *"Ye adulterers and adulteresses, know ye not that the friendship of the world is enmity with God? whosoever therefore will be a friend of the world is the enemy of God."* We must ask ourselves, "With whom do we feel most comfortable?" Are we most comfortable with those in the world or those in the Body of Christ? All that is in the world will pass away and is meaningless. II Peter 2 says:

> *"²⁰For if after they have escaped the pollutions [or sins] of the world through the knowledge of the Lord and Saviour Jesus Christ, they are again entangled therein, and overcome, the latter end is worse with them than the beginning. ²¹For it had been better for them not to have known the way of righteousness, than, after they have known it, to turn from the holy commandment delivered unto them. ²²But it is happened unto them according to the true proverb, The dog is turned to his own vomit again; and the sow that was washed to her wallowing in the mire"* (II Peter 2:20-21).

Every time we turn to the world, this is what we are doing, returning to our own vomit. That is what the world is to God. And that is why He declares to us, *"Love not the world, neither the things that are in the world."*

In Mark 4, Jesus made it very clear that for those on thorny ground, *"the cares of this world, and the deceitfulness of riches, and the lusts of other things entering in, choke the word, and it becometh unfruitful"* (Mark 4:19). All of these things speak of the world and are a temptation to all of us. And as we allow the things of the world to fill our life, it makes us unfruitful to the things of God.

I John 5:19 says, *"The whole world lieth in wickedness."* We see some of the casualties in the Bible. We see what happened to Saul in the Old Testament, how he started out good and ended up bad. We see Demas in II Timothy, *"For Demas hath forsaken me, having loved this present world"* (II Timothy 4:10). We cannot love this world. We must understand that God has placed us in this earth to be His precious people.

I pray that we would strive to make this the word of the Lord for our lives, that we would love neither the world and nor the things in the world. It says in Philippians 2, *"¹⁵That ye may be blameless and harmless, the sons of God, without rebuke, in the midst of a crooked and perverse nation, among whom ye shine as lights in the world; ¹⁶Holding forth the word of life"* (Philippians 2:15-16). We are to shine as lights unto this world, not to love it or be a friend to it. We are in this world, but not of it (John 15:19, 17:14-16). We are to be *"holding forth the word of life,"* being an example to others of the grace of God and the power of the cross.

"Then Job Arose"
Job 1:20

Day 9

Here in Job 1:20, we see one of the greatest examples of worship. Job lost all of his possessions, property, and children in one swoop because Satan accused him before God. God allowed Job to be tested in ways that many of us will never know. Nevertheless, Job's response to all of this is mind boggling. Job was quite the man of God and if anyone of us could respond the way he did, we would be true worshippers.

For years, I regarded Job the way many have. I was taught that it was all Job's fault, he was self-righteous, and brought all of that upon himself. However, it says in Job 1:22, *"In all this Job sinned not, nor charged God foolishly."* This verse clearly states that Job had nothing to do with what happened. You and I may have had nothing to do with what happened to us. Perhaps it's simply a divine test, as it was with Job's case. The Lord said to Satan, *"Hast thou considered my servant Job,"* (Job 1:8). God was the one who initiated it. How are we going to respond? Job's response was:

> *"Then Job arose, and rent his mantle, and shaved his head, and fell down upon the ground, and worshipped. ²¹And said, Naked came I out of my mother's womb, and naked shall I return thither: the Lord gave, and the Lord hath taken away; blessed be the name of the Lord"* (Job 1:20-21).

First, *"Job arose."* The easiest thing to do when trials come is to lie down, to quit, to backslide, to run from God. But instead, *"Job arose."* Second, he *"rent his mantle."* Clothes in the Scripture speak of our righteousness; it says in Revelation 19:8, *"for the fine linen is the righteousness of the saints."* Also, speaking of the bride in Psalms 45:13, it says, *"Her clothing is of wrought gold."* So, when Job, *"rent his mantle"*, he was saying that he had gained nothing in his walk with God, nothing without His righteousness.

Then he *"shaved his head"*. Hair in the Scriptures speaks of covering. Baldness was despised, but Job didn't care that he was despised. He was saying he had no covering but God, in spite of all that had happened to him. Then he *"fell down upon the ground and worshipped."* This is the ultimate definition of worship in the Hebrew and Greek; to fall prostrate before that which you're worshipping. That's exactly what Job did. He *"fell down upon the ground, and worshipped."*

Oh, that God would help you and me to respond the same way. No matter what goes on or happens to us, let us respond like Job, who *"sinned not nor charged God foolishly."* Instead, let us arise from the ashes and declare our righteousness as His. Today, let's not be afraid of the loss of reputation or people despising us, but let our only covering be the Lord; and worship Him despite what is happening to us.

"Not Living Unto Ourselves"
II Corinthians 5:15

DAY 10

One of the things that is permeating the body of Christ today is an all-about-me mentality, a selfishness. This is so alien to what Jesus wants. Jesus said in Matthew 11, *"Learn of me; for I am meek and lowly in heart"* (Matthew 11:29). *"Let this mind be in you,"* Philippians tells us, *"which was also in Christ Jesus"* (Philippians 2:5). The mind of Christ Jesus was in that He gave Himself, left all His glory, put upon Himself human flesh, and became like us. He humbled Himself even unto death.

The Bible says in Mark, *"For even the Son of man came not to be ministered unto, but to minister"* (Mark 10:45). In this day and age, it seems as though everything has been turned around backwards. In many ways it has become all about us rather than about the Lord Jesus. II Corinthians 5:15 tells us, *"And that he died for all, that they which live should not henceforth live unto themselves, but unto him which died for them, and rose again."* One of the things we learn if we are true disciples is that we are not living for ourselves.

Ask yourself today: is that what you're doing? The Bible tells us in II Timothy, *"¹This know also, that in the last days perilous times shall come. ²For men shall be lovers of their own selves"* (II Timothy 3:1-2). Judges 17 says, *"Every man did that which was right in his own eyes"* (Judges 17:6). In Genesis 11:4, when they built the tower of Babel, they said, *"Go to, let us build us a city and a tower, whose top may reach unto heaven; and let us make us a name, lest we be scattered abroad upon the face of the whole earth."* Let us make us a name. This statement is the essence of confusion, which is the definition of "Babylon." There is utter confusion when men live for themselves for they love, *"The praise of men more than the praise of God"* (John 12:43).

The Lord is trying to teach us to die to our own desires, wants, and needs and to live unto God. John tells us, *"Except a corn of wheat fall into the ground and die, it abideth alone: but if it die, it bringeth forth much fruit"* (John 12:24). God is desperate for a people willing to become servants and willing to die to themselves so that others might live. He wants a people who have the heart of Jesus. Let's decide today to *"not henceforth live unto"* ourselves, but live unto Him who died for us and rose again.

"Judah Shall Plow"
Hosea 10:11

DAY **11**

Here we find in the Scriptures one of the most tremendous truths, *"Judah shall plow"* (Hosea 10:11). The name *"Judah"* means *"praise."* In other words, we need to plow with our praise. As we go about our day and face all that we have to face, we must remember the admonition in Scripture when David says, *"I will bless the Lord at all times: his praise shall continually be in my mouth"* (Psalms 34:1).

The word *"plow"* in Hebrew means *"to scratch, to engrave, to dig."* We have to sometimes scratch and dig. We have to *"offer the sacrifice of praise to God continually, that is, the fruit of our lips giving thanks to his name"* (Hebrews 13:15). Sometimes it's hard to praise God, but yet, those of the tribe of Judah shall plow. The word *"plow"* also means *"to hold your peace, to be silent, or practice secretly."* Sometimes even though praise is not silent, it's peaceful. It's not done so others can see. We don't do what we do for men, but we do what we do for God. We do what we do in secret. So we must plow, scratch, dig, and press through with our worship. Some other translations read:

> *"Judah must plow"*
> *"Judah will be working the plow"*

This is our calling. We were born to worship Him, as Revelation 4:11 says, *"For thy pleasure they are and were created."* In Proverbs 20:4 it says, *"The sluggard will not plow by reason of the cold..."* There are always reasons, difficulties, and experiences in life that would cause us not to worship or to praise God. But we have to understand that when we praise, we break through the enemy's attack against us. When we praise we break through our circumstances.

I Corinthians 9:10 says, *"He that ploweth should plow in hope."* We plow in hope knowing that God *"inhabits our praises"* (Psalms 22:3). Psalms 8:2 says, *"Out of the mouth of babes and sucklings hast thou ordained strength because of thine enemies, that thou mightest still the enemy and the avenger."* In other words, praise is ordained strength and it will stop the enemy and the avenger. This is why we plow. This is why we dig. This is why we continue to lift up our voices.

Isaiah 28:24 asks, *"Doth the plowman plow all day to sow?"* In other words our plowing has a purpose. We plow, worship, and praise God no matter what we are going through because we know the breakthrough is coming.

It says in Amos 9:13, *"Behold, the days come, saith the Lord, that the plowman shall overtake the reaper."* The day is coming when Judah's plowing shall overtake even the seed being sown in the earth, because there will be such a groundswell of worship and praise coming from the body of Christ. I encourage you to learn how to worship and praise God liberally. Then use it to plow up all the rough places in your life. For in this He has given you strength.

"As For Me"
Psalms 55:16

Day 12

David declares in Psalms 55, "*As for me, I will call upon God; and the Lord shall save me*" (Psalms 55:16). This phrase "*as for me*" sets us apart from others. It's saying, "This is what I'm going to do. This is what I have decided. Even if it's different from others, I'm going to do it." David decides for himself to call upon the Lord and because of that, the Lord shall save him. Have you decided for yourself to call upon the Lord and say "*as for me*"?

It says in Joshua 24:15, "*But as for me and my house, we will serve the Lord.*" In other words, Joshua is saying, "I don't know what you're going to do with your house, but as for me and my house, we're going to serve the Lord." Every one of us needs to have this principle established in our lives. We need to make our own private decision that, as for us, this is what we're going to do regardless of what anybody else says or does.

In another place in Psalms David writes, "*But as for me, I will come into thy house in the multitude of thy mercy*" (Psalms 5:7). In other words, David is saying, "I've made the decision that I'm going to the house of the Lord. I'm going to belong to a local church. I'm going to have a pastor, a father ministry, in my life. And I'm going to love it, because this is the will of God for my life. I can't judge you for what God is doing with you; all I know is, as for me, this is what God has revealed." Have you come to a conclusion and a decision in your own life about this?

David also says in Psalms 26:11, "*But as for me, I will walk in mine integrity.*" This is a decision that every one of us must make if we're going to keep our "*vessel in sanctification and honour*" (I Thessalonians 4:4). We must be willing to make the kind of decision that says, "As for me, this is what I'm going to do."

One of my favorite passages of Scripture is Psalms 17:15, when David says, "*As for me, I will behold thy face in righteousness.*" I can say to you clearly, "As for me, I long to behold His face in utter and complete righteousness." He continues to say, "*I shall be satisfied, when I awake, with thy likeness.*"

As for me, I have been set on this path, and nothing can deter me from it. It's the narrow way that leads to life (Matthew 7:14). The word "*life*" used there in Matthew 7:14 is the Greek word "*zoe*" which means "life as God is living it right now."

As for me and my house, we will serve the Lord. As for me, I will come into His house in the multitude of His mercy. As for me, I will walk in my integrity. As for me, I will call upon God. But most importantly, as for me I will behold His face in righteousness and I won't be satisfied until I awake with His likeness. Beholding and looking into His lovely face is what transforms me into His glorious image (II Corinthians 3:18). As for me, I will call upon God and behold His lovely face. How about you?

"*Eat This Roll*"
Ezekiel 3:1

There are two places in Scripture where we find the principle of eating the Word of God. One is in Ezekiel chapters 2 and 3:

DAY 13

> "*When I looked, behold, an hand was sent unto me; and, lo, a roll of a book was therein;* ¹⁰*And he spread it before me; and it was written within and without: and there was written therein lamentations, and mourning, and woe.* ¹*Moreover he said unto me, Son of man, eat that thou findest; eat this roll, and go speak unto the house of Israel.* ²*So I opened my mouth, and he caused me to eat that roll.* ³*And he said unto me, Son of man, cause thy belly to eat, and fill thy bowels with this roll that I give thee. Then did I eat it; and it was in my mouth as honey for sweetness.*" (Ezekiel 2:9-3:3)

This roll, or scroll, represents the Word of God. He wants us to eat His Word. He's spread it before us, and it is written within and without. This means there is a living word and a written word, the spirit word and the natural word. Jesus said, "*The words that I speak unto you, they are spirit, and they are life*" (John 6:63).

Here, Ezekiel was commanded to eat this book. Eating the Word of God means giving yourself to sound doctrine and searching "*the scriptures daily, whether those things were so*" (Acts 17:11). It means you are "*laying up in store...a good foundation against the time to come*" (I Timothy 6:19). If Jesus truly is the Word, as it says in John 1:1, "*In the beginning was the Word, and the Word was with God, and the Word was God,*" then as we eat the Word, we're filling ourselves full with Jesus. Ezekiel was told to fill his bowels, or to satisfy himself, with the roll that He gave him (Ezekiel 3:1). When the Lord gives us revelation, His hidden truths out of the Scriptures, it should satisfy us and cause us to want more and more. It should create in us an unsatisfied satisfaction. If we give ourselves to the Word, it will give itself to us. We become living epistles "*known and read of all men*" (II Corinthians 3:2).

We find this same principle in Revelation 10, when John is told to go to the messenger of God and say, "*Give me the little book.*" The angel said to him, "*Take it, and eat it up; and it shall make thy belly bitter, but it shall be in thy mouth sweet as honey.*" It continues to say, "*And I took the little book out of the angel's hand, and ate it up; and it was in my mouth sweet as honey: and as soon as I had eaten it, my belly was bitter*" (Revelation 10:9-10). Our admonition is to "take it and eat it up. Eat this roll, the written and the living Word of God, the logos and the rhema word." As we give ourselves to it, it is sweet in our mouths and bitter in our bellies. It is wonderful going in, but bitter in our life's circumstances. Revelation is married to situation; so as we eat the Word, it is sweet to the taste, but then walking it out is another story. That's when sanctification and the dealings of God come in. But, nonetheless, once we overcome, that Word belongs to us forever. So, today, the admonition is, presented to us, "Take and eat it up. Eat this roll."

"Let Him Glory In The Lord"
II Corinthians 10:17-18

DAY 14

In this passage in II Corinthians 10:17-18, we hear the apostle Paul saying, *"¹⁷But he that glorieth, let him glory in the Lord. ¹⁸For not he that commendeth himself is approved, but whom the Lord commendeth."* The Bible says in Proverbs 20:6, *"Most men will proclaim every one his own goodness: but a faithful man who can find?"* Proverbs 27:2 says, *"Let another man praise thee, and not thine own mouth."*

One of the greatest distractions in the body of Christ today is that we have too many people boasting of what they're doing, boasting of their testimonies, and boasting of their experiences. This really is not the will of God. If we're going to glory or boast in anything, let us glory in the Lord.

The apostle Paul in Galatians 6:14, says, *"But God forbid that I should glory, save in the cross of our Lord Jesus Christ, by whom the world is crucified unto me, and I unto the world."* It is the Lord Jesus Christ, His cross, which has saved and redeemed us. We have nothing to boast in but that. How about you? If we take this all the way back to Jeremiah 9, we'll find this statement:

> *"²³Thus saith the Lord, Let not the wise man glory in his wisdom, neither let the mighty man glory in his might, let not the rich man glory in his riches: ²⁴But let him that glorieth glory in this, that he understandeth and knoweth me"* (Jeremiah 9:23-24).

Jesus said, *"And this is life eternal, that they might know thee the only true God, and Jesus Christ, whom thou hast sent"* (John 17:3). Knowing God is the end all. It is the greatest and most wonderful thing that we could ever esteem or run after.

Jeremiah 9:23 says, *"Let not the wise man glory in his wisdom."* *"For the wisdom of this world is foolishness with God"* (I Corinthians 3:19). Luke 16:15 says, *"That which is highly esteemed among men is abomination in the sight of God."*

Jeremiah 9:23 also says, *"Neither let the mighty man glory in his might."* David says in Psalms 147:10, *"[The Lord] taketh not pleasure in the legs of a man."* God doesn't need our strength. God doesn't need our abilities.

Jeremiah 9:23 continues saying, *"Let not the rich man glory in his riches."* Riches have a way of cutting us off, and *"the love of money is the root of all evil"* I Timothy 6:10. If we glory in our riches, then we're not glorying in Jesus, His provision, and faithfulness. We're glorying in our own abilities to provide for ourselves. He says, *"But let him that glorieth glory in this, that he understandeth and knoweth me."*

Over in Jeremiah 4:2 it says, *"The nations shall bless themselves in him, and in him shall they glory."* This is what the Lord wants for us as I Corinthians 1:31 says, *"That, according as it is written, He that glorieth, let him glory in the Lord."*

"If I Perish, I Perish"
Esther 4:16

Day 15

We find a tremendous truth in this passage of scripture. There are times in life when we are required to do things that seem beyond us, overwhelming us, and may cost us a great deal, even though we know deep in our heart, that it is the thing we must do. Too many times in life, people shrink back from what they have been asked to do. Here Esther has been told, under the direction of Mordecai, what she must do. The only way their situation could change was for Esther to go in before the king and stand for her people. It could have cost her life, but nonetheless, the fate of her people hung in the balance. Esther's response was finally *"if I perish, I perish"* (Esther 4:16). Some other translations of that verse read:

"If death be my fate, then let it come."
"Though I must die for it, let it be."

Revelation 12:11 tells us that *"they overcame him* [the devil] *by the blood of the Lamb, and by the word of their testimony; and they loved not their lives unto the death."* There are some occasions in life when all we can do is put ourselves on the line and stand. That's why in Ephesians 6:13 it says, *"Having done all, to stand."* Sometimes we just have to do it. It doesn't say it's going to be easy. God hasn't promised us a bed of roses. Many times we're required to lay down our lives as a sacrifice for other people. Though it may cost us dearly, it is the right thing to do. Jesus Himself left all the glory of Heaven, was clothed in human flesh in the incarnation, became the son of man, and died as our precious spotless Lamb of God to set us free and to save us. I believe that God is looking for that kind of heart in His people today.

He saw this in Abraham, when He said, *"Take now thy son, thine only son...and offer him there for a burnt offering"* (Genesis 22:2). In spite of the pain, the suffering, and the sacrifice, Abraham was going to offer his son because he knew it was the will of God. Abraham was about to plunge that knife into his son in obedience to God, and the angel of the Lord cried out to him, *"Now I know that thou fearest God, seeing thou hast not withheld thy son, thine only son from me"* (Genesis 22:12). I believe that this story is in the Scriptures for one reason. God wanted to know that at least one person was willing to do the same as Him, give up his only son. God many times requires of us a sacrifice, and it's really just a test to see if we will be faithful, honor the Lord, and do what is right. Even though it may cost us our very lives, we should respond like Esther, *"If I perish, I perish."*

So many times in the Scriptures, we find men and women standing and fighting against overwhelming odds. They lay their lives on the line to do the right thing, so that others might live. This is the true heart of God and should be the true heart of every believer. God help us to not be selfish, to not only care about ourselves and what's ours, but to also care for others. I like to call it the "I, me, and mine" syndrome.

Instead, let us have a Kingdom mentality and care more for our brethren than we do for ourselves. This truly is the will of God.

A great example of this is found in II Samuel 23 when those three mighty men broke through the host and brought the water from the well of Bethlehem to David. David was so moved by their sacrifice that in response he poured out that water before the Lord on the earth. These three men went in the jeopardy of their lives just because King David had sighed and wanted water. I believe that this passage is a type of the last great move of God on the earth. King David is a type of the King Jesus. The three men represent a company of people willing to go in the jeopardy of their lives and break through the host of the enemy to help facilitate the last great move of God. Jesus will pour water upon the whole earth through their sacrifice. The earth will be blessed, but their lives will have been in jeopardy and hung in the balance, willing to give their lives for the last great move of God. They settled it in their hearts when they said, *"If I perish, I perish."*

We must get to the place where we realize our lives are not our own. We belong to another. Let us echo Paul in Galatians 2:20, *"I am crucified with Christ: nevertheless I live; yet not I, but Christ liveth in me: and the life which I now live in the flesh I live by the faith of the Son of God, who loved me, and gave himself for me."* Paul also said *"I die daily"* (I Corinthians 15:31).

Psalms 116:15 says, *"Precious in the sight of the Lord is the death of his saints."* This is the reality of the Christian life. We are called to lay down our lives for one another, just as Jesus laid down His life for us. Though it may cost us our own lives, though the sacrifice may be great, though the odds might be overwhelming, there must come forth this courageous and valiant cry, *"If I perish, I perish."*

As I write this, I say to my own heart, "If death be my fate, then let it come, because what's more important to me is the will of God and the blessing upon God's people rather than my own personal safety." May God help you today to be like Esther, and go before the king for your brothers and sisters, or whoever it may be, with this refrain in your heart, *"If I perish, I perish."*

"Have Not I Sent Thee"
Judges 6:14

Day 16

We want to consider today the principle of God sending messengers, sending His people as prophets, and sending you and me with a message. Here in Judges 6:12,14 it says, *"And the angel of the Lord appeared unto him, and said unto him, The Lord is with thee, thou mighty man of valour. ¹⁴And the Lord looked upon him, and said, Go in this thy might, and thou shalt save Israel from the hand of the Midianites: have not I sent thee."*

The Lord sending us with a message, the Lord sending us with a purpose is what the Gospel is all about. We have not chosen Him but He has chosen us and ordained us that we should go forth and bear fruit. We can go all the way back to the book of Exodus where God called Moses, and said to him in Exodus 3:10, *"Come now therefore, and I will send thee unto Pharaoh, that thou mayest bring forth my people the children of Israel out of Egypt."* We have been sent with a message to bring God's people out of bondage, out of Egypt. Has He not sent us to save Israel from the Midianites, or in other words, to save God's people from their enemies? You and I have been sent.

In I Samuel 16:1 God says, *"How long wilt thou mourn for Saul, seeing I have rejected him from reigning over Israel? fill thine horn with oil, and go, I will send thee to Jesse the Bethlehemite: for I have provided me a king among his sons."* We have been sent by the Lord to anoint and to prepare God's people for the coming of the Lord and for service unto Him.

In Jeremiah 29:19 it says the Lord would rise up early, and send prophets to His people. Whether people would listen to them or not is another story, but He would rise up early and send them nonetheless. In Isaiah 6:8, Isaiah gets to hear what's going on in the throne room. He hears our great triune God saying, *"Whom shall I send, and who will go for us?"* Then you hear Isaiah saying, *"Here am I; send me."* Let this be our response to the Lord's request to send us and that we will go.

In Luke 10:2 it says very clearly there that *"The harvest truly is great, but the labourers* [Greek: "teacher"] *are few: pray ye therefore the Lord of the harvest, that he would send forth labourers into his harvest."* God needs laborers, teachers, who will say "Here am I; send me." Just as Jesus in Mark 11:1 *"sendeth forth two of his disciples."* The Lord wants to send you and me. In John 20:21, Jesus says, *"As my Father hath sent me, even so send I you."*

I want to finish with this passage where God is speaking to Paul concerning his calling in Acts 26:16-17, *"I have appeared unto thee for this purpose, to make thee a minister and a witness both of these things which thou hast seen, and of those things in the which I will appear unto thee; ¹⁷Delivering thee from the people, and from the Gentiles, unto whom now I send thee."* God has sent us, what will our response be? He has sent us to save His people, to deliver them, to bring them the anointing, and to bring them the Gospel. In the last days there will be a company of people as Malachi 4:5 says, *"Behold, I will send you Elijah the prophet before the coming of the great and dreadful day of the Lord."* You and I are that people. He has sent us!

"In His Sanctuary"
Psalms 96:6

Day 17

In Psalms 96:6 we see these words, *"Honour and majesty are before him: strength and beauty are in his sanctuary."* The word *"sanctuary"* in Hebrew means, "a sacred place; a consecrated, a dedicated, a holy place; or a holy place of Jehovah." The sanctuary is the place of God's presence.

I love what David says in Psalms 26:8, *"Lord, I have loved the habitation of thy house, and the place where thine honour dwelleth."* I can say to you I have loved the habitation of His house, and the place where His honor dwells. All through my life the only place where I've ever found total peace, total comfort, total forgiveness, and total contentment, is in the presence of our precious Savior in the sanctuary.

You know David says, in Psalms 77:13, *"Thy way, O God, is in the sanctuary."* The sanctuary is the place of His presence, the place where His honor dwells, and the place where His glory is. Oh how we should long to be there every day. Our heart should be homesick when we're away from it.

I pray that today a revelation hits you that the sanctuary of God becomes your home. He says in Isaiah 60:13, I will *"beautify the place of my sanctuary; and I will make the place of my feet glorious."* Isn't this like our God, to make everything beautiful and glorious in His presence?

I love what David said as well in Psalms 73:17, *"Until I went into the sanctuary of God; then understood I their end."* Many times we don't understand what's going to happen to the wicked, and those that seem to be so blessed in this life but are out of the flow of the things of God. Yet when we get in the presence of God, the place where His honor dwells in His sanctuary, we can understand their end. The word *"end"* there means "their here after; where they are going to be." One day all of us will stand before the judgment seat of Christ and be judged for what things we've done in our bodies. And we will receive a reward accordingly.

For me, my greatest joy is to be in the sanctuary. *"Lift up your hands in the sanctuary, and bless the Lord"* Psalms 134:2. Why don't you bless the Lord today! Go into the sanctuary of God. Strength and beauty are in that sanctuary. Jesus is there, because He is the sanctuary.

"Found Faithful"
I Corinthians 4:2

Day 18

We want to look today at the principle in Scripture about being found faithful. Here in I Corinthians 4:2 it says, *"Moreover it is required in stewards, that a man be found faithful."* It is required in stewards (another word for household manager, i.e. pastors, leaders, or Christians in their daily lives) to be found faithful. Paul said in I Timothy 1:12, *"That he [Jesus] counted me faithful, putting me into the ministry."* So there is a proving of ourselves to the Lord in being found faithful in order to be released into the ministry.

As we look at the world today, we find a plaguing problem. In Psalms 12:1, *"For the faithful fail from among the children of men."* Nevertheless Psalms 101:6 says, *"Mine eyes shall be upon the faithful of the land."* In Proverbs 20:6 it says, *"Most men will proclaim every one his own goodness: but a faithful man who can find?"* Who can find a faithful man? A faithful man is someone that will hold up the Word of the Lord, keep his testimony, lay down his life unto the death and proclaim, and be an example of the Gospel of Jesus Christ.

Jesus put it this way in Luke 16:10, *"He that is faithful in that which is least is faithful also in much."* So many times we disregard the least things, the natural things and don't count them as important. Yet I Corinthians 15:46 declares, *"Howbeit that was not first which is spiritual, but that which is natural; and afterward that which is spiritual."* God always looks at what we do in the natural to determine our spiritual reward. We are going to be judged according to the things we have done in our body. Have we been faithful? Have we honored the Lord with our lives? Are we faithful or do we proclaim our own goodness. In the gospel of Luke, Jesus says:

> *"⁴²Who then is that faithful and wise steward, whom his lord shall make ruler over his household, to give them their portion of meat in due season? ⁴³Blessed is that servant, whom his lord when he cometh shall find so doing. ⁴⁴Of a truth I say unto you, that he will make him ruler over all that he hath"* (Luke 12:42-44).

So we find that the faithful and wise servant is the one who, when the Lord is coming, is found doing the right thing, plodding on everyday, obeying the word, striving to be better with his walk, offering up his body as a living sacrifice, being faithful to God, faithful to His word, faithful to His people and faithful to the exhortation to take the Gospel to the nations. When the Lord comes, if He finds you so doing, the Bible says that Jesus will make you ruler over all that He has.

Today, let us give ourselves to be those faithful men and women. We will serve the Lord without looking for anything other than just a smile on His face. As Psalms 31:23 says, we will find that *"the Lord preserveth the faithful."*

"Three Hundred Foxes"
Judges 15:4

DAY 19

Here in Judges 15, there is a revelatory story about the end time harvest. God uses His remnant to bring about that harvest. Even though this is a true story that happened in the Old Testament, it has great spiritual implications for us today and for the *"last days"* saints. It says in verse 1, *"But it came to pass within a while after, in the time of wheat harvest, that Samson visited his wife."* Harvest time is the Feast of Tabernacles. It's a time of fullness, when God goes and gathers His remnant, His people, out from the earth. It goes on to say:

> *"And Samson went and caught three hundred foxes, and took firebrands, and turned tail to tail, and put a firebrand in the midst between two tails. ⁵And when he had set the brands on fire, he let them go into the standing corn of the Philistines"* (Judges 15:4-5).

I believe that this is speaking of the remnant, because the number three hundred in Scripture is representative of the faithful remnant. Samson here is a type of the Lord Jesus. He went and caught three hundred foxes. Foxes in Scripture normally would be a bad thing, but in this case, I believe it's talking about the sons of God. A fox can go in very quietly, get his provision, and get out without even being noticed. God wants His people to be *"wise as serpents, and harmless as doves"* (Matthew 10:16).

Jesus is going to catch Himself three hundred foxes. It is not an exact three hundred, but simply representative of a remnant of people. He will then take the *"firebrands and [turn] them tail to tail."* What this means is there will have to be unity within this remnant. You can't be doing your own thing. You must be joined to your brothers and sisters. Levi in the Old Testament was a part of God's priesthood and Levi's name means "to join". We must be joined to one another in purpose and vision.

As we are joined, He sets our tails on fire so that we will go and gather His remnant. Fire is not always a bad thing; it's simply the purging fire of God. It is the fire that excites and ignites. In this case, I believe it's the fire of God igniting the remnant to go and do the will of God. Every now and then, all of us need someone to set our tails on fire, to stir us up. Yes, we should learn to stir up ourselves. But we also know that we can ask the Lord to send His firebrand and light our tails on fire, so we can then be loosed. God wants to loose a remnant into His harvest. It says that Samson let them go into the standing corn of the Philistines. God wants us to go to the Gentiles and make disciples of all nations (Matthew 28:19).

We can't do this without a real, holy zeal and passion. The Bible says in Psalms 69:9, *"For the zeal of thine house hath eaten me up."* I pray today that we are eaten up with passion and desire. May the Spirit of God so satiate our souls and spirits that everywhere we go, we are living testimonies. May we become a living *"epistle written in our hearts, known and read of all men"* (II Corinthians 3:2). Jesus said of John, *"He was a burning and a shining light"* (John 5:35). It says in Hebrews 1:7 that He makes *"his ministers a flame of fire."*

I pray to God that we will be those ministers who are flames of fire, tail to tail. We will no longer be selfish or ambitious, doing our own thing, but will be joined to each other. As the Word of the Lord comes forth, we will go forth into the harvest field and begin to burn up *"both the shocks, and also the standing corn, with the vineyards and olives"* (Judges 15:5). We will bring the power and glory of God to the nations. God will use that fire to burn all of the foolishness out of them and bring them to a saving grace in the Lord Jesus. Are you one of the three hundred foxes? I pray that you are.

"Four Types Of Songs"
Ephesians 5:18-19

There are four types of songs revealed in the Scriptures: psalms, hymns, spiritual songs and lastly, as mentioned in Psalms 98:1, *"a new song"*. The first three of these types of songs are shown in Ephesians 5:18-19, *"¹⁸And be not drunk with wine, wherein is excess; but be filled with the Spirit; ¹⁹Speaking to yourselves in psalms and hymns and spiritual songs, singing and making melody in your heart to the Lord."*

Psalms are songs or scriptural choruses taken from the Bible. Hymns are songs written about God, His word and His works. We are to sing songs taken from the Bible. Such songs are the most powerful ones, because the Word of God is riddled with the power of God. Spiritual songs are supernatural songs. The Greek word for *"spiritual"* means "ethereal or supernatural." The Greek word for *"song"* is translated as an "ode or chant." It is obvious that this speaks of singing in a supernatural chant, in the Spirit, which I believe is to be singing in tongues. This is as spoken of in I Corinthians 14:15, *"What is it then? I will pray with the spirit, and I will pray with the understanding also: I will sing with the spirit, and I will sing with the understanding also."* Such spirit songs are supernatural and can only be sung by those baptized in the Holy Ghost with the evidence of speaking in tongues.

In Psalms 98:1, we are told to *"sing unto the Lord a new song."* In Psalms 40:3 it illustrates, *"He hath put a new song in my mouth, even praise unto our God: many shall see it, and fear, and shall trust in the Lord."* As psalms and hymns come to you directly from the Scriptures, a new song comes to you directly from God. He will put a new song, a song never heard before in your mouth and it will ultimately be as praise to God. David expresses in Psalms 28:7, *"With my song will I praise him."*

In Revelation 14:3, it talks about the 144,000 priests saying, *"And they sung as it were a new song before the throne."* We hear this many times in the book of Revelation. There is a new song coming to flow with the psalms, hymns and spiritual songs. In order that we may truly find God in our worship, let all these types of songs be a part of our walk with the Lord. This is important because God inhabits our true and full praises unto Him. Psalms 22:3 says, *"But thou art holy, O thou that inhabitest the praises of Israel."* Once our precious God comes down, we are changed forever.

It says back in Ephesians 5:19 *"making melody in your heart to the Lord."* This means that we are actually ministering to ourselves also as we worship God. We're supposed to use all these psalms, hymns, spiritual songs and new songs to admonish, not only ourselves, but also one another. In Colossians 3:16 it says *"Admonishing one another in psalms and hymns and spiritual songs, singing with grace in your hearts to the Lord."* We are also to sing them with grace in our hearts to the Lord. We can sing with grace if you've experienced grace. And if we've experienced grace, these four types of songs will be obvious to you. Sing them today. Deuteronomy 32:9 tells us, *"The Lord's portion is his people."* I exhort all of us to minister to Him today.

"Knowing The Time"
Romans 13:11

DAY 21

We desperately need to have an understating and a knowing of the time. Paul declares, *"And that, knowing the time, that now it is high time to awake out of sleep: for now is our salvation nearer than when we believed"* (Romans 13:11). We need to be as the children of Issachar who *"were men that had understanding of the times, to know what Israel ought to do"* (I Chronicles 12:32).

What kind of sleep has the body of Christ fallen into when Paul states, *"It is high time to awake out of sleep"*? I believe that there is selfishness and a personal gratification that has come forth and has been fostered among the people of God. There is too much self being preached and too much talk about us receiving blessings from the Lord.

Haggai 1:2 says, *"Thus speaketh the Lord of hosts, saying, This people say, The time is not come, the time that the Lord's house should be built."* However, it is time for the Lord's house to be built and come together. Ephesians 1:10 says, *"That in the dispensation of the fulness of times he might gather together in one all things in Christ."* God is gathering His people in this time. We see this is in the book of Zephaniah, *"At that time will I bring you again, even in the time that I gather you: for I will make you a name and a praise among all people of the earth, when I turn back your captivity before your eyes, saith the Lord"* (Zephaniah 3:20).

We know that, *"To every thing there is a season, and a time to every purpose under the heaven"* (Ecclesiastes 3:1). God has a time and now is not the time to be concerned about ourselves. Now is a time to be concerned about the Kingdom of God and building the house of the Lord. Haggai 1:4 says, *"Is it time for you, O ye, to dwell in your cieled houses, and this house lie waste?"* Is this a time for people to be so concerned about their own personal lives and not the Kingdom of God? We are moving into a day when the emphasis is no longer on "I" but on "us." God is looking for a people who will join with Him, rise up, and be concerned about the building of His house and Kingdom. Zechariah 10:1 says, *"Ask ye of the Lord rain in the time of the latter rain; so the Lord shall make bright clouds, and give them showers of rain."* God is waiting to send us the last great move of God. Do we know this or are we sleeping?

In the book of II Kings we find the story of Naaman getting healed from his leprosy. Gehazi began taking money, garments, etc. from Naaman. Elijah then asked Gehazi an important question, *"Went not mine heart with thee, when the man turned again from his chariot to meet thee? Is it a time to receive money, and to receive garments, and oliveyards, and vineyards, and sheep, and oxen, and menservants, and maidservants"* (II Kings 5:26)?

God's heart has gone with us and He is watching us. Is it a time for us to dwell in big houses? Is it a time for us to receive money, garments, and things? No, it is a time for us to be concerned about the building of the house and the Kingdom of God. Hear the Word of the Lord today, know the time in which we live and, *"Sow to yourselves in righteousness, reap in mercy; break up your fallow ground: for it is time to seek the Lord, till he come and rain righteousness upon you"* (Hosea 10:12).

"Pride Goeth Before Destruction"
Proverbs 16:18

DAY 22

Pride is the original sin. It is the sin that causes man the most trouble and the Scriptures are full of admonitions for us to not be proud, but to *"humble [ourselves] in the sight of the Lord"* (James 4:10). Obadiah 3 says, *"The pride of thine heart hath deceived thee."* Pride deceives us. It's too easy for us to get caught up in pride or be proud of something or someone. We must be careful and know that, as it states in Proverbs 6:16-17, *"16These six things doth the Lord hate: yea, seven are an abomination unto him: 17A proud look, a lying tongue, and hands that shed innocent blood."* In II Timothy 3:2, speaking of the last days, Paul says, *"Men shall be lovers of their own selves, covetous, boasters, proud."* This is one of the end time manifestations of satan and of the world as it grows closer and closer into darkness and evil.

Pride is a terrible thing. It separates us from God and from people and causes us to make fools of ourselves. *"In the mouth of the foolish,"* Proverbs 14:3 says, *"is a rod of pride."* It's foolish to be proud. It's foolish to be petty. It's foolish to hold grudges, to remain bitter, to think you're right and everybody else is wrong. This is not the will of God for us. I John 2:16 says, *"For all that is in the world, the lust of the flesh, and the lust of the eyes, and the pride of life, is not of the Father, but is of the world."* Pride is of the world. It manifests the things of the flesh and is not of the Father. The sweetest, most humble, loving, meek, and lowly person in the universe is Jesus. God cannot and will not use prideful people, as He says in I Peter 5:5, *"God resisteth the proud, and giveth grace to the humble."*

We must fight to stay free from pride. The Bible is very clear concerning this. It says in Proverbs 16:5, *"Every one that is proud in heart is an abomination to the Lord."* We must learn to humble ourselves. Jesus said, *"Take my yoke upon you, and learn of me; for I am meek and lowly in heart"* (Matthew 11:29). If we're going to be like Jesus, then pride will not be a characteristic found in our lives. On the contrary, we will be *"meek and lowly in heart."*

Pride destroys, divides, hurts, and separates. Pride is a sin, and God wants nothing to do with it. He resists it. And if we be found in pride, then God will be resisting us. So whatever has happened, no matter what the cause, there is not reason for us to be proud and haughty. We must *"be clothed with humility"* (I Peter 5:5). God, help us today to take the low seat and not be ambitious or proud or seek to be above others. Help us not to use our liberty for an occasion to the flesh, but help us seek to be lowly and humble in heart. Moses was the meekest man on the face of the earth; look how God used him. God will use you us if we'll fight the pride of life that comes from the world that tries to register in every one of our lives.

Humility is the key. The way up is down. God wants us to be free from this horrible affliction called pride. The only way to be delivered from it is to humble ourselves whenever it tries to raise its ugly head. James 4:10 tells us, *"Humble yourselves in the sight of the Lord, and he shall lift you up."* All we need to do is bow down to the Lord, give Him the situations and circumstances of our lives, and not allow bitterness and pride to find root in our lives. It will only bring destruction and chaos. It brought satan, or lucifer, down and it will bring us down. Let us seek to be like Jesus today. Let us seek to be like Moses and others who walked in humility with a tender heart, lowliness of mind, serving one another, helping one another, having a sweet spirit, staying sweet and low, never boasting, always seeking reconciliation, and always walking in humility. This is God's way. This is God's answer.

"Pride goeth before destruction, and a haughty spirit before a fall" (Proverbs 16:18). Don't let there be destruction in your life. Don't be destroyed because you refuse to bow. God called His people *"stiff-necked"* and *"uncircumcised"* in heart many times (Exodus 32:9, Leviticus 26:41), and Stephen said the same thing in Acts 7:51. How horrible it must be to be stiff-necked and hardened in our hearts and never walk in humility or see people through loving, gentle eyes.

So today, may God help us to not walk in pride, but to abase ourselves before Him in everything. Pray, "Lord Jesus, I humble myself in your sight. I want to be like you. I want your character in my life."

"Thou Knowest Me"
Psalms 139:2

Day 23

The Bible is very clear, when it says Jesus is the *"author and finisher of our faith"* (Hebrews 12:2). He knows *"the end from the beginning"* (Isaiah 46:10). Our precious Father knows everything about us, even the whispers of our hearts. He knows what we want before we even ask Him. There is nothing about us that He doesn't know.

Jesus said in Luke 14, *"For which of you, intending to build a tower, sitteth not down first, and counteth the cost, whether he have sufficient to finish it"* (Luke 14:28)? Our precious Savior counted the cost before He came into our lives. He knew everything that we would ever do, every sin we would ever commit, and yet He still came. It says in I Corinthians 11, *"...the Lord Jesus the same night in which he was betrayed took bread"* (I Corinthians 11:23). Jesus, knowing that the disciples would betray and leave Him, made a covenant with them beforehand. This means to us, *"If we believe not, yet he abideth faithful: he cannot deny himself"* (II Timothy 2:13). Our faithful God, who knows everything about us, is never deterred or upset. He sees our end from the beginning; He sees what we shall be, not what we are.

We need to be encouraged today. The Lord knows everything about us. He told Jeremiah, *"Before I formed thee in the belly I knew thee"* (Jeremiah 1:5). Before we were even formed in our mother's womb, Almighty God knew everything about us. Hebrews 4:13 tells us, *"All things are naked and opened unto the eyes of him with whom we have to do."* The book of Matthew says, *"There is nothing covered, that shall not be revealed; and hid, that shall not be known"* (Matthew 10:26).

We need to understand that, knowing all this, our God loves us. He loves us in spite of what our present condition may be. Do not give up hope and be dragged down by your weaknesses. There's no need to feel condemned and guilty. Hear the Word of the Lord in Psalms 139:

> *"¹O Lord, thou hast searched me, and known me. ²Thou knowest my downsitting and mine uprising, thou understandest my thought afar off. ³Thou compassest my path and my lying down, and art acquainted with all my ways. ⁴For there is not a word in my tongue, but, lo, O Lord, thou knowest it altogether. ⁵Thou hast beset me behind and before, and laid thine hand upon me. ⁶Such knowledge is too wonderful for me; it is high, I cannot attain unto it. ⁷Whither shall I go from thy spirit? or whither shall I flee from thy presence? ⁸If I ascend up into heaven, thou art there: if I make my bed in hell, behold, thou art there. ⁹If I take the wings of the morning, and dwell in the uttermost parts of the sea; ¹⁰Even there shall thy hand lead me, and thy right hand shall hold me. ¹¹If I say, Surely the darkness shall cover me; even the night*

> *shall be light about me. ¹²Yea, the darkness hideth not from thee; but the night shineth as the day: the darkness and the light are both alike to thee. ¹³For thou hast possessed my reins: thou hast covered me in my mother's womb"* (Psalms 139:1-13).

What a tremendous truth! It continues to say:

> *"¹⁵My substance was not hid from thee, when I was made in secret, and curiously wrought in the lowest parts of the earth. ¹⁶Thine eyes did see my substance, yet being unperfect; and in thy book all my members were written, which in continuance were fashioned, when as yet there was none of them"* (Psalms 139:15-16).

He saw our "*substance*", and sees it now, "*yet being unperfect.*" In His book it says, all your members were fashioned, when as yet there were none of them. He knows everything about us; He knew everything we would ever do, and He still loves us in spite of it. He is convinced that we will be fashioned.

All we need to do is continue. We continue to get up, dust ourselves off, repent, and go on with God. Jesus tells us in John 8, "*³¹...If ye continue in my word, then are ye my disciples indeed; ³²And ye shall know the truth, and the truth shall make you free*" (John 8:31-32).

"His Father Called Him Benjamin"
Genesis 35:18

DAY 24

This is the story of Rachel dying while giving birth to Jacob's last son, Benjamin. God had just been visiting Jacob again and spoke to him in Genesis 35:11 saying, *"A nation and a company of nations shall be of thee, and kings shall come out of thy loins."* God was speaking great promises to him. The story continues on:

> *"¹⁵And Jacob called the name of the place where God spake with him, Bethel. ¹⁶And they journeyed from Bethel; and there was but a little way to come to Ephrath: and Rachel travailed, and she had hard labour. ¹⁷And it came to pass, when she was in hard labour, that the midwife said unto her, Fear not; thou shalt have this son also. ¹⁸And it came to pass, as her soul was in departing, (for she died) that she called his name Ben-oni: but his father called him Benjamin."* (Genesis 35:15-18)

The word *"Ben-oni"* means "son of my sorrow, son of my pain." This was painful for Rachel, so she named this son after her own situation. Many times we name the situation we're in after our own pain and sorrows, while however, God has another name for it.

Jacob is a type and shadow of the body of Christ. Rachel's hard labour and travail to bring forth that last son speaks of the last day sons of God being birthed out of a great time of travail according to the promise of the Lord that kings will come out of the loins of the body of Christ.

Although Rachel, not knowing or believing that promise, neither having ever heard of it, spoke out of her own despair in her situation which we do as well many times. But when Jacob came upon it, he said, *"You will not call my son Ben-oni."* But he called him *"Benjamin,"* which means in the Hebrew "son of my right hand, son of my old age." This speaks to us of a company of overcomers who are going to come forth in the last days; a Benjamin company who are the sons of the right hand.

Psalms 45:9 tells us, *"Kings' daughters were among thy honourable women: upon thy right hand did stand the queen in gold of Ophir."* The queen is the bride. The queen in gold of Ophir stands at the right hand of her Husband. This is the bride of Christ; this is the overcomers; this is the son of the right hand. They will sit at the right hand of Jesus. Jesus sits at the right hand of the Father and the Holy Ghost at His left, but somebody needs to be on the right hand of Jesus. That place is reserved for the Benjamin company, the son of His old age. This is a mature group of people who have come forth and been matured and processed in the dealings of God to where they are of full age, having been perfected. Though they may have started out with a name like Ben-oni, son of pain and sorrows, they shall become the sons of the right hand, the sons of old age.

"Is Not My Help In Me"
Job 6:13

DAY 25

As believers, you and I have an enduring and wonderful witness inside of us that is independent of our own minds, of the world, of the flesh and independent of the devil. This witness is the Spirit of the living God. Job says here in Job 6:13, *"Is not my help in me?"* This is a tremendous truth for you and me, because we need not go any further than our own spirit to find the help that we need. Our help is in us!

I John 5:10 says, *"He that believeth on the Son of God hath the witness in himself."* That means the witness is in us. This is the same witness that Elizabeth found when she was greeted by Mary and the babe lept in her womb (Luke 1:41). There is a babe that will leap in our womb that will release peace (or lack of peace) to let us know what is of God or not of God. *"Out of his belly shall flow rivers of living water"* (John 7:38) and as Micah 3:8 tells us *"truly I am full of power by the spirit of the Lord."* All of this is found within us, within our human spirit.

In I John 2:20, it says, *"Ye have an unction from the Holy One, and ye know all things."* We have an unction and we need to let it function. We need to allow the Spirit within us to be released to flow over our minds, through our bodies to give us the strength, power, deliverance, encouragement and guidance that we need. I John 4:4 tells us that, *"greater is he that is in you, than he that is in the world."* What a tremendous revelation that within us is the greater One, the powerful One, the Almighty God! When we receive the Lord Jesus as our Savior we receive, Emmanuel, which means "God with us".

Is not my help in me? The answer is yes and we need not look any further than our own spirit to receive the help and encouragement that we need. I John 2:27 tells us *"the anointing which ye have received of him abideth in you, and ye need not that any man teach you."* It's not that we don't need the five-fold ministry to teach us. It means that we don't need anyone to teach us right from wrong because the anointing within us will teach us and speak to us.

Is not my help in me? Today, consider that, as you go about your day, you have become a partaker of the divine nature. The divine nature lives within you, which is the Spirit of the living God. He is truly in you and whatever you need, all of heavens resources, is found inside your human spirit. God lives there and He will help you. I Corinthians 6:17 states, *"But he that is joined unto the Lord is one spirit."*

Proverbs tells you that *"the spirit of man is the candle of the Lord"* (Proverbs 20:27). In your spirit is the candle of the Lord, it is where God lives. Release that Spirit within you today and allow it to take precedence within you, instead of your carnal mind. You will find, truly, that your help is in you and you don't need to look further than your own human spirit today.

"Truth Is Fallen In The Street"
Isaiah 59:14

DAY 26

Here in Isaiah 59:14-15, we find a drastic and terrible revelation, *"And judgment is turned away backward, and justice standeth afar off: for truth is fallen in the street, and equity cannot enter. ¹⁵Yea, truth faileth."* We are living in a day where truth is no longer something that people like to walk in. We've come into a time of lies and deception. These are hard days.

The word *"truth"* in Hebrew means: "stability, certainty, trustworthiness, faithfulness, to build up or support, to render firm or faithful, to be trusted or believed or be permanent." This is not really what we see happening. Earlier in Isaiah 59 it says, *"None calleth for justice, nor any pleadeth for truth"* (Isaiah 59:4). What a statement! Nobody is pleading for the truth.

In Jeremiah 7:28 it says none, *"receiveth correction: truth is perished, and is cut off from their mouth."* We are living in a day when people *"are not valiant for the truth upon the earth"* (Jeremiah 9:3). God help us. In verses 5-6 it says, they *"will not speak the truth: they have taught their tongue to speak lies... Thine habitation is in the midst of deceit; through deceit they refuse to know me, saith the Lord."*

God wants us as Zechariah 8:16 says to, *"Speak ye every man the truth to his neighbor."* We are to be called *"a city of truth"* (Zechariah 8:3). Jesus said in John 8:32, *"And ye shall know the truth, and the truth shall make you free."* Truth has the ability to make us free. This is why people don't walk in it because they want to remain in bondage and don't want to *"buy the truth"* (Proverbs 23:23). We pay a price for truth.

Truth is the answer for our lives. Proverbs 16:6 says, *"By mercy and truth iniquity is purged."* And in a day when few are valiant for the truth with nobody pleading for the truth, truth then is fallen in the streets. Let us be as Philippians 2:15-16 exhorts us to be, *"The sons of God, without rebuke, in the midst of a crooked and perverse nation, among whom ye shine as lights in the world. Holding forth the word of life."* Let us walk in firmness, stability, and trustworthiness. And even though it might cost us, we will speak the truth in love and not lie. We will buy the truth and sell it not! Rise up today! Let's be men and women of truth. Let's be valiant for the truth!

"He Is A Babe"
Hebrews 5:13

Day 27

In this great passage of Scripture in Hebrews 5:13 it says, *"For every one that useth milk is unskilful in the word of righteousness: for he is a babe."*

There are five levels of growth in our Christian walk: babes, children, young men, old men, and fathers. "Babes" is the least of all of them. And I think that far too many are still babes in Christ because they are unskilful in the word of righteousness and have need of milk and not strong meat because *"strong meat belongeth to them that are of full age, even those who by reason of use have their senses exercised to discern both good and evil"* (Hebrews 5:14). Peter tells us in I Peter 2:2, *"As newborn babes, desire the sincere milk of the word, that ye may grow thereby."* The Word of God is the answer to grow us up, mature us, and give us substance as Christians, if we would give ourselves to it.

Jesus taught the Word of God daily as well as the apostles, Paul and the early church. In the Old Testament you had what was called the morning and evening sacrifice. We are to come before the Lord every day; day and night if we can. Joshua was charged by the Lord, *"This book of the law shall not depart out of thy mouth; but thou shalt meditate therein day and night..."* (Joshua 1:8). Perhaps if we did this as well, we wouldn't be a babe. Paul tells the Corinthian church:

> *"¹And I, brethren, could not speak unto you as unto spiritual, but as unto carnal, even as unto babes in Christ. ²I have fed you with milk, and not with meat: for hitherto ye were not able to bear it"* (I Corinthians 3:1-2).

Paul was calling them immature because he had to feed them with milk. In other words, they were completely dependent upon somebody else to teach them. They didn't have any substance of their own.

God wants us to be *"nourished up in the words of faith and of good doctrine"* (I Timothy 4:6). We are to *"grow in grace, and in the knowledge of our Lord and Savior Jesus Christ"* (II Peter 3:18). We are to grow from the babyhood stage into hopefully the stage of fatherhood. We do this by going from *"faith to faith"*, *"glory to glory"*, *"strength to strength"*, and so on.

Paul said, *"For when for the time ye ought to be teachers, ye have need that one teach you again"* (Hebrews 5:12). They were still babes and needed to be taught. We need to ask ourselves today, are we able to nourish ourselves and others? Or do we need others to nourish us and constantly build us up? God wants us to grow up and be able to feed ourselves and others. We don't want to always be babes in Christ, but mature sons and daughters of the Lord, so that He might trust us with the word He has invested in us, so that ultimately we can help others do the same.

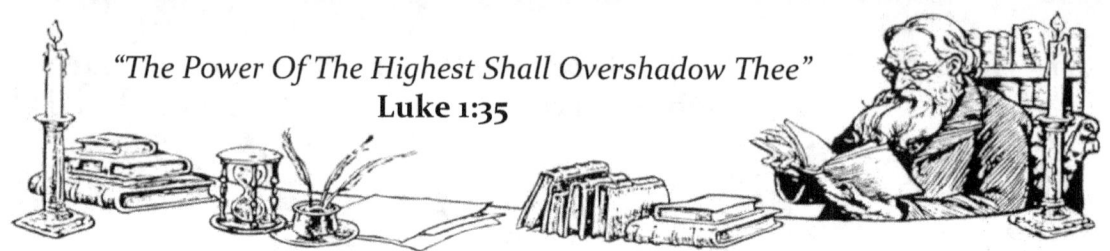

"The Power Of The Highest Shall Overshadow Thee"
Luke 1:35

Luke 1:35 says, *"The Holy Ghost shall come upon thee, and the power of the Highest shall overshadow thee: therefore also that holy thing which shall be born of thee shall be called the Son of God."* Wow, what a glorious truth and revelation found in this passage. We find such a tremendous revelation of God wanting to visit us in His glory, to *"overshadow"* us. This word *"overshadow"* in the Greek means "to envelop in a haze of brilliancy, to invest with supernatural influence, a shining cloud surrounding and enveloping persons with brightness." God wants to envelop us in a haze of brilliancy and glory. He wants to invest in us His supernatural influence.

We see this happening to Jesus in Matthew 17 when Jesus went up on the mount of transfiguration. He was transfigured before Peter, James, and John and it says while Jesus was speaking, *"a bright cloud overshadowed them: and behold a voice out of the cloud, which said, This is my beloved Son, in whom I am well pleased"* (Matthew 17:5. Jesus was enveloped in a haze of brilliancy and this is what He wants for us. And out of this cloud and glory there will be a voice always pointing us to Jesus to hear and listen to Him. It would behoove us then to walk in this overshadowing anointing.

Oh, that the power of the highest would overshadow you today; that right now He would envelop you in a haze of brilliancy and invest you with supernatural influence; that a shining cloud would surround and envelop you with brightness; so that everyone round about you would be ministered to and touched just as they were in Acts 5 by Peter's shadow when it says, *"Insomuch that they brought forth the sick into the streets, and laid them on beds and couches, that at the least the shadow of Peter passing by might overshadow some of them"* (Acts 5:15).

Peter was walking in such a haze of brilliancy and glory, that as he passed people, there was such a sphere of influence that touched, healed, and delivered them without Peter having to do anything. I believe God wants us to walk in this kind of glory, not for our benefit, but for the benefit of others; that when we walk into a room enveloped in a haze of glory, it invests us with supernatural influence and changes the temperature. This is never to bring glory to ourselves, but that Jesus may be glorified and others may sense the power and glory of God and hear His voice out of that cloud.

As that glory rests upon us, note also that there will be a holy thing born of us called the son of God. As the glory cloud rests on us, the Jesus within us is brought forth and matured. Today, submit yourself to the Lord. James 4:8 says, *"Draw nigh to God, and he will draw nigh to you."* Allow the glory of God today to descend upon you in a haze of brilliancy, power, and brightness filling you with His love, mercy, and grace. Wherever you go today, may you have the same impact that Peter had so that people will be healed and delivered.

"Therefore Michal Had No Child Unto The Day Of Her Death"
II Samuel 6:23

Day 29

Today we want to look at the story of Michal, the daughter of Saul, and how she judged David in an unrighteous way, when he danced before the Lord. David was rejoicing that the ark of God, a type of the manifest presence of God, was being brought back to Jerusalem. Michal judged David terribly as we read in II Samuel:

> "The daughter of Saul came out to meet David, and said, How glorious was the king of Israel to day, who uncovered himself to day in the eyes of the handmaids of his servants, as one of the vain fellows shamelessly uncovereth himself! ²¹And David said unto Michal, It was before the LORD." (II Samuel 6:20-21)

Michal accused David of dancing half-naked before the handmaids, acting foolishly, and uncovering him openly before them. This was certainly not the heart of David. He simply stripped himself of his kingly attire and danced with all of his might girded only with a linen ephod in response to God's glory and manifest presence coming into Jerusalem. God's glory meant everything to David. The revelation here is that in the presence of the King of Kings, there is no other king. What an example David is to all of us, especially those in leadership. But David doing a beautiful thing before the Lord and Michal's despising of it, reminds me of what Paul wrote in Titus 1:15 saying, *"Unto the pure all things are pure: but unto them that are defiled and unbelieving is nothing pure."*

The Bible says in Matthew 7:1, *"Judge not, that ye be not judged."* It is not the wisdom of God to be judging people critically. Too many times we judge after the outward appearance and we miss the mark. We don't really look for the inward heart of the situation. God does. He judges the heart (I Samuel 16:7) while most people judge after the outward appearance.

Paul said in I Corinthians 4:5, *"Judge nothing before the time."* We must be very careful about our judgments. As Jesus said in John 7:24, *"judge righteous judgment"*, meaning that we are not to judge others in an unrighteous way. The end result of this will be that we'll bear no fruit for the rest of our lives, just as it happened to Michal. How sad for a woman, who was born in this world to give birth to children, to offer to her husband that for which God gave her to him, and give him nothing! Michal suffered for the rest of her life because of this judgment.

How many times have we judged people in an unrighteous way or suspiciously? How many times have we judged a situation without knowing the facts? How many times have we judged someone without first looking into the situation or hearing both sides of the story? It is best then to hold our judgments to ourselves and not speak them into existence, especially in the way Michal did by attacking her husband.

God help us to have a soft and sensitive spirit, and a tender heart towards our brothers and sisters, even towards those in the world. God knows all of us are treated unkindly by the world, even accused daily by the devil day and night. Even more, we are also judged by our brothers and sisters; as it is well said by many that Christians are the only ones who shoot their wounded. There is nothing worse than being accused of something you didn't do, or being accused of something you would never dream of doing, even when the facts clearly show you didn't do it. Still others, because of hidden motives in their hearts, or suspicions, or simply because they decided to come against you, use words to cruelly crush and hurt you.

The word of the Lord to us today is we will bear no fruit if we judge people unjustly. May God helps us today to look with the eyes of Jesus upon everyone we come in contact with, to judge nothing before the time and wait on the Lord. Let us be patient and not judge unrighteous. Otherwise, we will end up like Michal, who judged her husband horribly and cruelly. This was certainly not the will of God.

I believe far too many of us, including myself, judge this way too often. We are not sensitive enough to the Holy Spirit leading us. We don't listen to the witness of the Holy Spirit telling us to be patient and not to say anything. Many times we speak before knowing all the facts. In Proverbs 29:11 it says, *"A fool uttereth his mind"* before hearing a matter. Let's not be fools and say something before we know the whole situation. I don't know about you, but I want to bear fruit the rest of my life. I don't want to have thorns as it says in Mark 4:18-19, or to allow those thorns to grow up, to choke and bear no fruit.

We want to bear fruit. We want to honor the Lord and glorify His name. Let's do it by simply not judging our brothers and sisters in an unrighteous way or cruelly. Matthew 7:2 reads, *"...and with what measure ye mete, it shall be measured to you again."* Let's be tender-hearted, kind, generous and loving towards others so that we always bear fruit unto the Lord!

"Four Wonderful Things"
Proverbs 30:19

In Proverbs 30:19, we find four principles from what Solomon says here:

"¹⁸There be three things which are too wonderful for me, yea, four which I know not: ¹⁹The way of an eagle in the air; the way of a serpent upon a rock; the way of a ship in the midst of the sea; and the way of a man with a maid." (Proverbs 30:19)

This obviously has natural repercussions, but I believe the Bible is a spiritual book. Therefore, this passage has great spiritual significance to us today. Four is the number of the new creation man and creation. So these four things sum up what happens in the new creation man's life. We are that new creation man being conformed to the image of Jesus Christ.

The first thing that Solomon finds too wonderful is *"the way of an eagle in the air"*. An eagle in the Scripture always speaks of the overcomer, riding upon the high places of the earth seated in heavenly places in Christ Jesus (Ephesians 2:6). *"Surely in vain the net is spread in the sight of any bird"* (Proverbs 1:17). Flying high in the heavenlies, rising up like an eagle, we are overcomers. We can see and have vision for the future; and we *"are not ignorant of the enemies devices"* (II Corinthians 2:11).

Secondly there's *"the way of a serpent upon a rock"*. This is simply Satan trying to use our flesh to control us, frustrate our purpose, and destroy us. The thing that's wonderful about it is; this new creation man sees through these schemes. He's not ignorant of his devices (II Corinthians 2:11), and he's able to deal with the serpent.

Thirdly there's *"the way of a ship in the midst of the sea"*. This speaks to us of guidance, and how even in troubled waters we can be guided by the Holy Spirit and the Word of God. In Genesis 28:15 God says, *"I am with thee, and will keep thee in all places whither thou goest."* Jesus said, *" I am with you alway, even unto the end of the world"* (Matthew 28:20). He will guide us. *"But the anointing which ye have received of him abideth in you, and ye need not that any man teach you"* (I John 2:27). We don't need anybody to guide us anymore. We simply need the Spirit of God within us. The overcomer has now learned and discerned the witness of the Spirit, because of habitual use (Hebrews 5:14).

Last, but not least it says *"the way of a man with a maid"*. Ephesians 5 tells us that the natural marriage between a man and a woman is simply a picture of the true marriage between Christ and His church. This man and His maid is Jesus and His bride. The overcomer, the new creation man, realizes that his highest calling is brideship and that the heavenly bridegroom has called him. *"For thy Maker is thine husband; the Lord of hosts is his name,"* Isaiah 54:5 tells us. The bridegroom is calling us and the overcoming, new creation man is responding.

Yes, these four things listed above are too wonderful to consider, like Solomon said. If we choose to receive these four principles today, they can be a reality to us and we can be conformed to the image of Jesus Christ.

"The God Of All Comfort"
II Corinthians 1:3-4

DAY 31

This will be one of my favorite devotionals to write, because I have experienced this revelation so many times personally. I have experienced the comfort of our wonderful, loving and precious God in every sense possible. Believe me when I say that my own personal image of God has been formed over years and years of studying the Word of God, being in His glorious presence, pastoring people, and seeing how our wonderful Father is always so near and dear in comforting His people when we need Him the most.

Paul states in II Timothy 1:12, *"I am not ashamed: for I know whom I have believed."* I have believed and seen God's hand gently helping me and countless others through the most difficult circumstances. I have heard His voice tenderly and lovingly speaking to me, as well as to others, in the hour of great need. I have watched God's people go through horrible circumstances and yet find Him and His abiding and loving presence. I have seen how Jesus, our true and great Shepherd of the sheep, carries His lambs in His arms, when necessary.

In II Corinthians 1:3-4 it states, *"Blessed be God... the Father of mercies, and the God of all comfort; ⁴who comforteth us in all our tribulation, that we may be able to comfort them which are in any trouble, by the comfort wherewith we ourselves are comforted of God."* The Greek word for *"comfort"* here means, "to call near, to give consolation, to exhort or to implore". When we need God the most, He is there calling us near. Just like when Adam and Eve sinned and hid themselves among the trees in the Garden of Eden, God came looking for Adam saying, *"Where art thou?"* (Genesis 3:9).

The Scriptures are full of admonitions that God is our God of comfort. We find this in Isaiah 40:1, where it says, *"Comfort ye, comfort ye my people, saith your God."* Isaiah 51:3 says, *"For the Lord shall comfort Zion: he will comfort all her waste places."* Psalms 94:19 says, *"Thy comforts delight my soul."* When we are going through our valley of darkness, our valley of the shadow of death, our hour of need and there is no one is there, that is when our God comes with His great and marvelous comfort. Today, perhaps everyone has left you alone. Know that Jesus was alone in John 16:32 when He says, *"Everyone... shall leave me alone: and yet I am not alone, because the Father is with me."* God the Father is always there when everyone else forsakes us.

Today, God wants to console you and exhort you. He wants you to draw near to Him. Matthew 5:4 says, *"Blessed are they that mourn: for they shall be comforted."* If you are mourning or sad today, you can rest assured that God is going to comfort you. This is the Lord we serve. Isaiah 52:9, *"Break forth into joy, sing together, ye waste places of Jerusalem: for the Lord hath comforted his people."* Also in Isaiah 51:12, God says, *"I, even I, am he that comforteth you."* He is the God of all comfort that comforts you in all of your tribulation. No matter what the trial, the valley, the wilderness, the desert or the dealing of God, He is near. He is the one that comforts you. Let Him comfort you today for that is His name, the God of all comfort.

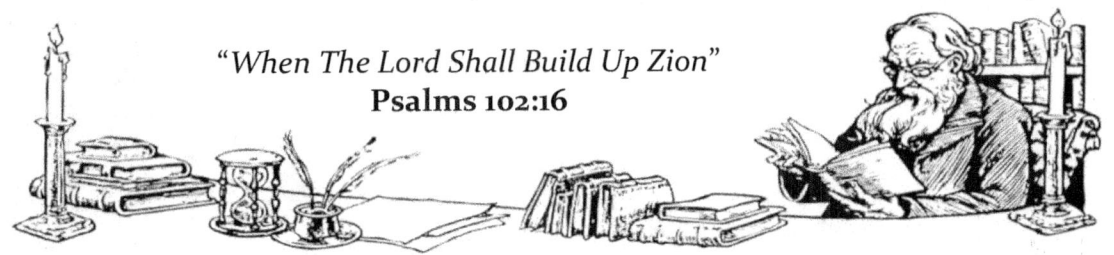

"When The Lord Shall Build Up Zion"
Psalms 102:16

DAY 32

The Bible says in Psalms 102:13, *"Thou shalt arise, and have mercy upon Zion: for the time to favour her, yea, the set time, is come"*. God is going to arise and have mercy upon Zion, because there is a time to favor her. There is a set time that only the Father knows. It continues to say in verse 16, *"When the Lord shall build up Zion, he shall appear in his glory."*

Zion is not only a mountain in Jerusalem, but it also speaks of a people and a kingdom. Most importantly, it speaks of that place in worship when we enthrone the Lord on our praises. In the deep places of worship, God comes down in His glory and rests between the cherubim upon the throne of our hearts. The Lord wants to appear in His glory out of Zion. He wants to give His glory to us. The Bible says in Isaiah 42:8, *"I am the Lord: that is my name: and my glory will I not give to another."* But He can give it to us, because we won't be another. He will give His glory to Himself, that which is in us that is of Himself, the Jesus part of us.

He wants to appear in His glory. Psalms 50:2 tells us, *"Out of Zion, the perfection of beauty, God hath shined."* It also says in Isaiah 60:1, *"Arise, shine; for thy light is come, and the glory of the Lord is risen upon thee"*. God wants to shine through His people, Zion. He wants to minister through them. The Bible declares in Isaiah 62:1, *"For Zion's sake will I not hold my peace."* He's going to come and build up Zion, because He wants the law to go forth from Zion (Micah 4:2). Not only does He want the law to go forth from Zion, but He wants His glory to shine forth from her. The book of Amos says, *"The Lord will roar from Zion"* (Amos 1:2). This is out of a people. Jeremiah 8:19 says, *"Is not the Lord in Zion? Is not her king in her?"* Yes, He is.

The book of Obadiah tells us, *"But upon mount Zion shall be deliverance, and there shall be holiness; and the house of Jacob shall possess their possessions"* (Obadiah 17). When God builds up Zion, this is what's going to happen to His people. They will possess their possessions and control their own destiny. The Bible is very clear that He's going to send the rod of His strength out of Zion (Psalms 110:2). Why? Psalms 132 says, *"For the Lord hath chosen Zion; he hath desired it for his habitation"* (Psalms 132:13). God wants to inhabit Zion. He wants His glory to inhabit it so He can shine out. He wants the world to see that His people are full of the glory. The Bible says in Isaiah 60:14, *"The sons also of them that afflicted thee shall come bending unto thee; and all they that despised thee shall bow themselves down at the soles of thy feet; and they shall call thee, The city of the Lord, The Zion of the Holy One of Israel."*

Zion will be known for being the people of God, the people that have manifested forth His glory. In Zechariah 9:9, it says, *"Rejoice greatly, O daughter of Zion; shout, O daughter of Jerusalem: behold, thy King cometh unto thee."* He's not only coming unto Zion, but He is appearing through Zion. It continues to say in Zechariah 9, *"When I have... raised up thy sons, O Zion, against thy sons, O Greece"* (Zechariah 9:13). God is raising up sons out of Zion today. Let Him *"build"* you up so He can appear in His glory.

"The Faithful God"
Deuteronomy 7:9

DAY 33

The Bible says in Deuteronomy 7:9, "*Know therefore that the Lord thy God, he is God, the faithful God, which keepeth covenant and mercy with them that love him and keep his commandments to a thousand generations.*" God is faithful. He is absolutely trustworthy and extremely loyal and reliable. He is the God that never fails, and never leaves or forsakes us (Hebrews 13:5). His Word is true. Because of this revelation, we can always depend on Him to do whatever He has said. Because He cannot lie, we can rest assured if He has said something, it will come to pass.

His faithfulness to us means He is perfectly loyal and consistently true to His name, His character, and His Word. This faithfulness is one of God's greatest moral attributes. The Hebrew word for "*faithful*" means "firmness, security, moral fidelity, stability, and trustworthiness". Some other translations of Deuteronomy 7:9 call Him "*the steadfast God*" and a "*trustworthy God.*"

Isaiah 49:7 says, "*Princes also shall worship, because of the Lord that is faithful.*" It says in I Corinthians 1:9, "*God is faithful, by whom ye were called unto the fellowship of his Son Jesus Christ our Lord.*" God is faithful, trustworthy, sure, and true. This is who He is; this is His character. One other Hebrew word for "*faithfulness*" means "to build up or support, to foster as a parent or a nurse, to be firm, to be permanent, to be true, certain, and assurance." This is who our God is!

The Bible says in I Corinthians 10:13, "*There hath no temptation taken you but such as is common to man: but God is faithful, who will not suffer you to be tempted above that ye are able.*" I Thessalonians 5:24 declares, "*Faithful is he that calleth you, who also will do it.*" God not only calls us, but He also will do the work in us. It says in II Thessalonians 3:3, "*But the Lord is faithful, who shall stablish you, and keep you from evil.*" We can depend on the trustworthiness and consistency of God to remain faithful, to establish us, and to keep us from evil.

In one of my favorite Scriptures, Paul tells us, "*If we believe not, yet he abideth faithful: he cannot deny himself*" (II Timothy 2:13). God's character is absolutely perfect; His moral integrity is absolutely tremendous. He cannot deny Himself, because if He did anything other than abide faithful, His character would be destroyed. It's who He is, the faithful God. Hebrews 2:17 says, "*Wherefore in all things it behoved him to be made like unto his brethren, that he might be a merciful and faithful high priest in things pertaining to God.*" He is the faithful God. David says in the book of Psalms 119:90, "*Thy faithfulness is unto all generations.*" Isaiah 11:5 tells us, "*Righteousness shall be the girdle of his loins, and faithfulness the girdle of his reins.*"

In Hosea 2:20 the Lord speaks to the bride, saying, "*I will even betroth thee unto me in faithfulness: and thou shalt know the Lord.*" We can remain connected to Him, because He is faithful.

Remember the story of Sarah. In Hebrews 11:11 it talks about Sara having Isaac when she was "past age", because she *"judged Him faithful who promised."* We can trust in His promise. In I Peter 4:19 it says, *"Wherefore let them that suffer according to the will of God commit the keeping of their souls to him in well doing, as unto a faithful Creator."* Revelation 19:11 tells us, *"I saw heaven opened, and behold a white horse; and he that sat upon him was called Faithful and True."*

And finally, in Lamentations 3:23, it says, *"...great is thy faithfulness."* Oh, how true. Experience it today. He is the faithful God.

"The Tongue Of The Learned"
Isaiah 50:4

DAY 34

In Isaiah 50:4 the Scripture declares, *"The Lord God hath given me the tongue of the learned, that I should know how to speak a word in season to him that is weary."* Oh what a blessing it is to receive a good word from God. *"A word fitly spoken is like apples of gold in pictures of silver"* (Proverbs 25:11). We need to learn how to speak a word in season to him that is weary. The only way to do that is to have the Lord God give you the *"tongue of the learned"*. To become the *"learned"* we must apply ourselves to the Scriptures, and we must study to show ourselves approved unto God (II Timothy 2:15). We need to be filled with the Word of God. We need to have it rooted down so deep within us that when we speak we are able to draw from a tremendous well of salvation and Word that is within us.

Jesus said that we should speak the Word of the Lord as people are able to hear it. We must be able to properly discern the word of the Lord for people's lives. This means that we must progress, in our personal lives, beyond just the cursory, elementary milk of the Word, and be able to handle and speak the meat of the Word. Hebrews 5:13-14 states, *"For every one that useth milk is unskilful in the word of righteousness: for he is a babe. But strong meat belongeth to them that are of full age, even those who by reason of use have their senses exercised to discern both good and evil."* We need discernment and the only way that we will obtain it is by fully giving ourselves to the Word of God, so that we become living epistles, known and read of all men (II Corinthians 3:2).

It was said of Jesus that no one had ever heard a man speak like Him before. That is because He only said the things that the Father was saying. We can do the same thing, as long as we make sure that we have prepared our work without and made it fit for ourselves in the field (Proverbs 24:27). This means that we have studied and filled ourselves with the Word of God so that when we speak, we speak according to the Word of the Lord and with His Words. When we simply speak the Scriptures to people, we encourage them, we bless them, and faith will arise in their hearts, because *"faith cometh by hearing, and hearing by the word of God"* (Romans 10:17).

The Bible says. *"To everything there is a season"* (Ecclesiastes 3:1). There is a season when in which we are to speak a word. We can speak a word out of season and it can be destructive, even though it may be a good word. We need to be like the children of Issachar. The Bible said they *"had understanding of the times, to know what Israel ought to do"* (I Chronicles 12:32). Do you have the tongue of the learned today? Have you studied and have you prepared? Have you laid a foundation against the time to come (I Timothy 6:19) so that when someone asks you, you are able to release a steady stream of the Word of God to them? God is looking for a people that will speak as an oracle of God, speak the Word in season and out of season to those that are weary (Isaiah 50:4). May God give you today the *"tongue of the learned"*, so that those you come in contact with will be encouraged and blessed by the words that you speak.

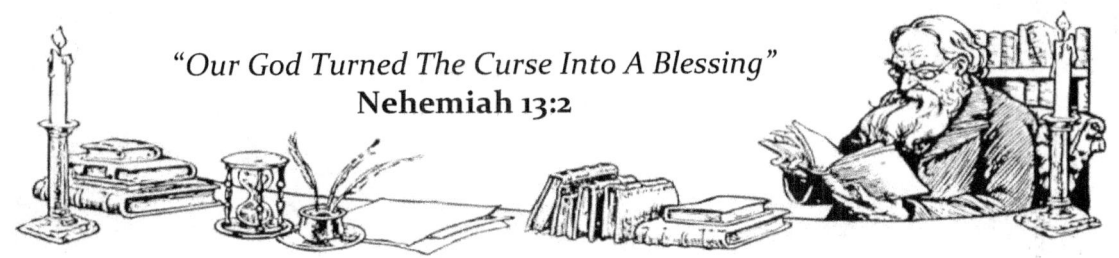

"Our God Turned The Curse Into A Blessing"
Nehemiah 13:2

DAY 35

One of the tremendous principles in Scripture is when Satan, or our enemies curses us; God is there to protect us and defend us. He *"turns the curse into a blessing"* for us. What a wonderful promise this is for us. No matter what the enemy can come up with, like Haman who wanted to destroy all of Israel and kill every Jew, God is there to protect us and defend us. The very noose that Haman prepared for the children of Israel, he was hung on himself. (Esther 5:14 - 7:10)

This is our God. He can take the evil the enemy does against us and turn it for good. The enemy may mean it for evil, but God means it for good. Never be afraid of a curse. Never be afraid of what the enemy may do because God is there to protect and keep us. In Numbers 23:7, Balak asks Balaam, *"Come, curse me Jacob, and come, defy Israel."* Balaam replies in verse 8, *"How shall I curse, whom God hath not cursed? or how shall I defy, whom the Lord hath not defied?"* Then in verse 20, he says, *"Behold, I have received commandment to bless: and he hath blessed; and I cannot reverse it."* There will be no reversing of the blessing of the Lord. No matter how hard the enemy tries to curse us, or even get prophetic ministry to curse us, God will *"[turn] the curse into a blessing."* What a blessed God we serve!

In Deuteronomy 23:5 it says, *"Nevertheless the Lord thy God would not hearken unto Balaam; but the Lord thy God turned the curse into a blessing unto thee, because the Lord thy God loved thee."* He *"turns the curse into a blessing,"* simply because he loves us. In II Samuel 16:13, we find the story of Shimei cursing David, *"And as David and his men went by the way, Shimei went along on the hill's side over against him, and cursed as he went, and threw stones at him, and cast dust."* David says before in verse 12, *"It may be that the Lord will look on mine affliction, and that the Lord will requite me good for his cursing this day."* David received his kingdom back that day, which had been stolen by his son, Absalom. God took the cursing of Shimei and turned it into a blessing for David because he did not respond in an evil way. Likewise, we can't react to others in the flesh. We have to follow David's example for our own life, knowing deep in our hearts, that whatever curse is pronounced against us, God can and will turn that curse into a blessing.

David says in Psalms 109:26-28, *"Help me, O Lord my God: O save me according to thy mercy: ^{27}That they may know that this is thy hand; that thou, Lord, hast done it.^{28}Let them curse, but bless thou."* They may curse us, but He is going to bless us. So, today, we have to keep in remembrance that what the enemy may mean for evil, God will use for our benefit if we keep our heart right, waiting and trusting the Lord.

"A Bundle Of Myrrh Is My Wellbeloved Unto Me"
Song of Solomon 1:13

DAY 36

The Song of Solomon is the story of two lovers. Many historians and theologians have tried to say that this is the story of Solomon and one of his brides or simply a story of a young man and woman. But I don't see it that way at all. I see it as the story of the bride and the bridegroom, the Lord Jesus Christ and His precious bride. All of the natural things spoken here have revelatory interpretations. They speak of something other than themselves. They speak of spiritual truths, not natural ones.

It says in Song of Solomon 1:13, "*A bundle of myrrh is my wellbeloved unto me; he shall lie all night betwixt my breast.*" Here is such a wonderful statement full of revelation. If we can understand this, it will bring great comfort to us and help us in our relationship with our Husband to be.

First of all, we need to understand that myrrh in the Scriptures always speaks of suffering, something bitter, or bitter experiences. How can your wellbeloved be to you a bunch of bitter experiences? Well, this makes up any relationship. A relationship is made up of good times, bad times, mountains, valleys, wonderful experiences, as well as not so wonderful experiences. In the context of all of it, we grow in relationship with one another. This is how it is with the Lord and His people. We grow as we go through hard times together, having the Lord Jesus as a bundle of myrrh.

It was said to David, "*the soul of my lord shall be bound in the bundle of life with the Lord thy God*" (I Samuel 25:29). The bundle of life is the Lord Jesus. But He is also a bundle of myrrh. In John 15:20, Jesus tells us, "*Remember the word that I said unto you, The servant is not greater than his lord. If they have persecuted me, they will also persecute you.*" In another place, the Bible says, "*If we suffer, we shall also reign with him*" (II Timothy 2:12).

Suffering is part of our growth and part of the process of growing closer to the Lord. As we find later in Song of Solomon, the watchmen say to the bride, "*What is thy beloved more than another beloved, O thou fairest among women? what is thy beloved more than another beloved, that thou dost so charge us?*" (Song of Solomon 5:9), and they begin to beat her. Religious people, Pharisees, those who don't understand the deep things of God, or those who have no care to be intimate with the Lord, will always resist us and retaliate. God allows this to happen. But we must stand strong in our love relationship with the Lord. We must be like David, who said in Psalms:

> "*One thing have I desired of the Lord, that will I seek after;
> that I may dwell in the house of the Lord all the days of my
> life, to behold the beauty of the Lord, and to inquire in his
> temple*" (Psalms 27:4).

We must be like Moses, saying "*shew me now thy way, that I may know thee,*" and, "*I beseech thee, shew me thy glory*" (Exodus 33:13, 18). We must be like the apostle Paul, when he said, *"That I may know him, and the power of his resurrection, and the fellowship of his sufferings, being made conformable unto his death"* (Philippians 3:10). We need to become love slaves. We need to become closer to our Husband. Ephesians tells us that natural marriage is simply a type of the mystery of Christ and His church (Ephesians 5:32). It is symbolic of the relationship Jesus is to have with His people, which is greater than a natural relationship of marriage.

You may go through hard, bitter experiences with the Lord in your relationship with Him, but *"the trial of your faith"* is *"much more precious than of gold that perisheth"* (I Peter 1:7). These things come to us simply to make us stronger. *"Tribulation worketh patience,"* Romans 5:3 tells us. These things *"worketh for us a far more exceeding and eternal weight of glory"* (II Corinthians 4:17). It helps us to grow, not only just in knowledge, but in the ways of the Lord. We begin to know Him intimately.

So, the bride here referred to Him as her well beloved, not just beloved, but well beloved. Is He well beloved unto you? Do you love Him? Is He the pearl of great price in your life? Today, let Jesus be your well beloved. Love Him, *"For the Lord's portion is his people"* (Deuteronomy 32:9). All that God is going to get out of all that He has created is a people. Choose today to be numbered with that people.

In Song of Solomon 1:13, the bride continues to say, *"He shall lie all night betwixt my breasts."* What is between your breasts? Your heart. Oh, that the Lord would live right in the middle of our chests; that the closest thing to our hearts is the Lord Jesus. And that we love Him, worship Him, adore Him, and give Him the honor due unto His name.

He has long sought for a bride for His Son. It should be the cry of every one of our hearts to be the bride, to be His beloved. Let Him *"lie all night."* Night speaks of the difficult times, the hard places. If we have Him deep in our hearts as the great treasure of our lives, we will survive anything. *"Love never fails"* (I Corinthians 13:8). Our love for the Lord must be strong and enduring, just as His is towards us.

I pray today that as you go about your day, that you would seek to *"love the Lord thy God with all thine heart, and with all thy soul, and with all thy might"* (Deuteronomy 6:5). This is the first commandment. What is Jesus to you today? Let Him become everything to you. Let Him become your beloved, your well beloved, your only beloved, your true love, and your true husband.

"He Satisfieth The Longing Soul"
Psalms 107:9

Oh what a tremendous God we serve. He puts in us His grace so that we will run after Him. He feeds us, provides for us and blesses us every day of our lives. We can't take credit for anything in our lives. David said in Psalms 37:25, *"I have been young, and now am old; yet have I not seen the righteous forsaken, nor his seed begging bread."* He not only blesses us and ministers to us, but He satisfies us. To me, satisfaction means after I've been very hungry and longed for food; then I sit down and have a meal. Then when I've reached my limit of how much I can eat, I sit back and sigh, being fully satisfied. God wants you today to sit back and be satisfied with His goodness. Psalms 107:9 says, *"For he satisfieth the longing soul, and filleth the hungry soul with goodness."*

To those who are hungry for God and long for Him today, He will fill them with goodness. Psalms 103:5 says, that God, *"satisfieth thy mouth with good things; so that thy youth is renewed like the eagle's."* Psalms 68:19 also says, *"Blessed be the Lord, who daily loadeth us with benefits."*

I don't know why somebody tried to tell us that our God doesn't want to bless us or take care of us because it is just not true. Psalms 22:26 says, *"The meek shall eat and be satisfied."* Psalms 36:7-8 declares, *"⁷How excellent is thy lovingkindness, O God! Therefore the children of men put their trust under the shadow of thy wings. ⁸They shall be abundantly satisfied with the fatness of thy house."* Please let the Word of God fill your heart and mind today and let all negativity and lies from the enemy be cast down.

Psalms 37:18-19 says, *"¹⁸The Lord knoweth the days of the upright: and their inheritance shall be for ever. ¹⁹They shall not be ashamed in the evil time: and in the days of famine they shall be satisfied."* God's upright people have this promise, that their inheritance will never be lost. They will never be ashamed and when the days of famine come, naturally or spiritually, they shall be satisfied. Psalms 63:5 declares, *"My soul shall be satisfied as with marrow and fatness; and my mouth shall praise thee with joyful lips."* Psalms 65:4, *"Blessed is the man whom thou choosest, and causest to approach unto thee, that he may dwell in thy courts: we shall be satisfied with the goodness of thy house, even of thy holy temple."*

What a wonderful God who satisfies us. Hear the word of the Lord out of Psalms 132:13-15, *"¹³For the Lord hath chosen Zion; he hath desired it for his habitation. ¹⁴This is my rest for ever: here will I dwell; for I have desired it. ¹⁵I will abundantly bless her provision: I will satisfy her poor with bread."* This is God's promise. Psalms 145:16 says, *"Thou openest thine hand, and satisfiest the desire of every living thing."*

Oh, open your heart today. Receive from the hand of God your provision and your needs being met. As Philippians 4:19 says, *"But my God shall supply all your need according to his riches in glory by Christ Jesus."* He wants to satisfy your soul today. Let Him!

"Then David Arose"
II Samuel 12:20

Day 38

In II Samuel 12, we find David repenting after the death of the baby, which he and Bathsheba had in their sin. The Bible says that we reap what we sow. There are some things that we simply must go through because of what we've done, even though God has forgiven and released us. The Lord told David He would not lay his sin to his charge, yet there was still some reaping that had to come to pass (II Samuel 12:13-14). David here gives us a perfect example of how we're to repent and come out of the foolishness we've fallen into:

> *"Then David arose from the earth, and washed, and anointed himself, and changed his apparel, and came into the house of the Lord, and worshipped: then he came to his own house; and when he required, they set bread before him, and he did eat"* (II Samuel 12:20).

The first thing David did was arise from the earth. As the prodigal son did in Luke 15, we have to come to ourselves and realize that what we've been doing is not of the Lord. Then, we have to get up and away from the earth, the flesh, the carnal things that we've been caught up with. We arise and leave the earth.

Next, we wash ourselves. We confess our sins and faults to God. The Bible declares, *"He that covereth his sins shall not prosper: but whoso confesseth and forsaketh them shall have mercy"* (Proverbs 28:13). I John 1:9 tells us, *"If we confess our sins, he is faithful and just to forgive us our sins, and to cleanse us from all unrighteousness."* We wash ourselves in the blood of Jesus and receive our forgiveness.

Then, David anointed himself. We ask God to fill us afresh with the Holy Ghost. Ephesians 5:18 says, *"And be not drunk with wine, wherein is excess; but be filled with the Spirit."* The actual Greek here reads, "be ye continually filled." There isn't just one infilling, but many infillings. David anointed himself and went into the presence of God.

David then changed his apparel. Our clothes speak of our righteousness, what we've attained to in God, or what we're doing in God. His apparel obviously was not godly, and he needed to change. His clothes were ones of mourning and darkness. We must change our apparel and leave behind the worldly and Babylonish garments (Joshua 7:21) that keep us from God. We need to put on the fine linen of the righteousness of the saints (Revelation 19:8).

David came into the house of the Lord. How amazing it is to me, after all these years of ministry, to still see people, after they've fallen into sin, rather than running to the Lord, running from Him. They stay away from church. We must learn to run to the *"secret place of the most High"* and *"abide under the shadow of the Almighty"* (Psalms 91:1) in our time of need. Go to the house of the Lord. Don't be embarrassed. Arise and go to the house of the Lord. It's just as much your house as anybody else's. It was not built for great people, but for the sick and the needy. Jesus said in Mark 2:17, *"They that are whole have no need of the physician, but they that are sick: I came not to call the righteous, but sinners to repentance."*

While at the house of the Lord, David worshipped. In the Hebrew, this word means he fell prostrate or bowed down. We worship God by falling prostrate before Him, bowing ourselves down. Romans 12:1 says, *"I beseech you therefore, brethren, by the mercies of God, that ye present your bodies a living sacrifice, holy, acceptable unto God, which is your reasonable service."* This word *"service"* here means "worship." Are you willing, after going through this darkness and receiving the Lord's forgiveness, to bow yourself down?

It continues to say that when David came to his own house, instead of being ashamed and condemned, he went home and faced the music; he faced Michal and his friends. They set bread before him, and he did eat. In other words, he began to eat the Word of God, which would eventually restore him. John 8:32 tells us, *"And ye shall know the truth, and the truth shall make you free."*

David's actions are a picture of true, godly repentance. My prayer for you is that God will help you learn from David's example of Godly repentance and apply it to your life.

"My Heart Is Fixed"
Psalms 57:7

DAY 39

Here in this passage, David says, *"My heart is fixed, O God, my heart is fixed: I will sing and give praise"* (Psalms 57:7). He also says in Psalms 108, *"'O God, my heart is fixed; I will sing and give praise, even with my glory. ²Awake, psaltery and harp: I myself will awake early"* (Psalms 108:1-2). David's heart was fixed on praising the Lord. Is yours? Can you say, *"My heart is fixed, O God, my heart is fixed..."* Can you say, "I am determined to sing and give praise"? Psalms 33:1-3 tells us:

> *"'Rejoice in the Lord, O ye righteous: for praise is comely for the upright. ²Praise the Lord with harp: sing unto him with the psaltery and an instrument of ten strings. ³Sing unto him a new song; play skilfully with a loud noise."*

The Bible declares, *"Oh that men would praise the Lord for his goodness, and for his wonderful works to the children of men!"* (Psalms 107:8). Do we need an engraved invitation to begin to praise our God? *"O bless our God, ye people, and make the voice of his praise to be heard,"* the psalmist declares (Psalms 66:8). Perhaps for those that are dead spiritually or have not been forgiven much (Luke 7:47) or don't have a revelation of who God is, praise is difficult or uncomfortable. But for those that love the Lord with an absolute abandon and liberty, their testimony is, as it says in Psalms 34, *"'I will bless the Lord at all times: his praise shall continually be in my mouth. ²My soul shall make her boast in the Lord: the humble shall hear thereof, and be glad. ³O magnify the Lord with me, and let us exalt his name together"* (Psalms 34:2-3). I will bless the Lord at all times. It's a matter of your will. It's a matter of your choosing to do it.

Today, let's decide to give praise to God. Let's fix our hearts. Let's determine in our spirits that we're going to rejoice. We're going to worship him all the day. David said, *"Seven times a day do I praise thee because of thy righteous judgments"* (Psalms 119:164). Seven is a perfect number, a number of completion. Psalms 150 admonishes us:

> *"'Praise ye the Lord. Praise God in his sanctuary: praise him in the firmament of his power. ²Praise him for his mighty acts: praise him according to his excellent greatness. ³Praise him with the sound of the trumpet: praise him with the psaltery and harp. ⁴Praise him with the timbrel and dance: praise him with stringed instruments and organs. ⁵Praise him upon the loud cymbals: praise him upon the high sounding cymbals. ⁶Let every thing that hath breath praise the Lord. Praise ye the Lord."*

"Praise ye," that's you and me. With our hearts fixed, we declare, *"Praise ye the Lord,"* so that others may hear of it, and be glad.

"Showers Of Rain"
Zechariah 10:1

Day 40

Zechariah tells us, *"Ask ye of the Lord rain in the time of the latter rain; so the Lord shall make bright clouds, and give them showers of rain, to every one grass in the field"* (Zechariah 10:1). In the last days, God is going to have a people who will be desperate for the rain, the manifest presence of God. Their hunger for the glory will cause Him to send bright clouds and give showers of rain to the earth with a mighty move of God.

The word *"showers"* in Hebrew means "to rain violently." Psalms 72 tells us, *"He shall come down like rain upon the mown grass: as showers that water the earth"* (Psalms 72:6). Oh, when the glory falls and that manifest presence begins to rain down upon us, it'll be just like dry ground soaking up water that's bringing it life, fruit, and hope. It also says in Hosea, *"...he shall come unto us as the rain, as the latter and former rain unto the earth"* (Hosea 6:3). He shall come unto us. We're talking about the Lord Jesus Himself, His true glory and manifest presence. He shall come unto us as the rain, as the latter and former rain, which is the last move of God.

Oh, that God would put in us such a hunger for rain today. As Jesus said upon the cross, let us say, *"I thirst"* (John 19:28). He was thirsty, because, for the first time in His life, God the Father had to look away from Him. He could not look at His Son in such suffering. This was the only time that he was without that manifest presence. Oh, how thirsty He must have been. Do you thirst today? God wants to send showers of blessing, if we would simply ask Him for it. It says in Ezekiel:

> *"²⁴And I the Lord will be their God...²⁵And I will make with them a covenant of peace...²⁶And I will make them and the places round about my hill a blessing; and I will cause the shower to come down in his season; there shall be showers of blessing"* (Ezekiel 34:24-26).

God is going to come down. He's going to come unto us like the rain, the latter and former rain, the last glorious move of God is waiting, and it will be showers of blessing. The word *"blessing"* here in Hebrew means "prosperity." There will be showers of prosperity coming to us. Oh, bless the Lord. All we need to do is ask *"of the Lord rain in the time of the latter rain"* and He will give showers.

Look for the Lord to bring showers of blessing to you today. As the Bible declares to us in Hebrews, let's *"lift up the hands which hang down"* and strengthen the *"feeble knees"* no matter what circumstances we are walking through (Hebrews 12:12). If you are thirsty today, then ask Him to "rain violently" upon you, bringing life.

"The Soul Of The Wounded Crieth Out"
Job 24:12

DAY 41

One of the hardest things to understand as a believer is that even after we're saved, filled with the Holy Ghost and have a walk with God, we can still be wounded and deeply hurt. Some come to the Lord and have never been healed from the wounds of the past. Others come to the Lord and are wounded even in the house of the Lord, as Zechariah 13:6 says, *"Those with which I was wounded in the house of my friends."*

Job 24:12 says, *"Men groan from out of the city, and the soul of the wounded crieth out."* Many times all you can do when you have been wounded or hurt by someone is groan. The word *"wounded"* in Hebrew means "pierced or polluted" and it comes from a root word meaning "to bore, to dissolve". These wounds are hard to deal with and they cause us to cry out and to groan.

Are you wounded? Has someone pierced you through with words? Has someone polluted your life by some terrible wrongdoing? In Proverbs 26:22 it says, *"The words of a talebearer are as wounds, and they go down into the innermost parts of the belly."* The belly is the spirit of man, the deepest place of man. Somebody who gossips, or tells a secret that we've given them, or has betrayed us, causes wounds that go down into the deepest part of our belly (spirit). The deepest part of our being is affected by it.

Jesus was wounded in the house of His friends. This is the hard part about being a believer, to understand that people can still hurt us. The more sensitive you are, the more able you are of being hurt. This is sad but even in Babylon and in many churches within the system you find that this goes on. The Scriptures say, *"For she hath cast down many wounded: yea, many strong men have been slain by her"* (Proverbs 7:26). This strange woman here is a type of the harlot of Babylon and false doctrine. No matter how strong or how powerful you are, the words of a talebearer will go down into the innermost parts of your belly and wound you.

Wounds are deep and it takes the grace of God, the Word of God and the Spirit of God to help us and make us free. Remember the story of the parable in Luke 10:30-34: *"30A certain man went down from Jerusalem to Jericho, and fell among thieves, which stripped him of his raiment, and wounded him, and departed, leaving him half dead."* Perhaps you may come across some wounded people today, left half dead. Our job is not to be as the priest or the Levite, but as the Samaritan who *"33went to him, and bound up his wounds, pouring in oil and wine."* Oil is a type of the anointing and wine is the joy of the Holy Ghost.

Wounds can be a terrible thing. They can hinder us from a real walk with God. They can hinder us from doing what we need to do, from becoming the people God has called us to be. If you are wounded today, let the precious Holy Spirit and the Word of God minister to you. The truth shall make you free; you don't have to stay wounded. Jesus was wounded for you. It's time to receive your deliverance today. Be healed in Jesus' name!

"River Of Thy Pleasures"
Psalms 36:8

Here in the book of Psalms David says:

DAY 42

> *"How excellent is thy lovingkindness, O God! therefore the children of men put their trust under the shadow of thy wings. ⁸They shall be abundantly satisfied with the fatness of thy house; and thou shalt make them drink of the river of thy pleasures."* (Psalms 36:7-8)

You and I are to be abundantly satisfied with the prosperity and fatness of the house of God, the tabernacle of God. As we do that He will make us drink from the river of His pleasures. The Hebrew word for "*pleasures*" means "agreeable, delightful." This seems so contrary to what most of us go through, but in John 10:10 it says Jesus has "*come that they might have life, and that they might have it more abundantly.*" In the Greek it literally reads "*super abundantly*" or "*life to the fullest.*"

God wants us to drink of the river of His pleasures, not the world's pleasures. We find in Titus 3:3, that we were those that served in diverse lusts and pleasures. In II Timothy 3:4 there are those that are lovers of pleasure more than lovers of God. In Luke 8:14 it talks about the thorns that choke the Word of God. One of the things thorns represent are the pleasures of this life. We're not interested in the pleasures of this life. Like Moses in Hebrews 11:25 we chose "*rather to suffer affliction with the people of God, than to enjoy the pleasures of sin for a season.*" What we want are the pleasures of God, the river of His pleasure.

In Job 36:10-11 it says, "*¹⁰He openeth also their ear to discipline, and commandeth that they return from iniquity. ¹¹ If they obey and serve him, they shall spend their days in prosperity, and their years in pleasures.*" God wants us to spend our days in prosperity and our years in pleasures, if we will simply open our ear to Him and serve Him, and not seek for the old man and the pleasures of this life. The pleasures of this life are just for a season, just for a short time and then they're gone.

In Psalms 16:11 the Bible is very clear when it says, "*Thou wilt shew me the path of life: in thy presence is fulness of joy; at thy right hand there are pleasures for evermore.*" At His right hand there are pleasures today, and there is fullness of joy. God wants you to inherit this, and to walk in it. It's His desire that we drink from the river of His pleasures. If we simply open our ear to His instruction, we will spend our years in pleasure and in prosperity.

Delight yourself today in the fatness of God's house, in the courts of the Lord, in the presence of the living God, and in the Word of God. He says you'll be abundantly satisfied, and that He'll make you drink of the river of His pleasure. What a wonderful God we serve. Who would have ever thought that pleasure would be a word that would be encouraged in the Scriptures, but remember it's the pleasure of God not the pleasure of this world.

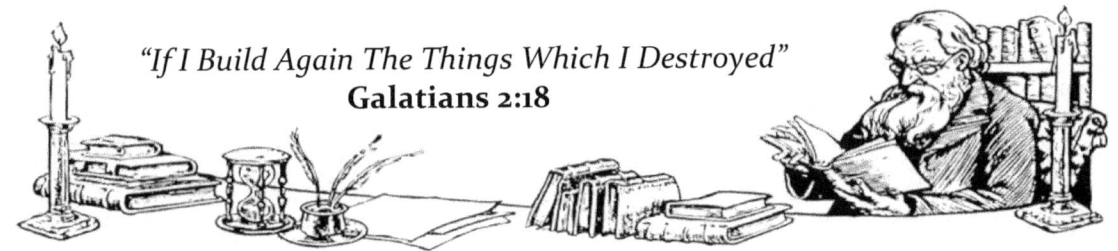

"If I Build Again The Things Which I Destroyed"
Galatians 2:18

DAY 43

In this passage of Scripture, Paul is speaking to us about continuing to live under the law after Christ Jesus has set us free. He says also to the Galatians:

> *"O foolish Galatians, who hath bewitched you, that ye should not obey the truth, before whose eyes Jesus Christ hath been evidently set forth, crucified among you? ²This only would I learn of you, Received ye the Spirit by the works of the law, or by the hearing of faith? ³Are you so foolish? Having begun in the Spirit, are ye now made perfect by the flesh? ⁴Have ye suffered so many things in vain? If it be yet in vain."* (Galatians 3:1-4)

How terrible it is to be delivered from the torment of the law and yet to allow ourselves to be brought back under it? This is what Paul is saying in verse 18 of Galatians 2, *"For if I build again the things which I destroyed, I make myself a transgressor."* Verses 19-20 continue, *"¹⁹For I through the law am dead to the law, that I might live unto God. ²⁰I am crucified with Christ: nevertheless I live; yet not I, but Christ liveth in me."* This is God's will for our lives, that we live free from the torment of the do's and do not's of the law.

In recent years, there has been a great emphasis on going back to our Jewish roots and rediscovering things out of the Jewish culture. While this is wonderful and can very much be a blessing, and can be historically enlightening, the truth is that God divorced himself from the Jewish nation because they were stiff-necked and uncircumcised in heart. They did not obey Him. They were willing to stay with the rules and regulations. They have hung on to those laws and have rejected the Messiah, who came to deliver the entire world. The law was simply a schoolmaster to bring us to Christ. Romans 10:4 states, *"For Christ is the end of the law for righteousness to every one that believeth."* Jesus put an end to it in His sacrifice, so that Jews and Gentiles can all live free now without the restrictions placed on them by the law.

If we build again those things which were destroyed, we make ourselves a transgressor. We are supposed to be dead to the law. So why would we allow ourselves to be brought back under bondage under the law? Colossians states:

> *"And you, being dead in your sins, and the uncircumcision of your flesh, hath he quickened together with him, having forgiven you all trespasses; ¹⁴Blotting out the handwriting of ordinances that was against us, which was contrary to us, and took it out of the way, nailing it to the cross...Let no man therefore judge you in meat, or in drink, or in respect of an holyday, or of the new moon, or of the*

> *Sabbath days: ⁱ⁷Which are a shadow of things to come; but the body is of Christ."* (Colossians 2:13-14, 16-17)

This is the problem. When we embrace the law, we allow ourselves to be put under the condemnation that comes from the "do's and don'ts" of the law and try to do good. However the law already proved we were incapable of doing so. We needed a savior then; we need a savior now and we will need a savior still. Paul goes on to say:

> *"Wherefore if ye be dead with Christ from the rudiments of the world, why, as though living in the world, are ye subject to ordinances, ²¹(Touch not; taste not; handle not; ²²Which all are to perish with the using;) after the commandments and doctrines of men?"* (Col. 2:20-22)

May the Lord help you today to no longer live under the law or the religious principles that Pharisaical people like to place upon you and me. Human beings are already used to guilt.

We almost don't need the enemy, the devil, because we are already good enough at condemning ourselves and feeling guilty. Jesus came that he might fulfill the works of the law and to take away the bondage of the law and the "Thou shalt not's." How many times in the Scriptures did Jesus say, "It was said unto you, but I say unto you...?" (Matthew 5-6). Our Jewish Messiah Jesus came not to bring us back under the law, but to deliver us from it and to set us free from condemnation and guilt.

So I ask you, why build again the things which have been destroyed? Stop building the things which have been destroyed. Stop living under the law. Stop living under guilt and condemnation. Stop forcing yourself to try to walk out in your flesh the things that you cannot do. There was only one sinless man, Jesus Christ. And as II Corinthians 5:21 states, *"For he hath made him to be sin for us, who knew no sin; that we might be made the righteousness of God in Him."* He became sin itself, that you and I could have the righteousness of God and have right standing with our Savior, God our Father.

I beg of you today, consider what Paul is saying. Who hath bewitched you, that you should not obey the truth? Did you receive the Spirit by works? Did you receive Jesus by the works of the law? Romans 3:20 says, *"by the deeds of the law there shall no flesh be justified in his sight."* We can never be justified by the law. We can only be justified through the grace of Jesus Christ.

Stop building the things which were destroyed. Stop making yourself a transgressor. Live free! *"If the Son therefore shall make you free, ye shall be free indeed,"* John 8:36 states. Jesus came that you might have liberty. He came that you might have life, and that more abundantly (John 10:10). Begin to live it today. Rejoice in your freedom. Praise God for His goodness and His deliverance. We are free by the grace of God!

"The Baptism Of The Holy Ghost"
Luke 24:49

DAY 44

In Luke 24:49 Jesus says, "*And, behold, I send the promise of my Father upon you: but tarry ye in the city of Jerusalem, until ye be endued with power from on high.*" Joel 2:28 says, "*And it shall come to pass afterward, that I will pour out my spirit upon all flesh; and your sons and your daughters shall prophesy...*" Acts 1:4 says, "*And, being assembled together with them, commanded them that they should not depart from Jerusalem, but wait for the promise of the Father, which, saith he, ye have heard of me.*" In Acts 1:8 Jesus says, "*But ye shall receive power, after that the Holy Ghost is come upon you: and ye shall be witnesses unto me both in Jerusalem, and in all Judaea, and in Samaria, and unto the uttermost part of the earth.*" The word "power" is the Greek word "*dunamis*" which means the miracle force, mighty power. You shall receive power after the Holy Spirit has come upon you.

I want us to look at every single Scripture where the baptism in the Holy Ghost took place. We see in the book of Acts:

> "*¹And when the day of Pentecost was fully come, they were all with one accord in one place. ²And suddenly there came a sound from heaven as of a rushing mighty wind, and it filled all the house where they were sitting. ³And there appeared unto them cloven tongues like as of fire, and it sat upon each of them. ⁴And they were all filled with the Holy Ghost, and began to speak with other tongues, as the Spirit gave them utterance*" (Acts 2:1-4).

This is the promise of the Father coming to pass. In Acts 10, Peter was asked by a man named Cornelius, an Italian man, to come to his house and preach the gospel. Peter had a great debate on whether he should go or not, but he finally went when God told him not to call unclean what He had made holy (Acts 10:28). The account reads:

> "⁴⁴*While Peter yet spake these words, the Holy Ghost fell on all them which heard the word. ⁴⁵And they of the circumcision which believed were astonished, as many as came with Peter, because that on the Gentiles also was poured out the gift of the Holy Ghost. ⁴⁶For they heard them speak with tongues, and magnify God...*" (Acts 10:44-46)

This is the baptism of the Holy Ghost bringing the Gentiles in. Then, in Acts 19, Paul traveling to Ephesus said to some disciples of John there, "*Have ye received the Holy Ghost since ye believed? And they said unto him, we have not so much as heard whether there be any Holy Ghost*" (Acts 19:2). Paul proceeds to lay hands on them and pray for them and they spoke in tongues and prophesied (Acts 19:6).

In Acts 8, showing that the baptism is a second experience to salvation, Phillip went down to Samaria preaching the Kingdom of God. It says, "*But when they believed*

Philip preaching the things concerning the kingdom of God, and the name of Jesus Christ, they were baptized, both men and women." It continues saying:

> "*¹⁴Now when the apostles which were at Jerusalem heard that Samaria had received the word of God, they sent unto them Peter and John: ¹⁵Who, when they were come down, prayed for them, that they might receive the Holy Ghost: ¹⁶(For as yet he was fallen upon none of them: only they were baptized in the name of the Lord Jesus.) ¹⁷Then laid they their hands on them, and they received the Holy Ghost.*" (Acts 8:14-17)

There is the baptism in the Holy Ghost. Now, the magician, Simon, saw that the baptism of the Holy Ghost had been given to them and saw them speaking in tongues. Because of that, he asked the apostles to be granted the same power to do what they were doing. Peter told him, "*Thy money perish with thee...*" (Acts 8:20) What Simon saw was people speaking in tongues.

Then, in Acts 9 we know the story of Paul on the road to Damascus, who gets saved and then Ananias prays for him, where he receives the Holy Ghost. It says scales fell off his eyes (Acts 9:18). Many people have wondered what happened to him; well, in I Corinthians 14:18 Paul says, "*I thank my God, I speak with tongues more than ye all.*" This means he spoke in tongues.

So, it is very clear to me that the baptism in the Holy Ghost is a second experience to salvation, but also, speaking in tongues is the evidence of this baptism. If you don't have it, receive the promise of the Father today.

"Give Me Children, Or Else I Die"
Genesis 30:1

In this hour in the body of Christ where we have seeker friendly churches, mega churches and this idea that big is God and where gain is being preached, I want to bring to you a contrary word, a word of caution and a true Scriptural principle that little is much when God is in it. We shouldn't despise the day of small things, or as Job 8:7 says, *"Though thy beginning was small, yet thy latter end should greatly increased."* Then as Jesus said in Luke 16:10, *"He that is faithful in that which is least is faithful also in much."* God watches how we react and how we handle the little things in life.

Here in Genesis 30:1 it says, *"And when Rachel saw that she bare Jacob no children, Rachel envied her sister; and said unto Jacob, Give me children, or else I die."* Rachel is a type of the local church or the church of Jesus Christ that is envious of Babylon that seems to be overflowing with people, overflowing with seeker-friendly churches and with mega churches, and are not content with the amount of people God has given them. God will give you as much as you can handle. Big is not God. Having a mega church, or having a multi-faceted, big-numbered church is not always the will of God.

Jesus is our example. By the time He went to the cross, He had nobody left walking with Him. When He was on the earth, He had about seventy people that followed Him wherever He went. So His church numbered about seventy. I've been a pastor for many, many years and I, like Rachel, have said *"Give me children, or else I die."* The real reason was envy or pride in me because I was embarrassed my church wasn't big enough and didn't have a lot of people.

We can apply this story to our personal lives when we look at the smallness of things in our lives. If we don't have lots of money in the bank or have a nice car or fancy clothes, then perhaps we feel we aren't spiritual enough or we haven't attained. This is nonsense. Paul says in I Timothy 6:5 of those with corrupt minds, *"supposing that gain is godliness."* Paul continues and says in verse 6, *"But godliness with contentment is great gain."* Moreover Paul says in Hebrews 13:5, *"Let your conversation be without covetousness; and be content with such things as ye have: for he hath said, I will never leave thee, nor forsake thee."*

We find this story amplified in I Samuel 1 when Hannah was tormented by the other wife of Elkanah, her husband, because she could not bear children. The other wife of Elkanah, whose name was Peninnah, *"⁶provoked her sore, for to make her fret."* Other pastors of churches may provoke us. Peninnah provoked Hannah. Why? Because the Lord had shut up Hannah's womb. Hannah was in great travail over this and wept and wept.

Are you weeping or are you fretting? Do you think that you are not spiritual enough? Do you think that you haven't done what was right? Years ago, the Lord spoke to me when I was going through the same thing. He spoke these words to me out of I Samuel 1:8. Elkanah, Hannah's husband, is a type of Jesus in this story. *"Then said Elkanah her husband to her, Hannah, why weepest thou? And why eatest thou not? And why is thy heart grieved? Am not I better to thee than ten sons?"* The Lord spoke to me and said, "Am I not better to thee than a multitude of people? Be faithful with what you have, son, and I will bless it." Let's not cry like Rachel, *"Give me children, or else I die."* Let's determine to be faithful in the least, and not despise the day of small things. Let's hold on and believe Job 8:7, *"Though thy beginning was small, yet thy latter end should greatly increase."*

"Shepherd Kings"
Jeremiah 23:4

DAY 46

In the last days we have a promise from God in Jeremiah 23:4, it says, *"And I will set up shepherds over them which shall feed them: and they shall fear no more, nor be dismayed neither shall they be lacking, saith the Lord"*. Jesus in Mark 6:34 had compassion of people because they are as sheep having no shepherd. The earth is in need of leadership today, not only leadership, but people and men of women of God with authority. I want us to consider this principal of Shepherd Kings as is found in the scriptures.

As far as I can see, there are four shepherd kings in the Bible: Moses, David, The Lord Jesus Christ, and those last-day pastors that God is raising up. All of them will be shepherds who have pastors' hearts, but also will have kingly authority to do the will of God. We find Moses in Exodus 3:1, was tending the flocks of his father-in-law. *"Now Moses kept the flock of Jethro his father in law, the priest of Midian: and he led the flock to the backside of the desert, and came to the mountain of God, even to Horeb"*. It was during that time when the Lord appeared to him sending him to Egypt to bring God's people out of the land. Then Moses left his shepherding and became the leader of the people of Israel. He was commander-in-chief of all the armies of Israel and king in Jeshurun. We read this in Deuteronomy 33:5, *"And he was king in Jeshurun, when the heads of the people and the tribes of Israel were gathered together"*. He was first a shepherd, then a king.

It was the same with David. He was a shepherd boy in Israel (I Samuel 16:11-13). It was David who wrote the Shepherd Psalm, and who in turn called upon the Lord to be his shepherd. Psalms 23:1 *"The Lord is my Shepherd, I shall not want."* God spoke to David, but he was rebuking him over his affair with Bathsheba and said in II Samuel 7:8 *"Thus saith the Lord of hosts, I took thee from the sheepcote, from following the sheep, to be ruler over my people, over Israel."* David, a shepherd, following the sheep, became Israel's most powerful king. He was first a shepherd, then a king.

In John 10:11 we hear Jesus speaking: *"I am the good shepherd: the good shepherd giveth his life for the sheep"*. Jesus is the shepherd of mankind, the shepherd of the people. Hebrews 13:20 speaks of that great shepherd of the sheep. He is also called in I Peter 2:25 the Shepherd and Bishop of our souls. I Peter 5:4 *"And when the chief Shepherd shall appear, ye shall receive a crown of glory that fadeth not away"*. At the end of the present age, Jesus will lay down the shepherd's crook and assume the scepter of the king for He is King of kings and Lord of lords, as it says in Revelation 17:14. Thus He is first a shepherd, then a king.

Lastly, as we saw in Jeremiah 23:4 that God is going to rise up shepherds over His people. In Ecclesiastes 12:11 it says, *"The words of the wise are as goads, and as nails fastened by the masters of assemblies, which are given from one shepherd."* He says that I will rise up pastors over them according to my heart. God is going to give shepherds to the people of the last days that will truly care for them. They will also have kingly authority to rule and reign, not only in the spirit realm, but here on earth; first a shepherd, then a king. Today be a shepherd and then a king.

"What God Leaves"
Zephaniah 3:12-13

DAY 47

In Zephaniah 3, we find this tremendous, prophetic passage: "*I will also leave in the midst of thee an afflicted and poor people, and they shall trust in the name of the Lord. ¹³The remnant of Israel shall not do iniquity, nor speak lies; neither shall a deceitful tongue be found in their mouth: for they shall feed and lie down, and none shall make them afraid*" (Zephaniah 3:12-13).

God is bringing forth a people. He's going to leave in the midst of the body of Christ an afflicted and poor people. Let's understand what this means. The word "*afflicted*" in the Greek simply means "humble" and the word "*poor*" is not speaking of natural poverty. Jesus said in Matthew 5, "*Blessed are the poor in spirit: for theirs is the kingdom of heaven*" (Matthew 5:3). If there ever was a time of need for humility in the body of Christ, it's now. There's so much arrogance of people professing their own greatness. There is so much self being taught. This is not the Lord; it's not the character of our God.

Jesus said in Matthew 11:28-29, "*²⁸Come unto me, all ye that labour and are heavy laden, and I will give you rest. ²⁹Take my yoke upon you, and learn of me; for I am meek and lowly in heart*". The character of Jesus is meekness and humility. So, if we're going to be in His image, then meekness and humility must be the character that we manifest. God is going to have a humble and meek people, a people that are not proud or arrogant, but rather a people who radiate the character and humility of the Lord Jesus. And because of that, "*they shall trust in the name of the Lord.*" Remember that a name reveals one's character. This company of people, this remnant in the midst of the body of Christ, will learn to trust in the character of their God.

This passage then goes on to say, "*The remnant of Israel.*" Remember, we are spiritual Israel, and this is a prophetic passage. They "*shall not do iniquity.*" Thank God there will be a time when we will overcome sin completely in our lives by the grace of God. We've been delivered from the penalty of sin; we're being delivered from the power of sin; eventually, we will be delivered from the very presence of sin (II Corinthians 1:10). The sanctification process is ridding the remnant of iniquity.

It continues to say that they will not speak lies, "*neither shall a deceitful tongue be found in their mouth.*" We will not be double minded; we will not say one thing and do another. The book of I John tells us, "*He that saith he abideth in him ought himself also so to walk, even as he walked*" (I John 2:6). We find in Revelation 14, that the one hundred forty-four thousand, which is a type of the overcoming army or the remnant, have no guile in their mouth (Revelation 14:5). There was no deceit in Jesus' mouth either (Isaiah 53:9). If we are to be like Him, lying and deceiving will no longer come through our mouths.

And finally, this remnant will "*feed and lie down, and none shall make them afraid.*" We will be able to come and eat out of the Word of God, drink from the wonderful Spirit of God, and rest in Him. And none: no demon, person, or thing shall make us afraid. What a picture of what God is leaving in the earth in these last days!

"I Will Not Go Out Free"
Exodus 21:5

This powerful story in the book of Exodus speaks of a Hebrew slave who after serving his time is now free to make his own choice and leave his master. This is a wonderful picture of us and our relationship with the Lord. I pray that as we read this today, our response will be the same as this Hebrew slave:

> *"²If thou buy an Hebrew servant, six years he shall serve: and in the seventh he shall go out free for nothing...if the servant shall plainly say, I love my master, my wife, and my children; I will not go out free: ⁶Then his master shall bring him unto the judges; he shall also bring him to the door, or unto the door post; and his master shall bore his ear through with an awl; and he shall serve him for ever."* (Exodus 21:2-6)

This needs to be the testimony of our lives, that even though we are free to do anything, we must not use our *"liberty for an occasion to the flesh"* (Galatians 5:13). The reason we don't is because we love our master. This slave says, *"I love my master. I will not go out free."*

There is much talk about us being free, such as John 8:36, *"If the Son therefore shall make you free, ye shall be free indeed."* This assuredly is true. But although we are free, we are still yoked unto the Lord. As a matter of fact, Paul calls us *"true yokefellow"* in Philippians 4:3. Jesus said in Matthew 11:29-30, *"Take my yoke upon you, and learn of me...For my yoke is easy, and my burden is light."* Even though the yoke may be easy and His burden is light, it is still a yoke. We are His servants and He is our master.

We need to plainly say, *"I love my master. I will not go out free."* We need to tell Jesus we don't want what the world has and we don't want what life can offer us. We have found the pearl of great price. We have found the joy of our lives in Jesus and walking with Him. In Song of Solomon 7:10 it says, *"I am my beloved's, and his desire is toward me."* His desire is toward us today.

Walking with Him, we have found that there is no greater master to serve than Him. *"For all that is in the world, the lust of the flesh, and the lust of the eyes, and the pride of life, is not of the Father, but is of the world,"* I John 2:16 says. Everything in the world can never compare to the glory, greatness, beauty and magnificence of our God. Paul says in I Corinthians 9:19, *"For though I be free from all men, yet have I made myself servant unto all."* We are free. We can do what we want, but we choose this day the Lord our God. We choose this day Him to serve.

Let Him take you today to the door, that heavenly, open door and bore through your ear with an awl that signifies that you belong to Him. You are His servant and He is your master forever. You will not hear the voice of the world calling. Your ears will always be open to hear only His voice.

"Give Me This Mountain"
Joshua 14:12

DAY 49

In Joshua 14 is the story of Caleb's great declaration of faith, when he stood and asked for the land that Moses had promised him. Caleb says here in Joshua 14:12, *"Now therefore give me this mountain, whereof the Lord spake in that day; for thou heardest in that day how the Anakims were there, and that the cities were great and fenced: if so be the Lord will be with me, then I shall be able to drive them out, as the Lord said."*

Caleb was eighty-five years old when this took place. Eighty is the number that means fulfilled life, and five is the number for grace. He had lived a fulfilled life of grace.

Forty five years earlier, only Caleb and Joshua had faith to go into the promised land, despite the Anakims, or the giants, being there. It says in Numbers 13:30, *"And Caleb stilled the people before Moses, and said, Let us go up at once, and possess it; for we are well able to overcome it."* This was Caleb's response. While the people are arguing with Moses, all full of doubt and unbelief, Caleb says they are well able. God said of Caleb, *"But my servant Caleb, because he had another spirit with him, and hath followed me fully, him will I bring into the land whereinto he went; and his seed shall possess it"* (Numbers 14:24). Notice how our faith affects our seed. What we do and what we believe will affect our children long after us. Some other translations of *"another spirit"* read, *"a different attitude"* or *"another mind."* It's important to realize that we need to believe God. What is the mountain in your life that you need to take? The Bible says:

> *"Not by might, nor by power, but by my spirit, saith the Lord of hosts. ⁷Who art thou, O great mountain? before Zerubbabel thou shalt become a plain: and he shall bring forth the headstone thereof with shoutings, crying, Grace, grace unto it"* (Zechariah 4:6-7).

It is by the grace of God that we will take our mountain. God wants us to be a people that learn how to possess the things that He has put out there before us. He has given us the land. Even though there may be giants in the land, He expects us to have another attitude, another mind that says, *"Give me this mountain."* Isaiah 57:13 tells us, *"He that putteth his trust in me shall possess the land, and shall inherit my holy mountain."* If we will put our trust in Him, we will possess the mountain. It says in Obadiah, *"But upon mount Zion shall be deliverance, and there shall be holiness; and the house of Jacob shall possess their possessions"* (Obadiah 17).

This is the glorious truth of this passage. When we say, "Give me this mountain," we show to God that there is a desire, a determination, and a willingness in us to do whatever it takes. As we wholly follow the Lord our God and put our trust in Him, we will get this mountain. What is your mountain? God wants you to have it. The Bible declares in Zechariah 8:12, that God *"will cause the remnant of this people to possess all these things."* Ask Him today to help you drive out the giants and possess that which God has promised you.

"And He Brought Forth His People With Joy"
Psalms 105:43

DAY 50

The Word of the Lord to us today is joy. God's desire is for all of us to have true joy; joy, being different from happiness, because happiness is temporal. Happiness is what's happening to us right now. But joy is one of the eternal traits of God. It is a deep and abiding principle that comes out of our spirits and has no relationship to our circumstances, to our souls, or to what's happening in our bodies.

God loves to give joy to His people. Because He has joy, He gives it freely to us. Joy is a wonderful part of the nature of God; therefore it endures regardless of our situation. Our precious God who loves us so much knows that in this life we need help in our journey with Him. Therefore, He has provided joy to make this journey easier. Joy comes from the Lord as Psalms 105:43 says, *"and He brought forth His people with joy."*

Joy is an eternal truth. And God wants all of us to experience His joy. As Romans 14:17 says, *"For the kingdom of God is not meat and drink; but righteousness, and peace, and joy in the Holy Ghost."* We find our joy in the Holy Ghost. The Kingdom of God is not a hard kingdom. Solomon said the way of the transgressor is hard (Proverbs 13:15). Jesus said in Matthew 11:30, *"my yoke is easy, and my burden is light."*

You and I, no matter what the circumstances, no matter how hard they may be, can have an abiding joy at all times. Isaiah says:

> *"For the Lord shall comfort Zion: he will comfort all her waste places; and he will make her wilderness like Eden, and her desert like the garden of the Lord; joy and gladness shall be found therein, thanksgiving, and the voice of melody."* (Isaiah 51:3)

No matter what circumstances in which we find ourselves, we can have joy. Isaiah 55:12 tells us, *"For ye shall go out with joy, and be led forth with peace."* We are to go out with joy, and inside we're to have joy. Joy abides when happiness fails. Joy is an unshakable belief that God is a good God, that He loves us and that He's true to His promises and always redeems and reconciles us.

Psalms 30:11 says, *"Thou hast turned for me my mourning into dancing: thou hast put off my sackcloth, and girded me with gladness."* So no matter what our situation, God turns our mourning into dancing. He puts off our sackcloth and girds us with gladness. He has given us, as Isaiah 61:3 tells us, *"the oil of joy for mourning, the garment of praise for the spirit of heaviness."* Praise is simply another eternal characteristic. It abides deep within us. If we will let it, we let out that abiding river of living water, the Holy Spirit, from within. And in that river is the joy of the Lord that abides continually.

Let that joy and that river come out of you. So no matter what you're going through, as James 1:2 says, *"My brethren, count it all joy when ye fall into divers temptations."* I Thessalonians 1:6 says, *"And ye became followers of us, and of the Lord, having received the word in much affliction, with joy of the Holy Ghost."* II Corinthians 8:2 tells us, *"How that in a great trial of affliction the abundance of their joy and their deep poverty abounded unto the riches of their liberality."*

We can have joy no matter what the situation, because it is a river that runs through us that's deep and eternal. Remember Jesus and what He endured; all of the trial that He went through, sweating drops of blood. Hebrews 12:2 says, *"Looking unto Jesus the author and finisher of our faith; who for the joy that was set before him endured the cross."* There is joy set before us. It is flowing out of us right now. Don't let anyone take it. Stay in the presence of the Lord, and allow that joy to flow through you no matter what the circumstance.

As Psalms 16:11 says, *"Thou wilt shew me the path of life: in thy presence is fulness of joy."* In His presence truly is fullness of joy. No matter where you are, no matter what you're doing, no matter what is happening, joy can remain a continual and constant presence in our lives as you come into God's manifest presence. All you need to do is open your heart and let it flow. *"Weeping may endure for a night, but joy cometh in the morning,"* Psalms 30:5 says. No matter what the situation or circumstance, joy always comes. So I say to you today, as Nehemiah says,

> *"Go your way, eat the fat, and drink the sweet, and send portions unto them for whom nothing is prepared: for this day is holy unto our Lord: neither be ye sorry; for the joy of the Lord is your strength."* (Nehemiah 8:10)

This is the word of the Lord to you today. Receive that joy, walk in that joy, and let it flow through you. For the Kingdom of God is righteousness, peace, and joy in the Holy Ghost. *"The joy of the Lord is your strength"*, Nehemiah 8:10 says. Release it today and walk in it. And as Jude 21 says, *"Keep yourselves in the love of God, looking for the mercy of our Lord Jesus Christ."*

Joy, God's unshakeable, undeniable, eternal presence that flows out of your spirit, let it flow out of you today. Open your heart and believe the word of the Lord. Allow God to lead you forth today with joy giving you strength for the journey.

"To Make Thee"
Acts 26:16

Here in Acts 26, Paul is recounting his calling from the Lord and his meeting with the glory of God on the road to Damascus:

Day 51

"And I said, Who art thou, Lord? And he said, I am Jesus whom thou persecutest. ⁶But rise, and stand upon thy feet: for I have appeared unto thee for this purpose, to make thee a minister and a witness both of these things which thou hast seen, and of those things in the which I will appear unto thee" (Acts 26:15).

We see in this passage the purpose for which the Lord is appearing to Paul. Perhaps this is the purpose He has appeared to us. The purpose of God is *"to make thee a minister and a witness."* Jesus said in Matthew 4:19, *"Follow me, and I will make you fishers of men."* This word *"make"* in Greek means "to purpose, to handle for oneself in advance, or to choose." God will choose for us what we should be doing. He will give us purpose and will handle us for Himself, preparing us for our future ministry and life. He wants to make us a minister and a witness. The word *"minister"* simply means "servant."

Being made into something is a process. It's the process of sanctification and the dealings of God and it is never easy. Jeremiah 18:4 says, *"And the vessel that he made of clay was marred in the hand of the potter: so he made it again another vessel, as seemed good to the potter to make it."* God is making us into another vessel and to do that He has to sometimes mar us.

It says in Isaiah 60, *"I will make the place of my feet glorious...I will make thee an eternal excellency, a joy of many generations"* (Isaiah 60:13, 15). We are the feet of God in the earth, and He wants to make us an *"eternal excellency."* He wants us to be conformed to the image of His Son. He says in Isaiah 41:15, *"Behold, I will make thee a new sharp threshing instrument having teeth: thou shalt thresh the mountains, and beat them small."* God is making us into a new, sharp threshing instrument. This is not our natural character; this is not who we naturally are. We need the dealings of God to mold and shape us into that man of God, *"throughly furnished unto all good works"* (II Timothy 3:17). It says in Hebrews 13:21 that He wants to *"make you perfect in every good work to do his will."* So the will of God then, as He's appeared to us for this purpose, is to make us a minister.

Another Greek word for *"make"* means: "to complete thoroughly, to adjust, to fit, to frame, to mold, to repair, or to restore." This is what God is doing. He's completing us thoroughly. He's making us into servants and witnesses. We must bow down to His wisdom and understanding (Proverbs 5:1) and allow the Holy Spirit to do His work within us. He has appeared to us for this purpose, to make us an *"eternal excellency"*; to make us a sharp threshing instrument; to make us fishers of men, and to make us His servants. Follow Him and allow Him to make you a minister (servant) of His today.

"That Holy Thing"
Luke 1:35

DAY 52

In Luke 1:35, the angel Gabriel has appeared to Mary and spoken to her about her birthing Jesus. It says in Luke 1:35, *"The Holy Ghost shall come upon thee, and the power of the Highest shall overshadow thee: therefore also that holy thing which shall be born of thee shall be called the Son of God."* When the power of the Highest overshadowed Mary, it was the insemination of God. It was Jesus Christ our Savior, Emanuel, God with us.

The Spirit of the Lord spoke to me and said that every one of us have been born again by incorruptible seed by the Word of God that liveth and abideth forever (I Peter 1:23), and that holy thing is in every one of us. I John 5:10 says, *"He that believeth on the Son of God hath the witness in himself."* I John 2:20, *"But ye have an unction from the Holy One."* I John 2:27, *"But the anointing which ye have received of him abideth in you, and ye need not that any man teach you."* Inside of us now, in seed form, is the Lord Jesus. It's a holy thing, which shall come forth and manifest itself forth one day unto the entire world. God is going to have a people, upon whom the glory of God shall be revealed. All of the sanctification process, all that we're going through now, is to prepare this carnal nature of ours to receive the divine nature completely. Peter already tells us we've been made *"partakers of the divine nature"* (II Peter 1:4). There is a divine nature inside of you already. *"Who is he that overcometh the world, but he that believeth that Jesus is the Son of God?"* (I John 5:5). Jesus Christ now lives in us, and greater is He that's in us than he that's in the world (I John 4:4).

There is a holy thing inside of you. *"The spirit of man is the candle of the Lord, searching all the inward parts of the belly"* (Proverbs 20:27). The spirit of man is where Jesus lives. It's that part of you that cannot have a demon, that cannot be corrupted, that cannot be touched by anything of this world, the flesh, or the devil. It belongs to God. It's the part of us that is all God that contacts the spirit world. It's a holy thing, it's in seed form, and it must *"grow in grace, and in the knowledge of our Lord and Saviour Jesus Christ"* (II Peter 3:18). To become a whole man, as Ephesians 4:11-13 says, *"And he gave some, apostles; and some, prophets; and some, evangelists; and some, pastors and teachers; ¹²For the perfecting of the saints, for the work of the ministry, for the edifying of the body of Christ: ¹³Till we all come in the unity of the faith, and of the knowledge of the Son of God, unto a perfect man."*

We are becoming a perfect, corporate man. That holy thing which is in all of us makes us the many membered son of God in the earth. Jesus has sat down at the right hand of the Father (Mark 16:19). He's done everything He's going to do except ever live and make intercession for us (Hebrews 7:25). Now, it's up to us. We must take what God has given us and submit it to the Holy Spirit, and present our bodies as a *"living sacrifice, holy, acceptable unto God, which is your reasonable service"* (Romans 12:1). We must allow the Lord to take us from glory to glory, strength to strength, and faith to faith, until that which is in us, that holy thing, has grown up and has become the son of God. That thing which shall be born of this many membered son is called the manifestation of the sons of God. (Romans 8:19)

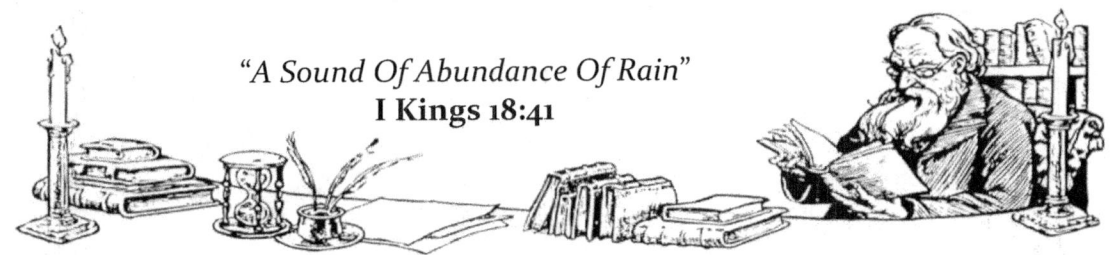

"A Sound Of Abundance Of Rain"
I Kings 18:41

DAY 53

This is the story of Elijah and how he prophesied that there would be no rain until he would pray to the Lord for rain to come. And for three and one half years there was no rain. Finally, though there had been no sign of rain, Elijah said to Ahab in I Kings 18:41, *"Get thee up, eat and drink; for there is a sound of abundance of rain."*

So Ahab went up to eat and drink while Elijah went to the top of Mount Carmel to pray. Elijah cast himself down on the earth and put his face between his knees. This is simply calling those things that are not as though they were. God gave an inward witness to Elijah that it was going to rain. Therefore Elijah spoke and confessed what he had heard in his spirit, and then he went and prayed earnestly that it might rain. James 5:17 says, Elijah *"was a man subject to like passions as we are"* but when he prayed earnestly that it would rain, it did. Likewise today, God wants to send us an abundance of rain, an abundance of the Holy Ghost, and an abundance of the glory to every local church and to every ministry. However, there needs to be a prophetic company of people who can hear the sound of the abundance of rain.

Can you hear the sound of the going in the top of the mulberry trees as David did in II Samuel 5:23-25? God basically told him, "When you hear that sound, move out." You need to be able to hear, as Job says, *"The noise of His voice."* Consider Acts 2:2, *"suddenly there came a sound from heaven as of a rushing mighty wind."* This was the sound of the Holy Ghost being poured out! We need to know the sound of God's voice. We need to be able to hear the rain falling before it even comes and we need to be able to prophecy it. And then, we need to do our part by praying, fasting and believing God to see it happen. We must never be afraid to confess what God has witnessed to our spirit. If we are sure and know it's true, then we ought to just pray and watch it happen.

It goes on to say in the story with Elijah praying for rain that it came to pass upon the seventh time that he sent his servant to look, the servant said in I Kings 18:44, *"Behold, there ariseth a little cloud out of the sea, like a man's hand."* It hadn't even begun to rain yet, but Elijah replied to the servant, *"Go up, say unto Ahab, Prepare thy chariot, and get thee down, that the rain stop thee not."* It goes on to say, *"And it came to pass in the mean while, that the heaven was black with clouds and wind, and there was a great rain."* Great rain will come when we hear the sound of rain. We must be close enough to the Lord in order to know and discern the times in which we live so that we may know what God is doing and that we may prepare ourselves for the abundance of rain. God wants to send the glory. He wants to send a mighty outpouring of the Spirit to His people in the last days.

Psalms 42:7 says, *"Deep calleth unto deep at the noise of thy waterspouts."* Can you hear the noise of His waterspouts? Can you hear the sound of the abundance of rain? Can you hear a rushing mighty wind that is about to bring the last great move of God? Let us earnestly pray for rain and prepare ourselves for the sound of the abundance of rain.

"Another Shall Gird Thee"
John 21:18

DAY 54

Jesus says is John 21:18, *"Verily, verily, I say unto thee, When thou wast young, thou girdedst thyself, and walkedst whither thou wouldest..."* Isn't that the truth? In youth we gird ourselves, walk where we want to go, and do what we want to do. Ultimately though, we must grow up in the Lord *"...but when thou shalt be old, thou shalt stretch forth thy hands, and another shall gird thee, and carry thee whither thou wouldest not."*

Jesus here is dealing with His disciple Peter, and helping him be restored to his walk with God. Even though Peter had denied Him three times, Jesus gave him three times to answer that he loved Him. Then Jesus' response after every one of Peter's answers was *"feed my sheep."* Peter did not yet have an understanding of the "agape" love of God. He only knew friendship love. Jesus was asking Peter if he loved Him with the God kind of love, but Peter would only say I love you Lord as a friend.

This is what it's like in our youth. The young man stage is probably the hardest stage for anybody to go through. *"I write unto you, young men, because ye have overcome the wicked one"* I John 2:13 tells us. Young men, because they have some authority and anointing but are still immature, can be very destructive. As such, they can become a hindrance to the things of God, and in particular to themselves. They haven't been matured and seasoned with age. Hebrews 5:14 says, *"Strong meat belongeth to them that are of full age, even those who by reason of use have their senses exercised..."* Strong meat belongs to them that are of full age. It does not belong to the youth because when we're young we do what we want to do. That's why Lamentations 3:27 says, *"It is good for a man that he bear the yoke in his youth."*

Isaiah 40:30 says, *"Even the youths shall faint and be weary, and the young men shall utterly fall."* Sometimes we need to fall, because in rising up out of the ashes of our weakness and failures, we then begin to understand how mighty and powerful the grace of God is. We find then how wonderful and complete the love of God is. For example, notice the difference between the prodigal's beginning and ending (Luke 15:11-32). He started out saying to his father *"give me"* and returned home saying *"make me"* after much failure. There was a world of the dealings of God in between them. Maturity lies in the words *"make me."* *"Give me"* is the language of the youth.

Back in John 21:18 Jesus basically says to Peter, "When you're old you're going to willingly stretch forth your hands and say, take me Lord where you want me to go" (John 21:18, paraphrased). Then Jesus says these great words *"and another shall gird thee."* In other words your life is not your own anymore. Your life is hid with Christ in God (Colossians 3:3). It's no longer you that lives but Christ that lives in you (Galatians 2:20). Then He will take you where you don't want to go, like John on the Isle of Patmos (Revelation 1:9). Patmos literally means "my killing." Patmos is the place of your personal killing and is the place where you get the revelation of Jesus Christ. Today, if you're young take heart, you won't always be that way. If you're old, mature, and of a full age, stretch forth your hands and let Jesus gird you and take you to a place you don't want to go; that place where you don't want to go is the place where you'll get the revelation of Jesus.

"The Labor Of The Foolish"
Ecclesiastes 10:15

In this passage of Scripture it reads, *"The labour of the foolish wearieth every one of them, because he knoweth not how to go to the city"* (Ecclesiastes 10:15). People that don't know where they are going always end up putting more work and effort into their journey and it just makes it harder for them.

In Acts 2:40 Peter said, *"Save yourselves from this untoward generation"* or a generation that doesn't know where they are going or a generation that doesn't have a purpose and doesn't have a mark set for them. As believers we are in a race as Hebrews 12:1 and I Corinthians 9:24 brings out. This race is leading us somewhere. It is the *"mark for the prize of the high calling of God in Christ Jesus"* (Philippians 3:14).

The word *"foolish"* in the Hebrew means "stupid or silly." In other words it represents for us those who have no knowledge of the Scripture, those who don't search the Scriptures, those who have not been taught, or those who are ignorant. The word *"labour"* in the Hebrew means "toil or a wearing effort; anguish and troublesome work." In other words, we tend to try harder when we don't get to where we are going and as such, we get weary. The word *"wearieth"* here means "to gasp, to be exhausted, to tire, to faint." It's easy to faint when we are trying so hard and seemingly getting nowhere. Sadly, this is the case for far too many people.

Proverbs 24:10 says, *"If thou faint in the day of adversity, thy strength is small."* We don't need to faint. We just simply need to know where we are going. We don't need to be foolish. We need to search the Scriptures and have a walk with God. We need to be a part of a local church, have a pastor and father ministry, and have a vision. Proverbs 29:18 says, *"Where there is no vision, the people perish."* Hosea 4:6 says, *"My people are destroyed for lack of knowledge."*

Let us get into the Word, let us begin to spend time with Jesus and get a personal vision; *"Thy word is a lamp unto my feet, and a light unto my path"* (Psalms 119:105). *"Lamp unto my feet"* means candlelight or just enough light to see where we are walking. *"Light unto my path"* means a spotlight or light for down the road to see where we are going. This is what the Word of God does for us. We need a candle for our feet, for our everyday walk and we need a spotlight to tell us where we're headed down the road.

Hebrews 11:10 says Abraham *"looked for a city which hath foundations, whose builder and maker is God."* Today, you should be running this race, going to this city, ultimately headed for the prize of the high calling of God. If you are weary today and laboring, cease from that and be a wise man. Read the Scriptures and submit yourself to those that God has brought into your life. Open your heart and give yourself in a new, intimate, and dynamic relationship with the Lord Jesus and Ecclesiastes 10:15 will not be said of you. Have a foundation built and made of God. Then you will know where you are going and you will know how to go to the city.

"Six Cities For Refuge"
Numbers 35:6

DAY 56

In the Scriptures we find that God provided for those who killed somebody accidentally, without malice or intent, a place to run to for safety. The cities of refuge were given so that people, who did not hate, were not mad, or didn't react in a violent way purposely could have a place to flee. Of course this speaks ultimately of the Lord Jesus Christ, who is our ultimate city of refuge. We run to Him and are safe. *"God is our refuge and strength, a very present help in trouble"* (Psalms 46:1). He's the strong tower to which we run into and are safe (Proverbs 18:10).

Here we read in Numbers 35:6, *"And among the cities which ye shall give unto the Levites there shall be six cities for refuge, which ye shall appoint for the manslayer, that he may flee thither."* In Joshua 20:7-9, we find that the Scriptures speak in particular about what these cities were. As we look at them and look at their names in specifically, it will give us a greater revelation of what this truth means.

We find the definition of this also in Deuteronomy 19:1-13. The Lord speaks here of the cities of refuge. I want us to take a look at the names of these cities listed in Joshua 20, and how as a type and shadow they apply to our lives when we went to the Lord Jesus for our own refuge.

The first place was called *"Kedesh"* which in Hebrew means "holy place, sacred, or consecrated." In other words, there is a secret place that we can run to, a city of refuge. The presence of God, a holy place that's sacred and consecrated, that no evil can enter therein. The second city *"Shechem"* means "strength, shoulder, or burden." In other words when we run to this city of refuge, Jesus will become our strength. He will shoulder our problems and carry our burdens for us. The third city was *"Hebron"* which means "united, communion, or joined together." This means that as we run to that city of refuge, we can join with the Lord in an intimate relationship. There we'll find not only peace and safety, but the love of God manifested.

The fourth city was *"Bezer"* which means "cut off, inaccessible, in a fortification." When we're in this city of refuge, when we're with the Lord hidden away from everybody else, we're inaccessible. There's a fortification round about us. We're cut off and cannot be touched. The fifth city was *"Ramoth"* which means "exultation, heights, or heavenly." When we go to this city of refuge and run to the Lord Jesus for safety, we are exalted and seated in heavenly places in Christ Jesus (Ephesian 2:6). We are taken to heights above the place where we are.

The last one was *"Golan"* which means "circle, circuit, hedged, or walled in." God hedges us or walls us in and becomes a safety net for us. He becomes a holy refuge, a holy place for the unclean. He becomes a shoulder for the weary, a secure refuge and stronghold for the hopeless. He becomes a high refuge, exalted for the humble. He is the perfect refuge. In Him we are safe forever, run to Him today.

"The Lord Is Gracious"
Psalms 145:8

DAY 57

One of the marvelous revelations of Scripture is to know who our God really is. There are many theologians and theological books and Ecclesiastes 12:12 says, *"Of making many books there is no end."* There are plenty of people trying to tell us about the Lord, who He is, who He was, but so many never let the Scriptures define our God for Him. The Bible is very clear; the Lord has defined Himself to us. Above all things, we need to know that He is gracious. Here in Psalms 145 David says:

> *"⁸The Lord is gracious, and full of compassion; slow to anger, and of great mercy. ⁹The Lord is good to all: and his tender mercies are over all his works."* (Psalms 145:8-9)

The word *"gracious"* is a Hebrew word used and translated as many different words in the Bible. It means "to bend or stoop in kindness to an inferior one." This is what the Lord does; He bends and stoops in kindness to us, inferior ones. Oh how I love Jesus! He is so gracious!

In Exodus 33:13 we see Moses crying, *"shew me now thy way, that I may know thee,"* and in Exodus 33:18 he says, *"I beseech thee, shew me thy glory."* God answers him by saying He will declare His name to Moses and pass by him. He then proceeds to tell Moses who He is in Exodus 34.

Let me tell you, I have read many thousands of books, many hundreds of commentaries; I have studied the Scriptures daily for forty three years and I have come to this conclusion: only the Word of God gives us a true revelation of God the Father. I have heard so many men preaching and screaming what God is going to do to people, trying to scare them by using hell and threatening people with it as a punishment. The image we get of God is that He is an angry God just waiting to plunge the world into darkness or burning fire. This is so far from the truth! My heart breaks, and oh, how it must break the Father's heart!

Years ago the Lord spoke to me to write a book called, "The God Manual." I argued with Him about it because I thought, "Everyone knows You; there is no need for me to write a foolish book called The God Manual." The Lord immediately answered me with Isaiah 1:2, where it says, *"The ox knoweth his owner, and the ass his master's crib: but Israel doth not know, my people doth not consider."* Jeremiah 2:32 says, *"Can a maid forget her ornaments, or a bride her attire? yet my people have forgotten me days without number."*

The Lord said to me, "They know what their pastor has told them of Me; they know what their parents have told them, what their grandmother has told them. They know what their denomination has told them. They know what their own minds and friends have told them. I want you to be led by the Holy Spirit to write a book letting Me define Myself through the Scriptures. Let Me reveal Myself in the Word to the people."

That book ended up being 1,200 pages and we taught 160 characteristics of God, over 270 times. The manifest presence of God came down in every meeting in such a fashion I had never known it before in all of my years of ministry.

So, here in Exodus 34, as God descended in a cloud, He proclaimed Himself to Moses. This is not Martin Luther, Saint Augustine, or any other early church father or great theologian; this is God Himself getting a chance to define Himself. This is not Charles Spurgeon or Moody or anyone else, but the Lord declaring who He is. So, it says in Exodus:

> "*⁶And the Lord passed by before him, and proclaimed, The Lord, The Lord God, merciful and gracious, longsuffering, and abundant in goodness and truth, ⁷Keeping mercy for thousands, forgiving iniquity and transgression and sin...*" (Exodus 34:6-7)

This is our God as described by Himself! He is gracious. The Lord is gracious, full of compassion; He is slow to anger and of great, great mercy.

Psalms 111:4 reads, "*He hath made his wonderful works to be remembered: the Lord is gracious and full of compassion.*" Psalms 112:4 reads, "*Unto the upright there ariseth light in the darkness: he is gracious, and full of compassion, and righteous.*" Psalms 116:5 reads, "*Gracious is the Lord, and righteous; yea, our God is merciful.*" This is what I want you to see. He bends and stoops in kindness to us, inferior ones.

Peter says, "*If so be ye have tasted that the Lord is gracious.*" (I Peter 2:2-3) Have you tasted that the Lord is gracious? Has He bent and stooped in kindness to you? He sure has to me! In forty three years of knowing Him I can only say to you that God has always, always, always bent and stooped in kindness to me. Psalms 37:26 says, "*He is ever merciful, and lendeth; and his seed is blessed.*" I have been blessed because of the graciousness of God. He is gracious! Receive and know this in your heart today. David said in the book of Psalms:

> "*⁷Will the Lord cast off for ever? and will he be favourable no more? ⁸Is his mercy clean gone for ever? doth his promise fail for evermore? ⁹Hath God forgotten to be gracious? hath he in anger shut up his tender mercies? Selah. ¹⁰And I said, This is my infirmity: but I will remember the years of the right hand of the most High. ¹¹I will remember the works of the Lord*" (Psalms 77:7-11)

Our God is gracious! Today I pray that as you go about your day these Scriptures come storming back to you and you remember the Lord is gracious. He has defined Himself out of His own mouth. He is full of compassion, slow to anger and of great mercy. The Lord is good to all. His tender mercies are over all His works.

"Our God Shall Fight For Us"
Nehemiah 4:20

DAY 58

Here in Nehemiah Chapter 4, we find the story of the people of God rebuilding the walls of the house of Jerusalem. And as they built, the enemy came out against them to frustrate their purpose in building. It was so that each man had to carry a sword in one hand while doing the work of building with the other hand (verse 17). We see also that they were separated far from one another (verse 19). Therefore, Nehemiah declares to them in verse 20, *"In what place therefore ye hear the sound of the trumpet, resort ye thither unto us: our God shall fight for us."*

Even though the enemy was coming against them, it would not be the end of the story. Though the people of God were out-numbered, out-maneuvered, and overwhelmed, the word of the Lord was to them that as they built the wall, He would fight for them. Likewise, as we build the wall of God in our own lives, we need to be persuaded of this promise, as it says in Exodus 14:14, *"The Lord shall fight for you, and ye shall hold your peace."* We don't need to do anything other than to stand back and let the Lord our God take over. We see this also in Joshua 23:10, *"One man of you shall chase a thousand: for the Lord your God, he it is that fighteth for you, as he hath promised you."* He has promised to fight for you today. You are not alone; you're never alone in this life. You have a God that not only loves you and cares for you, but a God who is willing and able to fight for you. It's a promise you can depend on!

In Deuteronomy 3:22 He says, *"Ye shall not fear them: for the Lord your God he shall fight for you."* Also, II Chronicles 20:17 says, *"Ye shall not need to fight in this battle: set yourselves, stand ye still, and see the salvation of the Lord with you, O Judah and Jerusalem: fear not, nor be dismayed; tomorrow go out against them: for the Lord will be with you."*

Many times in battle, God would tell the children of Israel to send Judah first. Judah in Hebrew means "praise." In other words this signifies that the power that comes from the presence of God would facilitate their deliverance! They didn't need to fight that battle. They simply needed to set themselves, stand still, and see the salvation of the Lord. You and I don't need to fight our battles. We need only to believe as Jesus said in Mark 5:36, *"Be not afraid, only believe."* If we believe, God will make sure that our enemy is defeated. Hezekiah said of the enemy in II Chronicles 32:8, *"With him is an arm of flesh; but with us is the Lord our God to help us, and to fight our battles."* The enemy has only an arm of flesh, but you and I have all the resources of heaven: the angelic host and the power of God as He comes down to fight for us.

Hear the word of the Lord today! Whatever you are facing, the Lord your God is going before you today. Follow the example of Scriptures. Worship the Lord in your circumstances and He shall fight your battles. Deuteronomy 20:4 says, *"For the Lord your God is he that goeth with you, to fight for you against your enemies, to save you."* Be at peace today! He will fight your enemies for you, to save you! All you need to do is what Psalms 37:7 tells you to do, *"Rest in the Lord and wait patiently for Him."* And as you do the Lord our God will fight your battles!

"Men As Trees Walking"
Mark 8:24

Day 59

In Mark 8:22-26, we find the story when Jesus went to Bethsaida to heal a blind man. After leading the blind man out of the town, Jesus spit on his eyes and the man looked up and said, "*I see men as trees, walking*" (Mark 8:24). The Jesus laid His hands on him a second time and the man "*saw every man clearly.*"

First of all, Jesus spat on the man's eyes. This represents the anointing of God coming upon the man. So when the man first opened his eyes, he saw into the spiritual realm and he saw men as God sees them: "*as trees walking.*" Then, when Jesus put His hands on the man's eyes again, he saw "*every man clearly*".

Jesus wants to "*anoint thine eyes with eyesalve, that thou mayest see*" (Revelation 3:18). I want to see as Jesus sees and if He has to spit in my eyes to do it, then, go ahead Jesus! I believe that this is the same eyesalve that Jesus used to supernaturally heal this blind man. Then the second time Jesus put His hands on him, he saw every man clearly. I don't know about you, but I'm tired of seeing all men clearly as they truly are: corrupt, vain, perverted, full of issues and problems. I'd rather see them as the Lord sees them, "*men as trees, walking.*"

The Bible says in Psalms 104:16, "*The trees of the Lord are full of sap.*" That means that they are full of anointing. And in Isaiah 61:3 it says, "*That they might be called trees of righteousness, the planting of the Lord, that he might be glorified.*" We are those trees. We're supposed to be walking, having a consistent and steady walk with the Lord. We are not to keep falling down, being overcome or tossed to and fro, but rather, walking in that dominion and authority that He has both promised and given to us.

Jesus at one point said in Matthew 12:33, "*Either make the tree good, and his fruit good; or else make the tree corrupt, and his fruit corrupt: for the tree is known by his fruit.*" It's up to us to make the tree good. He says in Matthew 7:18, "*A good tree cannot bring forth evil fruit, neither can a corrupt tree bring forth good fruit.*" It is up to us to be good fruit to the Lord; to be trees of righteousness.

In Psalms 1:3, if one gives himself to the Word of God, "*He shall be like a tree planted by the rivers of water, that bringeth forth his fruit in his season; his leaf also shall not wither; and whatsoever he doeth shall prosper.*" Psalms 52:8 says, "*But I am like a green olive tree in the house of God.*" And then in Hosea 14:8 it says, "*I am like a green fir tree. From me is thy fruit found.*" The color green Scripturally means "prosperous"; it speaks of prosperity, riches and honor. We are to be trees of righteousness, men as trees walking prosperously.

We need to plant ourselves by the rivers of water and have our eyes anointed with eye salve. Let Jesus spit on your eyes so that you can see your brethren and yourself as you really are through the anointing, not clearly, but rather, to see yourself and men as God intended you to see yourselves: as mighty trees walking. The word in the Greek for "*trees*" is "oak tree," one of the largest and mightiest trees. You are that tree; we are that tree. Let us be men as trees walking.

"Full Of Power By The Spirit"
Micah 3:8

DAY 60

Here in Micah 3:8 it says, "*But truly I am full of power by the spirit of the Lord.*" We no longer need to live lives of weakness and frailty. This is because God has provided for us an abundant source of power and a never ending level of strength from the third part of His Godhead, the Holy Spirit. Micah says "*truly I am full of power by the spirit of the Lord.*" Power comes from the Spirit of the Lord. That is the Holy Spirit of God, the aspect of the Godhead that is available right now for the body of Christ. It's this revelation that we're concerned with today.

In Zechariah 4:6 the Scripture says, "*Not by might, nor by power, but by my spirit, saith the Lord of hosts.*" The Spirit of God is what brings the power of God. Far too many Christians are powerless or don't seem to know anything about the power of God. This is related obviously to the baptism of the Holy Ghost. Isaiah 28:12 tells us this is the rest and the refreshing that God wanted to send. Jesus said to His disciples in Luke 24:49, "*but tarry ye in the city of Jerusalem, until ye be endued with power from on high.*" He says just before that "*And, behold, I send the promise of my Father upon you...*" He was speaking of the baptism of the Holy Ghost.

Then again in Acts 1:8 He says, "*But ye shall receive power after that the Holy Ghost is come upon you.*" The Greek word "*power*" there is "dunamis." It means "miracle force, dynamite, or God's awesome mighty power." We receive this miracle force, this dynamite, after we've received the Holy Ghost. It is imperative then that we receive this baptism of the Spirit, and this mighty powerful anointing that comes with it.

It is said of Jesus in Acts 10:38, "*How God anointed Jesus of Nazareth with the Holy Ghost and with power: who went about doing good, and healing all that were oppressed of the devil.*" He was anointed with the Holy Ghost and with power. You see power comes from the Spirit of God. It is the might of God, the aspect of God that brings His full force into the earth.

There are two words for "*power*" in the Greek. One is authority, "exousia", the other is "dunamis" which we looked at in Acts 1 which is "miracle force." "Exousia" means "authority." Jesus has given us both. We have the ability to grow in authority and also the ability to walk in the power of God. Jesus said in Matthew 28:18-19, "*All power is given unto me in heaven and in earth. Go ye therefore, and teach all nations.*" God has a commission for you and me. All power was given to Him. He gave it to the Holy Ghost who then gave it to us via the baptism of the Holy Ghost, and then with this power we are to go to the nations. We are to then go and lay hands on the sick, raise the dead, preach the Kingdom of God, and do miracles all for the Kingdom's sake.

Truly today, you are full of power by the Spirit of the Lord. Encourage the Spirit of the Lord in you today. John 7:38 tells us, out of our bellies shall flow rivers of living water. Psalms 46:4 tells us, "*There is a river, the streams whereof shall make glad the city of God.*" That river is flowing. Let it out, let it flow, and be continually filled with God's dynamite power by the Holy Spirit.

"There Is Hope Of A Tree"
Job 14:7

DAY 61

Here in Job 14:7 we find this verse, *"For there is hope of a tree, if it be cut down, that it will sprout again, and that the tender branch thereof will not cease."* This passage speaks of a great truth found throughout the Scriptures, that God requires the death of our flesh. God requires the carnal, Adamic nature, that rules and reigns in our soulish mind, to be put down. As Romans 8:13 tells us to *"mortify the deeds of the body"*. We can do this with hope, because *"there is hope of a tree, if it be cut down, that it will sprout again"*. Today, we can find comfort in this Scripture that it will sprout again.

In John 12:21, when those Greeks came to Philip, they said to him, *"Sir, we would see Jesus."* Philip told Jesus, and Jesus answered, *"The hour is come, that the Son of man should be glorified. ²⁴Verily, verily, I say unto you, Except a corn of wheat fall into the ground and die, it abideth alone: but if it die, it bringeth forth much fruit"* (John 12:23-24). The principle is that before there can be life, there must be death. Before there can be revelation, there must be death.

We look at John, the great apostle, and we find that he was sent to the isle of Patmos, as Revelation 1:9 says, *"I John... was in the isle that is called Patmos, for the word of God, and for the testimony of Jesus Christ"*. History tells us that they had tried to boil John to death first. They had tried to kill him but they couldn't. They sent him to Patmos as a last resort, but even there God was not finished dealing with that old carnal nature. So Patmos was his answer. The name *"Patmos"* means in the Greek "my killing." What happened to John on the Isle of Patmos? He got the revelation of Jesus Christ.

Jesus said, *"Except a corn of wheat fall into the ground and die, it abideth alone"*. We can choose to abide alone, be selfish, and have things the way we like them, or we can choose to *"die daily"* as Paul said in I Corinthians 15:31. To die daily is to die to ourselves, to our worldly ambitions, to our desires, to our wants and to our needs. It means to give ourselves to the Kingdom of God and to the people of the Kingdom of God. It is all for the cause of Christ, because *"if it die, it bringeth forth much fruit"*.

"For there is hope of a tree, if it be cut down, that it will sprout again, and that the tender branch thereof will not cease." No matter what we go through and the price we pay to die to ourselves, that tender branch, that river that flows out of our bellies will never cease to give us nourishment, hope, and help. There is hope for us today, that as we die to ourselves, His life and His fruit will manifest itself in us.

"The Everlasting Arms"
Deuteronomy 33:27

In Deuteronomy 33:27, the Scriptures declare, *"The eternal God is thy refuge, and underneath are the everlasting arms."* You and I need to remember that always underneath us, under girding us, ready to catch us when we fall, are the precious, everlasting arms of our Lord and Savior Jesus. What comfort this brings to us, that He is there to carry us and to provide comfort for us.

One thing is for sure. If we should fall, fear not. If we should blow it and make a terrible mistake, even if everyone we know turns from us, even after we have lost everything, underneath it all, His loving, precious arms will be there. He will be there to catch us, protect us, and set us gently back on the path of life once we have truly repented and made things right.

The arm or arms in Scripture are frequently used in a spiritual sense to denote power. It also represents salvation, His ability to deliver, support, and to conquer. But it also speaks of His great gentleness. Isaiah 40:11 tells us, *"He shall feed his flock like a shepherd: he shall gather the lambs with his arm, and carry them in his bosom, and shall gently lead those that are with young."* This is akin to Mark 10, when Jesus took the little children that came to Him. In rebuking His disciples, He said, *"Suffer the little children to come unto me, and forbid them not: for of such is the kingdom of God."* He then *"took them up in his arms, put his hands upon them, and blessed them"* (Mark 10:14-16). Oh, what a precious God, that *"underneath are the everlasting arms."*

Today, remember His everlasting arms as you go about your day. It says in Psalms 77:15, *"Thou hast with thine arm redeemed thy people, the sons of Jacob and Joseph. Selah."* In Isaiah 53:1, it says, *"Who hath believed our report? and to whom is the arm of the Lord revealed?"* We could say here, "To whom are the arms of the Lord revealed?" His arms underneath provide protection, comfort, strength, and courage. Never think that your God will ever leave you or forsake you (Hebrews 13:5). Today, know you cannot fall or miss it, because our God is too big. Underneath everything are His precious, glorious arms. Oh, bless the Lord today for all His goodness!

As the bride says in Song of Solomon 8:6, *"Set me as a seal upon thine heart, as a seal upon thine arm,"* let Him catch you today. Know assuredly He is always there and will never leave you or forsake you because *"underneath are the everlasting arms."*

"Wandering From Our Place"
Proverbs 27:8

DAY 63

Proverbs 27:8 says, *"As a bird that wandereth from her nest, so is a man that wandereth from his place."* God has appointed a place for His people Israel. *"But now hath God set the members every one of them in the body, as it hath pleased him"* (I Corinthians 12:18). When we wander from that place, it's like a bird wandering from its nest. We have no shelter, no protection, and no covering. The Bible is very clear that God has called us to a place, a local church, a family, a local body.

It says in Hebrews 10:25, *"Not forsaking the assembling of ourselves together, as the manner of some is."* Some people have gotten mad, angry, have been wounded, or simply stand in judgment of others and have left the local church. They've left their place. We should never leave our place, because when we do, the opposite of II Samuel 7:10 takes place. We no longer have protection from our enemies, we don't have a place of our own, and we're constantly moving, being tossed to and fro. God wants us committed and submitted to a local house, being *"perfectly joined together"* (I Corinthians 1:10).

Jeremiah 17:12 says, *"A glorious high throne from the beginning is the place of our sanctuary."* God has given us a glorious high throne, His glorious anointing and presence, in the place where we're called. Any time you put several people together there will always be things to work out. All of us have problems, insecurities, inferiorities, and issues that we must work out. That's why God has caused the local church to be in existence, because that's the community in which we work these things out. Therefore, we are not to leave it.

We need to learn how to wait on the Lord and stay in our place. Job 14:14 says, *"All the days of my appointed time will I wait, till my change come."* We need to wait, be at peace, and not go running off as Martha did in Luke 10:41, *"careful and troubled about many things"*. We need to be patient, be at peace, like Mary, and sit at Jesus' feet and hear His word. Then when He's ready for us to go, He speaks the word and we go.

Ecclesiastes 10:4 says, *"Leave not thy place."* Ecclesiastes 8:10 reads, *"And so I saw the wicked buried, who had come and gone from the place of the holy, and they were forgotten in the city where they had so done."* Wickedness will drive you from God's place. When you've come and gone from that place of the holy, you'll be forgotten.

Job 27:21,23, speaking of the wicked, says, *"The east wind carrieth him away, and he departeth: and as a storm hurleth him out of his place. ²³ Men shall clap their hands at him, and shall hiss him out of his place."* There will always be men and women that will create issues in our lives. Paul said, *"For Demas hath forsaken me, having loved this present world."* Some we can't keep, some we snatch by getting them out of the fire, and others we just simply have to learn to live with them and put up with them. We should never leave our place, just as a bird wanders from its nest; it loses its protection, provision, and peace. Don't let that happen to you. Let's be planted in the house of our God.

"Which Hope We Have As An Anchor Of The Soul"
Hebrews 6:19

DAY 64

Hope in the Scriptures is a tremendous revelation and every believer needs to have hope. It is the *"anchor of the soul"* as said in Hebrews 6:19, *"¹⁹Which hope we have as an anchor of the soul, both sure and stedfast, and which entereth into that within the veil."* Hope is the thing that ties us and grounds us to the Lord and to the things of God. Hope is one of the finest responses of which a believer is capable. It keeps us alive, even when the conditions of life seem almost unbearable.

One Hebrew word for hope means "to wait, to be patient." Another one means "a chord of expectancy." The Greek word for hope means "to anticipate, expectation, or confidence." My personal definition of hope is: the feeling of believing in the possibility of your desires coming forth and the possibility that events will turn out for the best.

Too many times we find hope vanishes from our lives when we're faced with overwhelming circumstances. As Proverbs 13:12 says *"Hope deferred maketh the heart sick."* Or as the body of Christ says in Ezekiel 37:11 *"Our bones are dried, and our hope is lost."* The word of the Lord today is to hope, to not give up, but continuing to believe, to wait on the Lord, and to be patient; to anticipate with expectation and confidence that God is going to make things turn out for the best in all of our lives.

This is to me the anchor of our soul. I Corinthians 13:13 says, *"And now abideth faith, hope, charity."* These three things are to abide in us. David said in Psalms 71:14 *"But I will hope continually."* I Peter 1:13 says, *"Wherefore gird up the loins of your mind, be sober, and hope to the end."* We read in Psalms 131:3, *"Let Israel hope in the Lord from henceforth and forever."* And then in the very sad and mournful book of Lamentations 3:26 Jeremiah declares, *"It is good that a man should both hope and quietly wait for the salvation of the Lord."*

You need to have hope today! Let faith arise in your heart today and in the midst of any situation know that God is watching and listening. He knows right where you are in your situation, and He has not forgotten you. David prayed in Psalms 119:49, *"Remember the word unto thy servant, upon which thou hast caused me to hope."*

Psalms 130:5 says, *"My soul doth wait, and in his word do I hope."* His Word is our anchor. His Word is the thing that grounds us and causes us to hope. We turn to it no matter what situation we're in today. Ephesians 6:17 says, *"And take the helmet of salvation, and the sword of the Spirit, which is the word of God."* This helmet of hope rests upon our head which really speaks of our soul and mind, which is the great battleground of Satan. We must have this helmet, this hope of salvation to withstand the devil's tactics and the overwhelming pressures of life. With this helmet of hope, however, it gives us the "mind of Christ" and causes us to remember His Word.

The Bible tells us in Jeremiah 17:7, *"Blessed is the man that trusteth in the Lord, and whose hope the Lord is."* Psalms 146:5, *"Happy is he that hath the God of Jacob for his help, whose hope is in the Lord his God."* We can hope; we can believe; we can anticipate; we can wait and be patient today because ultimately God is working all things together for good to us that love Him (Romans 8:28). We need to be as Abraham who, as Romans 4 says, hoped even when everything in the natural was against the promise of God because he was *"persuaded that, what he had promised, he was able also to perform"* (Romans 4:21). Remember Romans 8:25, *"But if we hope for that we see not, then do we with patience wait for it."* Hope is the essence of our walk with God. Hope is the essence of our daily living. We need hope.

Never despair, never quit, and never give up. No matter what life may bring us remember that within us burns a shining, eternal, and glorious flame. It is a flame of hope. Hope in His uncompromising, faithful Word. Hope in the mercy and love of our great God today. Hope in knowing that Satan and all his devils have been defeated. Hope in that God is working together, no matter what the situation, to bring good into our lives.

Is it any wonder that in Psalms 42:11 David says, *"Why art thou cast down, O my soul? and why art thou disquieted within me? hope thou in God."* The word of the Lord to us is *"hope thou in God."* Our hope is in God alone. With that as its foundation, it brings a total grounding of one's confidence and expectation in God's goodness and providential care even in the face of trouble, overwhelming circumstances, bondage, darkness, etc. In short, it gives us the assured expectation of salvation, and of all the blessings included in salvation, not only for this life, but for the life to come. This hope remains steadfast because of the finished work of our Lord Jesus, in His death and resurrection, and in the absolute truth and faith in the Word of God.

Therefore hear the word of the Lord today. Let faith and hope arise in your heart. Anticipate, wait, be expectant, and be patient for the promise of God. Ultimately, everything will turn to your good as you hope in God. He's faithful. He's always true. And He loves you.

So my beloved, do as Peter exhorted us to do in I Peter 1:13, *"gird up the loins of your mind, and hope to the end."* We all are *"prisoners of hope"* as Zechariah 9:12 says, believing today for something. No matter how bleak something may seem, *"hope thou in God."* Job tells us in Job 14:7, *"For there is hope of a tree, if it be cut down, that it will sprout again."* You will sprout again. You will come forth. God is working all things for good in your life! Hope thou in God!

"The Work Of God"
John 6:28-29

DAY 65

The Bible says in John 6, "*²⁸Then said they unto him, What shall we do, that we might work the works of God? ²⁹Jesus answered and said unto them, This is the work of God, that ye believe on him whom he hath sent*" (John 6:28-29). Many of us are asking, "How can we do the works of God"? We want to be used of the Lord. We want to glorify God by our works and show out of our works meekness and wisdom. How can we do this? We do it by believing.

The Bible says in Hebrews, "*But without faith it is impossible to please him: for he that cometh to God must believe that he is, and that he is a rewarder of them that diligently seek him*" (Hebrews 11:6). God rewards us when we believe Him. Psalms 103:7 tells us, "*He made known his ways unto Moses, his acts unto the children of Israel.*" The children of Israel didn't operate in the acts or works of God; they simply were recipients or saw them. But Moses, who knew His ways and believed God and was called the friend of God, did mighty works in the name of the Lord.

We can do wonderful, mighty works if we simply believe. That's why Jesus, in Mark 5, turned to the man who had just learned his daughter was dead and said, "*Be not afraid, only believe*" (Mark 5:36). Jesus said in Mark 9:23, "*If thou canst believe, all things are possible to him that believeth.*" If we have a desire to do the works of God, to be used by God all over the world or even in our own households, community, church, or city, it begins by believing. It's as simple as that. To do the works of God takes no more faith than "*as a grain of mustard seed*" (Matthew 17:20). All of us start out the same, but not all of us end up the same.

Some want their entrance to be an abundant entrance "*into the everlasting kingdom of our Lord and Saviour Jesus Christ*" (II Peter 1:11). We want our works to go before us. The Bible says that every man will be judged according to his works (Revelation 20:12-13). What will be your judgment? Will the works of God follow you? He's coming to reward us for all that we've done. So, what can we do that we might work the works of God that we might see people healed, delivered, made free, and prosper? We must start believing. Start at the beginning and have a simple faith in Jesus and a trust that is unshakable. Paul, at one point, discerned that a woman had faith to be healed and spoke to her and she rose up and was healed. He did mighty works. The Bible says in the book of Acts that great works were done through the hands of the apostles. How did they do them? The same way anybody does, by simply believing God.

Today, let's determine in our hearts to simply "*believe that he is, and that he is a rewarder of them that diligently seek him*" (Hebrews 11:6). Then we will see the mighty works as well and glorify God. Only believe.

"To Walk In All His Ways"
Joshua 22:5

In Joshua 22:5, Joshua declares to the people, *"But take diligent heed to do the commandment and the law, which Moses the servant of the Lord charged you, to love the Lord your God, and to walk in all his ways."* God doesn't want us to walk in just some of His ways, or the ones we like to pick and choose; He wants us to walk in all of His ways. The Word of God is not a buffet table for us to select what we want to do here and there, but we're to do all of His ways. Jesus said, *"If ye love me, keep my commandments."* (John 14:15). The ways of God are the commandments of God, the statutes, the testimonies of the Lord found in the Scriptures. We must have a hunger and a thirst to walk in those ways and to know them.

The Bible says in Psalms 103:7, *"He made known his ways unto Moses, his acts unto the children of Israel."* It's one thing to see the acts of God but it's another thing to know the ways of God, because if we know the ways of God we can perform the acts of God. We can do this by searching the Scriptures and asking God, just as Moses did. That's how he learned the ways of the Lord. If you go way back into Exodus 33:13, you hear him crying out to the Lord, *"Shew me now thy way, that I may know thee."* Is this the cry of our hearts? If it isn't, then we need to cleanse ourselves and repent for anything in us that would keep us from knowing His ways.

The Scriptures say in Genesis 24:27, *"I being in the way, the Lord led me."* When we're in the way of the Lord the Lord is leading us. The Bible also says in Proverbs 16:25, *"There is a way that seemeth right unto a man, but the end thereof are the ways of death."* We don't want to be walking our own ways, because as Jeremiah 10:23 says, *"it is not in man that walketh to direct his steps."* Psalms 37:23, *"The steps of a good man are ordered by the Lord: and he delighteth in his way."* We need to delight in the way of God. We need to do as Moses did and cry out *"shew me now thy way"* so that we can be in the way and so that the Lord can lead us. Then the acts of God will have no problem following.

Oh, that men would give themselves to the ways of God, instead of the ways of men. David said in Psalms 25:9, *"The meek will he guide in judgment: and the meek will he teach his way."* There must be an element of meekness and teachability in our spirit for us to learn the ways of God. There must be humility, because he that comes to God must not come boastfully or proudly, but humbly.

The perfect example of humility was John the apostle in Revelation 10. When God the Father spoke from heaven and said to him to go and take the little book out of the messenger's hand, he humbled himself and did it. Even though He was the last living apostle, he bowed without hesitation. Even though he had been boiled alive and suffered much at the hands of the gospel, he still was teachable and meek and saw His need for the Word of God. He knelt before the angel and he said, *"Give me the little book"* (Revelation 10:9). Why would John do that? Because He was hungry for the ways of God, he was still devoted to Jesus so much that the ways of the Lord meant more to him than his own way. God help us today to walk in the ways of the Lord our God. Let us be examples; let us be different; let us walk through this world as lights shining in dark places and let us walk in the ways of God.

"Altogether Lovely"
Song of Solomon 5:16

Day 67

In this wonderful passage in Song of Solomon 5, it says, *"His mouth is most sweet: yea, he is altogether lovely"* (Song of Solomon 5:16). As I was meditating on the Word of God one day, I realized, as the Spirit gave me revelation that *"altogether"* here means more than just how Jesus is altogether lovely. You see, there are three aspects to the Lord's body: the Lord's physical body, the Lord's body as the body of Christ, and then our own physical body, which is called His body as well.

In this case, it is speaking about the many-membered body of Christ. The word *"altogether"* in Hebrew means "the whole, all, any, every, or everyone." It comes from a root word meaning "to complete or to make perfect." So, Jesus being *"altogether"* means not only is He holy and perfectly complete, but His body, the many-membered son, is as well. The whole, all, or everyone is altogether lovely.

The word *"lovely"* means "delightful or an object of affection or desire." I pray to God that you and I can remember that the rest of our brothers and sisters should be delightful to us and an object of our affection or desire.

In Romans 12, it says, *"For as we have many members in one body, and all members have not the same office: ⁵So we, being many, are one body in Christ, and every one members one of another"* (Romans 12:4-5). We, being many, are one, altogether. The Bible also says in I Corinthians, *"For we being many are one bread, and one body: for we are all partakers of that one bread"* (I Corinthians 10:17). Just like all the ingredients that make the bread become one loaf, we become one as a body. We are altogether. Unity is something that we strive for and that God wants us to have. We are to endeavor *"to keep the unity of the Spirit in the bond of peace"* (Ephesians 4:3).

I want you to know that in God's eyes, we are altogether lovely just like His Son. If we're going to have the image of Jesus and be conformed to His image, we're going to need to see each other as altogether lovely. I Corinthians 12 tells us, *"¹²For as the body is one, and hath many members, and all the members of that one body, being many, are one body: so also is Christ. ¹³For by one Spirit are we all baptized into one body"* (I Corinthians 12:12-13). So, we are altogether Jesus, that is, the Jesus that's in a people here on earth. And we are altogether lovely.

My prayer to God is that you and I will see each other as delightful and as an object of affection or desire. Then it will be said, not only of the Lord Jesus Himself, but also of you and me, that we are altogether lovely.

"The Lord Shall Laugh"
Psalms 37:13

DAY 68

One of the most warming and joyful of all God's characteristics is that He loves to laugh. For most of the religious world everything about God is always solemn, sobering, and frankly bereft of any humor or lightheartedness. However, as we search the Scriptures and search for the image of God we see that God laughs. We just may come away surprised and blessed that our great and loving God is also full of rich humor, and is not the angry, depressed, sullen, somber, unhappy, boring, judgmental God that we've been taught He is. On the contrary we will find Him full of joy, full of wit, and full of humor, and that He really desires for us to be happy, joyful, and full of laughter as well.

It personally gives me great joy to know that my God laughs. If the truth be told, I have heard Him laughing while in His presence many times in my forty-three years as a believer. I have heard Him chuckle at my foolishness, or even while I'm repenting for something foolish that I've done. Oh, what a wonderful God He is. I trust that as you get to know Him better, His Word, and in His Spirit, we will find as so many others have, and as I believe the Scriptures declare, that He is a laughing, joyful, rejoicing, precious, and merry Father.

The word for *"laugh"* or *"laughter"* in the Hebrew means "to laugh outright in merriment, to make sport, or to play." In Psalms 37:13 it says, *"The Lord shall laugh at him: for he seeth that his day is coming."* Psalms 59:8 says, *"But thou, O Lord, shalt laugh at them; thou shalt have all the heathen in derision."* In other words God laughs outright in merriment all the time, especially at those that raise their fist at Him in defiance. It's like a little ant saying to our big human bodies "I defy you" as we crush that ant with our foot so easily.

"Rejoicing" in the Hebrew is the same word as laughter. In Proverbs 8:30-31 it says, *"and I was daily his delight, rejoicing always before him; ³¹Rejoicing in the habitable part of his earth; and my delights were with the sons of men."* Jesus was laughing with the Father when the earth was created. You and I need to laugh as well.

Nehemiah 8:10 says, *"the joy of the Lord is your strength"*? Psalms 16:11 says, *"Thou wilt shew me the path of life: in thy presence is fulness of joy."* Jesus said in John 15:11, *"These things have I spoken unto you, that my joy might remain in you, and that your joy might be full."* "For the kingdom of God is not meat and drink; but righteousness, and peace, and joy in the Holy Ghost" (Romans 14:17). "But the fruit of the Spirit is love, joy, peace" (Galatians 5:22). His character is full of joy. It's simply a part of who He is.

God is laughing. So many times in my life have I heard that great, profound, and deep laugh. Can you hear it right now? He wants to have sport with you. He wants to laugh out loud in merriment with you. As Zephaniah 3:17 says, *"he will rejoice over thee with joy; he will rest in his love, he will joy over thee with singing."* This is our God. He shall laugh. It's like in Luke 15:5 when He has found that lost sheep, *"he layeth it on his shoulders, rejoicing."* I'm sure He's laughing that He's got His son back. He's a laughing God. Rejoice today with your Father who loves you.

"Thou Turnest Man To Destruction (Depression)"
Psalms 90:3

DAY 69

The word *"destruction"* in Psalms 90:3 is actually the Hebrew word for depression. Psalms 90:3 reads, *"Thou turnest man to destruction; and sayest, Return, ye children of men."* Therefore, this verse could read, "Thou turnest man to *depression...*" God can actually use depression in our lives for His glory's sake. Remember as Romans 8:28 states, *"And we know that all things work together for good to them that love God, to them who are the called according to his purpose."* He will turn us to depression and then say, *"Return ye children of men,"* when He has accomplished the work that He wanted to do in us.

It's so easy for all of us to become discouraged, dismayed, distressed and disappointed at times. Yet there is a remedy for it in the Scriptures. Sometimes God allows us to go through these things so that we can find that remedy and then not only help ourselves, but others with whom we come in contact.

In Numbers 21:4 it says, *"...the soul of the people was much discouraged because of the way."* *"The way"* is our walk with God and it is easy to be discouraged by our own sin, our own faithlessness, our own weaknesses and the weaknesses of others. But we must keep our eyes on Jesus. We must lay aside that sin that so easily besets us and run with patience the race that is set before us (Hebrews 12:1) and not allow oppression and depression to grab hold of us.

In Isaiah 53:4 it says, *"Surely he hath born our griefs, and carried our sorrows."* Jesus has taken our depression from us. In the garden of Gethsemane, remember that He sweat drops of blood; He was in torment and agony. I believe that Jesus was very depressed. Yet Jesus triumphed over it and because He did, then you and I can!

Are you down today, depressed and dismayed? Psalms 42:5 asks, *"Why art thou cast down, O my soul? And why art thou disquieted in me? Hope thou in God: for I shall yet praise him for the help of his countenance."* The literal Hebrew rendering of the end of this verse reads, *"for His presence is salvation."* Our souls don't need to be cast down or disquieted, full of no-peace and torment. His presence is our salvation!

Hear me today. Hope thou in God and continue to worship and praise Him. For His presence and His glory will be our salvation. God will not leave us depressed. He will say *"Return, ye children of men."* His presence and glory will cause us to return and rise out of depression and He will restore our lives with peace and joy of the Holy Ghost.

"Confirmed Unto The End"
I Corinthians 1:8

DAY 70

Here in I Corinthians 1:8, we find the apostle Paul say, *"Who shall also confirm you unto the end, that ye may be blameless in the day of our Lord Jesus Christ."* There is so much controversy in the body of Christ about whether we're eternally saved or not, or whether the keeping power of the Holy Ghost is sufficient. I can only say to you, after 45 years of walking with Jesus, that my own Scriptural opinion is that God will absolutely keep us.

Psalms 138:8 says, *"The Lord will perfect that which concerneth me: thy mercy, O Lord, endureth for ever: forsake not the works of thine own hands."* And one of my favorite Scriptures is Genesis 28:15, when He tells Jacob, *"I am with thee, and will keep thee in all places whither thou goest, and will bring thee again into this land; for I will not leave thee, until I have done that which I have spoken to thee of."* Oh, what a tremendous truth this is! How it makes our hearts rejoice to know that we're not in this thing alone especially in the day to day fighting to overcome sin, to keep our hearts right, and to keep a sweet and humble spirit. Only the Holy Ghost and the Word of God and the precious grace of God will be able to see us through. It certainly won't be because of our own efforts.

But He has told us, promised us in His Word, that He would confirm us unto the end and that we would be blameless. Somehow, someway, the Lord Jesus is going to have a bride without spot or blemish or any such thing (Ephesians 5:27). He says in Song of Solomon 4:7, *"Thou art all fair, my love; there is no spot in thee."* In the book of Job, it says, *"And thou shalt know that thy tabernacle shall be in peace; and thou shalt visit thy habitation, and shalt not sin"* (Job 5:24). Zechariah tells us, *"In that day there shall be a fountain opened to the house of David and to the inhabitants of Jerusalem for sin and for uncleanness"* (Zechariah 13:1). Jesus said in Luke 18:8, *"When the Son of man cometh, shall he find faith on the earth?"* Faith for what? Faith that you're continuing to believe that the God who saved you is the God who can keep you and the God who will deliver you and ultimately make you free from every sin, sickness, disease, demon, personal problem, and weakness.

It says in the book of Jude, *"Now unto him that is able to keep you from falling, and to present you faultless before the presence of his glory with exceeding joy"* (Jude 24). Notice it says, *"unto him that is able,"* not you and me. And you and I will be presented faultless, confirmed to the end, before our precious Father, not because of what we've done, but because of what Jesus has already accomplished and what the Holy Spirit finished in our lives. Take courage today and keep this revelation deep in your heart. You've already been confirmed unto the end.

"For The Battle Is The Lord's"
I Samuel 17:47

DAY 71

One of the great things about walking with the Lord Jesus is we come to an understanding that we cannot fight our own battles. He must fight them. Also, we learn that He is more than willing to fight our battles.

In this passage, David is about to destroy Goliath, the great giant who all Israel feared. God wanted the people to know as He says in I Samuel 17:47, *"And all this assembly shall know that the LORD saveth not with sword and spear: for the battle is the LORD's, and he will give you into our hands."* David knew because he had already faced a lion and a bear alone, that spears and swords were not enough. Human strength cannot do it. Psalms 147:10 tells us that the Lord, *"takes no pleasure in the legs of a man."* Proverbs 21:31 says, *"The horse is prepared against the day of battle: but safety* (or victory) *is of the LORD."* Psalms 108:13 also states, *"Through God we shall do valiantly: for he it is that shall tread down our enemies."* We need to understand that we will win our battles only as we allow God's grace to work through us. It is He that will defeat our enemies as we trust him.

In II Chronicles 20:15 it says, *"Hearken ye, all Judah, and ye inhabitants of Jerusalem, and thou king Jehoshaphat, Thus saith the LORD unto you, Be not afraid nor dismayed by reason of this great multitude; for the battle is not yours, but God's."* This is when Jehoshaphat and the children of Israel were surrounded by armies and it was overwhelming to them. They thought they were never able to defeat their enemies. But as they began to pray and seek the Lord, the Spirit of prophesy came upon Jahaziel in the congregation. And this was the word of the Lord to them out of that prophecy. How can we overcome our enemies? We can do it if we understand that the battle is not ours, but God's.

In your situation today, hear the word of the Lord. The battle is not yours. Your flesh and earthly things cannot defeat spiritual things. II Corinthians 10:3-4 says, *"For though we walk in the flesh, we do not war after the flesh: (For the weapons of our warfare are not carnal, but mighty through God to the pulling down of strong holds)."* Our weapons are supernatural ones, mighty through God. God will fight our battles. We do not have to.

In Romans 8:37, it says, *"Nay, in all these things we are more than conquerors through him that loved us."* We are more than conquerors through Him. It is through Jesus that this battle will be won, not by us and not by standing in our own might. But as Ephesians 6:10 says, *"Finally, my brethren, be strong in the Lord, and in the power of his might. Put on the whole armour of God, that ye may be able to stand against the wiles of the devil."* We will be able to stand against the enemy, fight our battles when we know the Lord is there to do it for us. What we simply need to do is what Psalms 68:1 declares, *"Let God arise, let his enemies be scattered: let them also that hate him flee before him."* Let God arise in us and as we let Him, our enemies will be scattered.

David said in Psalms 56:9, *"When I cry unto thee, then shall mine enemies turn back: this I know; for God is for me."* Do you know that one thing? Are you confident? Are you fully persuaded that the Lord will fight your battle? Hear the word of the Lord:

> *"When thou goest out to battle against thine enemies, and seest horses, and chariots, and a people more than thou, be not afraid of them: for the LORD thy God is with thee, which brought thee up out of the land of Egypt. ²And it shall be, when ye are come nigh unto the battle, that the priest shall approach and speak unto the people, ³And shall say unto them, Hear, O Israel, ye approach this day unto battle against your enemies: let not your hearts faint, fear not, and do not tremble, neither be ye terrified because of them; ⁴For the LORD your God is he that goeth with you, to fight for you against your enemies, to save you."*
> (Deuteronomy 20:1-4)

What a tremendous word of encouragement. Our fight and struggles today are not ours alone. Our God will fight for us. Our God will take this battle into his own hands and deal with our enemies.

In Joshua 23:3 it says, *"And he have seen all that the LORD your God hath done unto all these nations because of you; for the LORD your God is he that hath fought for you."* Praise the Lord! The Lord your God is the one who will do our fighting. All we need to do is trust in Him, release Him, let Him arise and our enemies, though they be many, shall be scattered and broken and flee before us and Him as He arises in His manifest presence. We are not alone today. It may seem like it. The enemy might be whispering that to us. People may be telling us that. But we are not alone. God will fight for us.

Nehemiah 4:20 says, *"In what place therefore ye hear the sound of the trumpet, resort ye thither unto us: our God shall fight for us."* Our God always is ready to take our part. He is ready to take your part today. So shake off that heavy burden. Shake off that doubt and unbelief and embrace this word that the battle is the Lord's and He will give your enemy, that thing that distresses you so, into your hands.

What we need to do when faced with the enemy is simply let God arise. Believe me, the enemy will scatter. It is not up to us. It is what the Lord has already done through Jesus that will bring us the victory. Glory to God! Remember now, in the situation, that the battle is not yours. It is the Lord's. Give it to Him today. Release it to Him today and watch your enemies flee and scatter before you!

"Set Me As A Seal"
Song of Solomon 8:6

DAY 72

Our love relationship with the Lord Jesus is the greatest gift ever given to man. He, our heavenly Bridegroom, is calling us into a great relationship. He says in Hosea 2, "*I will even betroth thee unto me in faithfulness: and thou shalt know the Lord*" (Hosea 2:20). What an awesome thing that we might become the bride of Christ. In Song of Solomon 8:6, it says, "*Set me as a seal upon thine heart.*" I believe, today, Jesus is calling us to set Him as a seal upon our hearts, to remember Him, put Him first and to know Him intimately.

We can hear Paul saying, "*That I may know him*" (Philippians 3:10), and Moses saying in Exodus 33:13, 18, "*shew me now thy way, that I may know thee. ¹⁸I beseech thee, shew me thy glory.*" We see the bride say in Song of Solomon 1:4, "*Draw me, we will run after thee.*" We hear David saying in Psalms 42:1, "*As the hart panteth after the water brooks, so panteth my soul after thee, O God.*" He also says in Psalms 27:4, "*One thing have I desired of the Lord, that will I seek after; that I may dwell in the house of the Lord all the days of my life, to behold the beauty of the Lord.*" This is the cry of our hearts; this is the cry of the bride as she waits for her Husband.

Isaiah 54:5 tells us, "*For thy Maker is thine husband; the Lord of hosts is his name.*" The precious bride of Christ, who was called the queen in Psalms 45:9, will one day be seated at His right hand. In Revelation 19, it says, "*Let us be glad and rejoice, and give honour to him: for the marriage of the Lamb is come, and his wife hath made herself ready*" (Revelation 19:7). We are making ourselves ready now. The greatest way to do that is to fall more and more madly and helplessly in love with the Lord Jesus.

I know that some will mock this and laugh at it, but "*unto you therefore which believe he is precious*" (I Peter 2:7). Can't you hear the cry, "*O taste and see that the Lord is good*" (Psalms 34:8)? David in Psalms 116 tells us, "*I love the Lord, because he hath heard my voice and my supplications*" (Psalms 116:1). Oh, how I love the Lord Jesus. For forty-three years, He has done nothing but care for me and protect, defend, heal, deliver, and save me. David said in Psalms 86:15, "*But thou, O Lord, art a God full of compassion, and gracious, longsuffering, and plenteous in mercy and truth.*"

The bride says here in Song of Solomon 8:6, "*Set me as a seal upon thine heart,*" just as John laid his head on the breast of Jesus. The word "*seal*" means "to close up or to make an end." I want my relationship with Jesus to be closed up, to be a sealed thing. I want it to be pure. No longer will He have to ask, as He asked Simon Peter, "Do you love Me?" The word for love that Jesus uses is "*agapao,*" which is the God kind of love, whereas, Peter uses the word "*phileo,*" a friend kind of love. No longer will we answer, "Yes Lord, I phileo You, or like You as a friend." No, we love Him intimately. Our passion is unparalleled and rises up out of us like waters. Set Him as a seal upon your heart, today. Take Him in, "*for love is strong as death*" (Song of Solomon 8:6).

"What Is Man?"
Hebrews 2:6

The Bible says here in Hebrews 2:6, *"What is man, that thou art mindful of him? or the son of man, that thou visitest him?"* We must ask ourselves who are we that God should even be concerned about us; that He would even want to care about us or visit us? Some other translations of Hebrews 2:6 read:

> *"Why are people so important to you?"*
> *"What is man that you are so concerned with Him?"*
> *"What are people that you should take care of them?"*

Well for one thing Isaiah 55:9 says, *"For as the heavens are higher than the earth, so are my ways higher than your ways, and my thoughts than your thoughts."* Psalms 138:6 adds, *"Though the Lord be high, yet hath he respect unto the lowly."* How many times do we see in Scriptures a prophet or a man or woman of God ask this very same question? For example, consider Gideon's response when the Lord called him a mighty man of valor. He basically said, "Who, me?" (Judges 6:12-15). Moses told the Lord in Exodus 3:11 in response to God calling him, *"Who am I, that I should go unto Pharaoh, and that I should bring forth the children of Israel out of Egypt?"*

David said in Psalms 144:3, *"Lord, what is man, that thou takest knowledge of him! or the son of man, that thou makest account of him!"* Well the answer to this is simple, as Deuteronomy 32:9 says, *"For the Lord's portion is his people."* God created us for His pleasure (Revelation 4:11). Man is God's chief creation. God desires greatly to have fellowship with us and have habitation with us. Oh, how He longs for this in all of our lives. Job 7:17-18 says, *"¹⁷What is man, that thou shouldest magnify him? and that thou shouldest set thine heart upon him? ¹⁸And that thou shouldest visit him every morning."* What a tremendous revelation this is to you and me. God has set His heart upon us. He desires to visit us every morning.

I know this makes us feel unworthy and we can't understand why, but nonetheless we must receive this Scriptural truth in our hearts. This is the revelation that God wants to be with His people. We are His portion. We're all He's ever going to get out of this world. And though we may feel small and despised, yet we do not forget Him. Though we may say like David in I Chronicles 29:14, *"But who am I, and what is my people, that we should be able to offer so willingly after this sort?"* How many times have I thought, "why me"? It is simply because of God's grace, calling, and love for us.

"The heart knoweth his own bitterness" (Proverbs 14:10). We know we are nothing, but in Him we are everything. II Corinthians 4:7 says, *"We have this treasure in earthen vessels."* God wanted to do it this way. He invested in a people and gave His Son for us. What is man that He is mindful of him? We are simply His portion, His people, the sheep of His hand and it is a joy for Him to *"raiseth up the poor out of the dust, and lifteth up the beggar from the dunghill, to set them among princes, and to make them inherit the throne of glory"* (I Samuel 2:8). Amen!

"Stir Up The Gift Of God"
II Timothy 1:6

DAY 74

Here in II Timothy 1:6, the Bible declares, *"Wherefore I put thee in remembrance that thou stir up the gift of God, which is in thee by the putting on of my hands."* When Paul ordained Timothy and laid his hands upon him, the gift of God came in him. The book of Romans tells us that *"the gifts and calling of God are without repentance"* (Romans 11:29). So, when that gift came in him, it stayed in him. If we had been prophesied over or have had hands laid on us to receive the baptism of the Holy Ghost or any other gift, those gifts remains in us.

From time to time, we need to stir that gift up ourselves, as it says in Jude, *"But ye, beloved, building up yourselves on your most holy faith, praying in the Holy Ghost"* (Jude 20). Sometimes, we need to build up our most holy faith and stir ourselves, shaking ourselves from the doldrums of life and even of our walk with God. We need to bring to the surface the great, secret treasure that God has placed within us. As it says in II Corinthians, *"we have this treasure in earthen vessels,"* and we need to let that treasure flow out (II Corinthians 4:7).

It seems we need to be reminded of that so many times. Peter said, *"Yea, I think it meet, as long as I am in this tabernacle, to stir you up by putting you in remembrance"* (II Peter 1:13). A few chapters later, he says, *"This second epistle, beloved, I now write unto you; in both which I stir up your pure minds by way of remembrance"* (II Peter 3:1). God is asking you today to allow Him to stir up your mind by way of remembrance. That gift that He's given you is not to lay dormant. Don't let that talent that He's given you bring forth no increase (Matthew 25:14-25). He's coming for faithfulness (Luke 18:8). Be faithful to use that gift. Proverbs 18:16 tells us, *"A man's gift maketh room for him, and bringeth him before great men."* The gift itself will make room for us.

It says in Isaiah, *"And there is none that calleth upon thy name, that stirreth up himself to take hold of thee"* (Isaiah 64:7). We need to learn how to stir up ourselves and how to allow God the privilege by the Holy Ghost to flow out of us in a mighty way. The Bible says in Exodus, *"And they came, every one whose heart stirred him up, and every one whom his spirit made willing..."* (Exodus 35:21).

Is your spirit willing today? Is your heart stirred up? Do you see all around you the needs of people, the tears, loneliness, depression, and the oppression? Oh, how the world needs the gift of God. Too many times we hold back and hoard that gift when it is to be shared with the world. Everything that God has given us is not for us, but for someone else. God gave you that gift; be faithful with it. Stir up the gift of God in you right now. Stir it up. Begin to use it, proclaim it, and display it for all the world to see, that God may be glorified.

"Addicted To The Ministry Of The Saints"
I Corinthians 16:15

DAY 75

Let's look today at the principle of ministering to the saints. It is one of the truths in the Scriptures that is most profoundly ignored, even by local churches and pastors. But it is one of the principles in Scripture that we need operating in our lives, in our families, and in our local churches. Paul said in I Corinthians 16, "*I beseech you, brethren, (ye know the house of Stephanas, that it is the firstfruits of Achaia, and that they have addicted themselves to the ministry of the saints)*" (I Corinthians 16:15).

What does this mean, "*the ministry of the saints?*" The word "*ministry*" in the Greek means "a servant, to attend to, to do menial tasks for." There are people within the body of Christ that have that revelation, that servant mentality. To have a servant mentality is to have the ministry of Jesus, to have the same attitude that He had. The Bible is very clear concerning this principle. Paul also said in Romans 15, "*But now I go unto Jerusalem to minister unto the saints*" (Romans 15:26). His purpose in going was to serve the saints. It is our job to serve, attend to, and take care of the saints. Paul writes in another place:

> "*For as touching the ministering to the saints, it is superfluous for me to write to you: ²For I know the forwardness of your mind, for which I boast of you to them of Macedonia, that Achaia was ready a year ago; and your zeal hath provoked very many*" (II Corinthians 9:1-2).

This is the will of God for us: that we take on a servant's mentality and that we love ministering to the saints. The Bible tells us that, "*A bishop then must be…given to hospitality*" (I Timothy 3:2). It also says in Titus 1 that we should be "*a lover of hospitality, a lover of good men*" (Titus 1:8). "*Hospitality*" is a word that means you absolutely love to entertain strangers. Your willingness to do it is exuberant. It's not drudgery to you, but it is a blessing and your heart is absolutely given to it. I Peter 4:9 declares, "*Use hospitality one to another without grudging.*"

Wow, isn't this something? God wants us to serve one another, to attend to one another, and to minister to one another, to use hospitality and to entertain one another. This means calling people, checking up on them, inviting them to your house, going to lunch with them, inviting them to dinner, and getting to know them. The book of Proverbs tells us, "*A man that hath friends must shew himself friendly*" (Proverbs 18:24). God wants us to be, as Romans 12 says, "*Distributing to the necessity of saints; given to hospitality*" (Romans 12:13). This is an admonition of the Lord, that we be given to hospitality and that we be distributing to the necessity of the saints.

Have you ministered to the saints recently? Has someone ministered to you? Let this begin with us today. We will minister to the saints; we will show hospitality to one another without grudging; we'll be a lover of hospitality, given to it for Jesus' sake.

"He Was Zealous For His God"
Numbers 25:13

DAY 76

The Lord spoke to Moses in Numbers 25 saying:

"Phinehas, the son of Eleazar, the son of Aaron the priest, hath turned my wrath away from the children of Israel, while he was zealous for my sake among them, that I consumed not the children of Israel in my jealousy. ¹²Wherefore say, Behold, I give unto him my covenant of peace: ¹³And he shall have it, and his seed after him, even the covenant of an everlasting priesthood; because he was zealous for his God, and made an atonement for the children of Israel" (Num. 25:11-13).

Phinehas, because he made an atonement for the children of Israel and was not backslidden like the others, brought reconciliation for the people of Israel. Oh, how God wants us to be consumed with zeal for His house and for His people. David said in Psalms 119:139, *"My zeal hath consumed me."* It also says in John, *"And his disciples remembered that it was written, The zeal of thine house hath eaten me up"* (John 2:17).

Do you have zeal today? Are you stirred in your spirit? Are you zealous for your God, for His sake? Even though everybody around you may be falling back unto perdition (Hebrews 10:39) or are lackluster, slothful, and lukewarm, don't let somebody else set your temperature for you. You set the temperature wherever you are. Be zealous for the Lord, for His sake.

It says in II Corinthians, *"Your zeal hath provoked very many"* (II Corinthians 9:2). Our zeal has a tendency to provoke others. It stirs them up and causes them to reach for heights in God that they never would have before. Just by our very presence, we can create a stir. The Bible says when Peter walked along the street and his shadow fell upon the people, that many were healed and got their deliverance. Like Peter, we need to take our eyes off of men and place them on God. We need to allow what God's doing in us to bleed out of us and into others.

Oh, be zealous for the Lord today. Let the Spirit of God fall upon you afresh now. Let the anointing of God quicken you, make you alive. Let the Word of God fill your heart with joy and peace. When the Corinthians repented for their sin, Paul wrote to them and said, *"For behold this selfsame thing, that ye sorrowed after a godly sort, what carefulness it wrought in you, yea, what clearing of yourselves, yea, what indignation, yea, what fear, yea, what vehement desire, yea, what zeal"* (II Corinthians 7:11).

At one time, they were sinning but then were pure and clear in the matter, because zeal had overtaken them. Zeal for getting their hearts right had eaten them up. It says in Titus, speaking of Jesus, *"Who gave himself for us, that he might redeem us from all iniquity, and purify unto himself a peculiar people, zealous of good works"* (Titus 2:14). We are that peculiar people. Let's be zealous for His sake today. Let the zeal of the Lord of hosts eat you up. Let's be zealous for good works.

"My Dove, My Undefiled"
Song of Solomon 6:9

"My dove, my undefiled is but one; she is the only one of her mother, she is the choice one of her that bare her. The daughters saw her, and blessed her; yea, the queens and the concubines, and they praised her" (Song of Solomon 6:9).

DAY 77

One of the great truths in Scripture is the picture of the bride of Christ. For so many believers, the bride of Christ is the body of Christ at large. But after years of searching the Scriptures, I have come to a different conclusion. This is simply not the case. There is a *"wheel in the middle of a wheel"* (Ezekiel 1:16). God has a people within a people.

Jesus had the multitudes, the seventy that followed Him wherever He went, and the twelve disciples that He hand-picked. Out of the twelve, He chose three to go with Him on special occasions. And then He had one who laid his head on His breast at the last supper. That disciple, John, was called several times in the Scriptures the *"disciple whom Jesus loved"* (John 21:7). We know *"God is no respecter of persons"* (Acts 10:34), but yet John had a more intimate relationship than all the other disciples. He was the one who received the revelation of Jesus Christ. This separated him from his brethren.

Here in Song of Solomon 6, we see a beautiful picture of this bride. She is called, *"My dove"* (Song of Solomon 6:9). A dove has single vision and mates for life. God calls His bride His dove. He has a remnant within a people. His bride is His mate for life. She and He both have single vision for one another; they cannot see anybody else but each other. Their love is so strong; it's as strong as death (Song of Solomon 8:6). He then calls her *"my undefiled."* She's His pure one. She's the one who has sought to cleanse her life from *"all filthiness and superfluity of naughtiness"* (James 1:21).

It continues to say, *"...she is the only one of her mother, she is the choice one of her that bare her."* The mother, as found in Revelation 12, is not Israel, but the church. The manchild there, I believe, is the bride, the overcomers. And the rest of her seed (Revelation 12:17) is the thirtyfold Christians. Jesus said in Mark 4, *"And these are they which are sown on good ground; such as hear the word, and receive it, and bring forth fruit, some thirtyfold, some sixty, and some an hundred"* (Mark 4:20). The hundredfold believers are the bride of Christ. She is but one, chosen out of many. She is the choice one of her mother, the best of the lot. She's the one that's ascended above all the others.

It continues to say in Song of Solomon 6:9, *"The daughters saw her, and blessed her."* These daughters of the Lord are the other believers. Then it says, *"...yea, the queens and the concubines, and they praised her."* Queens are people with positions of authority and even royalty in the Kingdom of God. But similar to Queen Vashti (Esther 1), they're not the bride. Concubines are those who are not married, but have a relationship with someone. Far too many believers have a relationship with Him, but they're not married to Him.

Let's choose today to be: His dove, His undefiled, the only one, His choice one.

"What Doth The Lord Require Of Thee"
Micah 6:8

Day 78

Twice in the Scriptures we find this phrase, *"what doth the Lord require of thee."* Here in Micah 6:8 and in Deuteronomy 10:12-13:

> *"He hath shewed thee, O man, what is good; and what doth the Lord require of thee, but to do justly, and to love mercy, and to walk humbly with thy God?"* (Micah 6:8)

What a passage of Scripture! Even today, what is the Lord requiring of us as His people? Well the first is *"to do justly."* In other words, we do what is right and we do the honest thing. Second the Lord wants us *"to love mercy."* He wants us to be merciful people just like Him. He wants us to bless people with forgiveness and kindness. Thirdly, He wants us *"to walk humbly"* before Him. Some other translations of this verse read this way:

> *"only doing what is right, loving mercy, and walking without pride before God."*
> *"only to ask justly, to love loyalty, and to walk wisely before God."*

I tell you, if there ever was a need for these three things to be operating in a people it needs to be operating in the body of Christ. I've heard too many people say to me that they would rather trust somebody in the world than somebody in the church because the church has been so faithless, disloyal, and hasn't acted very justly. This should bring great shame to us and we should not want this to be our testimony. God has showed us what is good and what He requires of us. So today, we seek to do this. We are going to be just and we are going to love mercy. No matter what the situation is, we are going to do what is right.

You can always find the true character of a person because of what they do when they are by themselves and nobody is looking. This is when you become a real man or woman of God, when you *"do justly"* and do the right thing no matter who's looking or no matter what the situation requires.

God wants us to be forgiving, kind, and tender-hearted. Moreover, He wants us to love to give mercy. I tell you people will love to be around you if you love to give mercy because everybody desperately needs mercy.

Humility should be in our lives. Who wants to be around someone with a proud, arrogant spirit? Who wants to be around a know-it-all? I know I don't. There's nothing like being with someone who's just a humble precious person, who doesn't think more highly of themselves than they ought to think, but they simply walk wisely and without pride before God. Oh, that this would be in our own lives.

The second passage of Scripture akin to Micah 6:8 is found in Deuteronomy:

> "*¹²And now, Israel, what doth the Lord thy God require of thee, but to fear the Lord thy God, to walk in all his ways, and to love him, and to serve the Lord thy God with all thy heart and with all thy soul, ¹³To keep the commandments of the Lord, and his statutes, which I command thee this day for thy good?*" (Deuteronomy 10:12-13)

So here we have a few more things that God says to us of the things that He requires. The first is *"to fear they Lord thy God."* This shouldn't be very hard, for just being in His awesome presence and sensing His greatness and goodness should be enough to make any one of us bow before Him and have an awesome reverential fear of Him. Solomon said, *"The fear of the Lord is the beginning of wisdom"* (Proverbs 9:10).

Next, we are *"to walk in all his ways."* We don't have the right to pick and choose the ways we'll decide to walk with Him and the ways we won't walk with Him because Proverbs 21:2 says, *"Every way of a man is right in his own eyes."* Proverbs 16:25 adds that for the ways of a man, *"the end thereof are the ways of death."* Listen, we need to walk in all of God's ways and not just the ones that are easy.

We see this in the life of Moses. Psalms 103:7, *"He made known his ways unto Moses, his acts unto the children of Israel."* Because Moses knew God's ways, Moses did great miracles and mighty things. As one man, he led an entire nation out of bondage.

In addition, God wants us to love Him. Does God really have to ask us this? Sadly, yes. Jesus made this point in Luke 7:47, *"Her sins, which are many, are forgiven; for she loved much: but to whom little is forgiven, the same loveth little."* I don't know about you, but I owe everything I have and am to Jesus. He has loved me in all my years and I can't help but worship and praise Him and give Him the sacrifice of my life. David said in Psalms 116:1, *"I love the Lord, because he hath heard my voice and my supplications."* I don't know about you but this answers my own heart. I love the Lord!

Then He says *"to serve the Lord thy God with all thy heart and with all thy soul."* What the world needs are servants and people with a servant's heart. This is the greatest need in the body of Christ. Everybody wants to lead but nobody wants to serve. There are too many chiefs but not enough indians. Nobody wants to take the low part or the humble seat. But I found that if someone can't be faithful in the little things, he will never be faithful in the big things. God is looking for servants. Jesus said of Himself, *"the Son of man came not to be ministered unto, but to minister"* (Matthew 20:28). He requires of us that we be servants. The word *"minister"* in the Greek literally means "to do menial tasks." This means taking out the trash, cleaning, etc. I think we live in a day where we think too highly of ourselves and nobody is willing to be humble and simply serve.

Lastly, God requires of us *"to keep the commandments of the Lord, and his statutes."* As we love our God passionately, love mercy, do the right thing, walk humbly before Him and serve Him with all our hearts, God's grace will also teach us to keep the commandments and statues of the Lord. He will never ask us to do anything that He doesn't give us the ability to do. By God's grace today, begin to do these things and radiate His love and character in the earth, therefore glorifying His precious name!

"I Knew It Not"
Genesis 28:16

DAY 79

This to me is one of the most astounding truths in the Bible; that people will not know and do not know when the presence of God is within a place. Here in Genesis 28:16 it reads, *"And Jacob awaked out of his sleep, and he said, Surely the Lord is in this place; and I knew it not."* How many times has the Lord come to you and you have not recognized that it was Him. The Scriptures are full of admonitions of this happening; how people mistake the presence of God for something else. Or on the contrary, they think the presence of God is there when it is really not the presence of God. This is especially true in this charismatic world in which we live in, where so much is touted about people's gifts and abilities. But there is quite a difference between the true anointing, and talent or gifting. You and I need to know the difference.

In Ezekiel 44:23, God said of the sons of Zadok, the true priests of God, *"And they shall teach my people the difference between the holy and profane, and cause them to discern between the unclean and the clean."* It is our job as ministers to help people exercise discernment. The Hebrews were challenged about this, *"For when for the time ye ought to be teachers, ye have need that one teach you again...and are become such as have need of milk, and not of strong meat. But strong meat belongeth to them that are of full age, even those who by reason of use have their senses exercised to discern both good and evil"* (Hebrews 5:12, 14).

We need to teach God's people so that their senses can be exercised to discern between the holy and the profane, between strange fire and the glory, between true anointing and simple charisma. In John 12 when God the Father spoke to Jesus it says, *"The people therefore, that stood by, and heard it, said that it thundered: others said, An angel spake to him"* (John 12:29). There is a great deal of difference between the voice of God and thunder. Many don't know the difference and need to be taught.

We see this even in Samson's life. In Judges 16:20 it says *"he wist not that the Lord was departed from him."* Samson just assumed that the anointing and the presence of God would always be upon him. But he couldn't tell the difference because he was so backslidden in his heart and so full of sin. This is what sin does to us. Our hearts are *"hardened through the deceitfulness of sin"* (Hebrews 3:13).

Consider Michal, David's wife, when David came dancing before the Lord bringing the ark back into Jerusalem. What did she do in II Samuel 6:20-23? She despised David, accusing him of shamelessly uncovering himself. I guess it is matter of perspective as Titus 1:15 says, *"Unto the pure all things are pure: but unto them that are defiled and unbelieving is nothing pure; but even their mind and conscience is defiled."* She didn't recognize the glory or manifest presence of God represented by the ark of God. And because of it, she had no children or fruit the rest of her life.

God help us today to know the difference between thunder and His true voice. We need to know when God is there and when He isn't there. How sad it would be if the Lord was in the place we were and we knew it not.

"We Have This Treasure"
II Corinthians 4:7

Here in II Corinthians 4:7, Paul says, *"But we have this treasure in earthen vessels that the excellency of the power may be of God, and not of us".* You and I are simply earthen vessels that carry the treasure of God in us. I want to give you some other translations of this verse:

> *"But we have this treasure in jars of clay, to show that this all surpassing power is from God and not from us"*
> *"If you only look at us you might well miss the brightness. We carry this precious message around in the unadorned clay pots of our ordinary lives that is to prevent anyone from confusing God's incomparable power with us"*
> *"That this precious treasure, this light and power that now shines within is held in a perishable container, that is in our weak bodies, everyone can see that this glorious power in us must be from God, and is not in our own"*
> *"We have this wealth in vessels of earth so that we see that the power comes from God, and not from us"*
> *"But we have this treasure, the reflection of the knowledge of the glory of God in the face of Christ in earthenware containers in order that the super excellence of the power might be from God as the source, and not from us"*
> *"We are frail vessels of earth..."*

"There was a man sent from God", John 1:6 tells us. Our humanity is one of the things that endears us to God, but it is also one of the things that drives us crazy because of the Adamic nature. Nonetheless, the earthen part of us is not to be discarded. The Cherubims and the Seraphims both have the hands of a man, and the living creatures have the face of a man. In other words, the humanity that God created when He created mankind was originally a good thing. We do not need to extol or exalt the earthen vessel. We need to exalt the treasure.

I John 4:4 says, *"Greater is He that is in you than he that is in the world."* Micah 3:8 tells us *"truly I am full of power by the power of God."* Also, Job 36:8 reminds us *"He that is perfect in knowledge is with me."* All of this is happening in the realm of our spirit. It is where the treasure lies and shines through. Psalms 50:2 says, *"Out of Zion, the perfection of beauty, God hath shined."*

So we have this treasure in us. The Greek word for "*treasure*" means "a deposit, wealth literally and figuratively." In other words, there is a wealth of treasure in us that belongs to the Lord and goes to His glory and not to us. Proverbs 21:20 says *"There is treasure to be desired and oil in the dwelling of the wise."* There is treasure and oil, a type of God's anointing, in the dwelling of our earthen vessels. You and I need to extol that treasure and let it shine through. Proverbs 15:6 says, *"In the house of the righteous is much treasure."* In these earthen vessels is much treasure. In us lies the wisdom of God, the power of God, the authority of God, and the glory of God. You and I need to be aware and be conscious of this treasure, this deposit in us, by God, and let it out!

"The Three Gates We Must Pass Through"
Acts 12:8, 10, 13

DAY 81

Here locked away in this story in the book of Acts, is a story of our own personal walk with the Lord. Peter was imprisoned by the Pharisees and the angel of the Lord came and freed him. He had to pass through several gates on his way back to the house of the Lord. In every one of our lives, God finds us in prison; He brings light for us to pass through the gate. In addition, these three gates represent our journey from the Outer Court into the Most Holy Place.

These gates are indicative of our growth *"from glory to glory,"* (II Corinthians 3:18), *"faith to faith,"* (Romans 1:17), *"strength to strength,"* (Psalms 84:7), and *"vessel to vessel,"* (Jeremiah 48:11). There are dimensions of glory; *"In my Father's house are many mansions (or rooms)"* (John 14:2). As we go through these seasons in our lives, we are changed or likened to our precious Lord Jesus.

The passing through the first gate, we find here in Acts 12:7 that *"The angel of the Lord came upon him, and a light shined in the prison: and he smote Peter on the side, and raised him up, saying, Arise up quickly. And his chains fell off from his hands."*

Isn't this how we met Jesus, in a prison cell? A light shined in our prison, we were raised up quickly, and our chains fell off of our hands because of the salvation of the Lord Jesus. It goes on to say in verse 8, *"And the angel said unto him, Gird thyself, and bind on thy sandals. And so he did. And he saith unto him, Cast thy garment about thee, and follow me."* It is our job to gird ourselves and to bind our own sandals. Sandals speak of your feet and your walk with God. We must gird ourselves and bind our walk with God to our lives. Verses 9 and 10 of Acts 12 read,

> *"⁹And he went out, and followed him; and wist not that it was true which was done by the angel; but thought he saw a vision. ¹⁰When they were past the first and the second ward, they came unto the iron gate that leadeth unto the city."*

The first gate we must overcome is our own personal lives, our own personal chains. As we go on with God, eventually, we get the victory little by little. As we progress into authority and anointing, we come to the second gate, the *"iron gate that leadeth unto the city."* Iron always speaks of judgment in the Scriptures. It speaks of the principalities, powers, rulers of the darkness of this world, and spiritual wickedness in high places that control cities. When we've learned how to get the victory over ourselves we can then apply that victory to release others. The iron gate must be broken through. As we're walking in authority, all we need to do is go to the gate and it will open of its own accord.

Verses 12-14 of Acts 12 go onto say:

> *"¹²And when he had considered the thing, he came to the house of Mary the mother of John, whose surname was Mark; where many were*

> *gathered together praying. ¹³And as Peter knocked at the door of the gate, a damsel came to hearken, named Rhoda. ¹⁴And when she knew Peter's voice, she opened not the gate for gladness, but ran in, and told how Peter stood before the gate."*

The third and last gate we go through is the house of God. Once we've learned how to have authority over ourselves, then over the principalities of this world, then we must have authority in the house of God. We must be able to lead God's people, to minister to them, and to lay down our lives for them. Everything that happened to Peter wasn't for him; it was for someone else.

What is happening with you today isn't just for you. God is creating in you a man or woman of God and giving you authority in everything you go through. He is granting you His seal of approval, His anointing, as you break through the three gates in your personal life, the demons that surround cities, and then ultimately when you prevail in the house of God.

"Put Away The Strange Gods"
Joshua 24:23

Day 82

Here in this passage, Joshua says to Israel, *"Now therefore put away, said he, the strange gods which are among you, and incline your heart unto the Lord God of Israel"* (Joshua 24:23). Could it be that perhaps you and I have strange gods in our lives? This term *"strange gods"* literally means "to turn aside, to be a foreigner, to be profane, to commit adultery, to go to another, or to go away from." Every time you and I turn away from the Lord to some other god or idol or thing of any kind, in a sense, it is an act of adultery. We're going to another. We've turned aside and have become a foreigner.

In Deuteronomy 32:12, it says, *"So the Lord alone did lead him, and there was no strange god with him."* As long as the Lord is leading us there won't be a strange god with us. It says in Isaiah:

> *"¹¹I, even I, am the Lord; and beside me there is no saviour.*
> *¹²I have declared, and have saved, and I have shewed, when there was no strange god among you: therefore ye are my witnesses, saith the Lord, that I am God"* (Isaiah 43:11-12).

We are witnesses that He is God, the only God. *"For there is one God, and one mediator between God and men, the man Christ Jesus,"* I Timothy 2:5 tells us. There is salvation in no other than the Lord Jesus. All other gods are immaterial and foolish. All of the false messiahs and prophets have come and gone; they've died. Jesus died, but then rose again. He is the only God. We don't need to have a strange god within us. It says in Psalms, *"²⁰If we have forgotten the name of our God, or stretched out our hands to a strange god; ²¹Shall not God search this out? for he knoweth the secrets of the heart"* (Psalms 44:20-21). If we've forgotten the name of our God or stretched out our hands to some strange god, God will search this out. He knows everything, even the secrets of your heart. It's time to put away the strange gods, the strange, foreign things that cause us to make the Lord jealous. It's time to stop committing spiritual adultery, turning aside or away from Him.

The Bible clearly states, in Genesis 35, when Jacob was talking to his family, saying, *"²...Put away the strange gods that are among you, and be clean, and change your garments: ³And let us arise, and go up to Bethel..."* (Genesis 35:2-3). Let's put away the strange gods that are among us and be clean. Let's get washed in the blood of Jesus and change our garments. Let's put away these filthy garments of unrighteousness and put on the garments of salvation. Let us arise and go to Bethel. *"Bethel"* means "the house of God." We need to arise and go to the only house of true worship.

God promises us, in Psalms 81, *"...⁸O Israel, if thou wilt hearken unto me; ⁹There shall no strange god be in thee..."* (Psalms 81:8-9). Let's hearken to the Lord today. Let's hear His voice and let there be no other gods before us, nor within us.

"The Gospel Of Christ Without Charge"
I Corinthians 9:18

DAY 83

This I know will be a controversial word because we live in a day when charismatic preachers and television ministers have such an emphasis on prosperity and blessing in their teaching. There has also been a lifting up of ministers and an exaltation of men of God and their own well-being. This portrays a self-centered gospel and does not truly exemplify the life of Christ. Jesus said *"Learn of me for I am meek and lowly in heart"* (Matthew 11:29). There is too much emphasis on being monetarily paid and not being a true servant. Paul says here in I Corinthians 9:16, *"For though I preach the gospel, I have nothing to glory of: for necessity is laid upon me; yea, woe is unto me, if I preach not the gospel! What is my reward then? Verily that, when I preach the gospel, I may make the gospel of Christ without charge, that I abuse not my power in the gospel."*

Paul's reward for preaching was that he made the Gospel of Christ without charge. Today, let's consider what that statement means. We need to be like Paul in that we are not interested in making money or seeking our own gain off of the things of God. Jesus went into the temple and when He saw the buying and selling of doves, He overthrew the money changers and drove out all of the people that were using the things of God to make money for themselves. He told them that they had made His Father's house a den of thieves. Could it be that our own churches with all the publications, conferences, etc., have become just like those in the temple that Jesus drove out, where everything is about the money that is being made and how many people there are?

Remember in II Kings 5, after God used Elijah to heal Naaman of leprosy, that Naaman offered Elijah a gift in payment for his healing. Elijah refused, but his servant Gehazi secretly went to Naaman and lied to him saying that Elijah did want the gifts. Naaman gave them to him, and when Gehazi returned, Elijah said unto him, *"Went not mine heart with thee, when the man turned again from his chariot to meet thee? Is it a time to receive money, and to receive garments, and oliveyards, and vineyards, and sheep, and oxen, and menservants, and maidservants?"* (II Kings 5:26)

It is not a time to receive money! We are to present the Gospel of Christ without charge. Freely you have received, freely give; this is the Word of the Lord. After Abraham went and fought with the enemies of his brother-in-law, and Melchizedek blessed him, it says in Genesis 14: 22-23 that Abraham refused an offering from the king of Sodom. *"I have lift up mine hand unto the Lord, the most high God, the possessor of heaven and earth, ²³That I will not take from a thread even to a shoelatchet, and that I will not take any thing that is thine, lest thou shouldest say, I have made Abram rich."*

Let's have this testimony in us, that we will not take a thread to a shoelatchet, or anything for the gospel; or that we should say that anyone else has made us rich, because Jehovah Jireh is our provider. Let us make the Gospel available without charge. Let us be like Jesus.

"The Terror Of The Lord"
II Corinthians 5:11

DAY 84

Here in II Corinthians 5:11, Paul says, *"Knowing therefore the terror of the Lord, we persuade men; but we are made manifest unto God; and I trust also are made manifest in your consciences."* Knowing therefore the awesomeness and the fearfulness of God, it causes us to be stirred in our hearts to persuade men to turn to Him. The Bible speaks so greatly of Him in Nehemiah:

> *"Now therefore, our God, the great, the mighty, and the terrible God, who keepest covenant and mercy, let not all the trouble seem little before thee, that hath come upon us, on our kings, on our princes, and on our priests, and on our prophets, and on our fathers, and on all thy people, since the time of the kings of Assyria unto this day."*
> (Nehemiah 9:32)

The word *"terrible"* simply means "awesome, majestic and powerful." It's so powerful that it causes fear and dread to come upon you, not in a bad way, but in an awesome, respectful way. Psalms 47:2 speaks of Him in this way, *"For the Lord most high is terrible; he is a great King over all the earth."* Psalms 66:5 says, *"Come and see the works of God: he is terrible in his doing toward the children of men."* Earlier in verse 3 it says, *"Say unto God, How terrible art thou in thy works! through the greatness of thy power shall thine enemies submit themselves unto thee."*

In the Old Testament, it says in Deuteronomy 4:34 that God guides and instructs His people by a *"Mighty hand, and by a stretched out arm, and by great terrors."* It has been written many times that the terror of God was upon the cities. God is a great and marvelous good God, yet He is also righteous, awesome and holy. Anything that is not holy, righteous or pure is exposed in His great glory. They will cry out as in Revelation 6:16, *"And said to the mountains and rocks, Fall on us, and hide us from the face of him that sitteth on the throne, and from the wrath of the Lamb."* So knowing therefore the terror of the Lord, we persuade men to turn to God.

The Lord Most High is terrible. Jeremiah 20:11, *"But the Lord is with me as a mighty terrible one: therefore my persecutors shall stumble, and they shall not prevail: they shall be greatly ashamed; for they shall not prosper."* The Lord is with me, as a mighty and terrible one. Let all the earth know, let all our enemies know that the terrible God, the mighty, majestic, wonderful, and awesome God is coming out of His holy place.

Knowing this, it causes us to persuade men. For we must all appear before the judgment seat of Christ to give an account. Everyone will stand before the Lord ultimately and all the impurities, unrighteousness and sin will be exposed, just as it warns us in I Timothy 5:24, *"Some men's sins are open beforehand, going before to judgment; and some men they follow after."* Let our sins go beforehand and let us tell people that the day of judgment, holiness and wrath is coming. God is going to purge this world in righteousness. And knowing therefore the terror of the Lord, let us persuade and convince men.

"There Went With Him A Band Of Men Whose Hearts God Had Touched"
I Samuel 10:26

DAY 85

We find a principle in the Scriptures that it doesn't take a lot of people for God to move. Actually, if we look into the Scriptures in detail, we find that God rarely used a large number of people. Mostly it was either one person or a small group of people that He anointed and used to do His will.

In I Samuel 10:26, we find a passage of Scripture related to this when Saul was anointed king of Israel, *"There went with him a band of men, whose hearts God had touched."* It only takes a band of men whose hearts God has touched for His will to be accomplished. Other translations of this term *"a band of men"* include:

"A band of valiant men"
"Some true and brave men"
"Men of war"
"Powerful warriors"

In this day of TV Christianity and mega churches, we have a tendency to think big is God. But my contention is God is big, but big is not necessarily God. Just because something seems to be overflowing with people and it seems to have blessing upon it, doesn't make it the will of God. If Jesus is the true example for us, He died alone. He had nobody around Him. Even His disciples forsook Him.

No matter where you are or what you are doing, God will join people to you to fulfill His purpose. The word *"touched"* here in Hebrew simply means "to lay the hand upon, to lie with a woman, to violently strike." God will intimately touch the hearts of people around about you. God will touch people with His heart and they will come to you to be your friend and companion, as one of the translations reads, *"they became his constant companions."* It doesn't take a lot to stand with you. Jesus said, *"That if two of you shall agree on earth as touching anything that they shall ask, it shall be done for them of my Father which is in heaven"* (Matthew 18:19).

So there went with Saul a band of men whose hearts God had touched. God has valiant people in the earth even though it doesn't seem like that today. God does have an intimate relationship with many people. He has violently come into their lives in a good way, and they have the hand of God upon their lives. The anointing touches many lives, and as others see God in you, they will come. In Asa's day II Chronicles 15:9 says, *"for they fell to him out of Israel in abundance, when they saw that the Lord his God was with him."*

True devoted believers will always recognize other true devoted believers. There will be a witness in their spirit as to whom and what you are. They will recognize the anointing and seal of God in your life.

For many years in the past, I pastored small churches all over this country with my insecurities and ungodly expectations of myself as a pastor. Due to not having a great amount of members or a great amount of money in those churches, I thought that I was missing God and that I was unsuccessful. I equated success with numbers and money, and I equated blessing with riches and gain. But Paul in I Timothy 6:5 says, *"Perverse disputings of men of corrupt minds, and destitute of the truth, supposing that gain is godliness: from such withdraw thyself."* Hebrews 13:5 says, *"be content with such things as ye have: for he hath said, I will never leave thee, nor forsake thee."* God will bring the people into our lives that we need. God will bring the friends and loved ones who will walk with us and help us fulfill the will of God in our lives. There will be a band of men and women whose hearts God has touched. It doesn't take a great amount of people to fulfill the will of God.

Consider in Genesis 14:14-20 when Lot and his family were attacked, Abram took three hundred eighteen trained servants out of his own house and went and smote the enemies of Lot and recovered all Lot lost. God didn't do this for Lot as much as he did it for Abram, because Abram was a man of God. God will bring a band of men and women to you. It only takes a small remnant. Isaiah 1:9 says, *"Except the Lord of hosts had left unto us a very small remnant, we should have been as Sodom, and we should have been like unto Gomorrah."*

There is a remnant in the earth today. There is a group of people who worship like you, love Jesus like you do, and others will see it. Remember the story of Gideon in Judges 7? Gideon started out with 32,000 men, and God sent home everyone who was fearful and afraid; 22,000 left. Then God said 10,000 men were still too many so He brought them to the water to try them. In the end, the 32,000 men were narrowed down to a mere 300 men. That amount of men was just under 1% of what it originally was, yet with that band of 300 men, they conquered. God always has a remnant, and they will find you and help you fulfill your purpose in God. God is touching hearts all over the world today with intimacy, the Word of God, and His anointing, and they are responding and coming together.

Has God touched your heart? I know He has and He did it for a holy purpose and calling. Be encouraged today that you will fulfill your purpose in God. God will bring those faithful brethren to join you. Believe it and remember, *"there went with him a band of men, whose hearts God had touched."*

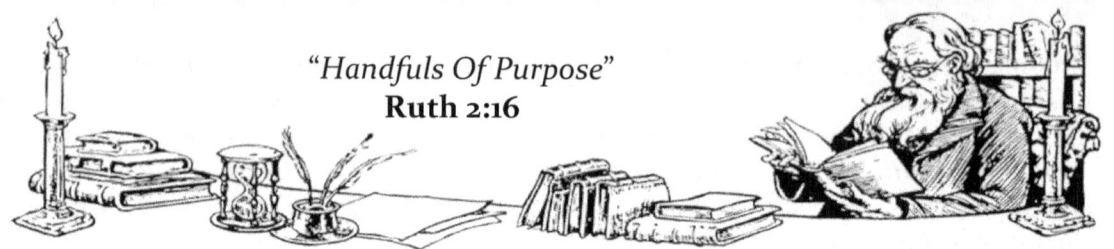

"Handfuls Of Purpose"
Ruth 2:16

DAY 86

Today, I would like to look at the story of Ruth and how it relates to us partaking of the Word of God in our lives. God's Word gives us revelation of Him, vision to see, light to walk, provision, sustenance as well as it gives us true purpose for all that God wants to do in our lives. Ruth is a type of the bride of Christ being married to Boaz, a type of Jesus. Ruth was a Moabite and not even of the people of God. She is a type of the Gentiles in these last days, who come into the Kingdom of God to become the bride of Christ. Let's pick up the story in Ruth 2:14, *"And Boaz said unto her, At mealtime come thou hither, and eat of the bread, and dip thy morsel in the vinegar. And she sat beside the reapers: and he reached her parched corn, and she did eat, and was sufficed, and left."*

Mealtime is when we come to the local church, to Bible school, or a teaching. The word *"come"* means "to draw near." Mealtime is the time for us to draw near and eat of the bread. Are you eating of the bread? The Bible says in Psalms 12:27, *"The slothful man roasteth not that which he took in hunting."* Every time you go to a meeting, you carry your little basket. Are you taking the bread? Are you gathering up the *"fragments that remain, that nothing be lost?"* (John 6:12) If you are, He'll reach over and give you parched corn. He'll give you the best of the revelation; He'll give you the best of the Word, a living Word that will suffice you.

It continues to say, *"And when she was risen up to glean, Boaz commanded his young men, saying, Let her glean even among the sheaves, and reproach her not"* (Ruth 2:15). She was only supposed to scrape through all the leftovers and pick up some of the principle wheat that had been discarded or not noticed by the reapers. He then said, *"Let fall also some of the handfuls of purpose for her, and leave them, that she may glean them, and rebuke her not"* (Ruth 2:14-16). These handfuls of purpose are handfuls of revelation. They are handfuls of written Word that will show us the way wherein we should walk. Today, He wants to let fall for you and me some handfuls of purpose. Habakkuk 2:3 tells us, *"For the vision is yet for an appointed time."* God's Word is full of vision. It says in Psalms 119, *"Thy word is a lamp unto my feet, and a light unto my path"* (Psalms 119:105). Proverbs 1:20 says, *"Wisdom crieth without."* In Luke 11, Jesus called the Word of God the *"wisdom of God"* (Luke 11:49).

Do you need purpose? Do you need a living Word? Come and glean near Jesus. Come get as close to Him as you can. Let Him see your heart. If your heart is right, He will reach and give you parched corn and command that His teachers, preachers, evangelists, apostles, and prophets leave for you some handfuls of purpose. They will leave for you the Word of God that will bless you and change your life. Oh, God, let handfuls of purpose fall for your people today.

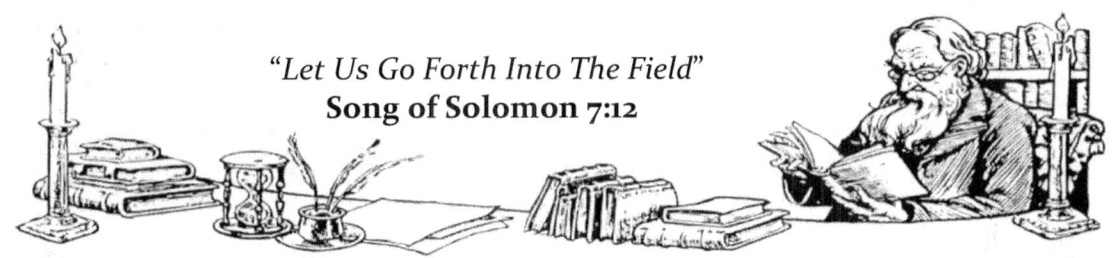

"Let Us Go Forth Into The Field"
Song of Solomon 7:12

The Bible says in Song of Solomon:

"¹¹Come, my beloved, let us go forth into the field; let us lodge in the villages. ¹²Let us get up early to the vineyards; let us see if the vine flourish, whether the tender grape appear, and the pomegranates bud forth: there will I give thee my loves" (Song of Solomon 7:11-12).

In this passage of Scripture, we find God's desire for the nations. Psalms tells us that His *"eyes behold the nations"* (Psalms 66:7). God cares and is concerned about the nations of this world. It says in John 3:16, *"For God so loved the world, that he gave his only begotten Son, that whosoever believeth in him should not perish, but have everlasting life"* (John 3:16). God is concerned that the nations hear the gospel and the truths of the Kingdom of God. Jesus said in Matthew 28, *"All power is given unto me in heaven and in earth. ¹⁹Go ye therefore, and teach all nations"* (Matthew 28:18-19). It is our job to make disciples of all nations.

The Bible says in Zechariah 2:8, *"After the glory hath he sent me unto the nations."* We have been sent to the nations, whether we go by ourselves or send someone else. God wants us to go into the field. Jesus tells us in Matthew 13 that the *"field is the world"* (Matthew 13:38). He's calling us to go and lodge in the villages and bring His presence and His Word. He tells us to *"get up early to the vineyards."* The vineyards are His. The Bible declares in I Corinthians, *"For the earth is the Lord's, and the fulness thereof"* (I Corinthians 10:26). He cares so deeply about the world. He wants to see if there's any fruit of His Word in the earth and if His people all over the nations are growing and prospering.

This is the word of the Lord to us today: we ought to be doing something to bring His presence and Word to the nations. It is there, He says, where He will give us His love. There we will find His pleasure and sense His glory and His delight raining down upon us as we take the gospel of His Kingdom to the nations.

The book of Nehemiah tells us to *"send portions unto them for whom nothing is prepared"* (Nehemiah 8:10). This is our job. The bride is asked in Song of Solomon 8:8, *"We have a little sister, and she hath no breasts: what shall we do for our sister in the day when she shall be spoken for?"* We have a little sister who has no nourishment. What will we do for her? God cares about the little sister.

I pray today that your heart be smitten with this word. I pray you begin to take on a Kingdom mentality, rather than a selfish one. I pray that you lose the doctrine of self that is so prominent in the charismatic movement, and respond like the bride, *"I am a wall, and my breasts like towers."* In other words, she is saying she will go because she has something to give them. Isaiah too was asked if he would go. The Lord asked him in Isaiah 6:8, *"Whom shall I send, and who will go for us? Then said I, Here am I; send me"* (Isaiah 6:8). Let us too go forth into the field!

"Eagles' Wings"
Luke 17:36

DAY 88

Here in Luke 17:37 Jesus said, *"Wheresoever the body is, thither will the eagles be gathered together."* The body here is the body of Christ; His shed blood, the perfect offering, and His sacrifice. The eagles are the blood-washed saints gathered around the atonement of His blood at the end of the present age. The eagles will be gathered together around the body of Christ. I believe these eagles are the manchild's wings, the overcomers in Revelation 12:14, when the woman is taken into the wilderness and given the wings of a great eagle to carry her and protect her. Also, God is spoken of as an eagle in Exodus 19:4 where it says, *"Ye have seen what I did unto the Egyptians, and how I bare you on eagles' wings, and brought you unto myself."* As we look at the Scriptures, we see this principle of the eagles' wings and the eagles being the overcomers.

In Revelation 4:7 and Ezekiel 1:10, 14 it talks about the living creatures having four faces, one of them being an eagle's face and another being a man's face. Therefore, I believe these are the overcomers, the eagles. In Psalms 103:5, one of our benefits of our salvation is *"that thy youth is renewed like the eagle's."* Also in Isaiah 40:31 it says, *"But they that wait upon the Lord shall renew their strength; they shall mount up with wings as eagles."* Those that wait on the Lord, and give themselves completely to Him, those who allow God's salvation to do a complete work, will mount up with wings as eagles.

Job 39:27-30 says, *"Doth the eagle mount up at thy command, and make her nest on high? ²⁸She dwelleth and abideth on the rock, upon the crag of the rock, and the strong place. ²⁹From thence she seeketh the prey, and her eyes behold afar off. ³⁰Her young ones also suck up blood: and where the slain are, there is she."* The eagle makes her nest on high, meaning she's seated in heavenly places. She dwells and abides on the rock, which is Christ Jesus. The strong place refers to the secret place of the Most High. It's from there she seeks to destroy her prey and her enemy. Her eyes behold afar off. She has vision for the future, and whereever the dead in Christ are, she is also there.

The same power that carried Israel from Egypt into the wilderness also will carry the perfected church into the wilderness in the beginning of the great tribulation. The Lord God will carry His redeemed, (60-fold believers represented by the woman) to this wilderness. It was in this wilderness that God took care of His people and bore them on eagle's wings. These eagle's wings now belong to the overcomers.

The eagle protects her young with its own body as Christ protects His saints. The eagle is of great courage, attacking beasts many times its own size. So is the Christian in conflict with Satan. The eagle uses great wisdom in taking its prey, sometimes filling its feathers with sand to blind its prey. The eagle builds its nest in the highest rock, which is Jesus. She has wonderful vision, sees afar off, and sees the end of the race. The eagle can behold the sun, and the eagle lives long. The eagle bitterly hates the serpent, Satan, and seeks to destroy it. The eagle also renews its youth. The eagle sheds its skin and becomes a new eagle. Just like the transfigured saints. Even today, the eagles are gathering. What a beautiful picture the Scriptures show us of what we can become in these passages. We are called to be part of this company.

"A King To Reign Over Us"
I Samuel 8:19

In the Old Testament, Israel refused to obey the voice of Samuel and the voice of God by saying in I Samuel 8:19, *"Nay; but we will have a king over us."* What is it about human beings that they want to have a king over them, to rule them? I believe every one of us has an innate sense for the need of authority in our lives that only Jesus can truly fill. However, through experiences in childhood, genetic influence and just the overall environment of life, we change and can become rebellious and open ourselves up to demonic possession. Therefore, our reaction to and relationship with authority is not as God intended it to be. What will we choose today?

We are supposed to be under a father ministry, under true pastors. Yet that has been perverted even in the church. We find this in Jeremiah 5:31, *"The priests bear rule by their means; and my people love to have it so."* I don't know about you, but I don't love having somebody rule and reign over my life. Yet it seems that there is something in all of us that desires authority. That is good, but for some people, that goes beyond just good and goes into bad, especially when we allow that authority to manipulate and control our lives. In II Corinthians 11:20 says, *"For ye suffer, if a man bring you into bondage, if a man devour you, if a man take of you, if a man exalt himself, if a man smite you on the face."* Is it possible that such a thing could happen? I believe that in the church there are men and women of God who started out good, but ended up bad. They have become selfish, manipulative and controlling. Somehow, we, as God's people, love to have it so. The reason is we don't want the responsibility to lead our own lives. We would rather somebody else guide us. We want a king over us, somebody else to tell us what to do and make the hard decisions for us.

In Galatians 2:4, Paul says, *"that because of false brethren unawares brought in, who came in privily to spy out our liberty which we have in Christ Jesus, that they might bring us into bondage."* What is so amazing is that there are people in the church who want to bring us into bondage. God was so upset with the shepherds of Israel that He said to them in Ezekiel 34:4, *"Neither have ye sought that which was lost; but with force and with cruelty have ye ruled them."* Have you ever been under a ministry that with force and cruelty you were ruled? We are not supposed to be unduly submitted to people who treat us that way. Yes, all of us should be submitted to one another. We should be submitted to the Lord Jesus and we should be submitted to our covering, the man whom God has put over us to shepherd us. But we are not supposed to let men ride over us.

It is not the will of God to have a king ruling over our lives. In I Peter 5:3, it says, *"Neither as being lords over God's heritage, but being ensamples to the flock."* God doesn't want His ministers being lords over God's heritage, but being examples. Paul told the Corinthians, *"our authority, which the Lord hath given us for edification, and not for your destruction"* (II Corinthians 10:8). I ask you today, do you want a king, or do you want the Lord Jesus to rule and reign in your life with His father ministries that guide, nurture and protect you?

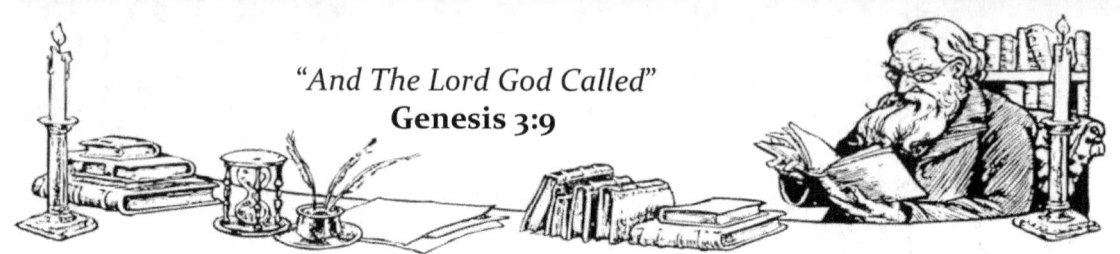

"And The Lord God Called"
Genesis 3:9

Day 90

In this devotion, today, I trust that God will reveal to all of us the great and holy calling that He has placed in all of our lives, both individually and corporately. There is no greater calling in one's life and upon one's heart than the call of God. As we go all the way back to the beginning, we find that it was not mankind that called upon God first, rather it was His great, loving heart that came calling to us. We find the first instance of this Scriptural truth in Genesis 3:9, *"And the Lord God called unto Adam, and said unto him, Where art thou?"*

God has been calling us for thousands of years and for the most part, we have refused to listen. This statement is true in all of man's history. It is not just the world that has refused to listen, but even His own people have outright rejected Him time and time again. It's no wonder why the Scriptures say in Matthew 22:14, *"For many are called, but few are chosen."* I believe few are chosen because few actually choose.

Remember what it was like when you first responded to God's call, how wonderful, how rich, how exciting and how fulfilling it was. The thing is, though, He has never stopped calling. That is why the Holy Spirit is so rightly called by so many as the hound of heaven. Like an old, faithful dog, God keeps coming back, reaching out to us, trying in every way to get our attention. Why some men don't respond will always remain a mystery to me. There is no reason why all of us shouldn't have a vibrant, glorious and intimate relationship with Him, not just once or twice a week, but every day and every moment. Life is simply too short. Now is the time, now is the day of salvation, and now is the time to respond to His gentle wooing.

In the Scriptures, we look at this tremendous revelation of the calling of God upon our lives. We can see the call of Samuel, *"And the Lord called as at other times, Samuel, Samuel"* (I Samuel 3:10). How many times has the Lord been calling to you and me? Exodus 3:4 says, *"And when the Lord saw that he [Moses] turned aside to see, God called unto him out of the midst of the bush."* God is calling to you, today. Does He have to call you out of a burning bush? Perhaps God was calling Moses long before Moses came upon that burning bush.

In II Chronicles 7:14 it says, *"If my people, which are called by my name, shall humble themselves, and pray, and seek my face."* You and I need to humble ourselves and hear the voice of God. Psalms 42:7 says, *"Deep calleth unto deep at the noise of thy waterspouts."* Are you listening? Are you hearing Him? God is calling. John 10:3 says, *"To him the porter openeth; and the sheep hear his voice: and he calleth his own sheep by name, and leadeth them out."* God is calling. Will you respond today? *"Faithful is he that calleth you, who also will do it"* (I Thessalonians 5;24). Proverbs 8:4 says *"Unto you, O men, I call; and my voice is to the sons of man."* God is calling, calling and calling, waiting for a people to respond to Him. He says in Isaiah 43:1, *"Fear not: for I have redeemed thee, I have called thee by thy name."* The Lord hath called you. Will you respond today? Will you give heed to His voice?

"His Eyes Behold The Nations"
Psalms 66:7

Here in Psalms 66, it says, "*He ruleth by his power for ever; his eyes behold the nations...*" (Psalms 66:7.) God's eyes are ever upon this world. "*For God so loved the world,*" John 3:16 says. His eyes are upon the nations. God is always thinking about what good He can do for the peoples of the earth. Every tribe, kindred, and tongue He cares about. Our job is to take His message, His presence, and His character throughout the earth.

It says in Zechariah, "*After the glory hath he sent me unto the nations...*" (Zechariah 2:8). This simply means we are to take the glory of God to the nations. As we follow the presence of the Lord, the majestic glory of God, it will lead us into the nations, where we will manifest His presence, His character, and His Word and bring the Kingdom of God to them. The fields are "*white already to harvest,*" the Bible says (John 4:35). In the book of Nehemiah, it says, "*...send portions unto them for whom nothing is prepared...*" (Nehemiah 8:10). Why? We are the ones who can do it. We are the ones with the provision to send to them. Song of Solomon 8:8 tells us, "*We have a little sister, and she hath no breasts: what shall we do for our sister in the day when she shall be spoken for?*" I believe this is the day that God has spoken of.

It says in Jeremiah, "*Make ye mention to the nations; behold, publish against Jerusalem...*" (Jeremiah 4:16). God wants us to publish His salvation. The book of Psalms tells us, "*Ask of me, and I shall give thee the heathen for thine inheritance, and the uttermost parts of the earth for thy possession*" (Psalms 2:8). This is our inheritance: the nations, the Gentiles, the unsaved peoples of the world. His eyes are upon the nations, because He cares for them and wants to bring them to Himself.

May God put that earnest care in every one of us. He wants us to behold the nations and be "*moved with compassion toward them,*" just as Jesus was when he saw the great crowd of people "*were as sheep not having a shepherd*" (Mark 6:34). All over the world today, there are people who are like sheep that have no shepherd. They are in desperate need of leadership, the Kingdom of God, the Word of the Lord, and the presence of God. It is our job; we are ambassadors for Christ. We're to make people know that they are "*reconciled to God*" (II Corinthians 5:20).

His eyes are beholding the nations; what are our eyes beholding? So many people think that somebody else should go, somebody else should be concerned for the nations. I know that not everyone is called to go to the nations, but we can sure help others and support them. Let's lift up our eyes today to the nations, the needy, and those in desperate want of the glory and the Word of God. As we behold the nations, God will say to us, "*Whom shall I send, and who will go for us?*" (Isaiah 6:8). My response is, "*After the glory hath he sent me unto the nations...*" (Zachariah 2:8).

"I Will Surely Buy It Of Thee At A Price"
II Samuel 24:24

DAY 92

II Samuel 24:24 says, *"...Nay; but I will surely buy it of thee at a price: neither will I offer burnt offerings unto the Lord my God of that which doth cost me nothing."* This is the story of David repenting for numbering Israel, how grieved his heart was at the loss of human lives, and how he needed to make this sacrifice to the Lord. So he sought to buy land to build an altar and make a sacrifice. The man who owned this property was willing to give it to him freely because David was the king, but David knew the price of his true repentance. He knew his relationship with the Lord depended on something far greater than that which costs him nothing. He wanted to show God that he was serious.

There are times in our lives when nothing less than that which causes a great sacrifice in our lives is the answer. Sometimes, it must cost us greatly. The Scriptures are very clear that salvation is free, and everything else in God after salvation costs us something. Sometimes, we just really have to pay the price as Proverbs tells us, *"Buy the truth, and sell it not"* (Proverbs 23:23). In Revelation 3 Jesus said, *"I counsel thee to buy of me gold tried in the fire"* (Revelation 3:18). This is what all of us must do. Sacrifice is part of what God requires of us.

The word *"sacrifice"* in Hebrew means "to slaughter." Sometimes, things in our lives have to be slaughtered. In the Greek, it means "to sacrifice by fire, to blow smoke at, or to kill." Some things can only be offered to the Lord by killing them. My life has been riddled with sacrifices and I know that God required them of me. It was my duty to give the sacrifice to Him when it was recquired.

In your life today don't take the path of least resistance. Don't take the way of the world or the easy way out. But as the Scriptures declare, with these sacrifices God is well pleased (Hebrews 13:16). Hebrews 13:15 says, *"By him therefore let us offer the sacrifice of praise to God continually, that is, the fruit of our lips giving thanks to his name"* (Hebrews 13:15).

We need to learn that everything isn't easy in the Christian Kingdom. Actually, some things are very hard. Jesus said, *"In the world ye shall have tribulation: but be of good cheer; I have overcome the world"* (John 16:33). God knows that every one of us has a breaking point. He knows that all of us allow and carry things in our lives that we don't want there. He knows we go through things that sometimes are beyond our control. All He asks is that we give Him everything. He has given everything and paid the ultimate price in the sacrifice of His Son. All He asks now is that we give Him the same.

Here David refused to take this property as a free gift from this man because he wanted to show God that it would cost him something. He knew what he had done was wrong and that he needed to pay the price for it. He was willing to do whatever it took to show God he was sorry.

Revelation 12 tells us, *"they overcame him by the blood of the Lamb, and by the word of their testimony; and they loved not their lives unto the death"* (Revelation 12:11). There must be this attitude in all of us, a willingness to sacrifice anything and everything for the Kingdom of God and for our precious Savior. Nothing is worth holding on to if God is requiring you to sacrifice it. We must be free and willing to die to ourselves, to situations, relationships, jobs, whatever it may be, whatever the price may be. We have to sacrifice it, die to it, and give it to the Lord.

You may be in a situation today where God is requiring a sacrifice of you. Don't hesitate. Realize that your walk with God is the most important thing in your life and that Jesus is the pearl of great price. Whatever He is requiring, give it to Him. Let it be said of you that you would never offer to the Lord anything that doesn't cost you something. Yes, it will hurt. Yes, it will cost you. Yes, you have to *"buy the truth."* But in the end, *"the truth shall make you free"* (John 8:32).

"Masters Of Assemblies"
Ecclesiastes 12:11

DAY 93

In the Scriptures, God calls Himself the Chief Shepherd and Bishop of our souls. Jesus calls Himself the Good Shepherd. Not only that, but as Ephesians 4:11-12 tells us, *"And he gave some, apostles; and some, prophets; and some, evangelists; and some pastors and teachers. ¹²For the perfecting of the saints, for the work of the ministry, for the edifying of the body of Christ."* The word pastor and shepherd are synonymous in the Bible. Jesus, being the Chief Shepherd, has delegated authority to under-shepherds who are to minister, to care for and to feed the flock of God.

Here in Ecclesiastes 12:11, it says, *"The words of the wise are as goads, and as nails fastened by the masters of assemblies, which are given from one shepherd."* The words of the wise are as goads. God gives words to shepherds. A true shepherd will always have the word of the Lord in his mouth for his sheep. John 10:11 says, *"The good shepherd giveth his life for the sheep."* It is written in Malachi 2:7, *"For the priest's lips should keep knowledge, and they should seek the law at his mouth: for he is the messenger of the Lord of hosts."* The priest's lips should keep knowledge. God wants His men and women to have knowledge and wisdom, to be properly trained and to teach the Word of God. I Peter 5:2 says, *"Feed the flock of God which is among you, taking the oversight thereof, not by constraint, but willingly; not for filthy lucre, but of a ready mind."*

In this day where so much emphasis is put on glorifying men, the cart has gone before the horse. It is the job of ministers and shepherds to feed the flock of God with words of wisdom. In Ezekiel 34:2 says, *"Should not the shepherds feed the flocks?"* Of course they should and they do it with *"the words of the wise"*. So those words of the wise are like goads, a stick that pushes an animal and keeps it in the flock.

God's Word is also *"as nails fastened by the masters of assemblies."* These doctrinal truths, these spiritual revelations that God gives us are to be fastened down into people's lives. The masters of assemblies are simply teachers and preachers. They are masters of the local churches. They are to take the Word of God and then fasten them, nail them in by teaching them, preaching to them, exhorting them and by prophesying to them, thereby feeding the sheep.

The masters are given from one shepherd. In other words, the Chief Shepherd, Jesus, give the under-shepherds the Word of God, and they take that word and then fasten that it into the lives of the people that God has entrusted to them.

Paul said in II Timothy 2:2, *"And the things that thou hast heard of me among many witnesses, the same commit thou to faithful men, who shall be able to teach others also."* This is the true principle of discipleship. The Chief Shepherd gives the masters of assemblies, the under-shepherds, the elders, pastors and teachers words of wisdom. Those words, like goads and as nails, are then used to fasten, mold and perfect God's people. Are you being molded and perfected today?

"When He Was Come Near"
Luke 19:41

DAY 94

In this passage of Scripture we find Jesus drawing near the city of Jerusalem and it says, *"And when he was come near, he beheld the city, and wept over it"* (Luke 19:41). How many times has the Lord drawn near you and me and we had not recognized it just as the two disciples did not recognize Jesus as they were walking to Emmaus in Luke 24:15-16, *"And it came to pass, that, while they communed together and reasoned, Jesus himself drew near, and went with them. But their eyes were holden that they should not know him"*

How many times have we not known it when Jesus has drawn near to us? Jacob said in Genesis 28:16, *"surely the Lord is in this place; and I knew it not."* How many times had the Lord called Samuel as a child and he knew it not? Samuel was not able to recognize God's voice until he finally got free from the bondage of men and came to know God personally (I Samuel 2:10). Isaiah 46:13 says, *"I bring near my righteousness; it shall not be far off, and my salvation shall not tarry."* Oh, how God longs to bring near His righteousness. He longs to come near you and me to bring His Word. Psalms 119:151 says, *"Thou art near, O Lord; and all thy commandments are truth."* He is never far away from us. The Lord neither sleeps nor slumbers.

The word for *"presence"* in the Hebrew is the same word translated elsewhere *"face."* It literally means "the turning of the face towards." Oh, that God would behold you today and you would let Him draw near. Let Him come close and don't be like the bride in Song of Solomon 5:2-3 who didn't get up from her bed right away when the Lord came to her in the night dripping with His anointing. She made an excuse that her shoes were off, representing she stopped walking with Jesus. She remained at first in her bed, which speaks of slothfulness or being too comfortable. Today, when the Lord comes dripping with His anointing, reaching for you, respond. The Lord came to His bride in Song of Solomon 5 to simply wake her up, knowing her condition. Rise up and meet Him today. The Lord knew that she would be condemned by not responding at first to Him. As such, she finally got up out of her bed to run after Him like never before.

He's just a breath away. His presence is hovering now, waiting for you. He told Moses years ago to tell His people to build a tabernacle so He could come and dwell with them (Exodus 25:8). God wants to draw near to you to inhabit you, *"For the Lord's portion is his people"* (Deuteronomy 32:9). Isaiah 55:6-7 says, *"Seek ye the Lord while he may be found, call ye upon him while he is near. Let the wicked forsake his way, and the unrighteous man his thoughts: and let him return unto the Lord."* Oh, let us return to the Lord today. Let us seek the Lord. Let us respond to His drawing near to us. Let's call upon Him because *"He is near that justifieth"* (Isaiah 50:8). It doesn't matter what your condition is. Let Him wash you clean if He has to. Let Him come near bringing, His righteousness and salvation. He is near and His commandments are true.

He is near and I pray He's not weeping over you like He did over Jerusalem because they didn't know their day of visitation, but rather He is rejoicing because like Samuel, you've answered the call.

"Where Is Mine Honor?"
Malachi 1:6

"A son honoureth his father, and a servant his master: if then I be a father, where is mine honour? and if I be a master, where is my fear? saith the Lord of hosts unto you, O priests, that despise my name. And ye say, Wherein have we despised thy name?" (Malachi 1:6)

DAY 95

The word *"honor"* in Hebrew is the word *"kabowd,"* which is also translated as *"glory."* It means *"weighty, heavy, and glorious."* Where is the weight of glory that we give to Him for all that He's done for us? In the Greek, the word *"honor"* means *"glory, praise, or dignity."* Our job as His people and as His servants is to honor Him.

The Bible tells us in Romans 13:7 to give *"honour to whom honour"* is due. It also says in I Samuel 2:30, *"Wherefore the Lord God of Israel saith...them that honour me I will honour."* It should be very simple to us. We should honor God with our lives. We should give Him the weightiest glory, dignity, and praise. In Psalms 104:1 David says, *"O Lord my God, thou art very great; thou art clothed with honour and majesty."* Our God is clothed with dignity, power, and awesomeness, but yet at the same time, He's humble, precious, loving, merciful, and compassionate.

So, what are the ways you and I can honor the Lord? How do we give Him honor? In the context of this passage, He's talking about the people offering polluted bread upon His altar, not really giving a true offering to Him. The Lord says to them, *"O priests, that despise my name"* (Malachi 1:6). To not honor the Lord is to despise His name, or His character. This really is insanity. David said in Psalms 26:8, *"Lord, I have loved the habitation of thy house, and the place where thine honour dwelleth."* The habitation of His house, the sanctuary, is the place where you and I honor the Lord with everything that's in us. We give Him glory and praise.

Let's look to the Scriptures to see how we honor the Lord. Proverbs 3:9 declares, *"Honour the Lord with thy substance, and with the firstfruits of all thine increase."* You and I show our honor for God by giving Him at least ten percent of our income, and really, it should be more than that. We honor the Lord by giving naturally to Him.

In Revelation 19:7, the Bible says, *"Let us be glad and rejoice, and give honour to him: for the marriage of the Lamb is come."* We need to be glad and rejoice that we have a heavenly Bridegroom that loves us and plans to marry us and share everything He has with us. Surely, He's due honor for that. It says in Revelation 4:11, *"Thou art worthy, O Lord, to receive glory and honour and power."* It also says in Revelation 5:13, *"Blessing, and honour, and glory, and power, be unto him that sitteth upon the throne."*

He's sitting on the throne today and He deserves all of the honor, worship, dignity, praise, and all of our good offerings. We owe Him everything. Let Him never have to say to us, *"Where is mine honor?"*

"Passing Through The Valley"
Psalms 84:6

Here in Psalms 84, it says:

> "*5Blessed is the man whose strength is in thee; in whose heart are the ways of them. 6Who passing through the valley of Baca make it a well; the rain also filleth the pools. 7They go from strength to strength, every one of them in Zion appeareth before God.*" (Psalms 84:5-7)

"Baca" in Hebrew means "weeping." The valley is a place that we all go through; it is a rite of passage for the believer. It speaks of a place of trial and testing, the dealings of God, adversity, temptations, and maybe even suffering. The valley is the place where we must learn to overcome. It is also the place of transition and change into deeper realms in God, in His Word, and in our own spiritual substance. It is where our revelation is married to our situation.

At one time, the enemies of Israel said, in I Kings 20, "*The Lord is God of the hills, but he is not God of the valleys.*" God answered them by saying, "*therefore will I deliver all this great multitude into thine hand, and ye shall know that I am the Lord*" (I Kings 20:28). God does not like our enemies saying things about Him or His people.

There are many times in our lives when we walk through valleys, hard experiences, deep, purging experiences. These are the valleys of life. The Scriptures speak of many valleys: "*Yea, though I walk through the valley of the shadow of death, I will fear no evil: for thou art with me; thy rod and thy staff they comfort me*" (Psalms 23:4). In Song of Solomon 2:1, the bride says, "*I am the rose of Sharon, and the lily of the valleys.*" Even in the midst of the valleys we can find that there will be a lily in our experiences. Isaiah declares, "*Every valley shall be exalted, and every mountain and hill shall be made low*" (Isaiah 40:4). Every valley shall be exalted, and blessed is the man who passing through the valley of weeping makes it a well. In Hosea, it says, "*the valley of Achor,*" which means "trouble," can become "*a door of hope*" for you. (Hosea 2:15).

We all don't understand it, and it may be hard to receive, but the valley is a very important place in the lives of believers. It is something we pass through. It is where we transition into something greater in God.

So, remember today to pass through the valley. It is not meant to be forever. We are simply going from "*strength to strength,*" "*faith to faith*" (Romans 1:17), "*vessel to vessel*" (Jeremiah 48:11). We will overcome. He will meet us in the valley, for He is surely the God of the valleys.

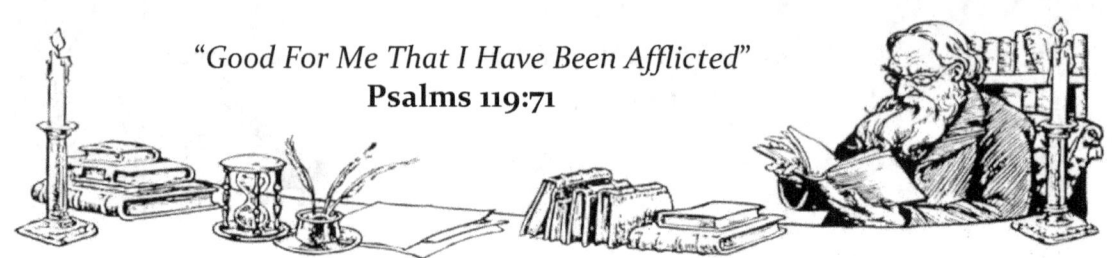

"Good For Me That I Have Been Afflicted"
Psalms 119:71

DAY 97

David says here in Psalms 119, *"It is good for me that I have been afflicted; that I might learn thy statutes"* (Psalms 119:71). The Hebrew word for *"afflicted"* means "chastised or punished." Can you say today that it was good for you to be afflicted? So many of us do not see that *"reproofs of instruction are the way of life"* (Proverbs 6:23). God corrects His people. The book of Job tells us, *"Behold, happy is the man whom God correcteth: therefore despise not thou the chastening of the Almighty"* (Job 5:17). We can be happy if we know what the end result will be, which is *"that I might learn thy statutes."* The only way to truly know the Word of God is to overcome something in our lives. Revelation must be married to situation. Whatever situation we are in today, there is a revelation that's going to be formed out of it. So, rather than being sad, let's see the end result and be happy about it.

Happy is the man whom God correcteth. Therefore, don't despise the chastening of the Lord. In both the Hebrew and Greek, the word *"chastening"* does not mean beating with a whip or a rod; it simply means "instruction and training." Our God is a good Father and He wants to bless us. He wants to train and discipline us. Moreover, Job 5 says, *"For he maketh sore, and bindeth up: he woundeth, and his hands make whole"* (Job 5:18). Every time God does something that seemingly hurts us, He then restores us. His purpose is never to hurt, but to cause us to grow and to know His Word and understand Him better.

It says in the next verse, *"He shall deliver thee in six troubles"* (Job 5:19). Six is the number for man and Satan, and as long as we are in this world, *"ye shall have tribulation,"* Jesus said (John 16:33). As long as we are men, and Satan is around, there will be trouble. There will be correction needed, but Job 5 continues to say, *"yea, in seven there shall no evil touch thee"* (Job 5:19). Seven is the number for completion. In other words, the day will come when we will have gone through enough and will no longer need the chastening of the Lord. The book of Hebrews tells us:

> *"⁵And ye have forgotten the exhortation which speaketh unto you as unto children, My son, despise not thou the chastening of the Lord, nor faint when thou art rebuked of him: ⁶For whom the Lord loveth he chasteneth, and scourgeth every son whom he receiveth"* (Hebrews 12:5-6).

Whom the Lord loves He chastens, teaches, disciplines, and instructs. The Lord loves you; He's not angry with you. He's simply trying to make you into a better man or woman of God. Hebrews 12 continues saying, *"⁷If ye endure chastening, God dealeth with you as with sons; for what son is he whom the father chasteneth not? ⁸But if ye be without chastisement, whereof all are partakers, then are ye bastards, and not sons"* (Hebrews 12:7-8). Do you want to be a bastard or a son, an illegitimate child or a full-grown son in the Lord? Is it good for you to be afflicted? Make your answer "Yes" today and become the man or woman of God He wants you to be.

"The Goodness Of God Endureth"
Psalms 52:1

DAY 98

Here in Psalms 52, David says, *"The goodness of God endureth continually"* (Psalms 52:1). In other words, there is no end to the goodness of God. David said in Psalms 27, *"I had fainted, unless I had believed to see the goodness of the Lord in the land of the living"* (Psalms 27:13). One of the words for *"fainted"* in Hebrew means "to be insane." I had almost gone insane, unless I had believed to see the goodness of the Lord in the land where I live. I don't know about you, but I don't need to see His goodness pie in the sky, by-and-by; I need to see it now.

Are you experiencing the goodness of the Lord in the land where you live? It's enduring continually. Psalms 65 tells us, *"We shall be satisfied with the goodness of thy house, even of thy holy temple"* (Psalms 65:4). David said in Psalms 107, *"Oh that men would praise the Lord for his goodness, and for his wonderful works to the children of men!"* (Psalms 107:8). Do we have to be begged and pleaded to praise God for His goodness? I don't think so. Psalms 31:19 says, *"Oh how great is thy goodness."* It says in Nehemiah 9:25, *"so they did eat, and were filled, and became fat, and delighted themselves in thy great goodness."*

His great goodness endures continually; there's no end to it. All we need to do is believe it. The Bible says in I John 4:16, *"And we have known and believed the love that God hath to us."* It's one thing to know something; it's another thing to believe it and walk in it. We don't need to just have something written in our notebooks or as a theory in our heads, but our revelation must be married to situation.

The goodness of God endures continually; it's always there. Why? God is good. He can't help Himself. David actually called the Lord in Psalms 144, *"My goodness, and my fortress."* (Psalms 144:2). I love the passage in Jeremiah, where he says, *"Therefore they shall come and sing in the height of Zion, and shall flow together to the goodness of the Lord"* (Jeremiah 31:12). We will all be flowing together to the goodness of the Lord in the last days. The book of Hosea tells us, *"Afterward shall the children of Israel...fear the Lord and his goodness in the latter days"* (Hosea 3:5).

When people see His great goodness in the last days, that's what will win people over. There is not going to be strong teaching on hell or judgment, but on the love of God and His goodness. People are desperate for just common goodness. There is so much hardness and separation in the world today; goodness is a forgotten fruit. It is actually called one of the fruits of the Spirit (Galatians 5:22). It also says in Ephesians 5:9, *"For the fruit of the Spirit is in all goodness and righteousness and truth."* Hallelujah! In the book of Nehemiah, the Holy Spirit is called *"thy good spirit"* (Nehemiah 9:20). Everything about our triune God is goodness. Jesus is the *"good shepherd"* (John 10:11). God our Father is a good father. Our triune God is full of great goodness.

Oh, that men would praise the Lord for His goodness! Would you do that today? Will you *"taste and see that the Lord is good"* (Psalms 34:8)?

"How That By Revelation He Made Known Unto Me The Mystery"
Ephesians 3:3

DAY 99

I want to look today at the principle of revelation as found in the Holy Scriptures. The Greek word for *"revelation"* means "to take off the cover, to disclose, an appearing, or manifestation." To take the cover off something means that you couldn't see it before. But when the cover is taken off, you now see it. The Hebrew word for *"revelation"* and *"reveal"* means "to unclothe."

In Matthew 16, Jesus asked the disciples, *"Whom do men say that I the Son of man am?"*, and, *"whom say ye that I am?"* Peter responded, *"Thou art the Christ, the Son of the living God."* Jesus then said, *"flesh and blood hath not revealed it unto thee,"* or taken the cover off so that you could see, *"but my Father which is in heaven"* (Matthew 16:13-17). Flesh and blood cannot reveal the Scriptures or the deeper truths of God to us. It takes the Father in heaven to reveal things to us. And how does He do that?

In Galatians 1:11-12, Paul says, *"But I certify you, brethren, that the gospel which was preached of me is not after man. ¹²For I neither received it of man, neither was I taught it, but by the revelation of Jesus Christ."* Jesus Christ is the one that brought the revelation. Paul says in Ephesians:

> *"How that by revelation he made known unto me the mystery; (as I wrote afore in few words, ⁴Whereby, when ye read, ye may understand my knowledge in the mystery of Christ) ⁵Which in other ages was not made known unto the sons of men, as it is now revealed unto his holy apostles and prophets by the Spirit;"* (Ephesians 3:3-5).

The Spirit of God is the one that takes the cover off. I Corinthians 2:9-10 says, *"But as it is written, Eye hath not seen, nor ear heard, neither have entered into the heart of man, the things which God hath prepared for them that love him."* Too many times, we stop at that verse and don't continue to the next one. Verse 10 tells us, *"But God hath revealed them unto us by his Spirit: for the Spirit searcheth all things, yea, the deep things of God."* We need to have the Spirit of revelation in our lives so that we can know the deep things of God and the things God has for us. They are exceedingly, abundantly above anything we could ever ask or think.

Remember, in Luke 2, the story of Simeon, of whom it says, *"it was revealed unto him by the Holy Ghost, that he should not see death, before he had seen the Lord's Christ"* (Luke 2:26). The word for *"revealed"* used here means a "divinely intimate" revelation or an "oracle" given to him by God. God wants to give us divinely intimate oracles. He wants to take the cover off things and let us see the deeper truths of His Scripture. And it does not come by men.

Daniel said, when he revealed the king's secret of the image that he saw in his dream, *"But as for me, this secret is not revealed to me for any wisdom that I have more than any living"* (Daniel 2:30). Revelation does not come by wisdom or intellect; it is given by the Spirit of God, who knows everything about God and takes the cover off for us. Deuteronomy 29:29 says, *"The secret things,"* or hidden realities, *"belong unto the Lord our God: but those things which are revealed belong unto us and to our children for ever, that we may do all the words of this law."* God wants us to know His secrets so we can do everything He has for us to accomplish.

Jesus said to the disciples in in Mark 4:11, *"Unto you it is given to know the mystery of the kingdom of God."* We can know the deeper truths of God, the hidden realities, and the mysteries of God that have been hidden for ages. They are *"now revealed unto his holy apostles and prophets"* and unto those of us that will allow the Spirit of God to take the cover off of the Word for us. We can know the things that have been hidden for ages.

Look at what happened to David when he gave the revelation of that dream to the king. Daniel said to him, *"there is a God in heaven that revealeth secrets, and maketh known to the king Nebuchadnezzar what shall be in the latter days"* (Daniel 2:28). Then in verse 47, *"The king answered unto Daniel, and said, Of a truth it is, that your God is a God of gods, and a Lord of kings, and a revealer of secrets, seeing thou couldest reveal this secret."* All of the other wise men and astrologers and mighty men could not reveal this secret, this dream, this vision that king Nebuchadnezzar had. And when Daniel did, it says that the king Nebuchadnezzar fell on his face and worshipped and said that God is the God of gods and Lord of kings. Verse 48 says, *"Then the king made Daniel a great man, and gave him many great gifts, and made him ruler over the whole province of Babylon, and chief of the governors over all the wise men of Babylon."* He did all of this simply because he was able to divine or take the cover off what others could not.

The Spirit of revelation is something for which each one of us needs to believe God, because we need to know the deeper things of God. Jesus said in Luke 10:21, *"I thank thee, O Father, Lord of heaven and earth, that thou hast hid these things from the wise and prudent, and hast revealed them unto babes."* You don't have to be a genius. You don't have to be a Greek scholar. You simply need to have the Spirit of revelation and the heart of a child, and God will reveal to you even the deepest of truths.

The Lord is waiting for a people to come forth who have been *"approved unto God, a workman that needeth not to be ashamed, rightly dividing the word of truth"* (II Timothy 2:15). Once we have approved ourselves unto God that we truly are disciples of His Word, that we love Him, and can keep His secrets, He then will reveal to us the deep and abiding mysteries that have been hidden.

Daniel prophesied that in the last days the books shall be opened. And we find that messenger in Revelation 10 standing with an open book in his hand and John was told to go and take it and eat it up. The open book represents somebody having revelation out of the Word of God. As John went and humbled himself and ate from that open book, he got the revelation of Jesus Christ.

Revelation is waiting for you and me as we spend time in the Word and in the presence of God. Hear the word of the Lord today. God wants us to see things we never saw before. Are you hungry for more? He wants to make known by revelation all of the deep things of God, the deeper truths, but most importantly, He wants to make known to us Himself.

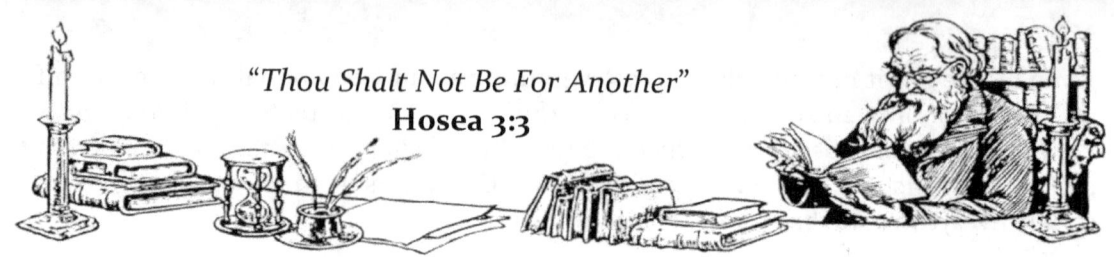

"Thou Shalt Not Be For Another"
Hosea 3:3

DAY 100

In Hosea 3, we see God speaking to Hosea to go and love a certain woman. This is a type of God going and loving us: His people. He says here in verse 3, *"And I said unto her, Thou shalt abide for me many days; thou shalt not play the harlot, and thou shalt not be for another man: so will I also be for thee."* First of all, God does not want us for another; He wants us for Himself. The Lord doesn't ask for a lot, but He does ask for commitment from us. He's our heavenly bridegroom, and He longs to be with us.

Hosea 11:4 says, *"I drew them with cords of a man, with bands of love: and I was to them as they that take off the yoke."* All day long we hear Him saying, *"Come unto me, all ye that labour and are heavy laden, and I will give you rest"* (Matthew 11:28). Psalms 42:7 says, *"Deep calleth unto deep."* This is His voice coming from the most holy place. It is His divine pull that is drawing us to be with Him. It is drawing us away from our other lovers and idols and is drawing us towards Himself.

In Jeremiah 29:13 he says, *"And ye shall seek me, and find me, when ye shall search for me with all your heart. And I will be found of you."* The Lord has sought for us. We have not chosen Him but He has chosen us. *"The Lord's portion is his people"* (Deuteronomy 32:9). We're all He's ever going to get out of this, and He's calling us today, drawing us to Himself. He wants us for Himself, not for another.

Is there another in your life today? Is there some idol, some thing that captivates you more than Jesus? Is there something that has become more to you than He is? Do you sense Him drawing you with the chords of His precious and holy love? He promises to her:

> *"¹⁹And I will betroth thee unto me for ever; yea, I will betroth thee unto me in righteousness, and in judgment, and in lovingkindness, and in mercies. ²⁰I will even betroth thee unto me in faithfulness: and thou shalt know the Lord."* (Hosea 2:19-20)

God wants us desperately to know Him. He wants the cry of our heart to be as Paul's in Philippians 3:10, *"That I may know him"* or as David's in Psalms 27:4, *"one thing have I desired of the Lord, that will I seek after; that I may dwell in the house of the Lord all the days of my life, to behold the beauty of the Lord."*

"Thou shalt not be for another man." *"Thou shalt have no other gods before me"* (Exodus 20:3). He alone is God, *"for thy Maker is thine husband; the Lord of hosts is his name; and thy Redeemer"* (Isaiah 54:5). Your heavenly Bridegroom is calling you with bands of love. Don't be for another because He promises to betroth us unto Him forever.

"He Careth For You"
I Peter 5:7

Day 101

What a glorious promise I Peter tells us, *"Casting all your care upon him; for he careth for you"* (I Peter 5:7). Oh what a wonder to know that the God of the universe, our great and glorious Savior, truly cares about us. Jesus says in Matthew 11, *"Come unto me, all ye that labour and are heavy laden, and I will give you rest"* (Matthew 11:28). Jesus wants to give us rest because He cares for us. The Bible says, *"In all their affliction he was afflicted"* (Isaiah 63:9). He knows what we are going through. He knows that *"we must through much tribulation enter into the kingdom of God"* (Acts 14:22).

Jesus says in John 10:14-15, *"I am the good shepherd, and know my sheep, and am known of mine. ¹⁵As the Father knoweth me, even so know I the Father: and I lay down my life for the sheep."* He laid down His life for us, and the Bible says that, *"he ever liveth to make intercession"* for us (Hebrews 7:25).

Truly, God cares for us. Don't ever doubt that. Even when earthly people and situations forsake us, He will not. The book of Psalms tells us, *"When my father and my mother forsake me, then the Lord will take me up"* (Psalms 27:10). When Israel went to battle in II Chronicles 32, Hezekiah said about the enemy, *"With him is an arm of flesh; but with us is the Lord our God to help us, and to fight our battles"* (II Chronicles 32:8). Glory to God! Our God cares about everything we are going through.

David said in Psalms 116:6, *"The Lord preserveth the simple: I was brought low, and he helped me."* How many thousands of times in my forty plus years of being a Christian has the Lord helped me and cared for me when no one else did?

He will care for us today. In Psalms 46:1, it says, *"God is our refuge and strength, a very present help in trouble"* (Psalms 46:1). This is our God. Isaiah declares, *"Fear thou not; for I am with thee: be not dismayed; for I am thy God: I will strengthen thee; yea, I will help thee; yea, I will uphold thee with the right hand of my righteousness"* (Isaiah 41:10). The Lord cares for you and me. Another Scripture in Isaiah reads, *"Can a woman forget her sucking child, that she should not have compassion on the son of her womb?"* Can parents actually do that? Can people forget? He says, *"yea, they may forget, yet will I not forget thee"* (Isaiah 49:15). This is our God. Psalms 111:5 says, *"He hath given meat unto them that fear him: he will ever be mindful of his covenant."* Why? Because He cares for us!

Consider the woman in Ezekiel 16, thrown to the side of the road. What did God do? While everyone else avoided her, He said that it was the time of love, spread His skirt over her and said, *"You are mine. I will take care of you now"* (Ezekiel 16:8).

Remember today, the Lord cares for you. Instead of looking to man or to our circumstances, lift up your eyes today and cast your care over to Him and He will sustain you. He will uphold you with His righteousness because He cares for you.

"Answering A Fool"
Proverbs 26:5-6

DAY 102

Here in Proverbs 26:4-5, we find this message, *"Answer not a fool according his folly, lest thou also be like unto him. ⁵Answer a fool according to his folly, lest he be wise in his own conceit."* I don't know about you, but these verses seem contradictory to me. On one hand, God tells us not to answer a fool and on the other hand, He tells us to answer a fool. I've struggled with this for many years until one day, when I was in the presence of God, He gave me the revelation. It's pretty simple.

First we must remember Ecclesiastes 3:1 which says, *"To every thing there is a season, and a time to every purpose under the heaven."* Moreover, Ecclesiastes 8:5 states, *"A wise man's heart discerneth both time and judgment."* A wise man will know when to speak and when to keep silent. Sometimes you answer a fool because if you don't, he'll think more highly of himself than he ought. He sometimes needs to be checked, humbled, or rebuked.

Then there are times that you don't answer a fool because it would be foolishness. There are times when we don't answer a fool because if we do, we would become like him. Proverbs 16:22 says, *"The instruction of fools is folly."* Proverbs 1:7 also states that, *"fools despise wisdom and instruction."* Likewise Proverbs 22:3 says, *"The simple pass on, and are punished."* Proverbs 29:9 states, *"If a wise man contendeth with a foolish man, whether he rage or laugh, there is no rest."* You see, when we begin to contend with a foolish man, whether we rage or laugh, there will be no peace, no joy and no rest because Proverbs 14:17 says, *"He that is soon angry dealeth foolishly."* Once we start dealing with the foolish, anger pursues us. So Proverbs 9:6 says, *"Forsake the foolish, and live, and go in the way of understanding."*

However, there are other times when we must answer a fool. The Bible says, in I Peter 2:15, *"For so is the will of God, that with well doing ye may put to silence the ignorance of foolish men."* There are times when we need to silence the ignorance of foolish men. There are times when we need to deal with them and not allow them to think that what they are saying means something. Psalms 5:5 states, *"The foolish shall not stand in thy sight."* The Bible is pretty clear in Proverbs 19:1, *"He that is perverse in his lips...is a fool."* Proverbs 29:11, *"A fool uttereth all his mind: but a wise man keepeth it in till afterwards."* There are times when you answer a fool because what he is saying is completely foolish and he is glorying in his ignorance. So we answer a fool according to his folly, lest he be wise in his own conceit. We stop him from thinking that what he is saying is meaningful because what he is saying is really stupid, foolish and ridiculous.

In conclusion, answer not a fool according to his folly, lest thou be like unto him. However, there will also be times when the witness of the Lord will be to answer the fool, lest he starts to think more highly of himself then he ought to and becomes wise in his own conceit. Remember that a wise man's heart discerns both time and judgment. May God give us the discernment today, whether to answer or not answer a fool.

"Let Him Deny Himself, And Take Up His Cross Daily"
Luke 9:23-24

Let's begin by looking at the words of Jesus:

DAY 103

> "*²³And he said to them all, If any man will come after me, let him deny himself, and take up his cross daily, and follow me. ²⁴For whosoever will save his life shall lose it: but whosoever will lose his life for my sake, the same shall save it.*" (Luke 9:23-24)

First of all, Jesus has said to all of us in Matthew 4:19, "*Follow me, and I will make you fishers of men.*" He said also in Matthew 11:28, "*Come unto me.*" We have responded to the call of God and now are walking with the Lord, saved and redeemed. However, we must learn to deny ourselves. Survival of the fittest is the cry of the world, but in the Kingdom of God, humility and denying ourselves is the hallmark of the Kingdom.

It is not easy to deny yourself because self-preservation is one of the greatest principles in humanity. But we must go against this and be like the Lord, who being in glory, left it all and came down and took upon himself the form of a man; He humbled himself. We need to humble ourselves and deny our selfish carnal nature.

Then Jesus tells us to take up our cross. This is not the Lord's cross, but our cross. Every one of us has a burden to bear. Every one of us, in each of our own personal walks with God, have dealings or things in our lives that we hate. Such dealings cause us to learn to live with what we hate in order to embrace that which we love. We need to take up this cross; we need to take up this burden. Remember Paul's thorn in the flesh, in II Corinthians 12:7-9:

> "*⁷And lest I should be exalted above measure through the abundance of the revelations, there was given to me a thorn in the flesh, the messenger of Satan to buffet me, lest I should be exalted above measure. ⁸For this thing I besought the Lord thrice, that it might depart from me. ⁹And he said unto me, My grace is sufficient for thee: for my strength is made perfect in weakness. Most gladly therefore will I rather glory in my infirmities, that the power of Christ may rest upon me.*"

Paul besought the Lord three times to be delivered from his thorn in the flesh, but the Lord said in verse 9, "*My grace is sufficient for thee: for my strength is made perfect in weakness.*" Jesus in the garden of Gethsemane said in Matthew 26:39, "*If it be possible, let this cup pass from me: nevertheless, not as I will, but as thou wilt.*" Just as Jesus and Paul did, we also need to take up our cross. This is a process that we need to walk through daily. This is not something we merely do every Sunday, or every Wednesday. It is something we do twenty-four hours a day. We take up the burden.

It says of Joseph in Psalms 81:6, "*I removed his shoulder from the burden.*" Joseph carried the burden of wearing the coat of many colors. He was then betrayed by his brothers and thrown into a pit. Later on, he had to endure the time he lived in Potiphar's house and then lastly, he persevered through imprisonment. He carried burden after burden until eventually, the weight of pressure no longer meant anything to him. The burden wasn't removed from him, rather his shoulder was removed from the burden; God removed Joseph from the burden.

"For whosoever will save his life shall lose it" (Luke 9:24). The life Jesus is speaking of here is the soulish carnal life. We don't need to conform to self-preservation. Rather, we need to deny ourselves. Jesus continues in verse 24, *"But whosoever will lose his life for my sake, the same shall save it."* We need to deny and lose ourselves and embrace the burden and the cross that the Lord has given us. We need to daily take up that cross and follow Him!

"Let Her Alone"
John 12:7

DAY 104

Today, as we look at this passage of Scripture in John 12, Mary has taken *"a pound of ointment of spikenard, very costly, and anointed the feet of Jesus, and wiped his feet with her hair"* (John 12:3). Then one of his disciples, Judas Iscariot, began to complain about her actions. Jesus then responded by saying, *"Let her alone."* I believe those three words carry great revelation. I believe it is more than past time for women to be allowed to minister and worship God freely and express themselves in the body of Christ.

If you look at the Scriptures, the first evangelists were women coming and proclaiming the resurrection of Jesus. Also, there were women apostles, prophets, and judges. And I believe that there were women teachers, Priscilla being one of them, as well as the *"great woman"* found in II Kings 4:8. In Psalms 68:11, it says, *"The Lord gave the word: great was the company of those that published it."* The actual Hebrew reads, "Great was the company of women that published it." It is time for women to begin to come forth under true coverings and begin to minister according as the Lord has called them to. Act 2:18 states that when God poured out the Spirit from on high on the day of Pentecost that, *"on my servants and on my handmaidens will I pour out in those days of my Spirit."* A handmaiden is a woman.

There is so much resistance and misunderstanding concerning the passages in the New Testament, particularly in I Corinthians 14 and in the book of I Timothy, concerning women keeping silent in the church. I think these simply mean women need to be subjected to men; they are not to *"usurp authority over the man,"* it says (I Timothy 2:12). That is the emphasis: not usurping authority. He would not tell women to prophesy in the church and then tell them to keep silent at the same time. Paul says in I Corinthians:

> *"34Let your women keep silence in the churches: for it is not permitted unto them to speak; but they are commanded to be under obedience, as also saith the law...36What? came the word of God out from you? or came it unto you only?"* (I Corinthians 14:34-36)

He says this to them facetiously. There is no law in the Old Testament that says women cannot speak out loud in the local church. The law Paul was referring to was the oral law of the Jews, the commandments and documents written by rabbis long after the Old Testament had been written. It was full of horrible statements about women, full of prejudice towards them.

The word of the Lord to you today, sisters and brothers, is *"let her alone"*. Let her be free to minister. Let her pour that costly ointment. Let her give voice to all that is crying out within her, that the Spirit of the Lord is moving in her heart for her to say and do.

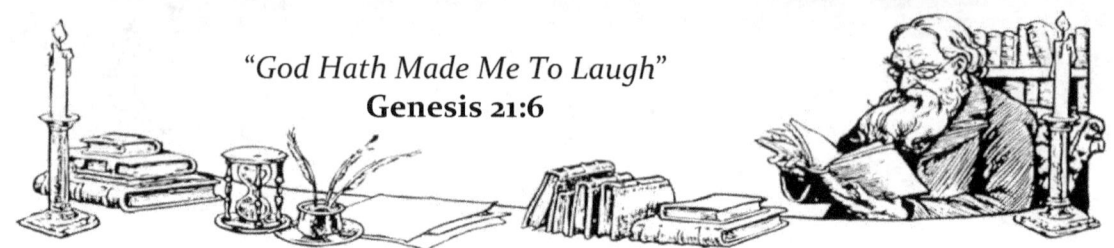

"God Hath Made Me To Laugh"
Genesis 21:6

DAY 105

Here in Genesis 21:6 we find Sarah saying, "*God hath made me to laugh, so that all that hear will laugh with me.*" Sarah herself had laughed foolishly when God had promised her a son, and then had Ishmael, defying the promise of the Lord and not obeying Him. However, God then answered, as He always does, and brought forth His promise. This was Sarah's response. Even though the deadness of her womb spoke so loudly, God intervened, for nothing is too hard for the Lord, nothing is impossible with our God. She had a child, the promised seed, Isaac. As that boy came out, she began to laugh, so that all would hear would laugh with her. They were not laughing at her, but with her.

Our God is a God of laughter, and He wants us to laugh as well. Ecclesiastes 3:4 says, "*A time to weep, and a time to laugh*" Have you laughed recently? I have found that people that don't laugh are miserable people; people that are joyless and never have any fun seem to be hard people. I have always loved to laugh; I love telling jokes and making people laugh. However, when I became a minister I tried to hide that and become religious. I will never forget, years ago in a ministers' meeting in Wisconsin, I was doing the "ministerial thing", shaking my head spiritually, having my eyes half shut trying to be spiritual and saying "Amen" in a deep voice. The voice of God came to me and said, "What are you doing?" I responded, "I don't know" and He said, "That's not you. I didn't create you that way. I created you a rejoicing and laughing person. Now be yourself." From that day, I have been delivered to be myself.

In Luke 6:21 Jesus said, "*Blessed are ye that hunger now: for ye shall be filled. Blessed are ye that weep now: for ye shall laugh.*" No matter what we are going through, eventually we will learn to laugh in that situation. Psalms 126:2 says, "*Then was our mouth filled with laughter, and our tongue with singing: then said they among the heathen, The LORD hath done great things for them.*" When was the last time your mouth was filled with laughter? Every time God moves for me or someone else I am simply overcome by laughter because I know it is not me, but my great God.

Job says: "*Behold, God will not cast away a perfect man, neither will he help the evil doers: ²¹Till he fill thy mouth with laughing, and thy lips with rejoicing.*" (Job 8:20-21) God wants to fill your mouth with laughing and your lips with rejoicing. Jeremiah 30:19 says, "*And out of them shall proceed thanksgiving and the voice of them that make merry*" God wants us to be merry, happy, and full of joy! This is His provision for us. Isaiah 65:18 says, "*But be ye glad and rejoice for ever in that which I create: for, behold, I create Jerusalem a rejoicing, and her people a joy.*" Wow! Psalms 118:15 says, "*The voice of rejoicing and salvation is in the tabernacles of the righteous*" This is what the Word of God declares! Psalms 40:16 says, "*Let all those that seek thee rejoice and be glad in thee: let such as love thy salvation say continually, The LORD be magnified.*"

The Lord hath made me to laugh. He made me to laugh, Sarah said, because He was true to His promise. Even though she blew it and made a terrible mistake, costing people great harm, yet still He came through for her in the end and she found herself laughing because of the goodness of God. Why don't you laugh today? Be free! Don't let religion bind you any longer. Be filled with laughter!

"A Wise Man Will Hear"
Proverbs 1:5

DAY 106

In the Scriptures we find two groups of people mentioned: the wise and the foolish. Jesus, in Matthew 25, spoke of five who were wise and five who were foolish. The five wise entered in, while the five foolish did not. The difference between the two, I believe, is, as it says in Proverbs 1:5, *"A wise man will hear, and will increase learning; and a man of understanding shall attain unto wise counsels."*

In other words, a wise man is a meek or teachable man. He is not someone who knows everything or even claims to. He is not arrogant or proud. It doesn't bother him to receive from someone else or to humble himself. In Proverbs 9:9 it says, *"Give instruction to a wise man, and he will be yet wiser: teach a just man, and he will increase in learning."* A wise man will receive instruction and become even wiser. This should be the heart of every one of us; that we would have a meek spirit just like Moses and like David. *"The meek will he guide in judgment: and the meek will he teach his way,"* David said in Psalms 25:9.

The Bible says in Proverbs 12:15, *"The way of a fool is right in his own eyes: but he that hearkeneth unto counsel is wise."* Do we have a problem receiving from other people? Is it easy for us to hear godly criticism? Can we handle a rebuke? I believe that if we can handle a rebuke, it tells us that we are a wise man or woman. We don't want to be a fool who is always right in his own eyes, who thinks he knows everything, and doesn't receive from anyone else. How terribly lonely life must be for people like that, always comparing themselves to others, coming out on top. This is not the heart of a true son of God.

Proverbs tells us to *"hear counsel, and receive instruction, that thou mayest be wise in thy latter end"* (Proverbs 19:20). We need to hear counsel and receive instruction. In another place in Proverbs, it says, *"For by wise counsel thou shalt make thy war: and in multitude of counsellors there is safety"* (Proverbs 24:6). There is safety in having counsel and covering over our lives. So much of what is said to be a covering today in the body of Christ is really nothing more than a façade. Men claim to have a board ruling over their ministry, or people claim that they are submitted to a pastor or a local church, but really they're no more submitted than a man on the moon. The pastor does not know them, and they don't know their pastor. They are not accountable to anybody. They basically do that which is right in their own eyes, which makes them very foolish.

I Peter 5:5 says, *"Likewise, ye younger, submit yourselves unto the elder. Yea, all of you be subject one to another, and be clothed with humility: for God resisteth the proud, and giveth grace to the humble."* There is no reason for us to be proud, a know-it-all, and not submit ourselves unto those who have been there before, who have gone through what we are going through now. We can receive great instruction from them. Paul, in Galatians 2:2, says, *"And I went up by revelation, and communicated unto them that gospel which I preach among the Gentiles, but privately to them which were of reputation, lest by any means I should run, or had run, in vain."* Even the great apostle Paul, who took nothing from anybody, made sure he submitted his revelation to elders, to those that were of reputation so that he would not be running in vain. All of us need counsel in our lives. If we would be wise men, we would receive instruction.

Solomon says, in the book of Proverbs, *"reproofs of instruction are the way of life"* (Proverbs 6:23). Reproofs, instructions, and corrections are the way of life. We need to bow down our ears to instruction (Proverbs 22:17). We need to humble ourselves and become receptive to wisdom coming from others so that our own lives can increase. Then we can be blessed and share that with others. The book of Hebrews tells us:

> *"Obey them that have the rule over you, and submit yourselves: for they watch for your souls, as they that must give account, that they may do it with joy, and not with grief: for that is unprofitable for you."* (Hebrews 13:17)

Are you truly submitted to a father ministry, to a local church, or to a pastor? Do you have a covering in your life? Do you hear counsel and instruction and reproof? Do you receive wisdom from that counselor or from that covering? If not, the Bible calls you a fool, because you only do what is right in your own eyes. In Proverbs 15:22, it says, *"Without counsel purposes are disappointed: but in the multitude of counsellors they are established."* Without counsel, instruction, and wisdom coming from someone other than ourselves, our purposes are disappointed. But when we submit ourselves to these wise men and women that rule over us, then we have purpose and have others watching for our souls.

Today, hear the word of the Lord. A wise man will hear. Let's be wise men and women and listen to what others have to say. Let's receive what others have to say. If it is critical and is something that we don't necessarily like hearing, but that rings true in our heart of hearts and in our spirit, if we would simply hear it, we will *"increase in learning"* and *"grow in grace, and in the knowledge of our Lord and Saviour Jesus Christ"* (II Peter 3:18). Jesus, Himself, was in the temple at the age of 12, talking with the doctors of the law and astounding everyone round about Him. Yet, He went home and submitted Himself to His own parents for another 18 years (Luke 2:41-52). If He can do it, we can do it too. Let's be wise men and women and hear.

"If Ye Bite And Devour One Another"
Galatians 5:15

DAY 107

The Bible says in Galatians, "*But if ye bite and devour one another, take heed that ye be not consumed one of another*" (Galatians 5:15). Far too many times in the body of Christ gossip takes place. People talk about one another behind each other's backs, criticizing and judging. They are not seeing their brothers and sisters through the Spirit. We must take heed, because if we continue to bite and devour one another, the Bible clearly says we will be "*consumed one of another.*"

In the Old Testament, when Israel was under siege, and there was no food left, they began to eat one another. God had to bring a great judgment before they would repent and deliverance could come.

In Psalms 55:12-14, David said his friend and acquaintance with whom he "*took sweet counsel together*" betrayed him. He said if it was an enemy who did it, he could have dealt with it without a problem. But it came from his friend. Nothing can be more discouraging than to know that the brother in whom you trusted has betrayed you, using bitter words against you, biting and devouring you behind your back. This is a shame and a sad state. Let it not be written of you and me that this was our testimony. Another chapter in Psalms reads "*...the workers of iniquity: ³Who whet their tongue like a sword, and bend their bows to shoot their arrows, even bitter words: ⁴That they may shoot in secret at the perfect...*" (Psalms 64:2-4).

Some people are always trying to find out other people's problems and sins, and then they repeat it to others. The Bible says of Jesus that no guile was found in his mouth (I Peter 2:21-22), and it says the same thing of the bride, the hundred and forty-four thousand (Revelation 14:5). If we're going to be like Jesus, our lips are going to have to be "*seasoned with salt*" and "*alway with grace*" (Colossians 4:6). Just like Jesus, we're going to have to let grace be poured into our lips (Psalms 45:2). Proverbs 18:8 tells us, "*The words of a talebearer are as wounds, and they go down into the innermost parts of the belly.*" Paul said in one place, their "*mouths must be stopped*" (Titus 1:11).

God, help us today to stop biting and devouring one another, judging unrighteously, saying things that we ought not, and uncovering one another's weaknesses. When we do this, it allows us to be built up in the eyes of whom we are speaking and tears down the other person. This is certainly not the will of God. The Bible clearly states, "*Honour all men. Love the brotherhood*" (I Peter 2:17). God wants us to speak kindly to one another.

No longer will it be said of you and me, as we submit ourselves to the Lord today, that we are biting and devouring one another. It says in James that "*the tongue is a fire, a world of iniquity*" (James 3:6). Give your tongue to Jesus today. Let's stop biting and devouring one another. Instead, let us "*exhort one another daily, while it is called Today*" (Hebrews 3:13).

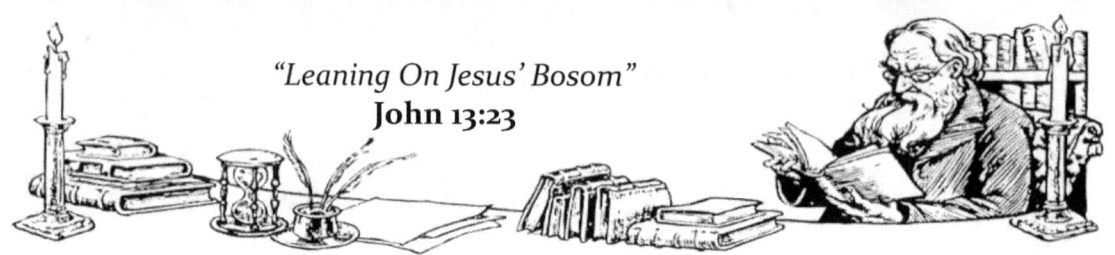

"Leaning On Jesus' Bosom"
John 13:23

DAY 108

In this precious passage of Scripture, we find the story of John, the apostle, leaning upon the breast of Jesus. What we want to do today is understand what this means and how it can be fulfilled in our own lives. Notice that at this last supper, the twelve disciples were there, but only one was lying upon the breast of Jesus. Many have heard me say, that Jesus had the multitude, the seventy, the twelve, the three, and the one, John. There are ranks within the body of Christ and there are ranks of intimacy, light or revelation, faith, authority, etc., but especially ranks of intimacy. Here we find a story of Peter with John laying his head on Jesus' breast, *"Now there was leaning on Jesus' bosom one of his disciples, whom Jesus loved"* (John 13:23-25).

God is no respecter of persons and Jesus loves all of us, but yet, at the same time, the Scriptures make it clear that this was the disciple whom Jesus loved. It can't be helped that we love some of our children more than another or feel closer to them. The reason is because they draw closer to us. John, unafraid of what people might think, leaned upon Jesus' bosom.

Remember Song of Solomon 1:13 says, *"A bundle of myrrh is my wellbeloved unto me; he shall lie all night betwixt my breasts."* The *"breasts"* in the Scripture speaks of the inner most part of someone, a place of great intimacy, a place of great depth, and a place of love. To lean your head upon that heart means you are submitting your soulish mind to the heart of God and you're looking for sanctification and deliverance. This is what the highest and truest disciple will do. He wants to be as his master and it is enough for him to have intimacy with God more than anything else.

The Bible speaks in Isaiah 40:11, *"He shall feed his flock like a shepherd: he shall gather the lambs with his arm, and carry them in his bosom, and shall gently lead those that are with young."* One of the names of God is "El Shaddai", or "the breasty-one, the nourishing one." It's the female part of God. As we lean upon the heart of Jesus, or upon the bosom of Jesus, we're laying upon that nurturing, motherly part of Him that draws us into greater depths of intimacy.

We see in this passage in John 13 that Peter asks John to ask Jesus a question. Later Peter would say in John 21:21, *"Lord, and what shall this man do?"* I believe he asked this in anger, jealousy, and ambition over John. Jesus replied in verse 22, *"What is that to thee? follow thou me."* There will always be those who misunderstand our intimate relationship with God and they will sense we have a greater intimacy with God than they have. They will either be jealous or persecute us for it, as the watchmen did in Song of Solomon 5. They began to wound and beat the precious bride.

For you and me today, we must not look at what others are doing, but have our eyes set upon the bosom of Jesus; the deepest part of God. *"Deep calleth unto deep"* (Psalms 42:7). We must respond and lay our head upon His heart to have greater intimacy with him. We will find, as we gently lie there, that He will gently lead us to become like John, *"one of his disciples, whom Jesus loved."*

"Be Thou An Example Of The Believers"
I Timothy 4:12

Day 109

Here in I Timothy 4:12, Paul says to his son in the faith, *"Let no man despise thy youth; but be thou an example of the believers, in word, in conversation, in charity, in spirit, in faith, in purity."* This is the Word of the Lord to all of us that are ministers and men and women of God. We need to learn to be examples to the believers. There is too much controversy in ministry today, and frankly, too much sin. I, of all people, have no stones to throw. But at the same time, it says in Acts 17:30, *"The times of this ignorance God winked at; but now commandeth all men everywhere to repent."*

Paul tells Timothy to be an example *"in word"* that means you don't share the Word of God deceitfully. You don't share things that glorify man and yourself, but you share things that promote the Kingdom of God. To be an example *"in conversation"* means that you live a lifestyle that is holy before the Lord. Also in your literal conversation, you speak of things that are true, honest, just, pure, lovely, and of good report (Philippians 4:8). To be an example *"in charity"* means you are walking in the love of God. To be an example *"in spirit"* means your attitude is right, and you're overflowing with the things of God. To be an example *"in faith"* means we are always men and women who believe God for all the things he's promised us. And finally, to be an example *"in purity"* means we are walking in holiness. The Bible says in Hebrews 12:14, *"Follow peace with all men, and holiness, without which no man shall see the Lord."*

In I Timothy 1:16, Paul says, *"Howbeit for this cause I obtained mercy, that in me first Jesus Christ might shew forth all longsuffering, for a pattern to them which should hereafter believe."* Paul was a pattern and an example for believers. He said in several places, *"Be ye followers of me"* (I Corinthians 11:1). The word *"followers"* in Greek means *"an imitator."* You and I need to be imitators of people who have a real walk with God.

The burden, brothers and sisters, is on us to walk as men and women of God that others might follow us. The Bible says in James 5:10, *"Take, my brethren, the prophets, who have spoken in the name of the Lord, for an example of suffering affliction, and of patience."* How many men of God in the Old Testament suffered affliction, but yet were patient and walked through it? Luke 21:19 tells us, *"In your patience possess ye your souls."* Men and women of God don't strive *"about words to no profit"* (II Timothy 2:14). They don't allow themselves to fall down into pettiness. They're an example; they are a pattern for others to follow. Peter says:

> *"The elders which are among you I exhort, who am also an elder, and a witness of the sufferings of Christ, and also a partaker of the glory that shall be revealed: ²Feed the flock of God which is among you, taking the oversight thereof, not by constraint, but willingly; not for filthy lucre, but of a ready mind; ³Neither as being lords over God's heritage, but being ensamples to the flock"* (I Peter 5:1-3).

How does he say we are examples to the flock? First, he says to feed the flock of God. We are to feed them the living Word of God, sound doctrine. He says to take the oversight thereof willingly. In other words, we're glad to be in the ministry and that God has called us to it. We don't do it for filthy lucre; we're not doing it for money, fame, or power, but simply for the Kingdom of God. He tells us to be of a ready mind. The book of II Timothy 4:12 says, *"Preach the word; be instant in season, out of season."* This means we're always ready to minister. Next, he says we should not be as lords over God's heritage. We don't seek to manipulate and control God's people. Paul said in II Corinthians 10:8, *"For though I should boast somewhat more of our authority, which the Lord hath given us for edification, and not for your destruction, I should not be ashamed."*

This is how you lead by example as Philippians 3:17 declares, *"Brethren, be followers together of me, and mark them which walk so as ye have us for an ensample."* We need to have men and women of God as examples to walk after as examples. It says in Hebrews 13:7, *"Remember them which have the rule over you, who have spoken unto you the word of God: whose faith follow, considering the end of their conversation."* The Spanish translation reads, *"Imitate their faith."*

Do you want somebody imitating you? Is your life worthy enough to be imitated? Are you an example? God, help us today to be true examples of ministry and discipleship. Let it be said of us, *"Now by this I know that thou art a man of God, and that the word of the Lord in thy mouth is truth"* (I Kings 17:24).

"Samuel Did Not Yet Know The Lord"
I Samuel 3:7

DAY 110

I want to talk today about being surrounded by the things of God and yet amazingly still not know God. Samuel had lived in the temple since he was weaned as a little child. He was now a teenage boy. Yet the Bible says, *"Now Samuel did not yet know the Lord, neither was the word of the Lord yet revealed unto him"* (I Samuel 3:7). I wonder how many of us have been in the temple for years and years and still do not yet know the Lord intimately and still do not yet have a real, holy walk with God. Jesus said in Matthew 7:22-23, *"Many will say to me in that day, Lord, Lord, have we not prophesied in thy name? and in thy name have cast out devils? and in thy name done many wonderful works? ²³And then will I profess unto them, I never knew you: depart from me."*

The problem is we can be like a rock in the midst of a rushing, flowing river for thousands of years. If we take that rock out of the water and break it open, we find that it is dry as dust within. How many people sit in church year after year and they are dry as dust on the inside? Well, if this is you, hear the word of the Lord today; you don't have to remain like this. Hear the voice of God calling to you like He did Samuel.

For many the outward manifestations of a local church or being part of the Kingdom of God is more important than the Lord Himself. The gifts become more important than the Giver. The work of the Lord becomes more important than the Lord of the work. How sad that you can be surrounded by the things of God and yet still not know Him.

In Ezekiel 44 when God contrasted between the sons of Zadok and the rest of the backslidden Levites, He told the Levites they could minister to the rest of the house but they would never minister to Him. Why? Because, they didn't know Him intimately. What is amazing to me is that you can cast out devils, prophesy in His name, and do wonderful things and still not know the Lord.

In John 21:4 we read, *"But when the morning was now come, Jesus stood on the shore: but the disciples knew not that it was Jesus."* How could the disciples not know it was Jesus after spending three and a half years with Him? Well, this can happen. Moreover, we can spend much time with Him and still not know Him intimately. Consider Israel and especially the Pharisees in Jesus' day, they did not recognize Jesus the Messiah when He came to them. Jesus said to them in John 5:39, *"Search the scriptures; for in them ye think ye have eternal life: and they are they which testify of me."*

God wants us to know Him and not just become the *"daughters of Jerusalem."* For many their parents have a true walk with God and they were just born into it without ever having a real walk with God. God wants every one of us to know Him intimately. When He calls, will you respond to Him today? Samuel responded by saying *"Speak, Lord; for thy servant heareth"* (I Samuel 3:9). Will you come today and sit at His feet and hear His Word and begin to know Him intimately?

"The Swelling Of The Jordan"
Jeremiah 12:5

DAY 111

One of the greatest truths about the end times is found in the book of Jeremiah 12:5. *"If thou hast run with the footmen, and they have wearied thee, then how canst thou contend with horses? And if in the land of peace, wherein thou trustedst, they wearied thee, then how wilt thou do in the swelling of the Jordan?"* I would like to speak with you today about the *"swelling of the Jordan"*.

The Jordan River would overflow its banks, rushing inland causing all of the beasts that were in the surrounding areas to come towards the city. As we read in Joshua 3:15, it says, *"(for Jordan overfloweth all his banks all the time of harvest)."* We need to understand that Jordan overflows all of its banks at harvest time. All of this is spiritual revelation and contains great truths about the end times.

There will be a last great move of God and it will be called the *"swelling of the Jordan."* The river of God will overflow its banks at harvest time. As it does, the first thing that we will experience is not the water, but the beasts. There will be warfare and demonic oppression like we've never seen before. But those that survive and who make it to the end will be the overcomers. So we will first face a demonic onslaught like never before. Then after that, the swelling of the Jordan, the glorious river of God will overcome God's people.

So it says here in Jeremiah 12:5, *"If thou hast run with the footmen, and they have wearied thee."* Footmen are the lowest class of the demonic kingdom. They are just demons. They are the ones that we deal with on a daily basis, that cause us to lust, to steal, have strife and contention, etc.

If we can't deal with those simple footmen and they have wearied us, then it says, *"How canst thou contend with horses?"* The horses are the four horses of the apocalypse that we find in the book of Revelation: war, poverty, famine and death. These are a greater level of demonic warfare that the world will be going through. Particularly, the sons of God must conquer war, poverty, famine and death. These are the horses we are going to have to contend with. They are spiritual horses as well as natural horses. To enter into the swelling of the Jordan and survive and become this overcoming army we must make it through.

Then it says, *"and if in the land of peace, wherein thou trustedst, they wearied thee, then how wilt thou do in the swelling of the Jordan?"* The land of peace is simply in places of prosperity and good times in our lives. Even in places of peace and in places of rest, we still have struggles with demons. We will still have struggles with our flesh and our carnal nature.

Finally, *"How wilt thou do in the swelling of the Jordan?"* The swelling of the Jordan is when the final demonic warfare comes rushing inland. Those beasts will try to overtake us and destroy us. We will never get to the water unless we survive the beasts. Paul says in I Corinthians 15:32, *"I have fought with beasts at Ephesus."* Those beasts were not human beings. They were devils.

So the *"principalities, powers, the rulers of the darkness of this world, and spiritual wickedness in high places,"* (Ephesians 6:12) are going to be unleashed. This is seen in Revelation 12:12 where is says, *"the devil is come down unto you."* Those that remain are going to have to stand up and resist the footmen, overcome them. Then they will have to contend with the horses (war, poverty, famine and death). They will need to make sure that in a land of peace they keep their testimony, being *"steadfast, unmoveable, always abounding in the work of the Lord"* (I Corinthians 15:58). Finally, when the swelling of the Jordan comes, they will survive and experience the last great move of God.

"All Flesh Shall See"
Isaiah 40:5

Day 112

The Scriptures declare in Isaiah 40:5, *"And the glory of the Lord shall be revealed* [or made clear]*, and all flesh shall see it together: for the mouth of the Lord hath spoken it."* All flesh shall see the glory of God. This is a tremendous truth and I want you to take encouragement today in knowing that even though you still may find weaknesses in yourself and may still be sinning, God has a plan and an expected end for you, which is perfection.

All flesh shall see the glory of God. This means that our flesh one day will not rule our lives. Paul encourages us in Romans 6:14, *"For sin shall not have dominion over you."* Philippians 3:3 says, *"For we are the circumcision, which worship God in the spirit, and rejoice in Christ Jesus, and have no confidence in the flesh."* Our confidence is in the Lord our God, not in our flesh. Jesus said in Matthew 26:41 says, *"The spirit indeed is willing, but the flesh is weak."* Even though our flesh is weak, and it seems to so consume us, we need to know and have faith that there is coming a day when God will deliver you and I completely from all our flesh. All flesh shall see the glory of God together.

Zechariah 13:1 tells us, *"In that day there shall be a fountain opened to the house of David and to the inhabitants of Jerusalem for sin and for uncleanness. ²And it shall come to pass in that day, saith the Lord of hosts, that I will cut off the names of the idols out of the land, and they shall no more be remembered."* God is going to cut off the idols out of our lives. He is going to remove from us our flesh. A fountain will be opened for sin and for uncleanness. Jesus said in Luke 8:18, *"When the Son of man cometh, shall he find faith on the earth?"* Jesus will be looking for faith in our lives for our final deliverance, faith for our full salvation. We have been delivered from the penalty of sin. We are being delivered from the power of sin every day by the Holy Spirit and by the Word of God. Eventually, we will be one day delivered from the presence of sin.

Titus 2:14 says that Jesus, *"gave himself for us, that he might redeem us from all iniquity."* God is going to deliver us one day not just from some iniquity, but from *all* iniquity. I Peter 4:1 says, *"For he that hath suffered in the flesh hath ceased from sin."* You and I have suffered in the flesh and we will eventually one day cease from all sin. Acts 2:17 tells us, *"And it shall come to pass in the last days, saith God, I will pour out of my Spirit upon all flesh."* God is pouring out His Spirit, in these last days, upon our flesh to help us be redeemed from all our sin and uncleanness. Glory to His holy name!

David says, in Psalms 16:9, *"My flesh also shall rest in hope."* You and I need to rest in hope that our flesh, that so bothers us, will one day no longer trouble us. Job 19:26 says, *"In my flesh shall I see God."* In our flesh, we shall see God. What a wonderful God we serve! Job 5:24, in talking about those who have received the chastening of the Lord, tells us, *"Thou shalt visit thy habitation, and shalt not sin."* Micah 7:19 says, *"He will turn again, he will have compassion upon us; he will subdue our iniquities; and thou wilt cast all their sins into the depths of the sea."* God is going to subdue our iniquities.

This is seen in the story of Jacob and Esau. Esau is a type of the man of the flesh and Jacob is a type of the man of the spirit. Esau burst through the womb first, but

Jacob, coming right after, *"took hold on Esau's heel"* (Genesis 25:26). You and I, the sons of God, will have our hands upon the man of the flesh, when we burst through the womb into the glorious liberty of the children of God.

Obadiah 17-18 says, *"But upon mount Zion shall be deliverance, and there shall be holiness; and the house of Jacob shall possess their possessions. ¹⁸And the house of Jacob shall be a fire, and the house of Joseph a flame, and the house of Esau for stubble. And they shall kindle in them, and devour them; and there shall not be any remaining of the house of Esau; for the Lord hath spoken it."* The man of flesh will be destroyed. Let us take heart today and know that one day all our flesh shall see the glory of God together!

"Behold The Man"
John 19:5

DAY 113

This is the story in Scripture when Pilate brings Jesus before the crowd of people and it says in verse 5, *"Then came Jesus forth, wearing the crown of thorns, and the purple robe. And Pilate saith unto them, Behold the man!"* (John 19:5)

Several years ago I was preaching in a church and as the worship was going on I was kneeling before the Lord in deep adoration being immersed in the glory and presence of God. While I was there just waiting on the Lord, the Holy Spirit spoke to me very clearly and strongly and said, "Turn to John 19:5." Now before that day I don't know if I ever recognized this passage. I had never preached on it and had never thought about it, so it was new to me.

So I turned to it, read it, and said to the Lord, "What are you trying to say to me?" And He said, "In the last days God the Father is going to be like Pilate and I'm going to present before the world just as Pilate presented Jesus, a many-membered son, the body of Christ, the bride of Christ, or that remnant of devoted believers who have given everything to Jesus and I am going to say to the world, Behold the man!" What a declaration.

To be this man, we have to follow in Jesus' footsteps. Jesus had to wear a crown of thorns and a purple robe. God's people right now are the many-membered son, the mystical body of Christ, and we are coming forth. Day by day, we are learning to die to ourselves, give ourselves to the dealings of God, and in order to be conformed into His image. We are being transformed by the renewing of our mind (Romans 12:2). Jesus is coming forth in us. But as we do, we are putting on that same crown of thorns and purple robe.

The crown of thorns fit upon Jesus' head which symbolizes the carnal soulish man. It represents the emotions, intellect, mind, and the affections of man. We must have this same crown upon our soulish man dealing and blocking our carnal nature from ever coming forth *"because the carnal mind is enmity against God"* (Romans 8:7). Instead, *"we have the mind of Christ"* (I Corinthians 2:16). The crown of thorns means that suffering has brought about in our lives the true mind of Christ.

Moreover, Jesus wore the purple robe. Purple in the Scriptures speaks of royalty and richness. In other words, to wear the purple robe means one has entered into royalty. Jesus said in Revelations 1:6 that He *"hath made us kings and priests unto God and his Father."* II Timothy 2:12 says, *"If we suffer, we shall also reign with him."* This people will have prevailed and overcome enough to have become royalty. It will be no longer them living, but Christ living through them (Galatians 2:20). They will be a living, breathing example of Jesus in the earth radiating His character. This will not be done singularly, but will be a corporate people. In Ephesians it says:

> "*¹¹And he gave some, apostles; and some, prophets; and some, evangelists; and some, pastors and teachers; ¹²For the perfecting of the saints, for the work of the ministry, for the edifying of the body of Christ: ¹³Till we all come in the unity of the faith, and of the knowledge of the Son of God, unto a perfect man, unto the measure of the stature of the fulness of Christ:*" (Ephesians 4:11-13)

Some other translations of verse 13 of Ephesians 4 read:

> "*...unto a full grown man*"
> "*...to reach the stature of manhood*"
> "*...to be of ripe age, to receive the fullness of Christ*"
> "*...to mature manhood ensured by nothing less than the full stature of Christ*"

This people or this corporate perfect man is going to come to "*the measure of the stature of the fullness of God.*" They will be perfect. The Greek word for "*perfect*" here simply means "complete, to finish." They would have finished their course, graduated, and entered into sonship. This is where the body of Christ is headed.

In John 21, we find Jesus after His crucifixion dealing with Peter and asked Peter three times if he loved Him more than everything else. Peter responded to Jesus by telling Him he loved Him, but used a different word for love. Jesus was using "*agape*", the God kind of love and Peter wasn't. Jesus was trying to lift Peter's level of love, and finally Jesus ended their conversation by saying in verse 18,

> "*Verily, verily, I say unto thee, When thou wast young, thou girdedst thyself, and walkedst whither thou wouldest: but when thou shalt be old, thou shalt stretch forth thy hands, and another shall gird thee, and carry thee whither thou wouldest not.*" (John 21:18)

This is indicative of all of our lives. When we were young we did what we wanted to do. We went where we wanted to go. But as we grow old and mature in God, we stretch forth our hands and let the Holy Ghost gird us. He then carries us where we don't want to go. Are you willing to stretch forth your hands today and let the Holy Spirit grow you up to manhood? Paul said in I Corinthians,

> "*But when that which is perfect is come, then that which is in part shall be done away. ¹¹When I was a child, I spake as a child, I understood as a child, I thought as a child: but when I became a man, I put away childish things.*"
> (I Corinthians 13:10-11)

Today we are still living in part waiting for that which is perfect to come. That which is perfect is not Jesus, but this many-membered son to come forth into fullness. When we become a man, we put away childish things. We no longer understand like children, speak as children, or think as children. We put away these childish things and become full grown mature men and women of God. And on that great day of the Lord, He's going to arise in a people and say to the world, "*Behold the man!*" (John 19:5)

"Stewards Of The Mysteries"
I Corinthians 4:1

DAY 114

Paul says here, "*Let a man so account of us, as of the ministers of Christ, and stewards of the mysteries of God*" (I Corinthians 4:1) Ministers are supposed to be stewards, in the Greek "household managers," of the mysteries of God. It's interesting that the Greek word for "*mystery*" which is "*mysterion*" means "that which is known only to the initiated."

Now what does that mean? That means in every one of our lives we're "*under tutors and governors until the time appointed*" (Galatians 4:2), and there comes a time in all of our lives where we reach a place where we've become "*approved unto God, a workman that needeth not to be ashamed, rightly dividing the word of truth*" (II Timothy 2:15). God then can trust us with His secrets and mysteries. We're initiated sovereignly into the deeper things of God. That's what the word mystery means.

Try as we might to explain the deep and truly tremendous ministries of God to others, many times they look at us like we're crazy and that we've lost our minds. The truth is that they've lost out with God because they haven't been initiated. They haven't proven themselves and haven't been accounted worthy, as Luke 21:36 says, "*to escape all these things.*" God cannot trust them because they haven't been approved unto God as a workman. They haven't proven themselves in searching the scriptures, sitting under the Word and giving themselves to a foundation. You and I need to be workmen, and become household managers of the mysteries of God. Every minister should be a steward of God's divine, hidden treasures and mysteries of the Word.

In Mark 4:13 Jesus had just finished a parable and said, "*Know ye not this parable? and how then will ye know all parables?*" Then He makes this statement in Matthew 13:11 speaking of the same parable, "*it is given unto you to know the mysteries of the kingdom of heaven.*" It is our right, privilege, and calling to know the mysteries of God. However, we cannot begin to understand them or receive them until we're initiated into the deeper things of God. At that point, because we're initiated, we can know then that which is only known by the initiated.

The Bible says in Ephesians 1:9 that He has "*made known unto us the mystery of his will.*" Paul said in I Corinthians 2:7, "*But we speak the wisdom of God in a mystery.*" The mystery is the wisdom of God; it's the deep things of God. Did you know that the Bible says "*great is the mystery of godliness?*" (I Timothy 3:16) Paul said, "*Behold, I shew you a mystery*" (I Corinthians 15:51). He also said we are called to "*make known the mystery of the gospel*" in Ephesians 6:19. Then in Colossians 1:26 he says, "*Even the mystery which hath been hid from ages and from generations.*" God wants the mysteries hidden from the foundation of the world to be revealed to His people.

Did you know there's coming a time that Revelation 10:7 says, when "*the mystery of God should be finished*"? There's coming a time when there'll be a people who will know Him from the least to the greatest (Hebrews 8:11). The knowledge of the glory of the Lord shall cover the seas (Habakkuk 2:14). There will be the secret things that belong unto the Lord our God, and unto those He chooses to reveal them to as Deuteronomy 29:29 tells us. You and I are called and ordained to understand the deep, precious truths of God, the hidden treasures, the unsearchable riches of Christ. It is given to us to know. We're supposed to know. As a matter of fact, we're called to be stewards of those mysteries.

So get initiated. Only God can give you that permit to go on from the foundations (Hebrews 6:3), and have great truths built upon it. Please, give yourself to the Word of God, so that God can give Himself to you; thereby giving you the understanding of the deep mysteries of God.

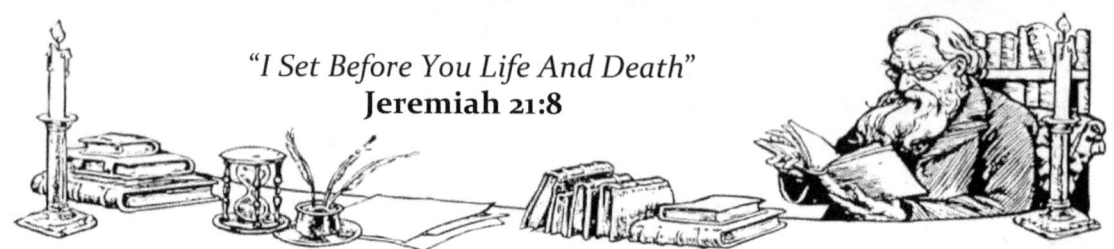

"I Set Before You Life And Death"
Jeremiah 21:8

DAY 115

One of the tremendous truths we find in the Scriptures is that God has laid many things before His people and given us a choice. We can choose which we way we will walk. Unlike the angels, we are free moral agents and can make choices about how our lives will be lead. The Bible says in Jeremiah 21, *"Thus saith the Lord; Behold, I set before you the way of life, and the way of death"* (Jeremiah 21:8). God has set before you and me the way of life and the way of death.

In Deuteronomy 30, it says, *"See, I have set before thee this day life and good, and death and evil"* (Deuteronomy 30:15). God has set before us these things, and we must choose which one we will walk after. God continues to say, *"I have set before you life and death, blessing and cursing: therefore choose life, that both thou and thy seed may live"* (Deuteronomy 30:19). God not only wants us, but our seed, to live. We have to make the choice; we have to choose life. The Bible says in I Corinthians, *"Whether life, or death, or things present, or things to come; all are yours"* (I Corinthians 3:22). Life and death is ours to do with as we see fit.

I want us to look at the ways we can choose life. Proverbs 12 declares, *"In the way of righteousness is life; and in the pathway thereof there is no death"* (Proverbs 12:28). We need to walk righteously before the Lord and keep in right standing with God at all times. It says in Proverbs 14, *"The fear of the Lord is a fountain of life, to depart from the snares of death"* (Proverbs 14:27). As long as you and I keep a holy fear of the Lord in our lives, we will never get caught in the snares of death. God has said, "All of this is yours, and I've set it before you." It is our choice. What are we going to do?

Proverbs 18 tells us, *"Death and life are in the power of the tongue: and they that love it shall eat the fruit thereof"* (Proverbs 18:21). We hold in our mouths the power of life and death by what we say and what we don't say. We need to keep a good confession before the Lord, because what a man believes in his heart, rules him. Proverbs 23 tells us that as a man *"thinketh in his heart, so is he"* (Proverbs 23:7).

The book of Romans tells us, *"For the law of the Spirit of life in Christ Jesus hath made me free from the law of sin and death"* (Romans 8:2). The Spirit of life in Christ Jesus that is in your soul right now has made you free from the law of sin and death. It also says in Romans, *"For sin shall not have dominion over you: for ye are not under the law, but under grace"* (Romans 6:14). You can walk free from sin and death by choosing life. The Bible says in I John 3, *"We know that we have passed from death unto life, because we love the brethren"* (I John 3:14). We need to love one another. I Peter 2:17 says, *"Honour all men. Love the brotherhood."* Jesus said in John 13, *"By this shall all men know that ye are my disciples, if ye have love one to another"* (John 13:35).

So, here we are; this is it. Choose life or choose death. It's up to you. Which one will you choose today? Paul prayed, *"so now also Christ shall be magnified in my body, whether it be by life, or by death"* (Philippians 1:20). Let's let Christ be magnified in our bodies, souls, and spirits by choosing life today.

"They Have Seen Her Nakedness"
Lamentations 1:8

DAY 116

This is an illuminating passage of Scripture about what happens to us when we sin and people's response to us when we are exposed. It says in Lamentations 1:8, *"Jerusalem hath grievously sinned; therefore she is removed: all that honoured her despise her, because they have seen her nakedness: yea, she sigheth, and turneth backward."* How many people are sighing today and turning backward because they have been exposed in some sin or something they were concealing has been revealed?

It is said that the body of Christ shoots its wounded. This is a sad state of being. Of all people on the face of the earth, we should be the most merciful, the most reconciling, and the most forgiving. Sadly, this doesn't seem to be the case.

Once people have seen our nakedness or have seen our fallen and weak self with all of our frailties and foibles, they have a tendency to remove themselves from us. All that used to honor us now despise us or set us at naught. Why? Because they've seen our nakedness.

We can't help but be who we are. We were created with our humanity. II Corinthians 4:7 says, *"we have this treasure in earthen vessels."* We are simply earthen vessels and when we are weak, He is strong (II Corinthians 12:10). The truth is *"every man at his best state is altogether vanity"* (Psalms 39:5). Without God we are all without hope and most miserable.

Romans 3:23 says, *"For all have sinned, and come short of the glory of God."* Therefore we need to be able to, *"Confess your faults one to another, and pray one for another, that ye may be healed"* (James 5:16). Healing will never take place until we stop removing people from our lives and stop despising them because we've seen their nakedness. Because by doing so, all we do is make them sigh and turn backward. Many people are no longer walking with the Lord today because at one time this happened to them. I pray that today the Lord will help us help each other and that once we see somebody broken and busted, we will help them. Let us act like the Good Samaritan did when he saw the one beaten, robbed, half-dead, and exposed. He went to where he was and helped him.

When Jesus found the bride in Ezekiel 16 laying there besides the side of the road in her own blood, instead of being a time to despise her, He said it was *"the time of love"* (Ezekiel 16:8). Moreover He said, *"Now when I passed by thee, and looked upon thee, behold, thy time was the time of love; and I spread my skirt over thee, and covered thy nakedness: yea, I sware unto thee, and entered into a covenant with thee, saith the Lord God, and thou becamest mine."* What good is love if it is never put to use when it is needed it most? So, when we see the nakedness of others, we need to follow the example that Jesus gave us and love them, pray for them and help them to receive their healing, just as He helped us to receive ours.

"Not Slothful In Business"
Romans 12:11

DAY 117

One of the things we learn as a Christian is that God expects us to be diligent, not only spiritually speaking, but also in the realm of putting down our soulish man and in the physical aspect. It is certainly a bad testimony when Christians are not faithful in their natural work. Paul says in I Corinthians 15:46, *"Howbeit that was not first which is spiritual, but that which is natural."* God does not want us to be slothful in business or being a bad example and testimony, giving the character of the Lord a bad name by the way we carry ourselves at our jobs, businesses or the work that we do. We are supposed to be *"fervent in spirit; serving the Lord"* as Paul declares at the end of Romans 12:11. I can be fervent in spirit because I am serving the Lord, not because of anything else.

Ecclesiastes 9:10 says, *"Whatsoever thy hand findeth to do, do it with thy might."* Proverbs 12:24 says, *"The hand of the diligent shall bear rule: but the slothful shall be under tribute."* There is a great deal of difference between the slothful and the diligent. Proverbs 13:4 says, *"The soul of the sluggard desireth, and hath nothing: but the soul of the diligent shall be made fat."* The diligent man will always have authority, will always rule and reign because he is *"fervent in spirit, serving the Lord."*

How are you at your job? What is your testimony there? What do the people say about you? Do they speak of you in glowing terms? You might be, you know, the only Jesus they will ever see. I Corinthians 10:31 says, *"...whatsoever ye do, do all to the glory of God."*

When you go to work today do it to the glory of God. Whatever your business may be, wherever your job might be, remember you are serving the Lord even in that capacity. So, be fervent in spirit; be full of the Holy Ghost. Before you even get to that job pray, read your Bible, worship the Lord, pray in the Spirit, prepare yourself so that when you get there you will not only be an example of faithfulness, but you will give glory unto the Lord by the way you do your job.

Remember the story of Joseph; no matter where he ended up, in the pit, in Potiphar's house, in the prison, the Bible says he prospered in every place that he was in. No matter what your job or business is, don't be slothful. Let the Lord speak to you today to be fervent in spirit because you are serving the Lord.

"The Glory In The Midst Of Her"
Zechariah 2:5

DAY 118

One of the glorious things that we have to look forward to in the coming days is found here in this passage in Zechariah 2:5, *"For I, saith the LORD, will be unto her* [the bride] *a wall of fire round about, and will be the glory in the midst of her."* Just as God did in the Old Testament, when He followed the children of Israel with a cloud by day and a fire by night, He will follow His people and will be a wall of fire round about them and a wall of protection around them. He will also be the glory in the midst of them.

We will have no glory of our own, but God will be our glory. Just as in the New Jerusalem, there will be no need of light, because *"the glory of God did lighten it"* (Revelation 21:23). In Isaiah 60:19 it also says, *"The sun shall be no more thy light by day; neither for brightness shall the moon give light unto thee: but the LORD shall be unto thee an everlasting light, and thy God thy glory."* God will be the glory in the midst of us.

Isn't it wonderful that the glory is simply the very essence of God, the very manifest presence of God Himself? He says in Zechariah 2:10, *"Sing and rejoice, O daughter of Zion: for, lo, I come, and I will dwell in the midst of thee, saith the LORD."* He will dwell in the midst of us by His glory. The Scriptures say in Psalms 102:16, *"When the LORD shall build up Zion, he shall appear in his glory."* He is going to appear in Zion, in glory. The earth is going to see a true representation of the glory and character of God through a people, via his manifest presence, saturating and satiating through us. Psalms 50:2 declares, *"Out of Zion, the perfection of beauty, God hath shined."* How is God shining? The answer is by His glory.

When you and I praise and worship the Lord and offer our hearts up to Him, our hearts literally enthrone His presence. Then He comes and rests between the cherubim and sits upon the throne of our hearts, in His glory. This was seen in the Old Testament when the Shekinah glory would come down and rest upon the mercy seat and speak to Moses. He is doing this again and will do it again within a people.

In Haggai 2:7 it says, *"And I will shake all nations, and the desire of all nations shall come: and I will fill this house with glory, saith the LORD of host."* God is going to fill His house with glory. Oh that you and I would get a revelation of this and would cry out to God for more of His glory, just as Moses did in Exodus 33:13 and 18, *"Shew me now thy way, that I may know thee...Shew me thy glory."* Isaiah 60:1-3, 7 says to us very clearly what is about to happen. God is going to speak to a people and say one day, *"Arise, shine; for thy light is come, and the glory of the LORD is risen upon thee. ²For, behold, the darkness shall cover the earth, and gross darkness the people: but the LORD shall arise upon thee, and his glory shall be seen upon thee...and I will glorify the house of my glory"* (Isaiah 60:1-2, 7). We are His house and He promises to be unto us a wall of fire round about us and the glory in the midst. Hallelujah!

"So Panteth My Soul"
Psalms 42:1-2

Here in Psalms 42 it reads:

> *"¹As the hart panteth after the water brooks, so panteth my soul after thee, O God. ²My soul thirsteth for God, for the living God: when shall I come and appear before God?" (Psalms 42:1-2)*

DAY 119

There is so much to say in these two verses. There should be a continual longing and desire for the Lord Jesus where the deepest part of our soul is crying out in thirst for Him. Some other translations of this verse read:

> *"I want to drink God"*
> *"Deep draughts of God"*
> *"Just as the deer longs for running streams, God, I long for you"*
> *"So I thirst for you"*
> *"So is my soul's desire for you"*

Oh, that God would give all of us this desire for the Lord, such a longing! The word *"panteth"* in the Hebrew is translated to two different English words. The first word means "to breathe hard after" and the second word means "above, the top, to highest, aloft to Jehovah or the Most High." So using the definitions of the words this verse could read, "As a deer goes after running water, so I breathe hard after you O God. My soul sails to the highest, aloft to Jehovah." This is what should be the cry of our hearts.

The word *"appear"* in the second verse means "to see or behold." The word, *"before"* means "the face, presence, the turning of the face towards". Many, many times that word is translated *"face"* or *"presence"* in the Old Testament. Therefore this verse should actually read, "When shall I come and behold the face of God". This should be the desire of our hearts, to behold His face. Our souls should be consumed with desire, thirsting to be with Him.

David said in Psalms 63:1, *"O God, thou art my God; early will I seek thee: my soul thirsteth for thee, my flesh longeth for thee."* Is your flesh longing, is your soul thirsting for Him? Psalms 84:2 says, *"My soul longeth, yea, even fainteth for the courts of the LORD: my heart and my flesh crieth out for the living God."* We want to behold a living God. We want to drink deep draughts of God. We want more and more and more until we overflow.

Lord, know that our hearts long and pant after you today. Let this come forth in all of our lives. Let our souls breathe hard after Him!

"When Ephraim Spake Trembling"
Hosea 13:1

Hosea 13:1 says that *"when Ephraim spake trembling, he exalted himself in Israel."* This passage of Scripture opens to us a tremendous viewpoint into what God is looking for in His people. When Ephraim spoke trembling, he exalted himself. As long as you and I stay in a place of humility and lowliness before the Lord and fear and honor Him, we will always be exalted. God always exalts the humble in heart.

The words *"trembling"* and *"tremble"* in Hebrew mean "fear or terror, to shudder with terror or reverential fear." This is not a fear as in being afraid of God, but a reverential, worshipful fear and being in awe as we behold Him. We fear Him in that we honor Him so greatly and are so overwhelmed by His presence and goodness that we are reverentially humbled by Him. The Scriptures are very clear that as long as we keep this kind of attitude, we will always have our provision and be exalted.

In Isaiah 66:2, it says, *"to this man will I look, even to him that is poor and of a contrite spirit, and trembleth at my word."* If there's anything we should have reverential fear towards or tremble at, it is the Word of God. We should approach it with great respect, awe, and wonder, for great is the Word of the Lord. God will look at those who have a poor and contrite spirit and who tremble at His Word. The word *"face"* in Hebrew is the same word translated *"presence"* and it means "a turning of the face towards." So, when He says He will look at them, it means He will put His manifest presence upon them as He sees in them humility, meekness, respect, hunger and an awesome fear for His Word.

Do you tremble at His Word? Do you honor the Word of the Lord so much so that it causes in you a reverence; causes you to shudder with terror that if you don't do it or complete it that somehow you will be cut off or separated from the presence of the Lord?

Ephraim spoke trembling. The name "Ephraim" means "double fruitfulness." He spoke trembling, and God exalted him. In Acts 7 we see the story of the glory of God appearing to Saul, who would later become the apostle Paul. As that glory descended upon him, the Bible says *"he trembling and astonished said, Lord, what wilt thou have me to do?"* (Acts 9:6). This is what should happen when the glory of God manifests itself to us or God reveals Himself to us in a mighty, powerful way.

In Acts 7:32, it says that Moses, when he saw that fiery, burning bush *"trembled, and durst not behold"* it. This is the awesomeness of God when we behold Him. As He came down in Exodus in all of His glory on the mountaintop, it says:

> *"18...all the people saw the thunderings, and the lightnings, and the noise of the trumpet, and the mountain smoking: and when the people saw it, they removed, and stood afar*

> *off. ¹⁹And they said unto Moses, Speak thou with us, and we will hear: but let not God speak with us, lest we die"* (Exodus 20:18-19).

To me one of the saddest verses in the Bible took place in Exodus right after this in verse 21, *"And the people stood afar off, and Moses drew near unto the thick darkness where God was."*. This is a reality of which we must be careful. When we see God in all of His greatness and glory, it can be overwhelming. Like David said in Psalms, *"My flesh trembleth for fear of thee; and I am afraid of thy judgments"* (Psalms 119:120).

Would to God our flesh would tremble when we read the Word of God, that it would convict us to walk circumspectly and to keep our hearts right. Our flesh should tremble at the presence of God. Psalms 114:7 says, *"Tremble, thou earth, at the presence of the Lord, at the presence of the God of Jacob."* Everything in us that radiates the earth or flesh should tremble and be in reverential fear; should shudder with terror at the awesomeness of the glory of God and the greatness of His power. It says in Job:

> *"¹At this also my heart trembleth, and is moved out of his place. ²Hear attentively the noise of his voice, and the sound that goeth out of his mouth. ³He directeth it under the whole heaven, and his lightning unto the ends of the earth. ⁴After it a voice roareth: he thundereth with the voice of his excellency; and he will not stay them when his voice is heard. ⁵God thundereth marvellously with his voice; great things doeth he, which we cannot comprehend"* (Job 37:1-5).

His voice is His Word, and you and I need to tremble and be awestruck as we hold it in our hands. In my own personal life, the first thing I do every morning when I rise is go in the presence of God, open my Bible, and reverentially, with fear and trembling, hold it before the Lord as I begin to read and search the Scriptures. If you want to be exalted, continue to humble yourself, to bow before Him, stay meek and lowly in His sight, and fall more in love with His Word.

The Bible is very clear in Psalms telling us to "*serve the Lord with fear, and rejoice with trembling*" (Psalms 2:11). If we're going to rejoice, we need to do it trembling. God is not interested in an arrogant, self-righteous, self-important people. We must see ourselves as who we are, the sheep of His hand, His humble people.

So the word of the Lord to you today is that Ephraim, even though he was doubly fruitful, *"spoke trembling"* and was exalted in Israel. Let you and I be exalted as we continue to tremble at the presence of the Lord and as we read the Word of God.

"That We May Be Able To Comfort Them"
II Corinthians 1:4

Today, I want us to look at this passage in II Corinthians:

"³Blessed be God, even the Father of our Lord Jesus Christ, the Father of mercies, and the God of all comfort; ⁴Who comforteth us in all our tribulation, that we may be able to comfort them which are in any trouble, by the comfort wherewith we ourselves are comforted of God." (II Corinthians 1:3-4)

First of all, we need to realize that God is the *"God of all comfort"* and He will comfort *"us in all our tribulation."* There is a reason for everything. *"The curse causeless shall not come,"* Proverbs 26:2 tells us. The book of Romans says, *"And we know that all things work together for good to them that love God, to them who are the called according to his purpose"* (Romans 8:28). Nothing happens to us that God has not ordained or allowed.

It says of Jesus that he *"took bread, and blessed it, and brake it, and gave it to the disciples"* (Matthew 26:26). You and I have been taken by the Lord. We did not choose Him; He chose us. Then He *"blessed us with all spiritual blessings in heavenly places in Christ"* (Ephesians 1:3). What a honeymoon. But then comes the breaking, the hardships, the dealings of God, the sanctification process. And all of this is for a reason: that He might give us to the disciples. All that God does for us is really not for us, but for others. What a tremendous truth if we could only receive it today.

God will comfort you in all your tribulation so that you may be able to *"comfort them which are in any trouble,"* by the comfort that you were comforted of God. There is nothing like talking to someone, when you're going through a hardship, problem, or struggle, who has been through that very same struggle and torment. They then have real life experience. They have partaken of the grace of God and overcame and can point the way for us. They can show us how to overcome ourselves.

So, we can comfort others with the comfort with which God comforted us. This is such a precious truth. Everything God does for you is for someone else. Can you receive that? Can you look then and see that whatever you are going through right now is really not for you? One day, you will be speaking to someone who will be going through that exact same thing, and you will then turn and give them the comfort and the grace that God gave you during that experience. They then will be comforted themselves.

Today, may our precious Jesus comfort our hearts with His love, grace, and Holy Ghost. Then we will one day truly be able to comfort those *"by the comfort wherewith we ourselves are comforted of God."*

"The Gift Of Grace"
I Corinthians 1:4

Day 122

Paul says to the Corinthians, "*I thank my God always on your behalf, for the grace of God which is given you by Jesus Christ*" (I Corinthians 1:4). This word for "*grace*" in the Greek means "the divine influence upon the heart and its reflection in the life." Oh, how we need His great grace and divine influence in our lives. Of all the attributes of God that we have seen thus far, this one is very near and dear to my heart. I have found that apart from His grace, I can do nothing.

If there ever was a time when people needed God's grace, it is now. Grace towards us is God's great heart. Anyone who teaches differently, as far as I'm concerned, shames His great character. He is a God of grace and mercy. He knows that, left to ourselves, we are absolutely incapable of being perfected in Him or walking in true holiness. God knows our human nature is an enemy against the Spirit of God (Romans 8:7), and that "*every man at his best state is altogether vanity*" (Psalms 39:5). Job, "*Yet man is born unto trouble, as the sparks fly upward*" (Job 5:7). Paul writes to the Romans, "*For I know that in me (that is, in my flesh,) dwelleth no good thing*" (Romans 7:18). It says in Psalms 103:14, "*For he knoweth our frame; he remembereth that we are dust.*" Jeremiah tells us, "*The heart is deceitful above all things, and desperately wicked: who can know it?*" (Jeremiah 17:9).

Our only hope is for the grace of God to help us and guide us towards a true, fruitful, and faithful walk with God. It's His gift to us, without which we are truly helpless. Many don't want there to be such an emphasis on grace, but Paul writes to Titus tells us grace teaches us to "*denying ungodliness and worldly lusts, we should live soberly, righteously, and godly, in this present world*" (Titus 2:12). Paul said to Timothy, "*Be strong in the grace that is in Christ Jesus*" (II Timothy 2:1). I don't know how someone can teach too much grace. It is our only hope for us to become like Jesus. God's grace is His ability enabling us when our ability is insufficient. Without it, we might never seek to be changed into His image (II Corinthians 3:18).

I refuse to let someone else's unscriptural opinion dictate my life. God decided to give us as a wonderful gift of grace, and every one of us should take full advantage of it. Let's set aside what we've heard or been taught, as we examine what the Bible says about grace. As we do, we will find that our precious and wonderful God has shed it upon us abundantly. Paul writes to the Ephesians saying, "*[8]For by grace are ye saved through faith; and that not of yourselves: it is the gift of God: [9]Not of works, lest any man should boast*" (Ephesians 2:8-9). He continues to say, "*Whereof I was made a minister, according to the gift of the grace of God given unto me by the effectual working of his power*" (Ephesians 3:7). Thank God for the gift of grace! Without it, you and I are helpless and hopeless. Today, I pray God shed His divine influence upon our hearts abundantly.

"Give Me, Make Me"
Luke 15: 12, 19

DAY 123

In Luke 15 we have the parable of the prodigal son, and there are many divine and precious truths that you and I can apply to our own personal lives. I don't know about you, but I know what it means to be the prodigal son. In this story we find these words, "give me" and "make me". It is the difference between maturity and foolishness, selfishness and generosity, commitment and self-centeredness, faithfulness and slothfulness, and backsliding and going on with God.

When the prodigal goes to his father and demands his inheritance, he says "give me the portion that is reserved for me" (Luke 15:12). "Give me" is such a self-centered and selfish way of looking at things. Sadly to say that in the Body of Christ today, this is what is being taught. It is all about us; I, me, mine, what I can get, and how I can get it to live the abundant life. What we don't understand is that when we say "give me" we are alienating ourselves from the Lord. It says in the Scripture that pride goes before destruction and a haughty spirit before a fall (Proverbs 16:18). God will not stand for selfishness or arrogance.

Coming back to the story, the father gives the son what he has asked for, and the son takes his journey into a far country and wastes his substance on riotous living. How many of us have done the very same thing? We have wasted the substance that God has given us because of our riotous living. We see here that the son enters into a great journey whereby he ends up being completely alone; he has spent his inheritance, and is now eating out of the troughs of pigs.

Hopefully it doesn't take us this long to realize our blunder; to realize our selfishness or self-centeredness. God help us today to have a kingdom mentality of "let us" being more concerned about our brother or sister than we are for ourselves.

And so, while in this pigpen, the prodigal son begins to consider what he had before. He decides he will return to his father and he says in Luke 12:19, "[I] *am no more worthy to be called thy son: make me as one of thy hired servants.*" The key to maturity is "make me" not "give me". I can say that I have seen many hundreds of brothers miss the mark because of ambition, jealousy, or pettiness. They never learned to say "make me as one of thy hired servants". This may not be considered a very lofty goal in some people's eyes, but that which is highly esteemed in the eyes of men is an abomination to God (Luke 16:15). God wants the attitude of our heart to reflect who and what we really are, and to reflect His glory.

We see that when the prodigal bows in his heart and says "make me", that his father does not lay this sin to his charge. He forgives and embraces him instead and throws a party to celebrate his return.

It must be known that when you say "give me" it is selfish, self-centered, and all about you; while "make me" is humble, in the fear of the Lord, and is all about you becoming a servant to serve others instead of receiving. Let us remember this as we go through today, that God is calling us to be His servant and to think of others over ourselves.

"I Will Now Turn Aside, And See"
Exodus 3:3

DAY 124

Exodus 3 tells the story of Moses and the burning bush, long after he had left Egypt, long after he had murdered the Egyptian, long after he had been married and had spent many years in the dealings of God. Forty years is the number of a generation, and is also the number in Scripture for trials and testing.

It says in Exodus, *"Moses kept the flock of Jethro his father in law, the priest of Midian: and he led the flock to the backside of the desert, and came to the mountain of God, even to Horeb"* (Exodus 3:1). It's important to know that the mountain of God *"Horeb"* means "waster." Moses had been leading a bunch of dumb sheep up the backside of a mountain. Going up a mountain is very difficult; living in the backside of the desert can never be a good thing. Being in a place called "waster" speaks of the great dealings of God in our lives, our trials and afflictions. We all have a Horeb, a wilderness, a desert, a place of "my killing."

Can you imagine doing the same thing: moving sheep up a mountain all day, every day for forty years? Some people think if they spend three and a half years in a Bible school they can have thirty years of ministry. Jesus had three and a half years of ministry and thirty years of doing nothing but being in the training of the Lord. Moses spent forty years training for forty years of ministry. John the Baptist was in the deserts until his showing unto Israel. Paul was in the deserts of Arabia for fourteen years before he brought his revelation out. We could go on and on. Joshua spent forty years under the tutelage of Moses. Elisha poured water on the hands of Elijah. This is the principle in Scripture of father ministry. God works through a father ministry in our lives to bring us forth to the place where we are ready.

It continues to say, *"the angel of the Lord appeared unto him in a flame of fire out of the midst of a bush"* (Exodus 3:2). This angel of the Lord, I believe, is a divine theophany, or a divine appearance. Jesus appeared to him in this burning bush. And Moses, *"looked, and, behold, the bush burned with fire, and the bush was not consumed."* This says to me that the fire of God is not a natural fire, but a spiritual one. It is a purging, remedial thing to rid us of the sin, darkness, and carnal nature in us.

Moses walked past that same bush every day for forty years and saw nothing, until one day, he saw that the very same bush was burning. It would be so easy to pass it by and just say, "Well, the heat of the desert caused it to catch fire. It's nothing important." It would be so easy to give up. The Bible says of Joseph, *"Until the time that his word came: the word of the Lord tried him"* (Psalms 105:19). It also says in Job, *"All the days of my appointed time will I wait, till my change come"* (Job 14:14). Your day will come, as it did for Joseph. He went from being a prisoner to be prime minister.

Moses then said, *"I will now turn aside, and see this great sight, why the bush is not burnt"* (Exodus 3:3). You and I must be ready to turn aside, to do the unordinary thing, and be ready to go when the master calls. Be watching for a burning bush. It will come at an hour that you think not (Luke 12:40).

"The Heart Of The Fathers"
Malachi 4:6

In the book of Malachi, we find this is the last word the Lord gave to His people for 400 years. So if this was the last word He spoke to them prophetically and He didn't speak again until right before the coming of Jesus, we need to take heed to what He said:

DAY 125

"Behold, I will send you Elijah the prophet before the coming of the great and dreadful day of the Lord: ⁶And he shall turn the heart of the fathers to the children, and the heart of the children to their fathers, lest I come and smite the earth with a curse." (Malachi 4:5-6)

In the last days before the coming of the Lord there will be a turning of the heart of the fathers to the children and the heart of the children to their fathers, lest God smites the earth with a curse. This is not only a natural principle but a spiritual one as well. Fathers not relating to children and children not relating to fathers is a curse as far as God is concerned. The problem is we don't have a lot of fathers. It's easy to have a child, but it is not easy to be a father.

Paul writing to Timothy says, *"²⁰For I have no man likeminded, who will naturally care for your state...But ye know the proof of him, that, as a son with the father, he hath served with me in the gospel"* (Philippians 2:20, 22). There are fathers in the gospel and there are women who are mothers in Zion whom God places in each one of our lives. I believe every believer should have a father ministry in their life, someone who disciples them just as Elijah discipled Elisha, Moses discipled Joshua, and Paul discipled Timothy, Titus, and many others. Therefore, we find this is a true Scriptural principle. God is a Father and has children and expects us to disciple others so that they may become sons.

I Corinthians 4:15 says *"For though ye have ten thousand instructors in Christ, yet have ye not many fathers: for in Christ Jesus I have begotten you through the gospel."* In Greek the word *"instructors"* here literally means "boy teachers." There are many of these in the body of Christ. Solomon said in Ecclesiastes 10:7, *"I have seen servants upon horses, and princes walking as servants upon the earth."* So many of the talented and outwardly beautiful are promoted; while those who have the true calling and seal of God upon their lives are overlooked. As such, we are left with boy teachers with no real substance of God in their life leading the body of Christ.

But change is about to come. God is turning the hearts of true fathers to the children and the children are turning their hearts to true fathers. Sadly, as I Corinthians 4:15 brings out; there aren't too many true spiritual fathers around. I think the best description of a father is found in I Thessalonians 2. Paul who was a great father in the Lord to so many says, *"But we were gentle among you, even as a nurse cherisheth her children: ⁸So being affectionately desirous of you, we were willing to have imparted unto you, not the gospel of God only, but also our own souls, because ye were dear unto us"* (I Thessalonians 2:7-8). This whole chapter in I Thessalonians 2 really gives a true description of a father ministry. And in these last days, God is turning the hearts of fathers to children and He's turning the hearts of children to fathers.

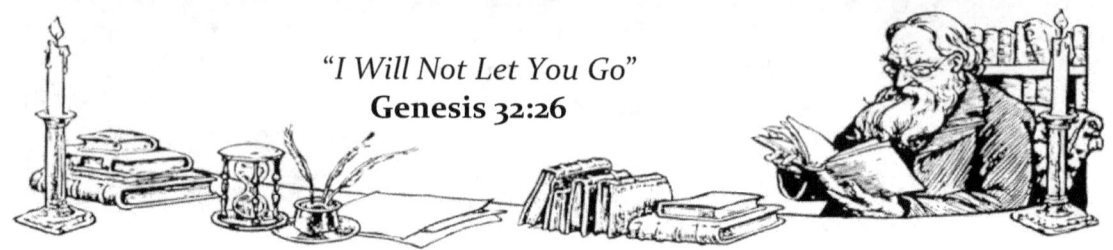

"I Will Not Let You Go"
Genesis 32:26

DAY 126

Just recently, in a time of worship and adoration, the Spirit of God fell upon me and the Lord spoke to me very clearly saying, "I want to see something from you." I thought, "Lord, I've walked with you over 40 years now. What more could You want to see from me?" And He said, "There are things yet to be redeemed in you, son. I want to see the middle of your soul." Then He took me to this passage in Genesis 32.

We all know the story of Jacob, how he betrayed his brother, how his name in the Hebrew means "deceiver and supplanter." At this time, he had not yet received his character change, his new name. And he met the angel of the Lord. That angel of the Lord, that messenger of the Lord, was none other than the Lord Jesus Himself. And Jacob wrestled with Him until the breaking of the day, as shown in Genesis 32:25-26, *"And when he saw that he prevailed not against him, he touched the hollow of his thigh; and the hollow of Jacob's thigh was out of joint, as he wrestled with him..."* So many times we find ourselves wrestling with the messenger of the Lord when it's really the message that our soul is wrestling with. When Jacob wrestled, God saw something in Him. Then God said, "I'm going to leave now, the day's breaking." And Jacob made this statement, *"I will not let thee go, except thou bless me."*

God is looking for something from you and me, and it's this: a determination, a willful passion that refuses to let go of God and His Word and His sanctifying process. God asked Him in verse 27, *"What is thy name?"* And he answered, *"Jacob."* In other words, "I'm still a deceiver and a supplanter." I don't know about you, but I myself would not and do not want to stay that way; I want to change. I want my character to be holy and righteous. I want it to be no longer I that live, but Christ that lives in me (Galations 2:20). I want people to see Jesus in me.

As Paul says in Romans 7, the things we want to do, we don't do, and the things we don't want to do, we end up doing (Romans 7:19). This seems to be our lifestyle. But there needs to be in us this cry: "I will not let you go!" It means "to put your hands upon, to lock in and not let go." Like Adonijah in I Kings 1, when he tried to take over the throne before Solomon did. When he was exposed, Adonijah knew that he was a dead man and he went immediately (verse 50) to the horns of the altar, *"But Adonijah, in fear of Solomon, went and took hold of the horns of the altar."* In the next verse he says, "I'm not leaving here, I'm not letting go, until he swears he will let me live." Which Solomon did; he let him live. Sometimes we have to grab hold of the altar when we're sentenced to death. Yet we know and are fully persuaded that grabbing hold and saying, "I will not let You go until you bless me" is the only way we can live.

Let that be our testimony today. Rise up on the inside and shout if you must, "I will not let You go!" Just like blind Bartimaeus in Mark 10:47, by the wayside begging and screaming, *"Jesus, thou Son of David, have mercy on me."* Everybody told him to be quiet. Yet he cried even louder. They're not blind. They're not begging, but you and I are. We want Jesus; we need Jesus. We need that character change, from Jacob to *"Israel"* which means "champion, favor with God and with man." Let God see that determination in our hearts today.

"Who Shall Separate Us From The Love Of Christ?"
Romans 8:35

DAY 127

Romans 8:35 states, *"Who shall separate us from the love of Christ? Shall tribulation, or distress, or persecution, or famine, or nakedness, or peril, or sword?"*

In this marvelous passage of Romans 8:35-39, we find one of the great truths of Scripture, that nothing can separate us from God because it is through Jesus that our salvation stands. But also, here I want us to see all the things the Apostle Paul mentions are certain things that we will face in our lifetime. Today, maybe you are facing one of these particular things. As we go over them and search them out, be encouraged today to know that they cannot separate you from the love of Christ.

The word *"separate"* in the Greek means, *"to put space between."* It comes from a root word that means, *"a space of territory, expanse, room."* Satan is constantly trying to put room or space between us and God. He is trying to separate us. Not only him but life, the world, the flesh and all that is in the world, the pride of life, and the lust of other things are trying constantly to separate us from the love of Christ. But it can't be done. No one or nothing can do these things. No one can put space between us and God.

The first thing Paul says is, *"shall tribulation?"* This word *"tribulation"* in the Greek means "pressure, anguish, affliction, trouble." Are you under pressure? Are you in anguish, affliction or trouble? You need to know today that it cannot separate you. It will not separate you because in II Corinthians 1:4 it says, *"[God] who comforteth us in all our tribulation."* Glory to God! Even though in Acts 14:22 it says, *"that we must through much tribulation enter into the kingdom of God,"* and Romans 5:3-5 declares, *"but we glory in tribulations also: knowing that tribulation worketh patience; ⁴And patience, experience; and experience, hope: ⁵And hope maketh not ashamed; because the love of God is shed abroad in our hearts by the Holy Ghost which is given unto us."* Can tribulation separate us? No! In fact, it brings us closer to Him and presses us into the Kingdom.

The second thing Paul mentions is distress. Distress in the Greek means, *"narrowness of room, calamity, anguish."* Do you feel crowded to the point where you can't breathe because of circumstances of life? The enemy may be chasing you or your own weaknesses are assailing you. Perhaps you are having problems with relationships. Or as Isaiah 28:20 states, *"For the bed is shorter than that a man can stretch himself on it: and the covering narrower than that he can wrap himself in it."*

No matter the circumstances, know this: just as in the Old Testament, when those that were in debt, discontented or in distress found David in the cave of Adullam, and he became a captain over them and they became a tremendous army, you and I go to Jesus in our distress and we find He will bless us. Nothing can separate us from Him. (I Samuel 22:1-2) In II Samuel 22:7 it says, *"In my distress I called upon the LORD, and cried to my God: and he did hear my voice out of his temple, and my cry did enter in his ear."* I Kings 1:29 it says, *"As the LORD liveth, that hath redeemed my soul out of all distress."* Psalms 118:5 also states, *"I called upon the LORD in distress: the LORD answered me, and set me in a large place."* David says in Psalms 4:1, *"thou hast enlarged me when I was in distress."* Psalms 120:1 also says, *"In my distress I cried unto the LORD, and he heard me."* Distress cannot separate us from the love of God.

Shall persecution? Persecution in Greek means *"to pursue or follow after."* It says in Mark 4:17 that persecution *"ariseth for the word's sake."* There will always be persecution. II Timothy 3:12 says, *"Yea, and all that will live godly in Christ Jesus shall suffer persecution."* Paul, in II Corinthians 4:9 says we are, *"persecuted, but not forsaken; cast down, but not destroyed."* We are to *"bless them which persecute you: bless, and curse not,"* as Romans 12:14 states. Persecution cannot separate us from the love of God. It cannot separate us or put space between us and Christ Jesus. None of these things can. Are you being persecuted today? Remember that persecution is appointed of God. Jesus said in John 15:20, *"The servant is not greater than his lord. If they have persecuted me, they will also persecute you."* Knowing this, we say as Paul does in II Corinthians 12:10, *"Therefore I take pleasure in infirmities, in reproaches, in necessities, in persecutions, in distresses for Christ's sake: for when I am weak, then am I strong."* Persecution won't separate us from God

The next thing Paul says is famine. *"Famine"* in the Greek means, *"destitution, scarcity of food, hunger, or dearth."* Famine cannot separate us either. In Job 5:20, it says, *"In famine he shall redeem thee from death."* Then in verse 22 of the same chapter it says, *"...in famine thou shalt laugh."* This is the word of God when it comes to scarcity, poverty, or dearth. Jesus states in Matthew 6:33, *"But seek ye first the kingdom of God, and his righteousness; and all these things shall be added unto you."* Everything that you need to eat, the clothing you need to put on, and all your needs will be met. David says in Psalms 37:25, *"I have been young, and now am old; yet have I not seen the righteous forsaken, nor his seed begging bread."* Famine cannot and will not separate us from the love of God in Christ Jesus. God will be faithful in these times to be there for us.

Can nakedness separate us from Jesus? Nakedness in the Greek means, *"absolute nudity."* It comes from a root word that means *"to strip."* This speaks to us of being naked and exposed. Satan will try to accuse and expose us as well as people will try to embarrass us, afflict us and shame us. But as Hebrews 4:13 states, *"...but all things are naked and opened unto the eyes of him with whom we have to do."* We need not worry about being naked or uncovered because God Himself will cover us as He did in Ezekiel 16:8, *"Now when I [God] passed by thee, and looked upon thee, behold, thy time was the time of love; and I spread my skirt over thee, and covered thy nakedness: yea, I sware unto thee, and entered into a covenant with thee, saith the Lord God, and thou becamest mine."* Nakedness will not separate us from His love reaching out and helping us.

Lastly, the sword cannot separate us. That word in the Greek means, *"a knife, war, fighting, punishment."* God shall redeem us from war, as Job 5:20 states, *"In famine he shall redeem thee from death: and in war from the power of the sword."* God will not allow the sword to thrust us. He will not allow the sword to separate us.

So if today these things are in your life, rejoice and be exceeding glad because nothing can separate you from the love of God which is in Christ Jesus.

"Commit Thy Way Unto The Lord"
Psalms 37:5

DAY 128

God's way, the narrow way (Matthew 7:14), is much better than our way. In Psalms 37:5 David says, *"Commit thy way unto the Lord; trust also in him; and he shall bring it to pass."* Why should we commit our way unto the Lord, because He knows the end from the beginning? We should pray as David, *"Teach me thy way, O Lord, and lead me in a plain path"* (Psalms 27:11). In Psalms 1:6, it says, *"The Lord knoweth the way of the righteous."* He knows what to do; He knows where we're going. We're not lost. God's too big to lose us. As it says in the book of Job, *"He knoweth the way that I take: when he hath tried me, I shall come forth as gold"* (Job 23:10).

What happens when we take the way of the Lord, many times, is that it may lead us to chastisement, sanctification, a dealing of God, tribulation, testing, or affliction. We don't like being tried. When revelation is being married to our situation, that's when we rebel, take the path of least resistance, and go somewhere else.

Rather than looking to Jesus for guidance, many people are depending on themselves for answers or simply have stopped listening to authority figures. They have no respect and don't submit themselves. It says in Jude 8, *"Speak evil of dignities"*. Because of rebellion, pride, ambition, or weakness, they fulfill Proverbs 14:12, which says, *"There is a way which seemeth right unto a man, but the end thereof are the ways of death."*

However, God *"made known his ways unto Moses, his acts unto the children of Israel"* (Psalms 103:7). We need to know the ways of God. We need to know what God wants. As David said, *"I will hear what God the Lord will speak"* (Psalms 85:8).

The Bible says in Psalms 25:9, *"The meek will he guide in judgment: and the meek will he teach his way"*. God has a place and a plan for us. He's given us *"an expected end"* (Jeremiah 29:11). Habakkuk 2:3 tells us, *"For the vision is yet for an appointed time, but at the end it shall speak, and not lie: though it tarry, wait for it; because it will surely come, it will not tarry."*

The problem is *"All we like sheep have gone astray; we have turned every one to his own way; and the Lord hath laid on him the iniquity of us all"* (Isaiah 53:6). But Jeremiah 10:23 tells us, *"O Lord, I know that the way of man is not in himself: it is not in man that walketh to direct his steps"*. We don't know where we're going. We need God's guidance. That's why David said, *"The steps of a good man are ordered by the Lord: and he delighteth in his way"* (Psalms 37:23).

You and I need to commit our way unto the Lord. We need to, as Jeremiah said, *"Stand ye in the ways, and see, and ask for the old paths, where is the good way, and walk therein, and ye shall find rest for your souls"* (Jeremiah 6:16). We need to allow Him to guide, lead, and teach us. Commit your way, today, unto the Lord!

"And The Lord Sent Nathan Unto David"
II Samuel 12:1

Day 129

In this story, we find David the king, *"the anointed of the God of Jacob, and the sweet psalmist of Israel,"* (II Samuel 23:1), the man after God's own heart (Acts 13:22), covering up great sins in his life. The word of the Lord to us today is, as it says in Proverbs, *"He that covereth his sins shall not prosper: but whoso confesseth and forsaketh them shall have mercy"* (Proverbs 28:13). The word *"covereth"* in Hebrew means "to cover (for clothing or secrecy), to conceal, or to hide." God does not want us hiding or covering our sins. In Numbers 32:23, it says, *"be sure your sin will find you out."* Some other translations of this verse read: *"You can be sure that your sin will track you down"*, *"Be sure your sin will catch up with you."* But this is clearly brought out in Galatians, saying:

> *"⁷Be not deceived; God is not mocked: for whatsoever a man soweth, that shall he also reap. ⁸For he that soweth to his flesh shall of the flesh reap corruption; but he that soweth to the Spirit shall of the Spirit reap life everlasting."* (Galatians 6:7-8)

The word *"deceived"* here in the Greek means "to cause to roam (from safety, truth, or virtue), to err, or to be seduced." God does not want us to roam from safety, truth, or virtue. He doesn't want us to err. The Bible says, *"Do not err, my beloved brethren"* (James 1:16). The word *"mocked"* in Greek means "ridiculed, to make mouths at, or to make fun of." God will not be mocked. Be sure your sin will catch up with you.

Read the story in II Samuel 12. Here the Lord sends Nathan to David. God will always send a man of God, someone in authority, to you to point out your sin. After Nathan tells him a parable, and David acts so self-righteous, Nathan looks at him and says, *"Thou art the man"* (II Samuel 12:7). What continues is God's response. In verse 10, He says *"Now therefore the sword shall never depart from thine house; because thou hast despised me."* The word *"despised"* here means "to disesteem, to think to scorn, to disdain, to treat contemptibly, or to treat someone as a vile person." David had reached a place of self-satisfaction. Thinking so highly of himself, that he thought he could disesteem God. He committed adultery, lied, covered his sin, had a man killed, and married the wife of one of his mighty men. How shameful.

All of us have sin in our lives from which we believe God for deliverance, but we cannot cover it or hide it in secrecy. It will find us out. God will send a Nathan to us and when He does, don't hide anymore. It is God's provision for deliverance in our life. So today the word of the Lord to us is to open our hearts and *"Having therefore these promises, dearly beloved, let us cleanse ourselves from all filthiness of the flesh and spirit, perfecting holiness in the fear of God"* (II Corinthians 7:1).

"A Man Sent From God"
John 1:6

DAY 130

Here we find in John 1:6, *"There was a man sent from God, whose name was John."* This seems like a simple Scripture with a plain revelation, but as we dig deeper and allow the Holy Spirit to speak to us, we can gain some insight into what the Lord wants us to see. God did not send a superman. He sent a man, a human being. The expectation on ministers sometimes is far greater than they can handle. Men are lifted up and elevated to positions they never should be, and thereby this causes them to fall. Paul said in II Corinthians 4:7 that we have this *"treasure in earthen vessels, that the excellency may be of God, and not of us."*

Men of God are just human beings. They are human in every way. Remember in Ezekiel 1 and in Revelation 5, when it talks of the cherubims and the living creatures. One of the things we'll find about them is that they have the hands of a man. They also have the face of a man. In other words, as ministers, our God-given humanity is what helps us relate to this world. God uses men and women so that not only are we able to give people spiritual blessings, but we can also reach out and touch them in a human sense and bring comfort and kindness to them. No matter how spiritual we may become, we still have the hands of a man. We never lose our humanity.

For so much of my ministry, I tried to be something other than who I was, because I wanted to please people. But try as I might, the things I wanted to do I couldn't do and the things I didn't want to do, I ended up doing (Romans 7:15). I finally realized that in my flesh, I could do nothing and I was desperate apart from the grace of God. Even though God called and sent me, I realized I was just a man with weaknesses like everyone else. All my issues did not go away when I entered the ministry. In fact, the warfare got greater. But I learned as Zechariah 4:6 says, *"Not by might, nor by power, but by my spirit, saith the Lord of hosts."*

Psalms 147:10 says, *"He taketh not pleasure in the legs of a man."* God is not interested in our talents, our intellect, or our greatness. This is why Paul wrote in I Corinthians 1:26, *"For ye see your calling, brethren, how that not many wise men after the flesh, not many mighty, not many noble, are called."* So who does He call then? He calls flawed vessels. Name anybody in the Scripture and it won't take very long for us to look into their lives to see that they had flaws. Some of them had great flaws. Consider David and Samson. But yet God called them, anointed them, redeemed them, and they served a great purpose in God.

By no means do we want to encourage anybody to sin. But at the same time, we need to know that there is provision for our sin. I John 2:1 says, *"And if any man sin, we have an advocate with the Father, Jesus Christ the righteous."* *"If we confess our sins, he is faithful and just to forgive us our sins, and to cleanse us from all unrighteousness"* (I John 1:9). So today I say to you, *"there was a man sent from God."* Let's cut these brothers some slack and have mercy upon them because they are human just like you and me. Elijah *"was a man subject to like passions as we are"* (James 5:17). But he prayed. Let's pray and believe God, understanding that apart from Him we can do nothing.

"The Entrance Of Thy Words"
Psalms 119:130

DAY 131

Here in Psalms 119:130 it says, *"The entrance of thy words giveth light; it giveth understanding unto the simple."* When God's word enters into our lives, it gives light and understanding. The word *"light"* in the Scripture is a type of revelation. It means that God has shined a light on a passage of Scripture that up until now was not understandable. His Word is the answer and is the light in our darkness. If you notice in verse 105 of the same chapter it says, *"Thy word is a lamp unto my feet, and a light unto my path."* We need His Word to enter into our life. When we need understanding, when we feel foolish, or we're in darkness, the answer is the Word of God.

Here in Proverbs 6:23 it says, *"For the commandment is a lamp; and the law is light."* This is just like when Peter says, *"We have also a more sure word of prophecy; whereunto ye do well that ye take heed, as unto a light that shineth in a dark place"* (II Peter 1:19). This is the Word of God. *"The entrance of thy words giveth light"* (Psalms 119:130). It shatters and dispels darkness, and brings revelation and truth to our hearts. Oh, that we would find a love for the truth. Jesus said, *"The words that I speak unto you, they are spirit, and they are life"* (John 6:63). He also said, *"flesh and blood hath not revealed it unto thee, but my Father which is in heaven. ¹⁸And upon this rock I will build my church"* (Matthew 16:17-18). That rock that the church is built on is the rock of revelation. Knowing something you did not know before. As God's Word enter into our hearts and minds, it brings with it light. For the law is a lamp and a light, and the entrance of those words gives light and understanding to the simple.

Psalms 19:7-8 says, *"The law of the Lord is perfect, converting the soul: the testimony of the Lord is sure, making wise the simple. ⁸ The statutes of the Lord are right, rejoicing the heart: the commandment of the Lord is pure, enlightening the eyes."* God's Word, His commandments, enlighten us. No longer do we need to stay in confusion, unbelief, or darkness. There is a light that is shining in a dark place and the Bible says we'd do well to take heed to it.

Have you taken heed to it? Do you see that light shining in the dark place? Run to it and be safe. Know that as you give yourself to the Word you're giving yourself to Jesus, because *"In the beginning was the Word, and the Word was with God, and the Word was God"* (John 1:1). As His words are read and they enter into your soul, they bring with them the light, the revelation, and the understanding that we need.

"The Blessing Of The Lord Maketh Rich"
Proverbs 10:22

Today we want to consider Proverbs 10:22 where it says, *"The blessing of the Lord, it maketh rich, and he addeth no sorrow with it."* Thanks be unto God that He doesn't add difficulties or sorrows to His blessings and goodness when it comes to us. On the contrary, our great God is a God that blesses His people because He loves them and He adds no sorrow to it!

DAY 132

Psalms 3:8 says, *"Thy blessing is upon thy people. Selah."* Psalms 5:12 says, *"For thou, Lord, wilt bless the righteous; with favour wilt thou compass him as with a shield."* Psalms 29:11 *"the Lord will bless his people with peace."* Proverbs 3:33 says, *"He blesseth the habitation of the just."* This is our God. He loves to bless His people. He loves to give and to minister to us. As a matter of fact, He *"daily loadeth us with benefits"* (Psalms 68:19). Psalms 103 lists these daily benefits, *"Who forgiveth all thine iniquities; who healeth all thy diseases; ⁴Who redeemeth thy life from destruction; who crowneth thee with lovingkindness and tender mercies; ⁵Who satisfieth thy mouth with good things; so that thy youth is renewed like the eagle's"* (Psalms 103:3-5).

The blessing of the Lord makes us rich! This is found in the New Testament as well in Ephesians 1:3, *"Blessed be the God and Father of our Lord Jesus Christ, who hath blessed us with all spiritual blessings in heavenly places in Christ."*

Are you walking in the blessings of God today? No matter what you are going through today, open your heart today and realize that you've been blessed *"with all spiritual blessings in heavenly places in Christ."* You don't need to justify or feel ashamed about the blessing of the Lord. It is a good thing. Jesus said in Luke 12:32, *"Fear not, little flock; for it is your Father's good pleasure to give you the kingdom."* God is your Father and every father wants to bless his children. It's the parent's job actually to lay up for the children (II Corinthians 12:14). We read in Psalms 132:13-15, *"For the Lord hath chosen Zion; he hath desired it for his habitation. ¹⁴This is my rest for ever: here will I dwell; for I have desired it. ¹⁵I will abundantly bless her provision."*

What a wonderful God we serve! How many times we struggle because of things we go through. Some might even call some of the things we go through a curse. But I want you to know that in Deuteronomy 23:5 it says, *"The Lord thy God turned the curse into a blessing unto thee, because the Lord thy God loved thee."* God turns the curse into a blessing for us. *"The blessing of the Lord, it maketh rich, and he addeth no sorrow with it."* God wants to *"pour you out a blessing, that there shall not be room enough to receive it"* (Malachi 3:10). Deuteronomy 2:7 says, *"For the Lord thy God hath blessed thee in all the works of thy hand: he knoweth thy walking through this great wilderness: these forty years the Lord thy God hath been with thee; thou hast lacked nothing."* God wants to abundantly bless your provision and He doesn't want you feeling sad, ashamed, sorry, or uncomfortable about it. Why? Because when He blesses you, it makes you rich and He adds no sorrow to it!

"My People Love To Have It So"
Jeremiah 5:31

Day 133

We read in Jeremiah 5:30-31, *"A wonderful and horrible thing is committed in the land; ³¹The prophets prophesy falsely, and the priests bear rule by their means; and my people love to have it so: and what will ye do in the end thereof?"*

Whatever these priests are doing is a horrible thing. Firstly, they prophesy falsely. Then it gets to the point that we see today, where it says, *"and the priests bear rule by their means."* In other words, the priests use their authority to put pressure on God's people. These priests manipulate, control, and force God's people into doing what the priests want them to do. We see this far too much in the body of Christ.

The Bible says in II Samuel 23:3, *"He that ruleth over men must be just, ruling in the fear of God."* In I Timothy 1:12 Paul said, *"he counted me faithful, putting me into the ministry"* You and I need to be counted faithful and we must emulate the ministry of the Great Shepherd, the Lord Jesus, who carried the lambs in His arms and gently leads those that are with young. Like Paul said in I Thessalonians 2:7, *"But we were gentle among you, even as a nurse cherisheth her children."* We need true pastors and shepherds, unlike those found in Ezekiel 34:2 where God says, *"Son of man, prophesy against the shepherds of Israel, prophesy, and say unto them, Thus saith the Lord God unto the shepherds; Woe be to the shepherds of Israel that do feed themselves! Should not the shepherds feed the flocks?"* There are too many men of God being fed and the people going without. It continues to say *"Ye eat the fat, and ye clothe you with the wool, ye kill them that are fed: but ye feed not the flock...but with force and with cruelty have ye ruled them. ⁴And were scattered, because there is no shepherd."* (Ezekiel 34:3-5)

It is not the will of God for pastors to lead people with force and cruelty. In II Corinthians 10:8 Paul says, *"our authority, which the Lord hath given us for edification, and not for your destruction."* Our whole purpose as men and women of God is, as Ephesians 4:11 outlines, *"For the perfecting of the saints, for the work of the ministry, for the edifying of the body of Christ."*

The sad thing about Jeremiah 5:31 is that when there are priests that do this, bearing rule by their means, it says that the people love to have it so. How sad! Then he says, *"and what will ye do in the end thereof?"* Well, in the end thereof you have a disillusioned, broken, faithless, wounded people who no longer are pressing toward the mark for the high calling (Philippians 3:14).

The Word of encouragement for you today is that He also promises in Jeremiah 3:15 saying, *"And I will give you pastors according to mine heart, which shall feed you with knowledge and understanding."* He has men and women of God after His own heart as He witnesses of David in Acts 13:22; and He will give these men and women to His people to feed them the knowledge and understanding of the Lord.

"For Yielding Pacifieth Great Offences"
Ecclesiastes 10:4

Day 134

One of the great things we learn in life is that learning to yield is the essence of getting along with other people. The Scriptures are very clear about this principle called yielding. Here in this passage of Scripture it fully reads, *"If the spirit of the ruler rise up against thee, leave not thy place; for yielding pacifieth great offences"* (Ecclesiastes 10:4). The spirit of a ruler can be any manipulating or controlling spirit. It can be some kind of authority figure rising up against you. It can be anybody, a family member, a preacher, a king, a friend, etc. It is simply somebody who is trying to manipulate, control, or push something on you.

The word for "*yielding*" is the Hebrew word "*marpe*" which means "a curative, a medicine, health, remedy, deliverance." It comes from a root word, "*rapha*", which means "to mend, a physician." The Greek word for "*yielding*' means: "to stand beside." A good dictionary definition is "to surrender or submit, to give way under pressure, to not be stiff, to bend, to be flexible." Some other translations of Ecclesiastes 10:4 read:

> *"For submission pacifieth great offences"*
> *"For gentleness allayeth great offences"*
> *"For reconciliation will mollify great offences"*
> *"Great harm by the healing touch may yet be assuaged"*
> *"Refer to him and you will pacify"*
> *"Yielding always pacifieth great offences"*

So when someone rises up against you and tries to control or manipulate your life, the first thing you do is *"leave not thy place."* In other words, don't be forced to move; don't be intimidated to be moved out of your God-given or rightful place. He says rather, *"for yielding pacifieth great offences."* What happens when we yield is we allow the healing power of God or His curative medicine to come in and help.

An old Chinese proverb says, "to yield is to preserve oneself." Another quotation says, "Forgiveness is the fragrance of the flower that clings to the heel that crushed it." In other words, no man should be able to force us so low as to make us hate him. Yielding is God's answer to controlling spirits, pushy people, and situations that are beyond our control. If we yield, we set in motion the cure, remedy, soundness, and the wholesome answer. We bring health to the situation.

Self-preservation may be the first law of nature, but self-denial is the first law of grace. A young Christian asked an elderly Christian once, "what are the three Christian virtues which are indispensable to the Christian walk?" The answer was, "the first is humility, the second is humility, and the third is humility." This, my friend, is the answer for life and for us to get along with people. You can truly gauge the character of a person by how he treats those who can do nothing for him and how he treats those who treat him unkindly.

When we yield, we allow the Holy Spirit to bring His precious grace, mercy, and reconciliation into a situation. We may be right, but our attitude wrong. Pride never helps anything. The best thing for us to do is to humble ourselves under the mighty hand of God and yield.

However in yielding, we are not to leave our place, give up or just allow anybody to intimidate or push us around or take over. This is never God's will. When the Lord said to turn the other cheek (Matthew 5:39), He meant that when somebody is retaliating while they are preaching the gospel. David many times asked the Lord about his enemy, "Shall I go up and go against them?" And God would tell him to go up and defeat them many times. Ecclesiastes 3:1 says, *"To every thing there is a season, and a time to every purpose under the heaven."* There's a *"time of war, and a time of peace"* (Ecclesiastes 3:8). Therefore I would say there is a time to yield and a time to not yield or give in.

Yielding is a spiritual principle. And as we allow it to take place, things will change in our lives for the better. I know there are people that have our number. They know the right buttons to push in our life. Moreover, there are those who are motivated to take control, ambitious and pushy people. There are unkind and unforgiving people that simply rub us the wrong way. We will never win in these battles when we respond in accordance with what they've done. We must yield and as we do, we pacify great offences. We stop terrible things from happening by being the one to yield.

Consider the story of Meshach, Shadrach, and Abednego in Daniel 3. They refused to bow down and were placed in the burning fiery furnace. When they came out of that fire alive not smelling like smoke, Nebuchadnezzar said:

> *"Blessed be the God of Shadrach, Meshach, and Abednego, who hath sent his angel, and delivered his servants that trusted in him, and have changed the king's word, and yielded their bodies, that they might not serve nor worship any god, except their own God."* (Daniel 3:28)

Rather than fight back and be rebellious they simply said they couldn't bow down and serve an idol. So they yielded their bodies up and God answered them and brought about a great deliverance and manifested His glory.

Paul in Romans 6 talks about yielding our members as servants to righteousness. This is our job, to yield our *"members as instruments of righteousness unto God"* (Romans 6:13). Many times, one of the most unruly members is our tongue many times. It is probably the greatest member that needs to yield. You and I can do it by the grace of God.

So hear the word of the Lord today. When the spirit of the ruler rises against you, simply yield without leaving your place. Be like Jesus who was *"meek and lowly in heart"* (Matthew 11:29). You will find that by doing so today you will be allowing the Spirit of the Lord to intervene, setting in motion the cure and resolution to any situation that comes your way.

"Walking in Integrity"
Proverbs 20:7

DAY 135

The Scripture says here that "*the just man walketh in his integrity: his children are blessed after him.*" The first part of this verse that says "*the just man walketh*" means that he lives his life before God and before men in integrity.

The Hebrew word for "*integrity*" means "completeness, innocence, perfection." Another dictionary definition means "a state or quality of being complete, undivided or unbroken, moral soundness, honesty, purity, and uprightness." This is integrity. Someone who has moral soundness and that is undivided and cannot be broken. They stay innocent and strive for perfection. The just man walks in this.

Proverbs 11:3 says, "The *integrity of the upright shall guide them.*" We need to allow the Spirit of God within us to lead us and guide us into all truth. In John 2:27 it tells us that by the anointing which we have received abides within us, that we need not that any man teach us because that anointing is able to teach us. This anointing, the Holy Ghost, will guide and help us stay morally sound, complete, innocent, undivided, and unbroken.

If there was ever a lack of integrity it is in the day that you and I live. We need people to be morally sound and honest. God help us as the sons of God, to be these men and women of integrity.

In Job 31:6, "*let me be weighed in an even balance, that God may know mine integrity.*" We should want the Lord to test and prove us. "*Search me, O God, and know my heart: try me, and know my thought, and see if there be any wicked way in me*" it says in Psalms 139:23-24. We should be willing for the Lord to deal with us so that our true moral soundness, our honesty, our integrity will come through.

It also says Psalms 25:21 to "*let integrity and uprightness preserve me*". It is hard to keep your integrity in this world where temptation and so much division lives. But you can do it because you can let integrity and uprightness preserve us. God will uphold you in your integrity (Psalms 41:12). He will stand with you and help you so that you don't lose your integrity.

Proverbs 19:1 says, "*Better is the poor that walketh in his integrity.*" I don't believe this means a poor man naturally, but the poor in spirit. It is better for us to stay humble and walk in our integrity than to be boastful, proud, and double hearted.

Finally in Job 27:5, Job says "*till I die I will not remove mine integrity from me.*" Job was one of the greatest men of God in the Bible, and would to God we would have this same confession of faith: till I day I will not remove my integrity from me. I will stay morally sound. I will stay pure. I will stay complete, undivided, unbroken, innocent, striving for perfection. I will be loyal. Let this be our life today, and the days to follow.

"How Sweet Are Thy Words"
Psalms 119:103

Day 136

In Psalms 119:103, it says *"How sweet are thy words unto my taste! Yea, sweeter than honey to my mouth."* Oh, what a revelation this is! When you and I give ourselves to the Scriptures, it is like honey in our mouth, so precious and so wonderful. Notice what David said:

> *"The law of the Lord is perfect, converting the soul: the testimony of the Lord is sure, making wise the simple. ¹⁰More to be desired are they than gold, yea, than much fine gold: sweeter also than honey and the honeycomb. ¹¹Moreover by them is thy servant warned: and in keeping of them there is great reward."* (Psalms 19:7, 10-11)

The Word is sweeter than honey and the honeycomb. He said in Ezekiel:

> *"Moreover he said unto me, Son of man, eat that thou findest; eat this roll, and go speak unto the house of Israel. ²So I opened my mouth, and he caused me to eat that roll. ³And he said unto me, Son of man, cause thy belly to eat, and fill thy bowels* [or satisfy thyself] *with this roll that I give thee. Then did I eat it; and it was in my mouth as honey for sweetness."* (Ezekiel 3:1-3)

The same thing happened in Revelation 10:9-11, when John the apostle was told by the voice from heaven to go take the little book out of the messenger's hand. It says in Revelation 10:9, *"And he said unto me, Take it, and eat it up; and it shall make thy belly bitter, but it shall be in thy mouth sweet as honey."* Then the angel said to John in verse 11, *"Thou must prophesy again before many peoples, and nations, and tongues, and kings."* This was the same as God said to Ezekiel. They both had to eat the book and then prophesy the Word of the Lord.

As we eat the Word of God, it is sweet to our mouth. Revelation is precious and wonderful. It is only when revelation is married to our situation that it becomes bitter because God is trying to work that revelation into our character and lives. Song of Solomon 5:16 says, *"His mouth is most sweet: yea, he is altogether lovely."* What comes out of the mouth of the Lord? The answer is simple; the Word of God. That is why we want Him to kiss us with the *"kisses of his mouth"* (Song of Solomon 1:2). We want the Word that is in Him to come into us. And how sweet are His words!

Finally, Psalms 141:6 says, *"They shall hear my words; for they are sweet."* Receive His Word, today. Receive that sweet honey of God's Word today in your life. Pray as Jesus taught us to pray, *"Give us this day our daily bread"* (Matthew 6:11). God has a daily Word for you and it will come to you sweet as honey. But know that when God begins to process that Word in your life, it will get bitter in your belly, but ultimately it will be turned back to sweetness as you see your own character being changed by His wonderful Word. How great is His Word and *"More to be desired are they than gold, yea, than much fine gold: sweeter also than honey and the honeycomb."*

"A Certain Damsel Possessed"
Acts 16:16

Day 137

In Acts 16:16 we find this passage, *"And it came to pass, as we went to prayer, a certain damsel possessed with a spirit of divination met us, which brought her masters much gain by soothsaying."* The word *"damsel"* here is another word for "slave girl." And the Lord has quickened me today to share this with you. So many times when we see magicians, fortune tellers, card readers, and people involved with cults, we have a tendency to have a dislike for them. But what we don't realize is that they are enslaved. This damsel was enslaved to her masters. And she brought them much money by fortune telling.

How many times have we seen or made disparaging comments about a fortune teller's house or any other cult's place of business not realizing that God created every human being and loves all people? Yes, I know that soothsaying and divination is an abomination to God and in the Old Testament they were to be stoned to death for participating in this. But at the same time, I know *"the law was given by Moses, but grace and truth came by Jesus Christ"* (John 1:17). Jesus has brought grace and truth and He said in many places, *"It hath been said...but I say unto you..."* (Matthew 5). Well it has been said that these people should be stoned to death, but I believe the word of the Lord is saying to us now that we need to see beyond this and see by the Spirit of God that these people who God loves are enslaved to darkness and enslaved to their masters. They have been taken over by a demon spirit and are only operating under such, as Paul said in Ephesians 2:2, *"ye walked according to the course of this world, according to the prince of the power of the air, the spirit that now worketh in the children of disobedience."*

We have all had our times past in all kinds of miserable and ungodly and unholy things. And thank God the blood of Jesus Christ washed us from our sin and saved us from our horrific and ungodly practices. Would to God that we would have the same spirit that Jesus had and the spirit every man and woman of God seems to have in the Scripture; a spirit of compassion and mercy and seeing beyond the obvious.

This damsel had a spirit of divination. There is no denying this. Paul was grieved by it and commanded that this demon come out of her in Acts 16:18. Well, her masters were furious. They used and abused her. Satan abuses and uses, and you and I must be the ones there to present the love and mercy of God, and show people that there is a way out and a way of grace, truth, and love. We need to show them God doesn't hate them. He simply wants to turn and save them. I tell you, if God can save me, as wicked and rebellious as I was, then He can save anybody. Do you remember how He saved the Apostle Paul who used to put Christians to death?

Perhaps you may run into a certain damsel today or someone with a spirit of divination. Just remember they are enslaved. They may be enslaved by Satan and enslaved by masters who are using them for their own gain. God help you as you preach the Gospel to these needy people.

"In Deep Waters"
Psalms 69:2

DAY 138

In Psalms 69 we read:

> *"Save me, O God; for the waters are come in unto my soul. ²I sink in deep mire, where there is no standing: I am come into deep waters, where the floods overflow me. ³I am weary of my crying: my throat is dried: mine eyes fail while I wait for my God."* (Psalms 69:1-3)

Have you ever been in this situation, where it feels like the deep waters have come into your soul? Have you ever felt like you're sinking in deep mire where there is no standing, like the floods are about to overflow you? Have you gotten weary of crying? Have your eyes failed? I want to say to you today, be of good cheer. God has heard your cry.

David said in Psalms 130:1-2, *"Out of the depths have I cried unto thee, O Lord. Lord, hear my voice."* Some other translations of that passage are:

> *"Help God, the bottom has fallen out of my life. Master, hear my cry for help."*
> *"From the depths of despair, oh Lord, I call for Your help."*
> *"Lord I am in great trouble, so I call out to You."*

All we have to do is remember that no matter what we go through, He said He would never leave us nor forsake us (Hebrews 13:5). The word *"depths"* means "a profound place, a deep dark place, an abyss, or a surging mass of water." It's root word means "to make an uproar, or to agitate something." There are always things in life sent to agitate us, to depress us, or to cause us to be overwhelmed. However, our God will not let it happen.

When He looks upon these places in our life Psalms 77:16 says, *"The waters saw thee, O God, the waters saw thee; they were afraid: the depths also were troubled."* Our circumstances will have to bow to Him. David said *"he drew me out of many waters"* (Psalms 18:16). God will draw us out somehow, but He will also use these depths while we're in it to teach us, to mature us, and to perfect us.

Psalms 71:20 says, *"shalt quicken me again, and shalt bring me up again from the depths of the earth."* The Lord will quicken you again, and bring you up from the depths of flesh. He will do it again and again because He loves you. Psalms 106:9 says, *"so he led them through the depths, as through the wilderness."* Whether you know it or not God is leading you, He's watching you, and His hand is upon you. In Psalms 78:15 it says He *"gave them drink as out of the great depths."* God will cause you to drink. *"Who passing through the valley of Baca make it a well"* (Psalms 84:6). This very thing that was sent to destroy you will not. This deep and profound place of darkness can actually become as Samson said, *"Out of the eater came forth meat, and out of the strong came forth sweetness"* (Judges 14:14). God will use this for His glory.

It says in Proverbs 3:20, *"By his knowledge the depths are broken up."* God's word will break up the depths in your life. It'll break up depths, the hard places, the stony places, and the pressing places in your life.

Last but not least in Isaiah 51:10 it says, *"Art thou not it which hath dried the sea, the waters of the great deep; that hath made the depths of the sea a way for the ransomed to pass over?"* God is going to help you, the ransomed, to pass over, pass through, and to overcome the depths and make it to the other side of freedom, deliverance, and joy.

"Rise Up, My Love"
Song Of Solomon 2:10

Day 139

Oh what a glorious and tremendous call is seen in Song of Solomon 2:10 when our Beloved Jesus speaks to His bride. *"My beloved spake, and said unto me, Rise up, my love, my fair one, and come away."* Oh to hear these words. One day all of us will hear these words when the Lord Jesus returns. He is going to say to His beloved bride, *"Rise up, my love."*

First of all, Jesus needs to be our beloved. *"Beloved"* in the Hebrew means "doubly loved." Jesus has to be more to us than just our Savior and Lord. He is our Husband. Remember, the Scriptures call Him the Bridegroom. Isaiah 54:5 says, *"For thy Maker is thine husband; the Lord of hosts is his name."*

He is our beloved. All of us must cultivate an intimate relationship with Jesus every day. John 17:3 says, *"And this is life eternal, that they might know thee the only true God, and Jesus Christ, whom thou hast sent."* This is the cry of the Scriptures, *"For the Lord's portion is his people"* (Deuteronomy 32:9).

God has longed to know a people and have intimacy with them. He told Moses to tell the children of Israel to build a tabernacle, *"that I may dwell among them"* (Exodus 25:9). Later Israel rejected Him and God had to leave the tabernacle because of their sin and perversion in the camp. Let this not that be the case with us. But rather let the Lord be welcome to come and visit at any time.

Oh to hear those words from Jesus, *"Rise up, my love."* Just as John heard in Revelation 4:1, *"Come up hither"*, this is the word of the Lord to us today. God is calling His beloved bride up higher. Rising up speaks of leaving something earthly and leaving something behind or rising from something else.

Throughout life, every one of us is involved in valley experiences, wilderness situations, and the dealings of God. But we are not going to remain in them forever. At some point it will come to an end. God has an expected end for us (Jeremiah 29:11) and that is to be with Him.

Our beloved Jesus is speaking to us today and saying, *"Rise up, my love."* We, on the other hand, must be His love. We must be His fair one; one that is holy, clean, and righteous. And then we must *"come away."* A day is coming when we will be allowed to come away from this earth, the world, the flesh, and the devil once and for all and embrace our precious Husband and say back to Him, *"My Beloved."*

"When Lust Hath Conceived"
James 1:14-16

DAY 140

I would like to share with you a tremendous revelation that came to me at a time of great need in my life. I've been a Christian over 40 years and have been in the ministry since 1975, yet, in much of my Christian life, I struggled with things that I just could not overcome. The older I've gotten and the longer I've stayed in the ministry, the more perplexing the guilt, condemnation, struggle, and anxiety that I endured has gotten. Simply because of sin that I couldn't conquer in my life, I was tormented.

Several years ago, while driving down the road, I had a mighty visitation of the Lord. I was struggling and concerned about my walk with the Lord. I wanted to do, as Paul said, what was good, but I found another law working in my members. That law was sin that had remained in my members. It wasn't the real me, but the sin in me that was still working in my members. On my way down the road that day, the glory of God descended on me in such a mighty way that I had to pull over onto the side of the road. Such an awesome dread and fear came into the car and God began to speak to me. He asked if I wanted my sons and daughters in the ministry to struggle as I've struggled. I said no. He then quoted to me Acts 17:30, *"having winked at the times of this ignorance, but now commandeth all men everywhere to repent."* I knew at that moment that it was time to repent. He wasn't asking, He was commanding. I told Him that I've tried so hard to stop. Then he told me the problem was that **I** was the one who was trying to stop versus yielding to Him for the grace to stop. *"The Spirit is willing, but the flesh is weak"* (Matthew 26:41). Then He took me to the book of James 1:14-16:

> *"But every man is tempted, when he is drawn away of his own lust, and enticed. Then when lust hath conceived, it bringeth forth sin: and sin, when it is finished, bringeth forth death. Do not err, my beloved brethren."*

The Lord said to me that in the times when you are drawn away, or enticed, before lust conceives, (it may be milliseconds) there is a short period of time when you need to bow to the grace of God. The Bible says that grace, in Titus 2:12, *"Teaching us that, denying ungodliness and worldly lusts."* He said, like he did in Zechariah 4:6, *"Not by might, nor by power, but by my spirit."* He reminded me of II Corinthians 12:9, *"My grace is sufficient for thee: for my strength is made perfect in weakness."*

So, when you are drawn away and tempted, before you yield to that, give yourself to Him. Allow His grace to flow through you and you'll find that He'll protect you. You will find victory over that sin. I've found that victory and walk in it today. I challenge you to do the same today. Take those moments and yield to the grace of God.

"Thou Understandest My Thought Afar Off"
Psalms 139:2

DAY 141

Here in this great passage of Scripture, we find how deep and abiding the Lord's knowledge is of every one of us. Nothing, not even one little thought, can be hid from Him. He, who formed us in the belly and knew us in the womb before our mothers brought us forth, knows everything about us. He is the Alpha and Omega, the beginning and the end. Psalms 139 says:

> "*¹O Lord, thou hast searched me, and known me. ²Thou knowest my downsitting and mine uprising, thou understandest my thought afar off. ³Thou compassest my path and my lying down, and art acquainted with all my ways. ⁴For there is not a word in my tongue, but, lo, O Lord, thou knowest it altogether. ⁵Thou hast beset me behind and before, and laid thine hand upon me. ⁶Such knowledge is too wonderful for me; it is high, I cannot attain unto it*" (Psalms 139:1-6).

He knows when we sit down, when we rise up, and "*understandest our thought afar off.*" Oh, how true this Scripture is. God knows everything about us. There is nothing that we can hide from Him. So, it is foolish then for us to think that we could harbor something and that He would not know about it. Psalms 90:8 says, "*Thou hast set our iniquities before thee, our secret sins in the light of thy countenance.*" As the book of Job puts it, "*Why, seeing times are not hidden from the Almighty, do they that know him not see his days?*" (Job 24:1). Our times are not hidden from the Almighty. Rather, the Bible tells us our times are in His hands (Psalms 31:15). He knows the end from the beginning of our lives.

Have this revelation in your heart. God can look upon you and see everything about you, and yet love you in spite of yourself. Oh, how great and how wonderful this knowledge is! It really is too high for us. It's hard for us to understand it. There is nothing that we can hide from Him. Hebrews tells us, "*Neither is there any creature that is not manifest in his sight: but all things are naked and opened unto the eyes of him with whom we have to do*" (Hebrews 4:13). All things are naked and open unto Him. This is the Word of God. This is the reality of life. Jesus knows everything about us, and the great thing is He loves us anyway.

Having this revelation and knowing that I cannot hide anything from the Lord, is very liberating to me. I know then that He even understands my thoughts and knows the inner workings of my heart. However, this is unlike Satan, because he cannot read our minds. He does not know our hidden thoughts; he can only plant thoughts there, watch our lives, and then surround us with demons that will try to bring those thoughts and desires and cause them to entice us into sin. God, however, looks right through us and nothing is hidden from Him.

Think not today that you can keep anything from Him. I Corinthians 4:5 says, *"Therefore judge nothing before the time, until the Lord come, who both will bring to light the hidden things of darkness, and will make manifest the counsels of the hearts."* We see this very clearly in Mark 10:17-22 when the rich young ruler comes to Jesus and says, *"¹⁷Good Master, what shall I do that I may inherit eternal life?"* Jesus tells him to obey the commandments, and he presumptuously and boastfully says, *"²⁰Master, all these have I observed from my youth."* Then one of my favorite passages of Scripture takes place in the next verse. It says, *"²¹Then Jesus beholding him loved him, and said unto him, One thing thou lackest: go thy way, sell whatsoever thou hast, and give to the poor."* Jesus could look at this self-righteous young man, and love him. He was rich and may have kept the law, but was still like all men.

"Verily every man at his best state is altogether vanity," Psalms 39:5 tells us. In sin did our mothers conceive us (Psalms 51:5). All of us, apart from the grace of God, are sinners. Jesus looked right through him and all the bluster and put his finger on the very thing that was the man's greatest problem. And he, hearing this,"²²*turned away very sorrowful because he had great many possessions"* (Mark 10:17-22).

Jesus can look right through everything we say and do. There's nothing we can hide from Him. Luke tells us:

> *"²For there is nothing covered, that shall not be revealed; neither hid, that shall not be known. ³Therefore whatsoever ye have spoken in darkness shall be heard in the light; and that which ye have spoken in the ear in closets shall be proclaimed upon the housetops"* (Luke 12:2-3).

What more can we say? Our great God, who knows everything, still loves us. He still reaches for us and cares for us in spite of ourselves. Settle this issue in your heart. He knows everything you're doing. He sees all that we do and even understands the inner workings of our minds. I don't know how more complete the Lord can be in understanding and knowing who we are. What's even more powerful and wonderful is that He loves us in spite of ourselves.

Dear friend, today, as you go through this day, know that you have someone who knows you intimately, knows everything about you, and yet is still merciful and caring. What a wonderful God you serve! What a precious Savior you have! He knows everything and yet still loves you and me. Rejoice and determine in your heart to never try to hide anything again because He already knows it, anyway. He understands your thoughts afar off.

"The Thoughts Of The Lord"
Micah 4:12

Here in Micah 4:12, it says, *"But they know not the thoughts of the Lord, neither understand they his counsel."* It is important for you and me to understand the thoughts of the Lord. He is thinking of you today. You are in His thoughts. What a marvelous truth!

Day 142

We have to remember, as it says in Isaiah 55:8-9, *"⁸For my thoughts are not your thoughts, neither are your ways my ways, saith the Lord. ⁹For as the heavens are higher than the earth, so are my ways higher than your ways, and my thoughts than your thoughts."* God's thoughts are higher than our thoughts, but nonetheless, He is thinking about us. It also says in Psalms 92:5, *"O Lord, how great are thy works! and thy thoughts are very deep."* David declares in another place in Psalms, *"How precious also are thy thoughts unto me, O God! how great is the sum of them! ¹⁸If I should count them, they are more in number than the sand: when I awake, I am still with thee"* (Psalms 139:17-18). What a glorious truth. God's thoughts towards you and me are great and many.

The book of Jeremiah tells us, *"For I know the thoughts that I think toward you, saith the Lord, thoughts of peace, and not of evil, to give you an expected end"* (Jeremiah 29:11). Oh my goodness, what a tremendous truth! This is contrary to what many preachers and people and theologians have said to us. God is thinking about us all the time, and His thoughts are of peace, and not of evil, to give us an expected end, an end of hope.

Psalms 33:11 declares, *"The counsel of the Lord standeth for ever, the thoughts of his heart to all generations."* Oh, blessed be the name of the Lord! It says in Isaiah, *"The Lord of hosts hath sworn, saying, Surely as I have thought, so shall it come to pass; and as I have purposed, so shall it stand"* (Isaiah 14:24).

Today, God is thinking of you a great number of thoughts. He's thinking about you; think about that! God bless you today and remember how precious His thoughts towards you are. Let it not be said of us, as it was said of those in Micah, that we know not the thoughts of the Lord. We know the thoughts of the Lord toward us. Even though they are higher than us, we can understand them because we know the Scriptures and His Holy Spirit. They are great and they are thoughts of peace, to give us a glorious and expected end.

"Men Ought Always To Pray"
Psalm 18:1

DAY 143

What a tremendous admonition from the Lord to us, His people, as He speaks this parable to us, *"that men ought always to pray, and not to faint."* The Bible encourages us to pray without ceasing. Paul said I Timothy 2:8, *"I will therefore that men pray everywhere, lifting up holy hands, without wrath and doubting."* Prayer is the answer instead of fainting. If we pray and get in the presence of God, then we won't faint or we won't give in to the situation that is tormenting us.

In Psalms 27:13, David said, *"I had fainted, unless I had believed to see the goodness of the LORD in the land of the living."* We don't need to wait for "pie in the sky by-and-by" to see God in heaven. We need to see God right now in the land of the living, where we live with our present circumstances. The word *"fainted"* in Psalms 27:13 means, "I almost went *insane*, unless I had believed to see". If we can condition ourselves and form a habit of praying instead of fainting, overreacting or reacting to bad situations, to the dealings of God, to trouble, etc., then eventually that habit will become a reality in our lives. The Bible says in Proverbs 24:10, *"If thou faint in the day of adversity, thy strength is small."* We need to stop fainting and start praying.

Every day, we need to go before the Lord and *"pray without ceasing,"* as I Thessalonians 5:27 exhorts. *"Praying without ceasing"* means to stay in an attitude of prayer by keeping an open and constant communion with the Lord.

It says of Enoch in Genesis 5:24, *"And Enoch walked with God: and he was not; for God took him."* The word *"walked"* in this verse means "to rest comfortably with God." As you and I get to the place where we rest comfortably with God, comfortable in His presence, and begin to know Him intimately, then He will become our dearest friend and compatriot. We will be able to tell Him everything and by doing so, those things that used to cause us to faint, those things that used to bring us down will no longer have that ability because of the overwhelming presence of God in our lives and because of our intimate relationship with the Lord Jesus.

Jesus said that we ought always to pray and not faint. That is the word for us today. Instead of fainting in our situation, let us arise and begin to pray and find the goodness of the Lord in the land of the living.

"In The Midst"
Mark 6:47

DAY 144

The Bible states in Mark 6:47, *"And when even was come, the ship was in the midst of the sea, and he alone on the land."* This passage of Scripture is very enlightening. It speaks to us of what we go through in our lives. So many times, we find ourselves in the midst of situations, dealings, temptations, and problems. And it takes place *"when even was come."* Doesn't it seem like it's always dark when we're in the middle of something? There's an absence of light, and Jesus seems to be elsewhere. You and I are on this ship, which represents the body of Christ, in the midst of the sea. We're in the midst of going on with God, when so many times, there's turmoil, trouble, persecution, and harassment.

It says in the following verse, Jesus *"saw them toiling in rowing; for the wind was contrary unto them"* (Mark 6:48). The word *"toiling"* in Greek means "to be in pain." Sometimes, as we struggle, we are in great pain. We're toiling and rowing, but the wind is contrary to us. The Bible says in Ecclesiastes, *"The labour of the foolish wearieth every one of them, because he knoweth not how to go to the city"* (Ecclesiastes 10:15). When something happens in our lives, we try to help the situation by doing more. We think if we could just pray more, fast more, or worship more, we might find our answer. But the truth is, though that may help, it's not the ultimate answer. He saw them toiling and rowing; He sees what we're doing. He sees the effort we're putting forth. He sees the trial of our faith.

It goes on to say that *"the wind was contrary unto them."* It seems like no matter what we do, the wind blows in another direction. It's blowing not the south wind, but the north wind, bringing with it judgment. Then it says, *"and about the fourth watch of the night he cometh unto them."* It is not the first, second, or third, but the fourth watch. Many times, the Lord will come at the last minute. Just remember that He will come.

The Bible says in Psalms 110:2 *"Rule thou in the midst of thine enemies."* This is the will of God for us. We need to know that even though Jesus has sent us forth *"as sheep in the midst of wolves"* (Matthew 10:16), and even though we *"walk in the midst of trouble,"* He will revive us (Psalms 138:7). This is God's promise to us.

In the meantime, you and I need to rule in the midst of our enemies. While we're in the midst, we need to take control, and *"stand still, and see the salvation of the Lord"* (Exodus 14:13). The Bible declares in Zephaniah 3, *"The Lord thy God in the midst of thee is mighty; he will save"* (Zephaniah 3:17). It says in Isaiah 12, *"Great is the Holy One of Israel in the midst of thee"* (Isaiah 12:6). In the midst of thee, Jesus will be there. It may be the fourth watch of the night, but He is coming. Have patience and wait; it will happen. You will be revived. Joel 2:27 tells us, *"And ye shall know that I am in the midst of Israel, and that I am the Lord your God, and none else: and my people shall never be ashamed."*

"He That Hath Mercy On The Poor"
Proverbs 14:21

DAY 145

The Bible tells us in Proverbs 14:21, *"He that hath mercy on the poor, happy is he."* There's something about giving that blesses us, because we're showing the nature of Jesus. In this day of economic crisis and trouble, there are many people all around us that are going without. There are homeless families being broken up and separated. We need to have mercy on the poor. It also says in Proverbs 14:31, *"He that oppresseth the poor reproacheth his Maker: but he that honoureth him hath mercy on the poor."* We honor God when we have mercy on the poor.

Jesus, help us to get a revelation today of helping and ministering to poor people. It is so important. Proverbs 19:17 tells us, *"He that hath pity upon the poor lendeth unto the Lord; and that which he hath given will he pay him again."* What a tremendous statement! If we would have pity on the poor, it's like we're lending unto the Lord, and we can rest assured we're going to get it back again. God will make sure of it.

It says in Proverbs 21:13, *"Whoso stoppeth his ears at the cry of the poor, he also shall cry himself, but shall not be heard."* We don't want to stop our ears or walk past someone who is in desperate need. This does not show the love of God. But if we will answer and give and consider them, we will be blessed in doing so. The Bible also says in Proverbs 28:27, *"He that giveth unto the poor shall not lack: but he that hideth his eyes shall have many a curse."* God is watching and knows how we respond to the poor and needy. If we give unto the poor, we personally will never lack.

Being poor is relative. It could be someone who simply has a need, but not necessarily someone that is destitute. It could be someone in a grocery store that is not able to pay for all of his groceries. It could be someone that doesn't have enough money to pay for his children's tuition. It could be someone that doesn't have enough provision to feed his household. Whatever it may be, as you and I give to them, we honor the Lord, and He is pleased with us.

In Proverbs 29:7, it says, *"The righteous considereth the cause of the poor: but the wicked regardeth not to know it."* You and I are the righteous; we need to consider the cause of the poor. Jesus said in Isaiah 41:17, *"When the poor and needy seek water, and there is none, and their tongue faileth for thirst, I the Lord will hear them."* God's eyes are on the poor. It says in Psalms 69:33, *"the Lord heareth the poor, and despiseth not his prisoners."* Glory to Jesus!

Let our eyes be open today. The answer for the poor is, as Jesus declares in Luke 6:20, *"Blessed be ye poor: for yours is the kingdom of God."* Let's participate in the kingdom by lending unto the poor today

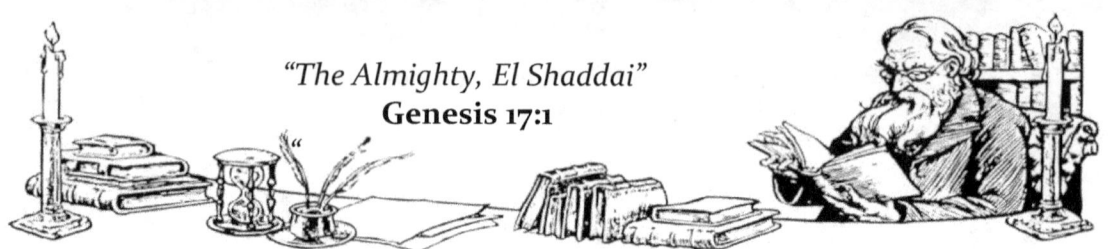

"The Almighty, El Shaddai"
Genesis 17:1

In Genesis 17:1 we find one of the definitions of God's great names. This name for God, El Shaddai, reveals Him as the source of all blessing, the One who is very intimate with His children. El Shaddai in Hebrew is a compound of the word *"El"* which means *"strength and mighty"* and *"Shaddai"* which means *"the almighty."* It's used forty-eight times in the Old Testament (thirty-one of which are found in the book of Job). The root of the word Shaddai means to be *"burly, powerful, impregnable, to ravish and The Almighty."* In other words there is nobody greater or better!

It also is related to the word *"Shadd"* which is the Hebrew word for *"breast."* Most of the time, El Shaddai is referred to as "The Breasted One." This reveals the intimate, motherly side of God's love. It reveals His nurturing, nursing, and intimate side where the sucklings receive from Him all that we need to live this life. The Greek word for Almighty is "the all ruling God, the absolute and universal sovereign."

At the last supper it is interesting that John *"leaned on his breast"* (John 21:20). You and I look to our God of love, as I John 4:8 tells us *"for God is love."* It is the unconditional love of the Father. In Genesis 17:1 it says *"I am the Almighty God."* He is the nurturing, motherly, intimate, and loving one. Today, God is calling us to receive from this female aspect of God's nature and to be nurtured and loved. John saw it and *"leaned on his breast"* being called *"the disciple whom Jesus loved."*

We see in Psalms 91:1, *"He that dwelleth in the secret place of the most High shall abide under the shadow of the Almighty."* As we, *"abide under the shadow of the Almighty"* we receive all of the things we need to live this life. We receive the unconditional love that only a mother has to her child. It is wonderful how God can be so powerful, so awesome and at the same time so nurturing and loving. It says in Isaiah 40:11 *"he shall gather the lambs with his arm, and carry them in his bosom."* We are simply the ones that He speaks of in Matthew 21:16, *"Out of the mouth of babes and sucklings thou hast perfected praise."*

We are those babes and sucklings that suckle at His breast, that receive from Him the nurturing love and goodness that only a mother can give. Our great God is not only male but also female. Man was created in His image and man was originally both male and female. Genesis 1:27 says, *"God created man in his own image, in the image of God created he him; male and female created he them"* (Genesis 1:27). Today, all of us need to get in touch with this side of God, the Almighty or El Shaddai. As we do, we will come away with a greater revelation and understanding of our God.

"The Blessing Of The Lord Maketh Rich"
Proverbs 10:22

DAY 147

Today we want to consider Proverbs 10:22 where it says, *"The blessing of the Lord, it maketh rich, and he addeth no sorrow with it."* Thanks be unto God that He doesn't add difficulties or sorrows to His blessings and goodness when it comes to us. On the contrary, our great God is a God that blesses His people because He loves them and He adds no sorrow to it!

Psalms 3:8 says, *"Thy blessing is upon thy people. Selah."* Psalms 5:12 says, *"For thou, Lord, wilt bless the righteous; with favour wilt thou compass him as with a shield."* Psalms 29:11 *"the Lord will bless his people with peace."* Proverbs 3:33 says, *"He blesseth the habitation of the just."* This is our God. He loves to bless His people. He loves to give and to minister to us. As a matter of fact, He *"daily loadeth us with benefits"* (Psalms 68:19). Psalms 103 lists these daily benefits, *"Who forgiveth all thine iniquities; who healeth all thy diseases; ⁴Who redeemeth thy life from destruction; who crowneth thee with lovingkindness and tender mercies; ⁵Who satisfieth thy mouth with good things; so that thy youth is renewed like the eagle's"* (Psalms 103:3-5).

The blessing of the Lord makes us rich! This is found in the New Testament as well in Ephesians 1:3, *"Blessed be the God and Father of our Lord Jesus Christ, who hath blessed us with all spiritual blessings in heavenly places in Christ."*

Are you walking in the blessings of God today? No matter what you are going through today, open your heart today and realize that you've been blessed *"with all spiritual blessings in heavenly places in Christ."* You don't need to justify or feel ashamed about the blessing of the Lord. It is a good thing. Jesus said in Luke 12:32, *"Fear not, little flock; for it is your Father's good pleasure to give you the kingdom."* God is your Father and every father wants to bless his children. It's the parent's job actually to lay up for the children (II Corinthians 12:14). We read in Psalms 132:13-15, *"For the Lord hath chosen Zion; he hath desired it for his habitation. ¹⁴This is my rest for ever: here will I dwell; for I have desired it. ¹⁵I will abundantly bless her provision."*

What a wonderful God we serve! How many times we struggle because of things we go through. Some might even call some of the things we go through a curse. But I want you to know that in Deuteronomy 23:5 it says, *"the Lord thy God turned the curse into a blessing unto thee, because the Lord thy God loved thee."* God turns the curse into a blessing for us. *"The blessing of the Lord, it maketh rich, and he addeth no sorrow with it."* God wants to *"pour you out a blessing, that there shall not be room enough to receive it"* (Malachi 3:10). Deuteronomy 2:7 says, *"For the Lord thy God hath blessed thee in all the works of thy hand: he knoweth thy walking through this great wilderness: these forty years the Lord thy God hath been with thee; thou hast lacked nothing."* God wants to abundantly bless your provision and He doesn't want you feeling sad, ashamed, sorry, or uncomfortable about it. Why? Because when He blesses you, it makes you rich and He adds no sorrow to it!

"Let Us Consider One Another"
Hebrews 10:24

DAY 148

Today we want to consider the principle of *"let us"*. This is found throughout the Bible either in actual words or in type and shadow. In the book of Hebrews, twelve times we find mentioned this term, *"let us."* Twelve is the number of divine government in Scriptures. In other words, to truly be Kingdom minded and understand the government of God, you and I need to have a corporate mindset. This term *"let us"* means having a mentality of others and not just ourselves; that we realize we are in a body and family and what we do matters and affects the body of Christ. Moreover, we need to get to the place where others are more important than ourselves.

The first instance of *"let us"* that I mention is found in Hebrews 10:24, *"And let us consider one another to provoke unto love and to good works."* For much of the world the *"I, me, mine"* mentality rules and reigns. And this is so not of Jesus. He wants us to consider one another as Hebrew 10:24 continues, *"to provoke unto love and to good work."* *"Let us"* means all of us. That means my brother and my sister. That means we are not just concerned about our own lives, but that we want our brothers and sisters to enter into everything that we have and hopefully our example, we provoke others to love and to good works.

The bride says in Song of Solomon 1:4, *"Draw me, we will run after thee."* In other words, she is saying whatever He does in her; she will use it to minister to others so they can run after Him too. Song of Solomon 1:4 continues, *"...we will be glad and rejoice in thee, we will remember thy love more than wine."* So this is the purpose of God that *"we, being many, are one body in Christ, and every one members one of another"* (Romans 12:5). Our concern then should be for one another.

Hebrews 3:13 says, *"But exhort one another daily, while it is called Today."* We need to be exhorting one another. We need to be encouraging one another. We need to be pressing in together and not separately. And as I Corinthians 12:23 says, *"And those members of the body, which we think to be less honourable, upon these we bestow more abundant honour; and our uncomely parts have more abundant comeliness."*

God wants us to know that everything that God does for us really is not for us but for others. Consider Joseph's life and all that he went through. It never really was for him. It was for the sake of the then known world. Everything that he suffered and all that he went through was never really about him, but so that he could have the answer for the world's famine. Actually his name was changed to an Egyptian name which literally means "savior of the world."

At the last supper in Luke 24:30 it says Jesus *"took bread, and blessed it, and brake, and gave"* it to the disciples. We are like that bread. God has taken and chosen you and me. Then He has blessed us wonderfully. But He does that for the purpose of breaking us. So with our broken lives and all that we've learned from the afflictions, suffering, and hardships of life, we can then feed and give that bread to others. So you see that everything that happened to us was never really intended for us, but intended for others.

Let us together press in. Let us together as a people behold our glorious Lord and manifest His character and name throughout the earth. Let the Lord deal with your heart today to be more concerned about your brothers and sisters, about their needs, helping them to make it, to know Jesus intimately, and to press on in God rather than living in a place of selfishness where all you care about is yourself and what happens to you and what you get out of life.

Focusing on prosperity seems to be the rationale of the body of Christ today. Most of what's on Christian television today teaches us we are the ones to be blessed. Too much of what is taught is all about us and lifting us up and not lifting up Jesus and His Kingdom. We need to have a corporate and Kingdom mentality.

May God help you today to let these two words *"let us"* resound deep within your spirit and move and motivate you to be a blessing to others. God spoke to Abraham in Genesis 12:2 and told him He was going to bless him that he might be a blessing. God has blessed you. Will you be a blessing? Will you reach your hand out to your brother and pick him up?

All those who could not cross the Jordan, the priests would carry them over the river unto their inheritance. We need to care for those uncomely parts. We need to care for our brother and sisters who are struggling. We need to be concerned that corporately, we together behold the Lord in all His glory. As Jesus said, *"By this shall all men know that ye are my disciples, if ye have love one to another"* (John 13:35).

So allow this term *"let us"* rise up today in your spirit. Let us do this together. Let us do it as a people. Let us get our minds off ourselves and on our brethren. *"Let us..."*

> *"Let us therefore fear..."* (Hebrews 4:1)
> *"Let us hold fast our profession."* (Hebrews 4:14)
> *"Let us therefore come boldly unto the throne of grace..."* (Hebrews 4:16)
> *"Let us go on unto perfection..."* (Hebrews 6:1)
> *"Let us draw near with a true heart in full assurance of faith..."* (Heb 10:22)
> *"Let us hold fast the profession of our faith without wavering..."* (Heb. 10:23)
> *"Let us consider one another..."* (Hebrews 10:24)
> *"Let us lay aside every weight, and the sin..."* (Hebrews 12:1)
> *"Let us run with patience the race that is set before us."* (Hebrews 12:1)
> *"Let us have grace..."* (Hebrews 12:28)
> *"Let us go forth therefore unto him without the camp..."* (Hebrews 13:13)
> *"Let us offer the sacrifice of praise to God continually..."* (Hebrews 13:15)

"I Will Make You"
Matthew 4:19

DAY 149

One of my favorite revelations from the Scriptures is that the Lord Jesus, God the Father and the Holy Spirit have promised to "*make me*" and there is no need for me to do it myself. The word "*make*" speaks of a time of dealing. It is God's time of working in me and creating in me the ability to do whatever it is He has called me to do. In Matthew 4:19, Jesus said, "*Follow me, and I will make you fishers of men.*"

I will share some of the things that God promises to make us into. These promises will have us go through wilderness experiences, afflictions, hard places and so on. Along with those challenging experiences, we will also have some mountain-top experiences and glorious times. All of these work together to mold and shape us into the very people that God has called us to be.

Deuteronomy 8:3 says, "*That he might make thee know that man doth not live by bread only, but by every word that proceedeth out of the mouth of the Lord doth man live.*" Thank God! He will make us to know this, because without the Word from His mouth, we will never grow up. He says in Proverbs 22:21, "*That I might make thee know the certainty of the words of truth.*" I'm so grateful that the Holy Spirit will not leave me to accomplish it all on my own. I'm grateful for that anointing that will teach me and share with me the revelation of God.

My heart's desire is that you run after Him, so that He can make you. He promises us in Genesis 17:6, "*And I will make thee exceeding fruitful, and I will make nations of thee, and kings shall come out of thee.*" I certainly cannot do that on my own. How about you? Deuteronomy 28:11 says, "*And the Lord shall make thee plenteous in goods.*" And in verse 13 of Deuteronomy 28 it says, "*And the Lord shall make thee the head, and not the tail.*" Glory to God!

I lived in abject poverty when I first met the Lord, and I tell you, I was always the tail. But now, He's made me as the head and not the tail, plenteous in goods. Let's believe this today and let Him do that in all of us. Deuteronomy 30:9 assures us, "*The Lord thy God will make thee plenteous in every work of thine hand.*" He's going to make everything that you and I touch plenteous. He's going to work it in us.

God tells us in Isaiah 41:15, "*Behold, I will make thee a new sharp threshing instrument having teeth.*" In other words, God will mold us and make us into instruments for His purpose, threshing the nations with the Word of God and the gospel of the Kingdom. Isaiah 60:15, "*I will make thee an eternal excellency, a joy of many generations.*" Think about that: you and I, living in eternal excellency throughout eternity. God will have molded and made you into a glorious being. It will take place as in Philippians 3:21, Jesus shall, "*Change our vile body, that it may be fashioned like unto his glorious body.*" And in Zephaniah 3:20, "*I will make you a name and a praise among all people of the earth.*" You will be made into a name and a praise among all the people of the earth. You will be known; you will be recognized, because the glory of the Lord shall be revealed through you.

If you will be faithful in just a few things, Matthew 25:21 says, "*I will make thee ruler over many things: enter thou into the joy of thy lord.*" You probably thought that you'd never amount to anything and that nothing good could come out of you, but the Bible says that He will make you ruler over many things if you'll just be faithful. Finally, in Hebrews 13:21: through Jesus Christ, God will, "*Make you perfect in every good work to do his will, working in you that which is wellpleasing in his sight.*" He will give you the ability, anointing and wherewithal to do all that He's asked you to do. He'll actually make you perfect in every good work to do His will.

Just like the prodigal son said in Luke 15:19, "*Make me as one of thy hired servants.*" We ought to come to a place of humility, submission and total reliance in God so that we may be made into what He's called us to be. Let us come to Him today saying, "Lord, make me."

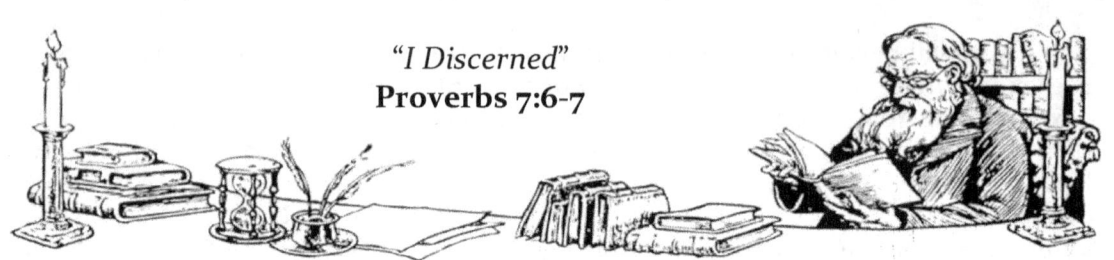

"I Discerned"
Proverbs 7:6-7

In Proverbs 7 is the story of the strange woman, who is a type of the harlot and the Babylonish church. Also, because she flatters with her words, she is a type of strange doctrine. I want to look today at this story about the young man who foolishly goes the way to her house (Proverbs 7:8) and is trapped. It says in Proverbs 7, "*⁶For at the window of my house I looked through my casement, ⁷And beheld among the simple ones, I discerned among the youths, a young man void of understanding*" (Proverbs 7:6-7).

The Biblical definition for "discernment" is to look through something. This is what God wants us to do in every situation. He wants us to use discernment, to look through something, to see to the other side of it, and to see all aspects of it. One of the Hebrew words for "*discern*" means "to know or to ascertain by seeing." You have to see something to know it; you have to see through it. Another Hebrew word for "*discern*" means "to separate mentally or distinguish." We have to be able to rightly divide every situation to discern it correctly. Paul said to "*judge nothing before the time*" (I Corinthians 4:5), but when we do judge, the Gospel of John tells us, "*judge righteous judgment*" (John 7:24). Ecclesiastes 8:5 says, "*A wise man's heart discerneth both time and judgment.*" He discerns what kind of judgment is to be meted out, because He sees, not only what happened, but why it happened. He sees the cause, not just the effect.

In I Kings 3, it says of Solomon, that he asked for himself "*understanding to discern judgment*" (I Kings 3:11). Oh, that all of us had the wisdom to pray his prayer. In Ezekiel 44, God wanted His holy priests, the sons of Zadok, to teach His people "*the difference between the holy and profane, and cause them to discern between the unclean and the clean*" (Ezekiel 44:23). If we ever needed discernment, it is in these last days. Jonah 4:11 says that in Nineveh, there were "*more than sixscore thousand persons that cannot discern between their right hand and their left hand.*" Jesus said in Matthew 16, "*O ye hypocrites, ye can discern the face of the sky; but can ye not discern the signs of the times?*" (Matthew 16:3).

We don't need to have a bunch of foolish, young men running around, going the way to the strange woman's house, giving heed to false doctrine and Babylonish principles. We need to "*by reason of use*" have our "*senses exercised to discern both good and evil*" (Hebrews 5:14). In the Greek, the word for "*use*" here means "habit or practice." So, by habitual using, we exercise our senses to discern both good and evil.

We're living in a day in which people "*call evil good, and good evil*" (Isaiah 5:20). In this day, we need discernment. We need the ability to look through and see every aspect of a situation, so that we can properly give a right judgment. Remember, "*A wise man's heart discerneth both time and judgment.*"

"Hold Your Peace"
Exodus 14:14

DAY 151

The Bible comforts and encourages us in Exodus 14:14, *"The Lord shall fight for you, and ye shall hold your peace."* When we trust in the Lord, we are kept in perfect peace. The Lord will fight for us; we don't need to fight for ourselves. We don't need to leave our place of peace. No matter what external circumstance comes our way, we ought to hold on to the peace of God that is within us. Once we let go of our peace, we will be overcome by our problems; turmoil will come into our lives. God wants us to hold on to our peace.

Jesus said in John 14:27, *"Peace I leave with you, my peace I give unto you: not as the world giveth, give I unto you. Let not your heart be troubled, neither let it be afraid."* Romans 14:17 states, *"For the kingdom of God is not meat and drink; but righteousness, and peace, and joy in the Holy Ghost."* And Romans 5:1 tells us, *"Therefore being justified by faith, we have peace with God through our Lord Jesus Christ."* So we have this peace, God has already given it to us and we need to hold on to it.

The circumstances and the forces of life will try to come and upset us; they will frustrate our purpose in building, cause us to be offended, cause us to backslide and cause us to be tempted and drawn away by our desires. However, you and I must find that river within us, *"There is a river, the streams whereof shall make glad the city of God, the holy place of the tabernacles of the most High"* (Psalms 46:4). Out of your belly, *"shall flow rivers of living water"* (John 7:38). Isaiah 66:12 also says, *"For thus saith the Lord, Behold, I will extend peace to her like a river."* God has extended peace like a river inside of us. All we need to do is let the river flow, and by doing that, we let peace flow. As it says in Philippians 4:7, *"The peace of God, which passeth all understanding, shall keep your hearts and minds through Christ Jesus."*

Now remember, we have peace with God through our Lord Jesus Christ and this peace of God that He's given to us, surpasses our understanding: our hearts and minds. The peace of God can surpass whatever your mind can come up with and whatever your heart can dream up. *"Let not your heart be troubled, neither let it be afraid."* Jesus also said, *"Ye believe in God, believe also in me"* (John 14:1). Believe in the God that is within you. Believe in the peace that passes all understanding and walk in that peace. Moreover, Isaiah 26:3 says, *"Thou wilt keep him in perfect peace, whose mind is stayed on thee: because he trusteth in thee."* We need to stay our minds on the Lord Jesus, and *"Set your affection on things above, not on things on the earth"* (Colossians 3:2).

Job 22:21 says, *"Acquaint now thyself with him, and be at peace: thereby good shall come unto thee."* Acquaint yourself with Jesus and spend time in His presence. Let the peace of God rule in your hearts and flow out of you. Let it rise up now and give you the sense of peace, satisfaction and confidence that is to come forth in your walk with the Lord. And as a final word: Colossians 3:15 says, *"And let the peace of God rule in your hearts, to the which also ye are called in one body; and be ye thankful."* Rule in the midst of your enemies today and stay in the peace of God.

"Riches And Honor Come From Thee"
I Chronicles 29:12

DAY 152

In I Chronicles 29:12 David says, *"Both riches and honour come of thee, and thou reignest over all."* Other translations read:

"Riches and glory come from you"
"You are the source for wealth and honor"

Proverbs 10:22 says, *"The blessing of the Lord, it maketh rich, and he addeth no sorrow with it."* Another translation reads, *"The blessings of the Lord bring riches, and they bring no sorrow with it".*

I have had a great struggle in my life believing that God wanted me to have riches and honor in my life. However, I tell you, they do come from Him. He came that we might have life, and have it more abundantly (John 10:10). That word "life" means life as God is living it now. I can assure you, God is not poor.

Psalms 35:27 says, *"Let them shout for joy, and be glad, that favour my righteous cause: yea, let them say continually, Let the Lord be magnified, which hath pleasure in the prosperity of his servant."* Some other translations read, *"He is happy when His servant prospers".*

God wants us to prosper; He wants us to have riches and wealth. However, one of the words for "prosperity" is shalom, which means safe, happy, whole, health and peace. God wants prosperity in all of our lives; as a matter of fact, He takes pleasure in it. This shows us God's real heart. That which gives Him pleasure is you and I prospering, spirit, soul and body, as well as in every other aspect in our life, which by the way includes financially. It gives Him great delight to see us safe, well, at peace and blessed.

III John 2 says, *"Beloved, I wish above all things that thou mayest prosper and be in health, even as thy soul prospereth."* My goodness! I tell you, He wants us to prosper; He wants us to have riches; He wants us to enjoy our life, and He doesn't want sorrow added to it.

Proverbs 21:20 says, *"There is treasure to be desired and oil in the dwelling of the wise."* Treasure to be desired! One of the Scriptures God used to transform my life in relation to the term "riches" was II Corinthians 8:9. I did not, and could not believe that this Scripture referred to material riches, until one day the Lord spoke to me and this became abundantly clear. He told me to look up the meaning of the word "rich", and I found that the Greek word in II Corinthians 8:9 means: to be wealthy, to be increased with goods, to wax rich, to make wealthy, possessions, abundance and money. So, I am without excuse, as I was that day. II Corinthians 8:9 declares, *"For ye know the grace of our Lord Jesus Christ, that, though he was rich, yet for your sakes he became poor, that ye through his poverty might be rich."* What a God we serve! Another translation reads:

"How, for your sake He became poor though He was rich, in order that you, through His poverty might grow rich"

"In order that by His poverty you might become rich and abundantly satisfied"

My goodness! What a God we serve. He wants riches and honor to come to us. Isaiah 60:5 says, *"Then thou shalt see, and flow together, and thine heart shall fear, and be enlarged; because the abundance of the sea shall be converted unto thee, the forces of the Gentiles shall come unto thee."* The Hebrew word for "forces" means riches. Another translation of this verse reads, *"and you shall possess the wealth of nations"*.

Riches and honor come from Him. Let's stop denying it. However, let's not make of this the only thing God does. Let's at least receive what belongs to us, for the Lord delights in the prosperity of His servant. Receive it today in Jesus name.

"The Old Lion Perisheth"
Job 4:11

Job 4:11 says, *"The old lion perisheth for lack of prey."* The Lord quickened to me that the old lion is the same lion spoken of in I Peter 5:8. It says there, *"your adversary the devil, as a roaring lion, walketh about, seeking whom he may devour."* The devil wants us as prey, to wreak havoc. He wants to eat from our carnal nature, our weaknesses, but we must *"resist him steadfastly in the faith"* (I Peter 5:9).

In John 14:30 Jesus said, *"Hereafter I will not talk much with you: for the prince of this world cometh, and hath nothing in me."* One translation reads, *"findeth nothing in common with me."* Do you find that you have anything in common with the devil? *"For what fellowship hath righteousness with unrighteousness and what communion hath light with darkness"* (II Corinthians 6:14)? There should be nothing in us that relates to the devil or wants anything from the devil.

The Bible says in James 4:7, *"Submit yourselves therefore to God. Resist the devil, and he will flee from you."* I John 5:18 says, *"We know that whosoever is born of God sinneth not; but he that is begotten of God keepeth himself, and that wicked one toucheth him not."* In the Greek the word *"keepeth"* means "guards." God doesn't want Satan have access into our lives, but it seems as if he's always around the outskirts. He's there whispering or roaring, trying to get in, trying to find something to feast on. Remember, he will perish if you are not prey.

I Peter 4:1 says, *"for he that hath suffered in the flesh hath ceased from sin."* Eventually we get tired of the enemy taking advantage of us, so we stand up and he flees. The Bible tells us we can bind the devil, loose him, resist him, and we can cast him out. We can deal with this old lion. He is *as* a roaring lion, but our God *is* the *"Lion of the tribe of Juda"* (Revelation 5:5).

Job 28:7-8 says, *"⁷There is a path which no fowl knoweth, and which the vulture's eye hath not seen: ⁸The lion's whelps have not trodden it, nor the fierce lion passed by it."* There is a path that you and I can walk that the enemy cannot get near, because of the divine shield of favor round us. We should grow in our understanding of our authority over the enemy. In II Corinthians 2:11 it says, *"Lest Satan should get an advantage of us: for we are not ignorant of his devices."* Once we have seen him and how he acts, we can deal with him accordingly.

In Luke 4:13 it says, *"And when the devil had ended all the temptation, he departed from him for a season."* In the Greek that reads "for a more opportune time." The enemy waits and watches until he finds our weaknesses and then tries to exploit them. As Jesus said to Peter, *"Simon, Simon, behold, Satan hath desired to have you, that he may sift you as wheat. But I have prayed for thee, that thy faith fail not: and when thou art converted, strengthen thy brethren"* (Luke 22:31-32). Even though he's waiting for a more opportune time, we're not ignorant of his devices. We're aware now. We can resist him steadfast in the faith. Resist him and he will flee. Have nothing in common with him. Understand what he's doing and where he's coming from, and you can guard yourself against the enemy.

"God That Cannot Lie"
Titus 1:2

DAY 154

The Scriptures say here in Titus 1:2, *"In hope of eternal life, which God, that cannot lie, promised before the world began."* In the world which you and I live in, trying to find one honest person can many times be difficult to say the least. The closer we get to the coming of the Lord, lying and dishonesty will grow increasingly. This is because in this last hour Satan who is the father of lies will be working furiously in the earth with his lying signs and wonders.

The Bible also speaks of a day in the book of Micah that *"all people will walk every one in the name of his god"* (Micah 4:5). Names always refer to character. So all those on the earth who will have Satan's image in their forehead will be like him in nature. Lies will come as easy to them as they do for the devil. Also because most of us have had dealings in times past with people in groups, families, or friends who have lied to us we almost expect it now.

In these last days it is so easy to see the worst in people, places, or things. Not to mention the fact that we have all lied at some point or another and loathe ourselves for it. It makes it hard for us when we come to the Lord to believe that He is unlike us. That His character, integrity, and honor is impeccable. However, He simply does not lie. The truth is He cannot because His nature goes against it.

The Bible says of God in Habakkuk 1:13, *"Thou art of purer eyes than to behold evil."* If God can't even bear to look at evil how can we ever imagine that He would be dishonest? He is simply not like us. *"For as the heavens are higher than the earth, so are my ways higher than your ways, and my thoughts than your thoughts"* (Isaiah 55:9). You and I need to have our hearts fixed on the fact that God cannot lie.

Let us look into the Word of God now. I Samuel 15:29 says, *"also the Strength of Israel will not lie nor repent: for he is not a man that he should repent."* God will not lie, the Strength of Israel can't. Here in Numbers 23:19 it says, *"God is not a man, that he should lie; neither the son of man, that he should repent."* God is not a man. It said the same thing in I Samuel. God is not like us. He doesn't think like us and He doesn't act like us. His character is so far above everything that we can think of.

In Psalms 89:34-35 He says, *"³⁴My covenant will I not break, nor alter the thing that is gone out of my lips. ³⁵Once have I sworn by my holiness that I will not lie unto David."* This is our God, He cannot lie, He will not lie. Hebrews 6:18 says, *"That by two immutable things, in which it was impossible for God to lie, we might have a strong consolation, who have fled for refuge to lay hold upon the hope set before us."* Another translation reads, *"It is impossible that God should prove false."* Do you hear this? It is impossible for God to lie.

II Timothy says 2:13 says, *"If we believe not, yet he abideth faithful: he cannot deny himself."* He cannot deny Himself. His character demands honesty out of Him. In

James 1:17 it says, "*Every good gift and every perfect gift is from above, and cometh down from the Father of lights, with whom is no variableness, neither shadow of turning.*" I Peter 2:22 says, "*Who did no sin, neither was guile found in his mouth.*" Romans 3:4, "*God forbid: yea, let God be true, but every man a liar.*" Our God does not lie, that is a simple fact. Actually Psalms 33:4 says, "*For the word of the Lord is right; and all his works are done in truth.*"

Folks, we need to believe the Word of God and let it speak to us. We cannot let what men have done, what our parents have done, and friends have done to us to cause us to think that God would be like them. He is not a man. Habakkuk 2:2-3 says, "*²Write the vision, and make it plain upon tables, that he may run that readeth it. ³For the vision is yet for an appointed time, but at the end it shall speak, and not lie.*" In the end we shall see that our precious God is not a liar, but He's a "*God of truth and without iniquity, just and right is he*" (Deuteronomy 32:4).

"Whom The Lord Knew Face To Face"
Deuteronomy 34:10

DAY 155

Out of all the Scriptures that I have looked at in the Bible, this one brings forth a revelation that is so dear to my heart, and, I believe, dear to God's heart. Today, I want to share with you the principle of face to face communion with God. Deuteronomy 34:10 says, *"And there arose not a prophet since in Israel like unto Moses, whom the Lord knew face to face."*

The Bible says in Proverbs 27:19, *"As in water face answereth to face, so the heart of man to man."* What does that mean? Well, the face of a person is the essence of that person. It's the presence of a person. When looking at somebody in the face, you can look into their heart. God wants you and Him to look at each other in the heart. Having face to face communion means becoming vulnerable before the Lord. It is important to note that in the Hebrew language, the word translated *"presence"* is also translated *"face"* elsewhere over 300 times. So, these words are interchangeable. Therefore Proverbs 27:19 can read, "As in water presence answers to presence." In other words, this is the real you and the real God meeting together.

Psalms 42:7 says, *"Deep calleth unto deep at the noise of thy waterspouts."* This is everything that we are, who we are, our soul, the essence of ourselves meeting with and coming face to face with the essence of who God is. No wonder David says in Psalms, *"My soul thirsteth for God, for the living God: when shall I come and appear before God?"* (Psalms 42:2). The actual Hebrew here reads, *"...when shall I come and behold the face of God?"* Beholding the face of God is beholding everything that He is. It's almost like making love and looking into the face of your lover, sharing such deep intimacy together.

Oh, that the Lord would help you today to lift up your eyes to *"set your affection on things above, not on things on the earth"* (Colossians 3:2). Lift up your eyes to where Christ is and look into the beautiful, tender, and loving eyes of your Husband-to-be.

Exodus 33:11 says, *"And the Lord spake unto Moses face to face, as a man speaketh unto his friend."* Just think; we can friends with the God of the universe, the Almighty God. It is so real and so available. All we need to do is get alone with God and begin to hunger and thirst for Him like David did.

Remember in John 12, the Greeks came and desired Philip, saying, *"Sir, we would see Jesus"* (John 12:21). Zaccheus, in Luke 19:3 *"sought to see Jesus who he was."* He wanted to see Jesus for who He was. In other words, we are not interested in seeing a religious Jesus or somebody else's idea of Jesus. We want to *"see Jesus who he"* is.

Is that what's in your heart? God will know it, just as any lover knows when the other really desires them and cares only for them. They can always see it on their face; the eyes never lie. The face can never really lie to someone who knows them well.

Man started off being able to walk with God in the garden and have great fellowship with Him. But because of the fall, he lost his ability to see God's face. Genesis 3:8 says, *"And they heard the voice of the Lord God walking in the garden in the cool of the day: and Adam and his wife hid themselves from the presence of the Lord God amongst the trees of the garden."* Too many times, we hide ourselves amongst the trees or that which is earthly and fleshly. We hide ourselves from the presence of the Lord. We find other things to do, anything other than meeting God face to face.

I have to tell you that, in all my years, I have noticed that intimacy is very difficult for men. It's very hard for men to look deep into a woman's eyes, whereas, the female always seems to have a capacity and an ability to do this. I envy this and pray that God releases that in my own life. I don't want to hear from the Lord, as He said to Moses, *"Thou canst not see my face: for there shall no man see me, and live"* (Exodus 33:20). God had to put His hand over Moses' face when He revealed Himself and walked by him.

But I read in the end of the book, Revelation 22 says, *"And they shall see his face; and his name shall be in their foreheads"* (Revelation 22:4). Somebody, somewhere, is going to do it. They're going to see His face as He is. They're going to know His presence fully and intimately. His name, or His character, shall be written in their foreheads, or in their minds. They will have the mind of Christ (I Corinthians 2:16).

I Corinthians 13:12 says, *"For now we see through a glass, darkly; but then face to face: now I know in part; but then shall I know even as also I am known."* A day will come when we will see Him completely face to face, presence to presence, heart to heart, and lover to lover. I John 3:2 tells us, *"Beloved, now are we the sons of God, and it doth not yet appear what we shall be: but we know that, when he shall appear, we shall be like him; for we shall see him as he is."* We shall see Him; this is what it's all about, beholding the glory of the Lord and being changed.

David says in Psalms 27:8, *"When thou saidst, Seek ye my face; my heart said unto thee, Thy face, Lord, will I seek."* Jeremiah, in Lamentations 5:21, says, *"Turn thou us unto thee, O Lord, and we shall be turned."* I say today, "Turn thou me unto thee, O Lord, and I shall be turned."

Will you pray that prayer as well; that you would desire to know God greater than you know Him today and see Him face to face? May this prayer of blessing help you towards that end! As it says in Numbers 6:24-26, *"[24]The Lord bless thee, and keep thee: [25]The Lord make his face shine upon thee, and be gracious unto thee: [26]The Lord lift up his countenance upon thee, and give thee peace."* Know God face to face today and the benefit is His grace and peace will upon you like never before.

"Let Them"
Psalms 149

Day 156

Here in this great Psalm we find a tremendous truth concerning releasing God's people to worship the Lord. I don't know what kind of church you're in or what kind of walk you have with the Lord, but the Lord wants His people to worship Him. The Bible tells us that the Father is seeking such to worship Him in Spirit and in truth (John 4:23). It says here in Psalms 149, *"Praise ye the Lord. Sing unto the Lord a new song and his praise in the congregation of saints"* (Psalms 149:1). God longs for His congregation and His people to praise and worship Him with liberty and freedom. *"Where the Spirit of the Lord is, there is liberty"* (II Corinthians 3:17).

Seven times the word "let" is used in this Psalm. Seven is the number of perfection. *"Let Israel rejoice in him that made him"* (Psalms 149:2). In other words, "let" means stop trying to prevent them from doing it. Release them. Pastors, leaders, and the watchmen in the church of Jesus Christ need to loose God's people to rejoice in Him that made them.

Then He says in Psalms 149:2 *"Let the children of Zion be joyful in their King."* Let them, release them, and free them to rejoice, to dance, and to worship in liberty and in truth. Then he says, *"Let them praise his name in the dance"* (Psalms 149:3). Dancing in the Spirit before the Lord is certainly scriptural and is a release for God's people as they worship the Lord in triumph. The next part of Psalms 149:3 says *"Let them sing praises unto him with the timbrel and harp."* That means worship leaders need to let people use instruments such as tambourines, shofars, etc. Let them be free to worship God and express themselves. *"For the Lord taketh pleasure in his people: he will beautify the meek with salvation"* (Psalms 149:4).

It then says, *"Let the saints be joyful in glory: let them sing aloud upon their beds"* (Psalms 149:5). We need to let the people of God be joyful in the glory of God. Let them enjoy that manifest presence of God. It is so rare that people get to experience corporate, glorious worship. When they do, when the glory falls, we need to let them be free. In the second half of verse 5 it says, *"Let them..."* for the sixth time, *"sing aloud upon their beds."* Don't try to hinder people from singing loud. *"The dead praise not the Lord"* (Psalms 115:17). Don't be nervous and don't allow those that don't like worship to interfere with the presence of God.

It then says, *"Let the high praises of God be in their mouth, and a two-edged sword in their hand"* (Psalms 149:6). Not just praises, but the high praises of God. The word *"praise"* in the Hebrew means "to make a show, to boast, to be clamorously foolish, to rave, to celebrate." Let God's people worship. Release them so that they can enter into high praises, not low praises, nor general praises. We are not satisfied with just the omnipresence of God; it is the manifest presence of God we are after. We want the glory to descend: the cloud of the Lord filling the house of the Lord. The leadership must release the people though. The pastor should be the first man to shout, dance, fall on his face, and sing aloud. Let them praise the Lord!

"Ought Not Christ To Have Suffered"
Luke 24:26

DAY 157

As a Christian for over forty years and a pastor since 1977, I have found that most Christians know very little about suffering. It is not taught or preached in the United States except in fundamental circles, where I believe it's taught in a wrong way. We need to understand suffering always precedes glory. If we're ever going to enter into God's glory, which we have been called to obtain, we need to walk through some suffering. This does not show a lack of faith our part. Actually, it's the will of God. Colossians 1 tells us, "*Who now rejoice in my sufferings for you, and fill up that which is behind of the afflictions of Christ in my flesh for his body's sake, which is the church*" (Colossians 1:24).

In Luke 24, the Bible says, "*Ought not Christ to have suffered these things, and to enter into his glory?*" (Luke 24:26). In other words, He is supposed to suffer and enter into His glory. There was no way the son of man could redeem the world without suffering. It says in Hebrews that Jesus "*for the joy that was set before him endured the cross*" (Hebrews 12:2). He kept this vision in front of Him all of the time. Job said, "*When he hath tried me, I shall come forth as gold*" (Job 23:10). The book of I Peter tells us, "*That the trial of your faith, being much more precious than of gold...*" (I Peter 1:7). Many people think he's talking about faith there, but he's talking about the trial. Please don't be under condemnation because of false doctrine that claims suffering is not of God. This is simply unscriptural and foolish. The Bible says in James 1, "*²My brethren, count it all joy when ye fall into divers temptations; ³Knowing this, that the trying of your faith worketh patience*" (James 1:2-3). The trial works patience. God allows suffering, because it works something in us.

Think back to the times in your life when you grew the most. Didn't it happen while you were in the dark places, valleys, and wildernesses? Paul says in II Corinthians, "*For our light affliction, which is but for a moment, worketh for us a far more exceeding and eternal weight of glory*" (II Corinthians 4:17). You're not going to get the exceeding, eternal weight of glory unless you go through the light affliction. You're not going to have patience worked into your life unless your faith has been tried. This is something you need to settle in your life.

Paul makes it very clear when he says in Romans, "*For I reckon that the sufferings of this present time are not worthy to be compared with the glory which shall be revealed in us*" (Romans 8:18). Our suffering can't be compared with what will be revealed in us. Believe that. It also says in I Peter 5:10, "*But the God of all grace, who hath called us unto his eternal glory by Christ Jesus, after that ye have suffered a while, make you perfect, stablish, strengthen, settle you.*"

Ought not Christ to have suffered these things and entered into His glory? Ought not you suffer so that you can enter into glory? May God help you today to receive this revelation. Don't be mad about it, but like Job, know that He knows what's happening with you, and when He has tried you, you will come forth as gold.

"God Is Preparing"
Ezekiel 1:1

DAY 158

In this first verse of the book of Ezekiel there is tremendous revelation found therein if you know some of the keys to understanding the Scriptures. If you know what numbers, names, and what words mean you can get a better understanding of this verse. There is a revelation in verse one that is very powerful. Ezekiel 1:1 reads, *"Now it came to pass in the thirtieth year, in the fourth month, in the fifth day of the month, as I was among the captives by the river of Chebar, that the heavens were opened, and I saw visions of God."* If you are in captivity today, I want you to know that this is the word of the Lord for you.

The word *"Chebar"* means: "as if made known, as if made clear, to have an abundance, to multiply". This is saying that in our captivity it should be clear and known to us what is happening in our lives. Job 24:1 says, *"Why, seeing times are not hidden from the Almighty, do they that know him not see his days?"* God knows what is going on. Our times are not hidden from the Almighty. He knows we are in captivity. Therefore, we should know that while being captive by this river Chebar something is about to happen.

An understanding of numbers will help us to understand the rest of this verse. Thirty is the number in the Scriptures for preparation for ministry. Four is the number for creation or the new creation man. Five is the number which represents grace. Let me take the privilege of giving the Sam Greene version of this verse: "In this time of preparation for ministry, God is creating, by His grace, a new man out of captivity."

In our captivity, God, by His grace, is preparing us for the ministry, bringing forth that new creation man in us. As we understand and see this we will see the heavens open, we will see Jesus and have visions of God. No more in captivity will we be disappointed, oppressed and depressed because it will be made known to us what is happening. We are simply there so God can prepare us and create in us, by His grace, that new creation man, prepared for ministry.

As we lift up our eyes to the heavens, today, I pray that the heavens open and that we will see visions of God, just as Stephen did on the day that he was stoned, as it says in Acts 7:55, *"..looked up stedfastly into heaven, and saw the glory of God, and Jesus standing on the right hand of God."*

So be encouraged today and realized that even though you might be in captivity, out of that captivity our precious Jesus is preparing you and I by His grace to be that new creation man, that many-membered Jesus in the earth.

"The Joyful Sound"
Psalms 89:1

Day 159

The Word declares in Psalms 89:15, *"Blessed is the people that know the joyful sound: they shall walk, O Lord, in the light of thy countenance."* In this Word today, I hope that I can help you hear, recognize, and respond to the sound of God. It is important that we don't mistake the voice of God for thunder or an angel as they did in John 12:28-29, but that we know the voice of God for what it is, the joyful sound.

Psalms 42:7 says, *"Deep calleth unto deep."* This means that the deepest part of God is calling out to the deepest part of our being, our spirits. Are we listening? Job 37:2,5 says, *"Hear attentively the noise of his voice, and the sound that goeth out of his mouth... God thundereth marvellously with his voice."* Oh praise the Lord that God is still speaking! He's thundering marvelously. Deep is calling unto deep. The sound of God can be heard.

In the Scriptures we find this sound in many forms and fashions. In Isaiah 30:30 it says, *"And the Lord shall cause his glorious voice to be heard."* Can you hear it today? *"The Lord's voice crieth unto the city"* Micah 6:9 says. My prayer is that the Lord can use this word to help you hear as the Scriptures declare, *"the sound of a going in the tops of the mulberry trees"* (II Samuel 5:24) or as the *"sound from heaven as of a rushing mighty wind"* (Acts 2:2). Revelation 1:15 describes *"his voice as the sound of many waters"* and I Kings 18:41 describes it as *"a sound of abundance of rain."* But more than anything Mark 2:1 says of Jesus, *"it was noised that he was in the house."* Can you hear the noise that Jesus is in your house today? The Scriptures declare that we are the house of God.

Paul said in I Corinthians 14:10, *"There are, it may be, so many kinds of voices in the world, and none of them is without signification."* The most significant voice to be heard is the voice of God. Remember way back in Genesis 3:8, it says Adam and Eve, *"heard the voice of the Lord God walking in the garden in the cool of the day."* Another translation reads, *"They heard the sound of the Lord walking in the garden, walking up and down."* God is walking up and down today in your spirit and He is speaking. Will you listen?

The deepest place in God's heart is calling out to the deepest place in our hearts and He wants His voice to be heard. So let's heed Job 37:2 which says, *"Hear attentively the noise of his voice, and the sound that goeth out of his mouth."* Respond to Him today and *"know the joyful sound."*

"The Communication Of Thy Faith"
Philemon 6

Day 160

Here in Philemon, we find Paul writing, *"That the communication of thy faith may become effectual by the acknowledging of every good thing which is in you in Christ Jesus."* We have great seminars on how to teach us to evangelize and preach the gospel. But I believe here in this verse of Scripture, Paul outlines for us the easiest and simplest way to tell others about our Savior.

How can we effectively communicate our faith? Well, Paul says *"by the acknowledging of every good thing which is in you in Christ Jesus."* All you and I need to do is acknowledge every good thing Jesus has given us and done in our lives. The easiest and most effective form of evangelism is simply telling your own story; telling what happened to you; telling how God met you, blessed you, and changed your life.

So many times when Jesus would heal people and minister to them, they wanted to go with Him and follow Him. But He would tell them to stay and go into their town and tell others about what God had done for them. This is the simplest form of bringing people to the Lord. In John 4 after Jesus met the woman at the well, she in turn went and told everyone in her town, *"Come, see a man, which told me all things that I ever did"* (John 4:29). In response to her communication to the town the Bible says, *"And many of the Samaritans of that city believed on him for the saying of the woman."*

If we want our faith to be communicated effectively, there is only one way to do it. It is to acknowledge to others the great things Jesus has done for us and if He did them for us, He can do those things for them. David wrote to others in Psalms 34:8, *"O taste and see that the Lord is good: blessed is the man that trusteth in him."* We know this for a fact because we've tasted ourselves that the Lord is good and are blessed because of it.

I've led countless people to Jesus in my life, not by following a "Roman Road" or some other scripted plan, but by simply telling others my own story. Years ago I was with a group in New Orleans, sent to preach the gospel. After one week of passing out tracts, our efforts were fruitless. While walking home one night, I noticed that most of our tracts were on the ground. Discarded by those we sought to help. The Lord spoke to me and said, "Don't just hand out tracts to anybody. I want you to only go to the ones I direct you to and tell them your story." So I did. Up to that point I had led no one to Jesus. But the next night nine people came to the Lord and it was absolutely glorious. Everything changed. I wasn't preaching out of a forced will, but was simply sharing the good news.

This is what the gospel means, "good news." It is also called "the glad tidings." You and I can tell the good news of the Kingdom of God. We can share our faith and it will be effective if we simply acknowledge every good thing that is in us in Christ Jesus.

"I Will Trust In Thee"
Psalms 56:3

Day 161

Here in Psalms 56:3 David says, *"What time I am afraid, I will trust in thee."* Who greater to trust in a time of trouble, in a time of fear, than the Lord our God? The Bible says in Psalms 118:8-9, *"⁸It is better to trust in the Lord than to put confidence in man. ⁹It is better to trust in the Lord than to put confidence in princes."* Leaders many times are very helpful and men can sometimes help us, but ultimately all can fail us and we need to always have our trust in the Lord.

Psalms 125:1 says, *"They that trust in the Lord shall be as mount Zion, which cannot be removed, but abideth for ever."* When we place our trust in the Lord, we will be like a mountain. Mount Zion, the great hill in Jerusalem, is a mighty fortress. God becomes that for us when we lift our hearts to Him.

Isaiah 26:4 says, *"Trust ye in the Lord for ever: for in the Lord JEHOVAH is everlasting strength."* He is everlasting strength. Psalms 144:2 says, *"My goodness, and my fortress; my high tower, and my deliverer; my shield, and he in whom I trust."* Blessed is the man, the Bible says over and over again, that trusts in Him. Isaiah 25:3 says *"Thou wilt keep him in perfect peace, whose mind is stayed on thee: because he trusteth in thee."* We can be kept in perfect peace because our trust is in Him. We don't need to be afraid, as long as we keep our minds upon Him and trust, believe, and have confidence in the Lord.

Psalms 34:8 says *"O taste and see that the Lord is good: blessed is the man that trusteth in him."* Paul says in II Corinthians 1:9-10, *"But we had the sentence of death in ourselves, that we should not trust in ourselves, but in God which raiseth the dead."* We don't need to be trusting in ourselves, because *"the heart knoweth his own bitterness"* (Proverbs 14:10). All of us know our own weakness and frailties. We need a higher source, and that source is God Himself.

Psalms 5:11 say, *"But let all those that put their trust in thee rejoice: let them ever shout for joy, because thou defendest them."* Our God is going to defend us. Our God is going to help us. We can put our trust in Him. *"Some trust in chariots, and some in horses: but we will remember the name of the Lord our God."* (Psalms 20:7). We don't trust in natural things, numbers, or strength. We will trust God's faithful character.

Lift up your eyes to heaven and trust in the Lord. The Lord says in Jeremiah 17:5-7, *Cursed be the man that trusteth in man, and maketh flesh his arm, and whose heart departeth from the Lord...Blessed is the man that trusteth in the Lord, and whose hope the Lord is."* From all of these above Scriptures we see that our God will always give us the victory and always cause us to triumph, because He is with us to defend us and protect us. We can rest at peace, knowing that nobody is mightier than our God. We can rest today in safety knowing that we can trust in the Lord our God.

"Who Shall Ascend Into The Hill Of The Lord?"
Psalms 24:3

DAY 162

Here in Psalms 24, the Lord gives us not only the goal, but how to reach the goal. The goal is to *"ascend into the hill of the Lord"* and *"stand in his holy place"* (Psalms 24:3). The hill of the Lord is Zion. Standing in His holy place is standing in the secret place, the manifest presence of God, the glory of God. How can we get there? It's just like in II Samuel 6, when David said, *"How shall the ark of the Lord,"* which is symbolic of the manifest presence of God, *"come to me?"* (II Samuel 6:9)

How can it? Well, first of all, in David's case, he missed it by making a little, wooden cart, and God had to judge him. Only the Levites could bear the manifest presence of God or the Ark of the Covenant. So, David had to go back and search the Scriptures. As he did, he found the way to carry the manifest presence of God. You and I can *"ascend into the hill of the Lord"* and *"stand in his holy place."* Let's look at the Scripture and see what it has to say.

In the following verse, he begins telling us who can and how we can ascend and stand. He first says, *"He that hath clean hands..."* (Psalms 24:4). What does this mean? It does not mean that your hands are washed with soap or cleaned with water. Hands in the Scriptures speak of our works. So, this is speaking of our works being clean and the reason for our works being right reasons. As it has been said before, you can say the right thing but have the wrong attitude. We must make sure that the motivation for our works be they natural or Spiritual have clean motivations. Our hearts should be pure and right so that the motivation for what we do is for the glory of God and not for the glory of man.

David then goes on to say, *"...and [he that has] a pure heart"* (Psalms 24:4). So many times the Scriptures admonish us to keep a pure heart. *"He that loveth pureness of heart, for the grace of his lips the king shall be his friend."* (Proverbs 22:11). Matthew 5:8 says, *"Blessed are the pure in heart: for they shall see God."* Having a pure heart, as I've said many times before, is one of the hardest things to keep in the Body of Christ. You have to fight against the world, the devil, *"the lust of the flesh, and the lust of the eyes, and the pride of life"* (1 John 2:16). Even for the Body of Christ, it is hard to keep your heart pure in the midst of all these things. However we can do it. We must do this if we want to stand in the glory of God and ascend to the hill of the Lord.

Next, David says, *"...who hath not lifted up his soul unto vanity"* (Psalms 24:4). We should not get involved in that which is vain or empty: things that glorify men instead of God and things that prosper the flesh rather than the Spirit. We must let our souls be lifted up, joined with our human spirit, so that that which is in our human spirit can flow through us. Vain, empty things are purposeless and do no good. They will take us out of the presence of God, the hill of the Lord, and cause us not to stand in His holy place. Let us be careful as we go throughout our day, to watch what we do and consider whether it is vain and meaningless.

The Bible says, "*...verily every man at his best state is altogether vanity*" (Psalms 39:5). Job said, "*Yet man is born unto trouble, as the sparks fly upward*" (Job 5:7). This is our nature. This is who we are and what we do with this Adamic nature that we have received is important. So, we must fight against it and say instead, as the Bible says in Psalms 25:1, "*Unto thee, O Lord, do I lift up my soul.*" In another psalm, David says, "*My soul is continually in my hand*" (Psalms 119:109). Let's lift up our souls unto Him and not consider vain purposes, but the purposes of God.

David continues in Psalms 24:4 to say, someone who has not "*sworn deceitfully.*" No deceitful words should come out of our mouths. We do our best to not say or do anything that would bring displeasure to the Spirit of God, for we will be judged for our every idle word (Matthew 12:36). "*Death and life are in the power of the tongue,*" the Bible says (Proverbs 18:21). We must watch our words carefully and keep a right confession and always say those things that are honest and of a good report and are a blessing to mankind. As we watch our mouths and our confession, we will see that we will ascend into the hill of the Lord and stand in his holy place, staying in the manifest presence of God. This is what we really desire if we love the Lord intensely.

In the following verse, the Bible says, he who does that "*shall receive the blessing from the Lord, and righteousness from the God of his salvation*" (Psalms 24:5). The blessing of the Lord is being in the hill of the Lord and standing in His holy place. Righteousness we have received, because "*he hath made him to be sin for us, who knew no sin; that we might be made the righteousness of God in him*" (II Corinthians 5:21). Let us enjoy the blessing of the Lord and the righteousness from the God of our salvation and ascend into the hill of the Lord and stand in His holy place.

Verse 6 continues to say, "*This is the generation of them that seek him, that seek thy face, O Jacob. Selah.*" Think about it. Those who do this are the generation that seeks Him, that seeks His face. I ask you today, "Are you seeking Him? Are you seeking His face? Do you want to ascend into the hill of the Lord and stand in His holy place?" Then simply do the things that verses 4-5 declare. Keep yourself in the love of God. Keep yourself in the presence of God and stand forever in His holy place, blessed by the glory of His presence.

"Holding On To Your Vision"
Habakkuk 2:2-3

In Habakkuk 2, the Lord says:

> "*Write the vision, and make it plain upon tables, that he may run that readeth it. ³For the vision is yet for an appointed time, but at the end it shall speak, and not lie: though it tarry, wait for it; because it will surely come,*" (Habakkuk 2:2-3).

DAY 163

As the vision is written and made plain before us on the tables of our hearts, we begin to run that read it. But we must understand that, like prophecies, visions are for an appointed time, and at the end, they shall speak and not lie. Though it tarry, wait for it. The key is the vision is for an appointed time, but in the end, it will speak.

We live by the bread of God, the Word of God, and every word that proceeds out of His mouth (Matthew 4:4). God gives us a personal vision and a corporate vision. The Bible says in Psalms 119:105, "*Thy word is a lamp unto my feet, and a light unto my path.*" The Hebrew word for "*lamp*" means "*candlestick.*" A candlestick gives off just enough light to see where you're walking; that's your personal vision. The Hebrew word for "*light*" here means "*spotlight.*" A spotlight can light an entire pathway. This is the broader vision for the body of Christ or the remnant.

Proverbs 29:18 tells us, "*Where there is no vision, the people perish.*" Without a vision, there is no hope for going on with Jesus. And once you get a vision, you need to understand that it won't come to fruition immediately. There is an appointed time. Remember it says in Job 14:14, "*all the days of my appointed time will I wait, till my change come.*" In Psalms 105:19, it says, speaking of Joseph, "*Until the time that his word came: the word of the Lord tried him.*" Ecclesiastes 3:1 declares, "*To every thing there is a season, and a time to every purpose under the heaven.*"

We need to hold fast and have faith in God. Don't give up on the vision that is yet for an appointed time. Hebrews 10:35-36 admonishes us, "*Cast not away therefore your confidence, which hath great recompence of reward. ³⁶For ye have need of patience, that, after ye have done the will of God, ye might receive the promise.*" It also says in Hebrews 6:12, "*That ye be not slothful, but followers of them who through faith and patience inherit the promises.*" Another place in Hebrews 10:23 reads, "*Let us hold fast the profession of our faith without wavering; (for he is faithful that promised).*" God has promised and given you a vision, and He will make sure that it comes to pass. Don't despair; don't begin to create Ishmaels in your life. Jeremiah 29:11 tells us, "*For I know the thoughts that I think toward you, saith the Lord, thoughts of peace, and not of evil, to give you an expected end.*"

The vision is yet for an appointed time, but at the end, it will speak. In Ecclesiastes 7:8 it says, "*Better is the end of a thing than the beginning thereof.*" The Bible says in Job 8:7, "*Though thy beginning was small, yet thy latter end should greatly increase.*" That vision will speak at the end, at the appointed time, and it won't lie. And though it tarries for a while, you wait for it. Have patience and confidence in God, because it will surely come. So today remember that vision will come to pass and God will be glorified.

"Unto Us"
Isaiah 9:6

Day 164

"Oh that men would praise the Lord for his goodness, and for his wonderful works to the children of men" (Psalms 107:8). Here we find in Isaiah 9:6 this beautiful phrase, *"For unto us a child is born, unto us a son is given."* He was not given just to anybody, but to us.

John 3:16 says *"For God so loved the world, that he gave his only begotten Son, that whosoever believeth in him should not perish, but have everlasting life."* God the Father personally gave us His Son because of the love He has for us. Unto us this great incarnation took place. Matthew 1:21 says *"thou shalt call his name JESUS: for he shall save his people from their sins."* Jesus was born for us to save us from our sins. II Corinthians 5:21 tells us: *"For he hath made him to be sin for us, who knew no sin; that we might be made the righteousness of God in him"*.

At the birth of child Jesus, the angels appeared, saying in Luke 2:14, *"Glory to God in the highest, and on earth peace, good will toward men."* God wants us to have peace on earth. His will toward men is good. He ensured both of these things for us by giving us His Son, *"For unto us a child is born, unto us a son is given."* Oh, that Son was given for you. He was given for me. Unto us He was given! He is now our Father, because unto us He was given. Jesus said in Matthew 6:9 *"Our Father which art in heaven, hallowed be thy name."*

Make it personal today in your life. Make your relationship with God an intimate one, because He wants to come unto you. He wants you to come unto Him. He said in Matthew 11:28, *"Come unto me, all ye that labour and are heavy laden, and I will give you rest."* He wants so desperately to have fellowship with you. God the Father has given everything He can to redeem mankind. All you have to do is receive it.

Jesus has sat down at the right hand of the Father as Romans 8:34 tells us, *"who is even at the right hand of God, who also maketh intercession for us."* He said on the cross in John 19:30, *"It is finished."* He did everything for you, even died on the cross. Paul said, *"To wit, that God was in Christ, reconciling the world unto himself, not imputing their trespasses unto them"* (II Corinthians 5:19).

Unto us a Son has been given. Unto us a Child is born. That little Child who astounded and confounded the lawyers in the book of Luke when He was just twelve years old grew up to be the Son of Man, the Son of God, and the Lamb slain from the foundation of the world (Luke 2:47).

He said in Exodus 12:3, *"a lamb for a house."* There is a lamb for your house today and a lamb for you personally. One of the Lord's covenant names for us is "Jehovah Jireh" and it literally means "the Lord shall provide." He has provided, for unto us, unto you and unto me, a Child is born. Unto us a Son has been given. Praise His glorious name. Receive Him today and receive His peace and good will for your life!

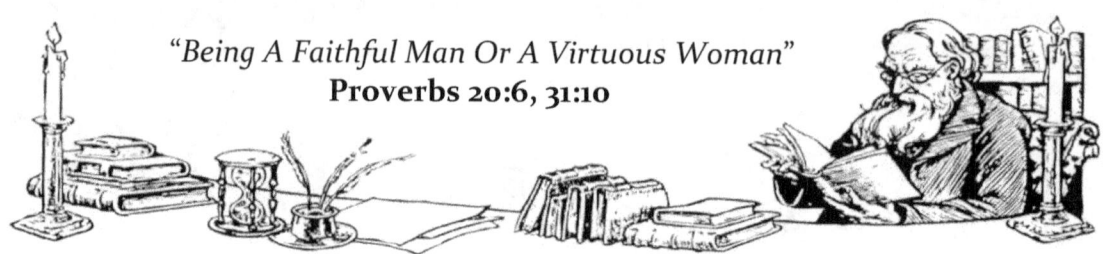

"Being A Faithful Man Or A Virtuous Woman"
Proverbs 20:6, 31:10

Day 165

It says in Proverbs 20:6, *"Most men will proclaim every one his own goodness: but a faithful man who can find?"* It also says in Proverbs 31:10, *"Who can find a virtuous woman?"* He mentions both men and women; God doesn't leave anybody out. The sons of God are made up of both men and women. He's looking for faithful men and virtuous women. Can He find that faithful man in you? The Lord says in Luke, *"Who then is that faithful and wise steward...Blessed is that servant, whom his lord when he cometh shall find so doing"* (Luke 12:42-43).

In other words, that steward is faithful day in and day out to do the will of God; he's diligent. He is, as it says in Romans 12:11, *"Not slothful in business; fervent in spirit; serving the Lord."* In Psalms 101:6, it says, *"Mine eyes shall be upon the faithful of the land."* You and I need to learn to be faithful men and women that God can trust and rely on. We don't ever want the Lord to doubt whether we will be faithful, or whether we'll do what He tells us to do. Just like Jesus, even if we don't really want to do it, our response is, *"Nevertheless not my will, but thine, be done"* (Luke 22:42).

The Bible says, *"Who can find a virtuous woman? for her price is far above rubies. "The heart of her husband doth safely trust in her, so that he shall have no need of spoil"* (Proverbs 31:10-11). Jesus is our Husband, and He wants to trust in you. This can just as easily apply to men as well as women, because we all hope to become the bride of Christ. It says of her in Proverbs 31, *"She seeketh wool, and flax, and worketh willingly with her hands"* (Proverbs 31:13). So much is said about her. It says in Proverbs 31:29, *"Many daughters have done virtuously, but thou excellest them all."*

God is looking for faithful men and women who will do His will in the earth. He's looking for people who will carry the torch of the gospel of Christ Jesus and teach the Kingdom of God to the nations. He wants a people who are an example of truth, righteousness, holiness, purity, and the love of God. All throughout the Scriptures, we find faithful men and women. It would behoove us then to search the Scriptures to see their examples. We see men like Joseph and David and women like Deborah, Priscilla, Jael, and Lydia.

"Who can find a virtuous woman?" Can God find you today? Will God see in you a measure of faithfulness and a willingness to do the will of God above all else? Will he see that you are not seeking things for yourself, but for the Lord and His righteousness? Brothers, how about you? Will He find you to be a faithful man? Will He find you diligently doing the same thing every day like Moses? He went up the backside of a mountain for forty years, but then one day, he turned aside to see the bush burning with fire.

Because we are faithful, God will bless us. Let us learn to be faithful men and virtuous women. Let's be faithful, so that when we stand before the judgment seat of Christ, we will hear Him say to us, *"Well done, thou good and faithful servant: thou hast been faithful over a few things, I will make thee ruler over many things: enter thou into the joy of thy lord"* (Matthew 25:21).

"A Garden Inclosed"
Song of Solomon 4:12

Here in the Song of Solomon we find a tremendous principle. *"A garden inclosed is my sister, my spouse; a spring shut up, a fountain sealed"* (Song of Solomon 4:12). First we need to define who this garden is. Well, the garden is called *"my sister, my spouse."* This is speaking of the bride of Christ. It says in verse 15 that she is, *"a fountain of gardens, a well of living water."* Today I would like to speak of God's bride being a garden enclosed.

She is a *"garden inclosed... a spring shut up, a fountain sealed."* Why would the Lord say this? I believe there is a time in all of our lives, like Paul says in Galatians 4:2, where we are *"under tutors and governors until the time appointed of the father."* This is a principle in the Word of God. John the Baptist spent time in the desert. Jesus did nothing for thirty years, but prepare Himself. Paul spent a long season in the deserts of Arabia. In a sense they were *"inclosed"*. They were a *"fountain shut up."*

As we look in Luke 10:38-42, we find that Martha and Mary are the typical examples within the body of Christ. Martha typifies those that are distracted with care, always going, always doing, and feeling the pressure to do the work of the Lord. Hence they get weary and frustrated. On the other hand there is Mary. Jesus says of her in Luke 10:42, *"Mary hath chosen that good part, which shall not be taken away from her."* She chose to sit at Jesus' feet and hear His word.

That *"good part"* is what we are looking at today. There is a time in every one of our lives where God makes us a garden inclosed, a spring shut up, and a fountain sealed. God does this in our lives so that He can do a great, intimate and deep work in our lives of sanctification, a work of growth in grace and a work of coming to the place where we know the Lord intimately. As II Peter 3:18 states, *"But grow in grace, and in the knowledge of our Lord and Saviour Jesus Christ."* Also I Peter 2:2 tells us, *"As newborn babes, desire the sincere milk of the word, that ye may grow thereby."* We must, as II Timothy 2:15 states, *"Study to shew thyself approved unto God, a workman that needeth not to be ashamed, rightly dividing the word of truth."* There needs to be a time of proving, a time of sitting under the word, a time of giving ourselves to the Lord and a time of a foundation being built in our lives. Psalms 11:3 says, *"If the foundations be destroyed, what can the righteous do?"*

So God has a time period for every one of us, where He closes and shuts us off, seals us up, where it is just Him and us. He gives us time to sit under the Word and search the Scriptures, time to learn how to pray and deal with the enemy, a time for intercession and a time to grow in our authority. He gives us time to get to know Him intimately, to grow in our worship and our ability to find His presence.

Finally, after we have been a garden inclosed, He wants to come into His garden, as Song of Solomon 5:1 tells us. He wants to say to others, *"O friends; drink, yea, drink abundantly"* (Song of Solomon 5:1). He wants to ultimately open up that garden for others to eat from what we have gathered, what we've attained to and what we've received during this time of separation to the Lord. Be a garden inclosed today, a spring shut up and a fountain sealed!

"The Fear Of Man Bringeth A Snare"
Proverbs 29:25

DAY 167

We see here that Solomon says in Proverbs 29:25, *"The fear of man bringeth a snare: but whoso putteth his trust in the Lord shall be safe."* For you and me, when we fear men and what they can do to us, it simply belittles what God can do for us. Our Lord is all-powerful and promises to protect us and keep us. Psalms 34:19 says, *"Many are the afflictions of the righteous: but the Lord delivereth him out of them all."*

In Psalms 118:6, David declares, *"The Lord is on my side; I will not fear: what can man do unto me?"* The Lord is on your side and *"If God be for us, who can be against us?"* (Romans 8:31). What can man do unto you? The answer is nothing. There is no need to fear men because what it does is it brings a snare. It brings a trap and bondage. You do not need to live your life in the fear of men.

In Psalms 56:4, David declares *"In God I will praise his word, in God I have put my trust; I will not fear what flesh can do unto me."* We need to put our trust, confidence, hope, and faith in the Lord today, then watch as He protects and keeps us. He loves us and because He loves us, He is going to keep and protect us. In addressing Israel's enemy in the promise land Deuteronomy 3:22 says, *"Ye shall not fear them: for the Lord your God he shall fight for you."* The Word of the Lord to us today is that the fear of man brings a snare. We don't need to be snared because God will fight for us.

Solomon said in Proverbs 1:17, *"Surely in vain the net is spread in the sight of any bird."* Since we are seated *"together in heavenly places in Christ Jesus"* (Ephesians 2:6), mounted up *"with wings as eagles"* (Isaiah 40:31), as we look down we can see the nets and snares the enemy tries to set and prepare for us. We simply then put our trust in the Lord and know that He is on our side and not fear what men can do to us because we know the Lord shall fight for us. David said in Psalms 27:

> *"The Lord is my light and my salvation; whom shall I fear? the Lord is the strength of my life; of whom shall I be afraid?" ²When the wicked, even mine enemies and my foes, came upon me to eat up my flesh, they stumbled and fell. ³Though an host should encamp against me, my heart shall not fear: though war should rise against me, in this will I be confident."* (Psalms 27:1-3)

No matter if the enemy is encamped around you. The Lord is your light and confidence. You do not need to fear man, *"for he hath said, I will never leave thee, nor forsake thee. So that we may boldly say, The Lord is my helper, and I will not fear what man shall do unto me"* (Hebrews 13:5-6). Boldly declare this today. God truly is your helper. Believe it! Walk free from any snares today, trusting in the Lord, knowing He is on your side, knowing He shall fight for you, and knowing He will never leave nor forsake you from this day forward.

"No Man, Lord"
John 8:11

DAY 168

In John 8, beginning in verse 3, we find the story of the adulterous woman who was caught in the act and brought to Jesus by the scribes and Pharisees. He stooped down and began to write on the ground, while they were telling Him that she should be stoned. He then said, *"He that is without sin among you, let him first cast a stone at her"* (John 8:7). They then left one by one until *"Jesus was left alone, and the woman standing in the midst."* Then it says in John 8:10-11, *"¹⁰When Jesus had lifted up himself, and saw none but the woman, he said unto her, Woman, where are those thine accusers? hath no man condemned thee? ¹¹She said, No man, Lord. And Jesus said unto her, Neither do I condemn thee: go, and sin no more."*

"No man, Lord" means there is no man that can condemn us. There is no man that God would allow to condemn His people. The Bible is very clear. It says in Isaiah 54:17, *"No weapon that is formed against thee shall prosper; and every tongue that shall rise against thee in judgment thou shalt condemn"*. Romans 8:1, tells us, *"There is therefore now no condemnation to them which are in Christ Jesus."* The word "no" used here in Romans, as well as in John 8, literally means in the Greek "not even one (man, woman, or thing), none, nobody, nothing." God does not want His people condemned.

It says in Psalms 37:32-33, *"The wicked watcheth the righteous, and seeketh to slay him. ³³The Lord will not leave him in his hand, nor condemn him when he is judged."* God is not going to condemn His people. In John 3:17, Jesus declares, *"For God sent not his Son into the world to condemn the world; but that the world through him might be saved"*. Proverbs 17:15 says, *"He that justifieth the wicked, and he that condemneth the just, even they both are abomination to the Lord."* Our God will not allow this. He doesn't want His people to be under condemnation. In Romans 8:34, it says, *"Who is he that condemneth? It is Christ that died, yea rather, that is risen again, who is even at the right hand of God, who also maketh intercession for us."* There is no man who can condemn you. Don't let them do it. The Bible says in Isaiah 50:

> *"⁸He is near that justifieth me; who will contend with me? let us stand together: who is mine adversary? let him come near to me. ⁹Behold, the Lord God will help me; who is he that shall condemn me? lo, they all shall wax old as a garment; the moth shall eat them up."* (Isaiah 50:8-9)

There is no man, Lord. There's no one here that can condemn us. The Word of the Lord to us today is that there is none without sin, none among us who has the right to throw stones. There is now no condemnation if you're in Christ Jesus. So, rejoice, lift up those hands that hang down, strengthen those feeble knees (Hebrews 12:12), and know that God will not allow condemnation. He didn't come to this world to condemn us, but to save us. And much more now, being saved, as Romans 5:9-10 tells us, shall we *"be saved from wrath through him"* and *"be saved by his life"*.

"Hath The Rain A Father?"
Job 38:28

DAY 169

Job 38:28 is a very interesting Scripture, and one that we would do well to understand. The rain, I believe, represents the manifest presence of God, His glory, or the Holy Spirit. We need to understand that when God talks about sending the rain, He's talking about sending His presence and the Holy Ghost. Zechariah 10:1 says, *"Ask ye of the Lord rain in the time of the latter rain; so the Lord shall make bright clouds, and give them showers of rain."* We can ask God for rain, and that rain really is not water. It is the rain of His presence, *"the former and latter rain,"* as He calls it in Joel 2:23. Also in Hosea 6:3, He says, *"he shall come unto us as the rain, as the latter and former rain unto the earth."* Jesus shall come unto us as the rain. So the manifest presence of God is the rain of God.

"Hath the rain a father?" I believe the answer to that is yes and has a two-fold revelation. Does the manifest presence of God have a father? Well first of all, God is the father of rain. Psalms 147:8 says, *"Who covereth the heaven with clouds, who prepareth rain for the earth."* Matthew 5:45 says He *"sendeth rain on the just and on the unjust."* He is the one who does it. Jeremiah 51:15-16 says, *"He hath made the earth by his power...he maketh lightnings with rain."* So God is the father and author of rain, and in this passage it's talking about His presence.

Secondly, when it comes to the presence of God, and you and I experiencing it, we need someone on the earth to be that father to bring the rain. Remember, it says in Psalms 68:9, *"Thou, O God, didst send a plentiful rain, whereby thou didst confirm thine inheritance, when it was weary."* All over the earth today people are weary and dry, like the valley full of dry bones in Ezekiel 37, desperate for the presence of God. They need the rain, the manifest presence of God, the glory of God. They're in a dry and thirsty land where no water is (Psalms 63:1). It is our job to be the ones; to be the father that brings the rain to those people; to bring the manifest presence of God to the nations of the world.

Just like Elijah, when he said in I Kings 17:1, *"As the Lord God of Israel liveth, before whom I stand, there shall not be dew nor rain these years, but according to my word."* God's going to have a people who are going to be able to bring the rain. The two witnesses in Revelation 11:6 *"have power to shut heaven, that it rain not in the days of their prophecy,"* and they also have power to release the rain. God is going to have a people who will release that rain. Leviticus 26:4, says, *"Then I will give you rain in due season, and the land shall yield her increase."*

God wants to give rain; He wants to give His manifest presence. He wants to visit the earth. He wants everyone to know Him intimately and to know His rich and glorious presence. That's why your prayer needs to be, as it declares in Isaiah 64:1, *"Oh that thou wouldest rend the heavens, that thou wouldest come down, that the mountains might flow down at thy presence."* Oh Lord, help us to be like fathers, to not think of ourselves and our own needs and wants and desires, but begin to take upon ourselves a Kingdom mentality, a corporate mentality, that cares about our brothers and sisters. Song of Solomon 8:8 says, *"We have a little sister, and she hath no breasts."* In other words, we have others in the body or Christ (little sisters) that have no ability to feed or nourish themselves or others. As I travel all over the world, I find people desperate for nourishment. Nehemiah tells us we are to *"send portions unto them for whom nothing is prepared"* (Nehemiah 8:10). It is our job then to bring the rain.

Hath the rain a father? Yes. Not only God the Father, but we need earthly, spiritual fathers, people who are willing to be pioneers and pay the price to bring God's presence to His people. Just like Peter did when he went to Cornelius' house (Acts 10), we need to go to the nations of the earth and bring God's holy presence to His precious sheep that are desperately thirsty for the real presence of God. Psalms 72 says:

> *"⁶He shall come down like rain upon the mown grass: as showers that water the earth. ⁷In his days shall the righteous flourish; and abundance of peace so long as the moon endureth."* (Psalms 72:6-7)

God wants the righteous to flourish and walk in an abundance of peace and He wants to come down like the rain upon them. But the rain needs a father. Are you willing to be that father? Are you willing to be the one that says like Isaiah did when asked, *"Here I am, send me"* (Isaiah 6:8)? Are you willing to bear the glory of God? Are you willing to take God's manifest presence to His people?

Whether it be at your job, to your family, on a missionary journey, or just to your church, take the presence of God and be willing to be a father. Take the responsibility that comes with being a father and bring the rain. Bring God's holy presence, His glory, so that people can know Him intimately and thirst no more.

Oh, how the earth is waiting and thirsty for fathers to bring them rain. Hath the rain a father? Perhaps God the Father is asking you that today wherever you are. Will you bring God's rain to the earth? Let that be your testimony for the rest of your life, in Jesus' name!

"The Manchild"
Revelation 12:5

DAY 170

It says here in Revelation 12:5, *"And she brought forth a man child, who was to rule all nations with a rod of iron."* She, spoken of here, is the *"woman clothed with the sun, and the moon under her feet, and upon her head a crown of twelve stars"* (Revelation 12:1). It says in verse 2, *"And she being with child cried, travailing in birth, and pained to be delivered"* (Revelation 12:2).

There is much controversy over who this manchild is. Most fundamentalists and evangelicals believe that this manchild is Jesus; I don't have any problem with that, because Jesus ultimately is the manchild. But if you read in Revelation 4:1, the voice that spoke to John said, *"I will shew thee things which must be hereafter."* "Hereafter" speaks of things in the future. Therefore everything after this verse is to take place in the future, not in the past. So, I don't believe that it would be speaking of Jesus as this particular manchild spoken of here, though He is the great and wonderful manchild.

The woman, who I believe is the church, not Israel, brings forth this manchild, who is to rule all nations with a rod of iron. Now, if we let the Bible define itself and compare *"spiritual things with spiritual"* (I Corinthians 2:13), there is a clear definition of who this manchild is. It says in Revelation 2:26-27, *"And he that overcometh, and keepeth my works unto the end, to him will I give power over the nations: ²⁷And he shall rule them with a rod of iron."* Remember that it said in Revelation 12:5, this manchild *"was to rule all nations with a rod of iron."* So, the manchild then is the company of overcomers. This is the group of hundredfold Christians that have pressed through and broken into all that God wanted them to have. They have the image of Christ, so that it is no longer they who live, but Christ who lives in them (Galatians 2:20). They have gone on unto perfection (Hebrews 6:1), or completion and graduation.

So now having overcome, God gives them this great privilege of being the firstborn, the manchild. It is given to them as an inheritance to rule all nations with a rod of iron. It says in Psalms 2, *"⁸Ask of me, and I shall give thee the heathen for thine inheritance, and the uttermost parts of the earth for thy possession. ⁹Thou shalt break them with a rod of iron"* (Psalms 2:8-9). This manchild is ruling the nations with a rod of iron, which represents the authority and judgment of God. They are the overcomers.

God, help us today to overcome, so that we'll put ourselves in a position to be this glorious manchild, who was *"caught up unto God, and to his throne"* (Revelation 12:5). This simply means the manchild was caught up into all of His authority, His power, and His goodness and glory.

"Lay Aside Every Weight"
Hebrews 12:1

Day 171

Hebrews 12:1 says, *"Wherefore seeing we also are compassed about with so great a cloud of witnesses, let us lay aside every weight, and the sin which doth so easily beset us..."* God is asking us here to lay aside the weight and sin that seems to so easily come upon us in life. It is easy to take the path of least resistance and give in to sin and temptation. But you and I must fight every moment of every day, stirring ourselves up in Jesus, so that sin will not have dominion over us. We can lay aside every weight and sin by the grace of God.

The Bible tells us to *"Cast thy burden upon the Lord, and he shall sustain thee"* (Psalms 55:22). If we would give the Lord these burdens of sin which so easily come, He will help us and sustain us. Jesus said in Matthew 11:28, *"Come unto me, all ye that labour and are heavy laden, and I will give you rest."* Laden with what, laden with sin and weights that bear us down, causing us to be depressed, oppressed, condemned, tormented, guilt-ridden, etc.? This is not the will of God for His people. God wants us to be free from these things.

Jesus said in Matthew 5:29-30, *"And if thy right eye offend thee, pluck it out...And if thy right hand offend thee, cut it off, and cast it from thee."* In other words, you and I need to put to death the motions of sin in our flesh. We need to lay aside the things that cause us to sin. God wants this for our lives. Paul wrote to the Romans:

> *"¹²Let not sin therefore reign in your mortal body, that ye should obey it in the lusts thereof. ¹³Neither yield ye your members as instruments of unrighteousness unto sin: but yield yourselves unto God, as those that are alive from the dead, and your members as instruments of righteousness unto God. ¹⁴For sin shall not have dominion over you: for ye are not under the law, but under grace."* (Rom. 6:12-14)

We are not under the law, but under grace. God does not want us being laden down and burdened down with sin. God wants us to lay aside habits and things in our lives that are unprofitable.

In Romans 13:12 it says, *"The night is far spent, the day is at hand: let us therefore cast off the works of darkness, and let us put on the armour of light."* It is up to us to come unto Him that are heavy laden and cast off the works of darkness. As we do, He will give us rest and sustain us. We must not let sin have dominion over us. We don't have to because, we are now the righteousness of God in Christ Jesus, for *"greater is he that is in you, than he that is in the world"* (I John 4:4). We have *"this treasure in earthen vessels"* (II Corinthians 4:7) that we must use to *"fight the good fight of faith"* (I Timothy 6:12).

Don't give up. Don't surrender. As Paul told the Corinthians *"quit you like men, be strong"* (I Corinthians 16:13). *"Wherefore lift up the hands which hang down, and the feeble knees; And make straight paths for your feet"* to God (Hebrews 12:12) so that it can be said of us that we've laid *"aside every weight, and the sin which doth so easily beset us, and let us run with patience the race that is set before us"* (Hebrews 12:1). And by doing so we *"ye may be blameless and harmless, the sons of God, without rebuke, in the midst of a crooked and perverse nation, among whom ye shine as lights in the world; Holding forth the word of life..."* (Philippians 2:15-16). Let this be our testimony today as we lay aside every weight and sin, in Jesus' name.

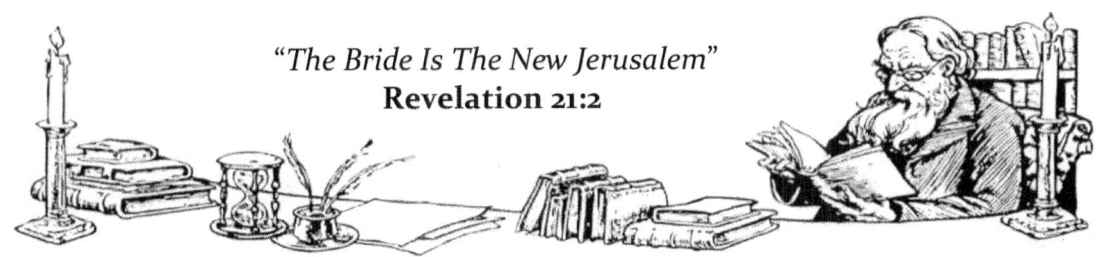

"The Bride Is The New Jerusalem"
Revelation 21:2

The Bible says in Revelation 21:

> "*²And I John saw the holy city, new Jerusalem, coming down from God out of heaven, prepared as a bride adorned for her husband…¹⁰And he carried me away in the spirit to a great and high mountain, and shewed me that great city, the holy Jerusalem, descending out of heaven from God, ¹¹Having the glory of God*" (Revelation 21:2, 10-11).

DAY 172

Oh, what a great picture of God's people, the bride of Christ, having the glory of God and existing in an everlasting, beautiful place with God in the New Jerusalem. Here, he says that this holy city, the New Jerusalem, was coming down from God out of heaven. One thing we realize about this is that it is coming down, not going up. We're seated in "*heavenly places in Christ Jesus*" (Ephesians 2:6). The bride is going to come from a heavenly place, not an earthly one. They will be coming down from God; they will have been with Him. They will be totally caught up in the things of the Lord and in the great and wonderful glory of God. They will be coming "*out of heaven.*" They are coming from a heavenly perspective. It is not a natural Jerusalem, but a heavenly Jerusalem; it is spiritual, not natural.

Galatians 4:26 says, "*But Jerusalem which is above is free.*" Hebrews 12:22 also says, "*But ye are come unto mount Sion, and unto the city of the living God, the heavenly Jerusalem.*" This is the bride of Christ. This is made up of Christian believers. Too much emphasis has been placed on natural Israel. Though we believe God will fulfill His promises to natural Israel, we must understand that Israel and Jerusalem have spiritual meanings as well. Jerusalem is now the people of God, whether Jew or Gentile, "*for there is no difference between the Jew and the Greek: for the same Lord over all is rich unto all that call upon him*" (Romans 10:12).

It continues to say in Revelation 21:2 that the holy city is "*prepared as a bride adorned for her husband.*" The key word here is "*prepared.*" She is prepared as a bride. Our job right now is to prepare ourselves to be His bride. It says in Revelation 19 that "*his wife hath made herself ready*" (Revelation 19:7). Are you being prepared as a bride adorned for her Husband?

God wants to carry us away in the Spirit to a great and high mountain. In Matthew 17, Jesus took Peter, James, and John "*up into a high mountain apart*" (Matthew 17:1). There upon the mountain, the glory of God fell, and Jesus was transfigured before them. The Lord is carrying us away, in the Spirit, up this mountain of the dealings of God and the trials of this life through which He's going to show the entire world His great city, the holy Jerusalem, descending out of heaven from God. We will appear to all men; it will be the manifestation of the sons of God. We will have the glory of God. This is what we were called to from the beginning, to obtain the glory of God. The new Jerusalem, the Bride, will have His glory. Are you prepared as a bride adorned for her Husband?

"Hope As An Anchor"
Hebrews 6:19

Day 173

The Bible is full of admonitions that tell us to hope in God. You and I need to understand that this word, *"hope"* in the Greek means *"expectation, confidence and to anticipate."* A dictionary definition of this word states that it is simply *"the feeling that what is desired is also possible"* or that *"events may turn out for the best."* In the Hebrew, it means *"to wait and to be patient."* You and I need to keep our expectancy.

In Hebrews 6:18-19 it states, *"to lay hold upon the hope set before us: ¹⁹Which hope we have as an anchor of the soul, both sure and stedfast, and which entereth into that within the veil."* Our hope is an anchor to our soul. It is sure and steadfast and it will be the very thing that causes us to enter into the most holy place.

I Corinthians 13:13 says, *"And now abideth faith, hope, charity, these three; but the greatest of these is charity."* Hope is abiding and is just as powerful as faith and love. We need to keep our hope in the Lord. We don't need to be like those dry bones in Ezekiel 37:11, *"They say, Our bones are dried, and our hope is lost: we are cut off for our parts."* Or as Proverbs 13:12 says, *"Hope deferred maketh the heart sick: but when the desire cometh, it is a tree of life."* We don't need to let our hope get deferred. We need to hope continually as the Bible says in Psalms 71:14, *"But I will hope continually, and will yet praise thee more and more."*

I Peter 1:13 tells us, *"Wherefore gird up the loins of your mind, be sober, and hope to the end for the grace that is to be brought unto you at the revelation of Jesus Christ."* Psalms 131:3 also says, *"Let Israel hope in the Lord from henceforth and forever."* Love, as described in I Corinthians 13:7, *"Hopeth all things, endureth all things."*

You and I need to use patience when it comes to the promise of God. David proclaims in Psalms 119:74, *"They that fear thee will be glad when they see me; because I have hoped in thy word."* The Word of God will build up your hope, and help you to keep it in your heart. As Romans 15:4 says, *"That we through patience and comfort of the scriptures might have hope."* The Word of God will cause your hope to be constant. The Bible says in Jeremiah 17:7, *"Blessed is the man that trusteth in the Lord, and whose hope the Lord is."*

Psalms 146:5 tells us, *"Happy is he that hath the God of Jacob for his help, whose hope is in the Lord his God."* Our hope is in a person; our hope is in Jesus. As David said in Psalms 130:5 *"I wait for the Lord, my soul doth wait, and in his word do I hope."* You can pass through all kinds of darkness and valleys, just as the bride does in Hosea 2:15, *"And I will give her her vineyards from thence, and the valley of Achor for a door of hope: and she shall sing there, as in the days of her youth, and as in the day when she came up out of the land of Egypt."* You can pass through that valley. Don't worry about your circumstances. God will bring that expectancy to pass for you.

Zechariah 9:12 tells us that we are, *"prisoners of hope."* We've got to believe. We've got to be persuaded that what He has promised, He is able also to perform (Romans 4:21). We need to just continue to believe God and hope, as Lamentations 3:26 says, *"It is good that a man should both hope and quietly wait for the salvation of the Lord."*

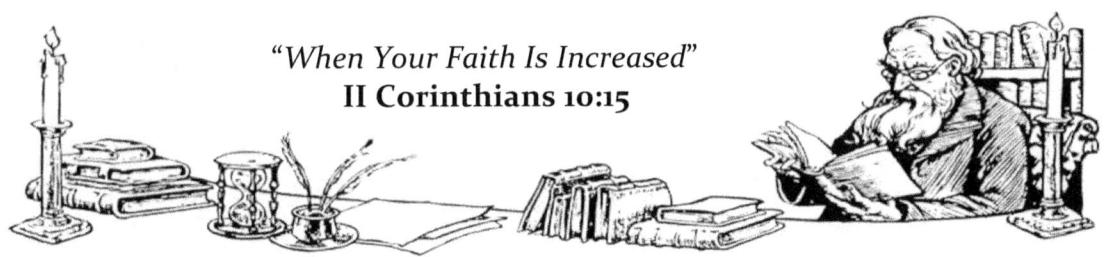

"When Your Faith Is Increased"
II Corinthians 10:15

DAY 174

Here in this passage, though Paul is speaking of giving, he says, *"but having hope, when your faith is increased."* One thing we need to know is the faith that God has given us can and should grow. As II Thessalonians 1:3 says, *"We are bound to thank God always for you, brethren, as it is meet, because that your faith groweth exceedingly."* God wants our faith to grow and not remain stagnant. In II Peter 1:5, it tells us, *"And beside this, giving all diligence, add to your faith."* He wants our faith added and increased today.

We find that from faith to faith we grow, as we see in Romans 1:17 when he says, *"For therein is the righteousness of God revealed from faith to faith: as it is written, The just shall live by faith."* Our faith grows and our ability in God grows. My prayer for us is like what is said in Luke 17:5, *"And the apostles said unto the Lord, Increase our faith."* We want our faith increased so we can believe God more and more. Not just for ourselves but for all those around us who are in desperate need because, *"without faith it is impossible to please him"* (Hebrews 11:6). *"Now faith is the substance of things hoped for, the evidence of things not seen"* (Hebrews 11:1). We need faith because faith moves God.

In I Thessalonians 3:10 Paul says, *"Night and day praying exceedingly that we might see your face, and might perfect that which is lacking in your faith?"* God wants to perfect that which is lacking in our faith. In other words He wants our faith to reach perfection.

Now in Acts 14:22, Paul tells those disciples there, and exhorts them, to continue in the faith. We have to continue. We have to keep pressing in by praying in the Holy Ghost, by giving ourselves to the Word of God, and by using our faith and believing God every day. That's how our faith will grow. As Jude 20 says, *"building up yourselves on your most holy faith, praying in the Holy Ghost."* *"So then, faith cometh by hearing, and hearing by the word of God"* (Romans 10:17).

In II Corinthians 8:7 Paul says, *"Therefore, as ye abound in every thing, in faith, and utterance, and knowledge."* God wants you to abound in faith. He wants your faith to grow exceedingly. Let that begin today. Let faith arise in your heart, so that He will find it in us. As Luke 18:8 says, *"When the Son of man cometh, shall he find faith on the earth?"* Let us be that people of faith!

"Pride Hath Deceived Thee"
Obadiah 3

DAY 175

We find here in Obadiah 3, it says, *"The pride of thine heart hath deceived"*. The Moffat translation says: *"The pride of thine heart hath played thee false."* The word *"pride"* in the Hebrew means "arrogance, pomp, and a swelling up." Basically, pride is just the arrogance of man thinking more highly of himself than he ought to think. The Scriptures are full of admonitions about pride.

It says in I John 2:16, *"For all that is in the world, the lust of the flesh, and the lust of the eyes, and the pride of life, is not of the Father, but is of the world."* Pride does not come from God our Father. That seed was not in him, but it was found in Lucifer, and was the original sin.

Proverbs 14:3 says, *"In the mouth of the foolish is a rod of pride."* Then in Proverbs 6, it says, *"These six things doth the Lord hate: yea, seven are an abomination unto him"* (Proverbs 6:16-17). The first on the list in verse 17 says *"a proud look."* Jeremiah 49:16, a mate scripture to Obadiah 3, says, *"The pride of thine heart hath deceived thee."* Pride deceives us into thinking that we are something that we are not and causes us to be arrogant and refuse instruction or council. We refuse to humble ourselves. Proverbs 29 tells us, *"A man's pride shall bring him low"* (Proverbs 29:23). Either we will humble ourselves, or God will have to humble us. Which choice do you want?

Pride is destructive. It says in Proverbs 16, *"Pride goeth before destruction and a haughty spirit before a it is fall"* (Proverbs 16:18). If you find yourself in pride or your spirit is haughty, that is not the Spirit of God. James 4:6 says that *"God resisteth the proud, but giveth grace to the humble."* God resists pride. He does not like it at all, because it is not His nature or His character.

Look at all the people in Scripture who lost out to pride. Saul started out humble, hiding himself in the woods when they wanted to make him king. At the end of his life, he said, *"I have played the fool, and erred exceedingly"* (I Samuel 26:21). Samson, once again, starts out good, but ends up full of pride in Babylon. His eyes were put out, his hands in chains, grinding and walking in circles. Look at Michal, David's wife. She despised him and bore no fruit the rest of her life.

The greatest example of pride is of Nebuchadnezzar in Daniel 4:

> *"³⁰The king spake, and said, Is not this great Babylon, that I have built for the house of the kingdom by the might of my power, and for the honour of my majesty? ³¹While the word was in the king's mouth, there fell a voice from heaven, saying, O king Nebuchadnezzar, to thee it is spoken; The kingdom is departed from thee. ³²And they shall drive thee from men, and thy dwelling shall be with the beasts of the field: they shall make thee to eat grass as*

> *oxen, and seven times shall pass over thee, until thou know that the most High ruleth in the kingdom of men, and giveth it to whomsoever he will"* (Daniel 4:30-32).

Seven times is perfection. God had to deal with Nebuchadnezzar until he broke the spirit of pride in his life. So, Nebuchadnezzar found himself with fingernails like claws of a bird. He found himself eating grass and living in the woods. He did eat grass as oxen and his body was wet with the dew, verse 33 says, until his hair was grown like eagle's feathers, and his nails like birds claws. But, at the end of days, he lifted up his eyes, and he repented and blessed the Lord God and honored Him that liveth forever. Then he said in verse 37, *"I, Nebuchadnezzar praise and extol and honor the King of Heaven, all whose works are truth, and His ways judgment: and those who walk in pride He is able to abase."* Don't have the Lord to abase you. Choose to humble yourself in the sight of the Lord today, be not deceived, and walk free from pride.

"How Shall We Sing The Lord's Song In A Strange Land"
Psalms 137:4

DAY 176

In this passage of Scripture we find a very important truth that we cannot sing the Lord's song in a strange land. The word *"strange"* in Hebrew here means "alien, foreign, or heathen." The Bible says in many places that we are to *"worship the Lord in the beauty of holiness"* (Psalms 29:2, 96:9). We are to sing praises of God in the sanctuary (Psalms 150:1). We are to lift up holy hands (Psalms 134:2). The heathen will only mock this as they were doing here in Psalms 137:

> *"By the rivers of Babylon, there we sat down, yea, we wept, when we remembered Zion. ²We hanged our harps upon the willows in the midst thereof. ³For there they that carried us away captive required of us a song; and they that wasted us required of us mirth, saying, Sing us one of the songs of Zion. ⁴How shall we sing the Lord's song in a strange land?"* (Psalms 137:1-4)

These Babylonish heathens wanted the children of Israel to make them laugh and foolishly give them happiness requiring them to sing one of the holy songs of Zion. But this cannot be done. And I find today that in too many churches, the mix of the world and the church has brought forth what the Bible calls strange fire and it is an unholy mixture. We cannot sing the Lord's true song in a strange land. Heathens, alien to the Kingdom of God, foreigners to the things of God, will never understand our songs; they will never understand the glory and presence of God. It is foreign to them.

God told Israel to not offer strange incense upon His altar in Exodus 30:9. And we find in Leviticus 10:1 that Aaron's sons offered strange fire before the Lord which was the exact thing God told them not to do. And when they offered that strange fire, they died instantly and were burnt to a crisp. Strange fire is very serious to the Lord. He doesn't like it. The Bible speaks of strange gods being among them. Proverbs 7 speaks of the strange, adulterous woman that we are to stay away from with all diligence.

But I want to talk to you for a moment here about the strange land. The strange land is the land of anti-Christ. It is anti the anointing. It is the place that is foreign to the presence of God and no wonder the children of Israel wept when they remembered Zion.

Just recently I was in a foreign nation and away from my precious church and the great and glorious worship that we have there. One place in particular did not worship. They did not know the Lord intimately and as I was ministering, trying to bring the people into the glory while they were resisting it, I had this thought, "Oh how I missed being in Zion." I missed my precious church back home and the glory of the presence of God there. When we worship, the manifest presence of God comes down in such a glorious and mighty fashion and we have true intimacy with God; the Lord is truly enthroned upon our praises. Singing these songs in this foreign land to these people who were not children of Zion and did not know the Lord intimately almost seemed alien to me. They didn't understand the glory. They didn't enter in and it was therefore not glorious.

In many churches today, we find that they allow people to play on their worship team that are not even saved, but because they are good musicians or singers. They overlook the fact that they don't know Jesus and don't have the Spirit of God. Moreover, they don't realize that when they play and sing with them, it is strange fire being offered upon the altar to the Lord.

I was in a church one time, preaching and before I got up to minister I found out that the worship leader, who was blind, was not saved. But because he was such a great musician, they paid him to come and lead the worship. Well obviously it was great music and there was great rhythm and everybody loved it, but it was void of the presence of God. The glory was not there.

God gave me the grace that day to share with those people about true worship. I ended up leading the musician to Jesus and he was so touched by Spirit of God that I know their worship in the church was transformed from that day on. That was a miracle. That doesn't happen often.

How desperately the world needs the presence of God and it can only come as we sing the songs of Zion. As we lift up holy worship unto God, God comes then and is enthroned upon our worship. This is Zion. And we don't need to be singing the Lord's song in a strange land.

The Bible says in Titus 3:10, *"A man that is an heretick after the first and second admonition, reject."* How many times have you given that which is holy unto dogs? For example, you've tried to tell somebody something holy and revelatory from the Scriptures and they look at you like you are crazy. They don't understand you because what you are sharing is foreign to them. They are either heathens or they are nominal Christians who are not pressing into the deeper things of God and do not know the Lord in an intimate fashion. We need to move on from this after the first and second admonition. We can't beg and plead those to come into the presence of God who don't want to come.

All I know is that the first time I entered into a meeting where people were worshipping gloriously, my spirit immediately witnessed and I knew I was home. As they sang the great chorus, "Alleluia," I rose in the Spirit and found myself before the throne of Almighty God.

How terrible and perverted it is to sing those songs in a place where they don't know the Lord they are singing about! How can we sing the Lord's song in a strange land? It's impossible. It cannot be done. Oh worship the Lord in the beauty of holiness. If you have been in a strange land, void of the presence and glory of God, come back to Zion today. Know that it is only there that you will find your own people of like precious faith. And as you worship, God will manifest Himself to you!

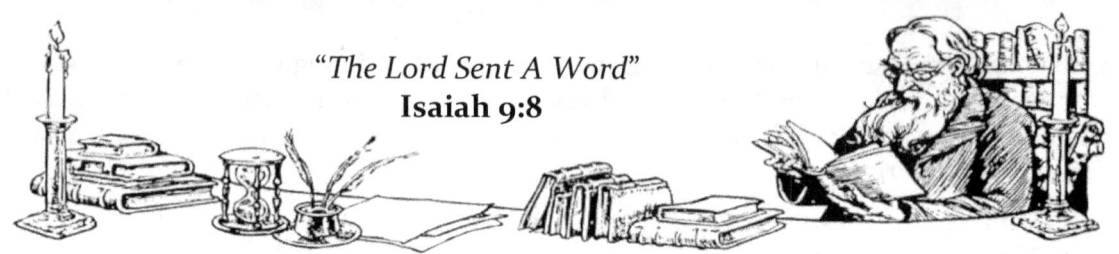

"The Lord Sent A Word"
Isaiah 9:8

DAY 177

In the book of Isaiah, it says, *"The Lord sent a word into Jacob, and it hath lighted upon Israel."* A tremendous truth is found in this passage. There is such revelation that may escape the eye of one who is not a true disciple.

The Lord sent a word into Jacob. Jacob's name means "supplanter and deceiver." A name always speaks of one's character. The only way God is going to deliver us and make us into an Israel, which means "champion," is by sending a word into us. John 8 tells us, speaking of the Word of God, *"And ye shall know the truth, and the truth shall make you free"* (John 8:32).

We clearly see in the Scriptures that the Word of God is what cleanses and changes us. It says in Psalms 119, *"⁹Wherewithal shall a young man cleanse his way? by taking heed thereto according to thy word...¹¹Thy word have I hid in mine heart, that I might not sin against thee"* (Psalms 119:9,11). The Bible also says, *"Sanctify them through thy truth: thy word is truth"* (John 17:17). Ephesians 5 tells us that He wants to *"sanctify and cleanse"* His people *"with the washing of water by the word"* (Ephesians 5:26). Paul declares in II Corinthians, *"Having therefore these promises, dearly beloved, let us cleanse ourselves from all filthiness of the flesh and spirit, perfecting holiness in the fear of God"* (II Corinthians 7:1).

God sent a word into Jacob. Speaking of Joseph Psalms 105:19 says, *"Until the time that his word came: the word of the Lord tried him."* God will send a word into you today, and it will try you. Your revelation must be married to your situation. That Word is working in you something powerful, mighty, and glorious. You will not remain the same. Oh, let the Word of God have its way. Let it *"have free course"* (II Thessalonians 3:1). Let it run within you, as it says in Psalms, *"He sendeth forth his commandment upon earth: his word runneth very swiftly"* (Psalms 147:15). Receive that Word. The book of James tells us to *"receive with meekness the engrafted word, which is able to save your souls"* (James 1:21). Let the Word of God do its job in you.

The Lord is sending His Word into your Jacob-nature; your carnal, Adamic nature that deceives and supplants. God sees that you are destined for greatness, destined to be a champion, and destined to be an overcomer. And once that Word is sent into Jacob, it says that it *"hath lighted,"* or come to be known, *"upon Israel"* (Isaiah 9:8). That Word will work itself out of you. That revelation will be married to your situation. It will change you so that you will no longer be a deceiver and supplanter, but a champion and one that has found *"favour with God and man"* (Luke 2:52).

You will be an overcomer and an example to many, simply because the Lord sent His Word into you, into the depths of your nature. The precious Word of God purifies us, as it says in Psalms, *"as silver tried in a furnace of earth, purified seven times"* (Psalms 12:6). That earth is your and my earth, the things of the flesh in our lives. It is purifying all that is in you, making you into Israel, a champion.

"The Lord's Prayer"
Matthew 6:9-13

Here in Matthew 6, we find the disciples asking Jesus to help them pray. He responds saying:

> "⁹After this manner therefore pray ye: Our Father which art in heaven, Hallowed be thy name. ¹⁰Thy kingdom come. Thy will be done in earth, as it is in heaven. ¹¹Give us this day our daily bread. ¹²And forgive us our debts, as we forgive our debtors. ¹³And lead us not into temptation, but deliver us from evil: For thine is the kingdom, and the power, and the glory, for ever. Amen." (Matthew 6:9-13)

DAY 178

First, this is how we're supposed to pray and how God wants us to pray. We start by saying, "*Our Father.*" There must be a revelation that He is your precious heavenly Father. "*Which art in heaven*" means He's on the throne; He sits on the circle of the earth; He's the ruler of the universe. He continues to say, "*Hallowed be thy name,*" because all of our prayer must be as incense, prayer followed by praise and worship. We don't ever want to go into His gates without thanksgiving or into His courts without praise (Psalms 100:4). He then says, "*Thy kingdom come.*" Is that the desire of your heart? "*Thy will be done in earth, as it is in heaven.*" God's kingdom coming simply means His rule and reign in a people here on the earth right now. It is not what's coming, but is right now. Oh, precious Jesus, let Your will that's done in heaven be done in our lives right now in the earth.

He continues, "*Give us this day our daily bread.*" You and I can ask Him for our provision. We don't have to worry. He says "*all things that pertain unto life and godliness,*" He's already given us (II Peter 1:3). He also says in Matthew 6:33, "*But seek ye first the kingdom of God, and his righteousness; and all these things shall be added unto you.*" Philippians 4:19 tells us, "*But my God shall supply all your need according to his riches in glory by Christ Jesus.*" But still we must ask.

Then He says, "*Forgive us our debts, as we forgive our debtors.*" The key to being forgiven is to forgive. If we can release other people from the things they owe us, then God will be of a more gentle nature to forgive us for our debts. And then we're to pray, "*Lead us not into temptation, but deliver us from evil.*" We're not to be asking the Lord to tempt us or asking for presumptuous foolishness, but we need to pray to be delivered from the evil of this world and our own minds and fallen nature.

And last, He says, "*For thine is the kingdom, and the power, and the glory, for ever.*" There must be a recognition that the Kingdom is His, that all power in heaven and earth has been given unto Him and unto Him belongs the glory forever and ever. And then He says, "*Amen.*" This is what's commonly known as the Lord's prayer, although I believe that's found in another passage in the gospel of John, but this is our instruction manual for how to pray. It begins by a revelation of our great heavenly Father, knowing intimacy with Him and ends with a final "*Amen,*" which means "so be it." May God bless you today to pray and to live this prayer.

"All My Springs Are In Thee"
Psalms 87:7

Day 179

David confesses something remarkable in his worship to the Lord in Psalms 87:7, *"All my springs are in thee."* "The word *"springs"* in the Hebrew means, "a source of satisfaction, our fountain." It comes from a root word that means "to be content, to have an eye on the center." Or in other words, David is saying to the Lord, "You are the source of my satisfaction. You are the fountain of my life. You cause me to be content. I found everything I need in you." Some other translations of this verse read:

> *"My source of life and joy are renewed."*
> *"You are the source of everything."*
> *"Zion is the source of all my blessings."*

Oh, that we would find our satisfaction in Him; that no other could take His place; that He becomes the pearl of great price to us, the great treasure of our lives hidden in a field. If you can say as Peter did in I Peter 2:3, *"If so be ye have tasted that the Lord is gracious"*, then there can be no turning back. There can be no other God before Him and there can be no other thing before Him. Knowing Him, knowing His heart and knowing how precious, wonderful, generous and glorious He is, how could one ever turn their eyes from Him? Truly, for me, He is the source of everything.

The crazy thing is that God delights in being our source. He delights in meeting all our needs. It's His pleasure to give us His Kingdom. He loves to show us mercy and kindness. What a marvelous great God we serve!

All my hope, all my joy, all my satisfaction is found in Him. In my forty-three years of walking with Jesus, I admit to you that I have sought my source of satisfaction in so many things, only to come up empty and dry, bewildered, haunted, condemned, or empty. However, there has never been a time where I have gone into the presence and secret place of the Most High God and have not been satisfied.

Psalms 145:15-16 says, *"¹⁵The eyes of all wait upon thee; and thou givest them their meat in due season. ¹⁶Thou openest thine hand, and satisfiest the desire of every living thing."* How many times has He opened His hand and satisfied your desire? We must certainly make Him the number one source in our life. The older we get, the more we realize the frivolousness and foolishness of youth and how much time we've wasted on other things and giving ourselves to things that really did not produce any lasting fruit in our lives. It is only as we grow older do we realize the things that are important, or really mean something, that we should be giving ourselves.

I tell you, find Jesus today as your source of satisfaction. Find Him today as the one who is everything to you and let all of your springs be in Him. Let there be nothing else. Let your eyes see nothing else but Him, for He is altogether lovely. He is our wonderful and glorious Husband!

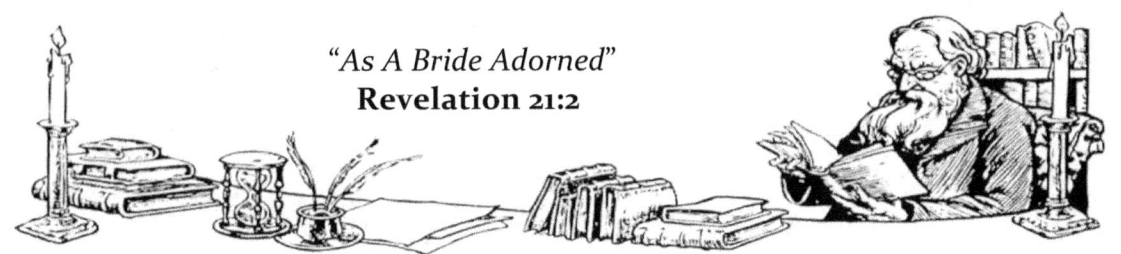

"As A Bride Adorned"
Revelation 21:2

DAY 180

Here in Revelation 21:2, the Scriptures say, *"And I John saw the holy city, new Jerusalem, coming down from God out of heaven, prepared as a bride adorned for her husband."* This revelation of God's bride is one of the most important principles in all of Scripture. God, our Father, has been seeking a bride for His Son. Of all the subjects one could teach or minister, this principle, as far as I am concerned, is the highest. Just like the Song of Solomon is called the *"song of songs"* (Song of Solomon 1:1). This is the teaching of all teachings.

God is calling a bride to Himself, to give to His Son. She will be adorned and ready for her Husband. In Song of Solomon 6:8-9, we find this principle, *"There are threescore queens, and fourscore concubines, and virgins without number. ⁹My dove, my undefiled is but one; she is the only one of her mother, she is the choice one of her that bare her. The daughters saw her, and blessed her; yea, the queens and the concubines, and they praised her."*

This dove, this undefiled woman, is the bride of Christ. Her mother is the church and she is the chosen one of her mother. There are sixty queens and eighty concubines, which are ranks within the body of Christ. There are virgins without number which are the rest of the body of Christ. Revelation 19:7 says, *"His wife hath made herself ready."* We need to be adorned for our Husband. We need to be this bride that is ready to meet with our Husband, Jesus.

This is seen in type in Genesis 2:22-25. Adam is the type of the church, God's body, and out from him is taken a bride, the woman who will be his wife. The bride of Christ will come out of the heart of the body to be given to God's Son to be wed. God has been calling and calling for His bride, every since God called after Adam, *"And the Lord God called unto Adam, and said unto him, Where art thou"* (Genesis 3:9)? The question we must ultimately answer is: Where are we in relation to our God and to our heavenly Bridegroom? God is calling a bride unto Himself. Oh, that you and I would receive this revelation and begin to walk in the brideship to which God has called.

Adorn yourself today with fine linen, clean and white. Proverbs 31:29 says, *"Many daughters have done virtuously, but thou excellest them all."* She is exceeding beautiful. She is a bride adorned for her Husband. In Ezekiel 16 we find this same principle in the woman cast out into the open field where everyone has forsaken her. But when the Lord passed by her, it was the time of love and He blessed her and ministered to her and she became *"exceeding beautiful, and thou didst prosper into a kingdom"* (Ezekiel 16:13). I believe this kingdom here speaks of the Kingdom of God.

We are called to be the bride of Christ. Not just a general Christian, but something far greater than that. Give ear, today, to the Word of God and become this bride that God the Father has been seeking for. *"For the Lord's portion is his people; Jacob is the lot of his inheritance"* (Deuteronomy 32:9). Let us give Him a bride for His Son.

"She Judged Him Faithful"
Hebrews 11:11

DAY 181

In Hebrews 11:11, we find this passage, *"Through faith also Sara herself received strength to conceive seed, and was delivered of a child when she was past age, because she judged him faithful who had promised."* Sara's story is a remarkable one. She was well past age as was her husband when she received strength to conceive seed and birth Isaac. She was able to do this even after first not believing and laughing at the promise of God. God even subtly rebuked her for it, but later as she began to consider His promise, she came to a place where faith arose in her heart. She judged Him faithful who had promised.

Therefore, *"Without faith it is impossible to please him"* Hebrews 11:6 says. *"For he that cometh to God must believe that he is, and that he is a rewarder of them that diligently seek him."* So, without faith, nothing is possible. When we come to God we must believe who He says He is and that He will reward us as we diligently seek Him. Sara herself received strength to conceive seed because she judged Him faithful who had promised.

How do you judge the Lord today? Hasn't He been faithful to you? Hasn't He always answered you? Hasn't He kept His promises? I Kings 8:56 says, *"There hath not failed one word of all his good promise"*. II Corinthians 1:20 says, *"For all the promises of God in him are yea, and in him Amen."* Sara judged God faithful because of a promise He made to her that she would conceive a seed and that the child would be a very important child. You and I need to judge Him faithful to the promises He has given us.

What has God spoken to you? What promise has He whispered to your heart? It may seem impossible today. It may seem like it will never come to pass in the natural. But the Bible declares, *"With God all things are possible"* (Mark 10:27) and *"There is nothing too hard for thee"* (Jeremiah 32:17).

All you and I need to do is to judge Him faithful, believe His Word, trust in Him, and we will receive the promise that He promised to us. Sarah judged Him faithful. Today, let the Word of the Lord be that you and I have judged Him faithful. Let us watch as the promises He gave to us come to pass.

"My Heart Is Fixed 2"
Psalms 57:7

Here in Psalms 57 David begins in verse 5 by saying:

"Be thou exalted, O God, above the heavens; let thy glory be above all the earth. ⁶They have prepared a net for my steps; my soul is bowed down: they have digged a pit before me, into the midst whereof they are fallen themselves. Selah. ⁷My heart is fixed, O God, my heart is fixed: I will sing and give praise" (Psalms 57:5-7).

The revelation of this verse is that our hearts must be fixed. He says, *"I will sing and give praise."* The Hebrew word for *"fixed"* means "to be erect, to stand, or be established." In other words, as Ephesians 6:13-14 says, *"Having done all, to stand. Stand therefore, having your loins girt about with truth."* You and I need to have a heart that's established, that's willing to stand and not be moved. Paul said in Acts 20:24, *"None of these things move me."* We will not be moved when our hearts are fixed. This is a matter of our will and a choice we make. We must determine today to be fixed, no matter what happens to us, no matter what goes on, no matter what the enemy tries, and no matter what our own minds bring to us. Let us pray today, *"O God my heart is fixed."* A heart that is erect, standing, and established in the Lord and His Word is a heart that is fixed. We will choose by our own will to sing and give praise no matter what. We see this also in Psalms 108:

"O God, my heart is fixed; I will sing and give praise, even with my glory. ²Awake, psaltery and harp: I myself will awake early. ³I will praise thee, O Lord, among the people: and I will sing praises unto thee among the nations" (Psalms 108:1-3).

This is what you and I need to do. We need to be alert, always be ready, standing fixed with a will that is determined to give God praise and glory for His greatness and His goodness. Psalms 112 is the Psalm of the man that fears the Lord and that delights greatly in His commandments. God begins to speak about this man and what will happen to him.

It says in Psalms 112:7-8, *"He shall not be afraid of evil tidings: his heart is fixed, trusting in the Lord. His heart is established, he shall not be afraid."* Once again *"fixed"* means "standing and established," even when evil tidings come to try to bring fear into our lives and threaten us. The established heart, the man that fears the Lord and delights greatly in His commandments, will not be afraid. He won't be moved. Why is that? Because his heart is fixed, trusting in the Lord. He is going to sing and give praise. Today let this be our testimony. God, our heart is fixed. We will sing and give praise and trust in the Lord.

"He That Hardeneth His Heart"
Proverbs 28:14

DAY 183

Here in Proverbs, it says, *"he that hardeneth his heart shall fall into mischief"* (Proverbs 28:14). God wants us to have pure, soft, tender hearts. He doesn't want us to have bitter, proud, or resentful hearts. This is indicative of the world and not of God.

The word *"hardeneth"* in Hebrew means "to be dense, tough, severe, harsh, and difficult, to be stubborn, or stiff-necked." When we harden our hearts, we become very dense and, dare I say, foolish. We become very tough so that no one can reach us, not even the Spirit of God. We become severe, harsh, and difficult with people. More importantly, we become stubborn or stiff-necked. This was the greatest hindrance Jesus found in the Pharisees and religious people. Even though trying to be religious, they were stubborn and stiff-necked, and refused the word of the Lord. They refused Jesus and the Spirit of God dealing with their hearts.

The Bible says in James, *"¹⁴But if ye have bitter envying and strife in your hearts, glory not, and lie not against the truth. ¹⁵This wisdom descendeth not from above, but is earthly, sensual, devilish"* (James 3:14-15). God does not want bitter envying and strife in our hearts. It's amazing that, even in the Christian community, we find that there is much pride, bitterness, and envy. It doesn't do much to share the gospel with the world when our hearts are like this. The world needs to see an example of the true character of Jesus. Jesus said in Matthew 11:29, *"Take my yoke upon you, and learn of me; for I am meek and lowly in heart."* The only people Jesus ever got upset with were religious, pharisaical, stubborn, proud, or stiff-necked people. He got upset with the ones who had hardened their hearts.

What they don't realize is that *"pride goeth before destruction, and an haughty spirit before a fall"* (Proverbs 16:18). James tells us, *"God resisteth the proud, but giveth grace unto the humble"* (James 4:6). Humility is the hallmark of the character of Jesus and should be the number one characteristic of the people of God. We don't want to *"fall into mischief."*

Proverbs 28:25 says, *"He that is of a proud heart stirreth up strife."* Isn't that the truth? How many times have all of us been in situations where someone, through pride, has stirred up a bunch of strife? It causes great problems between friends, family members, co-workers, etc. We need to make sure that if we strive to do anything, we strive to keep our hearts right.

The Bible says in Proverbs, *"The heart knoweth his own bitterness"* (Proverbs 14:10). We all know when we are proud, when our hearts are hardened and we refuse to listen. We must see that God cannot deal with us or reach us at this moment. It takes the grace of God and a miracle for us to bow down. How many people have left local churches and broken off fellowship with other people because of something they couldn't forgive or because of pride dwelling in them?

It says in Psalms 95, "*Harden not your heart, as in the provocation, and as in the day of temptation in the wilderness*" (Psalms 95:8). Don't harden your heart. Think right now: is there anything in your life right now in which you're being stubborn, difficult, stiff-necked, severe, or harsh? This is not the will of God. Today, let the Holy Spirit surround you and the love of God constrain you to act like Jesus. "*For where your treasure is, there will your heart be also*" (Matthew 6:21). Our treasure should be to have a heart like God and to keep our hearts right.

Paul said that we are to be "*kind one to another, tenderhearted, forgiving one another...*" (Ephesians 4:32). I Kings 8:61 says, "*Let your heart therefore be perfect with the Lord our God.*" God is looking for us to keep our hearts right. You may say, "I've tried and I've tried and I've tried, but I seem to have a problem." Well, I have the remedy for you.

David says in Psalms 51, "*Create in me a clean heart, O God; and renew a right spirit within me*" (Psalms 51:10). One day, as I was studying this passage, I realized something as the Spirit prompted me. I realized that if God needed to, He could create a brand new heart in me. He can create in us brand new hearts, soft hearts. So the next time your heart is hard and you can't seem to break it free, just pray this to the Lord, yield to Him, and allow Him to create in you a clean, right, and soft heart again, "*for God maketh my heart soft,*" Job said (Job 23:16). God will make your heart soft. We see in Saul's life that "*God gave him another heart*" (I Samuel 10:9).

Perhaps, that is you today. Let God give you another heart. If need be, let Him create in you a new, clean heart. Give Him the chance. Give the Almighty the ability to make your heart soft. For him that "*hardeneth his heart*" will always "*fall into mischief.*" You don't want that. You and I want our hearts to glorify God. So, as Proverbs 4:23 says, "*Keep thy heart with all diligence; for out of it are the issues of life.*"

"When I Shall Receive The Congregation"
Psalms 75:2

DAY 184

What a glorious and important truth we find in this passage of Scripture today, *"When I shall receive the congregation I will judge uprightly."* The Hebrew word for *"receive"* means "to take or accept." This Scripture says to us that we cannot begin to judge our brothers and sisters correctly, until we are flowing with the congregation or have received them into our hearts.

We have to accept our brothers and sisters as the Bible tells us, *"So we, being many, are one body in Christ, and every one members one of another"* (Romans 12:5). In describing the body of Christ in I Corinthians 12, it reveals to us that we are not islands unto ourselves but are all a part of the one body flowing together. One small member in the midst of the body should be flowing and relating with the rest of the body. As I Corinthians 12:21 says, *"the eye cannot say unto the hand, I have no need of thee: nor again the head to the feet, I have no need of you."*

Ask yourself today, have you received the congregation as David has? Have you taken them in and accepted the brethren? Paul declares in Romans 15:7, *"Wherefore receive ye one another, as Christ also received us to the glory of God."* Therefore, when we receive the congregation we do this unto the Glory of God.

We need to receive one another just as we are. We come to the Lord just as we are without one plea and we need to do the same with our brethren when they come to us. Jesus says in John 13:35, *"By this shall all men know that ye are my disciples, if ye have love one to another."* So many times in the Christian community, we don't see this happening. There is no love flowing from one to another. As a result, all men do not know that we are His disciples because we do not radiate the character of Jesus. Jesus said in the book of John:

> *"[12]This is my commandment, That ye love one another, as I have loved you. [13]Greater love hath no man than this, that a man lay down his life for his friends. [14]Ye are my friends, if ye do whatsoever I command you. [15]Henceforth I call you not servants; for the servant knoweth not what his lord doeth: but I have called you friends; for all things that I have heard of my Father I have made known unto you."*
> (John 15:12-15)

Jesus wants us to love one another as He has loved us. He wants us to receive everyone in the congregation without regards to race, gender, social strata, or any other reason. We are brothers and sisters the Bible tells us, *"Honour all men. Love the brotherhood. Fear God. Honour the king"* (I Peter 2:17). Hebrews 12:14 says, *"Follow peace with all men."* This should be our goal in life; to stay sweet, humble, and to receive the congregation. As we receive them and accept them we will then be able to discern a righteous judgment about men.

"Leaning Upon Her Beloved"
Song Of Solomon 8:5

"Who is this that cometh up from the wilderness, leaning upon her beloved?" (Song of Solomon 8:5). "Who is this?" What a question! I believe that this is speaking of the Bride of Christ and of her love relationship with her Bridegroom, the Lord Jesus. Notice where she's coming from: the wilderness.

Day 185

It seems that the wilderness or the desert is the place where all men, all prophets, and all those who have ever been used of the Lord have found their place. John was in the deserts until his showing unto Israel (Luke 1:80). Jesus was led of the Spirit into the wilderness (Matthew 4:1). Moses went to the dessert for forty years. The children of Israel spent forty years in the wilderness. I could go on and on. Paul was in the desserts of Arabia fourteen years. It seems that the wilderness is the place where we need to learn, be sanctified. The wilderness is where we need the processing of God to mold us, make us, and shape us into who we're called to be, which is to be conformed to the image of the Lord Jesus.

We find that coming up out of this wilderness speaks of overcoming. They haven't been lost or overtaken in the wilderness. They're coming up; they're rising out of the darkness and out of the wilderness, leaning upon their beloved. They've learned that by the grace of God they stand. That in their flesh they can do nothing, and without Him they can't survive.

Remember the story of Jacob in Genesis 32, how the Lord touched his leg and he walked with a limp the rest of his life (Genesis 32:25). The limp was there to remind him of when he went through the dealings of God, and that he was a supplanter and a deceiver. God wanted that little thing, that little limp in his life to remain, so that he would always remember that he was nothing apart from Jesus. Perhaps you and I limp. Perhaps you and I have something that reminds us of who we really are. Don't get me wrong, we are saints and sons of the living God, but yet we remember the rock from whence we were hewn (Isaiah 51:1).

So we embrace the wilderness as the Spirit leads us up into it. We fight through like Joseph. We see in Psalms 105:19 that *"Until the time that his word came: the word of the Lord tried him."* We wait, even in prison, until the call comes to go before Pharaoh and become prime minister. We're coming up, we're coming out, but we're changed and different. *"The sufferings of this present time are not worthy to be compared with the glory which shall be revealed in us"* (Romans 8:18). *"For our light affliction, which is but for a moment, worketh for us a far more exceeding and eternal weight of glory"* (II Corinthians 4:17).

Let patience have her perfect work in you (James 1:4). God is working something in you in the wilderness, and everyone is going to be surprised when they see you coming up out of it. They never thought you'd make it, but Jesus did. You know now that the way you got out, and the way you'll continue to stay out, is to lean upon your Beloved.

"The Difference Between The Holy And Profane"
Ezekiel 44:23

Day 186

The Lord here in Ezekiel gives us a line of demarcation between two kinds of priests: priests that are backslidden, who have left the Lord but still remain in the priesthood, and those priests that still continue to seek the Lord and love the Lord with all of their hearts. This is a very revelatory chapter but here in Ezekiel 44:23 we read, *"And they shall teach my people the difference between the holy and profane, and cause them to discern between the unclean and the clean."* Here, He is speaking to those priests who were His loyal priests. These priests were allowed to minister to Him and they were called the sons of Zadok. He says one of the primary things they are to do is teach His people the difference between the holy and profane and cause them to discern between the unclean and the clean.

If there ever was a day that this revelation is needed, it is now. So many people don't know the difference between the holy and the common (or profane) or the difference between the clean and unclean. We're living in the time that Isaiah said in Isaiah 5:23, *"Woe unto them that call evil good, and good evil; that put darkness for light, and light for darkness; that put bitter for sweet, and sweet for bitter!"* This seems to be the hour in which we live. It is beyond sad and it is heartbreaking; but there is a people like those in Jonah 4:11, the people of Nineveh, whom God sent Jonah to redeem and to help. The Lord said of these people that they could not *"discern between their right hand and their left hand."* We need to be concerned about the people in this world who are calling evil good and good evil. They can't discern between the right hand or the left and don't know the difference between holy and profane. The calling to the sons of Zadok, the true men and women of God, is for them to show the difference.

In Proverbs 17:15 it says, *"He that justifieth the wicked, and he that condemneth the just, even they both are abomination to the Lord."* You see this is what happens when evil men begin to rule and reign over us. The wicked get justified and the just get condemned; good is called evil and evil is called good. It is a slow process to wear us down. It causes an erosion in our own morals and in our own ability to stand before the Lord in purity and in holiness. We must be like Solomon, who in I Kings 3:9 said to the Lord *"give therefore thy servant an understanding heart to judge thy people, that I may discern between good and bad: for who is able to judge this thy so great a people?"* This is what the Lord has for us. We're to teach God's people the difference; the difference between the holy and profane and to discern between the unclean and the clean.

In this day of charismatic hoopla, anointing is misunderstood for charisma; gifts are exalted rather than the Giver of gifts and this is not the will of God. We are to teach the people the difference between strange fire and the real fire of the Lord. Come now today with an understanding heart and ask the Lord to help you to judge between the holy and profane, good and evil, the clean and the unclean.

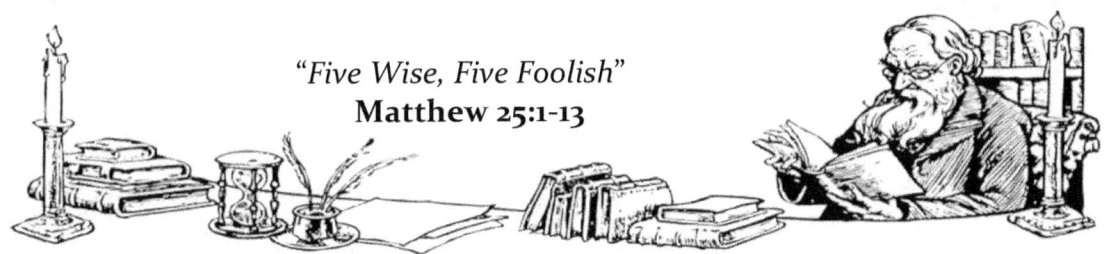

"Five Wise, Five Foolish"
Matthew 25:1-13

DAY 187

This parable of the ten virgins has been so misunderstood and so manipulated by religious people and Babylon to conform to their own theology. However, you and I are going to search the Scriptures to see whether these things are so. Matthew 25:1 begins by saying, *"Then shall the kingdom of heaven be likened unto ten virgins, which took their lamps, and went forth to meet the bridegroom."* This is talking about the Kingdom of Heaven and everybody that is in it. Virgins in Scripture always speak of the people of God. Today, it speaks of Christians. The lamp is our spirit. It is what God has done inside of us. It's the light that shines through us. Notice that all ten of them, all ten Christians went forth to meet the bridegroom. This is the call of God upon our lives, to become the bride of Christ, to meet the bridegroom, Jesus. Though many are called, few actually choose.

Verse 2 says, *"Five of them were wise, and five were foolish."* There is a difference in being wise in the Lord and foolish. *"They that were foolish took their lamps, and took no oil with them: ⁴ But the wise took oil in their vessels with their lamps"* (verses 3-4). Oil represents the Holy Ghost, the anointing. This says to me that half of the body of Christ has not received the baptism of the Holy Spirit, nor have they any oil of God. The wise take oil in their vessels with their lamps. Acts 1:8 says, *"But ye shall receive power, after that the Holy Ghost is come upon you."* The wise have received the baptism of the Holy Ghost. They have received the living Word of God and are marching forth.

Your lamp cannot be lit if there is no oil. The olive must be crushed before oil can flow. Jesus went to Gethsemane ("olive press"). We also must go through Gethsemane experiences, as it says in Acts 14:22, *"through much tribulation, we enter into the Kingdom of God."* The foolish took no oil but the wise did. *"While the bridegroom tarried, they all slumbered and slept"* (verse 5). This verse defines two kinds of sleeping in the Scriptures. One is resting in the will of God. The other is a sleep of slothfulness and slumber. We must be careful not to slumber.

"And at midnight there was a cry made, Behold, the bridegroom cometh; go ye out to meet him" (verse 6). It is always at midnight, the darkest hour of the day, which God moves. Verse 7 says, *"Then all those virgins arose, and trimmed their lamps"* Everyone went out to meet Him. However, the foolish had no oil and asked the wise for some oil. However, the wise could not give them any. The foolish want given to them something they can only get for themselves. You can't give what you don't have. They have refused the baptism of the Holy Spirit and the anointing. Now when they see that they need it, they want it given to them. However, Proverbs 23:23 tells us, *"Buy the truth, and sell it not."* We must go and buy for ourselves.

"And while they went to buy, the bridegroom came; and they that were ready went in with him to the marriage: and the door was shut" (verse 10). God forbid that it be said of us, that we didn't make it into the marriage supper of the lamb because we were fools. Saul said at the end of his life, *"I have played the fool, and have erred exceedingly"* (I Samuel 26:21). We don't need to be foolish. Today, we need to hear the Word of the Lord and be wise and be filled with His holy oil.

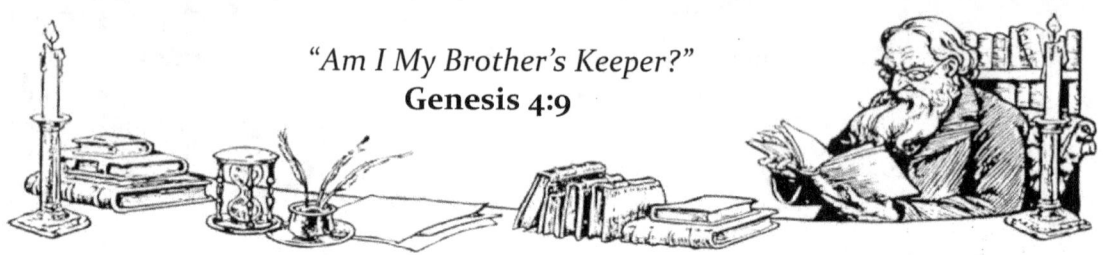

"Am I My Brother's Keeper?"
Genesis 4:9

Day 188

The Lord said to Cain in Genesis 4:9, *"Where is Abel thy brother? And he said, I know not: Am I my brother's keeper?"* Am I my brother's keeper? The answer to this obviously is yes. Remember in the book of Acts, they had *"all things common"* (Acts 2:44). They lived in a community and shared with one another. Are we our brother's keepers? I think so. We are one body in Christ. I Corinthians 12 tells us, *"For as the body is one, and hath many members, and all the members of that one body, being many, are one body: so also is Christ"* (I Corinthians 12:12).

We have been brought together supernaturally by God and we are now brothers and sisters. Remember what Jesus said, *"Who is my mother? and who are my brethren?...whosoever shall do the will of my Father which is in heaven, the same is my brother, and sister, and mother"* (Matthew 12:48, 50). Those who are around you, who hear the word of God and keep it, are your brothers and sisters. We are now our brother's keeper. How can I do that? Well, we can do that by following these Scriptural admonitions. In Ephesians 4:32 it says, *"Be ye kind one to another, tenderhearted, forgiving one another, even as God for Christ's sake hath forgiven you."* Hebrews 3:13 tells us, *"But exhort one another daily, while it is called Today."* It says in Hebrews 10:24, *"And let us consider one another to provoke unto love and to good works."* It says in Galatians 5:13, *"by love serve one another."* We are told in Romans 12:10, *"Be kindly affectioned one to another with brotherly love; in honour preferring one another."* Jesus said in John 15:12, *"This is my commandment...love one another, as I have loved you."*

It is very important to realize that we are our brother's keeper. What happens to our brother happens to us. A chain is only as strong as it weakest link. We must be our brother's keeper. We must learn to love each other, admonish each other, forgive one another, be tenderhearted, and be kind to one another.

Romans 15:1 tells us, *"We then that are strong ought to bear the infirmities of the weak, and not to please ourselves."* We need to be concerned about our brother's weakness and then reach out to help him. Yes, we are our brother's keeper. It says in Galatians 6:2, *"bear ye one another's burdens, and so fulfil the law of Christ."* The law of Christ is a commandment that we love one another, that we have an earnest care for one another. The Bible says, *"Love the brotherhood"* (I Peter 2:17). It also says in I Peter 1:22, *"see that ye love one another with a pure heart fervently."* In John 4:7, it says, *"Beloved, let us love one another: for love is of God; and every one that loveth is born of God, and knoweth God."* John also writes, *"Beloved, if God so loved us, we ought also to love one another"* (I John 4:11).

Thank you, Lord Jesus for my brothers and sisters today. They are my family. If anything happens to my brother or sister, I know I am responsible to be my brother's keeper. Cain should have known where Abel was. Cain did know; he was just hiding his sin. We must not do that. We need to have a Kingdom mentality. We need to encourage and edify our brother, because we are his keeper.

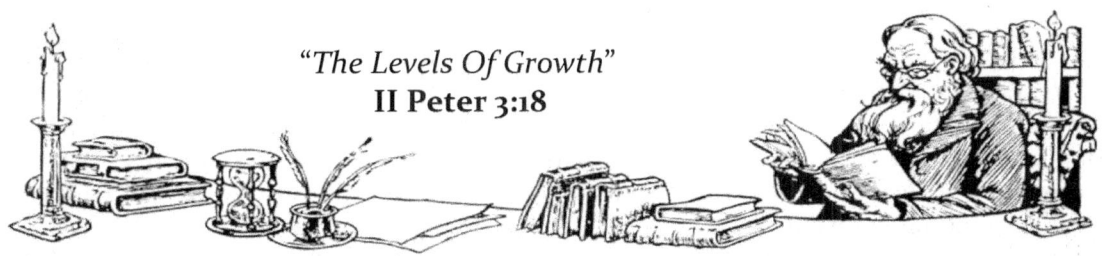

"The Levels Of Growth"
II Peter 3:18

DAY 189

It says here in II Peter 3:18 to *"grow in grace and in the knowledge of our Lord and Saviour Jesus Christ."* We are commanded by Jesus to come *"follow me and I will make you fishers of men"* (Matthew 4:19). The Lord has called us to His eternal glory in Christ Jesus. We must grow up in Him as Ephesians 4:15 says, *"But speaking the truth in love, may grow up into him in all things, which is the head, even Christ."* We must stop being children, tossed to and fro by every wind of doctrine.

I Peter 2:2 says, *"As newborn babes, desire the sincere milk of the word, that ye may grow thereby."* This is God's pattern and plan for our lives. There are levels of growth that we must go through, as is seen in the pattern of the tabernacle. There was the outer court, holy place and most holy place. The end of our faith and growth in God is found in the revelation of the most holy place.

God told Moses in Deuteronomy 2:3, *"Ye have compassed this mountain long enough."* How long have you been stuck in the same place? Are you growing? Are you maturing? Isaiah 28:20 tells us, *"For the bed is shorter than that a man can stretch himself on it: and the covering narrower than that he can wrap himself in it."* Far too many believers have not grown beyond the level that they've attained upon entering salvation.

Hebrews 6:1 exhorts us, *"let us go on unto perfection"*. God has a desire for us and an *"expected end"* (Jeremiah 29:11). That expected end is His image in our souls. How do we get there? Well, in I Samuel 2:19, Hannah brought Samuel a little coat every year. She would bring him the new little coat because Samuel was growing. The old coat could not fit him anymore. Likewise, we should be changing our garments. We should be growing in grace and in the knowledge of our Lord and Savior. We should be growing and maturing in the Lord, not staying steadfast in a realm of ignorance or complacency. Is your bed shorter than a man can stretch himself on it? Is your bed covering too narrow? It's time now to grow up.

Jeremiah 48:11 says, *"Moab hath been at ease from his youth, and he hath settled on his lees, and hath not been emptied from vessel to vessel, neither hath he gone into captivity: therefore his taste remained in him, and his scent is not changed."* In this verse is another example of our levels of growth in God. We are going from one vessel to another vessel. God empties our vessel out in order that we might become a new vessel. He then pours into that vessel a new level of growth and glory. This process continues on until we reach the final vessel: a vessel of glory, prepared for the Lord.

Psalms 84:7 tells us, *"They go from strength to strength, every one of them in Zion appeareth before God."* We go from one level of strength to another level of strength; we are always growing, always maturing. Proverbs 4:18 says, *"But the path of the just is as the shining light, that shineth more and more unto the perfect day."* The path of the just is as the shining light (revelation). We should be growing in revelation as each day goes by. Have you grown from where you were last year, last month, or even last week?

II Corinthians 3:18 says, *"But we all, with open face beholding as in a glass the glory of the Lord, are changed into the same image from glory to glory, even as by the Spirit of the Lord."* The Spirit of the Lord will help us go from one level of glory to another level of glory, until ultimately we will end up with the image of Christ in our souls. Romans 1:17 says, *"For therein is the righteousness of God revealed from faith to faith."* Paul told the Thessalonians, *"your faith groweth exceedingly"* (II Thessalonians 1:3). We are supposed to be going from one level of faith to another level of faith as we apply the wisdom that God gives us in each level.

Finally, Isaiah 28:10 says, *"For precept must be upon precept, precept upon precept; line upon line, line upon line; here a little, and there a little."* This is God's plan and revelation to us today of the levels of growth we are to pass through. One precept to another, one line to another, here a little, there a little, ultimately to end up with the image of Christ Jesus in us.

Are you growing in grace today? Make sure that you are sitting under the Word of God, spending time in prayer, worshipping the Lord Jesus, keeping your heart right, that you are always going upward and onward in Him. Today, let us be growing onward and upward in Him and as Jesus said to His disciples in Matthew 26:46, *"Rise, let us be going."*

"Blessed Are The Pure In Heart For They Shall See God"
Matthew 5:8

Day 190

One of the great principles found many times in Scripture is that God wants us to have a pure heart. Pure in the Greek means "clean or clear." For many years I thought that this Scripture meant that I would see God in heaven or in the future sometime if I kept my heart right. But then the Lord revealed to me one day that I can see God right now in my own situation if I kept my heart right or clean and clear from strife, contention, grudges, unforgiveness, bitterness, etc. I have found now in over forty years of walking with Jesus that keeping a right heart is one of the hardest things to do for any believer.

Truly I have been challenged over all these years and, as Paul prayed, I have found myself praying over and over again, *"And herein do I exercise myself, to have always a conscience void of offence toward God, and toward men"* (Acts 24:16). It is like when Paul told the Hebrews, *"Pray for us: for we trust we have a good conscience, in all things willing to live honestly"* (Hebrews 13:18). Conscience and heart here are the same thing. The definition of the word *"heart"* means, "the centermost part of your being." God wants the centermost part of our being to be pure, clean, and clear of all kinds of foolishness and darkness.

The Lord admonishes us in Proverbs 4:23 *"Keep thy heart with all diligence; for out of it are the issues of life."* Jesus said in Matthew 15:18, *"But those things which proceed out of the mouth come forth from the heart; and they defile the man."* You see, it is what comes out of our heart (mouth) that defiles us or blesses us. Proverbs 14:30 says, *"A sound heart is the life of the flesh."* Therefore, Jesus exhorts us that we will be blessed if we have a pure heart for we will continue to see God in our life. We will always be able to stay in constant communion with God if we keep our hearts clean and clear.

I Peter 1:22 says, *"See that ye love one another with a pure heart fervently."* Proverbs 22:11 adds, *"He that loveth pureness of heart, for the grace of his lips the king shall be his friend."* God will be our friend if we love pureness of heart and I believe we have to love having a pure heart. It is too easy many times to take the path of least resistance and give in to pettiness, grudges, anger, lust, unforgiveness, strife, contention, and so on. There is nothing on this earth that is worth losing out with God. There is nothing on earth worth losing our peace with God and our ability to see Him, having fellowship with Him and having constant communion with Him. So purity of heart should be the goal and aim of every one of us, *"For as he thinketh in his heart, so is he"* (Proverbs 23:7). Titus 1:15 explains, *"Unto the pure all things are pure: but unto them that are defiled and unbelieving is nothing pure; but even their mind and conscience is defiled."*

You will be tested every day. But if you decide to make a decision to walk with a perfect heart and keep your heart clean and clear, in the end, Jesus will always be your friend and always stand with you. In addition, II Samuel 22:27 says, *"With the pure thou wilt shew thyself pure."* God will show Himself pure to all who walk in this principle.

David prayed in Psalms 86:11, *"unite my heart to fear thy name."* Our heart consists of our spirit and soul. Jesus lives in our spirit which is full of purity, cleanness, peace, and righteousness. Our soul is made up of our mind, emotions, affections, intellect, etc. and this is where all our warfare happens. It is necessary then to make sure our heart (soul and spirit) be united together to stay clean and clear. If we have a problem with having a hard heart, God can help us, *"For God maketh my heart soft"* (Job 23:16).

Psalms 51:17 says, *"The sacrifices of God are a broken spirit: a broken and a contrite heart..."* The word *"contrite"* means *"crushed."* We must always seek to have a crushed heart. In other words, we would be crushed if our hearts were displeasing to the Lord or if there was anything hidden in our hearts that made God turn His face from us. Didn't Jesus say in Matthew 11:29, *"I am meek and lowly in heart"*?

Oh my brethren, let us have *"singleness of heart, fearing God"* (Colossians 3:22) because *"he that is of a merry heart hath a continual feast"* (Proverbs 15:15). Proverbs 17:22 says, *"A merry heart doeth good like a medicine."* Let's have a rejoicing heart like Hannah in I Samuel 2:1, *"My heart rejoiceth in the Lord"* and make the decision that we are going to keep a pure heart and to stay free from distractions that try to make us unclean before the Lord. Let us repeat David's prayer in Psalms 57:7, *"My heart is fixed, O God, my heart is fixed: I will sing and give praise."* Strive, fight, and do whatever it takes to keep your heart pure. Nothing is worth getting off that place of peace. Keep your heart pure and you shall see God.

"The Elder Shall Serve The Younger"
Romans 9:12

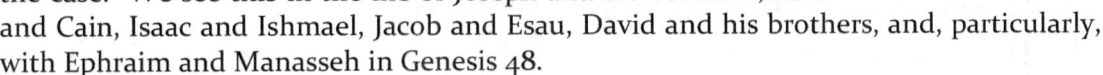

The Scriptures reveal a tremendous truth, how that by God's choice, in many cases, the youngest shall always rise above those who are the eldest, as Romans 9:12 states, *"The elder shall serve the younger."*

DAY 191

This is an unusual and enlightening truth. You would think that the firstborn or the eldest would be the one that God would shine His blessing on, but, over and over again, we see this is not the case. We see this in the life of Joseph and his brothers, Abel and Cain, Isaac and Ishmael, Jacob and Esau, David and his brothers, and, particularly, with Ephraim and Manasseh in Genesis 48.

Manasseh was the oldest, and Joseph wanted the blessing from his father to come upon this oldest son of his. However, the father placed the right hand, which is the right hand of blessing, upon the younger, Ephraim. The Bible says:

> *"¹⁷And when Joseph saw that his father laid his right hand upon the head of Ephraim, it displeased him: and he held up his father's hand, to remove it from Ephraim's head unto Manasseh's head. ¹⁸And Joseph said unto his father, Not so, my father: for this is the firstborn; put thy right hand upon his head. ¹⁹And his father refused, and said, I know it, my son, I know it: he also shall become a people, and he also shall be great: but truly his younger brother shall be greater than he"* (Genesis 48:17-19).

God chose Ephraim rather than the firstborn, Manasseh. There is a reason for this. It says in Job, *"Days should speak, and multitude of years should teach wisdom."* You would think that being older would make you wiser. He goes on to say, *"But there is a spirit in man: and the inspiration of the Almighty giveth them understanding. Great men are not always wise: neither do the aged understand judgment"* (Job 32:7-9). But being the elder doesn't always make you wiser.

For example, consider the response of the elder son in the parable of the prodigal son in Luke 15. In the end, it was the elder son who was full of pride and bitter towards the prodigal son and would not participate. The younger son, however, learned humility despite going through many more things. In the end, it seemed that the hand of God, the choice of God, was upon the younger son.

Paul said in I Timothy 4:12 *"Let no man despise thy youth."* You may be the younger, the one that nobody is putting their eyes upon, except the Lord. However, he declares very clearly, *"The elder shall serve the younger"* (Romans 9:12).

"Go Ye After It"
Joshua 3:3

DAY 192

As the children of Israel were getting ready to pass over the Jordan into the Promised Land, Joshua commanded the people, saying *"When ye see the ark of the covenant of the Lord your God, and the priests the Levites bearing it, then ye shall remove from your place, and go after it"* (Joshua 3:3). The Ark of the Covenant in Scripture is a type of the manifest presence of God and His glory. Wherever the ark was, God was. When David said *"How shall I bring the ark of God home to me?"* what he was saying was, "how shall I bring the manifest presence of God home to me?"

Do you see the manifest presence of God in your life? Do you know it? Do you know the difference between the anointing and charisma or talent? Do you know the difference between the gift of God and talent? There is such a difference, and in this charismatic world in which we live, there is much confusion regarding the two.

Joshua first said in the Scripture *"When ye see the ark of the covenant."* This tells us that it is necessary for you and me to see the manifest presence of God. You and I should be in places where God's glory falls regularly and where God's glory is at home.

Next the Scripture says *"and the priests the Levites bearing it."* This tells us that only the priests were allowed to carry it. In other words, in order for people to see the glory of God, there needs to be men and women of God that can carry the manifest presence of God upon them. And when we see this then we know that God is about to move. God is about to take us in to your promised land, to our inheritance.

Notice the commanding instruction that comes next in this passage, *"then..."* Only then (when you see them bearing it) *"...ye shall remove from your place, and go after it."* It is at that time when we see the glory of God and anointing being carried by those who have paid the price that we leave the place where we are and go after it.

Zechariah 2:8 tells us *"After the glory hath he sent me."* We are to go after it (not them, but it). In other words, we are not to follow men blindly or exalt them beyond measure, but to follow the glory because in following the glory, we are following God Himself.

Are you going after the glory today? Are you, as in Philippians 3:14, pressing *"toward the mark for the prize of the high calling of God?"* Have you said like David did in Psalms 27:4, *"One thing have I desired of the Lord, that will I seek after; that I may dwell in the house of the Lord all the days of my life, to behold the beauty* (or glory) *of the Lord."* Let this be our testimony; that not only have we seen the manifest presence of God, the ark of the Lord, and are in contact with ministers and brethren who carry the anointing, but that we are going after it. Go after the glory with everything that's in you today. Rise up and go after it!

"Be Of Good Cheer"
Matthew 9:2

DAY 193

In Matthew 9:2, the Bible says, *"And, behold, they brought to him a man sick of the palsy, lying on a bed: and Jesus seeing their faith said unto the sick of the palsy; Son, be of good cheer; thy sins be forgiven thee."* This man was brought sick of the palsy, lying on a bed. He couldn't move on his own. To us today, this represents being in a slothful state. Jesus' response to him was, *"Son, be of good cheer; thy sins be forgiven thee."* Many times, our physical ailments are derived from a deep-rooted spiritual problem, but the Lord who is in the midst of us, will help us.

He said to him, "Be of good cheer." The word *"cheer"* in the Greek means "to have courage, to be of good comfort, to have confidence, to be in fine spirits, or to be merry." Paul said in the book of Acts, *"I think myself happy"* (Acts 26:2). This is not mind over matter, but simply walking in a divine principle. In John 16:33, Jesus said, *"In the world ye shall have tribulation: but be of good cheer; I have overcome the world."* No matter where you are or what the situation may be, He is right behind you. He's there to say to you, "Be of good cheer."

In Mark 6, when the disciples were in the midst of the sea, toiling and rowing, trying to save their ship, Jesus came walking on the water toward them in the fourth watch of the night. When they saw Him approaching, they thought He was a spirit. Jesus then said to them, *"Be of good cheer: it is I; be not afraid"* (Mark 6:50). In other words, have courage. Have confidence. Speak to yourself. Be at peace.

The Bible says in Ecclesiastes 11, *"Rejoice, O young man, in thy youth; and let thy heart cheer thee in the days of thy youth"* (Ecclesiastes 11:9). God wants you to be happy; He wants you to have confidence and be of good comfort. When God was speaking to Paul in Acts 23, when Paul really needed a visitation from the Lord, it says, *"And the night following the Lord stood by him, and said, Be of good cheer, Paul: for as thou hast testified of me in Jerusalem, so must thou bear witness also at Rome"* (Acts 23:11).

Be of good cheer. So many times, we need a word from God. It says in the book of Proverbs, *"Heaviness in the heart of man maketh it stoop: but a good word maketh it glad"* (Proverbs 12:25). Time and time again, we simply need a good word to give us courage and good comfort and to cause us to have confidence.

The Word of the Lord to you today is to be of good cheer. Be in fine spirits. Be merry. Have courage. If you hear that still, small voice and become quiet enough, you will hear encouragement flowing to you from the throne of God.

"Wilt Thou Not Revive Us"
Psalms 85:6

DAY 194

The Hebrew words for *"revive, revived and reviving"* mean "live, to quicken literally or figuratively, to recover, to restore to life, to repair, to nourish up." Another Greek word used for "revive" means "preservation of life, sustenance to recover yourself" or in other words "to recover your life, to live again or to be alive again".

Here in Psalms 85:6, we see this principal, *"Wilt thou not revive us again: that thy people may rejoice in thee?"* I want you to know from my heart I believe that if someone is in need of reviving, this means they are dead either physically, soulishly or spiritually. The word *"revive"* itself gives the impression of having to activate or set something back into motion. It means, "To restore to life or consciousness, to bring back, to renew, and to return to life." This implies that only that which is dead needs to be revived.

In Christianity we hear the term *"revival"* used often to express a series of meetings at a church or a religious gathering. It doesn't seem clear to anyone that for this to happen the church or people had to have been in a state of death. We will see what the Scriptures say about this. If we find ourselves in need of revival, perhaps we will have discovered the way back to life. We will also learn how to stay in a vibrant state of well-being: spirit, soul and body. Therefore we will no longer need to be revived because we are staying and living in God's constant stream of life.

In view of the frequent modern use of the term revive and revival, it is worthy of notice that Paul addressed Timothy in II Timothy 1:6 saying, *"Wherefore I put thee in remembrance that thou stir up the gift of God, which is in thee."* Perhaps Timothy, like us, had let his passion, zeal and heart for God and God's purposes slip away. Like too many, he had fallen into a slothful sleep that leads to a spiritual death.

May God show us through His holy Word not only what this term, *"revival"* means, but also reveal to us the way to stay alive, fresh and vibrant in Him. *"Wilt thou not revive us again: that thy people may rejoice in thee?"* To say this in other words, the people aren't rejoicing in Him, so they need to be revived to do it. The answer to this is simple; we are the circumcision that worships God in the spirit. Paul says in Philippians 4:4, *"Rejoice in the Lord always: and again I say, Rejoice."* The Bible is clear that we are to be praising God at all times, as it states in Psalms 34:1, *"I will bless the Lord at all times his praise shall continually be in my mouth."*

It says in Habakkuk 3:2, *"O Lord, I have heard thy speech, and was afraid: O Lord, revive thy work in the midst of the years, in the midst of the years make known; in wrath remember mercy."* Let's ask the Lord today to revive the work in the midst of the years. Maybe you are old in the Lord, and maybe you have just let things slip. May you be quickened, revived, made alive again, recovered and restored to life by the Spirit of God today. Isaiah 57:15 says, *"For thus saith the high and lofty One that inhabiteth eternity, whose name is Holy; I dwell in the high and holy place, with him also that is of a contrite and humble spirit, to revive the spirit of the humble, and to revive the heart of the contrite ones."* God wants to revive you today; He wants to awake you out of your slumber. Let Him recover your life now. He will revive you again so that you may rejoice in Him.

"O Lord, Thou Hast Deceived Me"
Jeremiah 20:7

DAY 195

God, many times in Scripture, uses craftiness to deal with His people. He did this to prove them, or to simply see what they would do. It was never done with malice. Our God is righteous, just, and pure; His motives are always right. However, in dealing with mankind, many times He must do things that they don't understand. Many times He would ask a question just to see how His disciples would answer. Or He would hide and use testing and trials to prove them.

We find in Jeremiah 20:7, *"O Lord, thou hast deceived me, and I was deceived: thou art stronger than I, and hast prevailed: I am in derision daily, every one mocketh me."* The word *"deceived"* can simply be translated as "fooled". So, the scripture would read, *"O Lord, thou hast fooled me, and I was fooled."* How many times in my life has God asked me to do something, when He really intended me to do another? Really, He was just checking my life out.

So many details and instances in our lives seem to be a paradox. It's just like when those ten lepers came to Jesus in Luke 17. He told them after healing them to go to the priests. When the Samaritan came back to give glory to God for his healing, Jesus said in verse 17, *"Where are the nine?"* Jesus never really intended for the other nine to go to the priests. He wanted them to come and give him glory. He left the choice up to them.

Many times the choice is left up to us. Like in Joshua 5:13-15, Joshua saw a man with a sword drawn in his hand and went to him saying, *"Art thou for us, or for our adversaries?"* The man's answer was neither. The Lord will do this to see our reaction. In Luke 24, Jesus disguised himself on the road to Emmaus and walked with His two disciples for a long time. They never knew it was Him. Then He pretended like He was going to go further. Could it be true that God would deceive or fool us like this? Yes, because there was purpose behind everything He was doing. Never forget that *"all things work together for good, for those who are called according to his purpose"* (Romans 8:28).

God knows what He's doing. In Matthew 15, Jesus tested the woman of Canaan's faith by initially ignoring, rejecting, and not healing her. However, eventually He said in verse 28, *"O woman, great is thy faith: be it unto thee even as thou wilt."* He had even called her a dog in verse 26. He wanted her to press through with faith and belief. In John 20, Jesus appeared to Mary at the tomb and she didn't know it Him either. Also, in John 21, Jesus was unknown to His disciples as He stood there on the shoreline. Lastly, in I Samuel 16:1-6, the Lord speaks to Samuel to go and anoint David as king, but Samuel is afraid to go because Saul might find out. So God tells Samuel to go and make a sacrifice to the Lord at Jesse's house instead. That was not His original intent, but God has His ways and means. So, He sometimes fools us for a greater purpose and a greater end. Perhaps today you find yourself in a situation like one of these. Remember this word during these times and know that God is working all things for good. As Hosea says, *"then shall we know if we follow on to know the Lord."* His ways are truly higher than ours.

"Receive Not The Grace Of God In Vain"
II Corinthians 6:1

Day 196

Here in II Corinthians 6:1 Paul says, *"We then, as workers together with him, beseech you also that ye receive not the grace of God in vain."* This is one of the great truths of Scripture. So many times we frustrate and hinder the grace of God in our lives, because we've been taught a law orientated Gospel. Many people live under condemnation and guilt, and constantly put themselves back under dos and don'ts from which Jesus has already delivered them.

God has given His grace freely to you. *"For by grace are ye saved through faith; and that not of yourselves: it is the gift of God"* (Ephesians 2:8). His grace is the gift of God. It isn't a license to sin. Paul said *"God forbid"* (Romans 6:15) in that regard. On the other hand, Paul tells Titus that grace teaches us to *"deny ungodliness and worldly lusts"* (Titus 2:12). Therefore, he tells Timothy to *"be strong in the grace that is in Christ Jesus"* (II Timothy 2:1).

In Paul's writing to the Hebrews he says *"it is a good thing that the heart be established with grace; not with meats"* (Hebrews 13:9). Meats are talking about the law. We need to be established in grace, not the law. *"For Christ is the end of the law"* (Romans 10:4). When we try to be put back under the law we become like the Galatians who Paul wrote to in Galatians 2:21, *"I do not frustrate the grace of God: for if righteousness come by the law, then Christ is dead in vain."* You and I don't need to frustrate God's grace. That's His divine enablement and unmerited favor. It's our answer. It will see us through. It will get us to where we need to be.

In Galatians 5:4 he says, *"Christ is become of no effect unto you, whosoever of you are justified by the law; ye are fallen from grace."* *"Fallen from grace"* simply means we've stopped allowing the grace of God to have an effect in our lives. It certainly doesn't mean we've lost our salvation. It just means we've frustrated the grace of God. We understand then in Galatians when Paul said:

> *"O foolish Galatians, who hath bewitched you, that ye should not obey the truth, before whose eyes Jesus Christ hath been evidently set forth, crucified among you? ² This only would I learn of you, Received ye the Spirit by the works of the law, or by the hearing of faith? ³ Are ye so foolish? having begun in the Spirit, are ye now made perfect by the flesh?"* (Gal. 3:3)

Your flesh couldn't get the job done before, and it will not get the job done now. We need to understand as James 4:6 says, *"But he giveth more grace."* We're also to *"grow in grace, and in the knowledge of our Lord and Saviour Jesus Christ"* (II Peter 3:18).

So today, *"receive not the grace of God in vain"*. Do not frustrate the grace of God. Don't fall from grace. Embrace grace. Let your heart be *"...established with grace; not with meats"* and watch His divine enablement help you become an overcomer.

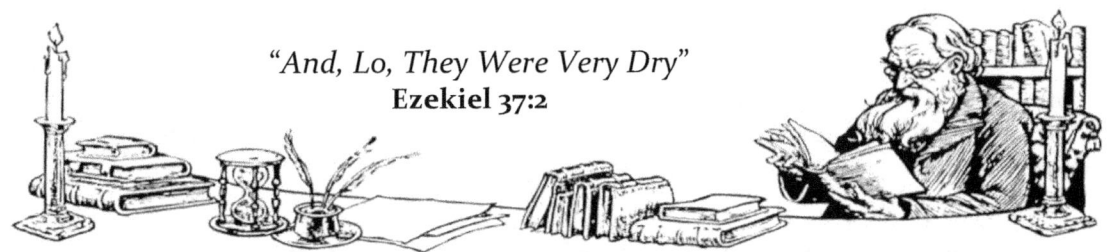

"And, Lo, They Were Very Dry"
Ezekiel 37:2

DAY 197

In this great passage about the valley of dry bones, we find some powerful truths related to the body of Christ and where they are at right now. As a pastor now since 1977, I have travelled all over the world and have ministered to almost every kind of situation known to man and have seen the state of the body of Christ in an intimate way. Well, Ezekiel 37 paints a great picture for us of the body of Christ.

In Ezekiel 37, the hand of the Lord comes upon Ezekiel, and sets him down in the midst of the valley full of bones. As He caused him to pass by them, the Bible says *"there were very many in the open valley; and, lo, they were very dry"* (Ezekiel 37:2). It's bad enough to be in a valley, but to be in an open valley, where everybody can see you, is even worse. It seems like the body of Christ is quite open in front of the world with all the television programs and T.V. ministries. We're open, showing all of our weaknesses and frailties, and the confusion and bickering and arguing. So much of what is being said is not of the Lord, and the lifestyles the world sees of us do not match up with the true lifestyle of the Bible.

This description in Ezekiel 37 describes the body of Christ in many ways today. We're in a valley and we are bones. These bones will become an exceeding great army eventually (Ezekiel 37:10), and that is the word of the Lord to us, but it is not until that prophetic wind of the Holy Ghost blows over the body of Christ and restores these bones. The Lord asks Ezekiel *"Can these bones live"* (Ezekiel 37:3)? The answer is yes; the truth is they will live again as the Holy Spirit moves mightily upon the earth. But at this point, they're simply dry.

This intrigued me many years ago, as I was searching the Scriptures and looked up the Hebrew word for *"dry."* I found it had three distinct meanings: "ashamed, confused, and disappointed." Isn't that the truth? How many Christians do you know that are one of these three things?

Because of a lack of teaching on grace, righteousness, and freedom from condemnation, so many people in the body of Christ walk around ashamed. They are ashamed of the sin in their lives, their weaknesses, and their inability to walk with God the way they should. What they don't realize is the Bible is full of admonitions that *"my people shall never be ashamed"* (Joel 2:26-27). We don't have to be ashamed, because we are *"made the righteousness of God in him"* (II Corinthians 5:21). He's committed to working in our lives to get us to the place where we will never be ashamed and will *"forget the shame of [our] youth"* (Isaiah 54:4) and one day walk free from *"the sin which doth so easily beset us"* (Hebrews 12:1).

"Dry" also means "confusion." How many people do you know who are confused? People are confused by leadership, bad teaching, by simply following the crowd, by not sitting under the Word of God and sound doctrine. Confusion is rampant, but it doesn't need to be. Habakkuk 2:2 says, *"And the Lord answered me, and said, Write the*

vision, and make it plain upon tables, that he may run that readeth it." The answer to confusion is sound doctrine, sound Bible teaching, sitting at Jesus' feet and hearing His Word as Mary did (Luke 10:39). People are confused because they are not taught the Word of God.

Ephesians tells us that we should *"be no more children, tossed to and fro, and carried about with every wind of doctrine, by the sleight of men"* (Ephesians 4:14). All confusion would end if God's people would do as they did in Acts 2. As soon as they were saved, water baptized, and received the baptism of the Holy Spirit; they began to sit under apostolic doctrine on a daily basis. It's interesting that Jesus taught the Bible daily; the disciples taught the Bible daily; Paul taught the Bible daily. Acts 19:9 says that Paul *"disputed daily in the school of one Tyrannus"* for two years. We know that in the Old Testament, there was a morning and an evening sacrifice. Yet, nowadays, most Christians go to church twice a week. God wants us to meet with Him every day.

Lastly, the word *"dry"* also means "disappointed." How many people have been disappointed? People are disappointed in themselves, in the body of Christ, and by leadership. They've had a bad experience with a pastor or a brother or sister and can't get over it and forgive. This is what is causing them to be dry bones in an open valley. God, help us. We don't need to be this way. If we would just look to Jesus, our disappointment would leave, and there would be no more disappointment. Remember in the Old Testament, it says in I Samuel:

> *"¹David therefore departed thence, and escaped to the cave Adullam: and when his brethren and all his father's house heard it, they went down thither to him. ²And every one that was in distress, and every one that was in debt, and every one that was discontented, gathered themselves unto him; and he became a captain over them: and there were with him about four hundred men"* (I Samuel 22:1-2).

I believe this is the answer. David here is a type of Jesus, and we need to go down to Him. Instead of being ashamed, confused, and disappointed, or in debt and discontented, we need to gather ourselves unto Him. In Ephesians, it says, *"That in the dispensation of the fullness of times he might gather together in one all things in Christ"* (Ephesians 1:10). We need to come and gather to the Lord. And as we do, He will become a captain over us, and we will then become, as these men did, one of the mightiest armies ever known on the face of the earth. David's mighty men became the greatest force really ever known in warfare.

So, here we are. Maybe you're ashamed. Maybe you're confused or disappointed. Maybe you're in debt, discontented, or in distress; and you're in an open valley, and everybody sees it. Go to Jesus today. You may have to go down and humble yourself to go to Him, but go down and gather yourself to Him. Because there are millions of others just like you, who are all those things, and they found their way to Jesus. And as they did, He became a captain over them. And as it says in Ezekiel, when he *"prophesied as he commanded me, and the breath came into them, and they lived, and stood up upon their feet, an exceeding great army"* (Ezekiel 37:10), God will breathe into you, breathe upon you, and you will live. And eventually, you're going to stand upon your own feet and be part an exceeding great army!

"Cease Ye From Man"
Isaiah 2:22

Day 198

One of the first things we learn as a believer is that once we come out of the world and into the Kingdom of God, God calls us *"out of darkness into his marvellous light"* (I Peter 2:9). We also realize that apart from Him, we can do nothing. Paul said in Romans 7:18, *"For I know that in me (that is, in my flesh,) dwelleth no good thing."* David said in Psalms 39:5, *"every man at his best state is altogether vanity"* and in Psalms 51:5, *"Behold, I was shapen in iniquity; and in sin did my mother conceive me."* Jesus said in Matthew 26:41, *"the spirit indeed is willing, but the flesh is weak."*

So we understand then that our flesh is vain and weak. We are born into sin and therefore we need to deal with our humanity. Therefore, Isaiah tells us to *"cease ye from man"* (Isaiah 2:22). We need to cease from all of the carnal and Adamic nature and know that the Scripture declares, *"Knowing this, that our old man is crucified with him, that the body of sin might be destroyed, that henceforth we should not serve sin. ⁷For he that is dead is freed from sin"* (Romans 6:6-7).

If you and I are dead, we are free from sin. This is why the Bible tells us to *"mortify the deeds of the body"* (Romans 8:13). Romans 6:11 tells us to *"reckon ye also yourselves to be dead indeed unto sin, but alive unto God through Jesus Christ our Lord."* You and I need to reckon ourselves dead. We need to cease from man. Why? Because Jesus said, *"The flesh profiteth nothing"* (John 6:63). There is nothing about it that is worth anything. Romans 8:7 says, *"The carnal mind is enmity against God."*

We must understand that God is looking for us to cease from that carnal nature of sin in all of us that tries to rise and control our lives. Paul calls it the *"motions of sins"* that still live in us (Romans 7:5). Even though we've been made free from sin and Jesus lives in our spirit, we all know that there are still parts of our soul that are inhabited by our canal nature.

This is why we are in the sanctification process being changed into His image day by day. The Word of God renews our minds and cleanses these areas in our soul so that we might say like Paul in Galatians 2:20, *"I am crucified with Christ: nevertheless I live; yet not I, but Christ liveth in me."* We would have ceased from man, ceased from our carnal nature, and ceased from that which has tried to rule and reign other than the Lord Jesus. Ceasing from man means we fully embrace Jesus as Lord in every area of our lives so we can say it is no longer us that live, but Jesus living through us. Let this be our testimony today!

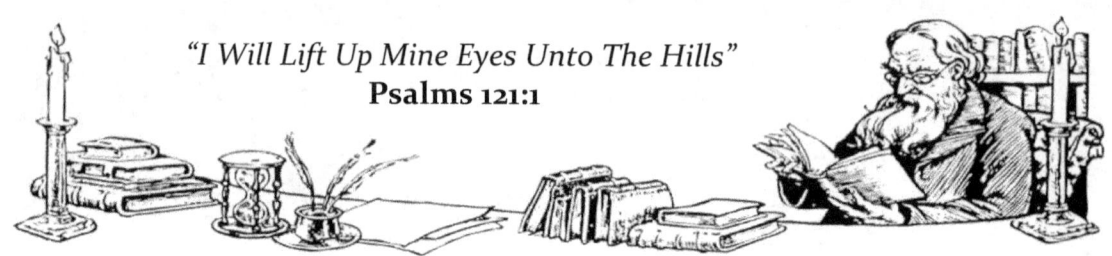

"I Will Lift Up Mine Eyes Unto The Hills"
Psalms 121:1

DAY 199

Here in Psalms 121 it says, *"I will lift up mine eyes unto the hills, from whence cometh my help"* (Psalms 121:1). So many people use this to speak of the natural beauty of the earth and how God has created the mountains and the hills, but most people forget the second verse. It says, *"My help cometh from the Lord, which made heaven and earth"* (Psalms 121:2). My question is: When has a hill ever helped anybody? Hills don't help people; they can't protect us in the sense of stopping the enemy. So, when you read verse 2, you understand what it is saying. He is asking a question in verse 1: From whence cometh my help; does it come from the hills? He answers it in verse 2. Our help comes from the Lord who made the very hills we're talking about.

It says in Jeremiah, *"Truly in vain is salvation hoped for from the hills, and from the multitude of mountains: truly in the Lord our God is the salvation of Israel"* (Jeremiah 3:23). Only in the Lord our God will our salvation come. We cannot expect natural things, even the great, majestic beauty of nature, to help us; only the God of our salvation can come to our aid. Many times when looking to buy a greeting card, I see that verse on the front of cards trying to encourage people. But they don't understand natural things cannot help us. No matter how powerful, majestic, and strong they may be, they can never compare to the salvation of the Lord. We need to stop looking at natural things no matter how great they may seem. Ultimately, they will not work. Salvation comes from the Lord.

Speaking of the Lord Jesus, Proverbs 8 tells us:

> *"²⁴When there were no depths, I was brought forth; when there were no fountains abounding with water. ²⁵Before the mountains were settled, before the hills was I brought forth: ²⁶While as yet he had not made the earth, nor the fields, nor the highest part of the dust of the world. ²⁷When he prepared the heavens, I was there..."* (Proverbs 8:24-27).

Jesus was there before anything was created. And He will be there after all that God has created has melted with a fervent heat. He remains the salvation of the earth. He remains your salvation. Lift up your eyes today, not to the hills, but to the Lord. *"Set your affection on things above, not on things on the earth"* (Colossians 3:2).

"The Least Of All Saints"
Ephesians 3:8

Today we want to look at a glorious truth in the Scriptures. Paul said of himself in Ephesians 3:7-8, *"Whereof I was made a minister, according to the gift of the grace of God given unto...Unto me, who am less than the least of all saints, is this grace given, that I should preach among the Gentiles."*

This was not just pretty pose to Paul, but this was actually what he believed about himself. In I Corinthians 15:9 he says, *"For I am the least of the apostles, that am not meet to be called an apostle, because I persecuted the church of God."* But by the grace of God we are who we are and being the *"least"*, which in the Greek literally means "far less, very little, short in size, amount or dignity" is what we should believe about ourselves.

I Corinthians 1:26 says to us, *"For ye see your calling, brethren, how that not many wise men after the flesh, not many mighty, not many noble, are called."* Many times it's the little things, the least of things that are chosen by God. It seems that He always chose, the younger or youngest of the brothers, over the first born. God has a passion for the least.

Look how many people in the Bible demonstrate this. Gideon in Judges 3:2 speaks of himself as the least in his father's house. Saul in I Samuel 9:21 said, *"Am not I a Benjamite, of the smallest of the tribes of Israel? and my family the least of all the families of the tribe of Benjamin? wherefore then speakest thou so to me?"* Moses basically told the Lord He couldn't speak (Exodus 4:10). Jeremiah said the same thing, "Why are you calling me" (Jeremiah 1:6)? Gideon later said "Who, me" (Judges 6:15)? I could say the same thing. But here's the glorious truth. By the grace of God, we are who we are.

Luke 16:10 tells us, *"He that is faithful in that which is least is faithful also in much: and he that is unjust in the least is unjust also in much."* You and I simply need to be faithful in where we are and God will do the rest. Little is much when God is in it. Recall the parable of the mustard seed in Matthew 13:32, *"Which indeed is the least of all seeds: but when it is grown, it is the greatest among herbs, and becometh a tree."* God takes that little thing, that least of all things, and uses it for His glory.

You have to believe and know this about yourself. For Paul, and even for me, this is not a joke. I know I am the least; I know I am nothing apart from the grace of God. But think of what God does with the least. It says in Matthew 2:6 about the birth of Jesus, *"And thou Bethlehem, in the land of Juda, art not the least among the princes of Juda: for out of thee shall come a Governor, that shall rule my people Israel."* Out of the least, came the Governor, the Savior. Remember, little is much when God is in it.

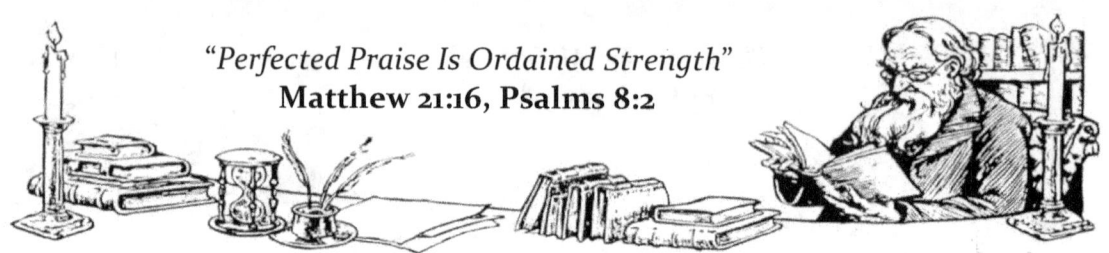

"Perfected Praise Is Ordained Strength"
Matthew 21:16, Psalms 8:2

Day 201

Here in Matthew 21, Jesus gives us one of the greatest tools to defeat Satan and to come out of the valleys, dealings of God, and the problems we have in our lives. He says here, "*Yea; have ye never read, Out of the mouth of babes and sucklings thou hast perfected praise?*" (Matthew 21:16). As we read this, remember that Jesus is referring to the Scripture in Psalms that declares, "*Out of the mouth of babes and sucklings hast thou ordained strength because of thine enemies, that thou mightest still the enemy and the avenger*" (Psalms 8:2). There are hundreds and hundreds of commentaries and theological books written to help us understand the Scriptures, but nothing is better than Jesus' interpretation of what a Scripture means.

When we see these two Scriptures side by side, Jesus defines for us what the Old Testament referred to as "*ordained strength*" as "*perfected praise.*" Perfected praise is ordained strength. Who knew that worshipping and praising God brings us the victory over Satan and his minions? Devils have to bow and flee as we begin to worship and glorify God. This is why we praise God, "*that thou mightest still the enemy and the avenger.*" Jehoshaphat sent the tribe of Judah (Judah means "praise) before the army, because their praise caused the enemy to flee (II Chronicles 20:21-22).

We can silence and quiet our enemies as we begin to simply worship and praise God. I know sometimes it is difficult to worship when we are going through something. That's why we are admonished to offer up "*the sacrifice of praise to God continually, that is, the fruit of our lips giving thanks to his name*" (Hebrews 13:15).

It is important to remember that the Scriptures declare, "*But thou art holy, O thou that inhabitest the praises of Israel*" (Psalms 22:3). As we begin to praise God, His presence falls and manifests itself, and He inhabits us. The enemy then, who cannot stand the presence of God, has to flee. Praise then becomes "*ordained strength*" for us. God tells us to use praise to silence the enemy.

So let's say, as David says in Psalms 34:1, "*I will bless the Lord at all times: his praise shall continually be in my mouth.*" Let us lift up "*holy hands, without wrath and doubting*" (I Timothy 2:8). Perfected praise is ordained strength.

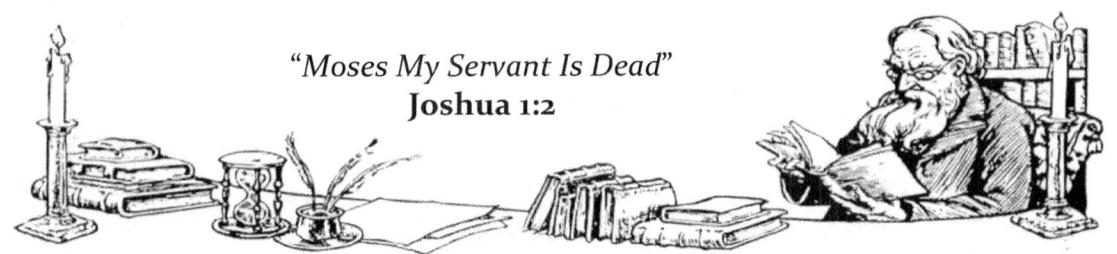

"Moses My Servant Is Dead"
Joshua 1:2

DAY 202

Here in this passage of Scripture lies a tremendous revelation that you and I cannot allow men or even the mere memory of men to hold us back. We cannot continue to live in another man's revelation. We must forge our own revelation in Jesus after we've sat under tutors and governors when the time appointed for us has come. Joshua 1:1-2 says, *"Now after the death of Moses the servant of the Lord it came to pass, that the Lord spake unto Joshua the son of Nun, Moses' minister, saying, ²Moses my servant is dead; now therefore arise, go over this Jordan, thou, and all this people, unto the land which I do give to them, even to the children of Israel."*

God had to speak to Joshua because Joshua had been serving Moses for forty years. Some brethren think that it's enough to spend just two years under a father ministry, but it isn't. We're not creating an assembly line here. We're actually bringing forth quality disciples to do the will of God. If it takes forty years for that to happen, then so be it.

Looking into Joshua's perspective, after forty years of standing under the shadow of Moses, you can only imagine how intimidating it was for him to step forward. Therefore, God had to remind him, *"Moses my servant is dead. Now therefore arise"* In other words, it is time for your leadership to come forth.

In Isaiah 6:1, it says, *"In the year that king Uzziah died I saw also the Lord sitting upon a throne, high and lifted up, and his train filled the temple."* So many times the memories of men or great ministries have passed on without leaving any inheritance or sons (in the Lord), to carry on the ministry. But, *"Moses is dead"* and in the year king Uzziah died, *"I saw the Lord high and lifted up, and I heard the voice of the Lord."*

This is what God wants for us: not to be as Samuel was when God called him many times and he thought it was the voice of Eli the high priest. Samuel kept going back and forth from the voice of God to the voice of Eli, until finally even back-slidden Eli said, "I think the Lord is calling you." We need to stop living in another man's revelation and begin to rise up and recognize that Moses is dead. What was in the past was glorious and we thank God for Moses and for anything that anyone has ever done for us in the past that helped bring us forth in God, but we cannot live in the past. God says in Isaiah 43:19. *"Behold, I will do a new thing."* We have to move on. The only way that God's people are going to cross over into the Promised Land is in their recognizing that it's their time to come forth.

God wants to manifest His glory in your life and in my life as we grow from grace to grace, faith to faith, glory to glory, strength to strength and vessel to vessel. And our growth will continue to go on until we reach the place where we've been approved unto God as a workman that needs not to be ashamed, a man of God thoroughly furnished unto all good works, ready to come forth in our own leadership and revelation. The Word of the Lord to you today is, *"Moses is dead; now therefore arise."*

"Cease From Strife"
Proverbs 20:3

DAY 203

Solomon declares in Proverbs 20:3, *"It is an honour for a man to cease from strife."* The Hebrew word for *"strife"* means "a contest, a quarrel, fighting, or discord." The Bible says, *"Only by pride cometh contention"* (Proverbs 13:10). Strife is something with which none of us want to deal. Galatians 5 tells us that strife is a work of the flesh. We want to do our best to stay away from strife; it's an honor to cease from it. God can help us, as we allow the Holy Spirit to control our lives and as we guard our mouths.

Proverbs 17:14 says, *"The beginning of strife is as when one letteth out water: therefore leave off contention, before it be meddled with."* What happens is water begins to come out of a faucet slowly, and then it begins to come faster. Strife begins with just a few words that come off as offensive, and then it proceeds with more words. Pride and contention come in *"where envying and strife is, there is confusion and every evil work"* (James 3:16). Many of us have a good heart and don't want to enter into strife. But we're drawn into it by the enemy, because he knows the buttons to push in our lives. Do not allow him to do this, but *"rule thou in the midst of thine enemies"* (Psalms 110:2).

It says in Philippians 2:3, *"Let nothing be done through strife or vainglory."* There's no need for pride to live in our lives; we don't need to prove anything. Let nothing be done through strife. The Bible says, *"He that is of a proud heart stirreth up strife"* (Proverbs 28:25). In Proverbs 29:22, it says, *"An angry man stirreth up strife."* It also says in the book of Proverbs 16:28, *"A froward man soweth strife."* So, we understand then that strife comes from anger, pride, and wickedness. God doesn't want this in our lives. When Paul was writing to the Corinthians, he said that they were a people full of strife and contention (II Corinthians 12:20). We don't want the man of God to find us that way. There's no reason for that.

The Bible is very clear when it says, *"For ye are yet carnal: for whereas there is among you envying, and strife, and divisions, are ye not carnal, and walk as men?"* (I Corinthians 3:3). Let it not be said of us that there's envying and strife among us. James says:

> *"But if ye have bitter envying and strife in your hearts, glory not* ¹⁶*For where envying and strife is, there is confusion and every evil work"* (James 3:14-16).

Bitter envying and strife is earthly, or of the fleshly carnal nature. And it comes from the devil. The Greek word *"strife"* there indicates selfishness. So, wherever we find pride, selfishness, or anger, we're going to operate in strife. God, help us, because then confusion and every evil work will be released in our lives. It is an honor to cease from strife. Let's decide today that we will cease from strife and honor our precious Savior.

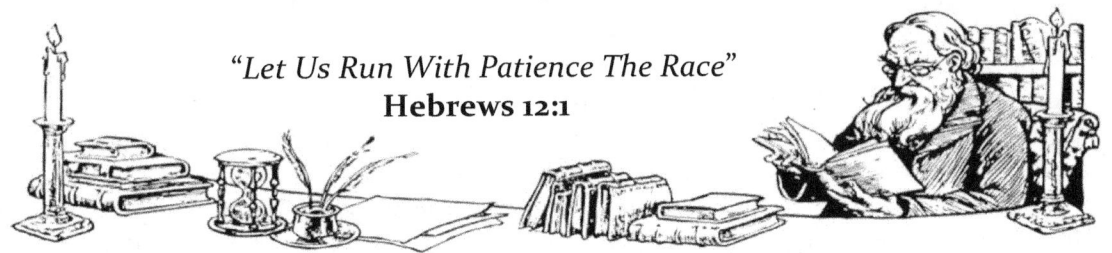

"Let Us Run With Patience The Race"
Hebrews 12:1

DAY 204

The Scripture declares here that every believer is running in a race. I marvel in that over forty-three years of being a Christian, there are still so many believers who have no idea that we are in a race and that we are running for a prize. Most people believe that this prize is heaven, but heaven was obtained for us by the cross of Jesus Christ, by that great uttermost sacrifice once for all as said in Hebrews 10:10 and as elaborated in verse 14, *"For by one offering he hath perfected for ever them that are sanctified."* To understand this race more, let's look at Paul talking about it in I Corinthians 9:24-27:

> *"Know ye not that they which run in a race run all, but one receiveth the prize? So run, that ye may obtain. 25And every man that striveth for the mastery is temperate in all things. Now they do it to obtain a corruptible crown; but we an incorruptible. 26I therefore so run, not as uncertainly; so fight I, not as one that beateth the air: 27But I keep under my body, and bring it into subjection..."*

First of all, we need to know that we are called to run in a race. Every believer after being born again is placed into this heavenly race. This race is called in other places, *"the narrow way"* (Matthew 7:14), *"the highway of holiness"* (Isaiah 35:8), and *"the path of the just"* (Proverbs 4:18), to name a few. Everything in our lives should be secondary to running this race that is before every believer. Hebrews 12:1 exhorts us to *"lay aside every weight, and the sin which doth so easily beset us, and let us run with patience the race that is set before us."* God's race is set before all of us.

What is this race for? Philippians 3:14 says, *"I press toward the mark for the prize of the high calling of God in Christ Jesus."* The Amplified version reads, *"I strain to reach the end of the race."* Are you straining to reach the end of the race today? Did you even know there was a race? Well whether you know it or not, you are in it and there is a prize to be won. The prize is the high calling of God in Christ Jesus. The high calling of God is not heaven, but it is brideship. The prize is knowing Jesus intimately. The Lord told Abraham in Genesis 15:1, *"I am thy shield, and thy exceeding great reward."*

The high calling of God is to have the image of Jesus in your soul. It is to be *"conformed to the image of his Son"* (Romans 8:29). II Corinthians 3:18 says we are to be *"changed into the same image from glory to glory, even as by the Spirit of the Lord."* This is what we are called to. This is the race we are running, every day being changed; every day going through the sanctification process; every day becoming more pure, holy, and more perfect before the Lord our God. For He said, *"Be ye holy; for I am holy"* (I Peter 1:16), and *"Be ye therefore perfect, even as your Father which is in heaven is perfect"* (Matthew 5:48).

So you are running in a race. How are you doing? Are you keeping up? Are you ahead? Are you lagging behind? Or have you stopped running altogether? The Lord wants to encourage you today to keep running; that there is a goal and a prize to obtain at the end of your walk with God. Remember how Paul said to Timothy, "*I have fought a good fight, I have finished my course, I have kept the faith*" (II Timothy 4:7). We want this to be our testimony. We want to finish our course God has set before all of us.

Matthew 7:14 says, "*Because strait is the gate, and narrow is the way, which leadeth unto life, and few there be that find it.*" Few find this abundant life that Jesus came for us to have, the fulfillment to the call of God upon our life. We are running after this.

In Ecclesiastes 9:11 Solomon said, "*I returned, and saw under the sun, that the race is not to the swift, nor the battle to the strong...*" It doesn't matter how fast you are or how strong you are. Psalms 147:10 says the Lord, "*taketh not pleasure in the legs of a man.*" It is not our earthly trying that is going to achieve this purpose. It is surrendering to the Spirit of God and giving ourselves to the Word of God and allowing it to work in our lives to help us fight this good fight of faith. We need to keep pressing on, straining to reach the end of the race for the prize.

For far too many people Ecclesiastes 10:15 is a reality, "*The labour of the foolish wearieth every one of them, because he knoweth not how to go to the city.*" When we don't know where we are going, we labor even harder and it wearies us. God doesn't want this to be the case in our lives. He wants us to run with purpose, run with wisdom, and run allowing the Spirit of God to operate in our lives.

Another translation of I Corinthians 9 says, "*So I run straight to the goal with purpose in every step*", "*So I run with a clear goal ahead of me*", "*I fight to win. I'm not playing around.*" Let this be our testimony and as Peter said in Acts 2:40, "*Save yourselves from this untoward generation.*" Don't be like this generation that is not heading towards anything. "*Untoward*" in the Greek means "warped, winding, perverse, or curved."

Today, don't take the path of least resistance. Stay on the narrow way, straining to reach the end. You have a purpose; you know where we are going. It is the prize of the high calling of God in Christ Jesus, "*so let us run with patience the race that is set before us.*" Determine in your heart today and God's grace will see you through.

"To Him That Overcometh"
Revelation 21:7

DAY 205

Eight times in the New Testament, we find the phrases "to him that overcometh" or "he that overcometh." Eight in the Scriptures is the number for new beginnings. "*Overcometh*" in the Greek simply means, "to subdue, to prevail over, to get the victory over, or to conquer." We are called to be overcomers. If we walk with the Lord faithfully, eventually, this will be what happens to us. After eight times of overcoming, we will become that new creation man with a new beginning to look forward to as true sons of God.

Revelation 21:7 says, "*He that overcometh shall inherit all things; and I will be his God, and he shall be my son.*" The true sons are overcomers. We see this pattern in the book of Revelation. It says in Revelation 2, "*To him that overcometh will I give to eat of the tree of life, which is in the midst of the paradise of God*" (Revelation 2:7). The tree of life is Jesus Himself. He said in John 6, "*Except ye eat the flesh of the Son of man, and drink his blood, ye have no life in you*" (John 6:53). He also said, "*I have meat to eat that ye know not of*" (John 4:32). We're not going to be eating at the marriage supper of the Lamb roast beef and mashed potatoes. We're going to be eating the deep things of God. Overcomers will be able to do this.

It also says in Revelation 2, "*He that overcometh shall not be hurt of the second death*" (Revelation 2:11). We need not fear the judgment of God that's going to come upon the world and the ungodly, because we will have overcome and will have been saved by grace.

In verse 17, it says, "*To him that overcometh will I give to eat of the hidden manna, and will give him a white stone, and in the stone a new name written, which no man knoweth saving he that receiveth it*" (Revelation 2:17). God's going to give them to eat the hidden manna that was in the golden pot. We will know the deep things of God. The white stone represents acquittal, or being justified. In that stone, God's going to give a new name, which no man knows. Name speaks of character. Our character will be different; it will be transformed by the presence of God.

Revelation 12:5 tells us, "*[26]And he that overcometh, and keepeth my works unto the end, to him will I give power over the nations: [27]And he shall rule them with a rod of iron.*" In Revelation 12, it says, "*And she brought forth a man child, who was to rule all nations with a rod of iron*". The overcomers will have power and authority over the nations. Glory to God! We can then preach the gospel freely and go anywhere we want to, taking the kingdom of God with us.

Revelation 3 declares, "*He that overcometh, the same shall be clothed in white raiment; and I will not blot out his name out of the book of life, but I will confess his name before my Father, and before his angels*" (Revelation 3:5). We shall be clothed in white raiment. It says in Revelation 19, "*And to her was granted that she should be arrayed in fine linen, clean and white: for the fine linen is the righteousness of saints*"

(Revelation 19:8). White raiment represents innocence and cleansing. It also says He will not take our name out of the book that He created at the foundation of the world. We will be in that book. Another one in verse 12 reads:

> *"Him that overcometh will I make a pillar in the temple of my God, and he shall go no more out: and I will write upon him the name of my God, and the name of the city of my God, which is new Jerusalem"* (Revelation 3:12).

God is making pillars, strong, foundational people that have the Word of God deep within them and the Spirit of God rolling out of them. They will be pillars in the temple of God; they will hold up the rest of the body. They will go no more out; they will not be leaving anymore, but will stay in the presence of God. He's writing upon them His name. That means they have the mind of Christ (I Corinthians 2:16) and the character of Jesus.

And last of all, in Revelation 3:21, it says, *"To him that overcometh will I grant to sit with me in my throne, even as I also overcame, and am set down with my Father in his throne."* What a glorious truth, that we could sit next to Jesus! Remember James' and John's mother said to Jesus, *"Grant that these my two sons may sit, the one on thy right hand, and the other on the left, in thy kingdom"* (Matthew 20:21). He told her, *"To sit on my right hand, and on my left, is not mine to give, but it shall be given to them for whom it is prepared of my Father"* (Matthew 20:23). Jesus is at the right hand of the Father, and I believe the Holy Spirit is at the left. But there's nobody at the right hand of Jesus. It says in Psalms 45 that the queen in gold of Ophir is at His right hand (Psalms 45:9).

We will sit with Him for all eternity simply because we overcame. Let the Lord help you today to overcome.

"Not Be Offended"
Luke 17:23

DAY 206

Here in Luke 17, we see when John first recognized that Jesus was the Son of God, he sent two of his disciples to follow the Lord. I've always wondered, why didn't John follow Jesus himself? If He really was the Lamb of God, what purpose was there for John's ministry any longer? I believe from that point on we find John backsliding. Ultimately he got his head cut off, after doubting whether Jesus was the one. He was obviously offended. Jesus answered them and said, *"Go your way, and tell John what things ye have seen and heard... ²³And blessed is he, whosoever shall not be offended in me."* (Luke 7:22-23).

The word *"offended"* in the Greek is *"skandalon"* it means *"a scandle, a snare, to give occasion to fall or stumble, to entice to sin, or to offend."* It's a scandal when someone is offended in you. John obviously was offended that Jesus is the son of God.

Jesus said in Matthew 18:6, *"But whoso shall offend one of these little ones which believe in me, it were better for him that a millstone were hanged about his neck, and that he were drowned in the depth of the sea."* God doesn't take pleasure in His little ones being offended. Offense brings a scandal. We must be careful to not let offense destroy us. Blessed is he who's not offended.

We need to keep ourselves from being offended. Because in Proverbs 18:19 it says, *"A brother offended is harder to be won than a strong city."* Paul said himself in II Corinthians 11:29, *"Who is weak, and I am not weak? who is offended, and I burn not?"* I believe offense causes us to burn with pride. It brings us to a place of scandal.

The truth is in James 3:2, it says, *"For in many things we offend all. If any man offends not in word, the same is a perfect man."* Most of the times, we offend people in word, nothing more than that. In John 6:53 when Jesus said, *"Except ye eat the flesh of the Son of man, and drink his blood, ye have no life in you."* Many of His disciples, when they heard this, said in verse 60, *"This is a hard saying; who can hear it?"* The next verse says, *"When Jesus knew in himself that his disciples murmured at it, he said unto them, Doth this offend you?"* We're not supposed to be offended by the Lord and shouldn't allow ourselves to be scandalized, given an occasion to fall, to stumble, or be enticed into sin because of something our brother has done. Blessed is he who's not offended.

Psalms 119:165 says, *"Great peace have they which love thy law: and nothing shall offend them."* II Corinthians 6:3 says, *"Giving no offence in any thing, that the ministry be not blamed."* Philippians 1:10 says, *"that ye may be sincere and without offence till the day of Christ."* Blessed is he, whosoever is not offended.

Does this offend you? Has someone offended you? Has God offended you? Has the Word, which brings offense, offended you? All I know is that Paul said, in Acts 24:16, something that I try to live my life by: *"And herein do I exercise myself, to have always a conscience void of offence toward God, and toward men."* I pray to God that is your testimony.

"Be Of Good Cheer 2"
Matthew 14:27

Day 207

Of all the sayings I've known in my life, one that has always blessed me, and one that I love repeating to other people is *"Be of good cheer."* I don't know why, but it always seems to leave a positive impact on the person I've spoken it to and it resonates back to me too. Today, I want you to be of good cheer and see in the Scriptures that this is the Lord's heart for all His disciples.

The word *"cheer"* in the Greek means "to have courage, to be of good comfort, to be confident, to exercise courage." Whatever you're facing today or whatever dealing you may be in, I want you to have courage. God wants you to be of good comfort and have confidence. So exercise your courage now and go throughout this day knowing that God wants you to be of good cheer. Let's read the story of when Jesus encouraged the disciples:

> *"24But the ship was now in the midst of the sea, tossed with waves: for the wind was contrary. 25And in the fourth watch of the night Jesus went unto them, walking on the sea. 26And when the disciples saw him walking on the sea, they were troubled, saying, It is a spirit; and they cried out for fear. 27But straightway Jesus spake unto them, saying, Be of good cheer; it is I, be not afraid"* (Matthew 14:25-27).

First of all, if Jesus has to walk on the water to get to you, He will, even if the wind is contrary. What are you in today? Are you in the midst of a situation? Is it tossing you around and is the wind blowing against you? Can you see Jesus walking on the water towards you? Listen to His voice as He tells you, *"Be of good cheer; it is I, be not afraid."* Why? Because He is going to stop that storm and He is going to help you walk on that water as Peter did.

In Matthew 9:2, they brought one sick of the palsy to Jesus and paralyzed. Sometimes we find ourselves paralyzed by life's circumstances, but yet Jesus said to that man when He saw their faith, *"Son, be of good cheer; thy sins be forgiven thee."* I tell you today that if you are paralyzed by a situation this is the word of the Lord to you, *"be of good cheer; thy sins be forgiven thee."*

Never forget what Jesus said in John 16:33, *"in the world ye shall have tribulation: but be of good cheer; I have overcome the world."* Tribulation is a fact of life, but in our tribulation Jesus wants us to be of good cheer because He has overcome the world. Because Jesus has overcome the world, you and I can overcome the world. Whatever you are facing today, hear the word of the Lord and let your heart be not afraid but *"Be of good cheer!"*

"The Lord's Message To His People"
Haggai 1:13

"*Then spake Haggai the Lord's messenger in the Lord's message unto the people, saying, I am with you, saith the Lord*" (Haggai 1:13). The Lord's message to you and me today through His Word and Spirit is, "*I am with you, saith the Lord.*" What a glorious testimony! Isaiah 41:10 says, "*Fear thou not; for I am with thee: be not dismayed; for I am thy God: I will strengthen thee; yea, I will help thee; yea, I will uphold thee with the right hand of my righteousness.*" What a precious truth to know, that He is with us!

Psalms 46:7 says, "*The Lord of hosts is with us.*" We need not be afraid because our God is with us. Speaking to Israel in Jeremiah 30:11 the Lord says, "*For I am with thee, saith the Lord, to save thee.*" Even when our enemies come against us, we can rest assured knowing that there is someone with us to help and save us.

In Haggai 2:4 the Lord says, "*Yet now be strong, O Zerubbabel, saith the Lord; and be strong, O Joshua, son of Josedech, the high priest; and be strong, all ye people of the land, saith the Lord, and work: for I am with you.*" We can be strong and go about the work that He has called us to, simply because He is with us.

The Lord of hosts is with you today! Receive this revelation in your heart as Paul did in Acts 18 when he was concerned about appearing before the synagogue, "*Then spake the Lord to Paul in the night by a vision, Be not afraid, but speak, and hold not thy peace: ^{10}For I am with thee, and no man shall set on thee to hurt thee*" (Acts 18:9-10).

What a glorious truth. I can say, in my own life, this has been true. The Lord has been with me in all of my forty plus years as a Christian. In the ups and downs of my life, He has always been there.

In Jeremiah 1:8 when God called Jeremiah, He said, "*Be not afraid of their faces: for I am with thee to deliver thee, saith the Lord.*" We can always be assured of the abiding presence of the Lord being with us to protect, keep, and help us.

In Genesis 26:24 it says, "*And the Lord appeared unto him the same night, and said, I am the God of Abraham thy father: fear not, for I am with thee, and will bless thee.*" This is God speaking to Isaac, carrying on the same thing He told Abraham, "*I am with thee.*" Later the Lord would say this very same thing to His servant Jacob, which is one of my favorite Scriptures, "*And, behold, I am with thee, and will keep thee in all places whither thou goest, and will bring thee again into this land; for I will not leave thee, until I have done that which I have spoken to thee of*" (Genesis 28:15).

Jesus left us these tremendous words at the end of the book of Matthew, "*and, lo, I am with you always, even unto the end of the world*" (Matthew 28:20). This is the message of the Lord to you, "*I am with thee.*" Receive it today!

"Course Of Nature"
James 3:6

Here in this passage, James is talking about the tongue, *"And the tongue is a fire, a world of iniquity: so is the tongue among our members, that it defileth the whole body, and setteth on fire the course of nature"* (James 3:6). This term *"course of nature"* literally means *"wheels of nature."* Some other translations read:

"The wheel of birth"
"The cycle of nature"
"The course of human existence"

The word *"course"* is the Greek word *"genesis."* So the *"wheels of nature"* are the laws of God or the laws of the spirit realm that are set in motion by the things that we do, be it giving, speaking, loving, being cruel and unkind, etc. What we do sets the wheels of nature in motion and they will continue until they come full circle and measure back to us what we've given out as Matthew 7:2 says, *"For with what judgment ye judge, ye shall be judged: and with what measure ye mete, it shall be measured to you again."*

In Genesis 8:22 it says, *"While the earth remaineth, seedtime and harvest, and cold and heat, and summer and winter, and day and night shall not cease."* As long as the earth remains, there will be these seasons in our life, *"seedtime and harvest, and cold and heat, and summer and winter, and day and night."* These all go in a circular fashion.

The words that we speak, be they positive or negative, as we continue to speak them, they continue to travel around the wheel of nature until it comes back around again. For example the words we said initially to bless others, will come around to ultimately bless us. We find this truth in Ecclesiastes 11:1 that says, *"Cast thy bread upon the waters: for thou shalt find it after many days."* As you give and cast your bread upon the water, it will come back to you after many days. The wheels of nature will start operating just as Luke 6:38 says, *"Give, and it shall be given unto you."*

Galatians 6:7 says, *"whatsoever a man soweth, that shall he also reap."* As we sow, speak, bless, are kind, generous, and continue to be so, we cause the wheels of nature to turn in a positive way. On the contrary, if we speak or do bad things, they will eventually come full circle and we will reap according to what we've done. The wheels of nature are always turning and we set them in motion.

Ecclesiastes 3:1 says, *"To every thing there is a season..."* Begin today to set the wheels of nature in motion by sowing blessing, goodness, love, peace, reconciliation, and faith and it will come back to you again as a blessing.

"Praising In The New Testament"
Acts 15:16

DAY 210

A strange and terrible doctrine has come forth in the body of Christ in recent years and it is a doctrine that limits how we are to worship. Some say that musical instruments shouldn't be used in worship in a New Testament church. Even others say clapping isn't allowed in the New Testament, only lifting up of hands. This seems rather silly to me because they try to separate the Old and the New Testament. Many places don't allow dancing. But the Bible says Jesus *"hath made both one"* (Ephesians 2:14). Both Old and New Testaments are the same Word of God. We can receive just as much from the Old Testament as we can from the New Testament. The Old is the New contained. The New is the Old revealed.

Here in Acts 15:16 it reads, *"After this I will return, and will build again the tabernacle of David, which is fallen down; and I will build again the ruins thereof, and I will set it up."* This is a quotation from Amos 9:11, it is a prophetic Scripture about God restoring the tabernacle of David in the last days in the New Testament. Well, if you have any understanding of the tabernacle of David, you know that they worshipped twenty-four hours a day there. They clapped and played every kind of instrument known to man, many of which David himself had created. They worshipped the Lord constantly and the glory of the Lord fell all the time. Therefore, it is ridiculous for anyone to think that we shouldn't be praising and worshipping God in the New Testament.

On the other hand, the New Testament is full of passages that exhort us to worship. In Acts 16:25, the Bible says that *"Paul and Silas... sang praises unto God."* I Peter 2:9 exhorts us, *"that ye should shew forth the praises of him who hath called you out of darkness into his marvelous light."* Hebrew 13:15 says, *"By him therefore let us offer the sacrifice of praise to God continually."* In Revelation 19:5 it says, *"Praise our God, all ye his servants, and ye that fear him, both small and great."*

The tabernacle of David is being restored in this hour; we are to worship God, with instruments, by clapping, by shouting, by dancing, by singing, and by lifting up holy hands, just as David did. Revelation 4:11 says, *"Thou art worthy, O Lord, to receive glory and honour and power: for thou hast created all things, and for thy pleasure they are and were created."* We were created for His pleasure. We were created to worship Him. Psalms 102:18 says, *"This shall be written for the generation to come: and the people which shall be created shall praise the Lord."*

So, today, hear the Word of God. Just as David established his tabernacle in the Old Testament, God is building again the tabernacle of David in these last days. It is the revelation of continual praise and worship, of clapping our hands, dancing, shouting and playing instruments. Hear His voice and worship Him today!

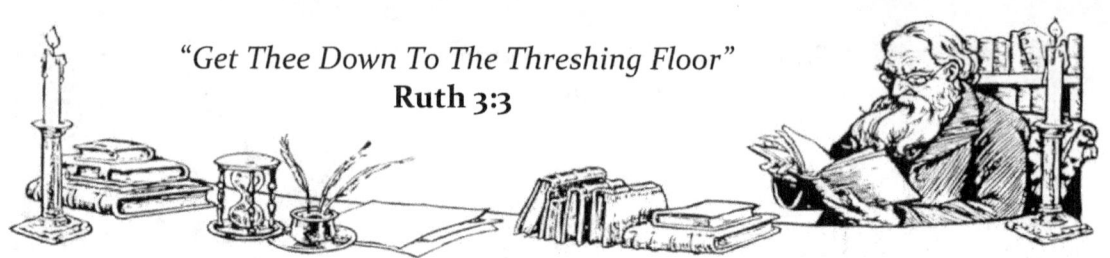

"Get Thee Down To The Threshing Floor"
Ruth 3:3

DAY 211

In the story of Ruth, we find many tremendous principles, especially those related to knowing God intimately. Ruth is a type of the bride of Christ. At one point in her journey, the word of the Lord comes to her to *"get thee down to the floor"* (Ruth 3:3). The *"floor"* here was the *"threshing floor."* As we will see in Scripture this speaks of a place where God wants to intimately deal with the sin in our lives.

We see this more clearly in I Chronicles 21, where David has numbered Israel and God has judged his sin. While Israel is being judged greatly for David's sin, having a great loss of lives, David now must go before the Lord and repent for his sin. Hundreds of thousands of lives have been lost because of David's sin. And the word of the Lord comes to David from Gad:

> *"¹⁸Then the angel of the LORD commanded Gad to say to David, that David should go up, and set up an altar unto the LORD in the threshingfloor of Ornan the Jebusite. …²⁴And king David said to Ornan, Nay; but I will verily buy it for the full price: for I will not take that which is thine for the LORD, nor offer burnt offerings without cost. ²⁵So David gave to Ornan for the place six hundred shekels of gold by weight. ²⁶And David built there an altar unto the LORD, and offered burnt offerings and peace offerings, and called upon the LORD; and he answered him from heaven by fire upon the altar of burnt offering* (I Chronicles 21:18, 24-26).

As we look at this, we see that David is in need of repenting for his great sin. It is obvious that David had an underlying sin of pride and ambition that God needed to root out from him. When we sin, God wants to root the sin out of us because many times, that sin will cost us our own lives and the lives of others, bringing damage to the body of Christ or to our family.

David was greatly sorry for his sin and desperately wanted God not to judge the people, but to judge him. God's answer was for him to get down to the threshing floor and buy it at full price from Ornan and sacrifice to God there. The word *"threshing floor"* in Hebrew means "to make even, an open and void place." The word *"threshing"* literally means "to trample, break and tread down." This is what they did with the wheat; they would break it, trample it, and tread it down to separate the chaff from the wheat. In David's repentance, God was separating the chaff from the wheat in his life, but he had to pay the full price.

God is coming to us and threshing out our lives, breaking up the chaff from the wheat, separating them, so we can have a pure life and a pure offering before the Lord.

It may be that we need to go down to the threshing floor, and there allow God to separate those things in our lives that are not of Him. This is not easy but we must buy it for the full price like David did.

It will cost us, but in the end we will be free from the chaff in our lives. We will be free from the ambitious and selfish things that cause other people problems, bringing hurt and damage to ourselves and others. This is not what we want as Christians. I know it is not what you want, and certainly it is not what God wants. The answer is to get down to the threshing floor and allow God to remove these things once and for all.

In Leviticus 26 it says:

> "^{5}And your threshing shall reach unto the vintage, and the vintage shall reach unto the sowing time: and ye shall eat your bread to the full, and dwell in your land safely. ^{6}And I will give peace in the land, and ye shall lie down, and none shall make you afraid: and I will rid evil beasts out of the land, neither shall the sword go through your land. ^{7}And ye shall chase your enemies, and they shall fall before you by the sword. ^{8}And five of you shall chase an hundred, and an hundred of you shall put ten thousand to flight: and your enemies shall fall before you by the sword. ^{9}For I will have respect unto you, and make you fruitful, and multiply you, and establish my covenant with you" (Leviticus 26:5-9).

This is what happens when you go down to the threshing floor, as God threshes us; it reaches to the great crop, the best fruit, bringing the best in us, and delivering us from the worst in us. Not only will God deliver us and separate that which is not of Him, but He will give us bread to the full, living in the land safely. We will have peace. None will make us afraid. He will rid the evil beasts out of the land which means any demons and tormenting things will be thrown out of our lives because we will have allowed God to thresh us. We will then chase our enemies and they shall fall before us by the sword, or the Word of God.

Get down to the threshing floor today! This is the Word of the Lord to us. Get down to the threshing floor. We must decide to go down and obey the Word of the Lord. Come with a repentant heart and allow the Holy Spirit to take His threshing instruments and tread down, break up, trample, and tear down the chaff in our life, so that all that is left is the pure vintage, the good, great crop which God is looking for to bear His fruit in the earth.

As we do this, we will become the people He wants us to become. He will have respect on us and establish His covenant with us and make us fruitful. No enemy will be able to stand before us. We must be like Ruth, David, and others paying the full price. It costs to go to the threshing floor because that is where God rids us of the evil, the Adamic nature, demons and all the other things that cause us to not walk fully with the Lord Jesus. So, today I admonish you, get you down to the threshing floor and pay the full price!

"Casting Their Garments"
Mark 11:7-8

This is the story of Jesus' triumphant entry into Jerusalem:

"*7And they brought the colt to Jesus, and cast their garments on him; and he sat upon him. 8And many spread their garments in the way: and others cut down branches off the trees, and strawed them in the way. 9And they that went before, and they that followed, cried, saying, Hosanna...*" (Mark 11:7-9).

I would like for us to consider today what it means to "*cast their garments on him...and spread their garments in the way*" for Jesus to walk on. "*Garments*" and our clothing in the Scripture speak of our righteousness and what we've attained to in God. Revelation 19:8 says "*fine linen is the righteousness of saints.*" Psalms 45:13 describes the bride as, "*all glorious within: her clothing is of wrought gold.*" In other words, she has the divine nature of God worked into her character. In Job's greatest time of need Job 1:20 says, "*Then Job arose, and rent his mantle, and shaved his head, and fell down upon the ground, and worshipped.*" By renting his mantle (or robe) and doing these things, Job was saying, "I have no covering, but the Lord. I have no righteousness besides His righteousness."

In Proverbs 6:27, Solomon said, speaking of adultery, "*Can a man take fire in his bosom, and his clothes not be burned?*" In other words, what you've attained to in God will be lost if you commit adultery. Nevertheless, you and I need to be aware that our clothing represents what we've attained to in God.

So when Jesus was on His triumphant entry into Jerusalem, these people cast their garments on Him. In other words, they were saying they have no righteousness apart from Him. II Corinthians 5:21 says, "*For he hath made him to be sin for us, who knew no sin; that we might be made the righteousness of God in him.*" We have been made righteous because of Him and we have no righteousness apart from Him. Then they spread their garments in the way. In other words, they were saying, "Lord Jesus, help me to walk with You. Cause my walk with You to be a good one. Help me attain to higher things in God."

Next it says they "*cut down branches off the trees, and strawed them in the way.*" Trees in the Scripture speak of earth and everything related to the flesh. You and I are to cut down the branches and flesh in our lives. For example Jesus said in Mark 9:43, "*And if thy hand offend thee, cut it off.*" God is not actually asking you to cut off your hand or anything else. But He is saying, "Cut these branches off." As these people cut down these branches they were saying of the sin and flesh in their lives, "We're giving these things to You Lord Jesus. As you pass by us in Your triumphant entry into our lives, the New Jerusalem, cleanse us from these things."

As we cast off our garments upon Him today, we say, "Lord we have no righteousness apart from You. We want to attain the very highest in You. The only way we can do that is cut off our branches, have You pass by, walk upon all these things, and tread upon us." Let Your will be done in our lives today, Jesus. We cast our garments before You, cut off the branches, so that You can be glorified in us!

"Clean Through The Word"
John 15:3

DAY 213

Here in John 15:3, Jesus says, *"Now you are clean through the word which I have spoken unto you."* The amazing truth in Scripture is that God cleanses us through His Word. The Word of God carries with it the sanctifying power and ability to cleanse us, not only from sin and degradation, but also from the carnal nature that so oppresses us. In speaking of the bride of Christ in Ephesians 5:26, Paul says, *"that he might sanctify and cleanse it with the washing of water by the word."* The Word of God is referred to as many different things. One of them is water, honey, bread, and meat. But today, we want to look at the fact that the Word of God is our cleansing agent; it has the ability to wash us clean from sin.

Jesus said in John 8:31-32, *"If ye continue in my word, then are ye my disciples indeed; ³² and ye shall know the truth, and the truth shall make you free."* You see, it is the truth, the Word of God that makes us free. Being set free is temporary, but being made free is permanent. God wants permanent change in our lives. This change can only come as we give ourselves to the Word of God. In John 17:17, the Lord says, *"Sanctify them through thy truth: thy word is truth."*

Our sanctification process is when the Word of God is applied to our lives. Chamber by chamber the Word of God invades our soul and delivers us from all of the things that are unclean and unrighteous. In Psalms 119:9 it says, *"Wherewithal shall a young man cleanse his way? By taking heed thereto according to thy word."* Our way can be cleansed as the Word of God is applied to our lives. The more we allow the Word of God into our lives, the more we are conformed into His image; more of him and less of us. It is so powerful, yet so simple.

If we would just give ourselves to the Scriptures, be rooted deeply in the Word of God, that very Word will give itself to us and begin to cleanse us and deliver us. I have seen it a thousand times in my life and ministry. Someone comes in very wicked, dark, and perverted. When they begin to sit under the Word of God, their lives begin to change; darkness becomes light as the Word of God dawns on them. They begin to understand who they are and who God is.

In Proverbs 16:6 states, *"By mercy and truth iniquity is purged."* Not only do we need mercy, but we need the truth. Jesus said in John 17:17, *"Thy word is truth."* When we take the mercy of God and apply it with the truth of God's Word, we will find freedom and deliverance from sin.

Lastly, in II Corinthians 7:1 it says, *"Having therefore these promises, dearly beloved, let us cleanse ourselves from all filthiness of the flesh and spirit, perfecting holiness in the fear of God."* The promises are the Word of God. The promises of God were given that we might be cleansed. The Word of God was given to us that we might be sanctified. So it behooves us, today, to give ourselves to the Scriptures so that Jesus can say to us, *"Now you are clean through the word which I have spoken unto you."*

"Jesus Beholding Him Loved Him"
Mark 10:21

DAY 214

Oh how this Scripture blesses me and ministers to my heart. For this is truly a definition of the way our God looks at us and cares for us. Here in this story, a man has come to Jesus and asked Him in Mark 10:17, *"Good Master, what shall I do that I may inherit eternal life?"* Jesus responded to him by telling him to obey the commandments. His foolish answer, in verse 20, was, *"Master, all these have I observed from my youth."* Jesus knew that was impossible because everything is naked and open before Him, as Hebrews 4:12 states. Despite all of this, it says in Mark 10:21, *"Then Jesus beholding him loved him."* Jesus saw through the man and through his apparent fallacy of his answer. Instead of reacting sarcastically or reacting negatively, Jesus just beheld the man and loved him. I am so glad that Jesus loves us when He looks at us and beholds us.

He looks at us with the look of love, just as he did to the woman laying in the street in Ezekiel 16. It says in Ezekiel 16:5, *"None eye pitied thee, to do any of these unto thee, to have compassion upon thee...to the lothing of thy person."* But when God passed by that woman, it says in verse 8, *"Now when I passed by thee, and looked upon thee, behold, thy time was the time of love; and I spread my skirt over thee, and covered thy nakedness: yea, I sware unto thee, and entered into a covenant with thee, saith the Lord God, and thou becamest mine."*

When He beholds us, He sees through us to the heart of our being. He knows us. He knows who we really are and what we are really like. He knows what makes us tick and what makes us do the things we do. He knows the end from the beginning. When He sat down to come into our lives, He counted the cost whether He had enough to finish it. He does have enough to finish it and He will finish what He has begun in us. Jesus is the *"author and finisher of our faith"* (Hebrews 12:2). Psalms 33:13 says, *"The LORD looketh from heaven; he beholdeth all the sons of men."* He beholds us and He loves us.

So much of the time we hear about the anger and the fury of the Lord. We hear about the great wrath that is coming upon the earth. Very little, perhaps, is heard of His great love for His people and His great tenderness. David says in Psalms 18:35, *"Thy gentleness hath made me great."* If it wasn't for His tender, loving-kindness and His mercy, where would we be? It's available to you today. God is beholding you. The Lord Jesus is looking right at you and as He does, His eyes are filled with love.

When He came to the city of Jerusalem, He saw the people like sheep without a shepherd. He even saw how they resisted Him so much. Despite that, He wept for Jerusalem and said in Matthew 23:37, *"O Jerusalem, Jerusalem, thou that killest the prophets, and stonest them which are sent unto thee, how often would I have gathered thy children together, even as a hen gathereth her chickens under her wings."* Let Him gather you today wherever you are, because in gathering you, He will carry you in His arms. As His presence falls upon you today and He turns His face towards you and is beholding you, know He is not angry. He loves on you as He beholds you today.

"Pattern Of The Early Church"
Acts 2: 41-47

In Acts 2 we begin to learn much concerning the manner and operation of the early church. We read:

> "⁴¹*Then they that gladly received his word were baptized: and the same day there were added unto them about three thousand souls.* ⁴²*And they continued steadfastly in the apostles' doctrine and fellowship, and in breaking of bread, and in prayers.* ⁴³*And fear came upon every soul: and many wonders and signs were done by the apostles.* ⁴⁴*And all that believed were together, and had all things common;* ⁴⁵*And sold their possessions and goods, and parted them to all men, as every man had need.* ⁴⁶*And they, continuing daily with one accord in the temple, and breaking bread from house to house, did eat their meat with gladness and singleness of heart,* ⁴⁷*Praising God, and having favour with all the people. And the Lord added to the church daily such as should be saved.*" (Acts 2:41-47)

We see in verse 41 the early church was not coerced into following Jesus. They came to Him gladly. Then it says that they continued steadfastly. I believe that the local church should follow this principle and the pattern. They continued steadfastly in the apostle's doctrine. Luke 24:53 tells us, *"And were continually in the temple, praising and blessing God."* Proverbs 8:34 says, *"Blessed is the man that heareth me, watching daily at my gates, waiting at the posts of my doors."* God wants us to continue in the temple, steadfastly watching daily at His gates.

Regarding the apostles doctrine, in verse 42 it says, *"And daily in the temple, and in every house, they ceased not to teach and preach Jesus Christ"* (Acts 5:42). Also, in Luke 19:47 it says, *"And He (that is, Jesus) taught daily in the temple."* Acts 6:4 says, *"But we will give ourselves continually to prayer, and to the ministry of the word."* The word of the Lord was the doctrine from those apostles as they were sharing it with the people. They continued steadfastly in the apostle's doctrine and in fellowship.

The word fellowship in verse 41 in the Greek is *"koinonia,"* which means "communion, sharing in common, partnership." The Bible says in I Thessalonians 5:11, *"Wherefore comfort yourselves together and edify one another, even as also ye do."* Malachi 3:16 states:

> *"Then they that feared the Lord spake often one to another: and the Lord hearkened, and heard it, and a book of remembrance was written before him for them that feared the Lord, and thought upon his name."*

It says in the book of Hebrews:

> "²³*Let us hold fast the profession of our faith without wavering, (for he is faithful that promised;)* ²⁴*And let us*

> *consider one another to provoke unto love unto good works: ²⁵Not forsaking the assembling of ourselves together, as the manner of some is; but exhorting one another: and so much the more, as ye see the day approaching"* (Hebrews 10:23-25).

And then in Acts 2:42, they continued in breaking of bread. Paul speaks of the Lord's Supper here in I Corinthians 11:23-26, *"²⁶For as often as ye eat this bread, and drink this cup, ye do shew the Lord's death till he come."* Then it says later on in verse 42, *"And in prayers."* Colossians 4:2 says we should *"continue in prayer, and watch in the same with all thanksgiving."* Ephesians 6:18 speaks of *"praying always with all prayer and supplication in the Spirit."* I Thessalonians 5:17 urges us to *"pray without ceasing."* And finally, regarding Jesus, in Luke 18:1 it says, *"And he spake a parable unto them to this end that men ought always to pray, and not to faint."*

The pattern of the early church is simple. These principles of the early church caused them to grow, as it says, *"And the Lord added to the church daily such as should be saved"* (Acts 1:47). This is the first part of it. Let us try to walk in these principles ourselves, so the Lord can add to us daily.

"Pattern Of The Early Church 2"
Acts 2:44-47

The Bible says in Acts 2:

> "⁴⁴*And all that believed were together, and had all things common; ⁴⁵And sold their possessions and goods, and parted them to all men, as every man had need. ⁴⁶And they, continuing daily with one accord in the temple, and breaking bread from house to house, did eat their meat with gladness and singleness of heart, ⁴⁷Praising God, and having favour with all the people. And the Lord added to the church daily such as should be saved*" (Acts 2:44-47).

DAY 216

This is the second part of the pattern of the early church. I believe, just as the first part was essential for every local church, this second part is as well. The legs that we will discover that we need to stand on are eternal, and I believe, they will help every local church and family in the Kingdom of God.

First, all that believed were together and had all things common. There must be a sense of unity and togetherness. We should be, as Ephesians 4:3 tells us, "*Endeavouring to keep the unity of the Spirit in the bond of peace.*" The early church was together in the Lord, having the same vision and purpose, and they had all things common. This is true Christianity: selling your possessions and goods and not keeping the money for yourself, like Ananias and Sapphira, who kept back part of the price (Acts 5:1-2). They parted them to all men, as every man had need. What a fellowship that would be if everyone cared about one another and met each other's needs. This is true community. God, help us to have this operating in our own lives, in our churches. Then, the world will see His love in us, just as Jesus said, "*By this shall all men know that ye are my disciples, if ye have love one to another*" (John 13:35).

Picking up again in Acts 2, it says they continued daily in the temple. There is so much to be said of daily teaching. In the Old Testament, they had the morning and evening sacrifice. Psalms 1:2 says, "*But his delight is in the law of the Lord; and in his law doth he meditate day and night.*" And Joshua 1:8 tells us, "*This book of the law shall not depart out of thy mouth; but thou shalt meditate therein day and night.*" Jesus, Paul, and the apostles all taught the Bible daily. Hebrews 10 admonishes us:

> "²⁴*And let us consider one another to provoke unto love and to good works: ²⁵Not forsaking the assembling of ourselves together, as the manner of some is; but exhorting one another: and so much the more, as ye see the day approaching*" (Hebrews 10:24-25).

We need to get a revelation that our family is now those that hear the Word of God and keep it (Matthew 12:48-50). It then says that they broke bread from house to house. That means they not only took communion on a regular basis, but they ate together. Breaking bread or eating a meal together opens up great doors of fellowship and reality among believers. We need to do this with gladness and singleness of heart, not with a double minded heart or any other motive other than being a blessing and getting to know our brothers and sisters.

It continues to say, *"Praising God, and having favour with all the people."* David said in Psalms 34:1, *"I will bless the Lord at all times: his praise shall continually be in my mouth."* We are to praise God at all times, and as we do that, it will create the favor of God. David said, *"...his favour is as a cloud of the latter rain"* (Proverbs 16:15). It then says that the Lord added to the church daily such as should be saved. As we have favor with all people, those people will come to the Lord Jesus when they see that true, living organism walking in the things of God, loving and caring for one another. This is truly what the local church should be, a family. This is pattern of the early church.

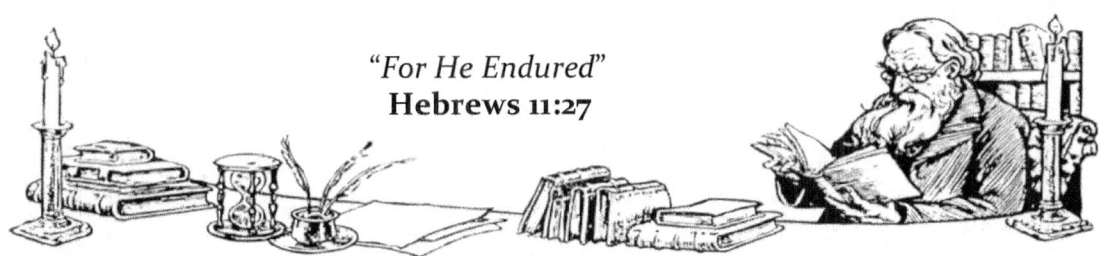

"For He Endured"
Hebrews 11:27

Day 217

This passage of Scripture in Hebrews 11 is speaking of Moses and all that he went through, *"By faith he forsook Egypt, not fearing the wrath of the king: for he endured, as seeing him who is invisible."* Another good word for *"endured"* is *"persevered."* Like Moses, you and I can learn to persevere and endure by seeing Him who is invisible for *"we walk by faith, not by sight"* (II Corinthians 5:7) and by doing so learn to overcome and be victorious in this life.

Many people don't want to endure or suffer hardship. But nonetheless it is the will of God for the overcomer to persevere and endure, for Jesus said, *"he that endureth to the end shall be saved"* (Matthew 10:22). This doesn't mean our eternal salvation, but our salvation when perfection comes to the body of Christ.

Paul told Timothy, *"endure hardness, as a good soldier of Jesus Christ"* (II Timothy 2:3). We are to learn to endure hardness as a good soldier. It isn't easy. The Lord never said it would be. Paul said in II Timothy 2:10, *"Therefore I endure all things for the elect's sakes, that they may also obtain the salvation which is in Christ Jesus with eternal glory."* Many times we endure, not for our sake, but for other's sake because we have a sphere of influence and what we do or don't do affects all those around us. When others see us not enduring or prevailing, we become bad examples, and their faith will be challenged.

The Bible says in James 5:11, *"Behold, we count them happy which endure."* Once we've endured, happiness will eventually come because James 1:12 says, *"Blessed is the man that endureth temptation: for when he is tried, he shall receive the crown of life, which the Lord hath promised to them that love him."* We just need to make it through to the other side. We need to endure and persevere. The easiest thing to do is give up and quit. Don't take the path of least resistance today. Let this word be burned into your memory. God wants you to endure. God wants you to persevere and He will help you to do it.

Moses endured by seeing Him who is invisible. It says of Abraham in Hebrews 6:15 *"after he had patiently endured, he obtained the promise."* Perhaps this is one of the things we need, patience; patience to survive the temptation and the stress. In the great chapter of love in I Corinthians 13, love is defined as that which *"beareth all things, believeth all things, hopeth all things, endureth all things. ⁸Charity never faileth"* (I Corinthians 13:7-8). Love never fails and neither does God. He wants us to endure. He wants us to overcome and persevere. And if we can keep our eyes on Jesus, endure till the end, then we shall obtain the promise.

"The Lord Hath Sought Him A Man After His Own Heart"
I Samuel 13:14

DAY 218

In the Scriptures, we find the phrase over and over again, that the Lord is seeking something. In I Samuel 13:14 we read, *"the Lord hath sought him a man after his own heart."* The reason why God was doing that was because He was displeased with Saul, who was the king at that time. He needed someone who had a heart like His own. This is still true today. God is desperately seeking and searching for those whose hearts are perfect towards Him (II Chronicles 16:9). He is seeking those whose hearts aren't interested in their own ambitions, their own desires, their own wants and needs, but are more concerned with the Kingdom of God and God's wants and needs.

The Hebrew word for *"sought"* and *"seeking"* mean "to search out, to strive after, to desire, to beseech." In other words, God is searching, striving, desiring and beseeching for someone who will have a heart like His. In Matthew 11:29, Jesus says, *"learn of me; for I am meek and lowly in heart."* God is looking for a people who are willing to be meek. Meekness is not weakness. Meekness simply means to be teachable and there is great strength in that. The Bible says that Moses was the meekest man on the face of the earth.

Lowly is another word for humble. God is looking for a humble people. He says in Isaiah 66:2, *"but to this man will I look, even to him that is poor and of a contrite spirit, and trembleth at my word."* He says also in Isaiah 57:15, *"I dwell in the high and holy place, with him also that is of a contrite and humble spirit."* God will dwell with those who have a humble heart just like His. You and I need to strive to have a conscience void of offence towards God and man, as Acts 24:16 states. Proverbs 22:11 states *"He that loveth pureness of heart, for the grace of his lips the king shall be his friend."* We need to strive to have a pure heart, a humble heart and not let pride, ambition or the praises of men rule us. Rather we must seek and desire to have a heart like God, a heart like the precious Lord Jesus, who humbled himself and became obedient unto death. God help us to have that revelation and to be like Him.

The Lord is seeking for men after His heart. Jeremiah 3:15 states, *"And I will give you pastors according to mine heart, which shall feed you with knowledge and understanding."* The world is in desperate need of leadership and in desperate need of true shepherds who pastor according to God's heart. We live in an age of seeker friendly churches, an age of large mega churches, big ministries, where everything in the body of Christ is about bigness, money, and numbers. Success is equated with gain. But gain is not godliness (I Timothy 6:5). You and I need to get this revelation that God is big, but big is not necessarily God. If success is determined by numbers then Jesus was a failure because when he left the earth, he had no one who was following him. All forsook him and fled, the Bible says.

God is looking for pastors who are willing to shepherd the sheep with His heart. By doing so, they will feed them with knowledge and understanding. If you are pastoring according to God's heart, then you will be doing that. If not, you won't. You would be pastoring them, not with godly knowledge, but with worldly and intellectual knowledge and your understanding would be askew and amiss.

In Psalms 19:14 David declares, "*Let the words of my mouth, and the meditation of my heart, be acceptable in thy sight, O LORD, my strength, and my redeemer.*" If God is looking for those men and women who are after His own heart, then we need to pray this prayer that David did in this Psalms. We must watch the words of our mouths. We must watch the meditations of our heart. What are we thinking about? Are we meditating on the things of God? Are we considering Him? Have we set our affections on things above and not on things of the earth, where Christ sits at the right hand of God (Colossians 3:2)? We must seek the Lord. We must guard our hearts so that we have a heart that is like His.

In Psalms 27:8, David says, "*When thou* [God] *saidest, Seek ye my face; my heart said unto thee, Thy face, LORD, will I seek.*" There must be a willingness in all of us to seek His face. Our hearts must respond and say, "*Thy face, LORD, will I seek.*" As in Psalms 84:2 states, "*My soul longeth, yea, even fainteth for the courts of the LORD: my heart and my flesh crieth out for the living God.*" Does your soul long and even faint for the courts of the Lord, the presence of the Lord? Does your heart and flesh cry out for the living God? Likewise David says in Psalms 42:2, "*My soul thirsteth for God, for the living God: when shall I come and appear before God?*" David is basically asking when shall he come and be with his precious Lord.

God is seeking, beseeching, longing and searching for men and women who want to have a heart like His. They are willing to pastor and be a leader according to His ways, seeking not the praises of men, but the praises of God. They are more interested in the things of Jesus, the things of the Kingdom of God, rather than the things that will better themselves or build them a name or a kingdom for themselves. We must shake ourselves from the flesh of this world, which exists in the body of Christ today and we must cry out, long and even faint for Him. Our hearts must cry out for the living God. God is seeking for a man after His own heart. I pray that He will find us worthy men and women, after His own heart.

"A God At Hand, A God Afar Off"
Jeremiah 23:23

Day 219

We read in Jeremiah 23:23, *"Am I a God at hand, saith the Lord, and not a God afar off?"* What does this mean? It means that God not only is present to help us in times of trouble, but He's also a God afar off in our deepest valley, our deepest trial, and our deepest struggle to help us. What a comfort to us that God has revealed himself to us to be a *"God at hand."* He's always within reach, always at hand to answer the cry of our needs, and to bless us when we need him.

Why should we be fretful or discontent when we're in a tough situation and it seems like He's a million miles away? Jesus said in Matthew 28:20, *"lo, I am with you alway."* What great courage this divine nearness should inspire in all of us. So many times we hear the enemy say, *"There is no help for him in God"* (Psalms 3:2). That He may be *"a God at hand,"* but He's not *"a God afar off."* In I Kings 20:28, the enemy said to the children of Israel, *"The Lord is God of the hills, but he is not God of the valleys."* I beg to differ with them. Jesus is a God of the valleys. In Psalms 23:4, it reads, *"Yea, though I walk through the valley of the shadow of death, I will fear no evil: for thou art with me; thy rod and thy staff they comfort me."* Yes, He's a God of the hills, He's the God at hand, but He's a God of the valleys as well. In Psalms 3:1-3, David writes, *"Lord, how are they increased that trouble me! many are they that rise up against me. ²Many there be which say of my soul, There is no help for him in God. Selah ³But thou, O Lord, art a shield for me; my glory, and the lifter up of mine head."*

God is not only right here, right now, but he's also going to be there tomorrow. Remember when Jesus was on the cross and what they said to him, in Matthew 27:40, *"If thou be the Son of God, come down from the cross."* Oh, how they mocked him, oh, how they mock us and say that there's no help for us. I declare to you today, that God is a God at hand and a very present help in times of trouble. He hears the whispers of our heart, but He also hears the great longing and cries when we are in a low place. Psalms 139:7-10, states:

> *"⁷Whither shall I go from thy spirit? or whither shall I flee from thy presence? ⁸If I ascend up into heaven, thou art there: if I make my bed in hell, behold, thou art there. ⁹If I take the wings of the morning, and dwell in the uttermost parts of the sea; ¹⁰Even there shall thy hand lead me, and thy right hand shall hold me."*

In Psalms 139:13, David goes onto say, *"For thou hast possessed my reins."* And he also says in Psalms 139:2-3, *"²Thou knowest my downsitting and mine uprising, thou understandest my thought afar off. ³Thou compassest my path and my lying down, and art acquainted with all my ways."*

He's a God at hand and a God afar off. Never forget that great passage in Genesis 28:15, *"And, behold, I am with thee, and will keep thee in all places whither thou goes* [at hand or afar off], *and will bring thee again into this land; for I will not leave thee, until I have done that which I have spoken to thee of."* So, today remember that God is with you in your high places and in your low places, both near and afar off. Bless His precious name!

"I Am My Beloved's"
Song Of Solomon 7:10

There are three places in the Song of Solomon where we find almost the seemingly same verse of Scripture. However, there is a slight variation that reveals a tremendous revelation to us concerning the bride of Christ.

DAY 220

The first of the three verses starts off in Song of Solomon 2:16, where the bride says to his Bridegroom Jesus, "*My beloved [Jesus] is mine, and I am his: he feedeth among the lilies.*" She starts out in a selfish way. All she seemed to be concerned about and emphasized most on was, "*My beloved is mine.*" Even though she also says, "*I am his,*" it is really all about her. When we first come into the Kingdom of God, there is quite a bit of selfishness in our lives. The emphasis is receiving from the Lord healing, deliverance, ministry, etc. We don't really have a Kingdom mentality yet. We don't really have the heart that the true bride is supposed to have. The emphasis is about what is "*mine*" and what we have and not what He has or wants.

But, as it always is in the processes of God, eventually, as we grow in grace and in the knowledge of our Lord and Savior, we pass from glory to glory, faith to faith, strength to strength, and vessel to vessel, we begin to grow. Then we get to the next verse of Scripture in Song of Solomon 6:3, which states, "*I am my beloved's, and my beloved is mine: he feedeth among the lilies.*" At first she said, "*My beloved is mine, and I am his.*" Now she says, "*I am my beloved's, and my beloved is mine.*" She is beginning to understand that it isn't all about her. Have you understood that yet, that it isn't all about I, me, mine and what is going on with you? The world doesn't revolve around us and neither does the Kingdom of God. We need to lose ourselves in the body. We need to let the greater include the lesser. The greater being the Kingdom of God, the body of Christ and the lesser being us, the single component within the body. So, in Song of Solomon 6:3, it is beginning to dawn on her that she belongs to Him and not He belongs to her.

Then as we continue on, we find the final stage in our lives, in Song of Solomon 7:10, "*I am my beloved's, and his desire is towards me.*" Remember, now, the principle of the Outer Court, the Holy Place and the Most Holy Place. The bride has gone from the Outer Court ("*my beloved is mine, and I am his*"), to the Holy Place ("*I am my beloved's, and my beloved is mine*"), now she reaches the third and final stage, the Most Holy Place, Kingdom living, the Kingdom living dimension, the knowing Him dimension, and brideship where she only says, "*I am my beloved's, and his desire is towards me.*" What a revelation of love! She has now entered into a love relationship towards Him. She realizes that she has not chosen Him, but He has chosen her. She leaves the "*mine*" and replaces it with, "*and his desire is towards me.*" In this stage of growth, it is all about Him, all about His desires, what He wants and what He is after. Where would you say you are today? Are you in the Outer Court, Holy Place, or Most Holy Place? I doubt if many of us are in the Most Holy Place. But at least we are on the journey and have left. God help you and me, today, to not say, "*my beloved is mine*" anymore, but to say, "*I am my beloved's, and his desire is towards me.*"

"The Garden Of Nuts"
Song of Solomon 6:11

DAY 221

I want to take a humorous look at this passage today, though surely it is not meant in a humorous way when the Lord is speaking of it here. But I think if you bear with me, you can see the typology within this passage of Scripture. Jesus is speaking of the bride of Christ in Song of Solomon 6:11, saying, *"I went down into the garden of nuts to see the fruits of the valley, and to see whether the vine flourished..."* I believe the garden of nuts is the bride of Christ, and that means you and me. Many people think we're nuts; many people think we're fruits.

I Peter 2:9 tells us, *"But ye are a chosen generation, a royal priesthood, an holy nation, a peculiar people"*. One of the Greek words for *"peculiar"* means "beyond usual or special (one's own)." We are God's own special people. We may be weird or nuts to the world, but yet we're still His peculiar people. It says in Deuteronomy 14:2, *"the Lord hath chosen thee to be a peculiar people unto himself"*. In Exodus 19:5, it says He has called us to be *"a peculiar treasure."* The word *"peculiar"* in Hebrew means "shut up, wealth, special, or jewel." While others may think us crazy, foolish, and nuts, we are His special jewels, His shut up wealth. You've got to look a little deeper; that nut may just be God's jewel.

Paul said in I Corinthians 4:10, *"We are fools for Christ's sake..."* I don't know about you, but I don't mind being a fool for Christ. It's easy. When the Lord Jesus has given you everything, redeemed you from a life of destruction, saved you, blessed you, set your feet upon a rock, and established your goings (Psalms 40:2), it's easy then to appear as fools to others. The Bible says, *"But God hath chosen the foolish things of the world to confound the wise..."* (I Corinthians 1:27). God has chosen the foolish things of the world. He has chosen you and me. We may be nuts, but we're chosen.

I Corinthians 3:18-19 tells us, *"¹⁸Let no man deceive himself. If any man among you seemeth to be wise in this world, let him become a fool, that he may be wise. ¹⁹For the wisdom of this world is foolishness with God"*. Luke 16:15 tells us, *"...that which is highly esteemed among men is abomination in the sight of God"*.

God enjoys you and me. He loves us. *"For the Lord taketh pleasure in his people,"* Psalms 149:4 tells us. We may appear crazy, nuts, foolish, and extremely peculiar and strange to others, but to Him, we are His special treasure, His shut up wealth, His own special people that are beyond usual. Has He come down into your garden of nuts today to see how the fruits flourish? I pray you're flourishing today, even as a fool, a nut, a fruit, or a peculiar treasure unto God.

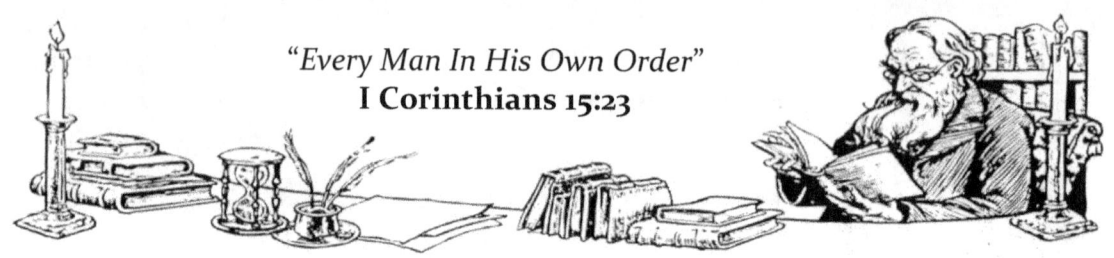

"Every Man In His Own Order"
I Corinthians 15:23

Paul writes to the Corinthians saying:

"²²For as in Adam all die, even so in Christ shall all be made alive. ²³But every man in his own order: Christ the firstfruits; afterward they that are Christ's at his coming" (I Corinthians 15:22-23).

The word "order" here in Greek means ranks. There are ranks within the body of Christ, ranks such as private, sergeant, lieutenant, captain, major, colonel, general and five-star general. In looking at these ranks, really what we are doing is revealing the remnant.

First of all, John tells us in Revelation:

"¹And there appeared a great wonder in heaven; a woman clothed with the sun, and the moon under her feet, and upon her head a crown of twelve stars... ⁵And she brought forth a man child, who was to rule all nations with a rod of iron: and her child was caught up unto God, and to his throne... ¹⁷And the dragon was wroth with the woman, and went to make war with the remnant of her seed..." (Revelation 12:1, 5 and 17).

In these verses, you have the manchild, the woman and the rest of the seed. These are ranks in the body of Christ. The woman is the Church, the manchild is the remnant and the rest of her seed are the remaining members of the Church. In Matthew 25:1 it says, *"Then shall the kingdom of heaven be likened unto ten virgins, which took their lamps, and went forth to meet the bridegroom."* "Virgins" in the Scriptures always speak of Christians and five of them here were wise and the other five were foolish. The five wise represent the remnant, and the five foolish, represent the Church. Matthew 20:16 says, *"So the last shall be first, and the first last: for many be called, but few chosen."* Everyone is called, but few actually choose to go on with God after their salvation. So, the few chosen are the remnant, and the many called are the rest of the believers.

In David's army, in II Samuel 23:8-39, there were David's mighty men, which were thirty-seven. There were the second three who didn't attain to the first three, and then there were the three that attained the highest degree in that army. You then had the rest of David's army, which are the general believers. So, you have four ranks here: the general believers, the thirty seven, the three who did not attain, and finally the three who attained.

In Proverbs 31:29 it says, *"Many daughters have done virtuously, but thou excellest them all."* The virtuous woman is the remnant and the many daughters are the rest of the body. Mark 4:20 talks about *"some thirtyfold, some sixty and some an hundred."* The hundredfold believers are the remnant, the sixty fold are a rank within the body of

Christ, and the thirtyfold are the rest of the Church. You have to ask yourself, where are you? Where do you belong in this great company?

Consider the book of Judges with the story of Gideon (Judges 6:11-7:25). God told Gideon that the people were too many and that He wanted him to send home those who were fearful. The army then was reduced from 32,000 men to 10,000 men. God then told Gideon to test the remaining people in the waters. He reduced the army again from 10,000 men to 300 men. The army of 300 men is representative of the remnant. The other 9,700 represent sixty-fold Christians and the 22,000 that went home represent the remainder of the body of Christ.

There are so many passages that it would take forever to show you all of them: but enough of this principle has been established now for you to see it. Just as at the mount of transfiguration, a multitude of believers were at the bottom of the mountain. Even all the disciples did not go to the top, only Peter, John and James (Matthew 17:1). Once again, we see the remnant, the disciples, and then the rest of the multitude. Please, hear the Word of the Lord. God has left us a very small remnant. Be a part of it!

"By Night"
Song Of Solomon 3:1

In Song of Solomon 3:1 it says, *"By night on my bed I sought him whom my soul loveth."* So many times in our life it seems like we grow in the Lord in the most troublesome times. Night time is the darkest part of the day, when there's no light. So it obviously speaks of a dark period, a time of the dealings of God, a time of pressure, or a time of struggle. However, that's the time when we need to seek Him whom our soul loveth, and if we love Him then we will seek Him.

DAY 223

David said, *"At midnight I will rise to give thanks unto thee"* (Psalms 119:62). It says in Acts 16:25, *"at midnight Paul and Silas prayed, and sang praises unto God"* (Acts 16:25). We find that as we worship God in the night season and as we seek the Lord, that the grace of God is there to deal with the situation we're going through. He gives songs in the night (Job 35:10). Life is hard, but the grace of God is stronger than life. So when you and I enter into a nighttime experience, we need to remember that this is not a time to draw back but a time to seek the Lord. This is a time when we seek the Lord while He may be found and call upon Him while He is near (Isaiah 55:6).

It's by night, during the darkness, during the hard places, there must be in us a determination to seek Him. Why? Because; He's the one whom our souls love. The Bible says that he who has been forgiven much loves much (Luke 7:47). I don't know about you but the Lord has been so gracious to me, so wonderful, and so precious. He is the pearl of great price to me (Matthew 13:46). He is the treasure in my heart, and because I love Him and honor Him, I will seek Him.

David said in Psalms 27:8, *"When thou saidst, Seek ye my face; my heart said unto thee, Thy face, Lord, will I seek."* David also said in Psalms 27:4, *"One thing have I desired of the Lord, that will I seek after; that I may dwell in the house of the Lord all the days of my life, to behold the beauty of the Lord, and to inquire in his temple."* *"In the secret of his tabernacle shall he hide me"* (Psalms 27:5). When you're in the night season, *"Yea, though I walk through the valley of the shadow of death, I will fear no evil: for thou art with me; thy rod and thy staff they comfort me"* (Psalms 23:4). Even Psalms 139:11-12 says, *"¹¹ If I say, Surely the darkness shall cover me; even the night shall be light about me. ¹² Yea, the darkness hideth not from thee; but the night shineth as the day: the darkness and the light are both alike to thee."* Darkness cannot keep Him from you. Night time will not keep the presence of God, the glory of God, and the word of the Lord from coming to you.

Make a decision that by night you're going to seek Him whom your soul loveth. You're going to seek Him because you love Him. He's important to you and He's your chief desire. Nothing in the night time or darkness can ever take away the joy and the desire in our heart for our lover, the Lord Jesus.

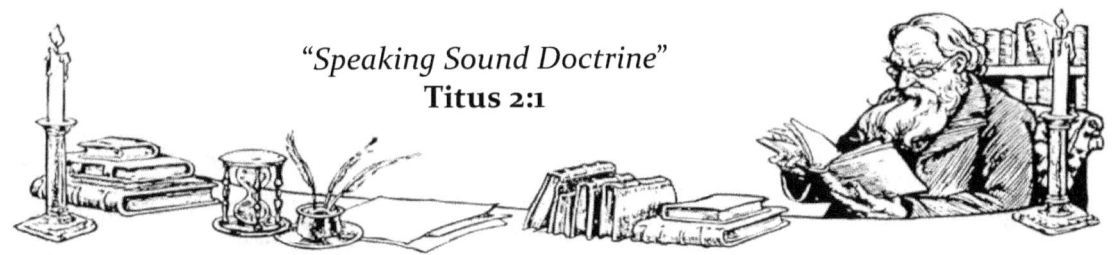

"Speaking Sound Doctrine"
Titus 2:1

DAY 224

Paul, in writing to his disciple Titus, speaks these tremendous words in Titus 2:1, *"But speak thou the things which become sound doctrine."* The word *"sound"* here in the Greek means "uncorrupt, true, safe and wholesome." The word for *"doctrine"* is "instruction, learning or teaching."

You and I are to speak, instruct and teach in an uncorrupt, true, safe and wholesome way. There are so many voices in this world today, and none of them are without significance. So many words are being preached. So many things are being said, but are they sound doctrine, are they wholesome, are they uncorrupt, and are they true? The Word of the Lord to us is that we need to speak the things which are suitable for sound doctrine. Paul writing to Timothy says, *"For the time will come when they will not endure sound doctrine; but after their own lusts shall they heap to themselves teachers, having itching ears; ⁴And they shall turn away their ears from the truth, and shall be turned unto fables"* (II Timothy 4:3-4).

I believe the time has come when many are not enduring sound doctrine. The Bible says that we have to endure sound doctrine. For many people, it is hard to sit under the Word of God and to give themselves to the Scriptures. They turn their ears away from the truth and toward fictions and fables. In these days of such "great conferences", ministers teach so many different things. If we keep attending these conferences, we will end up like those in Ephesians 4:14, *"Tossed to and fro, and carried about with every wind of doctrine, by the sleight of men, and cunning craftiness, whereby they lie in wait to deceive."*

This is not the will of God for us. He wants us to speak of things that are sound doctrine. In Titus 1:9, He encourages us, *"Holding fast the faithful word as he hath been taught, that he may be able by sound doctrine both to exhort and to convince the gainsayers."* It is so that we may be able to *"convince the* gainsayers" or in other words, "to convict the opposition."

You and I need to hold fast the faithful Word as we've been taught. As Paul wrote to Timothy in II Timothy 2:2, *"And the things that thou hast heard of me among many witnesses, the same commit thou to faithful men, who shall be able to teach others also."* By this sound doctrine that you and I have been taught, we then can turn, exhort and convince those that need to hear the Word of God.

God wants us nourished with good doctrine. Finally, in II John 9 it says, *"Whosoever transgresseth, and abideth not in the doctrine of Christ, hath not God. He that abideth in the doctrine of Christ, he hath both the Father and the Son."* You and I need to speak the things concerning sound doctrine. By doing so, we will convince and exhort all those around us, and by the grace of God, we will help people not to transgress, but rather abide in the doctrine of Christ so that they can know our wonderful God.

"Let Him Kiss Me With The Kisses Of His Mouth"
Song of Solomon 1:2

Day 225

The Song of Solomon is the love story between the Bridegroom Jesus and His bride. In this story we see many intimate moments played out between the bride and the Bridegroom. Of all the verses in this book, this one blesses me the most, for it tells the heart of the bride and her passion for Him. I pray that this same passion, love, and desire comes forth in every one of our lives for Jesus. I pray we find today a new place of love in our hearts for Him; that we experience a new and fresh devotion and a burning desire for intimacy with the Lord Jesus and say as she did in Song of Solomon 1:2, "*Let Him kiss me with the kisses of His mouth: for thy love is better than wine.*" Some other translations read:

> "*Let Him smother me with kisses of His mouth*"
> "*Kiss me full on the mouth*"
> "*Kiss me and kiss me again*"
> "*Oh, how I wish He would kiss me passionately!*"

Wow! Aren't these amazing terms? This should be the heart in every one of us, that He would kiss us full on the mouth and smother us with kisses of His mouth again and again, doing it passionately. Moreover, we should respond just as passionately by kissing Him back. No, we can't physically kiss the Lord, but we can do it spiritually speaking.

Our mouth speaks of our words, the Word of God, our breath, our worship, and our life. In other words, this means our life being intertwined with His life. It means our life speaking the Word of God, and most importantly our mouth touching His mouth. It is our life touching His life, our breath interweaving with His breath, the Holy Ghost. This is intimacy in the highest form.

A kiss is the most-tender thing two lovers can do between one another. It is sweet, passionate, and precious. The word "kiss" in Hebrew means "to fasten upon, to touch as a mode of attachment." We need to fasten upon the Lord with the intimacy that is rising in our hearts. As we do this, it is a form of attachment between us and Him.

Kissing is also worshipping Him with our mouth and praising Him. It is offering a sacrifice of praise and rejoicing in the Lord. As we do this, a mode of attachment comes, while we are telling the Lord how much we love Him. This is why Psalms 92:1 says, "*It is a good thing to give thanks unto the Lord, and to sing praises unto thy name, O Most High.*"

It also means "to equip with weapons." Praise is a definite force against the enemy. It is one of our tools and weapons against him. So, when we kiss the Lord, when we have passion and know Him intimately, it equips us with the best weapon of all, I believe. Knowing God intimately won't allow any demon, devil, circumstance, trial, or problem to ever stop us. We will know like Paul said in II Timothy 1:12, *"for I know whom I have believed, and am persuaded that he is able."*

So, fasten upon Him with your lips and worship Him intimately. The word *"beloved"* in Hebrew means "to boil in love towards." Are you boiling in love towards the Lord today? Is your heart raging with passion? Psalms 63:1 says, *"O God, thou art my God; early will I seek thee: my soul thirsteth for thee, my flesh longeth for thee"*

His love truly *"is better than wine."* The word *"better"* means "good in the widest sense." The word *"wine"* in Hebrew means "intoxication, banqueting, to be filled with joy." In other words, His love is better than any earthly intoxication and better than any earthly banqueting or earthly joy. It is better in the widest sense. Never forget that!

We see in the Gospel of Luke that Jesus was talking to the Pharisee that invited Him to his house and the woman, who was a sinner, brought an alabaster box of ointment to minister to Jesus. We read here:

> *"⁴⁴And he turned to the woman, and said unto Simon, Seest thou this woman? I entered into thine house, thou gavest me no water for my feet: but she hath washed my feet with tears, and wiped them with the hairs of her head. ⁴⁵Thou gavest me no kiss: but this woman since the time I came in hath not ceased to kiss my feet... ⁴⁷Wherefore I say unto thee, Her sins, which are many, are forgiven; for she loved much: but to whom little is forgiven, the same loveth little"* (Luke 7:44-47).

Why is it that those who love Jesus the most seem to be the ones that have been the greater sinners in this life? Maybe it is because we realize we are nothing without Him, and it is only by His grace that we stand. How desperate it makes us to let Him know we are so grateful and thankful for His love! In Song of Solomon 8:1 the bride says, *"when I should find thee without, I would kiss thee; yea, I should not be despised."* What do we do with Him when we find Him without? Well, we should kiss Him and pour out our love to Him by worshipping, honoring Him and praising Him.

Song of Solomon 8:1 reads *"I would kiss thee; yea, I should not be despised."* Who cares what people think? There will always be people who will judge us for our worship, like Michal despising David when he danced before the Lord with all of his might. Matthew 21:15 says that, *"when the chief priests and scribes saw the wonderful things that he did, and the children crying in the temple, and saying, Hosanna to the son of David; they were sore displeased."* Nonetheless, for those who love Him, He is everything. Their hearts' desire is that He would kiss them with the kisses of His lips. Only His lips will do. Only His love matters to them.

Psalms 2:12 says, *"Kiss the Son, lest he be angry, and ye perish from the way."* I admonish you today, kiss the Son. Let Him kiss you today and kiss Him back passionately and allow His love that is better than anything in this world fill you as you fall deeper in love with Jesus today!

"A Time To Dance"
Ecclesiastes 3:4

DAY 226

Here we find in Ecclesiastes 3:4 a marvelous Scripture that gives us a definition of how we are to worship and praise our God, *"A time to weep, and a time to laugh; a time to mourn, and a time to dance."* There is a time to dance. It is a time to rejoice before the Lord our God. The word *"dance"* in the Hebrew means "to stamp, to spin about wildly for joy, to twist in a circular fashion." The Hebrew word for *"rejoice"* means "to spin around under the influence of a violent emotion, to jump for joy." The word for *"rejoice"* in the Greek means "to spring up, to jump, to leap." So here we find that the word dance and rejoice are interchangeable many times. They mean the same thing.

God commands us to dance. He doesn't ask us. He commands it in the Scriptures. He says in Psalms 149:3, *"Let them praise his name in the dance."* God wants us to be liberated and loosed from all of our inhibitions and fears and dance before Him. Psalms 150:4 says, *"Praise him with the timbrel and dance."*

Zephaniah 3:14 says, *"Sing, O daughter of Zion; shout, O Israel; be glad and rejoice with all the heart, O daughter of Jerusalem."* God wants to hear us singing. God wants us to be glad and rejoicing or dancing with all of our hearts. Do we do this? I know that sometimes it is hard and we don't feel like dancing, but that is when Hebrews 13:15 says, *"let us offer the sacrifice of praise to God."* This is when we worship Him anyway because we know it is what God wants us to do. God wants us dancing. There's a time to mourn, but then there is a time to dance.

We find the story of David dancing before the people and it says, *"And David danced before the Lord with all his might; and David was girded with a linen ephod"* (II Samuel 6:14). And it then says as *"Michal Saul's daughter looked through a window, and saw king David leaping and dancing before the Lord; and she despised him in her heart"* (II Samuel 6:16). Think it not strange that some will despise, be critical, or judge you because of your freedom to dance.

Isn't it strange that dancing seems to be accepted everywhere except for the house of God? The Scriptures are very clear that we should dance before the Lord. People dance when they are happy, excited, or have overcome something. Shouldn't that be God's house? We're not talking about worldly, lustful dancing, but spiritual outbursts of praise and worship. God loves to see His people excited and rejoicing freely before Him. When God delivers you out of bondage, lifts a heavy burden off of you, sets you free, and gives you victory over the devil, it is right for you to rejoice in the dance. It's right to praise His name and play the tambourine. So folks, *"let us praise his name in the dance."*

Begin by doing it by yourself and then the liberty and freedom you find there will burst out with the general congregation. By dancing before the Lord, being free from inhibitions, we will bring others in. If you have never danced before the Lord or haven't danced in a while, hear the word of the Lord and offer up a sacrifice of praise by praising His name in the dance.

"The Fountain Opened"
Zechariah 13:1

Here in this passage, we find a tremendous truth about the coming days, *"In that day there shall be a fountain opened to the house of David and to the inhabitants of Jerusalem for sin and for uncleanness. (Zechariah 13:1).* There's coming a day when God is going to visit His people in a mighty visitation and wash them completely from all their sin and from all their uncleanness. Jesus said in Luke 18:8, *"When the Son of Man cometh, shall he find faith on the earth?"*

DAY 227

All of us have struggled with sin and weaknesses in our lives. Sometimes we're delivered instantly from some sins while others take us years in the dealings of God and the sanctification process to be delivered from them. But we must have hope, as I Peter 4:1 says, *"He that hath suffered in the flesh hath ceased from sin."* As long as you and I continue to repent, get up and believe God, there will ultimately be deliverance for us, because God's going to visit the earth with a mighty fountain of blood. A fountain shall be opened for sin and uncleanness. We've been delivered from the penalty of sin. We're daily being delivered from the power of sin. But soon we'll even be delivered from the very presence of sin itself.

In Micah 7:19 it says, *"He will turn again, he will have compassion upon us; he will subdue our iniquities; and thou wilt cast all their sins into the depths of the sea."* *"Subdue"* means *"to tread down, to conquer, to force under."* God is going to subdue all our iniquities. He's going to rid us of all these things that we could not stop doing no matter how hard we've tried. Zephaniah prophesied, *"I will also leave in the midst of thee an afflicted and poor people, and they shall trust in the name of the Lord.* ¹³*The remnant of Israel shall not do iniquity"* (Zephaniah 3:12-13). Could it be possible that there will actually come a time when we will be delivered completely from sin and iniquity? David said, *"Blessed are they that keep his testimonies, and that seek him with the whole heart.* ³*They also do no iniquity: they walk in his ways"* (Psalms 119:2-3).

This is an amazing truth. God has made provision for us as Titus 2:14 says, *"That he might redeem us from all iniquity."* Not just some, but all iniquity. The day is coming when you and I are going to be totally free from the bondage of sin and corruption, that which has plagued the human race from the beginning. The Adamic nature will be conquered and God will have a people in His image, free from the bondages and corruption of sin.

In Job 5:17, God says, *"Behold, happy is the man whom God correcteth: therefore despise not thou the chastening of the Almighty."* And He goes on to list the things that happens to us when we respond to the chastening of the Almighty. In Job 5:19 He says, *"He shall deliver thee in six troubles: yea, in seven there shall no evil touch thee."* The *"seventh"* or perfection is coming where there will be no more sin. Listen as He continues on in the next verse or so; *"and thou shalt visit thy habitation, and shalt not sin."* This is what's coming to all of us that will believe His Word!

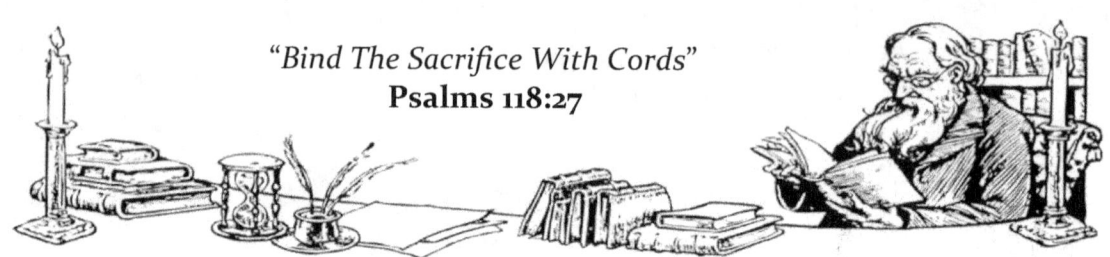

"Bind The Sacrifice With Cords"
Psalms 118:27

DAY 228

Psalms 118:27 says *"Bind the sacrifice with cords, even unto the horns of the altar."* Sometimes when you and I sacrifice something to the Lord and are going through difficult times we need to bind ourselves with cords to the horns of the altar as they did the animals in those olden days. It is so necessary for us to realize it is Scriptural for us to offer a sacrifice to the Lord and to actually become a sacrifice.

The word sacrifice means *"to slaughter."* There are times and things in our lives that God brings where we go through such dealings and trials where it seems like we're being slaughtered. We need to bind ourselves to the horns of the altar so we will remain there. In Psalms 50:5 it reads *"Gather my saints together unto me; those that have made a covenant with me by sacrifice."* God wants gathered to Him those that have made a covenant with Him by sacrificing.

We find that, in the Scriptures, Paul himself said *"Yeah, and if I be offered upon the sacrifice and service of your faith, I joy, and rejoice with you all"* (Philippians 2:17). Sometimes we are called to be offered up as a sacrifice for other people and it may be a slaughter, it may hurt but, nonetheless, it is the will of God.

We're also called to offer the sacrifice of praise to God continually, *"Let us offer the sacrifice of praise to God continually, that is, the fruit of our lips giving thanks to his name"* (Hebrews 13:15). In I Peter 2:5 it says *"Ye also, as lively stones, are built up a spiritual house, an holy priesthood, to offer up spiritual sacrifices, acceptable to God by Jesus Christ."* This is the will of God for us. Jeremiah 17:26 tells us *"And they shall come from the cities of Judah, and from the places about Jerusalem, and from the land of Benjamin, and from the plain, and from the mountains, and from the south, bringing burnt offerings, and sacrifices, and meat offerings, and incense, and bringing sacrifices of praise, unto the house of the Lord."*

There is a passage in the Old Testament found in II Chronicles 6:13 that says *"For Solomon had made a brasen scaffold, of five cubits long, and five cubits broad, and three cubits high, and had set it in the midst of the court: and upon it he stood, and kneeled down upon his knees before all the congregation of Israel, and spread forth his hands toward heaven."* In other words, Solomon was saying that he was the Lord's sacrifice. You and I are God's sacrifice in this earth. Jesus was our sacrifice and now we are the world's sacrifice. The only Jesus they'll ever see is us. We must *"bind the sacrifice with cords."* It's too easy to run when times are hard; too easy to try and get out of the dealings of God, to leave the place of the valley in which God has planted us. So hear the Word of the Lord today! Bind yourself with cords to the horns of the altar. Let us be the sacrifice. Let's climb on the altar ourselves and allow God to work His will in our lives so that it is no longer us that live, but Christ that lives and radiates through us (Galatians 2:20).

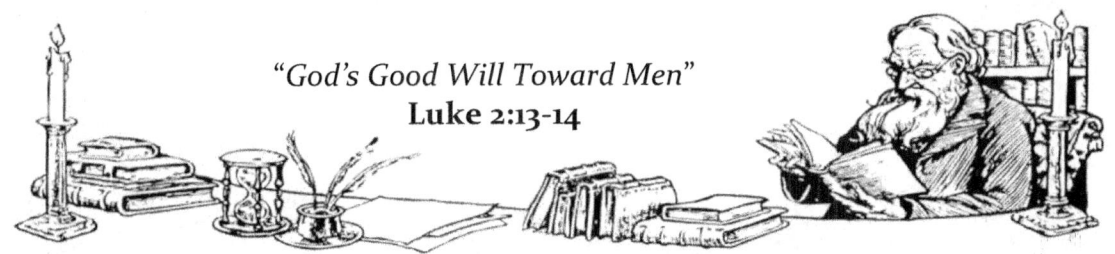

"God's Good Will Toward Men"
Luke 2:13-14

DAY 229

The Bible says here in Luke 2:13-14, *"And suddenly there was with the angel a multitude of the heavenly host praising God, and saying, Glory to God in the highest, and on earth peace, good will toward men."* This is the word of the Lord to us: peace and good will towards all men. John 3:16 says, *"For God so loved the world, that he gave his only begotten Son, that whosoever believeth in him should not perish, but have everlasting life."* II Peter 3:9 says that God is *"not willing that any should perish, but that all should come to repentance."*

God cares about His whole creation and has good will toward them. He wants them to have peace, especially those of us that are of the household of faith. Jesus says in John 14:27, *"Peace I leave with you, my peace I give unto you."* It is *"the peace of God, which passeth all understanding"* (Philippians 4:7).

God wants you to have peace. God wants you to have rest; like in Matthew 11:28, *"Come unto me, all ye that labour and are heavy laden, and I will give you rest."* Romans 5:1 says, *"We have peace with God through our Lord Jesus Christ."* We have peace through Jesus and this is God's will, not only for the body of Christ, but for the world. God does not take pleasure in wars or famine or in destruction. God would rather us walk in peace. He wants peace on earth. Then the Scripture in Luke 2:14 says, *"good will toward men."*

How many times did people come to Jesus and implore him to come to their house, their funeral, and pray for their family members? His answer was always, "I will". That's because Jesus said, in John 14:7, *"If ye had known me, ye should have known my Father also."* If Jesus is a true example of the Father, then that is exactly what the Father would have done in His place, *"I will."*

"Good will toward men." God's will is good and He wants us to be well. It says in III John 2, *"Beloved, I wish above all things that thou mayest prosper and be in health, even as thy soul prospereth."* God's will is good toward you. So many times we hear law-oriented preachers telling us that there is a God sitting up in heaven who has a club in His hand, ready to strike as soon as we make a mistake. My Bible tells me *"who shall deliver me from the body of this death"* (Romans 7:4). I thank God that it is through Jesus Christ. It goes onto say, in Romans 8:1, *"There is therefore now no condemnation to them which are in Christ Jesus,"* and in the Greek that reads, "No, not even one little condemnation."

God's will towards you is good. Stop listening to voices that tell you something to the contrary. *"For the Lord's portion is his people,"* (Deuteronomy 32:9). God cares for you; he loves you. He didn't have to die for you, but He did it because He wanted to. *"For the Lord taketh pleasure in his people"* (Psalms 149:4), and He will bless His people with peace. Let me leave you with this today: God is saying, "Peace, be still" (Mark 4:39), as He said to the boat that was rocking in the storm. *"Peace be still"* and know in your hearts that His will towards you is good.

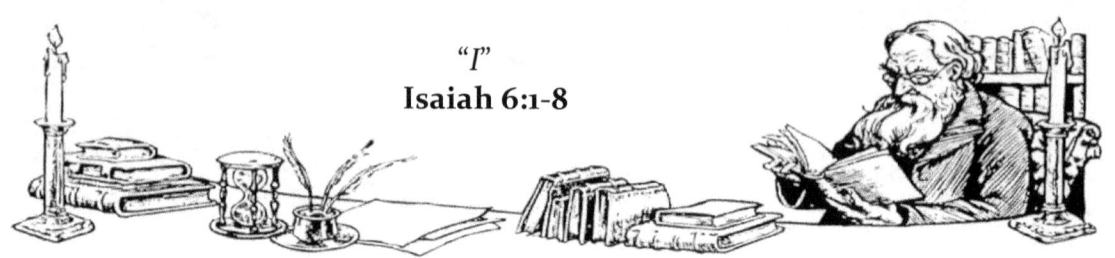

"I"
Isaiah 6:1-8

DAY 230

Here in this chapter of Isaiah's great visitation from the Lord and His ability to see in the realm of the Spirit, we find this personal pronoun "I" mentioned seven times in relation to seven different things. Seven is the number of perfection and so, I believe that this is a great revelation to us about the term "I."

> *"¹In the year that king Uzziah died I saw also the Lord sitting upon a throne, high and lifted up, and his train filled the temple. ²Above it stood the seraphims: each one had six wings; with twain he covered his face, and with twain he covered his feet, and with twain he did fly. ³And one cried unto another, and said, Holy, holy, holy, is the Lord of hosts: the whole earth is full of his glory. ⁴And the posts of the door moved at the voice of him that cried, and the house was filled with smoke. ⁵Then said I, Woe is me! for I am undone; because I am a man of unclean lips, and I dwell in the midst of a people of unclean lips: for mine eyes have seen the King, the Lord of hosts. ⁶Then flew one of the seraphims unto me, having a live coal in his hand, which he had taken with the tongs from off the altar: ⁷And he laid it upon my mouth, and said, Lo, this hath touched thy lips; and thine iniquity is taken away, and thy sin purged. ⁸Also I heard the voice of the Lord, saying, Whom shall I send, and who will go for us? Then said I, Here am I; send me"* (Isaiah 6:1-8).

I want us to look at the things that Isaiah says here in relation to this term "I". First of all he says *"I saw the Lord"*. You and I need desperately to see the Lord *"upon a throne, high and lifted up"*. When we do and we get a clue of what's going on in the heaven and we see the glorious atmosphere, the angels of God, and the cloud of glory our response should be like verse five, *"Then said I, Woe is me!"* When we come in contact with the glorious holiness of God it exposes all the uncleanness within us.

Isaiah then says, *"Because I am a man of unclean lips."* We must also realize that our tongue and our mouth are not as clean as they should be, nor are we carrying the gospel on our lips. Then he says, *"I dwell in the midst of a people of unclean lips"*. As we continue to watch and behold Him we see that He has a provision for us in our uncleanness. That provision is the glory. The glory will expose us but then the glory will also empower us! Verse 8 says, *"I heard the voice of the Lord, saying, Whom shall I send?"* When we hear the voice of the Lord it gives us fresh purpose and vision. Hearing Him is a must for us, it's personal. Then Isaiah said *"Then said I, Here am I; send me."*

Here are the seven "I's", the seven glorious revelations for us today: *"I saw the Lord, I said woe is me, I am undone, I am a man of unclean lips, I dwell in the midst of a people with unclean lips, I heard the voice of the Lord, then said I, Here am I; send me"*.

"At Midnight"
Matthew 25:6

DAY 231

We find in this tremendous passage what happens at midnight, *"And at midnight there was a cry made, Behold, the bridegroom cometh; go ye out to meet him"* (Matthew 25:6). The bridegroom here is Jesus and the call of the bride to go out and meet Him is made. Midnight, the darkest hour of the day, is when the cry is going to be made for the bride to go out to meet the bridegroom. As such, the bride must be preparing herself, getting ready for this. Are you preparing yourself today to go and meet Him?

Remember it was at midnight when the angel of death went out into the land of Egypt to smite all the firstborn. At midnight is when there is trouble. Job 34:20 says, *"The people shall be troubled at midnight."* In Acts 16, Paul and Silas had been captured, beaten, and thrown into the inner-most prison. They had suffered greatly. But the Bible says:

> *"²⁵And at midnight Paul and Silas prayed, and sang praises unto God: and the prisoners heard them. ²⁶And suddenly there was a great earthquake, so that the foundations of the prison were shaken: and immediately all the doors were opened, and every one's bands were loosed"* (Acts 16:25-26).

Likewise, you and I need to pray and sing praises at midnight, during our darkest hour. Midnight may be the darkest hour of the day, but it is always darkest before the dawn. David said in Psalms 119:62, *"At midnight I will rise to give thanks."* At midnight, you and I need to arise, shake off the darkness, not be troubled, not fear the angel of death or any other creature, but begin to pray, give thanks, and sing praises and God will move and send an earthquake to our situation. And not only will our bonds be loosed, but the prisoners around us will hear us and their bonds will be loosed too!

Are you rising to give thanks at midnight? Or do you curse the darkness? Hear the word of the Lord today. In your darkness God will give you *"songs of deliverance"* (Psalms 32:7). Job 35:10 says God *"giveth songs in the night."*

At midnight we need to arise and give thanks unto Him as I Thessalonians 5:18 says, *"In every thing give thanks: for this is the will of God in Christ Jesus concerning you."* At midnight the bride goes out to meet the bridegroom. We must shake ourselves from any sleepiness or foolishness; make sure we have oil in our lamps, and go out to meet Him. No matter how dark it is, Psalms 139 says, *"the night shineth as the day: the darkness and the light are both alike to thee"* (Psalms 139:12). There is no darkness so dark that God cannot still bring light.

Today, the call is out to go and meet Jesus at midnight. At midnight we will find Jesus, our bridegroom, closer than ever. What once was the darkest hour, light dawns, and our deliverance comes. Bless His holy name!

"I Will Heal Their Backsliding"
Hosea 14:4

DAY 232

Oh, what a wonderful promise we have in the Scriptures found here in the book of Hosea! God is dealing with the people who have been disloyal to Him and left Him. His response to them is His response to all those that are disloyal.

Hear the Word of the Lord today and remember this, not only for yourself, but for all your loved ones, your children, husbands, wives, family members, all those who are no longer, like Paul said in Philippians 3:14, *"pressing toward the mark for the prize of the high calling,"* running after Jesus with all their hearts. For all those who have become cold-hearted, lukewarm or just standing still and not really going on with God, this is the Word of the Lord for all of them. God says in Hosea 14:4, *"I will heal their backsliding, I will love them freely: for mine anger is turned away from him."* Bless the Lord!

The word *"backsliding"* here in Hebrew means "turning away, to retreat, to turn back." Too many times people turn away from the Lord because they have been offended or simply because they feel they can't walk the walk. Sometimes they may have had some bad experiences; other times they feel as if God doesn't meet their expectations or simply are overcome with sin. However, remember Jesus, who knows all things, knows everything about them. He counted the cost before He came into their life and He saved them (Luke 14:28) knowing everything about them. So here is the word of the Lord to them. God is going to heal their backsliding. Some other translations read:

> *"I will heal their disloyalty, their faithlessness, their waywardness"*
> *"I will love them lavishly"*
> *"My love will know no bounds"*
> *"I will forgive them for leaving me"*
> *"I will bring my people back to me"*
> *"I will love them with all my heart"*
> *"No longer am I angry with them"*

You see, even though others may be backslidden, they are still His people. We will always remain the sheep of His hand. Paul writes in II Timothy 2:13, *"If we believe not, yet he abideth faithful: he cannot deny himself."* Jesus said in John 10:28, *"And I give unto them eternal life; and they shall never perish, neither shall any man pluck them out of my hand."* David said in the book of Psalms:

> *"⁷Whither shall I go from thy spirit? or whither shall I flee from thy presence? ⁸If I ascend up into heaven, thou art there: if I make my bed in hell, behold, thou art there. ⁹If I take the wings of the morning, and dwell in the uttermost parts of the sea; ¹⁰Even there shall thy hand lead me, and thy right hand shall hold me. ¹¹If I say, Surely the darkness*

> *shall cover me; even the night shall be light about me. ^{12}Yea, the darkness hideth not from thee; but the night shineth as the day: the darkness and the light are both alike to thee. ^{13}For thou hast possessed my reins: thou hast covered me in my mother's womb"* (Psalms 139:7-13).

God, who knows everything, will never leave us nor forsake us. No matter where we are, His presence will still be there. He may be silent perhaps, but yet in the background He is watching, carrying, worrying, and leading us home. We read in Jeremiah:

> *"^{12}Go and proclaim these words toward the north, and say, Return, thou backsliding Israel, saith the Lord; and I will not cause mine anger to fall upon you: for I am merciful, saith the Lord, and I will not keep anger for ever. ^{13}Only acknowledge thine iniquity, that thou hast transgressed against the Lord thy God, and hast scattered thy ways to the strangers under every green tree, and ye have not obeyed my voice, saith the Lord. ^{14}Turn, O backsliding children, saith the Lord; for I am married unto you..."* (Jeremiah 3:12-14).

What a promise! He is married to us! All we need to do is acknowledge our iniquity, repent, return to Him and He will heal our backsliding. In the same chapter of Jeremiah 3:22 it says, *"Return, ye backsliding children, and I will heal your backslidings."* And they answer by saying, *"Behold, we come unto thee; for thou art the Lord our God."* He is our Lord and our God. If we will just return to Him He will heal our backslidings.

In Proverbs 14:14 it says, *"The backslider in heart shall be filled with his own ways."* This reminds me of the prodigal son in Luke 15 who leaves his father, takes his inheritance, and runs off. How did the father react? He didn't scream or try to prevent him from doing it. He simply let him go. However, the father goes outside, at the farthest point of the house on the highway, waiting for him to come back home.

I believe that the father in that story is a type and shadow of God the Father. The prodigal is us in many cases of our lives. The Father is waiting there, not standing in the house angry and spouting all kinds of judgments, rather, He is waiting patiently there for our return home. You see, He knows something. He knows that we were born of incorruptible seed and even when backslidden, that seed still remains in our hearts. He knows that eventually we will be filled with our own ways and we will come to ourselves and say like the prodigal said in Luke 15:18, *"I will arise and go to my father."* When he does return home, the Father greets him by throwing his arms around him, kissing him and hugging him. He then throws a party for him saying in Luke 15:32, *"It was meet that we should make merry, and be glad: for this thy brother was dead, and is alive again; and was lost, and is found."*

"Return, ye backsliding children, and I will heal you of your backslidings" (Jeremiah 3:22). What a great Savior we serve! What a precious and merciful Father we serve who vigilantly looks after us. The hound of heaven, the Holy Spirit, follows us until we come home. He will bring us home, for He is married unto us! Instead of giving up on like so many teach, He will ultimately heal the backslider!

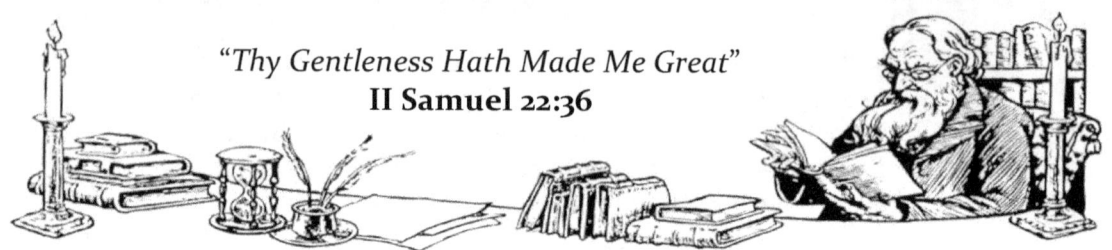

"Thy Gentleness Hath Made Me Great"
II Samuel 22:36

DAY 233

Here in II Samuel 22:36 it says, *"Thou hast also given me the shield of thy salvation: and thy gentleness hath made me great."* Thy gentleness hath made me great. The only way you and I will ever be great, that is, mature in God or perfected, is through His gentleness. The word *"gentleness"* here in the Hebrew means humility, royal mildness or meekness, to be humble in mind, especially saintly. My, my, my! Isn't this true of our God? Look at some other translations:

"And lowliness maketh me great"
"You stooped down to make me great"
"You touched me and I feel ten feet tall"
"Your willingness to help enables me to prevail"
"Thy mildness hath multiplied me"

Oh, what a great God! We find the same passage in Psalms 18:35. Without our precious Father stooping down to help us, we would have forever been lost in anonymity. Whatever we have, whatever we become or will be is because He will have made us that way. In II Corinthians 10:1 Paul says, *"Now I Paul myself beseech you by the meekness and gentleness of Christ."* Jesus said in Matthew 11:29, *"Take my yoke upon you, and learn of me; for I am meek and lowly in heart."* Arrogance is so foreign to Him; boastfulness is so unlike Him. We have too much arrogance and boasting in ministry today. There are too many peacocks prancing around when we should have some meekness and lowliness. In Zephaniah 3:12 He says, *"I will also leave in the midst of thee an afflicted and poor people."* Some other translations of II Corinthians 10:1 read:

"By the gentleness and consideration of Christ"
"By the quiet and gentle behavior of Christ"
"The mildness and modesty of Christ"
"By the gentleness and self-forgetfulness of Christ"

My goodness! Self-forgetfulness of Christ! Can we forget ourselves? My goodness! Isaiah 48:11 says, *"He shall feed his flock like a shepherd: he shall gather the lambs with his arm, and carry them in his bosom, and shall gently lead those that are with young."* His gentleness will make us great.

James 3:17 says, *"But the wisdom that is from above is first pure, then peaceable, gentle."* Coming from above is the gentle, precious, humble nature of our God. As we embrace His image, it will make us great. In Proverbs 29:21 it says, *"He that delicately bringeth up his servant from a child shall have him become his son at the length."* Another translation of this verse reads, *"If a servant is gently cared for in his early years, he will become your son."* You and I are servants of Christ, sons of God, but we are destined to be mature sons of God. He is delicately, gently bringing us up from a child, so that at the length we may be called the sons of God.

"His Compassions Fail Not"
Lamentations 3:22-23

DAY 234

Out of the Scriptures we find such a tremendous promise to us as the Lord's people, and even to the world: that our God is not only a God of goodness, mercy, and forgiveness, but He is moved with compassion. Lamentations 3:22-23 says, *"It is of the Lord's mercies that we are not consumed, because his compassions fail not. They are new every morning."*

The Greek word for *"compassion"* means "to have bowels for; to yearn; to feel sympathy; to feel pity; to be moved with an inward affection, the deep part of someone's emotions, for someone else; tender mercy." This is how our God feels for us. Today, hear the word of the Lord. The Lord's compassions for you will never fail. In fact, they are new every morning! Every morning He is watching and moved in His heart to help you in any way He can. In Matthew 14:14 it says, *"And Jesus went forth, and saw a great multitude, and was moved with compassion toward them, and he healed their sick."* He was moved with compassion for His people. God's compassion moves Him to heal us.

Again we find this in Mark 1:41, *"And Jesus, moved with compassion put forth his hand, and touched him, and saith unto him, I will; be thou clean."* This was Jesus' response to a leper asking Him if He can make him clean. This is our God. Psalms 111:4 says *"the Lord is gracious and full of compassion."* Over and over again we see that He is full of compassion! *"But thou, O Lord, art a God full of compassion, and gracious, longsuffering, and plenteous in mercy and truth."* (Psalms 86:15). Psalms 112:4 says *"he is gracious, and full of compassion."* Psalms 145:8 says *"The Lord is gracious, and full of compassion; slow to anger, and of great mercy."*

This is our God. He yearns for us and feels sympathy. The deepest part of His emotion is moved for you and me. He's sat where we've sat. He feels what we feel. He put upon Himself human flesh so that He could know what we go through, *"for we have not an high priest which cannot be touched with the feeling of our infirmities"* (Hebrews 4:15). Just like the father in Luke 15:20, *"But when [the prodigal son] was yet a great way off, his father saw him, and had compassion, and ran, and fell on his neck, and kissed him."* If you're a great way off today, the Father is watching and waiting. As soon as He sees anything from us, He will run to us and have compassion on us. He'll fall on our neck and kiss us. This is our God.

Oh how precious, merciful, and wonderful He is, that His heart yearns for us. We see this in Micah 7:18-19, *"He retaineth not his anger for ever, because he delighteth in mercy. ¹⁹ He will turn again, he will have compassion upon us; he will subdue our iniquities; and thou wilt cast all their sins into the depths of the sea."* As Jesus said to the Gadarene man in Mark 5:19, *"Go home to thy friends, and tell them how great things the Lord hath done for thee, and hath had compassion on thee."* Even if you are a great way off today, your heavenly Father is moved with compassion and full of great mercy!

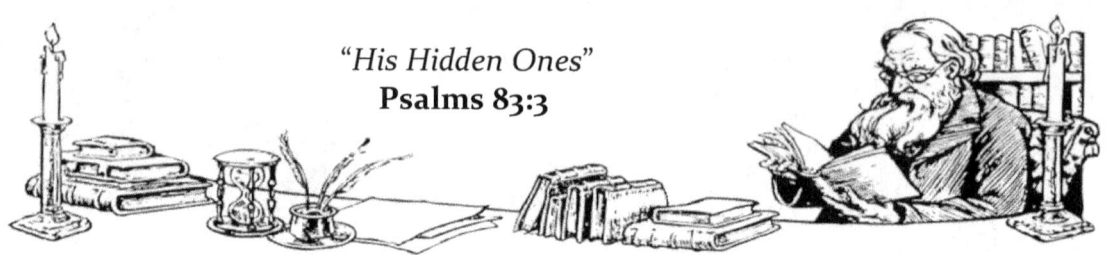

"His Hidden Ones"
Psalms 83:3

DAY 235

This is an illuminating revelation in Scripture. God has what are called *"hidden ones."* It is precious to know that God will hide us when the wicked in the world are oppressing and tormenting us. To be kept hidden and protected by Him is a joy. As we look at these hidden ones, let the true picture in the Scriptures come to show you what it means to be a *"hidden one."*

Psalms 83:3 reads, *"They have taken crafty counsel against thy people, and consulted against thy hidden ones."* Some other translations read:

> *"Your hidden and precious ones"*
> *"Your treasured ones"*
> *"Those you cherish"*
> *"Your sheltered one"*
> *"Those you love"*
> *"Thy protected ones"*
> *"Those of who you keep in a secret place"*

The word *"hidden"* means "to hide by covering over, to hoard, to reserve, to protect, to keep secret." God has a people that He is hiding, sheltering, protecting and keeping. They are to Him precious, treasured, cherished and loved. A great day is coming when He shall be revealed in glory through these hidden ones.

There was an Old Testament king who was hidden for many years because if he was found, he would have been killed. God is hiding us in the house of the Lord. You may be hidden, but the day is coming when the Lord is going to reveal His hidden ones and say, just as Pilate said about Jesus in John 19:5, *"...Behold, the man!"* The Lord spoke to me many years ago and said, "I will say unto the world one day, Behold, the many-membered man, the perfect man (as Ephesians 4:13 brings out), the sons of God."

God wants us hidden in Him. Colossians 3:3 says, *"For ye are dead, and your life is hid with Christ in God."* Your life is hidden with the Lord Jesus and He has anointed you for a reason. He hides us to deal with us, to teach us, to prepare us, to water us. We are a garden enclosed (Song of Solomon 4:12), so that He can work deep, deep in our souls, delivering us not only from the things that oppress us, but opening our souls chamber by chamber to fill them with His Word, His character, His presence and Holy Spirit.

In Exodus 33:21 God says, *"Behold, there is a place by me, and thou shalt stand upon a rock."* There is a place by Him where you and I can hide. It is called the secret place of the Most High and there abide under the shadow of the Almighty be protected by the wings of God (Psalms 91:1). We can be shielded and be hidden from the world. Yet all the while, He can deal with us and minister to us and bless us.

In Psalms 119:114 says, "*Thou art my hiding place and my shield.*" Psalms 32:7 says, "*Thou art my hiding place; thou shalt preserve me from trouble; thou shalt compass me about with songs of deliverance.*" He is our hiding place. Like a great eagle, He watches over us, nurtures us, protects us and shields us from the world, the flesh and the devil. Psalms 17:8 says, "*Keep me as the apple of the eye, hide me under the shadow of thy wings*" Psalms 57:1 says, "*yea, in the shadow of thy wings will I make my refuge, until these calamities be overpast.*" We need to run to the Lord, to that righteous tower and be safe. Psalms 91:1 says, "*He that dwelleth in the secret place of the most High shall abide under the shadow of the Almighty.*" Psalms 27:5 says, "*For in the time of trouble he shall hide me in his pavilion: in the secret of his tabernacle shall he hide me; he shall set me up upon a rock.*"

God is calling you now. Deep is calling unto deep (Psalms 42:7), drawing you into the secret place so He can hide you from the world, the flesh and the devil and minister His great grace to you. He wants to change you. Let's be one of God's hidden ones today, as we prepare to be displayed before the world, allowing the glory of God to shine through us, for "*Out of Zion, the perfection of beauty, God hath shined*" (Psalms 50:2).

"Chiefest Among Ten Thousand"
Song of Solomon 5:10

DAY 236

In this passage in Song of Solomon 5, the bride has gone searching for her lover, after He has tried to visit her. She did not respond immediately to Him when He was entreating her even though her *"bowels were moved for him"* (Song of Solomon 5:4). Therefore He withdrew himself. This caused her to get up and seek Him. This was God's intention all along. She says in verse 8, *"I charge you, O daughters of Jerusalem, if ye find my beloved, that ye tell him, that I am sick of love,"* (Song of Solomon 5:8). In other words, she was faint with desire for Him.

Is He the *"chiefest among ten thousand"* to you (Song of Solomon 5:10)? It says in Exodus, *"Who is like unto thee, O Lord, among the gods? who is like thee, glorious in holiness, fearful in praises, doing wonders"* (Exodus 15:11)? The Bible says He's the *"bright and morning star"* (Revelation 22:16). David said, *"For thou art great, and doest wondrous things: thou art God alone"* (Psalms 86:10). There is none like the Lord, absolutely none. The book of Jeremiah declares, *"Praise the Lord of hosts: for the Lord is good; for his mercy endureth for ever"* (Jeremiah 33:11).

Hebrews 2:9 tells us, *"But we see Jesus."* Our beloved Jesus is the chiefest; He is the greatest and the highest in our lives. He's everything to us. *"O taste and see that the Lord is good: blessed is the man that trusteth in him,"* the book of Psalms declares (Psalms 34:8). Peter tells us, *"Unto you therefore which believe he is precious"* (I Peter 2:7). Those of us that believe and know Him know just how precious and glorious He is. He is the chiefest and the greatest. He's our leader. He stands out among everyone else, a bright light shining in a dark place.

He said, *"And I, if I be lifted up from the earth, will draw all men unto me"* (John 12:32). As you and I lift Him up in our personal lives, in our souls, in our praise and worship, in our thought lives, and set our affection on things above (Colossians 3:2), we will see Jesus rising above all else. We will see Him *"high and lifted up,"* and His train filling the temple (Isaiah 6:1).

Notice that in Song of Solomon 5:7, *"The watchmen that went about the city found me, they smote me, they wounded me."* The watchmen represent leadership, perhaps even leaders in the body of Christ. They found her searching so desperately for her lover and smote and wounded her. Many times, even Christian leaders and pastors don't understand our desire and our passion for the Lord. They may ask us, as they did in verse 9, *"what is thy beloved more than another beloved, that thou dost so charge us?"*

Her answer was simply, *"My beloved is...the chiefest among ten thousand...¹⁶His mouth is most sweet: yea, he is altogether lovely. This is my beloved, and this is my friend, O daughters of Jerusalem"* (Song of Solomon 5:10-16). What would we answer somebody if asked why do we love Jesus the way we do? Well, to those in the bride, Jesus is the *"chiefest among ten thousand."*

"Judah Is My Lawgiver"
Psalms 60:7

Oh, what a glorious revelation this is! Judah is my lawgiver. What does this actually mean? Well, first of all we understand that the word *"Judah"* means "praise" in the Hebrew. So, what does this mean? It means then "praise is my lawgiver."

The Bible says in Colossians 2:20 that you and I are no longer under the restraints of touch not, taste not, and handle not. Christ is the end of the law the Bible says (Romans 10:4). Christ has fulfilled the law. We no longer live under those handwritings of ordinances that were against us (Colossians 2:14), but now we live in grace and truth that came by Jesus Christ. We live under grace, but in that grace is this wonderful revelation: as we worship and as we praise God, this is the lawgiver.

You might say "what do you mean, Brother Sam?" Well, what I mean is this: that the governing aspect of our lives now is our love for the Lord and our devotion to Him, as is given when we praise and worship Him. In other words, we decide not to sin now not because there's a word telling us not to, even though it's okay to do that. Our primary reason for not sinning is because of our love for the Lord. I worship God. I praise His glorious, mighty name and that very praise and worship governs me and keeps me from falling into sin or backsliding. It is now the lawgiver in my life. Plus, out of praise and worship we know that revelation flows.

In Genesis 49:10 it says, *"The sceptre shall not depart from Judah, nor a lawgiver from between his feet, until Shiloh come."* Shiloh is Jesus, and so, until the coming of the Lord, Judah is going to have the scepter, the rod of authority, in his hand, because he has attained to that place of worship. Psalms 50:2 says, *"out of Zion, the perfection of beauty, God hath shined."* Psalms 22:3 says, *"But thou art holy, O thou that inhabitest the praises of Israel."* God inhabits Judah and as He does, the rod of authority comes forth in him. As that rod of authority comes forth, the Word of God then flows freely from His presence.

The law then has now become praise and worship. It is the very thing that will keep you and me from going astray and from sinning. If we would just keep a worshipping heart, a thankful heart, we would never ever fall. I Thessalonians 5 says *"In every thing give thanks: for this is the will of God in Christ Jesus concerning you."*

Judah is our lawgiver. Out of praise and worship flows revelation and flows the Word of God. Some other translations of this verse read: *"Judah holds my royal scepter", "Judah is my royal scepter", "Judah is my hammer", "Judah, my scepter, will produce kings."* Judah produces kings because Judah has the Word of the Lord and Judah is praise. That is the lawgiver. That is the thing that restrains us, that governs us and that keeps us. *"Oh that men would praise the Lord for his goodness"* (Psalms 107:8). Rise up, enter into Judah today, and become a worshipper. As you do, the Word of God will flow freely from you and to you, and will keep you. No longer will you need rules and regulations. For that very praise is your rule.

"When I Cry Unto Thee, Then Shall Mine Enemies Turn Back"
Psalms 56:9

DAY 238

One of the great blessings of being a Christian is that we do not fight alone. In all of our battles, we have the God of the universe and all the resources of heaven standing behind and beside us to help us and fight for us. David says in Psalms 56:9, *"When I cry unto thee, then shall mine enemies turn back: this I know; for God is for me."* Some other translations read:

> *"The very day I call for help, the tide of the battle turns. My enemies flee!"*
> *"On the day I call for help, my enemies will be defeated. I know that God is on my side."*

You need to know that God is for you. You also need to know that there is nothing wrong with crying unto the Lord when your enemies come against you. He will cause them to turn back. The word *"enemies"* here in the Hebrew means "one of an opposite tribe, an adversary that hates you, or one that is hostile against you."

Psalms 60:12 tells us, *"Through God we shall do valiantly: for he it is that shall tread down our enemies."* In Micah it says *"the Lord shall redeem thee from the hand of thine enemies"* (Micah 4:10). It says in another place, *"Thou hast also given me the necks of mine enemies; that I might destroy them that hate me"* (Psalms 18:40). I love the story in II Samuel, when David goes to Baal-perazim. There the Lord breaks forth upon His enemies and brings deliverance to David and the people (II Samuel 5:20). The word *"Baal-perazim"* means "master of the breakthrough." He is the master of the breakthrough. Deuteronomy says, *"And it shall be, when ye are come nigh unto the battle, that the priest shall approach and speak unto the people, ³And shall say unto them, Hear, O Israel, ye approach this day unto battle against your enemies: let not your hearts faint, fear not, and do not tremble, neither be ye terrified because of them; ⁴For the Lord your God is he that goeth with you, to fight for you against your enemies, to save you"* (Deuteronomy 20:2-4).

Hallelujah! When our enemies come against us, God will come in and stand for us, and they must turn back. It says in Psalms 9:2-3, *"I will be glad and rejoice in thee: I will sing praise to thy name, O thou most High. ³When mine enemies are turned back, they shall fall and perish at thy presence."* Oh, praise the Lord! God is for you and me, and the enemies that are coming against us must turn back.

Psalms 27 says *"²When the wicked, even mine enemies and my foes, came upon me to eat up my flesh, they stumbled and fell. ³Though an host should encamp against me, my heart shall not fear: though war should rise against me, in this will I be confident"* (Psalms 27:2-3). You should be confident that the Lord will stand with you against any odds and turn back your enemies, because God is for you.

"The Angel Of The Lord Encampeth"
Psalms 34:7

DAY 239

Today I want to look at the subject of angels and how the angel of the Lord is sent to protect us, keep us and guide us in all our ways. In Psalms 34:7 it says, *"The angel of the LORD encampeth round about them that fear him, and delivereth them."* The Hebrew word for *"encampeth"* means, "to pitch a tent." The root word comes from the same Hebrew word for mercy, which means, "to bend or stoop in kindness to an inferior one." The angels, then, bend and stoop in kindness to us. They pitch a tent round about us to bring God's great mercy and deliver us in our lives. What a glorious truth this is!

Hebrews 1:14 says, *"Are they* [angels] *not all ministering spirits, sent forth to minister for them who shall be heirs of salvation?"* You and I are heirs of salvation and the angels of the Lord have been sent forth to minister for us. Jesus said in Matthew 18:10, *"Take heed that ye despise not one of these little ones; for I say unto you, That in heaven their angels do always behold the face of my Father which is in heaven."* All of us are given angels to watch over us, to protect us and to keep us. I imagine all of us have at least one angel. Some of us, perhaps, have more than others. But nonetheless, it is an angel's job sent from the Lord to protect, keep, guide and watch over us.

In Psalms 91:11 it says, *"For he shall give his angels charge over thee, to keep thee in all thy ways."* His angels have a job to do and it is to keep us in all our ways. Remember in Matthew 4:11, when Jesus was in the wilderness, it says that, *"Then the devil leaveth him, and behold, the angels came and ministered unto him."* Angels not only came then, but they came in the garden of Gethsemane and ministered to Jesus and encouraged Him there as well.

Oh that our spiritual eyes were opened today and we could see into the realm of the spirit and see that the spiritual realm is much more real than the earthly, natural realm, because that which happens in the spiritual realm controls and rules that which is in the earthly realm. All around us are angels protecting, keeping and watching over us and are there to minister for us and to us, if need be.

Abraham, when he sent his servant to look for his son a bride, said in Genesis 24:40, *"The LORD, before whom I walk, will send his angel with thee, and prosper thy way."* An angel is with us at all times and is there to prosper our way. Consider this today, before you go to work, before you get involved in today's activities or even at the end of the day, the angel of the Lord is with you and he's there to prosper your way, to help you along, to bring peace and prosperity into your life.

Remember in I Kings 19, how that Elijah was fed by an angel. An angel brought him food morning and evening. If only you and I could believe and know in our hearts that our angels are always there, ready to help us and assist us when we need it.

Hebrews 12:22 says, *"But ye are come unto mount Zion, and unto the city of the living God, the heavenly Jerusalem, and to an innumerable company of angels."* There are more angels, in the multiple millions perhaps, and they are sent for us, to help us.

One of the things I took note of as I was studying this was in Luke 16:22, which says, *"And it came to pass, that the beggar died, and was carried by the angels into Abraham's bosom."* I believe that at the moment we leave this life, we are met by the angels of God. Perhaps we are carried by the angels that are around us all of the time that we don't actually see or know. They are there ready to carry us into the very presence of God.

But why wait for then, when we can have them now and enjoy them. Peter enjoyed and received the benefits of his angels in Acts 5:19, when it says, *"But the angel of the Lord by night opened the prison doors, and brought them forth."* If you are in a prison today, you are not there alone. Remember when Daniel was in the lion's den, the angel of the Lord came and shut the lion's mouth. The angels are always there, waiting to assist, waiting to bless God's precious gift to us, always surrounding us and watching over us. We need not fear. The angel of the Lord encamps round about us and delivers us. They stoop in kindness, though we may seem to be inferior in this earthly form.

All the way back to the book of Exodus, when the children of Israel went forth through the wilderness, it says in Exodus 14:19, *"And the angel of God, which went before the camp of Israel, removed and went behind them."* The angel of the Lord went before them and behind them, to protect them in the front and guard them in the back. This is the will of God for every one of us. Right now, as we close this page, consider that the angel of the Lord is right there with you, encamping. The angel has pitched a tent. He is there to minister to you, to go before you, to prosper you, to lead you in the way, and to hold up your feet. Let him do it. Receive the angels of the Lord now and let them do their job in your life!

"Ready For The Marriage"
John 2:1-2

In John 2 we read:

DAY 240

> *"And the third day there was a marriage in Cana of Galilee; and the mother of Jesus was there: ²And both Jesus was called, and his disciples, to the marriage...¹¹This beginning of miracles did Jesus in Cana of Galilee, and manifested forth his glory; and his disciples believed on him"* (John 2:1-2, 11).

The word *"Galilee"* means "a circuit." In other words, this whole story is going to come full circle again. This natural story will find its fulfillment spiritual in the last days. The third day is coming. II Peter 3:8 says, *"That one day is with the Lord as a thousand years, and a thousand years as one day."* Therefore prophetically speaking, the third day from the resurrection of Jesus is dawning upon us. The third day is when God manifests Himself, comes for His people, and manifests Himself in His sons. Moreover, on the third day there is going to be a marriage. And who is going to be called to the marriage? Jesus and His disciples. You and I are called to this marriage. It is the marriage supper of the Lamb.

Matthew 25:10 says, *"And while they went to buy, the bridegroom came; and they that were ready went in with him to the marriage: and the door was shut."* What a horrible thing for the door to be shut and we are not allowed entrance into the marriage supper of the Lamb. But nonetheless, these were the five wise virgins that were escorted in because they bought oil, and paid the price and were ready. We find this again in Revelation 19:7, *"the marriage of the Lamb is come, and his wife hath made herself ready."* You and I need to make ourselves ready for the marriage supper of the Lamb because it's coming. But it seems too often that we hear excuses from the body of Christ. It says here in Matthew:

> *"²The kingdom of heaven is like unto a certain king, which made a marriage for his son, ³And sent forth his servants to call them that were bidden to the wedding...all things are ready: come unto the marriage. ⁵But they made light of it, and went their ways, one to his farm, another to his merchandise...But when the king heard thereof, he was wroth...⁸Then saith he to his servants, The wedding is ready, but they which were bidden were not worthy"* (Matthew 22:2-8).

You and I need to be ready. We need to be worthy of this wedding. In another passage of Scripture along the same lines, the Bible says, *"And they all with one consent began to make excuse"* (Luke 14:18). What is the excuse that you might use to not be ready? Let it not be said of you that you were not ready, but let it be said that you made yourself ready, paid the price, bought the oil, and did what was necessary because Jesus wants to manifest His glory. Just as He did with the beginning of miracles, the last miracle will be the bride.

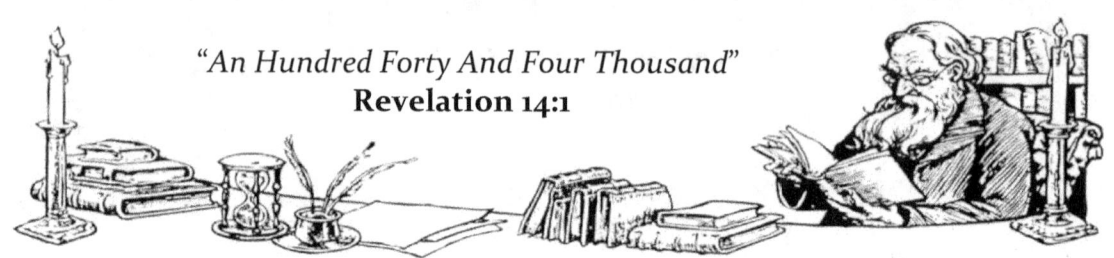

"An Hundred Forty And Four Thousand"
Revelation 14:1

Revelation 14:1 says, *"And I looked, and, lo, a Lamb stood on the mount Sion, and with him an hundred forty and four thousand, having his Father's name written in their foreheads."* What a glorious truth this is found here in the book of Revelation.

DAY 241

In most evangelical circles, they think this is speaking of the Jews. Furthermore, I refer you to Revelation 4:1 where the angel tells John, "I'm going to show you things to come." It is not speaking of the past, but it is speaking of the future. This 144,000 isn't an exact 144,000 people, but it is a company of people that are to come forth. The number twelve multiplied by twelve is equal to one hundred forty-four (12 x 12 = 144). Twelve in the Scriptures is the number for "divine government" or "complete government." So it means that this 144,000 are those walking in the divine government of God. I believe that this is speaking of the Kingdom of God.

As described in Revelation 14, the Lord is standing on Mount Zion. Zion is the place of worship. It is the place where our hearts enthrone the Lord. He sits between the cherubim and rests upon us. *"But thou art holy, O thou that inhabitest the praises of Israel"* (Psalms 22:3). He comes and rests in His love as we worship Him. Out of those worshippers, God is going to select 144,000, or those that are walking in God's divine government and kingdom and have His image. Why do we say that? It's because next it says, they have their *"Father's name written in their foreheads."*

The word *"written"* means "image." In other words, they have their Father's image in their foreheads. This simply means that this 144,000 have the mind of Christ. Their minds have been renewed and they have the image of Jesus written and worked into their lives. No longer are they ruled by the carnal Adamic nature. It goes on to say in verse 3 that they sang a new song, *"And they sung as it were a new song before the throne, and before the four beasts, and the elders: and no man could learn that song but the hundred and forty and four thousand, which were redeemed from the earth."*

"Redeemed from the earth" speaks of a remnant of people taken out of the earth. They sing a new song and are those worshippers who worship in Spirit and truth and have risen up to a place where they enter into the spiritual songs, as spoken of in Ephesians 5:19, *"Speaking to yourselves in psalms and hymns and spiritual songs, singing and making melody in your heart to the Lord."* Those who are walking in the government and Kingdom of God are worshippers. Verse 4 says, *"These are they which were not defiled with women; for they are virgins. These are they which follow the Lamb whithersoever he goeth. These were redeemed from among men, being the firstfruits unto God and to the Lamb."*

These were not defiled with women; this was not speaking naturally but spiritually. They haven't committed spiritual adultery, *"for they are virgins"*. Every believer is a spiritual virgin. And they are those who follow the Lamb. They are the firstfruits, the first ripened ones. They are the overcomers and they were taken from among men.

They are the remnant who follows the Lamb wherever He goes. This is their destiny and this is the choice they've made.

As we continue on to Revelation 14:5, it says, *"And in their mouth was found no guile: for they are without fault before the throne of God."* As Song of Solomon 4:7 says, *"Thou art all fair, my love; there is no spot in thee."* There is no fault or sin in them anymore, they've been totally redeemed. They don't lie or have deceit in them. They are walking in the Kingdom of God. Let us choose today to run after the Lord, to be a part of this 144,000.

"Our Banners"
Psalms 20:5

Day 242

We want to consider today the principle of banners in Scripture. In Psalms 20:5 it says, *"In the name of our God we will set up our banners."* Perhaps you didn't know it; we have banners to set up. The word *"banners"* in Hebrew means, "a sign, a signal; to be conspicuous, to flaunt." This definition implies that you want everyone to see these banners.

What are these banners that we want to flaunt to the world that in the name of our God we are to set up? In Psalms 60:4 it says, *"Thou hast given a banner to them that fear thee."* All those that fear Him, God has given to them a banner. It goes on to say in that verse, *"...that it may be displayed because of the truth. Selah."* Jesus is the *"way, truth and the life,"* John 14:6 states. Because truth has made us free, we can lift up a banner as a sign to the world and even be very conspicuous about it (and even flaunt it). We can lift up that banner to let the world know that our God is true and righteous altogether.

In Song of Solomon 2:4 it says, *"His banner over me was love."* Oh that we lift up the banner of love and tell people how much the world means to Him, how much we mean to Him and how desirous He is of our fellowship, our communion and habitation with Him.

In Song of Solomon 6:4 and 10, in talking about the bride of Christ, it says that she is, *"terrible as an army with banners."* When Israel would defeat an enemy, after they defeated them, they would march around them with their banners, very conspicuously and with them held very high, as a sign and a signal, that they were the victors and that God enabled them to be the victors. They also held up the banners to flaunt and to humble their enemy and to let them know that God was greater than they were.

In the name of our God, we will set up our banners. Name reveals character. So in the character of God we will lift up our banners. We will lift up the banner of the love of God, the banner of those that fear Him and the banner of those that walk in truth. We will be as terrible and mighty as an army with banners. We will be the people that walk with the banners of the Lord.

So today, lift up the sign, give the signal, be conspicuous and flaunt the banners of the Lord, the banners of truth, love, fear and of His character and awesome victory and delivering power. As Isaiah 13:2 says, *"Lift ye up a banner."* Let us lift up the banners today. In the name of our God, we will set them up. We will flaunt them in the earth and show them as a sign and a signal, that all will know that our God is the only true God.

"The Day Star Arise In Your Hearts"
II Peter 1:19

DAY 243

One of the wonderful names for Jesus is the *"day star"* or *"day spring."* We find it here in II Peter 1:19, *"We have also a more sure word of prophecy; whereunto ye do well that ye take heed, as unto a light that shineth in a dark place, until the day dawn, and the day star arise in your hearts."* The day star is the star that shines brightly in the morning and then it rises in our hearts at the coming of the Lord. The term *"day star"*, or *"dayspring"* in Hebrew is taken from the root word meaning, "to dawn; to be early at any task; earnestness; to search for painstakingly." The Greek word for *"day star"* means "a rising of light; the dawn; rising up; shooting out as a branch."

So, our *"day star"*, which shines through us from on high, is the Lord Jesus. It's spoken of in Luke:

> *"⁷⁸Through the tender mercy of our God; whereby the dayspring from on high hath visited us, ⁷⁹To give light to them that sit in darkness and in the shadow of death, to guide our feet into the way of peace."* (Luke 1:78-79)

This is our God. He is the *"day star"* and *"dayspring"*. Jesus, in Malachi 4:2, is called the, *"Sun of righteousness aris[ing] with healing in his wings."* In John 8:12, He declares, *"I am the light of the world."* He's come to give light to those that live in darkness. Those wise men in Matthew 2:1-9 followed His star in the east.

Jesus rose from the dead, as it says in Matthew 28:1, *"As it began to dawn toward the first day of the week."* He was the first to rise from the dead to show light to all the nations. In Job 38:12, it says, *"Hast thou commanded the morning since thy days; and caused the dayspring* (or the dawn) *to know his place."* The *"dayspring"* is the dawn of God; it is the glorious light of Jesus; it is the face of our God, the express image of our Father revealed to us in the form of a great light (morning light, dawn). So, you and I, out of our darkness, can begin to see our way through clearly.

Today, try to remember that the *"dayspring"* is coming to bless us and to bring light forever. It says in the New Jerusalem, that there will be no need for any light or any candle will the Lord God is the Light. He's the dawn for us. He is the *"day spring"*.

"Who Is A God Like Unto Thee"
Micah 7:18-19

DAY 244

There is no God like our God. That's why David said in Psalms 116:1, *"I love the Lord, because he hath heard my voice and my supplications."* It says in Micah 7:

> *"¹⁸Who is a God like unto thee, that pardoneth iniquity, and passeth by the transgression of the remnant of his heritage? he retaineth not his anger for ever, because he delighteth in mercy. ¹⁹He will turn again, he will have compassion upon us; he will subdue our iniquities; and thou wilt cast all their sins into the depths of the sea"* (Micah 7:18-19).

Oh, how marvelous and great is the forgiveness of God! Who else would do all this? He pardons our iniquity and passes by our transgression. He doesn't retain His anger, because He delights in mercy. He will turn again toward us and have compassion on us. More than that, He will subdue and help us get delivered from our iniquity. And then He will cast all our sin into the depths of the sea, never to be remembered again. This is why David writes in Psalms 103, *"²Bless the Lord, O my soul, and forget not all his benefits: ³Who forgiveth all thine iniquities"* (Psalms 103:2-3). In Psalms 68, he also says, *"Blessed be the Lord, who daily loadeth us with benefits, even the God of our salvation. Selah"* (Psalms 68:19). This is a daily provision for us.

Who is a God like unto Him? What a glorious, forgiving, merciful God. It says in Psalms 86, *"For thou, Lord, art good, and ready to forgive; and plenteous in mercy unto all them that call upon thee"* (Psalms 86:5). I don't know about you, but I want to start shouting right now, because the Lord is good! And He's ready, willing, and able to forgive us. He is plenteous in mercy to all that call upon Him. He does not disregard anyone. It says in Numbers 14, *"The Lord is longsuffering, and of great mercy, forgiving iniquity and transgression"* (Numbers 14:18). Praise the Lord! Who is a God like unto Him? Who would ever think that our God would be so kind and precious to us, to always forgive us time and time again?

Psalms 130 tells us, *"If thou, Lord, shouldest mark iniquities, O Lord, who shall stand? ⁴But there is forgiveness with thee, that thou mayest be feared"* (Psalms 130:3-4). Thank God, He doesn't mark our iniquities. We shouldn't mark each other's iniquities either, because if He did, none of us could stand. But there is forgiveness with Him, that He may be feared. I did not come to the Lord because of a fear of hell or judgment. I was in such terrible shape that, when I heard of the love and goodness of God, I couldn't believe my ears. So, I readily accepted the Lord Jesus as my Savior, and my life was changed. I never would have dreamed that God could be so good. Who is a God like unto thee, that forgives, pardons iniquities, and doesn't mark our sins? Oh, how I love the Lord, because He has heard my voice. Why don't you worship Him with me now? Thank God for His forgiveness and His goodness and remember that today he has loaded you with His benefits. Amen!

"Our Daysman"
Job 9:33

Day 245

Here in Job 9:33, Job says, *"Neither is there any daysman betwixt us, that might lay his hand upon us both."* This word *"daysman"* is an interesting Hebrew word. A *"daysman"* is "a mediator or an umpire; someone that goes between or advocates for someone else." It is from a Hebrew word which means "to be right or correct, to argue for, to justify or to decide." The word *"mediator"* in Greek means "a go between, an inner communicator, a reconciler or intercessor, someone in the middle." It speaks of one who mediates between two parties with a view to producing peace or one who acts as a guarantee to secure something that could not be otherwise obtained.

Jesus Christ is our *"daysman."* He is the one for whom Job cried out to. Job was desperate as he uttered in Job 16:21, *"O that one might plead for a man with God, as a man pleadeth for his neighbour!"* How many times have you wanted for somebody to plead your case? He says in Job 13:3, *"Surely I would speak to the Almighty, and I desire to reason with God."* And once again later on in Job 31:35, *"Oh that one would hear me! behold, my desire is, that the Almighty would answer me, and that mine adversary had written a book."*

God has given us a mediator as it tells us in I Timothy 2:5, *"For there is one God, and one mediator between God and men, the man Christ Jesus."* In Hebrews 7:22, Jesus is called the mediator of the better covenant, *"By so much was Jesus made a surety of a better testament."* We no longer need to plead for anyone, because I John 2:1 tells us, *"We have an advocate with the Father, Jesus Christ the righteous."*

So our daysman, or our mediator and umpire, is the go between, the One between us and the Father. Oh, how we need this in our lives. There is a daysman between us and He has laid His hands upon us both. He is our mediator, one who can take what you and I need before the Lord. The Catholic Church has their priests who act as mediators, but I do not believe that man was ever intended to be mediators between God and man. Jesus, the Lamb of God slain from the foundation of the world, is our mediator, for there is salvation in no other. There is no other name under heaven whereby men must be saved but by the name of Jesus Christ (Acts 4:12).

Jesus is the daysman. He will argue for us. He will try to convince for us. He will dispute for us. He is that go between, the reconciler, the intercessor and He has a view to produce peace. He wants to secure for us the things that we cannot obtain on our own. He is the daysman. Realize today that you have an advocate. You have someone to plead your cause, someone to stand for you to God the Father. O praise our precious daysman! No need to cry out, beg or plead for any other advocate or for someone to help us, He's already done it; He's become our daysman.

"He Hath Remembered His Covenant Forever"
Psalms 105:8

Day 246

One of the glorious truths we will look at today is that God's covenant that He made with us through His son Jesus is a covenant that cannot and will not be broken. Psalms 105:8 declares, *"He hath remembered his covenant for ever, the word which he commanded to a thousand generations."* It is irrevocable because God who cannot lie said it was so. In Psalms 111:5 it says, *"He hath given meat unto them that fear him: he will ever be mindful of his covenant."* He will not forget it. He will ever be mindful of His covenant.

The book of Ecclesiastes tells us *"I know that, whatsoever God doeth, it shall be for ever: nothing can be put to it, nor any thing taken from it: and God doeth it, that men should fear before him"* (Ecclesiastes 3:14). We need to realize that what God does is forever. Nothing can be put to it, and nothing can be taken from it.

In Isaiah 54:9-10, that great passage in which the Lord says Himself, *"neither shall the covenant of my peace be removed, saith the Lord that hath mercy on thee."* Before that He said, *"For the mountains shall depart, and the hills be removed; but my kindness shall not depart from thee."* Mountains departing and the hills being removed, all of that can happen; think of it. But His kindness shall not depart from you, nor can His covenant of His peace be removed. This is a covenant of peace. This is a covenant of joy. This is a covenant of grace. It's forever, and it was given to us by our great and wonderful God through the gift of His Son Jesus Christ. *"For by grace are ye saved through faith; and that not of yourselves: it is the gift of God"* (Ephesians 2:8). The gift of God is His covenant to us.

In Jeremiah 32:40, *"And I will make an everlasting covenant with them, that I will not turn away from them, to do them good."* He's made an everlasting covenant. Either everlasting is everlasting and forever is forever, or the Word of God is simply just not true. Eternal is eternal. Ever mindful means what it says. He hath remembered His covenant forever.

I really don't know how anyone could doubt or be in unbelief concerning this principle. It's revealed throughout the Scriptures. God who cannot lie promised before the world began. Hebrews 6:18 says, *"That by two immutable things, in which it was impossible for God to lie, we might have a strong consolation."* Over and over again the Word of God declares that our God never lies, He never betrays us, He never breaks His promises, and He will always be mindful of what He has said to us, period.

David in II Samuel 23:3 says, *"He that ruleth over men must be just, ruling in the fear of God."* Then he says in verse 5, *"Although my house be not so with God."* In other words David is saying he hasn't been completely all that he should be and then continues *"yet he hath made with me an everlasting covenant, ordered in all things, and sure."* David had the revelation of God's everlasting covenant. It is sure!

In other words, David is saying, "even though everything in my life is not perfect yet, even though I don't always do the right thing and always say the right thing, even though the Adamic nature, part of that carnal nature, is still living in me even though I hate it, He will not forsake me. He counted the cost when He came into my life. Even though I'm not there yet, '...*yet he hath made with me an everlasting covenant, ordered in all things, and sure.*"

Paul, describing the Last Supper, says of Jesus that in *"the same night in which he was betrayed took bread...this is my body, which is broken for you"* (I Corinthians 11:23-24). That communion table is a sign of the covenant between us and God and we're told to do it as often as we can in remembrance of this eternal covenant. The first part of that verse often gets overlooked. He did it on the night He was betrayed. He knew full well that the disciples were going to leave Him alone and forsake Him. Knowing that in the days ahead they would be tormented by this thought, before it happened, on the night He was betrayed He took bread and make a covenant with them. He did this before they were going to completely leave Him and forsake Him so that they would know that when they did, He still wouldn't forsake them. Oh how great is our God! Psalms 118:29 says, *"O give thanks unto the Lord; for he is good: for his mercy endureth for ever."* The Lord is good, gracious, full of compassion, full of loving kindness and tender mercies.

Just as we find in Genesis 9:15-16 when God destroyed the earth with water, and He saw the destruction that was made, He placed in the heavens a bow. He said that as long as that bow was there He will never destroy the earth like that again. Every time you and I see that rainbow, it is a symbol to us of the everlasting eternal covenant that our God has made with us. He hath remembered His covenant forever. He will ever be mindful of His covenant. His covenant of peace won't be removed. He's made an everlasting covenant with us, ordered in all things and sure. Every time we see the rainbow, He's saying remember, I'll be faithful to my covenant. Then in Psalms 89 David is speaking prophetically about Jesus and us His children:

> *"30If his children forsake my law, and walk not in my judgments; 31If they break my statutes, and keep not my commandments; 32Then will I visit their transgression with the rod, and their iniquity with stripes. 33Nevertheless my lovingkindness will I not utterly take from him, nor suffer my faithfulness to fail. 34My covenant will I not break, nor alter the thing that is gone out of my lips"* (Psalms 89:30-34).

Even if we forsake His law and keep not His commandments, He will never take away His lovingkindness or break His covenant. Jesus will remain faithful because He hath remembered His covenant forever. He wants us to remember it too when we need it the most. Perhaps that is today. Hear the word of the Lord. This is a glorious truth that was settled forever by Jesus dying on the cross once and for all. God will not break His covenant. He will ever be mindful of it. He said it was so. He doesn't lie so it is a settled fact. Let this be sealed in your spirit today, now and forever.

"The Face Of An Angel"
Acts 6:15

In Acts 6 is the story of the stoning of Stephen. At the end, it says, *"And all that sat in the council, looking stedfastly on him, saw his face as it had been the face of an angel"* (Acts 6:15).

DAY 247

Stephen was a man who started out as a deacon, a lowly brother that God exalted and used mightily. One of the great things about him was that, as these people were accusing him of all kinds of ungodly lies, he did not have the face of an angry man. There are but few angel faces to be seen in this selfish, sin-distorted, perverted world. Many times, the features of the soul stamp themselves on our countenance or face. But if the face or image of Jesus has been impressed upon the inner man, some of that glory will be seen without. In the midst of being charged with blasphemy, the sweet countenance of Jesus rested upon his face, and they saw the face of an angel. In this holy man's heart, there was no hatred or anger; he simply loved his enemies who were despitefully using and persecuting him.

Years ago, I was ministering to a woman who had terrible migraine headaches. Her mother committed suicide because she, like her daughter, also had migraines. I went to pray for her on a day when I was not feeling very spiritual and had just eaten a large lunch. I was feeling gluttonous, actually, so I was a little disturbed when I received her phone call. I was worried that I would not be ready to go and pray for her. But the Spirit of the Lord spoke to me, saying, "I'm going to show you something today."

As I went to her house and began to pray for her, laying my hands on her, I peered through one eye and noticed that she was staring right at me. I closed my eye quickly and continued to pray. But I peeped once again to find her still staring straight into my face. So, I kept my eyes closed after that and finished the prayer, "...in Jesus' mighty name."

This woman had been suffering her whole life; this was serious. After I had prayed for her, I looked at her and asked, "How do you feel?" She replied, "All the pain is gone," and we both began to worship and glorify God. I then asked her, "Why were you staring at me so intently?" I was thinking that there must have been a stain or crumbs of food on my face or stuck in my beard. But she told me, "Brother Sam, when I looked at your face, I saw the face of Jesus." You can imagine how astounded I was. I, Brother Sam, am the least of all saints and ministers, yet as she beheld me, the inner man and the glory of the Lord shone through.

A day is coming when the world is going to behold the face of Jesus. The world is going to say of a people that they have the face of an angel.

"The Little Foxes"
Song of Solomon 2:15

One of the things that plagues Christians, especially those of us who are really trying to go on with God, are the little things in our lives that seem to keep spoiling us and causing us trouble. Here in Song of Solomon 2:15 the Bible says *"the little foxes, that spoil the vines: for our vines have tender grapes."* We are the vine in this passage and the tender grapes are our spirit man. I Peter 2:11 says *"abstain from fleshly lusts, which war against the soul"*; the soul is the place of warfare and that is where the foxes dwell.

DAY 248

Foxes are a type of the devil or demons. The little foxes are there to spoil the vines. It's not the big things in life that cause us trouble but the little ones, the little foxes end up spoiling the vine. It's easy to do because our vines have tender grapes. What God has done in us is so precious and wonderful that our human spirit will not allow sin to get close to it, so it closes up and goes inward while we allow our carnal man to rule and reign. We are not to live in the knowledge of good and evil *"Because the carnal mind is enmity against God: for it is not subject to the law of God, neither indeed can be"* (Romans 8:17).

I want to talk about the result of allowing sin to linger in our lives. We think, because it is a little fox that it is not important and we can get by with it. So many times we allow little things to exist because they don't seem important enough to deal with. Over a long period of time they will begin to erode the righteousness of God, erode our own faith and bring guilt and condemnation in us. The Bible says in I Corinthians 5:6 *"Know ye not that a little leaven leaveneth the whole lump?"* It only takes a little leaven. What is the leaven in your life? May God shine His light upon you today and in His glory reveal all that is not of Him.

In Proverbs 7 we find the progression of sin in the young man, void of understanding, going away to the strange woman's house. Even though he was told not to do so, he does and verse 9 says *"In the twilight, in the evening, in the black and dark night."* In other words, deception starts at twilight (just enough light to deceive us). The twilight eventually will turn to evening and then to the black and dark night perhaps costing us our lives. We find in Proverbs 24:33 that it only takes *"a little sleep"* and *"a little slumber"* for these little foxes to grow up. We need to heed the admonition of Paul in Ephesians 4:26-27 where he says *"Be ye angry, and sin not"*. This means to be angry at sin, not letting *"the sun go down upon your wrath."* Or in other words, we never lose our righteous indignation against sin. Paul adds, *"neither give place to the devil."* We give place to the devil when we let the little foxes rule and reign. Enough of the little foxes today, let's give place to the Lord and not allow any fox to spoil our vines.

"The Little Chamber"
II Kings 4:10

In II Kings 4 it says:

"*⁸And it fell on a day, that Elisha passed to Shunem, where was a great woman; and she constrained him to eat bread. And so it was, that as oft as he passed by, he turned in thither to eat bread. ⁹And she said unto her husband, Behold now, I perceive that this is an holy man of God, which passeth by us continually. ¹⁰Let us make a little chamber, I pray thee, on the wall; and let us set for him there a bed, and a table, and a stool, and a candlestick: and it shall be, when he cometh to us, that he shall turn in thither*" (II Kings 4:8-10).

This great woman speaks of all women in the Scriptures that are teachers of the word of God, for "*she constrained him to eat bread.*" This woman fed Elisha. She ministered to him, and every time he came there he sat at her feet and ate bread. So she asked her husband if they could make a little chamber for him when he came. There were four pieces of furniture in this little secret chamber. They're all significant and have great meaning.

First, "*let us set for him there a bed.*" A bed is where you rest upon. It's something that speaks to us, like when God caused a deep sleep to come upon Adam and brought Eve to him (Genesis 2:21). Adam was resting in the Lord and waiting on God. She provided a little chamber where the man of God could rest in the Lord. Not only that, but where he could wait on the Lord.

Then she provided a table. A table is used to put things on, and I believe it was a table for studying. A place where he could study the deeper things of God and study the Scriptures to show himself approved unto God, a workman that needs not to be ashamed, rightly dividing the Word of truth (II Timothy 2:15).

Thirdly, she provided a stool. This reminds us of the word in the scriptures called the footstool, "*we will worship at his footstool*" (Psalms 132:7). This stool is for him to sit in the presence of God, to worship God, and like Mary sit at Jesus' feet (Luke 10:39). She not only heard His word, but she sat at His feet and worshipped Him there.

Lastly, she provided a candlestick, or in the Hebrew a lamp stand. A candle gives light and revelation. She prepared a place where the man of God could come and revelation would flow to him. Light would come to him on certain Scriptures, on prophetic anointings, and so on.

Notice that there were four pieces of furniture. Four is the number of creation, or the new creation man. The new creation man must have these four pieces of furniture operative in His life. He needs a bed to rest in the Lord, a table to study the Scriptures and give himself to the Word, a stool as a place of worship, and a candlestick for revelation. You and I need a little chamber, a secret chamber, where the new creation man can come forth in us.

"A Refining Fire"
Malachi 3:1-4

"²But who may abide the day of his coming? and who shall stand when he appeareth? for he is like a refiner's fire, and like fullers' soap: ³And he shall sit as a refiner and purifier of silver: and he shall purify the sons of Levi, and purge them as gold and silver, that they may offer unto the LORD an offering in righteousness." (Malachi 3:2-3)

He is like a refiner's fire, and fullers' soap. He will sit as a refiner and purifier of silver. God is going to refine and purify the sons of Levi, and purge them. Just like gold and silver is put under fire to get rid of the bad things, and cause the real ore to come to the surface, God will purify us with His fire, burning out the dross in our lives. He wants to burn out the stuff that is in us that does not radiate the character of God (which gold speaks of), and His redemption (which silver speaks of). Isaiah says:

"⁴When the Lord shall have washed away the filth of the daughters of Zion, and shall have purged the blood of Jerusalem from the midst thereof by the spirit of judgment, and by the spirit of burning" (Isaiah 4:4).

God is going to wash away the filth of the daughters of Zion, purging the sin from Jerusalem with a spirit of judgment and burning. So many people think that the fire of God is an evil thing, but remember the bush that Moses turned aside to see; it did not burn because it was a spiritual fire. That fire was remedial, it was there to cleanse and to heal, and to change. The fire of God for the believer is not a natural fire, but a spiritual one to burn away the dross, the iniquity, the sin, and the obstacles in our lives.

Thank God for His fire. Thank God that He is a refining fire and is purging us. Zechariah talks about the remnant, which will be brought through the fire, saying:

"⁹And I will bring the third part through the fire, and will refine them as silver is refined, and will try them as gold is tried: they shall call on my name, and I will hear them: I will say, It is my people: and they shall say, The LORD is my God" (Zechariah 13:9).

Once we have been brought through the fire and refined as silver, and tried as gold, then we're going to call on His name and say, "The Lord is my God." He will gladly answer saying, "These are my people."

Remember when the children of Israel took treasure from the nations they conquered, they were to either cleanse it by putting it through water or fire. You and I are put through the fire of God to be refined, purified and purged, so that we might become the holy army, the sons of God.

So today, if you find yourself in the fire, receive this word and let His fire refine you. Then, shall your offering be pleasant unto the Lord.

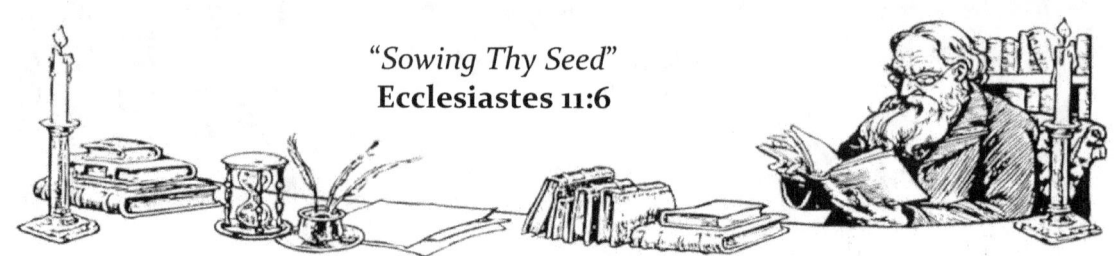

"Sowing Thy Seed"
Ecclesiastes 11:6

DAY 251

Ecclesiastes 11:6 says, *"In the morning sow thy seed, and in the evening withhold not thine hand: for thou knowest not whether shall prosper, either this or that, or whether they both shall be alike good."* The context of this passage begins with *"cast thy bread upon the waters"* (Ecclesiastes 11:1) which speaks of giving. I believe this is not just talking about sowing money, but sowing the seed of the Word of God into our lives. Jesus said in Luke 8:11, *"The seed is the word of God."*

This brings up the principle of the morning and evening sacrifice as found in the Old Testament. You and I need to be walking in this principle. Many people have no comprehension that the Bible teaches us that we are to be taught the Word of God daily. Did you know that Jesus taught daily? The apostles taught the Word of God daily. Paul taught the Bible daily in the school of Tyrannus (Acts 19:9). So in the morning, we need to sow the Word of God and in the evening we need to withhold not our hands. Jesus teaches us to pray in Matthew 6:11 *"Give us this day our daily bread."* There is a daily portion of God's Word that is waiting for you and me. But we must be prepared to receive it.

Starting off in the morning with the Word of God is the way we should live our lives. But then there must also be an evening sacrifice, where we spend time in the Word of God, for Solomon goes on to say, *"for thou knowest not whether shall prosper, either this or that, or whether they both shall be alike good."* In other words, all we are required to do is to be faithful as Jesus said in Luke 12:42-43, *"Who then is that faithful and wise steward, whom his lord shall make ruler over his household, to give them their portion of meat in due season? Blessed is that servant, whom his lord when he cometh shall find so doing."* God is looking for faithful and wise stewards so that when He comes, He shall find them doing the will of God, teaching faithfully.

I have personally taught the Scriptures pretty much daily since 1977 and have continued throughout the course of my life because Jesus said to His disciples, *"If ye continue in my word, then are ye my disciples indeed; And ye shall know the truth, and the truth shall make you free"* (John 8:31-32). Many people are not made free because they never give themselves to the truth.

Hosea 10:12 says, *"Sow to yourselves in righteousness, reap in mercy; break up your fallow ground: for it is time to seek the Lord, till he come and rain righteousness upon you."* Sow the Word of God into your life every morning. Read the Scriptures daily. Sit under daily teaching. And then in the evening withhold not thy hand.

Lastly, this Scripture also speaks of daily giving, sharing, and communicating our faith to others. We need to sow the Word of God in the morning and we need to sow the Word of God in the evening, never letting up. So let's begin today by sowing the Word of God morning and evening. As you do, you will be made free, blessed by the Lord and produce a harvest in your life. He will come and rain righteousness upon you!

"The God Of Peace Shall Bruise Satan"
Romans 16:20

DAY 252

Here in Romans 16:20 it reads *"The God of peace shall bruise Satan under your feet shortly."* If you read Jeremiah 30 we find that it says about the people of God that their bruise was incurable and that there was no healing balm for it. Then the Lord ends that chapter by promising them that He would bless them, heal them, and cure them. The answer is that the God of peace has bruised Satan under our feet already.

All the way back in Genesis 3:14-15, God and His promise of the Messiah says to the serpent *"Because thou hast done this, thou art cursed above all cattle, and above every beast of the field; upon thy belly shalt thou go, and dust shalt thou eat all the days of thy life."* That dust is the flesh of our lives and in verse 15 it reads, *"And I will put enmity between thee and the woman, and between thy seed and her seed."* Her seed in that Scripture is the promised Messiah, the Lord Jesus Christ. He goes on to say in that verse *"it shall bruise thy head, and thou shalt bruise his heel."* The Messiah bruised or destroyed the head (that is the government, kingdom, and works of Satan). The Hebrew word *"bruise"* means "bruised with stripes or a black and blue mark." Jesus has bruised Satan for you and me.

The Spirit of the Lord has anointed us *"to set at liberty them that are bruised"* as found in Luke 4:18. God has set at liberty those that have been bruised and wounded. In Isaiah 53:5 it says *"he was wounded for our transgressions, he was bruised for our iniquities."* Jesus took the punishment; Jesus paid the price and by doing so became the victor over Satan's kingdom and gained back all that we lost in God. I John 3:8 reads *"The Son of God was manifested that he might destroy the works of the devil."* We are now free to be set at liberty because of this; and because of the Lord's sacrifice no longer are our sicknesses incurable!

It would behoove every one of us to not only know but believe the love that God has for us and to believe that Satan is already a defeated foe. He has been bruised under our feet; Satan is now the one with black and blue marks and bound with fetters. You and I are free today and can walk free because Jesus was *"bruised for our iniquities."* It is already done. You and I are the redeemed of the Lord today!

"Gather Up The Fragments"
John 6:12

DAY 253

John 6:12 tells us to *"gather up the fragments that remain, that nothing be lost."* The word of the Lord for us today is that in our lives, there are many broken pieces, many things that are fragments that seem unnecessary and unfruitful. Many times we throw away the negatives in our lives because we don't feel that they are important or that they're doing us any good. But here Jesus tells His disciples to gather up the fragments that remain so that nothing be lost. God wants us to gather up everything in our life. You see, all things are working together for good to them that love God (Romans 8:28). So we must understand and know that nothing happens to us that the sovereign God has not allowed in our lives.

Gather up the fragments. It's interesting that this Hebrew word for *"fragments"* means, "a broken piece, something broken." A good dictionary definition defines it as "a part broken off, a portion that is unfinished or incomplete, or an odd piece." There are too many broken off parts in our life, too many portions that are unfinished or incomplete, or just odd pieces. And all the things that happen to us may seem odd, incomplete, and so many things are unfinished or broken off, be it relationships, plans, etc. But Jesus said to gather up all those fragments, that nothing be lost. Nothing is lost when it is used for the glory of God. God wants us to use all things for His glory.

It is interesting that these were barley loaves, which in Scripture, is a type of harvest time, the Word of God, poverty, or humility and lowliness. Barley was mainly for poor people and slaves, and was also food for horses, mules, and donkeys. And there was not only a spring harvest, but also a winter harvest of barley. Interesting, isn't it? Isn't that just like God? Behold the goodness and severity of God (Romans 11:22). In all the seasons of God, there are things happening to us. *"To every thing there is a season, and a time to every purpose under the heaven"* (Ecclesiastes 3:1).

We all have things that are incomplete or unfinished. And our tendency is to just forget about them and throw them away but we don't realize that we need all of those things to make the whole. Everything that happens to us, I believe, God has a purpose and a plan to teach us and to help us to grow into the image of His Son Jesus. Even if we don't think it is important to Him, it is important. There are fragments everywhere in all of our lives. Broken pieces, odd pieces, things we don't understand when we're going through them. That's why we always need to remember, as Hosea 6:3 tells us, *"Then shall we know, if we follow on to know the Lord."* God hasn't promised us that we would know everything about every situation. Sometimes, we just have to believe and wait until we're ready to receive that revelation, whatever it may be.

What is it in your life that has been broken off, is unfinished or is an odd or incomplete piece? Maybe, because it was poor, or something beastly, or came in the winter, you thought it was unnecessary to retain it or to comprehend it or to even count it as a part of your life and your maturation in God. I want you to know, Jesus is saying to us today, "*Gather up the fragments, that nothing be lost.*" Of all that we have, and all that we will lose or gain in this life, everything is important. It may have been a divorce, a bad relationship with your parents, a broken friendship, something that you went through that bothered you greatly or that you just pushed down and thought was unnecessary.

Another translation of this verse reads, "*Gather up now the fragments (the broken pieces that are left over), so that nothing may be lost and wasted.*" You and I need to gather up the broken pieces that are left over. They haven't gone away. Those pieces are still part of our soul, part of our human nature. And they're still living within us, even though we've pushed them down or shoved them away. They're still there and must be dealt with at some point. God doesn't want anything lost or wasted in our lives. But it's up to us to gather them up; let the Holy Spirit show us the reason for it; and then apply it and add it to our lives.

Other translations refer to these fragments as "leftovers," "scraps," and "broken bits." So many times, things just seem like leftovers and scraps, unnecessary and unimportant. But they really are important. The slightest hurt, the slightest abuse, the bad situation, the negative happening are all important. All of these things are important to us growing up in Jesus and becoming the people He has called us to be. We don't need to throw anything away. Everything is important.

Think back over your life now, and let the Holy Spirit bring the broken pieces, the incomplete pieces, and the broken off pieces, the scraps, or the leftovers. Don't let them be lost. Don't let them be wasted. Let all of it turn and rebound to the glory of God. Use everything that has happened in your life to make you a better person. And as you follow on to know the Lord today, understand that all things are working together for good for your life. For God is waiting for us to, "*gather up the fragments that remain, that nothing be lost.*"

"Ye Shall Find Rest Unto Your Souls"
Matthew 11:29

Day 254

Here in the gospel of Matthew 11:28-29, we find these comforting and precious words from Jesus. *"Come unto me, all ye that labour and are heavy laden, and I will give you rest. ²⁹Take my yoke upon you, and learn of me; for I am meek and lowly in heart: and ye shall find rest unto your souls."* God wants us to find rest in our lives.

The word *"rest"* signifies a fixed and secure habitation. In the Greek it means, "To repose, to take ease, peace, prosperity, quietness, relaxation." The Hebrew word means, "to desist from exertion, to settle down, to be quiet or to let alone; a settle spot."

Hebrews 4:9-11 tells us, *"There remaineth therefore a rest to the people of God. ¹⁰For he that is entered into his rest, he also hath ceased from his own works, as God did from his. ¹¹Let us labour therefore to enter into that rest, lest any man fall after the same example of unbelief."* There remains a rest for the people of God. God wants us to find rest for our souls. If we are going to do any laboring at all, any striving at all, it should be to enter into that rest. This is why the Lord says in Mark 2:27, *"The sabbath was made for man, and not man for the Sabbath."* In other words, God wanted a day of rest for His people, a day of quietness, a day of repose and inactivity. This inactivity is not so much natural as it is spiritual. We find, then, that as we go about our daily lives, there are all kinds of things around us that try to take the "rest" from our souls and get us out of a place of peace with God.

Today, hear the word of the Lord. I Kings 18:56 states, *"Blessed be the LORD, that hath given rest unto his people Israel."* Isaiah 30:15 also states, *"For thus saith the Lord God, the Holy One of Israel; In returning and rest shall ye be saved; in quietness and in confidence shall be your strength."*

This is what God wants for us, quietness and confidence. He doesn't want us to be full of anxiety, fear and torment. In Exodus 33:14, God responds to Moses' request for Him to go with His people by saying, *"My presence shall go with thee, and I will give thee rest."* God's rest comes from His precious and glorious presence. So as Psalms 116:7 states, *"Return unto thy rest, O my soul; for the LORD hath dealt bountifully with thee."* The Lord wants to deal bountifully with you today and give you rest.

"Wisdom Is The Principal Thing"
Proverbs 4:7

DAY 255

Solomon, apart from the Lord Jesus, was the wisest man on the earth and he shared with us in Proverbs 4:7 saying, *"Wisdom is the principal thing; therefore get wisdom: and with all thy getting get understanding."*

"Principal" in Hebrew means "the first in time, order or rank." Wisdom should be the first thing in time, in order and in rank in our lives. We should seek for it. We should run after it and give ourselves to it. The Bible says in Proverbs 3:13, *"Happy is the man that findeth wisdom, and the man that getteth understanding."* The man who gets wisdom is a happy man and is an understanding man. It says in Proverbs 8:11, *"For wisdom is better than rubies; and all the things that may be desired are not to be compared to it."* And Proverbs 14:33, *Wisdom resteth in the heart of him that hath understanding: but that which is in the midst of fools is made known."*

Solomon also said in Ecclesiastes 1:17, *"And I gave my heart to know wisdom, and to know madness and folly: I perceived that this also is vexation of spirit."* He gave his heart to know wisdom. Are you giving your heart to wisdom? Are you seeking to know the deeper things of God and to be wise in this earth? Remember the story of the wise and foolish virgins in Matthew 25. Those foolish were not let in to the wedding celebration. Wisdom is the principal thing and wisdom is far better than rubies and happy is the man that finds it. You and I need to give ourselves to it, just as Solomon did. If we love our own soul, we'll do it.

The Bible says in Proverbs 1:20, *"Wisdom crieth without; she uttereth her voice in the streets."* She is constantly trying to get our attention. And in Proverbs 8:12, *"I wisdom dwell with prudence, and find out knowledge of witty inventions."* Discernment, prudence and wisdom is so desperately needed in this life where there are too many fools doing foolish things.

We know, as in Psalms 111:10, *"The fear of the Lord is the beginning of wisdom: a good understanding have all they that do his commandments: his praise endureth for ever."* Beyond that, wisdom is the principal thing, but far too many believers seem to lack wisdom. *"Who is a wise man and endued with knowledge among you? let him shew out of a good conversation his works with meekness of wisdom,"* as it says in James 3:13.

You and I need to be endued with wisdom. We must apply ourselves to it; we must give ourselves to it. Then we will rise above all others and the foolish petty things of this world. Let us use discernment and look through things. Let us seek to know the deeper truth of things. Let us see beyond the obvious and try to find the depth in every situation.

In Psalms 90:12, Moses puts it this way, *"So teach us to number our days, that we may apply our hearts unto wisdom."* God help us today to see that wisdom is the principal thing and with all our getting, we choose to get understanding.

"*How Long Wilt Thou Forget Me, O Lord?*"
Psalms 13:1

Far too many believers think that God has forgotten them and left them alone in their situation. This is a prominent problem in the body of Christ. Today, I pray that the Lord enlightens you and reveals to you His everlasting love and faithfulness. David says here in Psalms 13:1, "*How long wilt thou forget me, O Lord? for ever? how long wilt thou hide thy face from me?*" He also says in Psalms 44:

DAY 256

> "*²³Awake, why sleepest thou, O Lord? arise, cast us not off for ever. ²⁴Wherefore hidest thou thy face, and forgettest our affliction and our oppression? ²⁵For our soul is bowed down to the dust: our belly cleaveth unto the earth. ²⁶Arise for our help, and redeem us for thy mercies' sake*" (Psalms 44:23-26).

So many times, it seems as if God has forgotten us in our affliction and oppression. But, folks, He has not! We have a mighty promise from God that He will never leave us or forsake us (Joshua 1:5, Hebrews 13:5). In Psalms 89, David asks, "*How long, Lord? wilt thou hide thyself for ever? shall thy wrath burn like fire?*" (Psalms 89:46). How many times have we said: "How long, O Lord?" Sometimes, it does seem like He is hiding Himself or has withdrawn Himself. It causes us to think that we're all alone in the situation, but the Lord has clearly stated in these other translations of Hebrews 13:5.

> "*For He himself has said, and the statement is on record, I will not, I will not cease to sustain and uphold you. I will not, I will not, I will not let you down.*"
> "*For He [God] Himself has said, I will not in any way fail you nor give you up nor leave you without support. [I will] not, [I will] not], [I will] not in any degree leave you helpless nor forsake nor let [you] down (relax My hold on you)! [Assuredly not!]*"

He will never leave or utterly forsake you. Though He may leave you for a moment, He will embrace you with everlasting love and kindness. It says in Isaiah 49, "*But Zion said, The Lord hath forsaken me, and my Lord hath forgotten me*" (Isaiah 49:14). The word "*forsaken*" means that He's left him. This is impossible. God, who cannot lie, swore by a promise to us through an immutable oath (Hebrews 6:17-18). He swore by Himself, so He cannot deny Himself (II Timothy 2:13). He will not leave us. But Zion still says, "*The Lord has forsaken me, and my Lord has forgotten me.*"

Is that the case for you today? Do you feel forsaken or forgotten? God's Word to you is, as it says in the following verses:

> "*¹⁵Can a woman forget her sucking child, that she should not have compassion on the son of her womb? yea, they*

> *may forget, yet will I not forget thee. ¹⁶Behold, I have graven thee upon the palms of my hands; thy walls are continually before me"* (Isaiah 49:15-16).

We are always in His thoughts. Others may forget us, but He will not. This is the promise of the Lord. So, what are we to think about this? Why do we wrestle with this all the time? David eventually found this in his own life; he says in Psalms 77:

> *"⁷Will the Lord cast off for ever? and will he be favourable no more? ⁸Is his mercy clean gone for ever? doth his promise fail for evermore? ⁹Hath God forgotten to be gracious? hath he in anger shut up his tender mercies? Selah"* (Psalms 77:7-9).

He then answers the question himself, saying, *"This is my infirmity"* or weakness. In other words, he is saying "I'm the one that has forgotten." God hasn't forgotten anything; He hasn't gone anywhere. David continues to say:

> *"¹⁰But I will remember the years of the right hand of the most High. ¹¹I will remember the works of the Lord: surely I will remember thy wonders of old. ¹²I will meditate also of all thy work, and talk of thy doings"* (Psalms 77:10-12).

This is our weakness. We may forget, but God will not forget us. Just like a mother nursing her little baby, who would never dream of turning that baby away, He could never do that to us. There may be some parents who would, but not Him. Why? We serve a faithful God who will never leave us or forsake us.

"To Do Thee Good At Thy Latter End"
Deuteronomy 8:16

The Bible says in Deuteronomy 8:16, *"Who fed thee in the wilderness with manna, which thy fathers knew not, that he might humble thee, and that he might prove thee, to do thee good at thy latter end."* Here we find a tremendous truth: God is going to do us good at our latter end. The book of Job tells us, *"Though thy beginning was small, yet thy latter end should greatly increase"* (Job 8:7). All of us may start small. There may be times in our lives when things don't seem to be going well, but we need to look to the end of a thing, not just the beginning thereof (Ecclesiastes 7:8). In Jeremiah, it says, *"For I know the thoughts that I think toward you, saith the Lord, thoughts of peace, and not of evil, to give you an expected end"* (Jeremiah 29:11).

God is going to give us an expected end. So many wonder about how their end is going to be. For you and me, as believers, we have something to look forward to: *"an expected end."* It is an end of hope. Jeremiah 31:17 says, *"There is hope in thine end, saith the Lord."* We, of all men, have hope. We have hope that the Lord Jesus will be faithful to what He has promised. Even though we may not understand everything that is happening today, all of the things in our lives will have meaning. One day, we'll find out, as it says in Hosea 6:3, *"Then shall we know, if we follow on to know the Lord."*

I Peter 1:9 it says, *"Receiving the end of your faith, even the salvation of your souls."* The end of our faith is just that: the complete salvation of our soulish man; that carnal nature being made like unto His glorious, wonderful image. We look unto Jesus, *"the author and finisher of our faith"* (Hebrews 12:2), the Alpha and the Omega, the beginning and the end, the first and the last (Revelation 1:8, 11). He is the one who begins this for us and He will be the one that ends it for us.

It says in Psalms 119, *"I have seen an end of all perfection"* (Psalms 119:96). The end of all perfection is that God is going to bring forth a people whose end is better than their beginning. Ecclesiastes 7:8 tells us, *"Better is the end of a thing than the beginning thereof."* Our end is going to be better! No matter how we started, or how it has been in the middle, ultimately, there is hope for our end.

"Mark the perfect man," Psalms 37:37 says, *"and behold the upright: for the end of that man is peace."* We have an expected end which is an end of peace. We can rejoice, because God always finishes what He begins. He has been with us in the beginning, will be with us at the end, and our end will certainly be far greater than our beginning.

In the book of Daniel, it says, *"But go thou thy way till the end be: for thou shalt rest, and stand in thy lot at the end of the days"* (Daniel 12:13). We shall rest and stand in our lot, and when the end comes we will have hope, because He will *"do thee good at thy latter end."*

"My Redeemer Liveth"
Job 19:25

Job said an amazing truth, *"For I know that my redeemer liveth, and that he shall stand at the latter day upon the earth"* (Job 19:25). First of all, Job said *"For I know."* You need to know this. Secondly you need to know He is your redeemer. Forget that He is everybody else's redeemer. He's your redeemer and He lives.

Paul said in Romans 5:10, *"For if, when we were enemies, we were reconciled to God by the death of his Son, much more, being reconciled, we shall be saved by his life."* So many times people seem to paint the picture to us that once we're saved we're pretty much on our own after that. But know that Jesus will always be your Savior. Paul said of the Lord in II Corinthians 1:10, *"Who delivered us from so great a death, and doth deliver: in whom we trust that he will yet deliver us."*

Jesus is our redeemer. Psalms 19:14 says *"Let the words of my mouth, and the meditation of my heart, be acceptable in thy sight, O Lord, my strength, and my redeemer."* Isaiah 47:4 says, *"As for our redeemer, the Lord of hosts is his name, the Holy One of Israel."* We read in Isaiah 54:5, *"For thy Maker is thine husband; the Lord of hosts is his name; and thy Redeemer the Holy One of Israel."* He's bought us with His blood. He paid the price and redeemed us from our past. One of the definitions for *"redeem"* is "to sever." He's severed us from our past.

Galatians 3:13 says, *"Christ hath redeemed us from the curse of the law, being made a curse for us."* We've been redeemed not only from our sin and ourselves, but from the curse of the law. I Peter 1:18-19 says, *"Forasmuch as ye know that ye were not redeemed with corruptible things, as silver and gold...But with the precious blood of Christ, as of a lamb without blemish and without spot."* You and I weren't redeemed with corruptible things but we were born again of *"incorruptible seed"* (I Peter 1:23) by the *"precious blood of the lamb."*

In II Samuel 4:9 David says, *"As the Lord liveth, who hath redeemed my soul out of all adversity."* Isaiah 43:1 says, *"O Israel, Fear not: for I have redeemed thee, I have called thee by thy name; thou art mine."* We need not fear. We are His. We have been redeemed. We are blessed because of the mercy of God. Luke 1:68 says, *"Blessed be the Lord God of Israel; for he hath visited and redeemed his people."* Revelation 5:9 says of Jesus, *"for thou wast slain, and hast redeemed us to God by thy blood out of every kindred, and tongue, and people, and nation."* Every color and strata of people has been redeemed by God because of the shed blood of Jesus Christ. Oh, that we would walk in this! Oh, that we would know this!

Isaiah 63:16 says, *"O Lord, art our father, our redeemer; thy name is from everlasting."* I pray today that you are doubtless about this because you see over and over again that God's grace has redeemed you. The Scriptures are full of these admonitions. David sang in Psalms 71:23, *"My lips shall greatly rejoice when I sing unto thee; and my soul, which thou hast redeemed."* Glory to God! Redemption is upon us. All we need to do is allow Jesus to redeem us and then walk in it.

"Betrayed By A Kiss"
Matthew 26:48-50

DAY 259

One of the hardest things we discover, as we walk with Jesus, is that occasionally even our brothers and sisters will betray us. Jesus experienced betrayal and His story leaves us great insight as to how to deal with betrayal. Jesus was betrayed by a kiss, as it says in Matthew 26, *"And forthwith he came to Jesus, and said, Hail, master; and kissed him. ⁵⁰And Jesus said unto him, Friend, wherefore art thou come?"* (Matthew 26:48-50).

In another Gospel it reads, *"Betrayest thou me with a kiss?"* How many times have you and I been betrayed by a brother or sister? Well, we need to take heart because Jesus Himself was betrayed. He said, *"Behold, the hour cometh, yea, is now come, that ye shall be scattered, every man to his own, and shall leave me alone: and yet I am not alone, because the Father is with me"* (John 16:32). Jesus understood that people would leave Him and betray Him, leaving Him alone.

In I Corinthians 11:23 it says, *"...the same night in which he was betrayed he took bread."* What an amazing truth! Just as Jesus said on the cross, *"Father, forgive them; for they know not what they do"* (Luke 23:34). Here on the night that He was betrayed by His closest disciples. These men and women had walked with Him for three and a half years, slept, ate, joked, and wept with Him, all betrayed Him.

How many people have you laid down your life for and to whom you have given everything, only to find that at some point they betray you, leave you, reject you, and turn away from you? Of all people, Jesus knows this. Isaiah 53:3 says, *"He is despised and rejected of men; a man of sorrows, and acquainted with grief: and we hid as it were our faces from him"*. We have done it to Him; others will do it to us. We need not to be concerned or think it strange when this happens to us.

In Psalms 41:9 David said, *"Yea, mine own familiar friend, in whom I trusted, which did eat of my bread, hath lifted up his heel against me."* Some other translations read *"Even my own familiar friend, whom I trusted and was confident"*, *"Who ate my bread and lifted up his heel against me"*, *"My most trusted friend has turned against me though he ate at my table."* You see, the only people that can betray us are those that are close to us. I could not care less what an enemy has to say about me; how about you? But when somebody who I have loved *"even my own familiar friend"* and have had fellowship with turns on me, it is hurtful. The Bible speaks of a day coming when *"ye shall be betrayed both by parents, and brethren, and kinsfolks, and friends. And ye shall be hated of all men for my name's sake"* (Luke 21:16-17). When this happens we must remember the example of the Lord Jesus, and not give in to vindictiveness or an answer of hardness. David experienced this (Psalms 55:12-14).

How many times have we walked in the house of God with someone with whom we took sweet counsel together, only to have found that they betrayed us? Joseph was betrayed by his brothers; David was betrayed by Absalom; Paul betrayed by Demas; Peter betrayed Jesus. You and I will know betrayal; so, let's know how to handle it, even when we're betrayed by a kiss. Let's respond as Jesus did, saying *"friend."*

"Add To Your Faith"
II Peter 1:5

Here in II Peter 1, we find this passage,

"*⁵And beside this, giving all diligence, add to your faith virtue; and to virtue knowledge; ⁶And to knowledge temperance; and to temperance patience; and to patience godliness; ⁷And to godliness brotherly kindness; and to brotherly kindness charity*" (II Peter 1:5-7).

DAY 260

Peter is admonishing and encouraging us that we are to add to our faith. Another translation of this reads, "*Supplement your faith.*" The word "*add*" in the Greek literally means "to furnish besides, to aid, to contribute, to fully supply." In other words, Peter is saying in verse 5 that we need to give all effort, diligence, and hard work to add and contribute or fully supply to our faith.

When we are born again, every believer begins with a seed and measure of faith and God wants to increase it. II Corinthians 8:7 says, "*Therefore, as ye abound in every thing, in faith, and utterance, and knowledge, and in all diligence, and in your love to us, see that ye abound in this grace also.*" In II Corinthians 10:15 Paul says, "*having hope, when your faith is increased.*" Colossians 1:23 adds, "*If ye continue in the faith grounded and settled, and be not moved away from the hope of the gospel...*"

Jesus is the "*author and finisher of our faith*" (Hebrews 12:2). He is there to begin our faith walk and He will be there till the end. Our job is to grow in faith as Romans 1:17 says we are to go from "*faith to faith.*" So God wants us to add to our faith.

Next, what are the things God wants to add to our faith? The first thing is virtue. The word "*virtue*" means "valor, manliness, moral excellence." God expects moral excellence out of us. This may seem overwhelming and beyond us, but by the Spirit of God we can achieve this if we continue in the faith. The Holy Spirit will add not only courage and manliness, but more importantly moral excellence to our lives. And who doesn't need moral excellence in their lives. Let the Lord add that today.

After virtue is knowledge. We can add knowledge to our faith. This is not just speaking of intellectual knowledge, but I believe this really speaks of the Word of God and knowing the Lord intimately. We need to add to our beginning faith an ongoing relationship with the Lord Jesus as II Peter 3:18 says, "*But grow in grace, and in the knowledge of our Lord and Saviour Jesus Christ.*" We increase in our Scriptural knowledge by sitting under the Word of God and giving ourselves to reading and studying the Bible.

Next we add temperance. The word "*temperance*" means "self-control, to be strong in a thing, to have your appetites controlled." Who doesn't need some temperance in their life? We are to add self-control to our life and be strong in the grace of God. We need to control our appetites.

God wants us to increase and grow in Him with these things manifesting themselves in our life. And as we spend time with Jesus, spend time in His Word, fellowship with the Holy Spirit, and worship in His holy presence, we are going to be changed as II Corinthians 3:18 says, *"into the same image from glory to glory."* You may not have much virtue today or much knowledge or temperance, but we can begin today to go from faith to another level of faith.

Then he says to add to your faith patience. Jesus said in Luke 21:19, *"In your patience possess ye your souls."* All of us need patience, *"who through faith and patience inherit the promises"* Hebrews 6:12 says. The Lord Jesus is the most patient being in the universe. He has great patience for you and me. Therefore allow Him to add that to your faith. If you are not very patient, the Lord will bring the dealings of God into your life to give you an opportunity to grow in this. This is the only way it can happen, by learning to be patient in every situation.

We then add to patience, godliness; godliness instead of worldliness. I Timothy 6:6 says, *"godliness with contentment is great gain."* The Bible speaks of the *"mystery of godliness"* (I Timothy 3:16). You and I, by allowing the Lord Jesus to live through our lives, can begin to walk in the state of godliness. Galatians 2:20 says, *"I am crucified with Christ: nevertheless I live; yet not I, but Christ liveth in me: and the life which I now live in the flesh I live by the faith of the Son of God, who loved me, and gave himself for me."* Let us determine in our hearts today to let Jesus live through us and not our old Adamic nature.

After godliness is brotherly kindness. Hebrews 13:1 says, *"Let brotherly love continue."* You and I need to love our brothers and sisters, being *"kind one to another, tenderhearted, forgiving one another, even as God for Christ's sake hath forgiven you"* (Ephesians 4:32). God wants us to walk as a family. Jesus said in Luke 8:21, *"My mother and my brethren are these which hear the word of God, and do it."* Our brothers and sisters are those in the Kingdom of God with us. And God wants us to be kind to them. And we can grow in this as we allow the Lord and His agape love to live through us.

And finally he says to add charity to our faith. Charity means God's agape love. God is love and by allowing the God within us to live through us, we can show the love of God to others. This is what God is after in all of our lives, that we would love others as He has loved us.

Peter finishes his thought in II Peter 1:8, *"⁸For if these things be in you, and abound, they make you that ye shall neither be barren nor unfruitful in the knowledge of our Lord Jesus Christ."* So beginning today, the Lord says to us, *"Add to your faith."* And as we do, we will neither be barren or unfruitful!

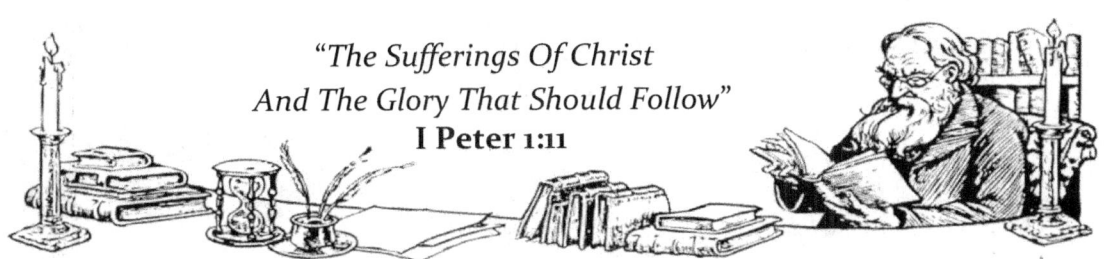

"The Sufferings Of Christ And The Glory That Should Follow"
I Peter 1:11

DAY 261

In this message today, we want to bring one of the most amazing truths found in the Scripture, one that is not heeded or listened to very much or is plainly ignored. I find that it is rarely preached about. That truth that I am speaking of is that the glory of God always follows or comes behind a time of suffering. Suffering is necessary for us to experience the glory. If this was only preached more, if this was only taught more, then God's people would be better prepared.

Here in I Peter 1:11 it says, *"Searching what, or what manner of time the Spirit of Christ, which was in them did signify, when it testified beforehand the sufferings of Christ, and the glory that should follow."* We see it say of Jesus again in Hebrews 11:2, *"who for the joy that was set before him endured the cross."* He realized that suffering would be followed by glory.

In Hebrews 2:10 it says, *"For it became him, for whom are all things, and by whom are all things, in bringing many sons unto glory, to make the captain of their salvation perfect through sufferings."* Glory and suffering go hand in hand. We go through suffering so that we can handle the weight of glory that God wants to give us. In II Corinthians 4:17 Paul says, *"For light affliction, which is but for a moment, worketh for us a far more exceeding and eternal weight of glory."* The light affliction is working for you an exceeding, eternal weight of glory.

We find that our lives can be very shallow if we've never gone through any real experience of suffering or hardship. For it's in those times that we learn how to truly trust God. We hew out of the rock ourselves a measure of faith, a measure of deep belief and trust in our great God. It brings with it, out of that suffering, great glory and substance in our lives. In Romans 8:18 Paul says, *"For I reckon that the sufferings of this present time are not worthy to be compared with the glory which shall be revealed in us."* This is our God. Hang in there! You may be suffering now, but glory is coming!

In Luke 24:26 Jesus says, *"Ought not Christ to have suffered these things, and to enter into his glory?"* There can be no entering into glory, unless you have suffered something. There are no overcomers unless they have overcome something. There is no testimony unless somebody has been tested. This is a simple principle. Suffering and glory go hand in hand and you and I need to rejoice, as I Peter 4:13 says, *"But, rejoice, inasmuch as ye are partakers of Christ's sufferings; that when his glory shall be revealed, ye may be glad also with exceeding joy."* Instead of being down about our sufferings, we are going to rejoice and be confident that it will all be worth it in the end. I Peter 5:10 says, *"But the God of all grace, who hath called us unto his eternal glory by Christ Jesus, after that ye have suffered a while, make you perfect, stablish, strengthen, settle you."* After you have suffered awhile, His glory will be released into your life. Suffering and glory go hand in hand. Let's rejoice today, as we see this principle worked out in our lives.

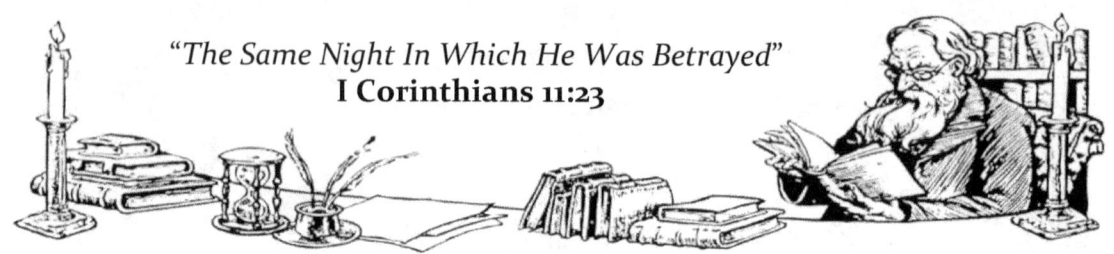

"The Same Night In Which He Was Betrayed"
I Corinthians 11:23

DAY 262

One of the most glorious truths in the Scriptures is found here in this passage. It says in I Corinthians 11:23-24, *"the Lord Jesus the same night in which he was betrayed took bread:* ^{24}*And when he had given thanks, he brake it, and said, Take, eat: this is my body, which is broken for you: this do in remembrance of me."*

This is what turned the tide for me when it came to my eternal salvation. I saw that I had nothing to do with my salvation, for truly as Ephesians 2:8 says, *"For by grace are ye saved through faith; and that not of yourselves: it is the gift of God."* My covenant with God does not stand on what I do or don't do; it stands between Jesus and the Father. Jesus is the firstborn in Psalms 89, where it says, *"Also I will make him my firstborn...My mercy will I keep for him for evermore, and my covenant shall stand fast with him"* (Psalms 89:27-28).

His covenant, as it says in II Samuel 23:5, is sure. It says in Isaiah 55:3, *"I will make an everlasting covenant with you, even the sure mercies of David."* Folks, the night in which Jesus was betrayed He purposely took bread knowing full well that everyone would forsake Him so that they would know later after they had fallen that they already had an eternal covenant with God and everything was taken care of. This is the grace of God in a nutshell.

Isaiah 54:10 tells us, *"For the mountains shall depart, and the hills be removed; but my kindness shall not depart from thee, neither shall the covenant of my peace be removed, saith the Lord that hath mercy on thee."* God's covenant is an everlasting covenant; it will never end. It is a sure covenant that God made with His Son, the son of man. You see, there was no man perfect enough to die for the sins of the whole world, therefore, Jesus is the *"Lamb slain from the foundation of the world"* (Revelation 13:8). He came, lived, and was *"in all points tempted like as we are, yet without sin"* (Hebrews 4:15). It says in II Corinthians 5:21, *"For he hath made him to be sin for us, who knew no sin; that we might be made the righteousness of God in him."*

The Bible also says, *"But God commendeth his love toward us, in that, while we were yet sinners, Christ died for us"* (Romans 5:8). On the night He was betrayed, He purposely took bread and formed a covenant with them to let them know He would never leave them or forsake them. He wanted them to know His covenant was sure no matter what they did, even to the point of betraying Him. A look at Peter is all it takes. He denied Him three times, cursed violently, and left Him, but yet, when the Lord appeared to the disciples, He asked Him, "Simon Peter, do you love me" (John 21:15-18)? He asked him this three times to counteract those three denials.

Our God is a covenant-keeping God. He hath remembered His covenant forever. He knows the *"end from the beginning"* (Isaiah 46:10). He knew everything you and I would do from the beginning. So, on the night He was betrayed, He purposely took bread, broke it, and gave it so that you and I would know that our eternal salvation, our eternal covenant, is forever sure. It's not a matter of what we do, but what He has already done. He's already taken the bread; He's already made the covenant with His Son, the Lamb of God.

"You Shall Be Free Indeed"
John 8:36

Day 263

John 8:36 tells us, *"If the Son therefore shall make you free, ye shall be free indeed."* When we are born again and washed in the blood of Jesus we are free from the bondage of sin. Romans 8:21 says we have been *"delivered from the bondage of corruption into the glorious liberty of the children of God."* God has come to deliver us and to make us free. By the anointing He breaks the yoke of bondage in our lives. The Bible says, *"For the law of the Spirit of life in Christ Jesus hath made me free from the law of sin and death"* (Romans 8:2).

II Corinthians 3:17 says, *"Now the Lord is that Spirit: and where the Spirit of the Lord is, there is liberty."* If the Spirit of the Lord is in you then there is liberty within you. I have come to find that people do not really like a truly free person because a truly free person has no insecurities, inferiorities, condemnation, and is at peace with himself and God. For some reason a free person tends to offend a lot of people. People who are not free are constantly trying to bring us into bondage by telling us, *"Touch not; taste not; handle not"* (Colossians 2:21).

Galatians 5:1 tells us, *"Stand fast therefore in the liberty wherewith Christ hath made us free, and be not entangled again with the yoke of bondage."* You and I have been made free indeed and we must stand fast in this. The enemy and especially religion are going to try to bring us under a yoke of bondage. Do not fall for this. Babylon screams their manmade laws, rules, and regulations, when God has come that you might not just be free but free indeed! Galatians 5:13 says, *"For, brethren, ye have been called unto liberty."* This is our calling. John 8:32 tells us, *"And ye shall know the truth, and the truth shall make you free."* The truth is that Jesus has already delivered us and the chains have already been broken.

Long ago I heard a story about a man who was in a prison cell with satan who proceeded to beat and torment the man. Jesus then came and opened up the cell, dealt with satan, unloosed the man's chains, and told him "you're free." However, the man never got up to leave the prison cell and eventually, satan recovered and came to beat the man once again. This is the kind of abuse we see in the world.

Why won't you get up today? Jesus has dealt with your enemy and broken the bonds of your yoke by His anointing. He has brought you into the glorious liberty of the children of God, called you to that liberty, and has made you free indeed! Take your freedom today and, *"Stand fast therefore in the liberty wherewith Christ hath made us free".*

"I Will Triumph"
Psalms 92:4

Psalms 92:4 says, "*For thou, Lord, hast made me glad through thy work: I will triumph in the works of thy hands.*" This is such a great revelation that you and I can triumph because of what God has done for us. The word "*triumph*" means, "to prevail, to win the victory over, to conquer." You and I are going to conquer, and win the victory over this world, our sin, flesh, and the devil.

Jesus said in John 16:33, "*In the world ye shall have tribulation: but be of good cheer; I have overcome the world.*" Because Jesus has overcome the world, you and I can overcome the world. I John 5:4 says, "*For whatsoever is born of God overcometh the world: and this is the victory that overcometh the world, even our faith.*" You and I are born of God and have already overcome the world. All we need to do is have faith in what Jesus has already done. Paul said in I Corinthians 15:57, "*But thanks be to God, which giveth us the victory through our Lord Jesus Christ.*"

In Colossians 2:15, Paul says, "*And having spoiled principalities and powers, he [Jesus] made a shew of them openly, triumphing over them in it.*" God triumphed over satan and all his host. God also became a man so that He can know what it is like to be a man, as Hebrews 4:15 says, "*For we have not an high priest which cannot be touched with the feeling of our infirmities; but was in all points tempted like as we are, yet with out sin.*" Jesus knows what we go through, even in our deepest and darkest despair. Luke 22:44 tells us that Jesus, "*being in an agony he prayed more earnestly: and his sweat was as it were great drops of blood falling down to the ground.*" He identified with our humanity and was tempted in all points, yet was without sin.

Paul tells the Corinthians, "*Now thanks be unto God, which always causeth us to triumph in Christ*" (II Corinthians 2:14). I love these absolute words found in the Scriptures like "*all*", "*every*" and "*always*". Always means always! All means all! I Thessalonians 5:18 says, "*In every thing give thanks: for this is the will of God in Christ Jesus concerning you.*" We can always give thanks because that we know that we will always triumph in the end. Psalms 108:9 states "*over Philistia will I triumph.*" He will triumph over all our enemies and make an open show of them. David declares in Psalms 47:1-3, "*He shall subdue the people under us, and the nations under our feet.*"

Revelation 5:5 says, "*Behold, the Lion of the tribe of Juda, the Root of David, hath prevailed.*" Jesus has overcome the world and has subdued the nations under us. Jesus has subdued our own flesh by conquering it Himself by not sinning. Philippians 3:21 says, "*He is able even to subdue all things unto himself.*" David wrote in Psalms 18:39, "*For thou hast girded me with strength unto the battle: thou hast subdued under me those that rose up against me.*" Glory to God! This is our God. We need to be of good cheer today and know that the triumphant God will help us to overcome and triumph. In Psalms 140:7 says, "*O God the Lord, the strength of my salvation, thou hast covered my head in the day of battle.*" Finally in Proverbs 21:31, "*The horse is prepared against the day of battle: but safety (victory) is of the Lord.*" Know today that you and I will triumph. Blessed be the name of the Lord!

"More Understanding Than All My Teachers"
Psalms 119:99

DAY 265

The Bible says in Psalms 119:99, "*I have more understanding than all my teachers: for thy testimonies are my meditation.*" This revelation is a precious truth, one that is very seldom talked about and very misunderstood. There comes a time in our lives, as the Bible says in Galatians, in which we are "*under tutors and governors until the time appointed*" (Galatians 4:2). We are to "*grow in grace, and in the knowledge of our Lord and Saviour Jesus Christ*" (II Peter 3:18). And at some point, we will reach a place when we will have more understanding than even our own teachers. In the following verse in Psalms 119, it says, "*I understand more than the ancients, because I keep thy precepts*" (Psalms 119:100).

It is the job of ministry to reproduce itself. Pastors should never be insecure and hold people back, but always encourage them to go forward and press onward to all they can be in God. They should be a great encouragement. They should not have a messiah complex, gobbling up all the glory, seeking flattery, loving "*the praise of men more than the praise of God*" (John 12:43).

When the day comes that you have more understanding than all your teachers, it'll probably be one of the saddest days of your life. You can no longer rest under the comfort of somebody else covering and protecting you. You're then sticking your own neck out to preach the truth. You will finally be initiated into the things of God yourself and have the ability to draw on the Scriptures. This is the will of God.

Paul said in II Timothy, "*And the things that thou hast heard of me among many witnesses, the same commit thou to faithful men, who shall be able to teach others also*" (II Timothy 2:2). This is discipleship: one father teaching a son, who will then teach his grandson, and so forth. This is how the Kingdom of God is to grow and prosper. Ephesians 4 tells us clearly the job of the fivefold ministry is "*For the perfecting of the saints, for the work of the ministry, for the edifying of the body of Christ: ¹³Till we all come in the unity of the faith, and of the knowledge of the Son of God, unto a perfect man, unto the measure of the stature of the fullness of Christ*" (Ephesians 4:11-13).

This is God's will, that the fivefold ministry will perfect, train, and disciple those who God places under them. It was a sad day for me when I realized I had quite a bit of Scriptural knowledge. It didn't make me proud or boastful, but rather, it was very humbling to know that God had invested such an inheritance in me. I also had to fight some fears and insecurities. It was so much easier when someone else was responsible, but now my turn had come. And perhaps your turn has come or is coming.

As we give ourselves to the precepts of the Lord, and "*hunger and thirst after righteousness,*" we shall be filled (Matthew 5:6). As we grow from "*faith to faith*" (Romans 1:17), "*glory to glory*" (II Corinthians 3:18), and "*from strength to strength*" (Psalms 84:7), we're going to grow in authority and understanding. And it may be that we'll surpass our teachers, but "*the disciple is not above his master: but every one that is perfect shall be as his master,"* the Bible clearly states (Luke 6:40). We don't ever want to usurp authority over anyone, but at the same time, we are not to deny who we are and what God has made us to be.

There will come a time in your life when your understanding will reach a higher pinnacle than your teachers. It does not denigrate them or make them any less. It simply means that they have done their job. They have fought a good fight and finished their course and have blessed the world now with a mighty teacher of the Scriptures (II Timothy 4:7).

"My Soul Is Weary Of My Life"
Job 10:1

DAY 266

We find here in the book of Job something pertinent that all of us go through, weariness. Job declares, *"My soul is weary of my life"* (Job 10:1). How many of us at different times in our lives have said the very same thing? We get burdened down by cares, failures, and disappointments. Life can be hard for all of us. There's no shame in being weary. The question is: what do you do when you're weary? If you are weary of life, then take heed to the Scriptures.

Here the word *"weary"* in Hebrew literally means "to loathe." This means that you loathe yourself for your weaknesses; another Hebrew word for *"weary"* means "to gasp or to be exhausted." The Greek word for *"wearied"* means "to feel fatigue or to work hard." It comes from a root word that means "a cut, toil (as reducing the strength), or pains." Our strength is reduced when we're weary. We feel fatigue and are worn out, weary from the journey of life. Another Greek word means "to fail in heart, to be weak, or to faint." This is not a weakness that is a detriment to your character; it is simply the sum of life's obstacles. Paul said in Galatians, *"And let us not be weary in well doing: for in due season we shall reap, if we faint not"* (Galatians 6:9).

The answer for us is found in the Scriptures, *"Thou, O God, didst send a plentiful rain, whereby thou didst confirm thine inheritance, when it was weary"* (Psalms 68:9). God has sent the rain, the glorious presence of God. Speaking of the baptism of the Holy Ghost and speaking in tongues, the book of Isaiah tells us, *"This is the rest wherewith ye may cause the weary to rest; and this is the refreshing..."* (Isaiah 28:12). The rest is the rain, the Holy Ghost. The Bible declares in Jeremiah, *"For I have satiated the weary soul, and I have replenished every sorrowful soul"* (Jeremiah 31:25). God wants to satiate, completely saturate, and encourage the sorrow in your weary soul. You don't have to remain this way; you don't have to be weary of your life, because the Scriptures clearly state:

> *"^{28}Hast thou not known? Hast thou not heard, that the everlasting God, the Lord, the Creator of the ends of the earth, fainteth not, neither is weary? there is no searching of his understanding. ^{29}He giveth power to the faint; and to them that have no might he increaseth strength. ^{30}Even the youths shall faint and be weary, and the young men shall utterly fall: ^{31}But they that wait upon the Lord shall renew their strength; they shall mount up with wings as eagles; they shall run, and not be weary; and they shall walk, and not faint"* (Isaiah 40:28-31).

Rise up; be not weary in well doing, your life is worth something. Let Jesus give you power and might, allow Him to renew your strength today that you may walk and not faint!

"I Was Brought Low, And He Helped Me"
Psalms 116:6

DAY 267

The Scriptures are very clear that there are times in our lives when we are brought into deep valleys, dark experiences, places of chastisement, and the dealings of the Lord. Every person finds himself on occasion in these places. But it is good to remember that there is no pit or hole so low that Jesus will not go lower still to help us. David experienced this and says in Psalms 116:6, "*I was brought low and He helped me.*" This is a marvelous truth. Some other translations read:

> *"I was in great need and He saved me"*
> *"I was at the end of my rope and He saved me"*
> *"When I was helpless"*
> *"When I was in serious trouble, He delivered me"*
> *"I was humbled and He delivered me."*

This is the definition of our God. He always helps and stands with the accused. The definition of "*low*" in the Hebrew means "to be feeble, to be oppressed, to be emptied, dried up; to be impoverished or to be made thin." There are times in all of our lives when we experience this. We see this in the book of Job:

> *"17Behold, happy is the man whom God correcteth: therefore despise not thou the chastening of the Almighty: 18For he maketh sore, and bindeth up: he woundeth, and his hands make whole. 19He shall deliver thee in six troubles: yea, in seven there shall no evil touch thee"* (Job 5:17-19).

There are times when it is necessary in everyone's life to be made sore, but God will eventually bind us up. Contrary to popular opinion, God does wound, but His hands make whole. The wonderful revelation here is that He will deliver us in six troubles. Six is the number in Scripture for man or Satan. In other words, six represents here the things we go through in life. But in seven, there shall no evil touch us. This is the word of the Lord to us today. There will come a day when there will be no more dealings, no more valleys, or experiences to go through. We will ultimately be delivered for the last time. We would have gone through all that man is supposed to go through in preparation for what God has for him. God uses trouble and experiences that bring us low, dry, impoverished, etc. so He can ultimately help us, deliver us, and make us whole. We see this principle in Hosea:

> *"1Come, and let us return unto the Lord: for he hath torn, and he will heal us; he hath smitten, and he will bind us up. 2After two days will he revive us: in the third day he will raise us up, and we shall live in his sight. 3Then shall we know, if we follow on to know the Lord: his going forth is*

prepared as the morning; and he shall come unto us as the rain, as the latter and former rain unto the earth" (Hosea 6:1-3).

Sometimes it is necessary for us to be torn. It is necessary for us to be smitten. But God promises us He will heal us. He has told us that He will bind us up and after two days revive us. Two is the number for witness and separation. In other words, God is doing right now whatever is necessary to make us into the image of Christ Jesus so we can be a true and right witness for Jesus on the earth. He must remove and cleanse the sin, flesh, and attributes in our life that are not of Him. This is not easy. It is not fun being brought low, but God will help us and revive us when He's completed His work in us.

Ultimately, He will revive us on the third day. The third day is a revelation when the sons of God come forth in the earth and shall live in His sight. Morning time speaks of resurrection. In other words, by dealing with us and bringing us low, God is helping us walk in resurrection power. We shall understand all of this as we simply make a decision in every season of life to follow on to know the Lord and as we do, His glory and presence will come to us encouraging us, helping us, and ultimately delivering us for the last time.

So whatever you are going through today or in this season of life, be encouraged that God has a great purpose in all of it. God knows where you are today. David said in Psalms 142:3, *"When my spirit was overwhelmed within me, then thou knewest my path..."* Every time your spirits is overwhelmed, you can rest assured that He will never leave you nor forsake you. You are not alone. He is there with you. Paul said in II Timothy 4:16-17, *"At my first answer no man stood with me, but all men forsook me...Notwithstanding the Lord stood with me, and strengthened me..."* Jesus experienced this and in John 16:32 said, *"every man...shall leave me alone: and yet I am not alone, because the Father is with me."*

David went on to say in Psalms 142:4, *"I looked on my right hand, and beheld, but there was no man that would know me: refuge failed me; no man cared for my soul."* All of us have had times like this, when there was no one around to help and we found no earthly help for our situation. But the Lord will be there to help us in those times, as David found out:

> *"⁵I cried unto thee, O Lord: I said, Thou art my refuge and my portion in the land of the living. ⁶Attend unto my cry; for I am brought very low... ⁷Bring my soul out of prison, that I may praise thy name"* (Psalms 142:5-7).

The word of the Lord to you today is, *"I was brought low, and He helped me."* God has a glorious end in all that He is doing. But today, wherever you find yourself or whatever situation you may find yourself in, never forget no matter how low you go, God always goes deeper still and will bind you up, will heal you, will bring your soul out of the prison, so you might praise His name and be the man or woman of God He created you to be! Blessed be the name of the Lord!

"Launch Out Into The Deep"
Luke 5:4

DAY 268

The Bible says in Psalms 42:7 that *"deep is calling unto deep at the noise of thy waterspouts."* There is always a call and a pull coming from the Most Holy Place and the mercy seat. It is drawing us ever onward and upward. It causes us to leave behind what we know and embrace what we don't know as we walk down this narrow way that leads to life (Matthew 7:14).

We need to launch out into the deep as Jesus said in Luke 5:4, *"Launch out into the deep, and let down your nets for a draught."* It's only in the deep that we find a draught of fish, or where we find the deep and revelatory truths of God. However, we must be willing to let go of where we are to embrace what we've never seen or heard before. We must trust the witness of the Spirit *"comparing spiritual things with spiritual"* (I Corinthians 2:13). We must be *"rightly dividing the word of truth,"* (II Timothy 2:15). We can rest assured that we can embrace all that there is in God.

It's time to launch out into the deep. It's time to stop hiding in another man's revelation. We need to begin to seek the Lord for ourselves; *"Seek ye the LORD while he may be found, call ye upon him while he is near,"* (Isaiah 55:6). You and I are called to go on to perfection (Hebrews 6:1) and to go on with the Lord. Paul says in Philippians 3:13-14, *"forgetting those things which are behind, and reaching forth unto those things which are before, I press toward the mark for the prize of the high calling of God in Christ Jesus"* (Philippians 3:13-14). The amplified version of verse 14 reads, *"I strain to reach the end of the race."* We must let go of where we've been to embrace where God wants to take us to.

In Luke 9:62, *"No man having put his hand to the plough, and looking back, is fit for the kingdom of God."* We cannot be like Lot's wife, frozen forever in a pillar of salt, when God has called us to go on with Him. In Isaiah 43:19 it reads, *"Behold, I will do a new thing; now it shall spring forth; shall ye not know it?"* We need to forget those things behind us. Are we willing to let go of where we are today to embrace what God has for us?

"Launch out into the deep." "Launch" in the Greek means "to put out to sea." We may not know where He's taking us, but He does. In I Corinthians 2:10 it says, *"But God hath revealed them unto us by his Spirit: for the Spirit searcheth all things, yea, the deep things of God."* The Holy Spirit wants to reveal the deep things of God to us. Psalms 92:5 says, *"O Lord, how great are thy works! And thy thoughts are very deep."* Daniel 2:22 reads, *"He revealeth the deep and secret things."* Jesus said in Mark 4:11, *"Unto you it is given to know the mystery of the kingdom of God."* I want to know what God has to say. As David said in Psalms 85:8 *"I will hear what God the LORD will speak."*

Hear me, my friends; the Lord is calling you upward and onward today. *"Follow me, and I will make you fishers of men,"* (Matthew 4:19); Can we follow the Lord today? *"Launch out into the deep,"* and find the great hidden, glorious, and revelatory truths that are waiting. So, today, embrace the Word of God with fullness.

"Peter Went Up To Pray And Became Very Hungry"
Acts 10:9-10

DAY 269

What a glorious truth we find here today in Acts 10:9-10, *"On the morrow, as they went on their journey, and drew nigh unto the city, Peter went up upon the housetop to pray about the sixth hour: ¹⁰And he became very hungry, and would have eaten."* Today, I want us to center upon the words, *"Peter went up... to pray... and became very hungry."* There is something about spending time in the presence of the Lord that makes us hungry. Not so much for physical food, but for spiritual food and spiritual nourishment.

Are you hungry today? *"Blessed are they which do hunger and thirst after righteousness: for they shall be filled,"* Matthew 5:6 says. Are you hungering and thirsting after righteousness? I tell you, the Bible is full of admonitions about being hungry. In Philippians 4:12, Paul admonishes us, *"both to be full and to be hungry."* Paul in the defense of his ministry, talking about what ministers go through, said in II Corinthians 11:27, *"in watchings often, in hunger and thirst."* In I Corinthians 4:11 he also said, *"even unto this present hour we both hunger, and thirst."* It is a part of the ministry to be hungry or to suffer hunger.

We need to stay hungry. We cannot be filled unless we are hungry. Peter went up to pray and as he prayed, he became very hungry. As we spend time in the presence of the Lord, God's glory and Word will come to us and will make us want Him even more. It will manifest in us an unsatisfied satisfaction that cries out with an insatiable desire for more and more and more of Jesus.

In Proverbs 27:7 it says, *"To the hungry soul every bitter thing is sweet."* It doesn't matter what the Lord gives us, we just know that whatever it is, we want it. So if it is bitter or sweet, we will eat it. God told Ezekiel to eat the roll (Ezekiel 3:1) and He told John to eat the little book (Revelation 10:8-10). When they ate it was *"in my mouth sweet as honey: and as soon as I had eaten it, my belly was bitter."* Nonetheless that roll, that little book was the Word of God.

When you go up to pray and God's presence comes, I trust that you are going to get very, very hungry. In Psalms 107:9 it says, *"For he satisfieth the longing soul, and filleth the hungry soul with goodness."* God wants to fill your hungry soul with goodness. He wants to fill you with Himself.

But we must have hunger. There must be within us desire. If we have to, let's go and pray and as we pray, we will become very, very hungry. In Psalms 146:7 it says that the Lord, *"giveth food to the hungry."* So it is imperative, then, that you and I be hungry today. Go up now to pray, and as you pray, you will become hungry!

"The Firstfruits Unto God"
Revelation 14:4

In Revelation 14, the Bible says:

> *"These are they which were not defiled with women; for they are virgins. These are they which follow the Lamb whithersoever he goeth. These were redeemed from among men, being the firstfruits unto God and to the Lamb"* (Revelation 14:4).

Day 270

The firstfruits are the first ripened fruits that need to be picked before the general harvest. To leave the firstfruits on the vine or tree, while waiting for the others to ripen, would mean those fruits would rot. So, God is gathering together a company of firstfruits, a group of people, unto Himself. They are the first ripened fruits out of the body of Christ. In Leviticus 23:10, the Lord said to Moses, *"When ye be come into the land which I give unto you, and shall reap the harvest thereof, then ye shall bring a sheaf of the firstfruits of your harvest unto the priest."* When the harvest was come, God wanted a particular sheaf of the firstfruits to be brought to the priests. It was not the whole harvest, but just a sheaf of the firstfruits. This is an example, once again, of the remnant within the body of Christ.

It says in Psalms 45:9, 13-14, *"Upon thy right hand did stand the queen in gold of Ophir. ¹³The king's daughter is all glorious within: her clothing is of wrought gold. ¹⁴She shall be brought unto the king in raiment of needlework: the virgins her companions that follow her shall be brought unto thee"* (Psalms 45:9-14). Notice, there are the virgins, her companions, and the queen, the bride of Christ, in gold of Ophir.

God has a remnant of people that He is bringing forth. They are the firstfruits, the first ripened company. The Bible says in Deuteronomy:

> *"⁸At that time the Lord separated the tribe of Levi, to bear the ark of the covenant of the Lord, to stand before the Lord to minister unto him, and to bless in his name, unto this day. ⁹Wherefore Levi hath no part nor inheritance with his brethren; the Lord is his inheritance"* (Deuteronomy 10:8-9).

God is separating the tribe of Levi, one tribe out of twelve, to carry His manifest presence, the ark, and stand before Him to minister unto Him. Malachi 3:17 tells us, *"And they shall be mine, saith the Lord of hosts, in that day when I make up my jewels; and I will spare them, as a man spareth his own son that serveth him."*

There are the jeweled, and there is the rest of the body of Christ. Won't you strive today to be those firstfruits unto God? Will you allow God to ripen you, cause you to come forth, and prepare you for the appearing of the Lord in His people? We can be the firstfruits unto God, the first ones who show His character and His nature to the earth.

"The Pearl Of Great Price"
Matthew 13:46

DAY 271

In today's passage, we find this parable:

> "A merchant man, seeking goodly pearls: ^{46}Who, when he had found one pearl of great price, went and sold all that he had, and bought it" (Matthew 13:45-46).

Jesus is the pearl of great price for you and me. There is no one in the universe more wonderful, precious, or glorious than He. When we find it, *"one pearl of great price"* we need to sell everything we have and pay whatever price required to purchase it.

"Great price" in this passage means "extremely valuable or very costly." Oh, how valuable He is! Paul wrote to Timothy, saying, *"But we have this treasure in earthen vessels"* (II Corinthians 4:7). It's that pearl of great price, the Lord Jesus, that we have in our "earthen vessels". In Colossians 2:3, it says, *"In whom are hid all the treasures of wisdom and knowledge."* In Him is hid all of the treasures of the universe and He is such a lovely, wonderful Savior.

Most of the time, we find Him in great trouble and difficulty. We find Him like a man dying of thirst in a desert who comes across living water, fresh and clean. Jesus shines so brightly in our dark world. He was, is and will be that pearl of great price for us for eternity. The Bible says, *"For where your treasure is, there will your heart be also"* (Luke 12:34). If He is your costly treasure, your heart will be there.

Nothing in this world can compare with Jesus; nothing can come close to the intimacy, joy, satisfaction, and comfort that come from being in a true relationship with Him. He truly is the pearl of great price. We have been seeking for all of our lives for something beautiful and wonderful. Men spend most of their lives searching; they try to find it in power, in money, in a man or woman, in business or things. We will never be satisfied until we find Him, the *"one pearl of great price."* There is only one. Some other translations of this verse read:

> "Finding one that is flawless, he immediately sells everything and buys it."
> "...having gone off, sold all, as much as he was possessing, having staked all that he had on one business venture which would either make him or break him..."
> "...though it costs all he has, he buys it."

The Bible says in Proverbs 23:23, *"Buy the truth, and sell it not."* We must pay the price for this pearl but oh, how worth it He is. Buy it today; buy Him today, the One that is flawless. He is the pearl of great price, *"In whom are hid all the treasures".*

"I Am"
John 8:58

DAY 272

Here in John 8:58, Jesus says, *"Verily, verily, I say unto you, Before Abraham was, I am."* This was referring to the voice of the Lord speaking to Moses in Exodus 3:14-15 proclaiming, *"I AM THAT I AM: and he said, Thus shalt thou say unto the children of Israel, I AM hath sent me unto you."*

Today, I want us to look at this tremendous principle of *"I am that I am."* In the Hebrew, this simply means "I will be what I will be. I will do what I will do." This is He, the almighty and eternal God that we serve, speaking of Himself. And He warns us in John 8:24, *"I said therefore unto you, that ye shall die in your sins: for if ye believe not that I am he, ye shall die in your sins."* Jesus is the great I Am and it infuriated the Pharisees, because they did not believe.

I want to quickly note to you some of the different times this revelation was brought forth in the Scriptures: where Jesus speaks of Himself as the *"I Am."* To start us off, in John 13:13 He says, *"Ye call me Master and Lord: and ye say well; for so I am."* He also said in John 8:23, *"I am from above: ye are of this world; I am not of this world."* In John 6:35, He said, *"I am the bread of life."* Now, understand that as each one of these things are spoken, they are the revelation of who the *"I Am"* is. The *"I Am"* is from above and not of this world. The *"I Am"* is the bread of life, or as Jesus says in John 6:51, *"I am the living bread which came down from heaven: if any man eat of this bread, he shall live for ever: and the bread that I will give is my flesh, which I will give for the life of the world."* This is who the great *"I Am"* is.

He can actually be whatever He wants, but He's chosen to restrict Himself to His Word and to the revelation found therein. In John 8:12 He says, *"I am the light of the world: he that followeth me shall not walk in darkness, but shall have the light of life."* And then in John 10:9, *"I am the door: by me if any man enter in, he shall be saved, and shall go in and out, and find pasture."* Jesus is the door to everything in life and to all things spiritual. He is the light and the revelation of the world, not just in the church, but in the world.

He says in John 10:10, *"I am come that they might have life, and that they might have it more abundantly."* The *"I Am"* is full of *"zoe"* or "life as God is living it right now." He said in John 11:25, *"I am the resurrection, and the life: he that believeth in me, though he were dead, yet shall he live."* This is the revelation of the *"I Am"*; He is the resurrection and the life. Revelation 1:18, *"I am he that liveth, and was dead; and, behold, I am alive for evermore, Amen; and have the keys of hell and of death."* Glory to God! In John 14:6, Jesus says, *"I am the way, the truth, and the life: no man cometh unto the Father, but by me."* And John 15:1, *"I am the true vine, and my Father is the husbandman."*

He is to be our Master and our Lord. Then in Matthew 28:20, *"Teaching them to observe all things whatsoever I have commanded you: and, lo, I am with you always, even unto the end of the world. Amen."* The *"I Am"* is always with us, He is always there for us. He said in the Amplified version of Matthew 18:20, *"For where two or three are gathered together in my name, there am I in the midst of them."* When you and I come together, *"I Am"* is right in the midst of us, overseeing us. He says in John 10:14, *"I am the good shepherd."* Bless His holy name. He is indeed a great shepherd. He is the chief shepherd and bishop of our souls.

He says in Revelation 1:17, *"Fear not; I am the first and the last."* And in Revelation 1:11, *"I am Alpha and Omega, the first and last."* He is the beginning and end; He is the author and finisher of our faith. The *"I Am"* really is everything. In Revelation 22:16 He says, *"I am the root and the offspring of David, and the bright and morning star."*

This is the revelation of the *"I Am."* There are many more in the Scriptures, but this is enough. You can refer to The God Manual for all the *"I Am"* scripture verses of Jesus. But these are enough to bring this revelation home to us. What a great God we serve!

"Where Would I Go"
John 6:68

Day 273

Here in John 6 Jesus reaches an impasse with His disciples and the multitudes when He says to them in verse 53 *"Except ye eat the flesh of the Son of man, and drink his blood, ye have no life in you."* It becomes a very tedious moment in the Scriptures because in verse 66 it states that *"From that time many of his disciples went back, and walked no more with him."*

In verse 67 Jesus says to the twelve, *"Will ye also go away?"* Jesus never begged anyone to walk with Him and He was never concerned about people leaving Him because He knew He was abiding in truth. We ought to follow that example. When we know we are in the will of God and walking in truth, it makes no difference whether people come or go.

Jesus asked His disciples, His closest friends on earth, *"Will ye also go away?"* and in verse 68 we see that Simon Peter replied *"Lord, to whom shall we go? Thou hast the words of eternal life."* Where would you and I go? I don't know about you but there is no place on the face of the earth to go other than to Jesus, especially having tasted and seen that the Lord is good. I Peter 2:7 says, *"Unto you therefore which believe he is precious."* Having known the glory of God and having known Him intimately how could we ever, ever turn away from Him?

Our Beloved is the greatest, most wonderful, altogether lovely being in the universe. Moreover, Peter added *"Thou hast the words of eternal life."* Where could we go to receive such wisdom, hidden treasures, and unsearchable riches of truth other than the Lord Jesus? Mark 4:11 says, *"Unto you it is given to know the mystery of the kingdom of God."* Where else could we learn these things that have been hidden from the foundation of the world? Where would we go and what would we do without Him? I could not imagine life without my precious Jesus. We find David saying the same thing in Psalms 139:7, *"Whither shall I go from thy spirit? Or whither shall I flee from thy presence?"* Where can you go from His Spirit? Is there any place to go from His presence? David found out there wasn't and continues:

> *"⁸If I ascend up into heaven, thou art there: if I make my bed in hell, behold, thou art there. ⁹If I take the wings of the morning, and dwell in the uttermost parts of the sea; ¹⁰Even there shall thy hand lead me, and thy right hand shall hold me. ¹¹If I say, Surely the darkness shall cover me; even the night shall be light about me"* (Psalms 139:8-11).

Where can we go? Even in hell He is there. If we say that darkness covers us, both darkness and light are alike to Him. The Lord will never leave us nor forsake us and we need to determine in our heart that we will never leave or forsake Him. Today, our response to our glorious, precious, wonderful Jesus should be *"Lord, to whom shall we go? Thou hast the words of eternal life."*

"If I Regard Iniquity In My Heart"
Psalms 66:18

Many years ago, I struggled with guilt and condemnation. No matter how much I tried to repent for the sin in my life, I could not be freed from that guilt, because I could not receive God's forgiveness. The Lord then spoke to me and literally said to me, "Why won't you believe my Word?" And then, out of nowhere, He told me to turn to this passage that I didn't even know existed. Perhaps I've read this passage of Scripture before, but it had never really registered with me until then. We find this glorious truth of God's mercy here in Psalms 66:18-20:

> "*18If I regard iniquity in my heart, the Lord will not hear me: 19But verily God hath heard me; he hath attended to the voice of my prayer. 20Blessed be God, which hath not turned away my prayer, nor his mercy from me.*"

In this passage of Scripture, we find the answer to guilt and condemnation and we see what happens to us when we repent, yet do not believe that we are forgiven. Remember that I John tells us, "*...we have known and believed the love that God hath to us*" (I John 4:16). It's one thing to know something, but you also have to believe it. You can't believe it if you don't know it. Even though the Scriptures are very clear about God forgiving us of all our sin, we still struggle with guilt and condemnation. Paul says in Romans 7, "*O wretched man that I am! who shall deliver me from the body of this death? I thank God [it's] through Jesus Christ our Lord*" (Romans 7:24-25). Earlier, he had said the things he wanted to do, he didn't do, and the things he didn't want to do, he did (Romans 7:19). Some have tried to say that this is Paul's life before he was saved, but I dare say if you ask any Christian, they could say the same thing as he did here.

We have all struggled with doing things that we weren't supposed to do. This is the tragedy of the Adamic nature in our lives. We need to learn and understand that we are no longer sinners; we are now saints. We have been saved by the grace of God. Ephesians 2:8-9 tells us, "*8For by grace are ye saved through faith; and that not of yourselves: it is the gift of God: 9Not of works, lest any man should boast*". Our salvation stands and rests upon what Jesus did at Calvary, not upon what we do or don't do. We could never save ourselves, nor can we keep ourselves. It is totally and completely by grace.

In Psalms 66 David says, "*If I regard iniquity in my heart, the Lord will not hear me*" (Psalms 66:18). This is just as it was for me on that day that I was praying and asking God to forgive me over and over again. I kept regarding in my heart my iniquity. In other words, God will not hear us because He's already forgiven us.

We must believe the Scripture that says, "*...the blood of Jesus Christ his Son cleanseth us from all sin*" (I John 1:7). We must believe the Bible when it says, "*If we confess our sins, he is faithful and just to forgive us our sins, and to cleanse us from all* *unrighteousness"* (I John 1:9). We must believe the book of Proverbs when it says, *"He that covereth his sins shall not prosper: but whoso confesseth and forsaketh them shall have mercy"* (Proverbs 28:13).

There are hundreds of Scriptures that say God forgives us when we repent. We need to not just know this in our heads, but we need to believe it in our hearts. We need to stop regarding iniquity in our hearts, because dwelling on our guilt blocks the forgiveness of God. The Lord spoke to me and said, "You are not allowing me to release my blood to forgive you when I have already paid the price for you."

David continues in Psalms 66:19 saying, *"But verily"* (or truly), *"God hath heard me..."* God heard you the first moment you began to repent and say you were sorry. God actually heard you from the moment your heart turned.

He knows the whispers of our hearts; His eyes are upon the hearts of men. David then says, *"...he hath attended to the voice of my prayer."* God does hear us when we pray. *"Men ought always to pray, and not to faint,"* Luke 18:1 says. We need to stop fainting and walking in guilt and condemnation. We need to know that when we pray, God hears our prayers and He answers us. He has attended to the voice of your prayer of repentance. You no longer need to regard in your heart the sin that you committed. You need to trust the Lord that His forgiving power has been released and that the blood of Jesus Christ has cleansed you from all sin. You are then free from punishment, guilt, and condemnation.

David ends this Psalms by saying, *"Blessed be God, which hath not turned away my prayer, nor his mercy from me"* (Psalms 66:20). My response to that is: praise the Lord! He will never turn away the prayer of the righteous, humble man with a truly repentant soul. I don't care if we do a thing seventy times seven in a day. If we offer to God a prayer of true repentance, He will hear us. Not only will He not turn away from us, but He will not turn His mercy from us either. You can be sure of one thing, *"his mercy endureth for ever"* (Psalms 136).

"I Determined Not To Know Any Thing Among You"
I Corinthians 2:2

Let us learn from Paul today when he says, *"For I determined not to know anything among you, save Jesus Christ, and him crucified"* (I Corinthians 2:2). We don't need to know everything about everybody. In fact, the knowledge of good and evil is one of the worst things that we can receive.

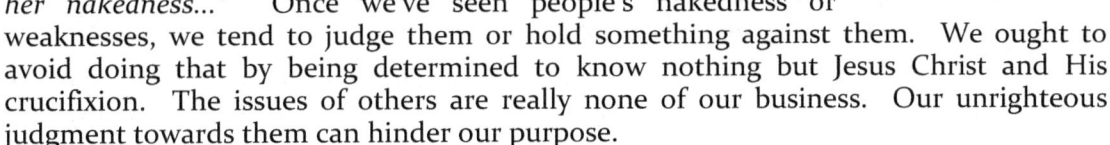

DAY 275

In Lamentations 1:8 it says, *"Jerusalem hath grievously sinned...all that honoured her despise her, because they have seen her nakedness..."* Once we've seen people's nakedness or weaknesses, we tend to judge them or hold something against them. We ought to avoid doing that by being determined to know nothing but Jesus Christ and His crucifixion. The issues of others are really none of our business. Our unrighteous judgment towards them can hinder our purpose.

Remember when God told Ananias to go pray for Paul in Acts 9:10-15? Ananias was reluctant to do so, because he knew of Paul and how he'd been killing Christians. What a hindrance that would have become for all of us, if we were in the same position as Ananias. However, if Ananias had not gone and prayed for Paul, two-thirds of the New Testament would not have been written.

All the issues and the past life stories of others are really none of our business. It's good to become close friends with people and to fellowship with them, but it is not necessary for us to know all the facts of their lives. If we knew too much about people, we would tend to judge them wrongfully. It is just human nature to do so. It should be enough for us to know whether or not someone has Jesus in their lives.

Years ago, a young man was introduced to me as "back sliding Joe." That statement always stuck in the back of my mind. I never trusted him. I judged him by those words. Later I was called upon to help ordain this young man to the ministry, but before I could lay my hands on him, I had to repent to him. I had to tell him that I was wrong for my judgments and that he had proven that he was well suited for the ministry. It would have been better for me not to know anything about him, save Jesus Christ and that He was crucified for this young man.

"For all have sinned, and come short of the glory of God," it says in Romans 3:23. *"...There is none that doeth good, no, not one"* (Psalms 14:3). *"All we like sheep have gone astray; we have turned every one to his own way; and the Lord hath laid on him the iniquity of us all"* (Isaiah 53:6). *"But we have this treasure in earthen vessels..."* (II Corinthians 4:7). All of us are made of earth and dust. *"If thou, Lord, shouldest mark iniquities, O Lord, who shall stand"* (Psalms 130:3)? None of us would. So it's best for us to determine not to know anything about our brother and sister, except only that which the Lord wants us to know. All we need to know in particular is that they're saved, and have received our precious Savior. Our lives then will be free from making unrighteous judgments. We then can love our brothers freely, without the torment of the knowledge of good and evil.

"My Strong Refuge"
Psalms 71:7

Day 276

The Scriptures proclaim that our great God is a refuge to His people in times of oppression, fear and distress, and that He is a refuge to us from our enemies. The Bible says we can literally run to Him and be safe. It declares that when all else in life fails us, He will be there for us as a great protector. He becomes a hiding place for us until the life storms pass. We need to not just know this in theory but in reality. When we have reached the end of our hope, when everything seems lost, He will always be that *"friend that sticketh closer than a brother."* (Proverbs 18:24).

Here in Psalms 71:7 David says, *"I am as a wonder unto many; but thou art my strong refuge."* Another translation reads, *"You are my secure shelter."* So many times we're like a wonder to so many people. They gaze at us, talk about us, question us, but it really doesn't matter because God is our strong refuge. No matter the storm, no matter the trial, no matter the situation, we have a place to run to.

There are five different words in the Hebrew for *"refuge."* One means "a force, security, majesty." Another means "a habitation, a dwelling place, an abode of God." Another means "a lofty inaccessible place." The fourth means "a shelter, a hope, a place of trust." Lastly, it means "a retreat, a place to flee to, and a place to escape, to vanish away, to lift up a standard." Psalms 46:1 says, *"God is our refuge and strength, a very present help in trouble."* God will always be there right in the midst of trouble. He will not leave us nor forsake us (Hebrews 13:5). You can rest assured He will come to your aid. In Deuteronomy 33:27 it says, *"The eternal God is thy refuge, and underneath are the everlasting arms: and he shall thrust out the enemy from before thee."* When we run to Him, to that strong tower, we find that the eternal God is our refuge, our hiding place, our place to retreat to, a place of trust, a shelter, and an accessible lofty place that no one can reach. Moreover, underneath it all are His everlasting arms holding us up. Psalms 142 says, *"I looked on my right hand, and beheld, but there was no man that would know me: refuge failed me; no man cared for my soul. ⁵I cried unto thee, O Lord: I said, Thou art my refuge and my portion in the land of the living."* (Psalms 142:4-5)

When others fail you, God will not. You can always go to Him. As Proverbs 14:26 says, *"In the fear of the Lord is strong confidence: and his children shall have a place of refuge."* You have a place to run to today, a place to go to when times get rough. Psalms 9:9 says, *"The Lord also will be a refuge for the oppressed, a refuge in times of trouble."* The word *"oppressed"* here means "crushed figuratively, afflicted, to collapse physically or mentally." Some other translations of this verse read: *"Jehovah is a tower for the bruised"*, *"The Lord defends those who suffer"*, *"He provides safety in the time of trouble."* The Lord will also be a refuge for the oppressed, those who are crushed, who are about to collapse physically or mentally. Run to Him now if that's you! Run to your refuge, to that lofty, inaccessible secret place, where no one can find you but Him for He is your refuge.

"I Will Speak, That I May Be Refreshed"
Job 32:20

DAY 277

The Bible says in Job 32:18, *"For I am full of matter..."* The word *"matter"* in Hebrew means, "words". The word continues to say in this verse, *"...the spirit within me constraineth me. ¹⁹Behold, my belly is as wine which hath no vent."* Jesus tells us in John 7:38, *"He that believeth on me, as the scripture hath said, out of his belly shall flow rivers of living water"*. This is out of your spirit. The belly is the innermost part of your being. It says Job's belly was *"as wine which hath no vent."* There's no place for the wine to go; it's bottled up on the inside. That's why the book of Job says, *"He cutteth out rivers among the rocks"* (Job 28:10). *"There is a river,"* Psalms 46:4 tells us, *"the streams whereof shall make glad the city of God."* God not only wants you to have wine, which is the Holy Ghost, but He wants that wine to have a vent, or else it will burst inside of us. What releases the words within us? What releases the Spirit and revelation of God from within us? Haven't you ever felt so tied up in knots inside, wanting to speak, but unable to do so? Have you ever felt like you weren't worthy enough to do so?

God wants you to open your mouth. Job continues to say, *"I will speak, that I may be refreshed: I will open my lips and answer"* (Job 32:20). Flowing out of you is the Word of the Lord and the Spirit of God. The only way to release it is to speak. This principle is true even of the baptism of the Holy Ghost with the evidence of speaking with other tongues. Isaiah 28 tells us, *"For with stammering lips and another tongue will he speak to this people"* (Isaiah 28:11). Some other translations of the Bible use the word *"strange"* in place of the word *"stammering."* God not only speaks to you, but He speaks through you. Job's belly was as wine which had no vent; it was not open. We need to speak in tongues to open that gateway.

Finally, he says that he will speak so he can be refreshed. It says, *"This is the rest wherewith ye may cause the weary to rest; and this is the refreshing: yet they would not hear"* (Isaiah 28:12). The rest of God comes from the baptism of the Holy Ghost with the evidence of speaking in tongues. Refreshing comes as we speak His glories, worship in His holiness, study His Word, proclaim it, and move in the prophetic realm. Are you full of matter? Are you full of words, but yet don't know how to get those words out of you? Speak, today, that you may be refreshed. Open your lips and answer. The Bible tells us in Psalms 81:10, *"Open thy mouth wide, and I will fill it."* This is our God; He will help us. Your belly needs a vent, and that vent comes when you open your mouth and begin to speak in an unknown tongue. When you do speak, it's going to cause that new wine that's in a bottle within you to then flow out of you. It will be like when the *"waters issued out from under the threshold"* and everything the river touched, it healed (Ezekiel 47:1, 9).

Begin to speak today. Yearn with all your heart and say, *"Let the words of my mouth, and the meditation of my heart, be acceptable in thy sight, O Lord, my strength, and my redeemer"* (Psalms 19:14). God wants to give you to be refreshed.

"For My People Is Foolish"
Jeremiah 4:22

The Bible says in Jeremiah 4:22, *"For my people is foolish, they have not known me; they are sottish (stupid) children, and they have none understanding: they are wise to do evil, but to do good they have no knowledge."* Today I want us to take a look at how God has no joy in the fool or the foolish. To gain a better understanding of what He is saying here, we need to look at both the Hebrew and Greek language and learn what these words mean.

There are a few Hebrew words for *"foolish"*. The first word we see means "stupid, wicked, a disgrace", while the second means "silly, to be fat; a stupid or a dull person." The last meaning is to be "perverse, to lack or despise wisdom, to be quarrelsome." We can conclude then that a fool's only authority is himself. The Greek words we find for *"foolish"* have very similar meanings to that of the Hebrew. They simply mean "mindless, stupid, ignorant, egotistical or rash, unintelligent, sensual, not understanding, dull, stupid, or heedless, an absurd person."

God is not interested in the foolish. The Bible clearly says in Proverbs 17:21, *"the father of a fool hath no joy."* It does not give God the Father joy when He sees that His people act silly or stupid. In verse 25, we see that it says *"a foolish son is a grief to his father"*, and Proverbs 19:13 says *"a foolish son is the calamity of his father."* He takes no pleasure in fools (Ecclesiastes 5:4) because He says in Proverbs 1:22 *"How long, ye simple ones, will ye love simplicity?"* Psalms 75:4 states *"I said unto the fools, Deal not foolishly."*

God does not want us to deal foolishly with our lives. He can take no pleasure in fools. He tells us in Proverbs 9:6 to *"forsake the foolish, and live; and go in the way of understanding."* Proverbs 10:1 adds, *"a wise son maketh a glad father: but a foolish son is the heaviness of his mother."* A wise son does not want to be a calamity to his Father or bring him grief; he wants Him to take pleasure in him. In Matthew 25 the parable of the ten virgins is found. Five were wise and five were foolish. The five foolish do not make it in when the Bridegroom came because they had not prepared their lamps.

We want to be God's wise children, so we need to take heed to this word today. We do not want to be seen as stupid, silly, fat, perverse, or dull in the eyes of our Father. We do not want to be considered a fool whose only authority is ourselves. This is not what we want. The Bible says in Proverbs 26:10, *"The great God that formed all things both rewardeth the fool, and rewardeth transgressors."* There will be a reward and a judgment for being foolish.

Finally we see in Deuteronomy 32:5-6, *"They have corrupted themselves, their spot is not the spot of his children: they are a perverse and crooked generation. Do ye thus requite the Lord, O foolish people and unwise?"* Today we want to remember that we want to be that wise son that makes the heart of our Father glad. We want to forsake the foolish. We want to live on and go in the way of understanding.

"Follow His Steps"
I Peter 2:21

Day 279

The word we will be looking at today is in I Peter 2:21, *"Follow his steps."* Jesus set the example for all of us and He is the chief son, the pattern son. We must walk in His steps to become like Him, to achieve all that God has for us. For this to happen, we need to have a desire to be directed in His steps, to follow His example.

Proverbs 16:9 says, *"A man's heart deviseth his way: but the Lord directeth his steps."* Too many times people tell us to prepare our future, to write a plan for ourselves, but the Spirit goes *"where it listeth"* (John 3:8). We don't know exactly what we should be doing because Jeremiah 10:23 tells us, *"O Lord, I know that the way of man is not in himself: it is not in man that walketh to direct his steps."* The way of man is not in himself. We need to follow the example of the Lord Jesus and follow His steps.

In I Kings 19:7 it reads, *"And the angel of the Lord came again the second time, and touched him* (Elijah)*, and said, Arise and eat; because the journey is too great for thee."* Haven't you discovered that the journey is too great for you? It can be overwhelming to be responsible for knowing what to do, nonetheless, the Bible says in Psalms 33:23, *"The steps of a good man are ordered by the Lord: and he delighteth in his way."* Good men's steps are ordered by the Lord and they don't let their own pride direct them. Proverbs 21:29 says, *"A wicked man hardeneth his face: but as for the upright, he directeth his way."* Let the Lord direct your steps. Let the Lord provide your vision for you. I Thessalonians 3:11 reads, *"Now God himself and our Father, and our Lord Jesus Christ, direct our way unto you."*

We need to let the Lord Jesus direct our way. In Isaiah 61:8 it says, *"For I the Lord love judgment, I hate robbery for burnt offering; and I will direct their work in truth."* God wants to direct us, to lead us, and our prayer should be, as in Psalms 27:11, *"lead me in a plain path,"* or as Moses said in Exodus 33:13, *"Shew me now thy way, that I may know thee."* Isaiah 30:21 says, *"And thine ears shall hear a word behind thee, saying, This is the way, walk ye in it, when ye turn to the right hand, and when ye turn to the left."* In Proverbs 3:6 it says, *"In all thy ways acknowledge him, and he shall direct thy paths."*

Let us choose today to bow to the wisdom of God. Let us follow the example of Jesus' steps. If we follow in His steps, then we can be assured of peace, prosperity protection, and provision because, as it says in Psalms 33:23, *"The steps of a good man are ordered by the Lord: and he delighteth in His way."*

"The Lord Calling As At Other Times"
I Samuel 3:10

DAY 280

This is a tremendous story about the calling of God on our lives, and in particular, Samuel's life. Samuel as a child was dedicated to the Lord and to the ministry. He served Eli, the man of God, who was not a bad man, but he was not a man that would teach or correct his children. Because of that, Samuel grew up not knowing the Lord, and therefore, did not respond when God came to him and called him three times, then it says in I Samuel 3:10, "*And the Lord came, and stood, and called as at other times, Samuel, Samuel.*"

When the Lord called Samuel the first three times, instead of answering the Lord, he went to Eli. So often in our lives our revelation is in another man. What we have we've gotten from somebody else and that's fine. We're "*under tutors and governors until the time appointed*" (Galatians 4:2). However, we're ultimately to be released to Jesus Himself. We're meant to have our own walk with the Lord. God called Samuel, but he ran to Eli and said, "*Here am I.*"

It's a terrible thing to confuse the voice of God with the voice of a mere human being or as something so natural, like the sound of thunder. In John 12:29, Jesus stood on the side of the road and the voice of God spoke, but rather than hearing the voice of God, some people said "*It thundered*". If you don't know the difference between thunder and the voice of God, you're in trouble. Eli, not knowing the voice of God, told Samuel to go lay back down. Samuel went three times and asked Eli, even though it was the Lord that called him. Twice Eli told him to go lay back down.

After the third time Samuel heard God's voice, even Eli, in his backslidden state, perceived that it could be the Lord (I Samuel 3:8-9). The Bible then says in verse 10, "*And the Lord came, and stood, and called as at other times, Samuel, Samuel. Then Samuel answered, Speak; for thy servant heareth.*" How many times has the Lord stood, right beside us, calling our names and asking for us? If we're in bondage to other men, or to a system, we can't hear His voice. God is calling your name today. Perhaps He's standing right there beside you, and you can't hear Him because you're too caught up in your circumstances or in a religious system; you're simply confused, or haven't really been taught correctly. Hear His voice today.

David said, "*I will hear what God the Lord will speak.*" We need to hear what God the Lord is saying. Just as Jehoshaphat said in I Kings 22:7, "*Is there not here a prophet of the Lord besides, that we might enquire of him?*" It seems there are so many voices in this world and Paul said, "*none of them is without signification*" (I Corinthians 22:7). Yet there is only one voice, the voice that's majestic and powerful, the voice of the Lord that's upon the waters (Psalms 29:3), and the voice of the Lord that breaks the cedars (Psalms 29:5). Let that voice pierce through all this religion, confusion, dealings, and hardship. Then, as at other times, as He's calling you, you will answer as Samuel did, "*Speak; for thy servant heareth.*"

"Forget Not All Of His Benefits"
Psalms 103:2

DAY 281

O what a wonderful thing that every day, our precious Savior always meets us and greets us with benefits! Here in Psalms 103, we find a list of benefits that God gives us, and in Psalms 68:19 we read, *"Blessed be the Lord, who daily loadeth us with benefits, even the God of our salvation. Selah."* Every day God greets us with wonderful things! The word *"benefits"* in Hebrew means "to treat a person well, to deal bountifully with, to reward them." Can you imagine this? Every day God rewards us. Every day He deals bountifully with us. Every day He treats us well. This is His desire. Oh, receive it today!

Have you allowed God to give you these benefits? He daily wants to load you with them, not just give you some, but daily load you with them. A load is a great amount that is hard to carry, because it is too great a weight. God wants this in our lives. He wants us to live life abundantly. John 10:10 says, *"I am come that they might have life, and that they might have it more abundantly."* In the Greek this reads, "Super-abundantly." This is why Jesus came!

Let's see those benefits given in Psalms 103. We don't want to ever forget these benefits with which God wants to load us. In verse 3a it says, *"Who forgiveth all thine iniquities."* Praise God! What a wonderful thing! God will forgive us for all our sin. I John 1:9 says, *"If we confess our sins, he is faithful and just to forgive us our sins, and to cleanse us from all unrighteousness."* Proverbs 28:13 says, *"whoso confesseth and forsaketh them shall have mercy."* I John 1:7 says, *"the blood of Jesus Christ his Son cleanseth us from all sin."* You can rest assured today that all your iniquities will be forgiven as you confess and turn from them. God wants to daily load you with His forgiveness.

Then Psalms 103:3b goes on to say, *"Who healeth all thy diseases."* Not "some" of your diseases or "most" of them, but "all" thy diseases. Jehovah Rapha, God our Healer, wants to heal us of every physical malady that we have. Open your heart today and receive it. Remember the leper that came to Jesus and said in Matthew 8:2, *"Lord, if thou wilt, thou canst make me clean."* Jesus immediately answered in Matthew 8:3 saying, *"I will; be thou clean."*

For those who wonder whether it is the will of God to heal or not, my answer is Jesus just told us, *"I will."* Every person that came to Jesus and said, "Heal my daughter", "Come, pray for my servant that is sick", Jesus always said, "I will" and He went and healed them all. Hebrews 13:8 says *"Jesus Christ the same yesterday, and today, and forever."* He is still healing. He is still delivering. Oh, if you are sick today, let Him heal you of that disease; He wants to load you down with this benefit.

Psalms 103:4a continues, *"Who redeemeth thy life from destruction."* Thank God that we no longer have to live according to the dictates of this world or under the torment of Satan. We are not of this world; we are in it, but not of it. We have been delivered out of the kingdom of darkness into the Kingdom of His dear Son and into the Kingdom of light. We have been redeemed from destruction and will not be destroyed by our enemies. Praise the Lord!

Then Psalms 103:4b says, *"who crowneth thee with lovingkindness and tender mercies."* There is no one greater than our God for loving us. He is the most wonderful, precious, tender, merciful, loving, and kind being in the universe. The words the Bible finds to describe Him are not just "loving" or "kindness", but "loving kindness," combining them both. God wants to crown us with His loving kindness. He wants to pour it out upon our head and let it pour down our spirit, soul and body, all the way down to the ground and into the deepest part of us. He wants to crown us with His loving kindness and tender mercies.

He is not just merciful, but His mercy is tender. God tenderly deals with us in everything. Bless His holy name! Receive today His loving kindness for you; don't resist it. I John 4:16 says, *"And we have known and believed the love that God hath to us."* Don't just know it, believe it and receive it today.

He goes on to say in Psalms 103:5, *"Who satisfieth thy mouth with good things; so that thy youth is renewed like the eagle's."* Our provision is going to be sure. Matthew 6:33 says, *"But seek ye first the kingdom of God, and his righteousness; and all these things shall be added unto you."* Philippians 4:19 says, *"But my God shall supply all your need according to his riches in glory by Christ Jesus."* We can know that our provision will be sure, for He will satisfy our mouth with good things, and because of that, our youth will be renewed like the eagles.

Anxiety, depression, heaviness, oppression will not come near us today. We will just shake that stuff off. Our youth will be constantly renewed as we meet with God every morning and receive His precious benefits. In Lamentations 3:21-22 it says, *"It is of the Lord's mercies that we are not consumed, because his compassions fail not. They are new every morning: great is thy faithfulness."* Great is His faithfulness. Every morning He meets us with His mercy.

In Psalms 116:12-13 David says, *"What shall I render unto the Lord for all his benefits toward me? I will take the cup of salvation, and call upon the name of the Lord."* Take His cup of salvation today and receive His daily load of benefits for you. Oh, what a blessing, what a storehouse of treasure it is! Receive it, take it and call upon the name of the Lord; call upon His character. Worship Him and praise Him; this is how we render and answer to the Lord for all of His benefits towards us!

"I Had Great Bitterness"
Isaiah 38:17

Day 282

Here in Isaiah 38, the Scriptures declare, *"Behold, for peace I had great bitterness: but thou hast in love to my soul delivered it from the pit of corruption: for thou hast cast all my sins behind thy back"* (Isaiah 38:17). Far too many people, instead of having the peace of God, have to live with great bitterness. It is a pit of corruption that comes to us because of unrepentant sin, circumstances, or many other problems.

Hannah, in I Samuel 1, was *"in bitterness of soul, and prayed unto the Lord, and wept sore,"* for her lack of having a child (I Samuel 1:10). Bitterness is a cancer that can destroy us. In the Old Testament, God brought His people to the waters of Marah, which literally means "waters of bitterness", to try them there (Exodus 15:23). In other words, God allows bitterness in our lives to see how we're going to respond.

In Exodus 1:14, Pharaoh made the lives of the Israelites *"bitter with hard bondage."* Our lives may be bitter with hard bondage, either because we are bound up with some sin or temptation, or we live in a pit of corruption of guilt and condemnation because of unrepentant sin, or some character trait that distresses us.

It says of Peter in Luke 22:62 that he *"went out, and wept bitterly."* Why? He denied the Lord. Instead of peace, we can have great bitterness. It says in John, *"Peace I leave with you, my peace I give unto you"* (John 14:27), and Romans 5:1 declares, *"we have peace with God through our Lord Jesus Christ."* We should have peace, but for many, instead of peace, we're locked into bitterness.

The book of Hebrews tells us we should look diligently *"lest any root of bitterness springing up trouble you, and thereby many be defiled"* (Hebrews 12:15). Bitterness wants to corrupt us, defile us, and destroy us. Therefore we need not be bitter toward anyone or anything. We shouldn't live in a pit of corruption when we're to have the peace of the living God. Paul wrote to the Ephesians, saying, *"Let all bitterness, and wrath, and anger, and clamour, and evil speaking, be put away from you, with all malice"* (Ephesians 4:31). Proverbs 14:10 says, *"The heart knoweth his own bitterness."* The book of James tells us, *"But if ye have bitter envying and strife in your hearts, glory not, and lie not against the truth. ¹⁵This wisdom descendeth not from above, but is earthly, sensual, devilish"* (James 3:14-15). God doesn't want us walking in bitterness or in the pit of corruption. God has delivered us and cast all of our sins behind our back, because He loves us.

Remember today, that in love to your soul, God is reaching to you, wanting to deliver you of your bitterness. It would be great if every one of us could fulfill Proverbs 27:7, which says to *"the hungry soul every bitter thing is sweet."* It would be great if we would look at the bitterness of our lives and understand that it is not meant to stay, but that it is used to work God's character into our lives. Revelation 10:10 says, *"And I took the little book out of the angel's hand, and ate it up; and it was in my mouth sweet as honey: and as soon as I had eaten it, my belly was bitter."* The Word of God, being worked into our lives, creates many bitter experiences as we are obedient to it and die to ourselves. God uses bitterness to glorify His name in us and change us. So rise up today and instead of having great bitterness, let the peace of God consume you.

"Thou Hast Been My Help"
Psalms 63:7

DAY 283

What a wonderful revelation we find here that, you and I are not alone. Psalms 63:7 says, *"Because thou hast been my help, therefore in the shadow of thy wings will I rejoice."* God wants to help you, don't you ever forget that. You are not alone. And Psalms 46:5 speaks more of how God is towards you, the one He loves, *"God is in the midst of her; she shall not be moved: God shall help her, and that right early."* God's not only going to help you, but He's going to do it as soon as He possibly can. That's why it says in Psalms 46:1 that, *"God is our refuge and strength, a very present help in trouble."*

He's a present help. You will never have to worry that He's not going to come and minister to you. He assures you in Hebrews 13:5, *"I will never leave thee, nor forsake thee."* He also declares in John 10:29 that no man shall pluck you out of His hand. Why can't we believe this? Why does Zion say in Isaiah 49:14, *"The Lord hath forsaken me, and my Lord hath forgotten me."* David said the same thing in Psalms 77:9, *"Hath God forgotten to be gracious? hath he in anger shut up his tender mercies? Selah."* The answer is: no, He is our help. The Bible boldly states in Psalms 124:8, *"Our help is in the name of the Lord, who made heaven and earth."* Your help is in the name, the character of God.

"Happy is he that hath the God of Jacob for his help, whose hope is in the Lord his God" (Psalms 146:5). Are you happy knowing that your God is your help? Is your hope in Him to help you? Isaiah said, *"Fear thou not; for I am with thee: be not dismayed; for I am thy God: I will strengthen thee; yea, I will help thee; yea, I will uphold thee with the right hand of my righteousness"* (Isaiah 41:10). "Yes, I will help you," is the Lord's answer to you.

So many religious people argue over what they think the will of God is. A leper said to Jesus in Mark 1:40, *"If thou wilt, thou canst make me clean."* Jesus said, "I will". Whether it is the will of God to heal, deliver, prosper or set someone free, argumentative religious people wouldn't be able to know, because they never experience the goodness of God. And the goodness of God, as the Bible puts it in Psalms 52:1, *"endureth continually."* He wants to help you, even amidst the reaping of your own mistakes. God says in Hosea 13:9, *"O Israel, thou hast destroyed thyself; but in me is thine help."* Even when you've blown it completely, having messed up and embarrassed yourself, He is your help. He's a friend that sticketh closer than a brother (Proverbs 18:24). When everyone else has gone and left you, He will remain and He will stretch down His hand and help you, like He did for that woman in Ezekiel who was tossed to the side of the road. When He passed by her, He said, *"This is the time of love. I have entered into a covenant with you and you became mine"* (Ezekiel 16:8).

God loves you at your worst. He wants to help you at your worst. That's why Hebrews 4:16 says, *"Let us therefore come boldly unto the throne of grace, that we may obtain mercy, and find grace to help in time of need."* Are you in a time of need today? Are you being surrounded by enemies tormenting and condemning you? In II Chronicles 32:8, Hezekiah says, *"With him is an arm of flesh; but with us is the Lord our*

God to help us, and to fight our battles. And the people rested themselves upon the words of Hezekiah king of Judah." You need to rest yourself upon the Word of the Lord today; rest upon the fact that our help is in the Lord our God. He will help you. Psalms 115:9-11 says:

> *"⁹O Israel, trust thou in the Lord: he is their help and their shield. ¹⁰O house of Aaron, trust in the Lord: he is their help and their shield. ¹¹Ye that fear the Lord, trust in the Lord: he is their help and their shield."*

In Psalms 121:1-2, it says, *"I will lift up mine eyes unto the hills, from whence cometh my help. ²My help cometh from the Lord, which made heaven and earth."* I don't know about you, but no hill has ever helped me. Your help comes from the Lord, not from natural things. Your help comes from the creator God, the loving Savior, the precious Holy Ghost. Your help is in the name of the Lord.

"A Lion In The Midst Of A Pit"
II Samuel 23:20

DAY 284

In II Samuel 23:20, it says, *"And Benaiah the son of Jehoiada, the son of a valiant man, of Kabzeel, who had done many acts..."* It says, *"He was more honourable than the thirty, but he attained not to the first three"* (II Samuel 23:23). He was still one of the mighty men of David whose numbers included thirty seven men.

If are going to be in the remnant, we have to do what Benaiah did. It says, *"he slew two lionlike men of Moab: he went down also and slew a lion in the midst of a pit in time of snow"* (II Samuel 23:20). First of all, God requires that we go down. To go up, we must first go down (Isaiah 37:31); to experience life, we have to experience death (John 12:24-25). God may call us down into a pit, and we don't understand why we're in the pit. It's full of lions and darkness. But we have to understand *"the curse causeless shall not come"* (Proverbs 26:2). Paul tells us, *"And we know that all things work together for good to them that love God, to them who are the called according to his purpose"* (Romans 8:28). God may bring you into a pit, but it has "purpose" written all over it. Don't throw away your pit; it may be the place of your deliverance.

In this passage it is speaking of a natural lion. But I Peter 5:8 says, *"your adversary the devil, as a roaring lion, walketh about, seeking whom he may devour."* I believe, in this case, it's speaking of satan. Sometimes, the Lord will bring us into the midst of a pit, in the midst of darkness. What do we find there? We find a lion; we find satan trying to attack us. Are you in the midst of a pit right now? Is the lion roaring and screaming at you? God sent you there for a purpose. It was not so that you would be overcome, but so that you could become an overcomer.

Benaiah's name means "Jehovah has built." God was trying to build in Benaiah's life. He was trying to cause him to be a man of God *"throughly furnished unto all good works"* (II Timothy 3:17). He slew the lion in the midst of the pit. In the middle of your situation, right at the highest point of darkness, God will enable you to slay that lion. *"Resist the devil, and he will flee from you"* (James 4:7). John says, *"For this purpose the Son of God was manifested, that he might destroy the works of the devil"* (I John 3:8). You are also a son of God; you have been manifested to destroy the works of the devil.

God has called you into a pit and asked you to slay the lion. And notice it was in a time of snow. Job says, *"Hast thou entered into the treasures of the snow?"* (Job 38:22). There was treasure to be found in this pit. He overcame the lion, just like Samson did when he slew the lion that *"roared against him"* (Judges 14:5). He later passed by the lion's carcass to find a swarm of bees and honey therein. He and his family ate of the honey from the lion's carcass, for *"Out of the eater came forth meat, and out of the strong came forth sweetness."* *"The eater"* is our pit. God will give you great revelation when you learn to stay in that pit. He will give you *"meat in due season"* (Psalms 104:27), when you choose to fight, overcome, and slay the lion, instead of running away. Then perhaps, we can find the treasures of the snow. Out of the eater comes forth meat; there is meat to be had out of this pit. Out of this strong enemy will come forth the sweetness of God. You can do it, because Jehovah is building you.

"How Dreadful Is This Place"
Genesis 28:17

This is the story of Jacob and his dream of beholding a ladder set up on the earth. The story account reads:

> "*¹²And he dreamed, and behold a ladder set up on the earth, and the top of it reached to heaven: and behold the angels of God ascending ¹³And, behold, the LORD stood above it, and said, I am ¹⁴And thy seed shall be as the dust of the earth*" (Genesis 28:12-14).

After giving him some promises, God awakened Jacob out of sleep (Genesis 28:16). So many times you and I, being in church, or sitting under our father-ministry or local ministry, fall asleep. It is not the sleep of resting in God, but a sleep of slothfulness. Solomon says, in Proverbs 19:15, "*Slothfulness casteth into a deep sleep*" whereas Genesis 2:21 says, "*God caused a deep to fall upon Adam.*" This latter was a sleep of rest in God. Whichever sleep you are in, there comes a time when you should awake out of your sleep.

Jacob awaked out of his sleep. Paul wrote to the Romans saying, "*And that, knowing the time, that now it is high time to awake out of sleep: for now is our salvation nearer than when we believed*" (Romans 13:11). Jacob awaked out of sleep after he had this awesome dream and said, "*Surely, the Lord is in this place and I knew it not*" (Genesis 28:16). The entire time he had been there he didn't even know that the Lord was in that place. I wonder how many people are going to church, and are a part of a religious system, never realizing that God is not there. What about people who are in a place where God IS moving and the glory IS falling, but they don't perceive it?

The Bible says in Genesis 28:17, "*And he was afraid, and said, How dreadful is this place!*" The word "*dreadful*" here means "awesome." Suddenly, you open your eyes and realize how awesome is that place, how awesome is the glory, how awesome is the Word. He goes on to say, "*this is none other but the house of God, and this is the gate of heaven.*" This IS the house of God, or as the enemies of God will say to the sons of God in the last days, "You are Zion, the city of the Lord" (Isaiah 60:14). This is the house of the Lord and the gate of heaven. Jacob would later call that place Bethel, which means "house of God." Our local churches should be awesome places, places where angels are ascending and descending with the Lord standing above them.

The ladder reached up to heaven. We have to be able to pierce the heavenlies and get into the glory of God, allowing that door in heaven to be opened (Revelation 4:1). Isaiah saw the door was opened as the seraphim began to cry holy, holy, holy; "*And the posts of the door moved at the voice of him that cried, and the house was filled with smoke*" (Isaiah 6:4). When we begin to worship the Lord and praise Him, being in a place where the ladder reaches the heavens, God will come down and stand above it. We will then awake out of our sleep and will see that the Lord is in this place, even if we knew it not. It will then dawn on us, and we will become very fearful in the sense of being awestruck, and we will know how awesome is this place. It truly is the gate of heaven, it is house of God.

"I Will Arise And Go To My Father"
Luke 15:18

DAY 286

Here in Luke 15 is a powerful passage on repentance and redemption and how one that is lost can be found again. More importantly, I want us to see the emphasis on the Holy Spirit today. The prodigal son, after spending much time away from the Lord and from his father, realizes his mistake and says, "*I will arise and go to my father*" (Luke 15:18). For many of us, our earthly fathers were not all they should have been. Therefore, when we come to Jesus, our relationship with our heavenly Father is clouded with uncertainty. Therefore, we need to relearn what a true father is like. Our heavenly Father is far greater than any earthly father.

Jesus said in Matthew 6:9, "*After this manner therefore pray ye: Our Father...*" God is our Father. What a wonderful truth! Out of all the religions in the world, none have a testimony like this, in which God, the creator of the universe, is their Father. But He is ours.

Jesus also said in Matthew 5:48, "*Be ye therefore perfect, even as your Father which is in heaven is perfect.*" He is your Father. In Isaiah 63:16 it says, "*Doubtless thou art our father...thou, O Lord, art our father, our redeemer.*" I rejoice today that my father is not my earthly father, who was not a very kind man. He jaded my opinion of what a father or an authority figure should be like. But I can now understand when Isaiah says, "*But now, O Lord, thou art our father; we are the clay, and thou our potter; and we all are the work of thy hand*" (Isaiah 64:8). The longer we go on with Jesus, the more we understand how great and marvelous our God is and what it means to us that He alone is our Father.

It says in Psalms 103:13, "*Like as a father pitieth his children, so the Lord pitieth them that fear him.*" Oh, praise the Lord! Aren't you glad that "*unto us a child is born, unto us a son is given...and his name shall be called Wonderful, Counsellor, The mighty God, The everlasting Father*" (Isaiah 9:6)? This is our God, the everlasting Father. We see this again in Psalms 89:26, when David, as a type of the Lord Jesus, says, "*He shall cry unto me, Thou art my father, my God, and the rock of my salvation.*" We have a Father and He's the rock of our salvation.

He's a wonderful God. He is the potter, and we're simply the clay in His hands (Jeremiah 18:1-4). No matter what hole we may end up in, He will always be there, like the father in Luke 15, waiting for his son to come home. We will simply arise and go to our father.

So, decide today that you will have a great relationship with your Father. If you think you are far away or separated from Him today, just say these words, "I will arise and go to my Father."

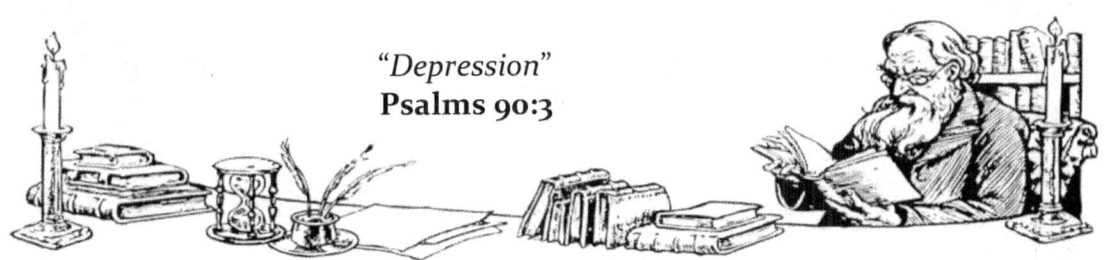

"Depression"
Psalms 90:3

DAY 287

This is the second time I am bringing up the subject of depression in this devotional because one of the things I have found as a pastor over the years is that most of God's people go through depression. Again, Psalms 90:3 states, *"Thou turnest man to destruction* [Hebrew: "depression"] *and sayest, Return, ye children of men."* Many of God's people are tormented with depression, agitation, compulsions and personal difficulties. Many people are also just sad and sorrowful. However, Jesus said in John 10:10, *"I am come that they might have life, and that they might have it more abundantly."*

The Bible is full of examples of people who were depressed and weary. Elijah went through depression. I Kings 19:4-5 says, *"But he* [Elijah] *himself went a day's journey into the wilderness, and came and sat down under a juniper tree: and he requested for himself that he might die; and said, It is enough; now, O Lord, take away my life; for I am not better than my fathers."* This was right after Elijah had done one of the greatest miracles ever known on the face of the earth by calling down fire from heaven! However, I have found that after some of my greatest victories come times of aloneness and depression. We need to remember to immediately replenish ourselves after a time of anointing. If we do not, then we can become like Elijah and become very depressed. Elijah even requested for himself that he might die. This was a mighty man of God. So anybody can be depressed. You are not alone. There is nothing wrong with you. You are just a human being and human beings wrestle with depression. Elijah also said, *"I am not better than my fathers."* Elijah was being too introspective. That kind of introspection will always destroy peace. We need to be careful about too much introspection in our lives by asking too many questions about ourselves.

We see another example in Mark 14, when Jesus went into the garden of Gethsemane. Gethsemane means "olive press". There is no anointing without the olive being crushed. If you want the glory and anointing of God, expect suffering, expect Gethsemane, expect crushing. It says in Mark 14:33 that he *"began to be sore amazed* [or deeply depressed or distressed], *and to be very heavy."* This was the Lord Jesus experiencing this. Jesus said to the disciples in verse 34, *"My soul is exceeding sorrowful unto death."* Then He asked God, the Father, if it was possible to escape the cross. You are not alone when you want to escape and run from the things that God has purposed for you to overcome. Even Jesus, because He was the son of man and had humanity, was touched by depression. Ultimately, though, He bowed and said in verse 36, *"Nevertheless not what I will, but what thou wilt."* This must be the case with us.

I want to assure you today that God wants to deliver you from your depression. Isaiah 53:5 says, *"But he was wounded for our transgressions, he was bruised for our iniquities: the chastisement of our peace was upon him."* Peace is for our soulish man, for our minds. He was chastised that you and I might have a sound mind. Let God deliver you. If He has turned you to depression, it is not forever. Hear His voice that says, *"Return ye children of men."* Today, come back into abundant life.

"He Sent A Man Before Them, Even Joseph"
Psalms 105:17

DAY 288

In today's word, I want to consider the man Joseph, whose name in the Hebrew means "addition." There are four major Scriptures about him. There is his story that's told in Genesis, and then he is mentioned in Psalms 105, Psalms 81, and Acts 7. I want to consider the last three and encourage you to read the story of Joseph starting in Genesis 37.

Psalms 105:17 says, *"He sent a man before them, even Joseph, who was sold for a servant."* First of all, God did not send a superman, he sent a regular man. He sent a man full of *"like passions"* like you and me (James 5:17). He sent him *"before them."* In other words, God always has a pioneer, someone He sends before. It isn't easy being that pioneer, but nonetheless, it was the call of God on his life.

"Even Joseph, who was sold for a servant." Joseph was betrayed by his brothers because he wore the coat of many colors. This coat was symbolic of the fact that he was a chosen and blessed son. And because of that they sold him into slavery.

Psalms 105:18 continues saying, *"Whose feet they hurt with fetters: he was laid in iron"*. He was put in prison, sold to Potiphar's house, and he had a tremendous time of difficulty living out the life that God had chosen him to live. But no matter where he found himself, whether he was betrayed, sold, or accused, he always prospered. And this pattern would continue throughout his life, because *"until the time that his word came: the word of the Lord tried him"* (Psalms 105:19).

Joseph's life teaches us so many times. For one, there is a timing to the Word of God. *"To everything there is a season, and a time to every purpose under the heaven,"* (Ecclesiastes 3:1). There is a time when the Word will come for our lives as it did Joseph's life. The meaning and purpose of our lives will be made known. But until that time when the Word is fulfilled, the word of the Lord will try and test us like it did Joseph. When that time is over, the blessing of God and the call of God is fulfilled in our lives. Psalms 81 says:

> *"⁵This he ordained in Joseph for a testimony, when he went out through the land of Egypt: where I heard a language that I understood not. ⁶I removed his shoulder from the burden: his hands were delivered from the pots"* (Psalms 81:5-6).

Years ago, when trying to understand what this meant, I thought it should read, "I removed the burden from his shoulder." But God made me understand that the word of the Lord trying him was causing his shoulder to be strong enough to handle any burden, until the day came when the burden no longer affected Joseph. He walked right out from under it and his hands were delivered from the pots. He was completely and utterly delivered. As it says in Acts, God *"delivered him out of all his afflictions, and gave him favour and wisdom in the sight of Pharaoh king of Egypt; and he made him governor over Egypt and all his house"* (Acts 7:10).

So this is the will of God for us as well. The word of the Lord will try us and test us. We'll be in afflictions. Our hands will be in pots and our shoulders encumbered with a burden. That word will work in our life, change our soul, our carnal nature, and until we become more and more like Jesus, and more and more like the sons of God that we were created to be. As this happens in our life we can begin to really understand what God is doing.

Up until this point, I'm sure Joseph had no idea what was happening. But yet, he never quit. He continued to prosper in every place. He was a man. He was a man just like you and me, someone who could feel betrayed and hurt. But yet, he still believed God and never gave up. And when his time came, the Bible says in Psalms 105:20, *"The king sent and loosed him; even the ruler of the people, and let him go free."* The king here represents God the Father. He went from prison rags to a prime ministers' suit of clothes in seconds.

The word of the Lord is trying you until the time that your word comes. Your word could come today. It could come in the next ten minutes. It may be at the end of this week, or next week, next month or years from now. But it is coming. And when it comes, in seconds you're going to be transferred from where you are to where you are called to be. Do not give up. It's easy to surrender in the midst of the dealings of God. It's easy to surrender and not want to be a pioneer and someone that goes before everybody else. It is a lonely road, but nonetheless, it may be the calling of God.

The next verses say, *"²¹He made him lord of his house, and ruler of all his substance: ²²To bind his princes at his pleasure; and teach his senators wisdom"* (Psalms 105:21-22). What a change and a transformation. He is now no longer an abused servant, but a ruler and a teacher. This is how God works. Psalms 66:12 says, *"Thou hast caused men to ride over our heads; we went through fire and through water: but thou broughtest us out into a wealthy place."*

God has a call on your life. Perhaps you are a pioneer, one who has gone before others. Remember the story of Joseph. His name meant "addition." But when Joseph finally became what God had called him to be, his name was changed. This speaks of his character being transformed. His name was changed to an Egyptian name meaning "savior of the world." He went from a prisoner to the prime minister of Egypt overnight and all that Joseph went through was preparation for the day when Joseph would be a savior to the world. What a glorious end.

Let Joseph's life encourage your heart today. You may be in the middle of the dealings of God. You may be in a season where God's Word is trying you. Don't give up. You're going to make it. You are changing. God is watching and rooting for you. Joseph's end was glorious. The end justified the journey. The same will be said of you as you follow on to know the Lord and allow God's Word to finish the work He sent it to do!

"Moses Drew Near"
Exodus 20:21

DAY 289

This is the story in Exodus 20 when God revealed Himself to all of Israel in all of His glory. *"¹⁸And all the people saw the thunderings, and the lightnings, and the noise of the trumpet, and the mountain smoking: and when the people saw it, they removed, and stood afar off. ²¹...and Moses drew near unto the thick darkness where God was"* (Exodus 20:18, 21).

This, to me, is one of the saddest passages in the whole Bible. When the people actually saw the Lord, for who He was and what He was, rather than rejoicing and running toward Him, they removed themselves and stood afar off. I remember when Peter, in Luke 22:54, *"followed afar off."* It was when Jesus stood before Pilate and was being accused. Peter kept his distance. How many times have others, because of a situation where God has shown them something about themselves, or they have seen an aspect of the Lord's character that begins to challenge them, stand afar off? Rather than pressing in and allowing their character to change, they remove themselves and stand afar off.

Out of at least three million Israelites only Moses drew near. However, God had only come to prove and test them. He wasn't there to scare them. Psalms 50:3 says that it is *"very tempestuous round about him."* I liken this to the eye of a hurricane. Yes, you have to go through a lot of boisterousness and storms, but when you reach the center, it is still and quiet. In I Kings 19:12, when there came a wind, an earthquake and a fire, there eventually came a *"still small voice."* What this signifies is that you and I will eventually break through into the heart of God and see Him for what and who He is. Where Jesus is there is great stillness and peace. Psalms 16:11 states, *"Thou wilt shew me the path of life: in thy presence is fullness of joy."* In His presence is fullness of joy!

When the children of Israel saw God for who He was, *"they removed, and stood afar off."* But *"Moses drew near unto the thick darkness where God was."* Have you drawn near to Him? Or have you removed and stood afar off? Are you following after the Lord? *"As the hart panteth after the water brooks,"* (Psalms 42:1) is your heart and soul panting after Him? David said in Psalms 63:8, *"My soul followeth hard after thee."* My prayer is that you and I would have such a heart that we would want to be as close as John was at the Last Supper when he laid his head upon Jesus' breast.

Sometimes when God comes down in all of His glory it can be a frightening thing. However, *"Unto you therefore which believe he is precious"* (I Peter 2:9). We have *"tasted that the Lord is gracious"* (I Peter 2:3). Since you and I love Him so, there is only one course of action for our lives and that is to draw near to Him. James 4:8 states, *"Draw nigh to God, and he will draw nigh to you."* Draw near to Him, today. Even though you may see thunder, lightning, and hear voices and see the mountain smoking, don't worry about it. It is just your heavenly Father in all of His awesome glory and power. If you just press through, you will find that sacred, wonderful and precious heart. It is the secret place of the Most High and there you will abide under the shadow of the Almighty (Psalms 91:1). So let's arise today, and draw near to the thick darkness, where God is.

"What You Do In The Dark"
Ezekiel 8:12

DAY 290

"Then said he unto me, Son of man, hast thou seen what the ancients of the house of Israel do in the dark, every man in the chambers of his imagery? for they say, The Lord seeth us not; the Lord hath forsaken the earth." (Ezekiel 8:12)

I want to talk to you about secret sin and it's effects. This is clearly borne out in Scripture. Here I want you to see the ancients, the elders of Israel. God says if you only could see what they do in the dark, in the chambers of their imagery. All of us have a secret place inside of us where we think things that we don't want anybody to know. It's a place where we contemplate things that, really in the light of the glory of God, we shouldn't. God is trying to bring those things out of us. He's trying to help us get delivered from them.

In Psalms 19:12 David prayed, *"cleanse thou me from secret faults."* We would pray to God that this would be our prayer today. In Psalms 90:8 he says, *"Thou hast set our iniquities before thee, our secret sins in the light of thy countenance."* The Bible says *"Neither is there any creature that is not manifest in his sight: but all things are naked and opened unto the eyes of him with whom we have to do"* (Hebrews 4:13). There is nothing we can keep secret from Him, even in the chambers of our imagery. God sees and knows everything and yet He still loves us.

So it's time now. *"And the times of this ignorance God winked at; but now commandeth all men everywhere to repent"* (Acts 17:30). It's time for you and me to grow up. We need to be *"Casting down imaginations, and every high thing that exalteth itself against the knowledge of God, and bringing into captivity every thought to the obedience of Christ"* (II Corinthians 10:5). We need to repent, clear our minds, and let the washing of the water of the word take place (Ephesians 5:26). Let Him sanctify us through His Word, because His Word is truth (John 17:17).

In Obadiah 6 it says, *"How are the things of Esau searched out! how are his hidden things sought up."* Esau is the man of the flesh. So God searches out our flesh. The Bible says, *"Be sure your sin will find you out"* (Numbers 32:23). In II Kings 17:9 it says, *"And the children of Israel did secretly those things that were not right against the Lord their God."* Lord, help us. We do not need to be doing things secretly that we know are not right before the Lord.

Though I have thankfully progressed beyond most youthful indiscretions, it hasn't been so long that I cannot feel your pain and I understand that all of us have these things. We cannot allow them though, because everything we do affects those around us. Consider Achan, who caused the children of Israel to be destroyed in battle, simply because of his foolishness (Joshua 7).

Paul says we *"have renounced the hidden things of dishonesty, not walking in craftiness, nor handling the word of God deceitfully"* (II Corinthians 4:2). We've renounced the hidden things of dishonesty. We simply make our prayer today *"cleanse thou me from secret faults"* and let my mind be renewed by the Spirit and by the Word of God. God help you today to be delivered and walk in liberty.

"God Is Not A Man"
Numbers 23:19

DAY 291

What a revelation this is to have! Far too many people look at God as someone they can relate to here on earth, either as an authority figure or their earthly father. As such, too many times we attribute to God things that don't belong to Him. Numbers 23:19 says, *"God is not a man, that he should lie."* Men lie, but God cannot lie. The Bible is clear about this.

In Hosea 11:9 the Lord says this, *"I will not execute the fierceness of mine anger, I will not return to destroy Ephraim: for I am God, and not man; the Holy One in the midst of thee."* God doesn't act like us. He doesn't think like us. He doesn't perform like us. Men can be mean, hard, cruel, and unforgiving. But God cannot do any of those things because *"God is love"* (I John 4:16). He is God and not man. Stop thinking of the Lord in the ways you think. The Bible says:

> *"For my thoughts are not your thoughts, neither are your ways my ways, saith the Lord. For as the heavens are higher than the earth, so are my ways higher than your ways, and my thoughts than your thoughts."*
> (Isaiah 55:8-9)

God is not a man. He doesn't act or think like us. We need to put on the *"mind of Christ"* (I Corinthians 2:16) so that when we consider the Lord, stand before Him, or worship Him, we worship Him for who He is. He is God. He is the Lord that proclaimed Himself to Moses in Exodus 34:6, *"The Lord, the Lord God, merciful and gracious, longsuffering, and abundant in goodness and truth."* In I Samuel, the Lord said to Samuel when choosing the next king of Israel:

> *"Look not on his countenance, or on the height of his stature; because I have refused him: for the Lord seeth not as man seeth; for man looketh on the outward appearance, but the Lord looketh on the heart."* (I Samuel 16:7)

The Lord simply doesn't see things the way we see things. How many more Scriptures do we need to look at before we begin to understand this? God doesn't see how we see. He doesn't think like we think because *"He is altogether lovely"* (Song of Solomon 5:16).

Let's read Numbers 23:19 again in its entirety, *"God is not a man, that he should lie; neither the son of man, that he should repent: hath he said, and shall he not do it? or hath he spoken, and shall he not make it good?"* He will make it good. This is the Word of God. So let's lay aside all these thoughts today that contradict the Word of God and that render God to the boundaries of a man. He is unlimited in His love and unsearchable because He is high above all. Remember today that God is not a man. God is a spirit whose ways and thoughts are always higher than ours.

"My Word Like As A Fire"
Jeremiah 23:29

God's Word is His cleansing agent that burns the dross in our lives. His Word truly is like a fire, burning all of the garbage and uncleanness in the lives of His people. Isaiah 4:4 tells us He will wash away *"the filth of the daughters of Zion"* and purge *"the blood of Jerusalem from the midst thereof by the spirit of judgment, and by the spirit of burning."* How God does this, many times, is through His Word. God's fire, as I've said before, is not a natural fire, but yet burns the chains of our lives.

Remember in Daniel 3, Shadrach, Meshach, and Abednego were cast into a burning fiery furnace, but it didn't consume them, because they were the people of God. It simply burned their bonds off, and they were set free. While they were in that fire, Nebuchadnezzar saw the Lord Jesus walking in the midst of them. When they came out, they didn't even smell like smoke. This is the fire of God, and this is like His Word in our lives.

Jeremiah 23:29 says, *"Is not my word like as a fire? saith the Lord; and like a hammer that breaketh the rock in pieces?"* I don't know how many times I've read the Word of God, and something began to burn deep within me, a hunger, a passion, and a desire to be better than I am today. That Word would provoke and challenge me. Remember Jeremiah said, *"I will not make mention of him, nor speak any more in his name. But his word was in mine heart as a burning fire shut up in my bones, and I was weary with forbearing, and I could not stay"* (Jeremiah 20:9). A man of God, who has been called of God, has the seal of God, and has the Word of God living and breathing in his soul, has to speak. God's Word in our hearts is a burning fire shut up in our bones. So many times I have stood to minister and felt like my whole body was a flame of fire. He did say He would make *"his ministers a flame of fire"* (Hebrews 1:7). I think this happens because of the Word of God in us and the anointing upon us.

His Word was in my heart like a burning fire. Do you feel it now? Even as you read this word, is His Word burning in you, stoking the fire. Proverbs 26:20 tells us, *"Where no wood is, there the fire goeth out."* You and I need to keep putting that Word in us, so that fire remains strong.

In Luke 24, in the story of the disciples on the way to Emmaus, it says, *"And they said one to another, Did not our heart burn within us, while he talked with us by the way, and while he opened to us the scriptures?"* (Luke 24:32). Oh, how many times has my heart burned within me as He opened the Scriptures to me and as He spoke with me. His Word is like a mighty fire. Remember in Genesis 3:24, He placed a placed a flaming sword in front of the Garden of Eden. If you and I are ever to get back to the garden, to what Adam once had, we're going to have to pass through that flaming sword. Ephesians tells us *"the sword of the Spirit...is the word of God"* (Ephesians 6:17). We'll have to pass through that fiery Word. May God blow His torch upon you today and burn up the dross with His Word.

"The Way Of The Fool Is Right In His Own Eyes, But He That Hearkens Unto Counsel Is Wise"
Proverbs 12:15

DAY 293

When you and I hearken unto counsel, we submit ourselves to elders, father ministries, pastors and leadership within the body of Christ. I Peter 5:5 tells us, *"Likewise, ye younger, submit yourselves unto the elder. Yea, all of you be subject one to another, and be clothed with humility."* God actually wants the younger to submit to the elder and everybody to be under authority. There is such safety and such joy being under authority. However, there are some people who will not hear counsel.

Proverbs 6:23 says, *"Reproofs of instruction are the way of life."* In Proverbs 20:18 it says, *"Every purpose is established by counsel: and with good advice make war."* We need to have good advice and we need to be submitted to authority. Paul says in I Corinthians 4:15, *"For though ye have ten thousand instructors in Christ, yet have ye not many fathers."* "Instructors" in the Greek means a "boy teacher." A boy teacher cannot help me. I need a man who has experience, a man who knows the Lord intimately and who could say he's sat where I have sat. Proverbs 19:20 says, *"Hear counsel, and receive instruction, that thou mayest be wise in thy latter end."* I believe we were all born with an innate desire to have authority over our lives. When we go without it, rebellion can come in. Proverbs 15:22 says, *"Without counsel purposes are disappointed: but in the multitude of counsellors they are established."* Our purpose will be established as we are submitted to others.

Paul told the Galatians that what he had received he did not receive from men, but from the Lord Himself. Even though he was sure it was from the Lord, he still went and submitted himself to Peter, James, John and the local church in Jerusalem. He did this because he didn't want to run in vain (Galatians 2:2). We need counsel in our lives; we need other people, a multitude of them to keep us safe. Proverbs 11:14 tells us, *"Where no counsel is, the people fall: but in the multitude of counsellors there is safety."* I'm not saying we're supposed to submit ourselves to everything, but a true pastor will lead you, exhort and edify you.

Proverbs 24:6 says, *"For by wise counsel thou shalt make thy war: and in multitude of counsellors there is safety."* This doesn't mean we run off to every prophetic ministry that comes along trying to get a word of prophecy to change your life, for II Peter 1:19 says, *"We have also a more sure word of prophecy; whereunto ye do well that ye take heed."* However, we need wise counsel. Hebrews 13:17 says, *"Obey them that have the rule over you, and submit yourselves: for they watch for your souls, as they that must give account, that they may do it with joy, and not with grief: for that is unprofitable for you."* God wants us to have wise counsel.

Finally, Proverbs 9:9 says, *"Give instruction to a wise man, and he will be yet wiser: teach a just man, and he will increase in learning."* Let us humble ourselves, as John did in Revelation 10. Even though he was the oldest and most well respected Apostle of his time, when he heard a voice from heaven telling him to go and take the little book from the messenger, he humbled himself and said, *"Give me the little book"* (Revelation 10:9). Let's have purpose and counsel in our lives. Let's be under authority, because a man who is under authority is going to have great authority.

"Thy Comforts Delight My Soul"
Psalms 94:19

DAY 294

Today, I want you to consider this passage of Scripture with me. Psalms 94:19 says, *"In the multitude of my thoughts within me thy comforts delight my soul."* In the multitude of our thoughts, many times we don't find delight, we find the opposite. We may find anxiety, fear, or just an all-around state of oppression. However, let this verse of Scripture be a revelation to your heart as you allow His comforts to delight your soul.

The word *"comfort"* in Hebrew means "consolation or to give solace." The Greek word means "to call near, to be of good comfort, to exhort, to implore." God wants to give consolation and comfort to our souls.

His comforts delight our souls. The soul is the place of all warfare (James 4:1). Our souls need comfort, peace, and rest. Well, God has said He wants us to have that comfort. Consider these passages. In Isaiah 40:1, it says, *"Comfort ye, comfort ye my people, saith your God."* Another place in Isaiah tells us, *"For the Lord shall comfort Zion: he will comfort all her waste places"* (Isaiah 51:3). Then in verse 12, it says, *"I, even I, am he that comforteth you"* (Isaiah 51:12). Glory to God! Isaiah 49:13 reads, *"The Lord hath comforted his people, and will have mercy upon his afflicted."*

David, of all people, and Isaiah both had great turmoil in their lives. Despite that, they found comfort in their God. You and I need to find His comforts. The Bible declares that He is *"the God of all comfort"* (II Corinthians 1:3). It says in II Corinthians 7:6, God *"comforteth those that are cast down."* The book of Hosea tells us, *"Therefore, behold, I will allure her, and bring her into the wilderness, and speak comfortably unto her"* (Hosea 2:14). God is alluring you today. He is drawing you and me ever closer to Him so that He might give consolation, rest, solace, and peace. Whatever the condition of your heart today, know this: the Lord is there to comfort you.

It says in II Thessalonians 2:16-17, *"¹⁶Now our Lord Jesus Christ himself, and God, even our Father, which hath loved us, and hath given us everlasting consolation and good hope through grace, ¹⁷Comfort your hearts, and stablish you in every good word and work."* Matthew 5:4 tells us, *"Blessed are they that mourn: for they shall be comforted."* The Bible tells us in John, *"And I will pray the Father, and he shall give you another Comforter, that he may abide with you for ever"* (John 14:16). God has given us the Holy Ghost, His precious presence as our comforter. *"Thy comforts delight my soul."*

Let your soul be delighted today as God surrounds you with solace and rest, consolation and peace. As Isaiah 61:2 says, He wants to *"comfort all that mourn."* Let the Comforter, the precious Holy Ghost fill you today and comfort your heart.

"In Your Patience Possess Ye Your Souls"
Luke 21:19

Day 295

If there is one characteristic or virtue in life most of us lack, it is patience. Oh, how we need to be more patient. And as we search the Scriptures concerning this, we will let the Word of God define it for us. Patience is not a gift. It is something that must be learned through discipline and trials. What it produces is something rather remarkable. Our God is a God of patience, and we want to be like Him. So why don't we see if we can be an imitator of Him and learn the beauty and joy of patience?

Luke 21:19 says, *"In your patience possess ye your souls."* Let us first define what this word *"patience"* means. The actual Greek word means "to be long-spirited, forbearing, to be longsuffering, to patiently endure, to stay under, to remain, to persevere, and to bear trials." Another Greek word for *"patience"* means "cheerful endurance, constancy, and patient continuance." I love this dictionary definition that defines it as "bearing pains or trials calmly or without complaint, being kind and tolerant, not hasty or impetuous, steadfast despite opposing difficulty or adversity, the capacity or habit of being patient, calmly tolerating delay, diligent persevering, calm endurance." I don't know about you, but that can't be said of me most of the time. I have a struggle with being calm while enduring and being gentle, moderate, and cheerful in the midst of storms and trials. But one thing we know about our God: He is a very patient God. The Lord is longsuffering, just as the Bible says over and over again. It says in James, *"...Behold, the husbandman waiteth for the precious fruit of the earth, and hath long patience for it"* (James 5:7). Jesus is our example. He is the one we need to look towards to learn how to become patient.

As it says in Luke, *"In your patience,"* or in cheerful endurance, or in longsuffering, *"possess ye your souls."* You see, when we are patient, we receive the will of God. The Bible says in Hebrews 10:36, *"For ye have need of patience, that, after ye have done the will of God, ye might receive the promise."* In Revelation 13:10, it says, *"Here is the patience and the faith of the saints."* The book of Hebrews also tells us:

> *"¹¹And we desire that every one of you do shew the same diligence to the full assurance of hope unto the end: ¹²That ye be not slothful, but followers of them who through faith and patience inherit the promises. ¹³For when God made promise to Abraham, because he could swear by no greater, he sware by himself, ¹⁴Saying, Surely blessing I will bless thee, and multiplying I will multiply thee. ¹⁵And so, after he had patiently endured, he obtained the promise"* (Hebrews 6:11-15).

We need to follow the Lord Jesus and those *"who through faith and patience inherit the promises,"* or inherit what they need. We have need of patience. The saints are supposed to have patience and faith working together.

In Psalms 130:5, it says, *"I wait for the Lord, my soul doth wait."* How hard is it to wait patiently? Another Psalms reads, *"I waited patiently for the Lord"* (Psalms 40:1). Psalms 37:7 tells us, *"Rest in the Lord, and wait patiently for him."* Elsewhere we read:

> *"We give thanks to God always for you all, making mention of you in our prayers; ³Remembering without ceasing your work of faith, and labour of love, and patience of hope in our Lord Jesus Christ, in the sight of God and our Father"* (I Thessalonians 1:2-3).

Finally, in Romans 8:25, the Bible says, *"But if we hope for that we see not, then do we with patience wait for it."* In your patience possess ye your souls. Oh, that God would help us to bear pains and trials calmly without complaint, to not be hasty or impetuous, but to calmly tolerate delay. This is something that will not come as a gift to us; it has to be earned. We earn it through the dealings of God. We earn it as we walk through hard places and allow God to add it to our lives. James tells us:

> *"Take, my brethren, the prophets, who have spoken in the name of the Lord, for an example of suffering affliction, and of patience. ¹¹Behold, we count them happy which endure. Ye have heard of the patience of Job, and have seen the end of the Lord; that the Lord is very pitiful, and of tender mercy"* (James 5:10-11).

Well, what will bring this patience into our lives? Romans 5:3 says, *"we glory in tribulations also: knowing that tribulation worketh patience."* God allows troubles, adversity, persecution, and trials of our faith so that patience can be worked into us. It says in James, *"³Knowing this, that the trying of your faith worketh patience. ⁴But let patience have her perfect work, that ye may be perfect and entire, wanting nothing"* (James 1:3-4). We are to be, as Romans 12:12 says, *"Rejoicing in hope; patient in tribulation; continuing instant in prayer."* So, patience yields a tremendous fruit. It causes us to possess this carnal nature, to take hold of this soulish nature that wants so desperately to do its own thing and to say what it wants to say.

You and I need to be patient. In Revelation 3:10, it says, *"Because thou hast kept the word of my patience, I also will keep thee from the hour of temptation."* If we will keep the word of His patience, He will keep us. James 5:7 tells us, *"Be patient therefore, brethren, unto the coming of the Lord."* We need to be patient unto the coming of the Lord. *"Blessed is the man that endureth temptation: for when he is tried, he shall receive the crown of life"* (James 1:12). If you and I will simply have faith and patience, we will possess the promise of God.

So, today, when things happen that are not good, that disturb or upset you, do not overreact. Rest in the Lord and wait patiently for Him, knowing that as you are patient, and as you allow the Holy Spirit entrance, you are beginning to possess your soul. May God help you to do this and in your patience, possess your soul.

"A Lively Hope"
I Peter 1:3

Day 296

The Apostle Peter here in I Peter 1:3 says, *"Blessed be the God and Father of our Lord Jesus Christ, which according to his abundant mercy hath begotten us again unto a lively hope, by the resurrection of Jesus Christ from the dead."* You and I have been begotten again, or born again, into a lively hope because of Jesus' resurrection.

The word *"lively"* means "quickened, to live." The word *"hope"* in the Greek means, "to expect, confide; trust, to anticipate with pleasure or confidence." Because of the resurrection of Jesus, we have been quickened to live. We can have confidence and we can trust in what God is doing; we can expect that we will also be resurrected. Colossians 1:27 says: *"To whom God would make known what is the riches of the glory of this mystery among the Gentiles; which is Christ in you, the hope of glory."* Christ in us is the down payment or the hope of future glory. Galatians 5:5 states as well, *"For we through the Spirit wait for the hope of righteousness by faith."* We can only access this hope by faith.

In I Corinthians 15:19-20 it says, *"If in this life only we have hope in Christ, we are of all men most miserable. But now is Christ risen from the dead..."* If we didn't have Jesus, there would be no hope. So thanks be unto God that He was resurrected on the third day, led captivity captive, gave gifts unto men (Ephesians 4:8), and has given us a hope, unshakeable for the future. That is why in I Peter 3:15 it says, *"...and be ready always to give an answer to every man that asketh you a reason of the hope that is in you..."* There is a hope that lies in every one of us and we need to be ready to give an answer to every man who asks us of that hope.

It is a lively hope, a quickened hope. Titus 2:13 tells us, *"Looking for that blessed hope, and the glorious appearing of the great God and our Savior Jesus Christ."* We need to be looking and waiting for the hope to be materialized. We cannot give up. We cannot surrender. We need to press through.

Finally, in Hebrews 6:18-19 it says, *"That by two immutable things, in which it was impossible for God to lie, we might have a strong consolation, who have fled for refuge to lay hold upon the hope set before us. ¹⁹Which hope we have as an anchor of the soul..."* God has bought us again to a lively hope, a quickened hope and an exciting hope because of the resurrection of Jesus. Today, let this principle dawn on your heart. He has caused us to come alive with expectation, confidence and anticipation of His glory and all that entails. A lively hope is what we have. Amen.

"Make Excuse"
Luke 14:18

Day 297

In Luke 14, we find a tremendous story. Jesus says in verse 16, "*A certain man made a great supper, and bade many...*" That great supper is the marriage supper of the Lamb. It continues to say he "*sent his servant at supper time to say to them that were bidden, Come; for all things are now ready*" (Luke 14:17). In the last days, as the marriage supper of the Lamb is about to take place, God is going to send forth the Spirit of the Lord saying, "Come, for all things are ready." It says in Revelation 19, "*the marriage of the Lamb is come, and his wife hath made herself ready*" (Revelation 19:7). You and I need to be like the wise virgins in Matthew 25. It says, "*They that were ready went in with him to the marriage: and the door was shut*" (Matthew 25:10). We want to be ready.

Luke 14 continues to say, "*And they all with one consent began to make excuse...*" (Luke 14:18). As a pastor now for over forty years, I have seen every kind of excuse used by the people of God. They try to excuse themselves from going on with God, sitting under sound doctrine, coming to prayer meetings, fasting, and any other thing that they don't really want to do. There seems to be no end to the excuses that human beings can come up with.

How about you? Have you made excuses for not attending meetings, not being faithful, and not really walking with the Lord? Have you sought to justify yourself? Listen to how these individuals justified themselves. The first one said, "*I have bought a piece of ground, and I must needs go and see it: I pray thee have me excused*" (Luke 14:18). That means his possessions spoke louder to him than Jesus. The next one said, "*I have bought five yoke of oxen, and I go to prove them: I pray thee have me excused*" (Luke 14:19). This one allowed his job to take precedence over his walk with God. The third one said, "*I have married a wife, and therefore I cannot come*" (Luke 14:20). This, I would say, is the crowning excuse. Many people let their spouses keep them from going to meetings and going on with God. This is not good enough to make it into brideship. We need to be ready; we need to stop making excuses. Look at what these excuses did. Luke 14 says:

> "*²¹So that servant came, and shewed his lord these things. Then the master of the house being angry said to his servant, Go out quickly into the streets and lanes of the city, and bring in hither the poor, and the maimed, and the halt, and the blind. ²²And the servant said, Lord, it is done...*" (Luke 14:21-22).

God has gone to those who have been bidden, and they've made excuses. Has He come to you? Do you hear the call of the bridegroom? Answer it today. Let's stop making excuses. Let's not allow our possessions to possess us, our jobs to control us, or even our families to manipulate us. Only Jesus is our Lord. We have no excuse.

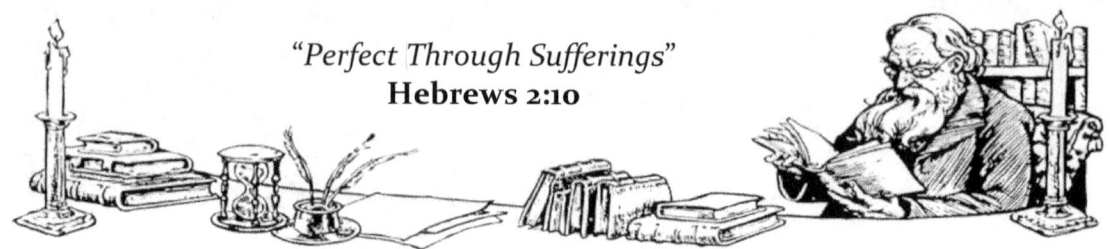

"Perfect Through Sufferings"
Hebrews 2:10

Day 298

Hebrews 2:10 says, *"For it became him, for whom are all things, and by whom are all things, in bringing many sons unto glory, to make the captain of their salvation perfect through sufferings."* This is a tremendous revelation that suffering brings perfection. Here we find that even in the case of the Son of the living God, we find this principle at work. The captain of our salvation was made perfect through suffering. Perfect in the Greek means "complete, mature." As Christians, we are made complete and mature through suffering.

This is an amazing truth that so many people miss. They throw away their negatives and they don't realize that the negatives have been sent to them to bless, help, and perfect them. Paul said in Romans 8:18, *"For I reckon that the sufferings of this present time are not worthy to be compared with the glory which shall be revealed in us."* These sufferings and things we experience are simply sent to us to make us perfect and present us faultless before the presence of the living God (Jude 24). James tells us in James 1:2-4:

> *"²My brethren, count it all joy when ye fall into divers temptations; ³Knowing this, that the trying of your faith worketh patience. ⁴But let patience have her perfect work, that ye may be perfect and entire, wanting nothing."*

Patience comes as we fall into diverse temptations and trials. It is sent to us to perfect us. II Corinthians 4:17 tells us, *"For our light affliction, which is but for a moment, worketh for us a far more exceeding and eternal weight of glory."* I know the phrase *"light affliction"* is debatable, but compared to the reward it brings, it doesn't even compare. Our afflictions won't last forever. There is an end to them. But while we're suffering them, let's remember that they are working *"for us a far more exceeding and eternal weight of glory."* This suffering is maturing us. It is to help us *"grow in grace, and in the knowledge of our Lord and Saviour Jesus Christ"* (II Peter 3:18). Peter writes:

> *"...if need be, ye are in heaviness through manifold temptations: ⁷That the trial of your faith, being much more precious than gold that perisheth, though it be tried with fire, might be found unto praise and honour and glory at the appearing of Jesus Christ."* (I Peter 1:6-7)

We want to be found unto praise and honor when the Lord Jesus comes. The trial of our faith and the sufferings that we go through are much more precious than gold that perishes. Why? It is because trials and sufferings make us perfect and complete. They allow God to finish His work in us. As we see this principle of suffering and glory today, follow Jesus' footsteps and be perfected as He was. Don't throw away your negatives for we can't have a picture without a negative. Selah! Think about it.

"Wash You, Make You Clean"
Isaiah 1:16

DAY 299

There is an aspect to our walk with God that is absolutely essential and that is the daily repenting and cleansing of ourselves from our sin. There must be in us a desire to be clean, to wash ourselves. Isaiah 1:16 says, *"Wash you, make you clean; put away the evil of your doings from before mine eyes; cease to do evil."* This is the word of the Lord to us, that we wash ourselves.

Hebrews 12:1 says *"Let us lay aside every weight, and the sin which doth so easily beset us."* There must be in us an ability to cry out to God as David did in Psalms 51:10-11, *"Create in me a clean heart, O God; and renew a right spirit within me. "Cast me not away from thy presence; and take not thy holy spirit from me."*

In II Samuel chapters 11 and 12, David had committed adultery, lied, deceived and caused a man to be murdered. Later, he reaped the benefits of what he had sown in the death of his child with Bathsheba. After he had lost that child, the Scriptures say, *"then David arose from the earth, and washed, and anointed himself, and changed his apparel, and came into the house of the Lord, and worshipped"* (II Samuel 12:20). This is what every one of us must do. We must learn to wash ourselves in the blood of Jesus, because the blood of Christ cleanses us from all sins (I John 1:9).

In Jeremiah 4:14 it says, *"O Jerusalem, wash thine heart from wickedness, that thou mayest be saved. How long shall thy vain thoughts lodge within thee?"* This reminds us of James 4:8 where God commands, *"Cleanse your hands, ye sinners; and purify your hearts, ye double minded."* It is our job to cleanse our own hands and to purify our own hearts.

II Corinthians 7:1 exhorts, *"Having therefore these promises, dearly beloved, let us cleanse ourselves from all filthiness of the flesh and spirit, perfecting holiness in the fear of God."* Let us cleanse ourselves.

Another way to wash ourselves is by the Word of God. Psalms 119:9 states, *"Wherewithal shall a young man cleanse his way? by taking heed thereto according to thy word."* Also in 119:11, *"Thy word have I hid in mine heart, that I might not sin against thee."* It is our job to hide the Word. It is our job to wash and cleanse ourselves, to deal with the naughtiness and vain thoughts and imaginations in our lives. It's up to us.

Jesus said in John 15:3, *"Now ye are clean through the word which I have spoken unto you."* We see the bride in Revelation 19:14 is *"clothed in fine linen, white and clean."* My prayer is that you will be that bride clothed in fine linen, innocent and righteous before the Lord, white and clean. Wash you today and make you clean.

"Brought Up The Ark Of The Lord With Shouting"
II Samuel 6:15

DAY 300

In the Scriptures, the ark of the Lord that God told Moses to build is a type of the manifest presence of God. Wherever we find this ark going, the glory of the Lord went with it. Remember when the ark was taken from the children of Israel, the Word of the Lord was *"Ichabod, saying, the glory is departed from Israel: because the ark of God was taken"* (I Samuel 4:21). When the ark left, the glory left. So the ark is a type and shadow of the glory of the Lord or the manifest presence of God.

In II Samuel 6:9, David asks, *"How shall the ark of the Lord come to me?"* He initially tried to bring the ark on a new cart, which was not after the set due order, and somebody died because of it. David had to search the Scriptures to realize that he shouldn't put the ark on a cart and that only the priests were allowed to carry and transport the ark. So they carried the ark on the priest's shoulders. II Samuel 6:15 then says, *"So David and all the house of Israel brought up the ark of the Lord with shouting, and with the sound of the trumpet."* In other words, every time the ark comes and the glory falls, shouting follows. The manifest presence of God does this for us. We see this elsewhere in I Samuel 4:

> *"And when the ark of the covenant of the Lord came into the camp, all Israel shouted with a great shout, so that the earth rang again. ⁶And when the Philistines heard the noise of the shout, they said, What meaneth the noise of this great shout in the camp of the Hebrews? And they understood that the ark of the Lord was come into the camp. ⁷And the Philistines were afraid, for they said, God is come into the camp. And they said, Woe unto us! for there hath not been such a thing heretofore."* (I Samuel 4:5-7)

Wherever the ark was, God was. When the manifest presence of God comes and the glory falls, it means God Himself is there manifesting Himself. We're not satisfied with just the omnipresence of God (the presence of God that is everywhere). As true worshippers and disciples of the Lord, we long and yearn for the manifest presence of God. We want Jesus to be in the house. We want Jesus to be in the midst. So wherever the ark is, the glory is and wherever the ark is, God is.

This is true even in our own personal lives. I tell you when God's glory falls, our first response is going to be a shout of praise. No matter how hard I might try to withhold myself and to keep myself from shouting praises, when the glory falls, the first thing that resounds in my heart is to offer up a mighty shout unto the Lord. This happens because something in me is responding to Him.

Psalms 42:7 says, *"Deep calleth unto deep at the noise of thy waterspouts."* In other words, when God's glory falls, it is the depth of God's heart reaching out to the depth of our hearts. True worshippers will always respond to God's overflowing glory by shouting praise, honor, and thanksgiving unto the Lord, for wherever the ark is, God is.

In II Chronicles 5, when Solomon had finished all the work for the house of the Lord, he told the priests to bring up the Ark of the Covenant and when they did it says:

> "[13]*It came even to pass, as the trumpeters and singers were as one, to make one sound to be heard in praising and thanking the Lord; and when they lifted up their voice with the trumpets and cymbals and instruments of musick, and praised the Lord, saying, For he is good; for his mercy endureth for ever: that then the house was filled with a cloud, even the house of the Lord;* [14]*So that the priests could not stand to minister by reason of the cloud: for the glory of the Lord had filled the house of God"*
> (II Chronicles 5:13-14).

Wherever the ark is, God is there resting between the cherubim. And where God is, His glory is. And when His glory is there, there is only one response as Psalms 47:1 says, *"shout unto God with the voice of triumph."*

"If Sinners Entice Thee"
Proverbs 1:10

Day 301

Solomon declares in Proverbs 1:10, "*My son, if sinners entice thee, consent thou not.*" This is the work of the enemy. He has been watching you your entire life to see where your weaknesses are. But the Bible says, "*We are not ignorant of his devices*" (II Corinthians 2:11). We know that Satan comes "*to steal, and to kill, and to destroy*" (John 10:10). In Nehemiah 4, as the people were rebuilding the wall, the enemy tried to frustrate their purpose in building. Today, don't allow him to do this.

We have the ability to "*consent thou not.*" The Bible tells us that "*sin shall not have dominion over you*" (Romans 6:14). We do not have to give in to our baser inclinations; we do not have to sin. This has been the religious thinking for many years in the body of Christ. I remember being told as a young believer that I would never stop sinning. People said I just had to get used to it and keep repenting. What kind of faith is that? I believe that a people will come forth who will have conquered sin. Remember the story of Jacob and Esau. Esau was the man of the flesh and he came through the womb first before Jacob. It always seems that the man of the flesh, the man of sin, always comes through first. But the Bible tells us that baby Jacob, as he was coming forth, grabbed hold of the heel of Esau. I believe that God's overcoming army is going to grab hold of the heel of sin. They will eventually conquer it, as Jacob did, getting the firstborn blessing and superseding his brother.

Don't give in to your baser inclinations. All of us are tempted. It says in James 1, "*But every man is tempted, when he is drawn away of his own lust, and enticed. ¹⁵Then when lust hath conceived, it bringeth forth sin*" (James 1:14-15). It says of Delilah and Samson, that "*when she pressed him daily with her words, and urged him, so that his soul was vexed unto death,*" that he gave in to her (Judges 16:16). All of us have areas in our lives of weakness, and the enemy knows this. He sends people and situations into our lives to try to drag us down and entice us to make us fall.

When we know Satan's devices, we will know how to defeat him. James 4:7-8 says, "*Resist the devil, and he will flee from you. ⁸Draw nigh to God.*" Isaiah 59:19 declares, "*When the enemy shall come in like a flood, the Spirit of the Lord shall lift up a standard against him.*" Allow the Spirit of the Lord a chance to lift up a standard. When lust comes, there is a conception period. You still have time, even if you have been enticed and drawn away, to allow the Spirit of God and His grace to flow up and out of you.

"*My son, if sinners entice thee, consent thou not*" (Proverbs 1:10). Don't do it. It says in James, "*Do not err, my beloved brethren*" (James 1:16). Paul told Timothy, "*Keep thyself pure*" (I Timothy 5:22). You can do it, because God's grace is able to teach you how to deny ungodliness and worldly lusts, and to live soberly and righteously in this present world (Titus 2:11-12).

"If The Foundations Be Destroyed, What Can The Righteous Do?"
Psalm 11:3

Day 302

In life, all of us need a foundation, a starting place, a beginning place, something to stand upon, and something to hold us up. Everything has to have an under-girding or a support base. Christians are no different.

In Hebrew, the word for *"foundation"* means "a basis of support, and purpose." It comes from a root word that means "to place, apply, or to lie something upon." I Corinthians 3:11 says, *"For no other foundation can any man lay than that which is laid which is Jesus Christ,"* The foundation of God begins with Jesus Christ and salvation, but after salvation God wants to lay a foundation in our lives of the Word of God. I believe that the foundations are simple, basic truths, such as God eternally loves us, God is merciful, God is for us and not against us, etc. In fact Psalms 11:3 tells us we really can't do anything without them, *"If the foundations be destroyed, what can the righteous do?"*

In Ezra 6:3, the Bible declares, *"Let the foundations thereof be strongly laid."* God wants a strong foundation in every Christian's life. So the will of God for every Christian after they get saved is to sit under sound doctrine and allow God to lay an awesome foundation of the Word of God in their hearts and lives. He wants the basis of support in our lives to be the Word of God, because without it we will falter. Jesus clearly brought this out:

> *"⁴⁷Whosoever cometh to me, and heareth my sayings, and doeth them, I will shew you to whom he is like: ⁴⁸He is like a man which built an house, and digged deep, and laid the foundation on a rock: and when the flood arose, the stream beat vehemently upon that house, and could not shake it: for it was founded upon a rock. ⁴⁹But he that heareth, and doeth not, is like a man that without a foundation built an house upon the earth; against which the stream did beat vehemently, and immediately it fell; and the ruin of that house was great"* (Luke 6:47-49).

This is the problem. Without a foundation, we cannot stand up under trials, testings, and temptations that come to all of us. Every sacrifice shall be salted with fire. Everybody will be tried. It is part of the dealings of God so He can mature us, and conform our character into His. So we need that foundation laid upon a rock. And that rock is the Word of God. God wants to personally lay this foundation, as He says in Zechariah 4:9, *"The hands of Zerubbabel* (a type of the Lord Jesus) *have laid the foundation of this house; his hands shall also finish it."* Jesus is attempting to lay a foundation in every life; a foundation of the Word of God and of sound doctrine. Hebrews 6 clearly defines for us what a foundation of the Word of God consists of:

> "¹*Therefore leaving the principles of the doctrine of Christ, let us go on unto perfection; not laying again the foundation of repentance from dead works, and of faith toward God, ²Of the doctrine of baptisms, and of laying on of hands, and of resurrection of the dead, and of eternal judgment. ³And this will we do, if God permit*" (Heb. 6:1-3).

Here the Scriptures name the six major doctrines that comprise the doctrine of Christ. God wants His people deeply grounded, founded, and established in His Word so they can grow. Notice in Hebrews 6:1-3 that we cannot go on to perfection (all that God has for us) until we have a foundation in the Word. Also, only God knows when that's done because He is the One who grants the permit. In Hebrews 5:12-14, the verses preceding Hebrews 6:1-3, he is rebuking the Hebrew Christians because they had been saved awhile and still were not established in the basic principles of the doctrine of Christ. When you don't have a foundation, you're a baby in the Lord. You are unskillful in the Word. Therefore it would behoove all Christians to know these principles of the doctrine of Christ. Because ultimately it is our job as Isaiah says:

> "And they that shall be of thee shall build the old waste places: thou shalt raise up the foundations of many generations; and thou shalt be called, The repairer of the breach, The restorer of paths to dwell in" (Isaiah 58:12).

This is our calling. Colossians 3:16 exhorts us, "*Let the word of Christ dwell in you richly.*" As we allow God to lay a foundation in our life and are in a deep intimate walk with Jesus, we then have the basis and support to face anything in life. And the winds, the storms, and the rains, though they may beat vehemently upon our house will never shake it because it is founded upon a rock.

I would encourage you today to give yourself even more to the Word of God and to consider that without the foundations, "*what can the righteous do?*" Nothing! Remember that the book of Hebrews 11:10 tells us that Abraham "*...looked for a city which hath foundations, whose builder and maker is God.*" You and I are looking for that city which hath foundations. It is in the Word of God. It is in the Scriptures. Without it, what can the righteous do? They are helpless.

But if God's people do give themselves to Jesus and His Word, they will build such a strong, powerful, and mighty fortress underneath them that can never be shaken. II Timothy 2:19 tells us, "*Nevertheless the foundation of God standeth sure, having this seal, The Lord knoweth them that are his.*" God knows us. He knows the ones who have a foundation. He will stand by them, strengthen them, support them, comfort them, and bless them.

So hear the word of the Lord today. Give yourself like never before to the Word of God, knowing it is the basis and support of everything you will face for the rest of your life and will fill you with His glorious purpose so you can fulfill all the will of God and be like those in Psalms 1:2-3, "*But his delight is in the law of the Lord; and in his law doth he meditate day and night. And he shall be like a tree planted by the rivers of water, that bringeth forth his fruit in his season; his leaf also shall not wither; and whatsoever he doeth shall prosper.*" Let the foundations be strongly laid in your life, Amen!

"Delivered From The Power Of Darkness"
Colossians 1:13

Day 303

Satan has been defeated and is being defeated every day in our lives. As II Corinthians 1:10 says Jesus has delivered us, daily delivers us, and in whom we trust will yet deliver us. Here we find in Colossians 1:13, *"Who hath delivered us from the power of darkness, and hath translated us into the kingdom of his dear Son."* Thanks be unto God for this deliverance and this translation. We've been delivered from the power or authority of darkness.

It says in Matthew 28:18, *"And Jesus came and spake unto them, saying, All power is given unto me in heaven and in earth."* *"Power"* is the Greek word *"exousia"* which means *"all authority."* It says in I John 3:8, *"For this purpose the Son of God was manifested, that he might destroy the works of the devil."* The word, *"destroy"* in Greek means *"to loosen, to break up, to dissolve."* Romans 16:20 says, *"And the God of peace shall bruise Satan under your feet shortly."* That word *"bruise"* in Greek means: *"to crush completely, to shatter, to break in pieces."* God is doing it for us right now.

God's already dealt with the devil because Colossians 2:15 tells us, *"And having spoiled principalities and powers, he made a shew of them openly, triumphing over them in it."* Also we see in Hebrews 2:14, *"that through death he might destroy him that had the power of death, that is, the devil."* So He's done it already, but He's doing it on a daily basis in our personal lives.

In Isaiah 10:27 it says, *"And it shall come to pass in that day, that his burden shall be taken away from off thy shoulder, and his yoke from off thy neck, and the yoke shall be destroyed because of the anointing."* The anointing of God in our lives is breaking the yokes of bondage. The yokes that the enemy has tried to put on us have no power, because God has divested him of his power. Now He's finishing that work in our personal lives. Deuteronomy 33:27 says, *"The eternal God is thy refuge, and underneath are the everlasting arms: and he shall thrust out the enemy from before thee; and shall say, Destroy them."*

Remember in Job 4:11, *"The old lion perisheth for lack of prey."* We're not giving him anything. We're not giving place to the devil. We're not letting the sun go down on our wrath (anger toward sin) (Ephesians 4:26-27). We're submitting ourselves to God, we're resisting the devil, so he will flee from us. We've been delivered from the power of darkness.

I love Psalms 17:4. It says, *"Concerning the works of men, by the word of thy lips I have kept me from the paths of the destroyer."* Thank God you can be kept from the paths of the destroyer by giving heed to the Word of God. Acts 10:38 says, *"How God anointed Jesus of Nazareth with the Holy Ghost and with power: who went about doing good, and healing all that were oppressed of the devil; for God was with him."* God wants to deliver you of that oppression. He has delivered you. Ultimately He will put an end to Satan. Remember this out of Revelation 12:11, *"And they overcame him by the blood of the Lamb, and by the word of their testimony; and they loved not their lives unto the death."* We are not afraid of the kingdom of darkness because we've been translated out of it into the Kingdom of His dear Son.

"Willing To Justify Himself"
Luke 10:29

Today we want to look at a principle in the Scriptures of not justifying ourselves, but allowing God to justify us. In this particular story we read:

> *"And, behold, a certain lawyer stood up, and tempted him, saying, Master, what shall I do to inherit eternal life? ²⁶He said unto him, What is written in the law? how readest thou? ²⁷And he answering said, Thou shalt love the Lord thy God with all thy heart, and with all thy soul, and with all thy strength, and with all thy mind; and thy neighbour as thyself. ²⁸And he said unto him, Thou hast answered right: this do, and thou shalt live. ²⁹But he, willing to justify himself, said unto Jesus, And who is my neighbour?"* (Luke 10:25-29)

DAY 304

The reason why he justified himself in verse 29 was in reality he hadn't loved his neighbor as himself and had not really been doing the will of God. So he had to justify himself and try to make himself look good to Jesus. The Bible says in Jeremiah 3:11 that, *"backsliding Israel hath justified herself."* You and I do not need to justify ourselves. Job 9:20 says, *"If I justify myself, mine own mouth shall condemn me."* Jesus said to the Pharisees in Luke 16:15, *"Ye are they which justify yourselves before men."*

God forbid that we justify ourselves because the Bible clearly says in Isaiah 50:8 *"He is near that justifieth me"* and in Romans 8:33 it says, *"It is God that justifieth."* We don't need to justify ourselves. This is what backsliders do. God is our justifier and He is near.

The Bible says in Luke 7:35, *"But wisdom is justified of all her children."* In wisdom, all we need do is allow God to be our justifier. We don't need to make excuses. We don't need to try to cover our weaknesses or mistakes because we simply know that Jesus justified us by His blood. I John 1:9 states, *"If we confess our sins, he is faithful and just to forgive us our sins, and to cleanse us from all unrighteousness."* Moreover, Isaiah 53:11 says, *"By his knowledge shall my righteous servant justify many; for he shall bear their iniquities."*

He has justified us and He will be the one that stops the weaknesses and inconsistencies in our lives. Rather than being willing to justify ourselves, let's allow God to justify us. Let God take your part. Today, He is near that justifies you.

"Ye Are Gods"
John 10:34

DAY 305

We want to look today at a very controversial Scripture, that there's been much confusion over. I teach and believe in the manifestation of the sons of God and that God will have an overcoming army in the last days. They will be created in His image and will have progressed to the point as Hebrews 6:1 says, *"let us go on unto perfection."* Perfection simply means completion. God is going to have a people in which it is no longer them that lives but Christ that lives in them (Galatians 2:20). They will fulfill the promise that Jesus gave saying, *"greater works than these shall he do"* (John 14:12).

I believe that this world is going to see the true ministry of Jesus once again in the earth. Jesus' ministry was only three and a half years. Three and a half years is not a number that speaks of perfection. Seven speaks of perfection. So I, in my humble belief, believe that there is yet a three and a half year ministry of Jesus to take place on the earth. Not by the Lord Jesus but by the many membered son Jesus. For most people we're the only Jesus they'll ever see. Jesus has sat down at the right hand of the Father, He said "It is finished" (John 19:30). So the only way the ministry of Jesus can be finished is through a people.

Now let's look at this controversy. John 10:34 says, *"Jesus answered them, Is it not written in your law, I said, Ye are gods?"* There's been great controversy over this principle as people have taught the "Ye are gods" doctrine. Some people have taken this way out of context and made it seem to say more than it does. To me, the answer is simple: we need to compare spiritual things with spiritual (I Corinthians 2:13), and rightly divide the word of truth (2 Timothy 2:15). Isaiah says every scripture has it's mate (Isaiah 34:16) or as II Peter 1:20 says, *"no prophecy of the scripture is of any private interpretation."* No verse or Scripture can be interpreted alone or by itself. We need to contrast and compare, and rightly divide the Word of God.

Jesus is simply quoting an Old Testament passage, and as we look at the Old Testament passage the New Testament passage becomes ever clearer. The new is the old revealed the old is the new contained. Too many people throw away the old covenant, but He "hath broken down the middle wall of partition" and made both one (Ephesians 2:14). We only have one Bible, one Word of God, and they're not separate. The covenants are separate but the Word is not.

This passage is taken from Psalms 82:6, *"I have said, Ye are gods; and all of you are children of the most High."* So we see here the reference Jesus is referring to. Notice the second part. At the very most, we are children of the most High God, yet, godlike in nature as Adam was before the fall, having dominion, and being able to rule and reign with Christ on the earth. Even with all that, there is only one mediator between God and man, the man Christ Jesus (I Timothy 25). There is only one God, the Most High God, the Lord Jesus Christ. We don't want to be Him nor shall we ever, but we will be like Him. We will be "in His image." He will always be the only Most High God; but He truly desires for us to be like Him and walk in His authority, as well as having the dominion He originally gave Adam.

"Turned Into Another Man"
I Samuel 10:6

Day 306

This is the story of Samuel anointing Saul to be captain over God's people or anointing him king. He says to him in I Samuel 10:6, "*And the Spirit of the Lord will come upon thee, and thou shalt prophesy with them, and shalt be turned into another man.*" Notice in verse 9 as well, "*and it was so, that when he had turned his back to go from Samuel, God gave him another heart.*" I want us to see in the Scriptures today about how God can change our character. God will turn us into another man; God will give us another heart.

Psalms 51:10 says "*Create in me a clean heart, O God.*" God can actually create a brand new heart in you, if He so desires. The Scriptures are full of admonition of people who's hearts have been turned or changed. We find this principally in the revelation of names in the Scripture. (This is found in my book on names if you want to look at it for further study).

Throughout the Scriptures, many people started out with one name, but then their name was changed. The name always reveals the character of someone. What happens when God changes someone's name is that He changes their character. There is always a process that happens between the times that their name changes, but nontheless God wants to turn us into another man. We may start out as one thing, but we are not going to end up the same way. Thank God! Our character needs to be changed, and made like unto His glorious character.

We are striving and believe to go from glory to glory, even as by the Spirit of the Lord, to be changed into that same image. From where we are now to where we will be ultimately, there is a long road, but God is working on changing our character.

Let us consider some of the people in Scripture who were given a name change. What about Abram to Abraham? "Abram" means "*exalted father*" and "Abraham" means "*father of a multitude.*" Abram was caught up in himself being an exalted father, being a high and lofty one. However, ultimately God dealt with him and gave him a Kingdom mentality and changed his perspective to that of a father of a multitude. The emphasis was no longer on him, but on the multitude or God's people.

Let us consider Jacob whose name means "deceiver, surplanter." His name was changed to Israel which means "a prince with God, a champion." Jacob, as we see in Genesis 32, wrestled with the angel and when God asked him who he thought he was Jacob replied he was "deceiver, surplanter." God's response was that he was no longer that man, because he had allowed Him to change him, and that he shall now be called Israel for he has been given power with God and with men.

How about Joseph? Joseph's name means "addition" and was changed to his Egyptian name which means "savior of the then known world." Everything was about Joseph in the beginning; the coat of many colors and who he was. But God dealt with him through many processes and then his name was changed to that of a savior.

God wants to turn our hearts into another man and He wants to give us another heart. Let's allow Him to do that today. Let Him change our character and conform us into His image.

"To The Uttermost"
Hebrews 7:25

DAY 307

The word *"uttermost"* in Greek means "full ended, entire, completion". I don't think that there is any question that it means to the uttermost or that God will go to wherever is needed. It says here in Hebrews 7:25, *"Wherefore he is able also to save them to the uttermost that come unto God by him."*

I want us to consider this word *"uttermost"* today and its revelation in the Scriptures. God's salvation for us is an uttermost salvation; a full-ended, entire, and complete salvation. It has been said that the word "gutter most" can be used; I know that was true in my case. This term is used by those of us who know we came from the gutter, and from the "gutter most" He is able to save us.

It also says in Psalms 2:8 that He has given us the heathen for our inheritance, and the uttermost parts of the earth for our possession. Full-ended, complete, and entire, God has given to us the whole world as an inheritance.

Let's consider Acts 1:8 which says *"Ye shall be witnesses unto me both in Jerusalem, and in all Judaea, and in Samaria, and unto the uttermost part of the earth."* Psalms 2:8 declares that the farthest parts of the earth is given to us, all we have to do is ask Him for them. This is what our God has given us, the uttermost parts of the earth for our possession and to take to them His wonderful glorious gospel.

David's prayer in Psalm 139: 8-10 says, *"If I ascend up into heaven, thou art there: if I make my bed in hell, behold, thou art there. ⁹If I take the wings of the morning, and dwell in the uttermost parts of the sea. ¹⁰Even there shall thy hand lead me, and thy right hand shall hold me."*

To the uttermost He is there and His salvation is to the uttermost. He has given us the uttermost parts of the earth to be His witness and for an inheritance. Our God has a full-ended, entire, and complete salvation for us; complete in every form and fashion. It is said in Matthew 12:42 *"The queen of the south shall rise up in the judgment with this generation, and shall condemn it: for she came from the uttermost parts of the earth to hear the wisdom of Solomon; and, behold, a greater than Solomon is here."*

The uttermost parts of the earth are waiting to hear about our *"uttermost"* salvation. Today let us remember that His salvation is complete; that He is always there, that He is ever present, and that even there His hand will lead us. Thanks be unto God for His uttermost salvation!

"He Thanked God And Took Courage"
Acts 28:15

DAY 308

Oh what a word from the Lord today for you! Paul had been on a long journey sailing for many, many days, and in Acts 28:15 it says, *"And from thence, when the brethren heard of us, they came to meet us as far as Appii forum, and The three taverns: whom when Paul saw, he thanked God, and took courage."* Paul, upon seeing the brethren, took courage.

The Bible says that we are to *"exhort one another daily, while it is called Today"* (Hebrews 3:13). I hope this is what you are doing because it helps our brothers and sisters to take courage in times of great stress and trouble in their lives. All of us get weary and all of us get down. Even Jesus in John 4:6 got weary but He sat down on a well of living water. You and I are called to be a blessing to our brothers and sisters and to encourage them. But sometimes it is unfortunate that we don't have brothers or sisters around us or we are not members of a local church family, which all of us should be. We should all have a pastor and father ministry in our lives.

Paul took courage by simply seeing his brothers and sisters of like precious faith. Let that be so for us, that when our brethren see us, their hearts are gladdened and encouraged. We see this in Isaiah's time, *"they helped everyone his neighbour; and every one said to his brother, Be of good courage"* (Isaiah 41:6).

I pray today that you are exhorting and encouraging your brothers and sisters, blessing them, strengthening them, and helping them. How many times have you needed a word from the Lord? Proverbs 12:25 says, *"a good word maketh it* (our hearts) *glad."* How often have I needed just a simple hand on my shoulder or a kind word from an authority figure or simply a smile from a friend so I could take courage as Paul did?

It is our job to bear the burdens of one another and to meet each other's needs. We are our brother's keeper. God wants us to stay in a place of encouragement. He says in Joshua 1:9, *"Have not I commanded thee? Be strong and of a good courage; be not afraid, neither be thou dismayed: for the Lord thy God is with thee whithersoever thou goest."* Be strong and of a good courage today! It's time for us to rise up now, shake ourselves from our circumstances, and understand that it is *"not by might, nor by power, but by my spirit"* (Zechariah 4:6) that anything is going to get accomplished. We need to take courage and know that the Lord our God is God.

Not only do we have Jesus, our precious Father and the Holy Ghost to help us, but we have our brothers and sisters. Paul took courage when he saw the brethren. I pray today that when someone sees you, they will be heartened and take courage and will be stirred in their spirit to press on even harder. Be a blessing today and help someone. Tell them, "be of good courage."

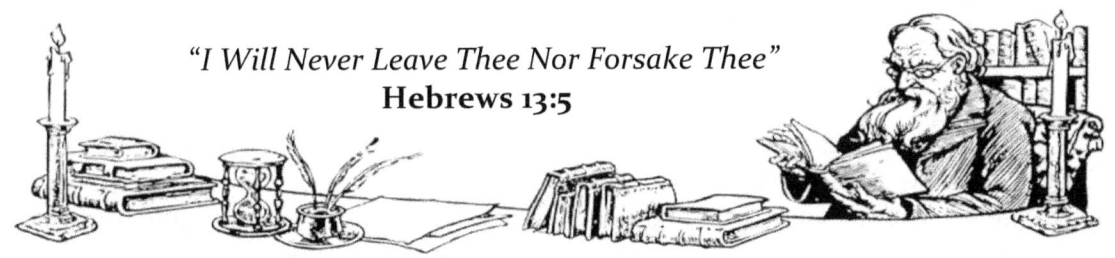

"I Will Never Leave Thee Nor Forsake Thee"
Hebrews 13:5

Day 309

Just the other day in teaching in my Bible class I made an amazing discovery. As I looked into the Greek language of this particular verse, it changed my life! As I read these words, *"I will never leave thee nor forsake thee"* I saw that the actual Greek language reads, *"I will not, I will not, I will not leave thee or forsake thee."* I don't know how more expressive, adamant, or conclusive God could be when it comes to Him never forsaking His people. Oh, what a glorious, wonderful, precious Savior we have! He has blessed us with an eternal salvation and saved us with an everlasting redemption. Bless His holy name! Hear the word of the Lord today! Hear Him say this directly to you, *"I will not, I will not, I will not leave thee nor forsake thee."* What a statement!

In the Greek He says it three times to emphasize to us the utter greatness of His promise and the absolute immutability of what He is saying. We know that the Bible says in Hebrews 6:18 that, *"it is impossible for God to lie"*, and in I Kings 8:56 it says, *"there hath not failed one word of all his good promise."* The Bible is very clear that He will never forsake us.

Let's read the following Scriptures: Joshua 1:5 reads, *"...as I was with Moses, so I will be with thee: I will not fail thee, nor forsake thee."* I Samuel 12:22 says, *"For the LORD will not forsake his people for his great name's sake: because it hath pleased the LORD to make you his people."* The Lord will not forsake His people for His great name's sake. A name in the Scriptures represents the character of that person. So in other words, God is not going to forget us because His character won't allow it!

Paul wrote in II Timothy 2:13 saying, *"If we believe not, yet he abideth faithful: he cannot deny himself."* As a Christian, He lives in you now by the Spirit of God. You've been born by the incorruptible seed of the Word of God and Jesus now lives inside of you. God will never forsake that Jesus inside of you, for He cannot forsake Himself. You see, His name is on the line when it comes to you. In Exodus it says:

> *"⁹And the LORD said unto Moses, I have seen this people, and, behold, it is a stiff-necked people: ¹⁰Now therefore let me alone, that my wrath may wax hot against them, and that I may consume them: and I will make of thee a great nation. ¹¹And Moses besought the LORD his God, and said, LORD, why doth thy wrath wax hot against thy people, which thou hast brought forth out of the land of Egypt with great power, and with a mighty hand? ¹²Wherefore should the Egyptians speak, and say, For mischief did he bring them out, to slay them in the mountains, and to consume them from the face of the earth? Turn from thy fierce wrath, and repent of this evil*

against thy people...the LORD repented of the evil which he thought to do unto his people" (Exodus 32:9-12, 14).

It wasn't as if God was really going to slay them or consume them from the face of the earth. He was testing Moses to see what his response would be. Like Moses, if we have a close relationship with the Lord and His Word, and have spent quality time with Him over the years we will know that He is a true, faithful and a loving God. He learn that His character is impeccable. His integrity is true, and His honesty is without question. He never lies!

He will not forsake His people for His great name's sake. God will not allow His character to be slandered, nor allow His name to be trodden in the mud. But Christians do that when they think that they can cross a line and God will quit on them and say things like, "God brought us out, but He couldn't take us in." This is not true! Here the word of the Lord, right from the Lord's mouth Himself, *"I will not, I will not, I will not leave thee."* I don't know what else the Lord can say.

In John 10:29 He said, *"...no man is able to pluck them out of my Father's hand."* Ecclesiastes 3:14 says, *"I know that, whatsoever God doeth, it shall be for ever: nothing can be put to it, nor any thing taken from it: and God doeth it, that men should fear before him."* You see, when God does something, it is forever. In Psalms 89:34-35 says, *"My covenant will I not break, nor alter the thing that is gone out of my lips. Once have I sworn by my holiness that I will not lie unto David."*

God always finishes what He starts, and His promises never fail. Psalms 138:8 says, *"The LORD will perfect that which concerneth me."* He will do it! So, take courage today. Even though the Christian life can be hard and sometimes our weaknesses and frailties seem to speak louder than anything, one thing is certain and constant and that is the faithfulness of God. He will not, He will not, He will not leave you nor forsake you! Do not listen to religious people; do not listen to the doubters and the naysayers and the Pharisees. You have the Word of God, not the word of men to depend on.

Isaiah 54:10 says, *"For the mountains shall depart, and the hills be removed; but my kindness shall not depart from thee, neither shall the covenant of my peace be removed, saith the LORD that hath mercy on thee."* That's enough for me! It doesn't say "saith any man." But is says, *"Saith the Lord."* So no matter where you find yourself today, remember He will not, He will not, He will not leave you nor forsake you!

"The Heavens Declare His Glory"
Psalms 19:1

DAY 310

Psalms 19:1 says, *"The heavens declare the glory of God; and the firmament sheweth his handywork."* God's glory is the essence of who He is and it shines throughout all the earth. The Bible says in Psalms 97:6, *"The heavens declare his righteousness, and all the people see his glory."* Whether people want to acknowledge it or not is another story. But God's glory is revealed in His handiwork: in the sun, moon and stars. Oh, how glorious our God is! How glorious is the creation that He has made!

My wife and I were recently ministering in Africa and we stood before Victoria Falls, one of the wonders of the world. We beheld the majesty of God! I have stood in many places and have looked and beheld the greatness, the massive awesomeness of God. The earth declares it and the earth reveals it. The Bible says in I Chronicles 16:24, *"Declare his glory among the heathen; his marvelous works among all nations."* The heathen, the nations need to see the glory of God and His marvelous works!

Numbers 14:21 declares, *"But as truly as I live, all the earth shall be filled with the glory of the Lord."* There is coming a day when the whole earth will be filled with the glory of God. Isn't that what the seraphim cried in Isaiah 6:3? It says, *"And one cried unto another, and said, Holy, holy, holy, is the Lord of hosts: the whole earth is full of his glory."* I believe that the earth is full of His glory right now. Many just can't behold it or see it because of religion. Babylon has kept them from seeing it. They may be bound with sin or demons, or just ignorance. But Isaiah 40:5 says, *"And the glory of the Lord shall be revealed, and all flesh shall see it together: for the mouth of the Lord hath spoken it."* God has spoken that the glory of the Lord shall be revealed, not only in nature and creation, but ultimately in a people. Psalms 72:19 says, *"Blessed be his glorious name for ever: and let the whole earth be filled with his glory; Amen, and Amen."* Habakkuk 2:14 also says, *"For the earth shall be filled with the knowledge of the glory of the Lord, as the waters cover the sea."*

There is coming a day when the glory of God will go from one end of the earth to another and no one will be able to gainsay against it. Psalms 102:15 says, *"So the heathen shall fear the name of the Lord, and all the kings of the earth thy glory."* All the kings of the earth are going to have to bow down when they see the glory of God as it is revealed. Verse 16 then says, *"When the Lord shall build up Zion, he shall appear in his glory."* The great thing that is coming is that God is going to appear in His glory and that will be within a people. Isaiah 60:1 echoes this truth, *"Arise, shine; for thy light is come, and the glory of the Lord is risen upon thee."* Not only is His glory declared in the heavens, but His glory will be declared within a people. They shall have His glory and the earth will once again see the glory of God.

"Ask For The Old Paths"
Jeremiah 6:16

DAY 311

In the book of Jeremiah the Bible declares, *"Thus saith the Lord, Stand ye in the ways, and see, and ask for the old paths, where is the good way, and walk therein, and ye shall find rest for your souls"* (Jeremiah 6:16). There are many definitions and names for God's path in the Scriptures. It says in Proverbs 4, *"But the path of the just is as the shining light, that shineth more and more unto the perfect day"* (Proverbs 4:18). This path of the just is to lead us to perfection. Everything we go through walking down this path makes us more and more like Him. Isaiah tells us:

> *"And an highway shall be there, and a way, and it shall be called The way of holiness; the unclean shall not pass over it; but it shall be for those: the wayfaring men, though fools, shall not err therein"* (Isaiah 35:8).

The highway of holiness is for the remnant, those in the body of Christ who are willing to stay morally clean and demon-free. The Bible says in Matthew 7, *"Because strait is the gate, and narrow is the way, which leadeth unto life, and few there be that find it"* (Matthew 7:14). Job 28 declares, *"⁷There is a path which no fowl knoweth, and which the vulture's eye hath not seen: ⁸The lion's whelps have not trodden it, nor the fierce lion passed by it"* (Job 28:7-8). God has a path which no demon knows. It's a narrow way, a highway of holiness that is like a shining light that shines more and more unto the perfect day (Proverbs 4:18). We need to ask for these old paths. I know it's not fashionable today to be one who gives himself to the Word of God and worship and to walk a devoted life of holiness before the Lord. It may not be popular, but it is still the way of the Lord.

In Psalms 16:11, it says, *"Thou wilt shew me the path of life: in thy presence is fulness of joy; at thy right hand there are pleasures for evermore."* This is not a path of the dead, but of the living. On this path, we can find His manifest presence, which will help and encourage us and give us true joy and pleasure. It also says in Psalms 23, *"He restoreth my soul: he leadeth me in the paths of righteousness for his name's sake"* (Psalms 23:3). God's name, or His character, is on the line here. This shows us He will do everything He can to help us become truly righteous.

"Ask for the old paths, where is the good way." Our prayer today should be, as it says in Psalms 17, *"Hold up my goings in thy paths that my footsteps slip not"* (Psalms 17:5). David said in Psalms 25:4, *"Shew me thy ways, O Lord; teach me thy paths."* It says in Ezra 8, *"Then I proclaimed a fast there, at the river of Ahava, that we might afflict ourselves before our God, to seek of him a right way for us, and for our little ones, and for all our substance"* (Ezra 8:21). You and I need to be asking for the old paths, because therein is the good way. It may be old fashioned; it may not be popular. But God is the *"Ancient of days"* (Daniel 7:9), and His paths lead us to the good and right way.

"Awake, O North Wind"
Song of Solomon 4:16

DAY 312

"*Awake, O north wind; and come, thou south; blow upon my garden, that the spices thereof may flow out*" (Song of Solomon 4:16). Today, we are going to look at this north and south wind. However, before we do, it is vital to understand certain keys to the Scripture, because they unlock great and deep spiritual truths to us. North in the Scripture always speaks of judgment. South in the Scripture speaks of prosperity and the blessing of the Lord. So we find here the principle of the dealings of God in our lives as well as the blessing and prosperity of the Lord.

Paul says in Philippians 4:12, "*I know both how to be abased, and I know how to abound.*" Romans 11:22 says, "*Behold therefore the goodness and the severity of God.*" The town of Bethany, which was Jesus' favorite place to go, means; "house of fruitfulness and house of affliction." There is both the right hand and the left hand of God. It says of God in Isaiah 45:7, "*I form the light, and create darkness: I make peace, and create evil.*" These are the ups and downs of the way God deals with us. Song of Solomon 2:6 says, "*His left hand is under my head, and his right hand doth embrace me.*"

God's dealings come in this fashion. He brings the north wind. He will work in our lives with pressure, tribulation, affliction, trouble and temptation. He brings judgment into his garden, which is the bride of Christ. He says, "*Awake, O north wind.*" Then He says, "*Come, thou south.*" The south always represents blessing, prosperity and the goodness of the Lord.

So we find here in this passage that God is calling for both the north and the south wind in the bride's life. At the end Song of Solomon 4:16 says, "*Let my beloved come into his garden, and eat his pleasant fruits.*" If our Beloved is going to come into our garden and find pleasant fruit, find fruitfulness, find perfection, and find maturity, then you and I are going to have to understand that God Himself is going to call for the north and the south wind to blow upon His garden.

The reason He does this is so that the "*spices thereof may flow out.*" As we endure the chastening of the Lord, as we endure the dealings of God, as we go through the pressures of life, God then immediately brings the south wind. He doesn't leave us in a bad place for long. As Hosea 6:1 says, "*Come, and let us return unto the LORD: for he hath torn, and he will heal us; he hath smitten, and he will bind us up.*" Do you see the principle? He tears and then He heals. He smites and then He binds us up.

"*And we know that all things work together for good to them that love God, to them who are the called according to his purpose*" (Romans 8:28). Nothing happens to us that God has not ordained or called for in our lives. He's calling for the north wind and the south wind. We must experience both, because without it, the spices, the fruits of the Spirit, the characteristics of God, the image of Christ Jesus and the nature of our Lord can never flow out of our lives. So today, let God open up your eyes to this principle that He is working in every one of us.

"The Noise Of His Tabernacle"
Job 36:29

DAY 313

"Also can any understand the spreadings of the clouds, or the noise of his tabernacle?" This is a tremendous passage about what should be going on in every local church and every tabernacle where worshipping the Lord takes place. There should be a noise in His tabernacle. Another translation reads, "how He thunders from his dwelling place."

I don't know what kind of worship you have at your church or what worship you have in your own personal life, but my Bible tells me in Psalms 66:8, *"Make the voice of his praise to be heard."* It also says in Psalms 118:15, *"The voice of rejoicing and salvation is in the tabernacles of the righteous."* In Psalms 100:1 it tells us, *"Make a joyful noise unto the Lord, all ye lands."* Then in verse 4 it reads, *"Enter into his gates with thanksgiving and into his courts with praise."* There should be a noise coming out of the house of God. The Bible says in Joel 3:16, *"The Lord also shall roar out of Zion."*

The Philistines in I Samuel 4:6, when they heard that the ark had come into the camp, said, *"What meaneth the noise of this great shout in the camp of the Hebrews? And they understood that the ark of the Lord had come into the camp."* They understood the noise because the ark of God represents the manifest presence of God. Therefore, it brought forth a shout. In Numbers 23:21, it says, *"the shout of a king is among them."* Too many people live under a Babylonish edict that says, God gets nervous when we shout or lead worship extravagantly. You know God is moving in a place when you hear noise coming from His house.

Remember the elder brother, in Luke 15:25, *"as he came and drew nigh to the house* (his father's house), *he heard musick and dancing."* This is what should be indicative of every local church. Even in our own personal life, we should be making His praise to be heard. Why? Because Psalms 48:10 says, *"According to thy name, O God, so is thy praise unto the ends of the earth."* He is certainly worthy of all our praise and worship. There ought to be a noise coming from every tabernacle.

The word noise in Job 36:29 means, "a crashing or loud clamor." It also means "crying, shouting, stir." It comes from a root word that means "a tempest; by implication, devastation: desolate (-ion), destroy, destruction, storm, waste ness." This is what should be coming out of the house of God; a mighty sound of praise and worship. Because in Psalms 29:9, *"In his temple doth every one speak of his glory."* Are you speaking of His glory? Are you making the voice of His praise to be heard? Can the prisoners hear you, like in Acts 16 with Paul and Silas in the inner prison?

Isaiah 68:6 says, *"A voice of noise from the city, a voice from the temple, a voice of the Lord that rendereth recompence to his enemies."* Then in Ezra 3:11-13 it says:

> *"And all the people shouted with a great shout, when they praised the Lord, because the foundation of the house of the Lord was laid. But many of the priests and Levites and chief of fathers, who were ancient men, that had seen*

the first house, when the foundation of this house was laid before their eyes, wept with a loud voice; and many shouted aloud for joy: so that the people could not discern the noise of the shout of joy from the noise of the weeping of the people: for the people shouted with a loud shout, and the noise was heard afar off."

In Mark 2:1 Jesus *"entered into Capernaum after some days; and it was noised that he was in the house."* Is there noise coming out of your house? It should be the noise of His tabernacle. So, today in your daily worship *"make the voice of his praise to be heard."*

"God's Place For Us"
II Samuel 7:10

God says here in II Samuel 7:10, *"Moreover I will appoint a place for my people Israel, and will plant them, that they may dwell in a place of their own, and move no more; neither shall the children of wickedness afflict them any more, as beforetime."*

DAY 314

This is a tremendous Scripture about our place in God. Men do not appoint our place in God. We do not appoint our place. Only God appoints our place. Another translation of this Scripture reads, *"And I will provide a place for my people Israel and I will plant them so that they can have a home of their own and no longer be disturbed. Wicked people will not oppress them anymore as they did at the beginning. I will give them rest from their enemies."* What a promise when we are in our place!

I believe God has appointed a place, a local church for every one of us. The word *"place"* in Hebrew means, "a standing spot, locality, an open place" and it comes from a root word that means "to abide, to accomplish, to be clear." The word *"plant"* means "to strike as with a hammer, to fix or to fasten." God wants to fix and fasten us in a local church, a standing spot, a locality that is to be our place. He goes on to say, *"I will appoint that place."* God appoints our place, not others. As a confirming Scripture, I Corinthians 12:18 says, *"But now hath God set the members every one of them in the body, as it hath pleased him."*

In Mark 6:39-40, *"³⁹And he commanded them to make all sit down by companies upon the green grass. ⁴⁰And they sat down in ranks, by hundreds, and by fifties."* The word *"companies"* means "ranks." I believe that this is a type of local churches that God has placed. Numbers 22:17 says of the children of Israel *"as they encamp, so shall they set forward, every man in his place by their standards."* God has a place for His people. Being in the place of God brings the protection of God, the peace of God, deliverance from our enemies, and gives us a place of our own. Haggai 2:9 says, *"And in this place will I give peace, saith the Lord of hosts."* Proverbs 15:3 states, *"The eyes of the Lord are in every place, beholding the evil and the good."* Isaiah 60:13 says, *"I will make the place of my feet glorious."*

Once again, looking back into II Samuel 7:10, God will plant us, fix us, fasten us down like a hammer does to a nail, *"That they may dwell in a place of their own."* We can have our own place, not somebody else's. Then He says that we are to, *"move no more."* We are not to be tossed to and fro, we're not to put the assembly of ourselves together as the manner of some do, but we are to abide in God's place. Then He said, *"Neither shall the children of wickedness afflict them any more."*

We can rest assured that when we are in God's place, we will come forth, prosper there and no longer live in need. Neither shall the children of wickedness, be they human, spirits or demons, neither shall they touch or harm us anymore. Why not? It is because we are in God's place. When you're in that place, you live in God's peace. He that is planted in the House of the Lord God *"shall flourish in the courts of our God"* (Psalms 92:13). I encourage you today to be a part of a local church. Be planted in the House of the Lord God and so shall you flourish.

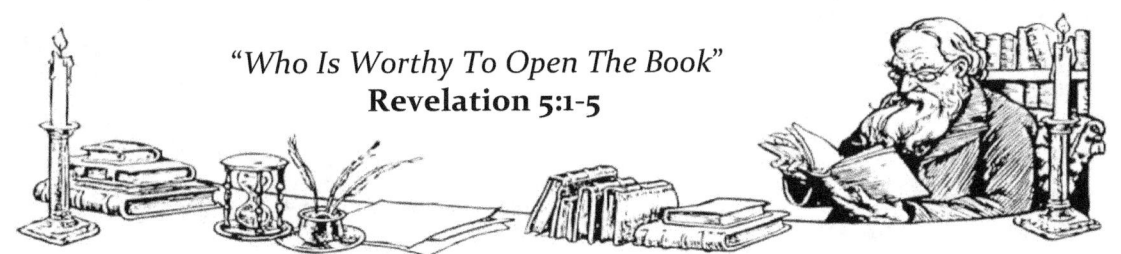

"Who Is Worthy To Open The Book"
Revelation 5:1-5

"And I saw in the right hand of him that sat on the throne a book written within and on the backside, sealed with seven seals" (Revelation 5:1). I believe that this book is the word of God. It's sealed, but as Daniel prophesied in the last days the books will be open (Daniel 7:10). We also see in Revelation 10 a messenger with an open book in his hand. It says in I Samuel 3:1, *"there was no open vision."* We need to understand that revelation is the rock that the church is built on. *"Flesh and blood hath not revealed it unto thee, but my Father which is in heaven"* (Matthew 16:17). God is going to open the book, but He has to do it first through a person, the Lord Jesus Christ. As we receive Him and give ourselves to the Word revelation will begin to flow in our lives as well.

"And I saw a strong angel proclaiming with a loud voice, Who is worthy to open the book, and to loose the seals thereof?" (Revelation 5:2). In other words, who is able to loose these hidden truths and revelations waiting from the foundation of earth? *"And no man in heaven, nor in earth, neither under the earth, was able to open the book, neither to look thereon"* (Revelation 5:3). No human being, no preacher, no teacher, no pastor, no minister, no prophet can do it. It takes revelation. It takes the Lord Jesus, the great door opener, to do this for us.

In verse 4 John says, *"And I wept much."* In the Greek this means he was pouring out his heart. He was weeping uncontrollably when he saw that the book, the Holy Bible, the Word of God, was not able to be loosed and the seals taken off. How he wept! How I weep today because so many people do not understand the Scriptures and don't have a revelation of what God is trying to do. Their ignorance is appalling. Even so, there it is waiting for us. Jesus has loosed the seals. Revelation is available if we simply would bow and seek the Lord, and *"Study to shew thyself approved unto God, a workman that needeth not to be ashamed, rightly dividing the word of truth"* (II Timothy 2:15). He admonished us in I Peter 3:15 to be ready to give an answer to all that ask us of the hope that lies within us. We cannot do this if we don't have a foundation. Revelation 5:3-4 says:

> *"And no man in heaven, nor in earth, neither under the earth, was able to open the book, neither to look thereon.*
> *⁴ And I wept much, because no man was found worthy to open and to read the book, neither to look thereon."*

How sad this is, how terrible it would be. Although next we see, *"And one of the elders saith unto me, Weep not: behold, the Lion of the tribe of Juda, the Root of David, hath prevailed to open the book, and to loose the seven seals thereof"* (Revelation 5:5). The Lion of the tribe of Judah, the Root of David, Jesus Christ our Lord has prevailed. The book is open, and He's loosed the seven seals thereof. Seven represents the number of perfection. Knowing the Word of God completely is offered to us now, because of what the Lord Jesus has done. Jesus has opened the book and we no longer need to weep. We now need to give ourselves to the Word. Dedicate yourself today, like the noble Bereans who searched the Scriptures daily to see if these things were so (Acts 17:10-11).

"Honour All Men"
I Peter 2:17

DAY 316

One of the great truths found in Scripture that is marvelous is that we should love and honor all men. *"God is no respecter of persons"*, Acts 10:34 says, and He loves everybody. Man was created in the image and likeness of God. This is all men, not just Christians. And all men are due respect and honor no matter what color, gender, or social strata they are. The greatest plague on humanity has been prejudice and racism. Men have enslaved one another for years and have sought to be dominant over one another showing a great lack of mercy and common care for their fellow humanity. Peter here tells us that this is contrary to the will of God as it says, *"Honour all men."* Some other translations read:

> *"Show respect for all men"*
> *"Treat everyone you meet with dignity"*
> *"Show proper respect to everyone"*
> *"Pay honor to all"*
> *"Bow properly to everyone"*
> *"Be respectful to all"*

How hard is it really to honor all men? If we realize that we are who we are by the grace of God and that God created us and our neighbor the same, there should be in us a willingness to love and respect everyone. The Bible says, *"For God so loved the world, that he gave his only begotten Son"* (John 3:16). In another place it says, *"while we were yet sinners, Christ died for us"* (Romans 5:8). So there is no reason for any Christian or person to hate or dislike the world. We all were once part of the world ourselves and we are now free from the demons and things of the world that controlled us, only by the grace of God.

Christ has dignified humanity by becoming human. Therefore we should honor common humanity even to the humblest person because of His example. We as Christians must set the example by breaking down all the barriers that divide us as people, be it race, creed, gender, social or political barriers. We are the ones that set this example.

Proverbs 24:23 says, *"These things also belong to the wise. It is not good to have respect of persons in judgment."* Deuteronomy 16:20 says, *"That which is altogether just shalt thou follow, that thou mayest live."* When Peter had that great revelation to go to the Gentiles, he opened his mouth and said in Acts 10:34-35:

> *"³⁴Then Peter opened his mouth, and said, Of a truth I perceive that God is no respecter of persons: ³⁵But in every nation he that feareth him, and worketh righteousness, is accepted with him."* (Acts 10:34-35)

What a glorious truth! Also in verse 28, Peter says, "*God hath shewed me that I should not call any man common or unclean.*" Wouldn't the world be a different place if this were a reality in all our lives?!

Leviticus 19:18 says, "*Thou shalt love thy neighbour as thyself.*" You might ask, "How can we do this?" Well, Romans 5:5 tells us "*because the love of God is shed abroad in our hearts by the Holy Ghost which is given unto us.*" God's love has been shown to us. God expects therefore that we show His love to others.

Romans 13:10 says, "*Love worketh no ill to his neighbour: therefore love is the fulfilling of the law.*" Galatians 5:14 tells us, "*For all the law is fulfilled in one word, even in this; Thou shalt love thy neighbour as thyself.*" If only we could do this, what a great thing that would be.

To honor someone is to treat him properly as a human being to give him his due. This is what God is requiring of us. It says in Romans 13:7-8:

> "*⁷Render therefore to all their dues: tribute to whom tribute is due; custom to whom custom; fear to whom fear; honour to whom honour. ⁸Owe no man any thing, but to love one another: for he that loveth another hath fulfilled the law.*"

So many people despise and reject their fellow humans because of their color, race, gender, or social status. Proverbs 17:5 says, "*Whoso mocketh the poor reproacheth his Maker.*" God loves everyone. God created everyone. Therefore every human being deserves respect, dignity, and honor. And we as believers must show the way. We must shine as lights in the midst of a crooked and perverse generation (Philippians 2:15). You and I show the love of God and prove we are true Christians by honoring all men, showing respect, and by giving to everyone his proper dignity. Oh, how the world would change if every one of us simply abided by, "*thou shalt love thy neighbor as thyself.*"

Each person loves himself. Human nature is survival of the strongest. We take care of ourselves before anybody else. But if we all honored one another, wars would cease, slavery would cease, prejudice would cease, and there would be harmony in the earth.

In the original earth, there was that harmony until man fell because of pride. God is trying to restore that now through His believers. We must set an example. Love everyone. Honor all men so that one day when we stand before the Lord, we can hear Him say to us, "Well done thou good and faithful servant. You've been an example of My character and My goodness in the earth."

Remember at that great time when the angels came to announce the birth of Jesus they said "*Glory to God in the highest, and on earth peace, good will toward men*" (Luke 2:14). If God has good will toward every man, you and I should have the same and treat others accordingly. May God help us from this day forward to show respect to give them their due, and honor all men.

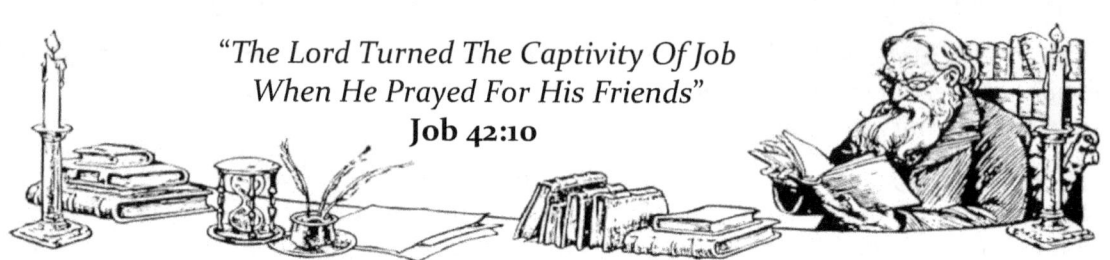

"The Lord Turned The Captivity Of Job When He Prayed For His Friends"
Job 42:10

DAY 317

The book of Job is the oldest book in the Bible. It was the earliest one ever found. We don't know much about Job but I have learned, having now studied the Scriptures for over forty years, that Job is one of the greatest patriarchs of the Scriptures. Job 42 tells us, "*And the Lord turned the captivity of Job, when he prayed for his friends*" (Job 42:10). In the Hebrew this reads, "*And the Lord reversed the fortunes of Job.*" Do you need a reversal of fortune? Do you need your captivity turned? Well, begin to forgive and release people.

The Bible says that we are in the hands of the tormentors if we don't forgive (Matthew 18:34-35). God Himself called these friends "*miserable comforters*" (Job 16:2). They were men that "*darkeneth counsel by words without knowledge*" (Job 38:2). They were not men of God; they came to accuse and frustrate Job. Job became very angry and self-righteous with them, but God required that Job forgive them and pray for them. He said to them, "*my servant Job shall pray for you: for him will I accept*" (Job 42:8). In other words, He's saying, "I'm not going to forgive you until Job prays for you and forgives you." What power we hold without even realizing it. John 20:23 tells us, "*Whose soever sins ye remit, they are remitted unto them; and whose soever sins ye retain, they are retained.*" If we would start walking in the authority that God has given us, there would be a great display of the power and glory of God. It all begins by simply praying for our friends.

Remember the story of David in II Samuel 15:1-14, when his son Absalom took over his kingdom and he had to flee. Shimei, a servant of Saul, came cursing David and calling him a bloody man (II Samuel 16:5-7). David's faithful man Abishai said, "*Why should this dead dog curse my lord the king? let me go over, I pray thee, and take off his head*" (II Samuel 16:9). But David said, "*Let him alone, and let him curse; for the Lord hath bidden him. ¹²It may be that the Lord will look on mine affliction, and that the Lord will requite me good for his cursing this day*" (II Samuel 16:11-12). Because David allowed Shimei to curse, that day David was restored to his kingdom.

Perhaps you and I are not walking in the Kingdom of God like we should, because we haven't allowed cursing to take place. We've allowed our miserable comforters to get under our skin and we haven't prayed for them. Jesus said, "*Pray for them which despitefully use you*" (Luke 6:28). This is the calling of God. Jesus Himself said on the cross, "*Father, forgive them; for they know not what they do*" (Luke 23:34). How ironic. It seems so unnatural to pray for people who have hurt, disturbed, or harmed you in some way. But yet, this is showing the love and greatness of our God. When we do this, God moves mightily. Stephen, while being stoned, said, "*Lord, lay not this sin to their charge*" (Acts 7:60). When he said this, he fell asleep, and I believe he didn't feel those stones hitting him. The Lord will turn our captivity when we simply forgive and pray for our friends. They need for us to do it, and we need to do it for God's blessing's sake.

"The Lord Thy God In The Midst"
Zephaniah 3:16-17

Here in this prophetic Scripture, we read:

"In that day it shall be said to Jerusalem, Fear thou not: and to Zion, Let not thine hands be slack. ¹⁷The Lord thy God in the midst of thee is mighty; he will save, he will rejoice over thee with joy; he will rest in his love, he will joy over thee with singing" (Zephaniah 3:16-17).

What a tremendous passage of scripture. Remember now, that Israel is a spiritual term and that we are now spiritual Israel. So when the Old Testament speaks of Zion and Jerusalem, Jerusalem speaks of us and Zion speaks of the church of the living God, the church of the first born. This is speaking to us now just as it did to the natural Israel then in the Old Testament times, but even more so to us, because this is a prophecy of the end times.

What day is this verse referring to? I believe it is speaking of the day of the Lord. *"It shall be said to Jerusalem, Fear thou not."* Fear is going to vanish, because God is going to arise in an overcoming army that no longer is going to be overcome and overtaken by the things that have tormented them. We are called to be that army that will not fear any longer.

"And to Zion, Let not thine hands be slack." Zion, that great worshipping and overcoming group of people that enthrone the Lord with their worship, will never see their hands slack or not doing the works of the Lord. We will enter in to the greater things just as Jesus promised in John 14:12, *"Greater works than these shall he do; because I go unto my Father."* Hands are related to works in the Scriptures.

Then in Zephaniah 3 verse 17, He says, *"The Lord thy God in the midst of thee."* Jesus said in Matthew 18:20, *"For where two or three are gathered together in my name, there am I in the midst of them."* We know that there's the omnipresence of God and then there's the manifest presence of God. This here speaks of His manifest presence. The Lord our God is in the midst of us, radiating His glory and presence. How many times have you and I been in a time of worship when the presence and the glory of God have come down so powerfully and so strongly, that the only thing we could say was, "The Lord thy God in the midst of us is mighty"? Because His might, power and awesomeness is revealed in His glory.

It goes on to say in verse 17, *"He will save."* You and I will never need to fear about losing our salvation, because He has not only once been our Savior, but He continues to save us. It assures us in Romans 5:10, *"Much more, being reconciled, we shall be saved by his life."* Because He's ever living to make intercession for us, you and I can call on Him to save us every day. No matter what religion tells us, He's not just our Savior once, He's our Savior forever.

Verse 17 continues on saying, *"He will rejoice over thee with joy."* The Lord rejoices over His people. His portion is His people. It brings Him great joy when He sees us growing, maturing and overcoming. Then, *"He will rest in his love."* Oh, what a place of rest and intimacy this will be for God with His people, in that place where He loves us and we love Him, where we say just as in Song of Solomon 7:10, *"I am my beloved's, and his desire is toward me."* God wants to rest in His love and be so intimate with us.

It finally ends in verse 17 saying, *"He will joy over thee with singing."* Can you believe that? Our precious God sings and He sings over us, just like a mother sings over her child to help him go to sleep at night. If you listen quietly and distinctly, you'll hear God singing over you songs of joy, peace, love and mercy. *"The Lord thy God in the midst of thee"* is a tremendous revelation. Believe it today.

"A Stone's Throw"
Luke 22:41

DAY 319

This is the story of Jesus in the garden of Gethsemane, how He led His disciples into the garden of Gethsemane and told them to abide in a certain place. In Luke 22:41 it says, *"And he was withdrawn from them about a stone's cast, and kneeled down, and prayed."* In Matthew 26:39, it says that Jesus *"went a little further."* This brings to us the principle of going just a little bit further than everybody else. I believe the overcomers, the bride, will proceed further in God than the rest of the body of Christ.

Remember Mark 4:20 says, *"Some thirtyfold, some, sixty and some an hundred."* We make the choice where we will be. Matthew 20:16 says, *"many be called, but few chosen."* In the Greek, it reads, "few choose". It is our choice for how far we go in God. We can be like the other disciples at the last supper or like John who leaned on Jesus' breast. Therefore, twice in the Scriptures we find that John was called the disciple whom Jesus loved. Because John pressed further, he was given the revelation of Jesus.

In the book of Ezekiel, chapter 47: 1-5, we read about his vision of the waters flowing out from under the threshold of the house, that there were waters up to the ankles, waters up to the knees, waters up to the loins, and finally it speaks of waters to swim in. When we have waters to the ankle, we still have control of our situation. Waters to our knees signify that even though we are being caused to bow the knee and be broken, we still have control. Even in waters to the loins we still have the ability to guide and direct ourselves, even though the waters (the Holy Ghost) are supposed to be delivering us. The loins speak of the loins of our mind as well as the loins of our physical body (sexual perversion). But God ultimately wants us to go further and be in waters to swim in. We decide how far we are going to go.

This is also seen in the story of the ten lepers in Luke 17:17. Only one leper, the Samaritan, returned to give glory to God. Jesus asked him, *"but where are the nine?"* I believe that question is still being asked today. Just like when the Lord asked Adam, *"Where art thou?"* (Genesis 3:9). In Genesis 22, we find the story of Abraham taking his son Isaac up to the mountain to sacrifice. Abraham says in Genesis 22:5, *"Abide ye here with the ass; and I and the lad will go yonder and worship."* The young men were not allowed to go up the mountain. They were to abide there. Only Abraham and Isaac went up. Are you willing to go beyond what everybody else is doing?

In Luke 14:10, speaking of the wedding and how we should not boastfully sit up at the front, Jesus says, *"Friend, go up higher."* I say to you today, *"Friend, go up higher."* When John's disciples came to Jesus in John 1:38, they asked Him, *"Rabbi, where dwellest thou?"* If you really want to know where He abides, you will find Him at the shepherds' tents (Song of Solomon 1:8). Well, Jesus answered John's disciples by saying in John 1:39 *"Come and see."* Are you willing to come and see? Are willing to go from glory to glory, strength to strength and faith to faith? Are you willing to be emptied from vessel to vessel until ultimately you reach the height, where deep is calling unto deep (Psalms 42:7). This is where the sound of the Lord is heard in the most holy place. I pray, today, that you will go a stone's throw further.

"What Seek Ye?"
John 13:8

Day 320

Today, we begin in John 1:38: *"Then Jesus turned, and saw them following, and saith unto them, What seek ye?"* Jesus did not say who seek ye, but what seek ye? In other words, He is saying, "what is it in Me ye seek?" This opens up a wide door of all kinds of things that we could explore. There is so much in Jesus worth seeking. But let me ask you today, *"What seek ye?"*

Jesus said in another place, *"What went ye out for to see?"* (Matthew 11:8). What is the reason we are seeking Him? What is the reason we come out to see Him. Remember that the Greeks in John 12:21 said: *"Sir, that we would see Jesus."* Zacchaeus climbed that sycamore tree because he wanted to see Jesus, the real Jesus. That is what brought me into the Kingdom of God as a fifteen year old teenager. I wanted to see the real Jesus; not the religious Jesus, not the Hollywood Jesus, not my mother's, or my grandmother's Jesus. I wanted to see and get to know the real Jesus myself.

The Bible says in Isaiah 55:6-7, *"Seek ye the Lord while he may be found, call ye upon him while he is near". Let the wicked forsake his way and the unrighteous man his thoughts: and let us return unto the Lord".* What seek ye? Ask yourself today, what is it that you seek from the Lord?

David admonishes us in I Chronicles 16:11 *"Seek the Lord and His strength, seek His face continually."* We could be seeking Him for strength, we could be seeking Him for answers, we could be seeking Him for provision, for miracles, or for healings. But, like Zacchaeus in Luke 19, I wonder if our main priority should be to really know Him. Jesus tells us in Luke 11:9 to *"seek and ye we will find."* If you and I will just seek Him, yearn after Him, and seek to know the real Jesus, we will find the real Jesus. We should not live in another man's revelation of Jesus, but have our own personal revelation of Him. This can only come if we spend time in the presence of God, sitting there like Mary at His feet, hearing His Word, worshipping Him, and having intimacy with Him.

Hosea 10:12 says, *"sow to yourselves in righteousness, reap in mercy; break up your fallow ground: for it is time to seek the Lord, till he come and rain righteousness upon you"* Are you ready? Is it not the time to break up that fallow ground in your life, the hard places, and the things that are keeping you from Him? Seek ye the Lord.

Jesus said in Matthew 6:33, *"But rather seek ye the kingdom of God; and all these things shall be added unto you."* It seems that all things stand or fall on whether or not we seek the Lord. But what are we seeking. *"What seek ye"* Jesus is asking? These disciples in John 1:38 wanted to know *"Rabbi, where dwellest thou?"* And the Lord's answer to them in John 1:39 was *"Come and see."* If you want to know where the Lord's dwelling then you have to go after Him. You have to run after Him and seek Him with all your heart.

"Let The Dead Bury Their Dead"
Luke 9:60

DAY 321

Today, we want to consider this principle that Jesus mentions in here Luke, *"And he said unto another, Follow me. But he said, Lord, suffer me first to go and bury my father. ⁶⁰Jesus said unto him, Let the dead bury their dead: but go thou and preach the kingdom of God"* (Luke 9:59-60). We have to ask ourselves, "What is the most important thing that God requires of us?" Here Jesus considers going and preaching the Kingdom of God to be preeminent.

I like what Elisha did when Elijah came to him and threw his mantle on him. He went and burned all the objects of his employment, said goodbye to his family, and left. He then went after Elijah and ministered unto him. For you and me, we need to let the dead bury their dead. Some other translations of this verse read:

> *"Jesus refused. 'First things first. Your business is life, not death. And life is urgent: Announce God's kingdom!'"*
> *"Let the spiritually dead bury their own dead."*

We need to understand that there are some people who just do not respond to the Lord, the things of God, or to the Kingdom of God. The Bible says, *"The dead praise not the Lord, neither any that go down into silence"* (Psalms 115:17). Many times, that may be those of our own family. Remember that Jesus said in Mark 3:

> *"Who is my mother, or my brethren? ³⁴And he looked round about on them which sat about him, and said, Behold my mother and my brethren! ³⁵For whosoever shall do the will of God, the same is my brother, and my sister, and mother"* (Mark 3:33-35).

Luke 14:26 says, *"If any man come to me, and hate not his father, and mother, and wife, and children, and brethren, and sisters, yea, and his own life also, he cannot be my disciple."* This doesn't mean we should hate our family, but the word "hate" here simply means "to love less." Our families cannot control our lives. He doesn't want spiritually dead people, who have no desire for Him, to hinder us.

You and I need to understand that not everybody wants the Lord like we do and not everyone responds to the glory or the presence of God. It says in Titus, *"A man that is an heretick after the first and second admonition reject"* (Titus 3:10). So, we have to decide what is most important for us. It should be the Lord Jesus and His kingdom. We cannot control what other people do even though we love them and care for them. Think about how God the Father feels. He *"gave his only begotten Son, that whosoever believeth in him should not perish, but have everlasting life"* (John 3:16). He's done everything He can do. What more can we do? We can share the gospel with them and love them, but we can't let them hinder us. So, today, make up your mind and settle it in your spirit. Let the dead bury their dead; let's go announce the Kingdom of God!

"Cares Of This Life"
Luke 21:34

DAY 322

"*³⁴And take heed to yourselves, lest at any time your hearts be overcharged with surfeiting* (or gluttony) *and drunkenness, and cares of this life, and so that day come upon you unawares. ³⁵For as a snare shall it come on all them that dwell on the face of the whole earth.*" (Luke 21:34-35)

One of the greatest problems Christians have is the word "care." The Bible says to "*Cast thy burden upon the Lord, and he shall sustain thee: he shall never suffer the righteous to be moved*" (Psalms 55:22). God wants us to cast all our cares on Him. I Peter 5:7 says, "*Casting all your care upon him; for he careth for you.*" Care is a tricky subject, because there's good care and then there's bad care.

Remember in Luke 10 when Martha was running around trying to fix a meal for Jesus, while Mary sat at His feet and heard His word. Jesus said, "Martha, Martha..." Why did He say that? Because she got mad at Mary and got frustrated because she was sitting down and not working. Then He said, "*thou art careful and troubled about many things*" (Luke 10:41). The word in the Greek means she was "distracted with care." That's what care will do to us, distract us from the things that are important. Even good care will do this. Martha wasn't really being evil, but it was a good care that was taken too far. That's why we need to "*take heed to yourselves, lest at any time your hearts be overcharged*" (Luke 21:34), because the enemy wants to overcharge our hearts.

Paul is pretty clear when it says, "*be careful for nothing; but in every thing by prayer and supplication with thanksgiving let your requests be made known unto God.*" (Philippians 4:6) Once again the Bible is absolute and emphatic. Nothing. We're supposed to cast our care upon Him, and not be careful for anything. This almost seems ridiculous. Most people would say, "Oh come on, we have to care. It's only natural that we care." Well, all I can tell them is that the cares of this world are seeking to destroy us, destroy the work of God, and destroy the Word of God in your life. Jesus said in Mark 4:19, "*the cares of this world, and the deceitfulness of riches, and the lusts of other things entering in, choke the word, and it becometh unfruitful.*" You see this is the desire of care; it wants to choke the word in our lives so that it becomes unfruitful.

Are you distracted with care? Are you overcharged with some concern or anxiety? You're to be anxious with nothing. You're to be overcharged with nothing. Our God is able to provide, help, and to sustain you. We've seen many times how "*he satisfieth the longing soul*" (Psalms 107:9). So why should you care? The Lord is on your side. The Lord is your helper. There is no need to be distracted with care from the calling of God and from the work of God. Far too many people allow care, even good care, to cause the Word of God in them to be choked, and it becomes unfruitful when it was so unnecessary. Today, cast all your care upon Him. He really does care for you.

"I Flee From The Face Of My Mistress Sarai"
Genesis 16:8

DAY 323

This is a story found in the Scripture about Hagar, who became a wife to Abram, because Abraham and Sarah could not wait for the promise of God and decided that they knew better than God in how to fulfill His promise. So, Hagar became his wife and bore him a son named Ishmael. And when she had conceived the child, Sarah despised her and began to torment this young lady. The Bible says in Genesis 16:6 that *"when Sarai dealt hardly with her, she fled from her face."*

Hagar did not do anything wrong. What happened here was Hagar bore the brunt of somebody else's mistake. I think in so many of our lives, others have made mistakes and we are living out the judgment of it. We blame and condemn ourselves, and our lives, many times, are burdened with all kinds of hardship because of what somebody else did, not what we have done.

The word of the Lord to you today is that you are not a mistake. You didn't do anything wrong. Somebody else made the mistake, and you happened to be the one that was punished for what they did. God is not angry with you or holding it against you. It was not your fault. Continuing in Genesis 16:

> "...⁷*the angel of the Lord found her by a fountain of water in the wilderness...*⁸*And he said, Hagar, Sarai's maid, whence camest thou? and whither wilt thou go? And she said, I flee from the face of my mistress Sarai*" (Genesis 16:7-8).

In other words, the Lord asks Hagar, "Where have you come from and where will you go?" This question is very intriguing. The principle here for us is we cannot proceed in life or go anywhere until we've dealt with where we've come from. Ecclesiastes 3:15 tells us, *"God requireth that which is past."* For many people, their past rules their future as well as their present life. And in many cases, this destroys their future. Too many of us think that we're a mistake and we live lives unloved, uncared for, insecure, feeling inferior and not good enough because of what somebody else has done.

Please hear Jesus today. You are not a mistake. You were *"fearfully and wonderfully made"* (Psalm 139:14). God knew you before you were in the womb and He has a plan, a great and mighty plan for your life. He even had a great plan for Ishmael. Ishmael's coming into being was wrong. But Ishmael was not the reason for that happening; he was the result.

If this is the word of the Lord for your life, right now, why don't you go back and make amends and make peace with your past. We don't want to be like Lot's wife (Luke 17:32). When she looked back, she became a pillar of salt (Genesis 19:26). In other words, she was frozen in the past and preserved forever in a position of looking back. She allowed her past to keep her dead and never going on in God. Likewise, we must deal with our past, the unfortunate situations of our childhood, our upbringing, our parents and our families, etc., so we don't find ourselves always looking back living in the past.

I, myself, suffered greatly with a family that was broken, full of hardship, poverty, abuse, you name it. I could not go anywhere until I decided I was not a mistake. Too many times in my life, people have told me I was nothing, that I was a mistake, and would amount to nothing. Life did not hold a lot of promise for me. But the day I met Jesus Christ as my Savior and was washed in His precious blood, everything changed. God then began to require of me to deal with my past, because I could never go on until I dealt with it.

As Psalms 139:15 says, *"My substance was not hid from thee, when I was made in secret, and curiously wrought in the lowest parts of the earth."* I had to realize that He was there for me, and He knew me when I was in my mother's womb. God was my Father. God and His people are now my family. Jesus said, *"Behold my mother and my brethren,"* as he pointed to His disciples when His mother and brothers tried to interrupt Him in a meeting (Mark 3:31-35).

I had to realize I was not a mistake. God had created me and I was created for His pleasure (Revelation 4:11). I was not somebody else's mistake. And all that happened to me in my early childhood, all the abuse and violence and perversion I had to fight my way through, was not the result of anything I had done, but the result of mistakes others had made. So I decided by the grace of God not to live any longer under the torment of somebody else's mistake in the past.

In verse 9-10, the angel then said to Hagar, *"9Return to thy mistress, and submit thyself under her hands...10I will multiply thy seed exceedingly."* God will bless you and prosper you, if you just go back, and once and for all deal with your past. You are not a mistake. You are simply the product of somebody else's mistake. Let God redeem you today, restore you, and give you a great hope and expectation for the future. You are not a mistake. You are God's child. You're the apple of His eye and He loves you intensely.

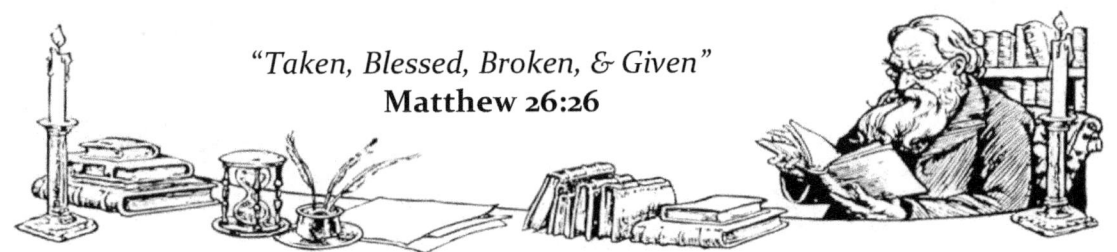

"Taken, Blessed, Broken, & Given"
Matthew 26:26

DAY 324

Matthew 26:26 says, *"And as they were eating, Jesus took bread, and blessed it, and brake it, and gave it to the disciples."* In this wonderful passage of scripture we find one of the greatest definitions of our walk with God, the Lord bringing us in, and what our ultimate purpose in God is.

Years ago, the Lord spoke to my heart saying that you and I are like that bread that has been taken. We did not choose the Lord, but He chose us. The Lord has taken us from the world, out of the kingdom of darkness and into the Kingdom of His dear Son. He took us, thank God, and then after we were born again and filled with the Holy Ghost, He began to bless us. During that great honeymoon time with Jesus, we experienced that great blessing of the Lord when we began to understand what it was like to be a Christian and to walk in the Kingdom of God. Oh, how wonderful it was having a relationship with the Lord and learning how to get free.

Then, the Bible says, He broke that bread. This is the part where many Christians have a problem. They love being taken, they love being blessed, but the ultimate purpose of God is to break that bread. Breaking here speaks of humbling, discipline, chastisement, correction, the dealings of God, temptation, and testing. The whole purpose depends upon us. If we allow God to break us, we will be changed. This is the sanctification process. Justification is free and is instantaneous the moment we receive Jesus. Glorification is when Jesus comes again and our bodies are made like unto His glorious body. That will also be instantaneous. This middle part of our salvation process called sanctification, takes a lifetime. This is the process of the breaking, the dealings of God, and our burden of being conformed and transformed to the image of Jesus Christ.

Are you experiencing the breaking today? For years, as I experienced the breaking, I did not really realize what purpose it was working in me. Everything that God does in us is not really for us, but for someone else. And all the times I would go through deep dealings, deep struggles, and trials, I never realized that it would one day benefit somebody else as I spoke to them about the comfort I received and how I had sat where they sat. For the breaking leads us to the next point.

After the breaking of the bread, Jesus gave that bread to the disciples. We are simply taken, blessed, and broken to be given away. All that God does in us, is for somebody else. So in Mark 6:41 it says: *"And when he had taken the five loaves and the two fishes, he looked up to heaven, and blessed, and brake the loaves, and gave them to his disciples to set before them."* You and I have been taken, thank the Lord for that. We have been blessed. Glory to God! We are in the breaking process in preparation of the greatest gift to mankind. You and I are to be given away as living epistles, as living truth to the world. This is your purpose and my purpose today. So endure the taking, the blessing and the breaking, so that you can be given.

"After Six Days"
Matthew 17:1

Here in this wonderful passage in Matthew, the Bible says:

"And after six days Jesus taketh Peter, James, and John his brother, and bringeth them up into an high mountain apart, ²And was transfigured before them: and his face did shine as the sun, and his raiment was white as the light." (Matthew 17:1-2)

What a glorious revelation. This is the mount of transfiguration. The number six in Scripture is referred to spiritually as the number for man and Satan. That is why 666 simply means the fullness of Satan in the fullness of man. It is man at his height, in his secular humanism, filled with the devil. That is the spirit of antichrist. But thank God after six days comes the seventh. Seven is the number for perfection, and this is where we're headed, to the seventh day. God bless the seventh day. It is the day of rest.

Notice, here, that Jesus takes Peter, James, and John on this seventh day. Peter, James, and John are only three out of the twelve apostles. The twelve apostles were out of the seventy disciples who walked with the Lord all the time. And the seventy came out of the multitude. These three represent a remnant of people that God has taken or chosen. I pray that you and I will be one of them. And He *"bringeth them up."* Right now God is bringing us up. We are growing *"in grace, and in the knowledge of our Lord and Saviour Jesus Christ"* (II Peter 3:18). We are going on unto perfection (Hebrews 6:1), going from *"glory to glory"* (II Corinthians 3:18), from *"faith to faith"* (Romans 1:17). We are rising up, as it says in Ephesians 4:13, *"unto a perfect man."*

He is bringing them up into a high mountain. Going up a mountain is never easy. Years ago, in Jamaica, I was climbing the backside of a mountain and fell and tumbled all the way down the mountain. What a journey downward it was. But even more so, what a journey back upward it was. Going up a mountain is hard; it is never easy. That is why Jesus is bringing us up; we are not just walking by ourselves. The Lord is bringing us up the mountain of transfiguration. He shall *"change our vile body, that it may be fashioned like unto his glorious body"* (Philippians 3:21).

If you're climbing the mountain today, grab hold of the hand of Jesus, because He is bringing you up. He is going to get you to the top of that mountain. And when you get there, you will find that it is a *"high mountain apart."* It will separate you from your brothers, just as Jesus, in the garden of Gethsemane, was a stone's throw away from the disciples (Luke 22:41). Many times, it is just a stone's throw away, but it is enough of a separation to make us feel alone. But we are like the Lord, who said, *"Ye shall be scattered, every man to his own, and shall leave me alone: and yet I am not alone, because the Father is with me"* (John 16:32). Those seeking great things, seeking the light of God, to be changed, for their face to shine like the Lord Jesus, so that it is no longer them that live but Christ that lives in them (Galatians 2:20), will be apart. But He is bringing us up. Six days are almost over, and the seventh is coming. Rejoice!

"Jesus Wept"
John 11:35

DAY 326

We have seen in the Scriptures that our God laughs, rejoices, gets angry, shows great mercy, and shows great compassion. We've seen as well that He's a jealous God. So it should not be a shock to us that He also weeps, since one of the most important characteristics of our being is found in crying, weeping, having sorrow for something, or shedding tears because of some occurrence or concern or loss. Jesus has these emotions as well. In John 11:35 it simply says, *"Jesus wept."*

We're created in the image of God. If we can weep or shed tears of sorrow most certainly He can. The Bible says in Isaiah 63:9, *"In all their affliction he was afflicted."* In Hebrews 4:15 it says, *"For we have not an high priest which cannot be touched with the feeling of our infirmities."* Isaiah 53:3 says He was a *"man of sorrows, and acquainted with grief."*

Jesus wept in John 11 not because He was weeping for Lazarus. He was weeping because His people, His closest disciples, Martha and Mary His friends, did not believe that He was the resurrection and the life. The word *"wept"* in the Greek means "to shed tears." I like this definition of weeping that calls it "expressing grief." It's an overpowering emotion, to shed tears.

Our weeping God; He weeps, He cries, He grieves. Hebrews 5:7 says, *"Who in the days of his flesh, when he had offered up prayers and supplications with strong crying and tears unto him that was able to save him from death, and was heard in that he feared."* It says in this verse that Jesus offered up the prayers with strong crying and tears. It should not be a shock to us that our precious God is moved and He weeps.

It says in Genesis 6:6, *"And it repented the Lord that he had made man on the earth, and it grieved him at his heart."* In Judges 10:16 it says, *"his soul was grieved for the misery of Israel."* In Matthew 26:37-38, when He took His disciples to the garden, it says He *"began to be sorrowful and very heavy. ³⁸Then saith he unto them, My soul is exceeding sorrowful, even unto death: tarry ye here, and watch with me."*

Our weeping God, who sheds tears for us, is weeping today over this world. He is weeping over the religious ones who cannot see His true greatness, His glory, and His grace. Oh that we would turn our hearts and not be as Proverbs 17:25 says, *"A foolish son is a grief to his father."*

Let's not make the Lord weep anymore. Let us be those that stop it by believing that Jesus is the resurrection and the life. Moreover, as it says in Proverbs 10:1, *"A wise son maketh a glad father."* Let's please His heart today.

"Dwelling Among The Tombs"
Mark 5:3

In this passage of Scripture we read:

"And they came over unto the other side of the sea, into the country of the Gadarenes. ²And when he was come out of the ship, immediately there met him out of the tombs a man with an unclean spirit, ³Who had his dwelling among the tombs; and no man could bind him, no, not with chains." (Mark 5:1-3)

First of all, you need to know that the word *"Gadarenes"* means "reward at the end." There is going to be a reward at the end of this story! Secondly, the word *"tombs"* in the Greek means "place of remembrance." How many of us dwell among the tombs in our lives? In other words, how many of us have places of remembrance that still haunt us, torment us, or condemn us? They could be things that happened in our childhood, instances with parents or loved ones; perhaps a divorce or a broken relationship. It could be a failure from the past or anything.

But these places of remembrance lodge in our soulish realm and they will hinder our future just as the Lord said to Hagar as she was running from her situation, *"whence camest thou? And whither wilt thou go?"* (Genesis 16:8). In other words, you cannot go on with God until you deal with what has been. Ecclesiastes 3:15 says, *"God requireth that which is past."* We don't need to be dwelling among the tombs and places of remembrance. God wants to help us and move us on from our past. Paul told the Philippians, *"This one thing I do, forgetting those things which are behind, and reaching forth unto those things which are before"* (Philippians 3:13). We need to forget those things which are behind. We need to allow the Holy Spirit today to come in and purge, wash, and cleanse our minds from these places of remembrance.

Moreover, we don't need to dwell among the tombs. When we do, we will act like the man in the story. *"And always, night and day, he was in the mountains, and in the tombs, crying, and cutting himself with stones"* (verse 5). What these places of remembrance do to us causes us to cry and to cut ourselves with stones. Cutting ourselves with stones speak of always being self-critical. We condemn ourselves and will remain in guilt.

God does not want us dwelling among the tombs. Hear the Word of the Lord today. Jesus said in Luke 9:62, *"No man, having put his hand to the plough, and looking back, is fit for the kingdom of God."* This is not speaking of heaven but the Kingdom of God which is God's rule and reign in our lives while on earth. God cannot rule and reign in our lives when we choose to remain and live in the past, dwelling in these places of remembrance. So I ask you today, forsake the places of remembrance. Forget those things which are past and reach forth to the things which are before you. And leave behind the places of remembrance forever.

"The Mount Of Transfiguration"
Matthew 17:1-2

This is a tremendous revelation about the remnant in the Scriptures. We read the story in Matthew:

> *"And after six days Jesus taketh Peter, James, and John his brother, and bringeth them up into an high mountain apart, ²And was transfigured before them: and his face did shine as the sun, and his raiment was white as the light."* (Matthew 17:1-2)

Notice that Jesus only took Peter, James, and John up the mountain with Him. He took neither all of the disciples nor the seventy, and did not take the multitudes. This shows us there is a remnant or a people within a people.

The passage begins with *"And after six days."* What comes after six? Seven. The seventh day is the day of perfection, harvest, and when God is going to shine through a people where He is going to say, *"Arise, shine; for thy light is come, and the glory of the Lord is risen upon thee"* (Isaiah 60:1). In the Greek it is called the *"parousia"* or the appearing of the Lord within a people. The first coming of the Lord is not when every eye shall see Him. But it will be the coming of the Lord in a people. Isaiah 60 continues, saying that the nations shall come *"to the brightness of thy rising."* This is speaking of others coming to the people of God because of the brightness of Jesus and His glory shining through them.

Even today, God is calling for a people within a people. He is taking out a remnant and a people like He did Peter, James, and John. Three is the number in Scriptures for "Godhead and resurrection." We need to have a revelation of the full Godhead (Father, Son, and Holy Ghost). This means we need to be baptized in the Holy Ghost. We need to be saved and we need to have intimacy with the Father. We need to be walking in a lifestyle that radiates His character.

Then it says that Jesus *"bringeth them up into an high mountain apart."* Going up a mountain is never easy. It can be very dangerous, treacherous, and hard especially when we feel that we are alone. You and I are going up this same hill. It is the hill of mount Zion. But Jesus is there with us. He's the one who *"bringeth them up."* He's going to bring us up.

Moreover, it is a high mountain apart. This mountain is high. We are seated in heavenly places in Christ Jesus (Ephesians 2:6). Psalms 149:6 says, *"Let the high praises of God be in their mouth, and a two-edged sword in their hand."* We are to be ever going up mount Zion, living in the manifest presence of God, with Him seated upon the thrones of our hearts. Mountains in Scripture speak of kingdoms, but they also represent obstacles. So when God is bringing us up, there may be obstacles in the way, but we will overcome them by His hand.

This mountain is apart. Not everyone will enter into this. It can be a lonely journey fighting and overcoming and going up while most stay at the bottom of the mountain. Jesus was alone in the garden of Gethsemane, a stone's throw away from His disciples. Many times we are only a stone's throw away from others pressing on. Or we will feel like Abraham who went to sacrifice Issac and said, *"I and the lad will go yonder and worship."* Where you need to go may be just a little way further, but you and I are hearing the call of God to make it to the top. We have to remember that we are not alone and that the Lord will be with us (Deuteronomy 31:8).

At the top it says that Jesus was *"transfigured before them: and his face did shine as the sun, and his raiment was white as the light."* The Greek word for *"transfigured"* means "metamorphosed." Not only did this happen to Jesus, but I believe He did this for Peter, James, and John to show that the same thing will happen to a remnant in the last days. I believe the many-membered son, the body of Christ that is going up this same mountain, will be transfigured on the seventh day and their face will shine with the glory of God. Paul says in Philippians 3:21, *"Who shall change our vile body, that it may be fashioned like unto his glorious body."* Let's look for the mount of transfiguration spiritually today. Let's go up this mountain as a body. Let's make sure we're in the remnant because the seventh day is coming.

"In His Favor Is Life"
Psalms 30:5

DAY 329

Psalms 30:5 says, *"For his anger endureth but a moment; in his favour is life."* Having God's favor brings us great life. The word *"favour"* in Hebrew means *"to delight in, or acceptable."* It comes from a root word that means *"to be pleased with, to satisfy a debt, graciousness, or kindness."* This is our God. The word for *"favour"* that I love the most means *"to bend or stoop in kindness to an inferior one."* I don't know about you but I am an inferior one, and He's stooped in kindness to me.

Psalms 5:12 says, *"For thou, Lord, wilt bless the righteous; with favour wilt thou compass him as with a shield."* God's favor is a shield round about us protecting us. He has stooped in kindness to us who are inferior ones, and has surrounded us with His favor. The Lord Jesus speaking in Proverbs 8:35 says, *"For whoso findeth me findeth life, and shall obtain favour of the Lord."* When we seek the Lord we find Him, and then we find true life (Jeremiah 29:13). How many people are living today without true life, the life that God intended them to have? His favor brings this life to us.

In Psalms 41:11 David said, *"By this I know that thou favourest me, because mine enemy doth not triumph over me."* We know that God's favoring us because our enemy cannot, does not, will not triumph over us. *"Thanks be unto God, which always causeth us to triumph"* (II Corinthians 2:14). The favor of God is the fact that He delights in us, and that He's pleased with us, surrounds us and protects us as a shield.

Proverbs 16:15 says, *"In the light of the king's countenance is life; and his favour is as a cloud of the latter rain."* Every time the glory falls, that's simply His favor setting His seal upon your life. I pray right now that that favor invades wherever you are. That His mighty, holy presence just descends upon you as you read this, and you're wrapped in the favor of God.

Proverbs 19:12 says, *"The king's wrath is as the roaring of a lion; but his favour is as dew upon the grass."* Is there anything more beautiful than waking up in the morning and stepping outside and seeing the grass glistening with that precious dew? This is what we have from the Father.

In Psalms 85:1 it says, *"Lord, thou hast been favourable unto thy land: thou hast brought back the captivity of Jacob."* Because He shows us His favor, He delivers us from our captivity. Proverbs 1:8-9 says, *"My son, hear the instruction of thy father, and forsake not the law of thy mother: For they shall be an ornament of grace unto thy head, and chains about thy neck."* An ornament of favor unto thy head; this is our God.

David prayed in Psalms 106:4, *"Remember me, O Lord, with the favour that thou bearest unto thy people: O visit me with thy salvation."* My prayer for you today is that He would visit you with His salvation, with the favor that He always has blessed His people. He says in Isaiah 60:10, *"but in my favour have I had mercy on thee."* May you experience that right now, in Jesus' name.

"I Shall Not Want"
Psalms 23:1

Day 330

One of the greatest provisions for being a Christian is that as we walk with the Lord Jesus, He promises to meet our needs. Let this word be personal to you today. David said in Psalms 23:1, *"The Lord is my shepherd; I shall not want."*

The truth is we are not to want. *"I shall not want"* the Bible says. The Hebrew definition for *"want"* means: "to lack, to fail, to abate, to decrease, to make lower." God doesn't want us lacking, failing, abating, or decreasing. He does want us to be decreasing only in the sense of walking in humility, but never in the sense of our provision.

The Word of God is pretty clear that He does not want us to not have our provision. Matthew 6:33 says, *"But seek ye first the kingdom of God, and his righteousness; and all these things shall be added unto you."* What are those things? The things that we eat, the things that we put on, and our daily needs are met according to His riches in glory. As it says in Philippians 4:19, *"But my God shall supply all your need according to his riches in glory by Christ Jesus."* The work *"supply"* there in the Greek means: "to cram a net full, to level up a hollow, to furnish or to satisfy; to give a major portion to or to complete." So God's supply is an overwhelming supply. It wants to cram the net full. That's what he meant in John 10:10 when he said, *"I am come that they might have life, and that they might have it more abundantly."*

So my God shall supply all your need according to His riches in glory. II Peter 1:3 says, *"According as his divine power hath given unto us all things that pertain unto life and godliness."* His divine power has given us all that we need to live this life, and walk in godliness. What more could we ask for? God our provider is so precious to us and He is such a good Father. He takes care of us, watches out for us, and makes sure all our needs are met. Some other translations of Psalms 23:1 say:

> *"The Lord shepherds me; therefore can I lack nothing."*
> *"The Lord shepherds me I shall never be in need."*
> *"The Lord takes care of me as His sheep. I will not be without any good thing."*
> *"Because the Lord is my shepherd; I have everything I need."*

This is just absolutely precious. It reminds me of what the Bible really says about us not wanting in Psalms 34:9, *"O fear the Lord, ye his saints: for there is no want to them that fear him."* There truly is no want to His saints that fear Him. Let this saying sink down into your ears today. Then in verse 10 of Psalms 34 he says, *"They that seek the Lord shall not want any good thing."* All we need to do is seek the Lord, fear the Lord, and we won't want for any good thing. How much more explicit or expressive can God be than that? We are not to go wanting. We are not to be without. Our daily needs are supposed to be met, and we need to believe this.

I know that in the Christian world that we live in there is far too much emphasis on prosperity, far too much emphasis on gain is godliness, and far too much emphasis on the saint rather than the Savior. In spite of that, we can't throw the baby out with the bath water. God is our Shepherd, and because of that we shall not want. He's the Good Shepherd that cares for His sheep.

Isaiah 41:11 says, *"he shall gather the lambs with his arm, and carry them in his bosom, and shall gently lead those that are with young."* What a savior! Oh my! He is truly as I Peter 2:25 says, *"the Shepherd and Bishop of your souls."* He takes care of us. He makes sure that we have everything we need.

In James 1:4 it says, *"But let patience have her perfect work, that ye may be perfect and entire, wanting nothing."* We should want nothing. I don't know how much more I can say about this except that Psalms 84:11 says, *"No good thing will he withhold from them that walk uprightly."*

This is a revelatory truth that all of us need not only to walk in, but to share with others, about the bountiful goodness, provision, and grace of our God. It never ceases to amaze me how many times I've gone through things in my life, and wondered where my provision was going to come from. Sometimes it was at 11:59 pm or at the last minute, but nonetheless, it always came. That's because our God is faithful, so very faithful.

He says in Proverbs 28:27 says, *"He that giveth unto the poor shall not lack."* When we give as Luke 6:38 says, *"Give, and it shall be given unto you; good measure, pressed down, and shaken together, and running over, shall men give into your bosom"* we simply set in motion this great principle that God established.

Finally, David said in Psalms 37:25, *"I have been young, and now am old; yet have I not seen the righteous forsaken, nor his seed begging bread."* I have been young and now I'm old, and I have not seen myself forsaken nor seen myself ever having to beg for bread. The reason being Jesus Christ, my precious, glorious, wonderful, loving Savior is my Shepherd. Because He's the Good Shepherd that lays down His life for His sheep (John 10:11), I shall not want.

Believe the word of the Lord today. Allow faith to arise in your heart and peace that your provision is sure for He is your shepherd that cares for you. You shall not want!

"A Zeal Not According To Knowledge"
Romans 10:2

Day 331

Here in Romans 10:1-2 is Paul's great prayer for his people, in which he says, *"Brethren, my heart's desire and prayer to God for Israel is, that they might be saved. ²For I bear them record that they have a zeal of God, but not according to knowledge."*

Is it possible to have a zeal of God that is not according to knowledge? Ecclesiastes 10:15, *"The labour of the foolish wearieth every one of them, because he knoweth not how to go to the city."* Too many times in our lives, we get excited and stirred, but yet really, we're moving on emotion and not by the Spirit or the Word of God. We always need to examine ourselves to see whether we be in the faith. We need to ask ourselves, "What am I doing?" and "Is the Lord's breath upon what I'm doing?" It's good to have zeal, but it's good to have zeal with knowledge. Proverbs 29:18 tells us, *"Where there is no vision, the people perish: but he that keepeth the law, happy is he."* We need vision and we need zeal, but we also need to keep the law and the Word of the Lord operating and working in our lives.

Look at the story in II Samuel 18 of the young man who wanted to give tidings to the king, yet Joab in verse 22, questioned him, *"Wherefore wilt thou run, my son, seeing that thou hast no tidings ready?"* But basically, the young man reacted, "I don't really care, I want to go anyway." This seems to be the testimony of many believers. They're not willing to sit at Jesus' feet under His Word as Mary did in Luke 10, but they have been moved by religious preaching and religious guilt and condemnation to make them want to go and do. In Luke 10:41-42, Jesus said to Martha, who was always serving and working, *"⁴¹Martha, Martha, thou art careful and troubled about many things: ⁴²But one thing is needful: and Mary hath chosen that good part, which shall not be taken away from her."*

While Martha was running around, caring about everything, Mary was sitting at Jesus' feet and hearing His Word. You can either go or you can sit and then go. You cannot give people what you do not have. It is better to sit and wait in the presence of God and as the Word of the Lord and the vision of the Lord comes to you, you can then run with that vision, but once you're finished, come back and sit before the Lord again.

Jesus said, *"Thou art careful and troubled with many things"*. In the Greek that reads, "She was distracted with care". It's too easy to be distracted with care because there's great zeal in our lives, as said in Psalms 13:19, *"The desire accomplished is sweet to the soul,"* yet we never seem to accomplish anything and merely run in circles. The Lord spoke to Moses in Deuteronomy 2:3 telling him he had compassed that mountain long enough, it was time to go on. And as Paul said in the book of Galatians 4:17-18, *"¹⁷They zealously affect you, but not well; yea, they would exclude you, that ye might affect them. ¹⁸But it is good to be zealously affected always in a good thing, and not only when I am present with you."* Yes, it's good to be zealously affected, but once again, that zeal must be directed by the Spirit and the Word of the Lord. Make sure your zeal is toward the Lord today and not toward selfish or hidden motivations or even religious motivation, and that it is according to knowledge that will glorify God.

"Ye Are My Friends"
John 15:14

DAY 332

Oh, how I love the Word of God, for it declares such glorious and precious truths. Today, let us consider this principle that Jesus spoke of in John:

> "*Greater love hath no man than this, that a man lay down his life for his friends. ¹⁴Ye are my friends, if ye do whatsoever I command you. ¹⁵Henceforth I call you not servants; for the servant knoweth not what his lord doeth: but I have called you friends.*" (John 15:13-16)

What a thing that God would call us friends. Several men in the Scriptures were called God's friends. There was Moses in Exodus, where it says, "*And the Lord spake unto Moses face to face, as a man speaketh unto his friend*" (Exodus 33:11). This speaks of great intimacy and vulnerability for one another. Also, it says in the book of Isaiah, "*But thou, Israel, art my servant, Jacob whom I have chosen, the seed of Abraham my friend*" (Isaiah 41:8). In James 2:23, Abraham was "*called the Friend of God.*"

The word "*friend*" in the Greek means "dear, a friend, actively fond of, an associate, a comrade, or a clansman." This is what God wants for us, that we would know Him with such intimacy and such friendship. Who would ever believe that the God of the universe would want to be friends with such a one as you and me? You are not friendless today. He has called you His friend. What a privilege that is!

Proverbs 22:11 tells us, "*He that loveth pureness of heart, for the grace of his lips the king shall be his friend*". Oh, praise the Lord! The king shall be our friend if we simply do what He commands and continue to keep our hearts pure and right. The bride declares in Song of Solomon 5:16, "*His mouth is most sweet: yea, he is altogether lovely. This is my beloved, and this is my friend, O daughters of Jerusalem.*" The great God we serve is a loving, compassionate, tenderhearted, merciful, yet righteous God. He wants to share all that He is with us as true friends do. He wants us to be dear to Him. He is actively fond of us. He is our comrade. He is our clansman.

The Scriptures are full of admonitions of how God is friends with a people. I want you to know today that there is no one closer. Proverbs 17:17 tells us, "*A friend loveth at all times, and a brother is born for adversity.*" There is no one that loves more than Jesus, and He is born for adversity. Whatever you are experiencing today, remember, "*Ye are my friends*". You are the friend of God. What a privilege and revelation to our hearts today!

"The Bones Of Elisha"
II Kings 13:20-21

DAY 333

This is a story tucked away in the Scriptures that brings forth an amazing and revelatory truth for us as believers. It is a story that a man, having lived his life and gone onto be with the Lord, can still yet be speaking. As the Scriptures say, in Hebrews 11:4, *"he being dead yet speaketh."* The anointing that's upon our lives can last beyond our lives if we walk uprightly before the Lord. The Scriptures we are talking about today from II Kings reads:

> *"²⁰And Elisha died, and they buried him. And the bands of the Moabites invaded the land at the coming in of the year. And it came to pass, as they were burying a man, that, behold, they spied a band of men; and they cast the man into the sepulchre of Elisha: and when the man was let down, and touched the bones of Elisha, he revived, and stood up on his feet"* (II Kings 13:20-21).

In these verses, Elisha was still having an impact in the world after his death. Would to God, every father ministry and minister seek to have an impact well beyond his life. The real reason for pastors and father ministries is to leave an inheritance to their spiritual children's children. In II Timothy 2:2 it says, *"And the things that thou hast heard of me among many witnesses, the same commit thou to faithful men, who shall be able to teach others also."*

God is bringing forth a new priesthood that has the spirit of Elisha. Elisha had a father ministry, the Bible says in II Kings 3:11, that he *"poured water on the hands of Elijah."* Elisha served Elijah faithfully. Then, when Elijah was taken up in II Kings 2:10, he said, *"If thou see me when I am taken from thee, it shall be so unto thee."* That means that when you see me, who I really am, then you can have my mantle. Paul said to Timothy in Acts 26:4 that he has seen *"my manner of life."* The reason Elijah was doing what he was doing wasn't for material possessions or fame or power, but simply for God's sake. So, Elisha followed in Elijah's footsteps. The truth we find here is that the seed in Elisha lived beyond his life. Notice that in Genesis it says that everything that God created, the seed was in itself. The holy thing that was in Elisha still lived even though his bones were dead. Remember the bones in Ezekiel 37:2, *"there were very many* (bones) *in the open valley; and, lo, they were very dry."* The word dry means "ashamed, confused, and disappointed."

When the enemy comes against you, like they did this man in II Kings 13:20-21, and tries to kill you and toss you into a grave, hopefully it is one where a man like Elisha was buried. Many of us are tossed into a grave or sepulcher, only to be overwhelmed, start to backslide, and quit. But if we're tossed in a grave where a man like Elisha is buried, we must remember that his bones are satiated with the anointing and glory of God. We find then that as this man's body touched the bones of Elisha, the seed of anointing that was in Elisha brought that man back to life. There can be no resurrection until there is a death. In the last days, God wants the sons of father ministries to die, and as they die, the ministry of that father will bring forth and anoint them. It will cause them to have a mighty anointing to minister throughout the earth.

Perhaps you need a father ministry. Do you have one? It would be glorifying God to have more Elishas throughout the earth today. As Elisha prayed one time, as he walked past the water of the Jordan in II Kings 2:14, *"Where is the Lord God of Elijah?"* I ask today, where are the Elishas whose bones will live after them, *"[they] being dead yet speaketh,"* and have an impact in their world?

"I Love The Lord"
Psalms 116:1

Day 334

This day I want it to be known, and I want you to let it be known, that I love the Lord and that you love the Lord. The Bible says that *"Many waters cannot quench love"* (Song of Solomon 8:7). Many waters, many things, can never quench the love that we have for Him. I pray today that you're consumed with an overwhelming passion, and a heart of love, for our precious Jesus.

The Bible says in Psalms 31:23, *"O love the Lord, all ye his saints."* David says in Psalms 18:1, *"I will love thee, O Lord, my strength."* Psalms 116:1 says, *"I love the Lord, because he hath heard my voice and my supplications."* He didn't have to respond when we called to Him. He didn't have to receive us. He doesn't have to be as I John tells us, *"God is love"* (I John 4:8, 16), but He is. Our God is a good God, a precious God, a wonderful God and because of that, we love Him.

Jesus said, *"He that has been forgiven much loves much"* (Luke 7:47). I don't know about you but He's forgiven me for quite a bit, and I love Him so. I love Him for all the years of forgiving me, for all the years of sustaining me, providing for me, caring for me, supporting me, and encouraging me. I love Him because He's tender and gentle, precious, kind, merciful, and compassionate.

In Song of Solomon 1:2-4 it says, *"² Let him kiss me with the kisses of his mouth: for thy love is better than wine."* In the Hebrew that reads *"loving you is better than wine."* Loving Him is better than any earthly intoxication or anything in this universe. Nothing can compare to having a walk of love with Him. It goes on to say, *"Because of the savour of thy good ointments thy name is as ointment poured forth."* His character is what His name represents. It pours forth like oil, and that's why *"the virgins love thee"* (Song of Solomon 1:3).

Oh how we love the Lord. It says in I John 2:15 *"Love not the world, neither the things that are in the world. If any man love the world, the love of the Father is not in him."* We must be so careful to watch worldliness and carnality in our lives. We must check ourselves and *"Examine yourselves, whether ye be in the faith"* (II Corinthians 13:5). If we're not careful, the Bible says our love can wax cold (Matthew 24:12). Don't let this happen today.

This morning or this evening, wherever you are and whenever it is you're reading this; open your heart now to the precious Holy Spirit. As His presence now floods down and fills you where you are, let that passion roll up out of you. Let it storm through your mouth in praises and honor to Him, and simply say with me with your whole heart, "I love the Lord."

"Boast Not Of Thyself Of Tomorrow"
Proverbs 27:1

DAY 335

Here we find a very enlightening and important truth, that you and I should not be presuming upon the Lord about tomorrow or the future. It says here in Proverbs 27:1, *"Boast not thyself of tomorrow; for thou knowest not what a day may bring forth."* We shouldn't ever be boasting of tomorrow because we really don't know what can happen today. So many people tell us to make a five year plan when it comes to our future. But James tells us:

> *"¹³Go to now, ye that say, Today or tomorrow we will go into such a city, and continue there a year, and buy and sell, and get gain: ¹⁴Whereas ye know not what shall be on the morrow. For what is your life? It is even a vapour, that appeareth for a little time, and then vanisheth away. ¹⁵For that ye ought to say, If the Lord will, we shall live, and do this, or that."* (James 4:13-15)

When it comes to our plans for the future, we should be saying the same, *"if the Lord will."* This is the problem with trying to plan and do things in the future. It doesn't do us well. We need to constantly be before the Lord and let our prayer be, *"Give us this day our daily bread"* (Matthew 6:11). We need to stay in the Word for, *"Thy word is a lamp unto my feet, and a light unto my path"* (Psalms 119:105).

Jesus says in Matthew 6:34, *"Take therefore no thought for the morrow: for the morrow shall take thought for the things of itself. Sufficient unto the day is the evil thereof."* Every day brings us a new set of circumstances and we cannot presume about tomorrow. We can hope and believe with faith, but we certainly can't walk in presumption and be boasting about what is going to happen tomorrow.

It says in Ecclesiastes 11:6, *"In the morning sow thy seed, and in the evening withhold not thine hand: for thou knowest not whether shall prosper, either this or that, or whether they both shall be alike good."* We really don't know what is going to happen tomorrow. We don't know what is going to happen next week, next month, or next year. So it is foolish for us to boast about what we are going to do in the future.

Let the Word of the Lord rise up in our hearts today and let the only thing that comes out of our mouths concerning our plans be, "if the Lord wills" or "by the grace of God we'll do this or that," with no more boasting, and with no more presumption. It only leads to trouble and we don't need any more trouble in our lives. We don't know what a day is going to bring forth, so today we simply say like James tell us to, *"if the Lord will."*

"Tasting That The Lord Is Gracious"
I Peter 2:3

Day 336

It says in I Peter 2:3, *"If so be ye have tasted that the Lord is gracious."* Have you found the Lord to be gracious? Have you found the Lord's grace and mercy to overwhelm your life? I know that in my forty-three years of walking with the Lord that I certainly have. If we look into the Scriptures we find that He is defined by this very word, gracious. This is our God. When God told Moses that He would pass by him defining Himself to him, He said He would place him in the cleft of a rock and declare His name (Exodus 33:19,22). As God declared Himself when He passed Moses in Exodus 34:6, He said, *"The Lord, The Lord God, merciful and gracious"*.

In Nehemiah 9:17 it says, *"Thou art a God ready to pardon, gracious and merciful, slow to anger."* In Nehemiah 9:31 it says, *"For thou art a gracious and merciful God."* Hallelujah! Have you tasted that the Lord is gracious? Jonah, when he was arguing with the Lord, was mad because God, in His graciousness, delivered Nineveh. In Jonah 4:2 he said, *"For I knew that thou art a gracious God."* Even Jonah, who was angry, knew that God's heart was pure grace.

John 1:17 says, *"For the law was given by Moses, but grace and truth came by Jesus Christ."* Has anyone ever shown more grace than the Lord Jesus? He is kind to the poor, kind to the harlots, kind to the adulterers. The only anger we've ever seen in Him was with the Pharisees and the religious people. You need to taste; you need to eat of the Lord's grace today.

Paul said in II Timothy 2:1, *"Be strong in the grace that is in Christ Jesus."* He told Titus that grace teaches us to deny ungodliness and worldly lusts (Titus 2:12). Be strong in God's grace. Don't let people try to keep you from the grace of God. The grace of God doesn't mean slippery, easy grace or greasy grace, as some people call it. They make a mockery of the character of God when they say such terrible things. How horrible it is when people don't have a revelation of God's grace. In Psalms 145 David says, *"The Lord is gracious, and full of compassion; slow to anger, and of great mercy. ⁹The Lord is good to all: and his tender mercies are over all his works."* (Psalms 145:8-9)

The Lord is gracious. It doesn't matter what some preacher says, or what some denomination says, or some law-bearing person would say to try to lay a trip on you. Our God is gracious! You and I need to begin to taste that graciousness. We don't need to be like David in Psalms 77:9 who said, *"Hath God forgotten to be gracious?"* He would later say in Psalms 77:10, *"This is my infirmity: but I will remember the years of the right hand of the most High."* In other words, I will remember my life and how gracious He has been. As I look back on my life, I see nothing but the Lord being gracious. I can certainly say as David said in Psalms 34:8, I have seen that the Lord is good, and like Peter, I have tasted that the Lord is gracious. How about you?

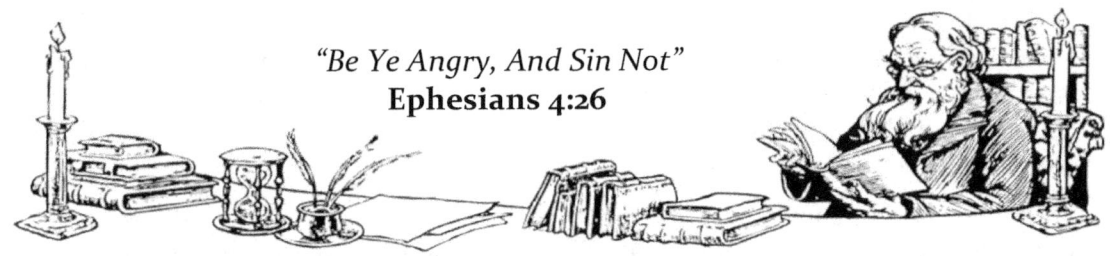

"Be Ye Angry, And Sin Not"
Ephesians 4:26

Reading this verse in context, we find the Apostle Paul exhorting the Ephesians 4:24-27:

DAY 337

> "²⁴And that ye put on the new man, which after God is created in righteousness and true holiness. ²⁵Wherefore put away lying, speak every man truth with his neighbor: for we are members one of another. ²⁶Be ye angry, and sin not: let not the sun go down upon your wrath: ²⁷Neither give place to the devil."

This is one of the most misunderstood Scriptures in the Bible. Too many people have taught falsely about this passage. God does not speak out of two sides of His mouth. He does not tell us to be angry, and then not sin, because anger is a fruit of the flesh. As it says in verse 31 of Ephesians 4 *"Let all bitterness, and wrath, and anger, and clamour, and evil speaking, be put away from you."* So what is God really saying in this passage? I believe this is a different kind of anger. It is a righteous indignation and not a fleshly or sinful anger. The actual Greek translation of this verse reads:

> *"Be constantly angry with a righteous indignation, and stop sinning. Do not allow the sun to go down upon your irritated, exasperated, and bittered anger. And stop giving an occasion for acting, giving opportunity to the devil."*

"*Angry*" in the Greek means: "to provoke or enrage, to become exasperated; a violent passion, justifiable abhorrence." "*Wrath*" in Greek means "rage." God wants us in an almost violent way, a righteous indignation, to look at our sin and to stop doing it. We should never let the sun go down upon our righteous indignation because when we do we give place to the devil and allow sin find root in us.

We must be constantly vigilant, constantly diligent, and aware that with a righteous indignation and hatred toward sin we can and will be free from sin. The Bible declares that *"...he that hath suffered in the flesh hath ceased from sin"* (I Peter 4:1). Far too long we've suffered, put up with sin, and allowed these little foxes to spoil the vine. But if we would just rise up with righteous indignation, and an anger to the sin in our lives, we would see it cease and leave us.

In Ecclesiastes 3:1-11, in the great passage about the seasons of life, I want to point out that there is a time to kill, a time to break down, a time to cast stones, a time to hate, and a time of war. God has made everything beautiful in its time (Ecclesiastes 3:11). There is a time to hate the sin in your life. I believe that when you and I start hating and despising the things that cause us to be separated from God, that causes the Lord to be displeased with us, we will start growing in the Lord tremendously.

James 4:7 states that when we *"resist the devil...he will flee from us."* Once the devil sees that he's dealing with a person who's serious about not sinning, who's serious about stopping all of the things in their his life that brings him out of fellowship with Jesus, he will eventually flee from him.

There must come forth in us what is found in Matthew 11:12, *"And from the days of John the Baptist until now the kingdom of heaven suffereth violence, and the violent take it by force."* *"Violence"* here in the Greek means: "to force, to press, to seize, to crowd oneself into." Sometimes we have to take things by force. Sometimes we need to get violent, shake ourselves, and command our souls what to do.

In II Corinthians Paul talks about the things that godly sorrow and repentance works in our lives and says:

> *"For behold this selfsame thing, that ye sorrowed after a godly sort, what carefulness it wrought in you, yea, what clearing of yourselves, yea, what indignation, yea, what fear, yea, what vehement desire, yea, what zeal, yea, what revenge! In all things ye have approved yourselves to be clear in this matter."* (II Corinthians 7:10-11)

The word *"indignation"* means "to be moved upon with anger." Godly indignation is worked in us when godly sorrow is working in us. When we really get sorry for our sin and truly repent, what happens is a true godly righteous indignation enters us and causes us to resist and reject that sin. This is what God wants.

We need to be like David when he came upon Goliath. Goliath was tormenting the people of Israel and David said in I Samuel 17:26, *"who is this uncircumcised Philistine, that he should defy the armies of the living God?"* We need to look at our own lives and say, "What is this sin or who is this devil that is defying Jesus in my life?"

When Jesus went into the synagogue and saw people selling doves, sheep, etc., along with the changers of money in John 2:13-17, He sat down and made a scourge of small cords and He drove all of them out of the temple. He overthrew the tables and poured out the money and said that the Father's house was to be a house of prayer. We are God's house and the temple of the Living God and we don't need these things living in our lives. We must make a scourge of small cords and begin to whip these things out of our lives.

When the disciples saw Jesus do this, it says they *"remembered that it was written, The zeal of thine house hath eaten me up."* May the zeal of the Lord eat you up today! Be ye angry, and sin not, let not the sun go down upon your righteous indignation and by doing so you won't give place to the devil!

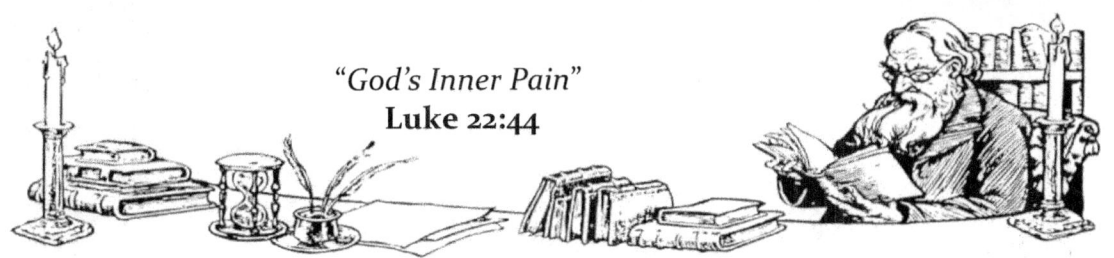

"God's Inner Pain"
Luke 22:44

Luke 22:44 speaks of Jesus in the Garden of Gethsemane. I want us to see that God has severe emotions, going through great agony when it comes to His people, whether it may be anger, sorrow, and trouble and grieving. Nonetheless, He experiences all of this. Hebrews 4:15 tells us, *"For we have not an high priest which cannot be touched with the feeling of our infirmities."* The word "infirmities" here means weaknesses. That is why the Father sent Jesus to the earth in the incarnation, so that He would know what we go through, feel what we would feel, and have compassion upon us.

Luke 22:44 says, *"And being in an agony he prayed more earnestly: and his sweat was as it were great drops of blood falling down to the ground."* Being in agony. I believe Jesus was tormented, pressed and oppressed in the garden of Gethsemane, as He wrestled with the thought of going to the cross and submitting to the will of God.

The Gospel of John tells us Jesus wept. We have already seen in other places that He laughs; if He laughs, we need to understand there is a time for laughing and there is a time for weeping. The account says that the Jews said, *"Behold how he loved him!"* and then, *"Jesus therefore again groaning in himself cometh to the grave."* (John 11:36 and 38) Now, you see, Jesus wasn't groaning because Lazarus was dead, but because His friends didn't even believe He was the resurrection and the life nor had power to deliver.

In John 12:27 Jesus says, *"Now is my soul troubled; and what shall I say? Father, save me from this hour: but for this cause came I unto this hour."* Jesus' soul was troubled. We know in John 4 He became weary and sat on a well. He has emotions and feelings and inner pain, just like we all do.

In Genesis 6:6 it says, *"And it repented the Lord that he had made man on the earth, and it grieved him at his heart."* Think of that! His own creation grieved Him at His heart. How sad this must be! And yet we think God is sitting on the circle of the earth having no connection with what we feel or go through. This is hardly the case. In Isaiah 63:9 it says *"In all their affliction he was afflicted..."* Every time we go through a hard place, He is right there with us. He is afflicted; He is troubled.

Oh, how I love Hosea 11:8 where it says, *"How shall I give thee up, Ephraim? How shall I deliver thee, Israel? How shall I make thee as Admah? How shall I set thee as Zeboim? Mine heart is turned within me, my repentings are kindled together."* God had inner pain as He watched His people doing wrong things and going against Him. Still, with compassion and mercy He reaches out to us. In Mark 3:5 *"When he had looked round about on them with anger, being grieved for the hardness of their hearts, he saith unto the man, Stretch forth thine hand. And he stretched it out: and his hand was restored whole as the other."* He was grieved for the hardness of the hearts. They should have known better.

What a God we serve! What a precious, wonderful and marvelous Creator! He feels what we feel. He has pain. The chastisement of our pain was upon Him; He suffered for us and by His stripes we were healed (Isaiah 53:5). He was wounded for our transgressions. Oh, how great a God He is!

"I Sought For A Man"
Ezekiel 22:30

DAY 339

God is looking for men and women of commitment, integrity, faithfulness and diligence. He desires a people that are steadfast, immovable and abounding in the work of the Lord. In Ezekiel 22:30, God speaks, *"And I sought for a man among them, that should make up the hedge, and stand in the gap before me for the land, that I should not destroy it: but I found none."*

God is looking for a man from among us, those of the remnant, ones who are a part of that people within a people. God wants those who will be a bridge over troubled waters, someone who will stand in the gap for others who cannot stand for themselves. God has however, *"found none."* What a sad statement. God could not find a man among the body of Christ to stand in the gap for the world, the church and for his brothers and sisters. God's search for such a man is declared perfectly in Isaiah, *"⁷And he laid it upon my mouth, and said, Lo, this hath touched thy lips; and thine iniquity is taken away, and thy sin purged. ⁸Also I heard the voice of the Lord, saying, Whom shall I send, and who will go for us? Then said I, Here am I; send me"* (Isaiah 6:7-8).

Once we've had our sin purged and once we've gotten rid of the Uzziahs in our life (Isaiah 6:1), we're going to hear Him say, *"Whom shall I send, and who will go for us?"* Isaiah quickly said, *"Here am I; send me."* The question is: can God send you, will you go for Him? *"We have a little sister, and she hath no breasts: what shall we do for our sister in the day when she shall be spoken for?"* (Song of Solomon 8:8). Will you go? Will you, *"Send portions unto them for whom nothing is prepared"*? (Nehemiah 8:10).

Now it is high time that we awake out of our sleep, for now is our salvation nearer than when we first believed (Romans 13:11). God is looking for people He can send, a people who will go for Him. Like in Luke 17:11-19, when the ten lepers were healed and only one returned to give glory to God, Jesus said, *"Where are the nine?"* He called out to Adam in Genesis 3:9, *"Where art thou?"* He asks you, "Where are you?" Are you prepared to sell out for the Kingdom of God, to give your life to His service?

In Exodus 32:26 Moses stood in the gate of the camp and said, *"Who is on the Lord's side? let him come unto me."* All the sons of Levi came to him. True priests will gather themselves and come to the Lord. They will come to His side and say, "You don't need to ask for a man; I'm Your man. I will go." Jesus said to Peter in John 18:21:

> *"Verily, verily, I say unto thee, When thou wast young, thou girdedst thyself, and walkedst whither thou wouldest: but when thou shalt be old, thou shalt stretch forth thy hands, and another shall gird thee, and carry thee whither thou wouldest not".*

Are you willing to be girded by the Lord, to go where you don't want to go? Let the Lord deal with your heart today. Choose to be His servant. Hear His voice when He speaks and run the race with patience. Be one who goes for Him.

"Lord, Is It I?"
Matthew 26:22

Here at the last supper Jesus addresses the disciples:

> *"Verily I say unto you, that one of you shall betray me. ²²And they were exceeding sorrowful, and began every one of them to say unto him, Lord, is it I?"* (Matthew 26:21-22).

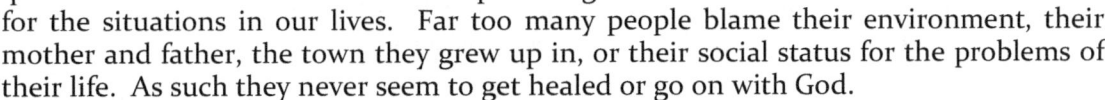

DAY 340

"Lord, is it I?" I believe that this phrase is something that should live in every one of us. We should ask ourselves this question all the time. We need to stop looking to blame others for the situations in our lives. Far too many people blame their environment, their mother and father, the town they grew up in, or their social status for the problems of their life. As such they never seem to get healed or go on with God.

I like what it says here, *"and began every one of them to say."* Can you imagine if every one of us in the body of Christ began to genuinely ask, *"Lord, is it I?"* In other words, we examine ourselves first instead of blaming others. In addition, James 5:16 says to confess our *"faults one to another, and pray one for another"* that we *"may be healed."* All pride, arrogance, and jealousy would leave the body of Christ overnight. We should examine ourselves whether we are in the faith (II Corinthians 13:5) and try our own spirits (I John 4:1). We are so busy trying and examining everybody else, when we really need to do some self-examination, check our own hearts out, and look to our own souls to see if we are the ones causing the problem.

In II Samuel 12, after David sinned with Bathsheba, committed murder, and then lied about it, the Lord sent Nathan to speak to him. The prophet came to him and gave him a parable about a little lamb. David was so furious toward the man who stole the little lamb. He acted so self-righteous here. He wanted to destroy that man. Yet the finger of the prophet pointed to him and said, *"Thou art the man"* (II Samuel 12:1-7).

How many times has that finger pointed itself at us? Do you feel the conviction of the Holy Ghost? Are we hardened to the deceitfulness of sin? Are we allowing pride to take root in us and prevent us from hearing the voice of our spirit? Proverbs 20:27 tells us, *"The spirit of man is the candle of Lord, searching all the inward parts of the belly."* The Spirit of the Lord will convict us of sin and unrighteousness. That is His job. That is what He came for, not to condemn, but to convict. You and I should simply stop and ask ourselves this question, "Is it me, Jesus? Did I do it? Did I cause this thing? Lord, is it I?" Every one of them began to say, "Is it I?" They were all convicted, when He said, *"One of you shall betray me."* Every time we betray, we are standing in pride and *"God resisteth the proud, but giveth grace to the humble"* (James 4:6).

Why don't we clothe ourselves with humility (I Peter 5:5) and with a spirit of submission and repentance today? We should examine ourselves first in every situation, "Lord is it I? Did I do this? Did I cause this?" We don't need to do anything else apart from what the witness of the Holy Spirit tells us. The Bible says in I John 5:10, *"He that believeth on the Son of God hath the witness in himself."* Let the witness of the Spirit guide us and deal with us. For the rest of our lives may we continually say, "Lord, is it I?"

"Apes And Peacocks"
I Kings 10:21

DAY 341

I know that as you read this today, it may sound quite unusual, *"apes and peacocks."* However, as strange as it sounds, it is a message of great meaning and conviction. This devotion today will illustrate what happens to people who start out with hearts that are on fire for Jesus, but over time, draw back in deception, leaving God to find no pleasure in them. I Kings 10:22 states, *"The king had at sea a navy of Tharshish with the navy of Hiram: once in three years came the navy of Tharshish, bringing gold, and silver, ivory, and apes, and peacocks. ²³So king Solomon exceeded all the kings of the earth for riches and for wisdom."*

King Solomon started out as a tender hearted, wonderful brother who once before, having been given the choice by God, chose to receive wisdom over gaining all the riches of the world. Therefore, being pleased with the humility of Solomon's heart, God gave him both wisdom and riches. God blessed him immensely.

God's heart towards Solomon was good, but as Solomon waxed richer and richer, and as his kingdom expanded, he became bored in his walk with the Lord. He began to give himself to the lusts of the world. He started not only importing gold and silver, but apes and peacocks. I Kings 10:1 tells us, *"But king Solomon loved many strange women."* The word *"strange"* in the Scriptures speaks of *"strange fire."* It speaks of those things which are foreign and alien to the Lord our God. God tells us in II Corinthians 6:17 that we are to, *"Come out from among them, and be ye separate, saith the Lord, and touch not the unclean thing; and I will receive you."* We're not to have anything to do with the world. We are in the world, but we are not of it.

Ultimately, riches brought Solomon down so low in selfishness that he would have the people bring him gold and silver. In today's prosperity teaching, where it's all about "I, me, mine" and "being blessed," it can become awfully sickening. Much of preaching we find today has an overemphasis on great prosperity and excess.

Don't be mistaken, God does want us to prosper. He does not, however, want us to live in the excess of it. Solomon began to live in excess. He had apes and peacocks brought to him. *"Apes"* speak of the beastly nature in man. It speaks of the carnal nature and of those things that are riddled with lust. And *"peacocks"* speak of something proud. This speaks of showing off in arrogance and pride. King Solomon ended up walking in pride and arrogance with a beastly nature.

The Bible says in I Kings 11:9, *"And the Lord was angry with Solomon, because his heart was turned from the Lord God of Israel, which had appeared unto him twice."* Can you imagine the Lord appearing to you twice, yet you still draw away from Him? Let this not be your story. Don't be concerned about the apes and peacocks of life. Be content with the things that you have. For He hath assured us in Hebrews 13:5, *"I will never leave thee, nor forsake thee."* He is all that we need and He should be all that we want. Let us continue to walk with the Lord with a selfless and humble heart.

"A Very Small Remnant"
Isaiah 1:9

DAY 342

Isaiah 1:9 says, *"Except the Lord of hosts had left unto us a very small remnant."* The remnant in the Scriptures is one of the most enlightening and revelatory truths found in the Bible. Most people either do not know about it or they have never heard of it. Some think that just the idea of there being a remnant is heresy and some think that it's foolishness. Nonetheless, in all my years of studying the Scriptures, I have found that without a shadow of a doubt, God has a people within a people, or a *"wheel within a wheel"* as spoken of in the book of Ezekiel 1. The beautiful truth about the remnant of God is, I believe, the present truth of this last hour.

It is a much needed Word. Throughout the Word of God, this principle is taught and described either within types and shadows, or by outright declarations. It is a truth that we need to know and understand. There is a high calling (Philippians 3:14), a holy calling (II Timothy 1:9) and a heavenly calling (Hebrews 3:1) found in the Scriptures. And just like there's more to walking with God, there is more to the Scriptures and there is more to God than what is typically taught in the body of Christ.

Without any question, this devotion seeks to show that God is bringing forth a people that in the last days will be conformed unto His image, as spoken of in Romans 8:29, *"For whom he did foreknow, he also did predestinate to be conformed to the image of his Son, that he might be the firstborn among many brethren."* Like in Ephesians 5:7, they will not have any spot or blemish, *"That he might present it to himself a glorious church, not having spot, or wrinkle, or any such thing; but that it should be holy and without blemish."* Also as described in Matthew 5:48, they will be, *"Perfect, even as your Father which is in heaven is perfect."* They are in the company of overcomers found within the body of Christ at large. They are a people within a people who have given themselves over completely to the Lord. They will be rewarded accordingly as promised in Revelation 2:26-28, *"²⁶And he that overcometh, and keepeth my works unto the end, to him will I give power over the nations."*

We can see this truth so plainly if we can put aside our religious bias. Consider the fact that Jesus had the multitudes, then He had the seventy, then the twelve (disciples), then He had the three (Peter, James and John) and then lastly, He had the one, John. He had John who laid his head upon Jesus' breast at the last supper. John had the revelation of Jesus Christ. He was the one and only one whom the Bible says, "Jesus loved."

The Bible speaks of thirty fold, sixty fold and a hundred fold in Mark 4:20, *"And these are they which are sown on good ground; such as hear the word, and receive it, and bring forth fruit, some thirtyfold, some sixty, and some an hundred."* *"For many be called, but few chosen,"* Matthew 20:16, or in the Greek, this reads, *"Few choose."* *"Few"* is the remnant that will choose to give themselves wholly to Jesus and His Word.

Paul declared that every man would be raised in his own order (I Corinthians 15:23). The Greek word for *"order"* is "rank." So there are ranks within the body of Christ. There is a remnant and by the grace of God, we need to have this principle established in our lives so that it may transform our lives and our walks with God. It says in Song of Solomon 6:8-9:

> *"⁸There are threescore queens, and fourscore concubines, and virgins without number. ⁹My dove, my undefiled is but one; she is the only one of her mother, she is the choice one of her that bare her. The daughters saw her, and blessed her; yea, the queens and the concubines, and they praised her"*.

She, this *"choice one,"* is the remnant. You and I need to understand this principle if we are ever going to achieve what God wants us to achieve: perfection, the image of Christ Jesus in our soul. Today let us therefore, as Paul does in Philippians 3:14, *"Press toward the mark for the prize of the high calling of God in Christ Jesus."* Let us choose today to press towards that high calling, which is to be in that remnant of God in Christ Jesus our Lord.

"A Man Shall Be As A Hiding Place"
Isaiah 32:2

Day 343

Here in the book of Isaiah this verse of Scripture says, *"And a man shall be as an hiding place from the wind, and a covert from the tempest; as rivers of water in a dry place, as the shadow of a great rock in a weary land."* Can this be true? Could it actually be that a man could be a hiding place for others? We know this is true in our personal lives. All of us have had times when a human being, a person, a pastor, a mother, a father, or a friend became for us a hiding place.

I believe a day is coming when God is going to have a perfect man as found in Ephesians 4:13. It will be a company of devoted men and women, a remnant of people, who will be that many membered man. As Pilate said when he put Jesus before the multitude, *"Behold the man!"* (John 19:5), God is going to say to the world "Behold the many membered man!" They are the spiritual body of Christ. They are the bride of Christ.

This company of people will have achieved a place where *"I live; yet not I, but Christ liveth in me"* (Galatians 2:20). They will have the image of Christ Jesus, and as Obadiah says in that day, *"saviours shall come up on mount Zion"* (Obadiah 21). Saviors here speak not of just the one Savior Jesus Christ, but saviors like Joseph who will one day have the image of Jesus completed within them. Joseph's Egyptian name literally means "savior of the world." Joseph was given that name because he saved the then known world from famine. He wasn't the savior but he was like a savior.

God is going to have men who will be a *"hiding place from the wind, and a covert from the tempest"*. The wind and the tempest are the great, horrific events that are going to take place on the earth. There will be a spiritual people who will radiate the love of God, the love of Jesus, and the character of God.

They will also be as rivers of water in a dry place. They will bring the presence and glory of God to people who are desperately thirsty for the things of God and the presence of God. They will also be *"the shadow of a great rock in a weary land"*. They will become the shadow to those who are dried, like that valley of dried bones in Ezekiel 37. They will be that prophetic company that prophesies over the dry bones and brings them to life, where the dried bones become an exceeding great army.

Yes, a man can be a hiding place from the wind and tempest, and a company of people shall be that many-membered man in the last days. Why don't you prepare and ready yourself to become that man?

"When The Philistines Heard That They Had Anointed David Over Israel"
II Samuel 5:17

DAY 344

II Samuel 5:17 reads, *"But when the Philistines heard that they had anointed David king over Israel, all the Philistines came up to seek David..."* In the Hebrew, this reads *"all the Philistines came up to attack David."* Why did they come to attack him? Well, they came to attack him because they heard that David had been anointed. The Philistines were the enemies of God, the enemies of God's people, and especially the enemies of those that had the anointing. Our enemy hates the anointing and will do anything he can to thwart and stop God's power and glory from finding a home in us. Therefore, as we press on in God, especially as God anoints us for His holy purpose, we have to be aware that stopping the anointing is the enemy's aim and goal.

The sad thing is many times the enemy will use our friends to resist what God is doing in our lives. David said in Psalms 55:14-16 that it was his friend who at first he took sweet counsel together with, whom later became his enemy after he was anointed king over Israel. You see, it could be our very friends and loved ones who seek our harm or start accusing us, once God begins to anoint us, use us, and bless us. This happens for many reasons. But primarily they wrestle with jealousy and ambition over the lives of those whom God anoints. Instead of rejoicing that God is using others, they get jealous and find themselves being an enemy of the anointing.

Please know that when David was anointed, that was the sign of God's seal of approval over his life as a leader. When God anoints you, it is a sign that God has sealed you, called you, and approved you. Just like God the Father did at the baptism of Jesus in the river of Jordan, He will do for you. God the Father confirmed His Son by speaking out of heaven while the Holy Ghost in the form of a dove lighted upon him and said, *"This is my beloved Son, in whom I am well pleased"* (Matthew 3:17).

When people hear about this in others, they have a tendency to respond like they did to Moses and say, *"Who made thee a prince and a judge over us?"* (Exodus 2:14) Or like they said to Jesus, *"Is not this the carpenter's son?"* (Matthew 13:55) They will try to relegate you to something natural and unimportant simply because you have the anointing of God. This is not a good thing on one hand but on the other it is. God will use it to keep us always seeking His face and to keep us humble.

We never need fear the Philistines or the enemies of God when they hear we are anointed. All of the enemies of the anointing, those who are full of ambition, fear, jealousy, will come up to seek those with the anointing. Consider how they responded to David at the battle with Goliath. David showed up simply obeying his father's instructions bringing food and seeking the welfare of his brothers. The Bible says that his brothers came against him and said, *"Why camest thou down hither? and with whom hast thou left those few sheep in the wilderness? I know thy pride, and the naughtiness of thine heart"* (I Samuel 17:28). They said this as if a few sheep were important. But David's answer was, *"Is there not a cause?"* Yes there is a cause and it is doing the will of God. Don't worry about what other people say as long as you and I know that our hearts are right and we are doing the best we can.

You must know that there will be attacks. Paul said in I Corinthians 11:19, *"For there must be also heresies among you, that they which are approved may be made manifest among you."* Saul was insanely jealous of David. We see how this motivated Saul to try to kill David. Once a good brother, Saul became a vengeful, bitter, resentful, and jealous old man who resisted God's true anointing.

Over the many years I've walked with Jesus I have watched brothers who became jealous when they compared themselves with others. Paul tells us in the New Testament that when we compare ourselves with others we are not wise (II Corinthians 10:12). We must be careful to not fall into the same trap. But we must never be afraid or ashamed of the anointing of God because it truly is the seal of God upon our life. It is His gift to us.

So the word of the Lord to us today is, when the Philistines hear we are anointed, what are we going to do? God wants us to rise up and continue to obey and walk after Him with all our hearts no matter what people say for ultimately *"we shall all stand before the judgment seat of Christ"* (Romans 14:10). We must all stand alone. Nobody else will answer for our lives but us.

People will hear that God has anointed you. People will know eventually that you have the gifting of God in your life. Never fear. Never shrink or fall back. Keep pressing onward because as you do, Jesus will meet you and you will understand what it means to flow in the anointing and glory of God. The enemies of God will have to bow and understand that you've had nothing to do with it but God Himself had everything to do with it.

When Samuel came to Jesse's house to anoint one of his sons, Jesse brought before Samuel all of his other seven sons. And Samuel said that none of these were God's choice but did he have any more sons. Jesse said that he had one more lad that was keeping the sheep. We may look to everybody else to be a little lad without much strength, but to God we are everything, *"for the Lord's portion is his people"* (Deuteronomy 32:9). So let the Philistines hear. Let the world and the devil know that God has anointed us and His anointing will carry us through.

"Not Destitute Of His Mercy And Truth"
Genesis 24:27

Day 345

A wonderful and glorious revelation is found here in Genesis 24:27, *"And he said, Blessed be the Lord God of my master Abraham, who hath not left destitute my master of his mercy and his truth."* God has not left destitute His people of His mercy and truth.

Proverbs 16:6 tells us, *"By mercy and truth iniquity is purged."* Too many people line up on either side of the coin. Some people are all mercy, while others are all full of the law and truth. However, we need both of these. It takes both mercy and truth. James 2:13 tells us that, *"mercy rejoiceth against judgment."* However, God doesn't forsake judgment, but He wants a balance of both of them. By mercy and truth iniquity and sin are purged in our lives. God gives us His mercy to forgive us, and the truth to deal with us, and help us to overcome whatever sin or problem we face. Oh, how precious our God is!

Psalms 98:3 says, *"He hath remembered his mercy and his truth toward the house of Israel."* God has remembered His mercy and His truth. There are times when God would want to react to us just with His law and deal with us accordingly. Yet, He always remembers His mercy. Thanks be unto the Lord. Psalms 89:14 says, *"Justice and judgment are the habitation of thy throne: mercy and truth shall go before thy face."* When the word *"face"* is mentioned in the Scriptures, it is synonymous with His presence. Wherever the presence of God is, mercy and truth have gone before! What a marvelous thing that God not only deals with us in truth, but yet abundantly sheds upon us His mercy.

Psalms 86:15 says, *"But thou, O Lord, art a God full of compassion, and gracious, longsuffering, and plenteous in mercy and in truth."* There is no end to His mercy. Psalms 36:5 states, *"Thy mercy, O Lord, is in the heavens; and thy faithfulness reacheth unto the clouds."* You can never use up the mercy of God.

In Psalms 25:10, it says, *"All the paths of the Lord are mercy and truth."* Everything that God does, every path that He might tread down, His mercy and truth are upon it. In Proverbs 20:28, it says, *"Mercy and truth preserve the king: and his throne is upholden by mercy."* God is preserved by the fact that He is merciful. He is God. He can do anything He wants to. He is the ruler and sovereign Almighty God of the universe. Yet He chooses to stoop in kindness to inferior ones like us. His character cannot allow Him to do anything less than that. It is who He is.

Psalms 57:3 says, *"He shall send forth his mercy and his truth."* What do you need today? His mercy and truth are available. Psalms 85:10 says, *"Mercy and truth are met together; righteousness and peace have kissed each other."*

We finish in Proverbs 3:3-4 and let this be the testimony of our lives today. *"Let not mercy and truth forsake thee: bind them about thy neck; write them upon the table of thine heart. ⁴So shalt thou find favour and good understanding in the sight of God and man."* May it be said so for us today, that we will never be destitute of His mercy and His truth.

"The Good Shepherd"
John 10:12

DAY 346

"I am the good shepherd: the good shepherd giveth his life for the sheep." We want to look today at the principle of Jesus being our shepherd. Psalms 80:1 says, *"Give ear, O Shepherd of Israel, thou that leadest Joseph like a flock; thou that dwellest between the cherubims, shine forth."* The Shepherd of Israel is the Lord Jesus. Peter calls Him in I Peter 5:4 our *"chief Shepherd"* and in I Peter 2:25 our *"Shepherd and Bishop of your souls."* Psalms 23:1 says, *"The Lord is my shepherd."*

A shepherd keeps his sheep, feeds them, takes care of them, disciplines them, guards and protects them. The Bible is very clear that God has chosen to call us sheep for a reason. We need all of those things in our life. In Isaiah 40, it says about Him in verse 11, *"He shall feed his flock like a shepherd: he shall gather the lambs with his arm, and carry them in his bosom, and shall gently lead those that are with young."* Our precious Savior feeds His flock like a shepherd and then gathers them into Him arms, carries them in His bosom, and gently leads those that are young.

John 10:14 says, *"I am the good shepherd, and know my sheep, and am known of mine."* There is no one greater than the Lord Jesus. He knows His sheep and they know Him. This should be the case for every believer, that they have a working, intimate relationship with their Lord and Savior, with their true Shepherd. Oh, how badly we need a Shepherd!

Ezekiel 34 brings out what happens when we are forsaken by earthly shepherds and by earthly leaders. But later on in the passage it tells us what God will do, *"Behold, I, even I, will both search my sheep, and seek them out. *12*...and will deliver them out of all places where they have been scattered in the cloudy and dark day"* (Ezekiel 34:11-12).

If you've been scattered and you are in a cloudy and dark day, you can rest assured, Jesus is looking for you. He is coming to get you. The passage continues:

> *"13And I will bring them out from the people, and gather them from the countries, and will bring them to their own land... 14I will feed them in a good pasture, and upon the high mountains of Israel shall their fold be: there shall they lie in a good fold, and in a fat pasture shall they feed upon the mountains of Israel. 15I will feed my flock, and I will cause them to lie down... 16 I will seek that which was lost, and bring again that which was driven away, and will bind up that which was broken, and will strengthen that which was sick"* (Ezekiel 34:13-16).

This is our God, our true Shepherd. *"The good shepherd giveth his life for the sheep"* (John 10:11). He lays it down. He seeks them out and He feeds them in a good pasture. Then He causes us to rest, to find peace in Him. Today, I pray that you would open your heart to the good Shepherd, the chief Shepherd and Bishop of your soul and let Him have access to you, so that you may lie down and rest.

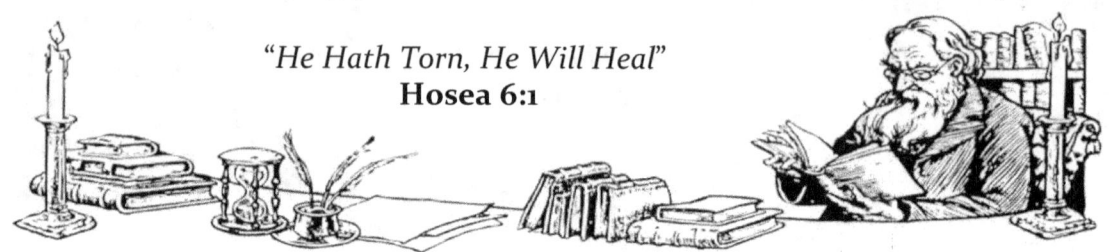

"He Hath Torn, He Will Heal"
Hosea 6:1

DAY 347

In Hosea 6:1 it says, *"Come, and let us return unto the Lord: for he hath torn, and he will heal us; he hath smitten, and he will bind us up."* This is such great irony, and such a great problem for many people. Romans 11:22 says, *"Behold therefore the goodness and severity of God."*

There's a right hand and a left hand of God. The right hand is the hand of blessing and the left hand is the hand of judgment. As Song of Solomon 2:6 says, *"His left hand is under my head, and his right hand doth embrace me."* God will be dealing with our soulish man with the left hand, while he caresses and blesses us with the right hand.

It says here *"for he hath torn."* In the Hebrew that means "to pluck up, or to pull off." God will pluck up and pull off the things in our lives that are not necessary. Then He will heal us. *"To every thing there is a season, and a time to every purpose under the heaven"* (Ecclesiastes 3:1). *"And we know that all things work together for good to them that love God,"* (Romans 8:28). *"The curse causeless shall not come"* (Proverbs 26:2). If there's a dealing of God in your life, know that there is purpose written all over it. God will eventually bring you to a season of blessing, as Psalms 66:12 says, *"Thou hast caused men to ride over our heads; we went through fire and through water: but thou broughtest us out into a wealthy place."* This is the irony of God. On one hand He will deal with us, and on the other hand He will bless us.

It then says back in Hosea 6:1, *"he hath smitten."* This word *"smitten"* in the Hebrew means "to strike or to beat." He will beat out of us those things that are not of the Lord. Then He will ultimately bind us up. Job 5:18 says, *"For he maketh sore, and bindeth up: he woundeth, and his hands make whole."* Isn't this what a father does to discipline his child? He doesn't want to, but he does it for the child's benefit. Afterwards he hugs and blesses the child. So that the child will know that it was for his good and not chastisement out of a need to beat or hurt someone.

Ultimately Job 5:19 says, *"He shall deliver thee in six troubles: yea, in seven there shall no evil touch thee."* So the whole purpose of making sore and binding up is so that no evil will ever touch us. He wants us to inherit the throne of glory (I Samuel 2:8). So, He must kill and then make alive, bring down to the grave and then bring up, make poor and then make rich, bring low and then us lift up (I Samuel 2:6-8). This is the purpose of God. In Isaiah 45:7 God says, *"I form the light, and create darkness: I make peace, and create evil: I the Lord do all these things."* We need to have a revelation of the sovereign God. We need to know that everything He's doing is for our good. He may use light and darkness, peace and evil, goodness and severity. So, today remember that even though we may be going through a dealing, He is *"working all things together."*

"The Journey Is Too Great For Thee"
I Kings 19:7

DAY 348

For each one of us, after we are born again by the blood of Jesus and the Word of God, we begin a unique journey with God. Though no one's journey is the same and all are individually tailored by our sovereign God, we see in Scripture a pattern that all who press on will experience. Therefore it is imperative that true disciples learn these patterns so they can be prepared, and know how to respond. Hopefully, many will be spared disappointment, hopelessness, and defeat. We will truly know the ways of God, knowing that in the end His desire for us is that we be victorious overcomers, and be like Enoch who had a true walk with God (Genesis 5:24).

One pattern is found in the story of Elijah in I Kings 19:7. The Lord spoke to Elijah and said *"the journey is too great for thee."* The word for *"journey"* in this story in the Hebrew means "a course of life, a trodden road, a mode of action." An angel told him he couldn't do it on his own and charged him to eat *"a cake baken on the coals, and a cruse of water at his head"* (I Kings 19:6). Elijah needed the cake and water to survive what he was about to face. You and I need to know the same thing for our life. The cake on the coals represents the living and fresh Word of God and the water is God's glory and manifest presence.

Jesus told the disciples in Luke 9:3 to *"Take nothing for your journey, neither staves, nor scrip, neither bread, neither money; neither have two coats apiece."* In other words, we need to be dependent totally on the Lord in this journey. God meets us like He did the Apostle Paul in Acts 9:3, *"And as he journeyed, he came near Damascus: and suddenly there shined round about him a light from heaven."* You and I started our journey when we met the Lord Jesus by a glorious light and found Him.

Paul says that one of the traits of a minister in II Corinthians 11:26 is *"in journeyings often."* This sure is the truth, but all of our journeys ultimately come down to one journey which is called throughout Scripture *"the narrow way"* (Matthew 7:14), *"the path of life"* (Psalms 16:11), and *"the highway of holiness"* (Isaiah 35:8), to name of few. All of us take it and all of us need to know that at the end of this journey is life as God is living it. Matthew 7:14 says, *"Narrow is the way, which leadeth unto life."*

Truly this journey is too great for us; we need Jesus and the Holy Spirit. We need the Word of God and the power of God to help us make it. We find that even in the gospel of John, Jesus got weary in His journey, *"Jesus therefore, being wearied with his journey, sat thus on the well"* (John 4:6). It is inevitable that you and I will get weary from our journey because it is too great for us, but this should not deter us or depress us. We simply need to do as Jesus did when we get weary, sit on the well of living water that springs up out of us to give us the courage to go on. We need to rise and eat the cake baking on coals. We need to eat the living Word of God, the precious truth that will give us hope and help us to go on. Then we need to drink from the cruse of water, drinking in the Spirit of God, allowing God's glory to fill our lives. This will give us the strength we need to continue on this journey. So arise and eat today and receive strength for your journey.

"Emmanuel"
Matthew 1:23

DAY 349

In Matthew 1, we find this great, tremendous truth about the name of our Lord Jesus. It says in verse 23, *"Behold, a virgin shall be with child, and shall bring forth a son, and they shall call his name Emmanuel, which being interpreted is, God with us."* What a powerful revelation. God is with us. He's with us in the form of the Lord Jesus, Emmanuel.

The Bible says in Psalms 46:7, *"The Lord of hosts is with us; the God of Jacob is our refuge. Selah."* As we go through our day, there are many things that will try to get us off our faith. The forces of life are against us and want to *"separate us from the love of God, which is in Christ Jesus our Lord"* (Romans 8:39). They can't, but they still try. You and I need to constantly put ourselves in remembrance that the Lord is with us.

In Isaiah 8:10, it says, *"Take counsel together, and it shall come to nought; speak the word, and it shall not stand: for God is with us."* There are people who take counsel together against us. But if our hearts are right with God, then we can know assuredly that God is with us. We are born of *"incorruptible seed"* (I Peter 1:23) and have been *"partakers of the divine nature"* (II Peter 1:4). Emmanuel, the Lord Jesus, is with us.

Numbers 14:9 states, *"Only rebel not ye against the Lord, neither fear ye the people of the land; for they are bread for us: their defence is departed from them, and the Lord is with us: fear them not"* (Numbers 14:9). All you and I need to do is not to rebel against the Lord or fear the people. David said in Psalms 27:1, *"The Lord is my light and my salvation; whom shall I fear? the Lord is the strength of my life; of whom shall I be afraid?"* We need not fear anyone, because the Lord is with us.

Please know in your heart of hearts today that Jesus is with you. He will *"never leave thee, nor forsake thee"* (Hebrews 13:5). Jesus said in John 10:29, *"No man is able to pluck them out of my Father's hand."* He is the ever-present God, *"our refuge and strength"* (Psalms 46:1). In II Chronicles 13:12, it says, *"And, behold, God himself is with us for our captain."* Behold, God is with you! He's your captain. He will never leave you.

Emmanuel is one of the great names of our Lord and Savior Jesus Christ, but it is also a revelation of His character and who He is. He is the God that is with us. It says in Romans 8:31, *"What shall we then say to these things? If God be for us; who can be against us?"*

"With Patience Wait"
Romans 8:25

Day 350

I don't know about you, but one of the hardest things in my life for me to overcome is my lack of patience. I don't know why, but it seems like patience is one of the hardest virtues for me to have added into my life, *"But if we hope for that we see not, then do we with patience wait for it."* In the world that you and I live today, patience is a lost virtue; everything is fast food, right now, everybody expects things yesterday rather than waiting for them. We have lost our ability to wait.

Hebrews 10:36 says, *"For ye have need of patience, that, after ye have done the will of God, ye might receive the promise."* You have need of patience. I know this has been a word for me; how about you? Are you patient? Are you at peace waiting for the Word of God to come to pass in your life? The Greek word for *"patience"* means "to be long-spirited, forbearing, and longsuffering, to patiently endure, to have fortitude." This can be difficult at times for all of us, but patience is one of the characteristics of the Holy Spirit, of God Himself. He is a great and loving, patient Father. James says:

> *"⁷Be patient therefore, brethren, unto the coming of the Lord. Behold, the husbandman waiteth for the precious fruit of the earth, and hath long patience for it, until he receive the early and latter rain. ⁸Be ye also patient; stablish your hearts: for the coming of the Lord draweth nigh."* (James 5:7-8)

Our husbandman, the Great Lord Jesus, has long patience while He is waiting for the fruit in our life. Then James says we should also be patient while we are waiting for the coming of the Lord. It is so easy to take the path of least resistance and become impatient, and get anxious with God and with our brothers and sisters.

II Timothy 2:24 says, *"And the servant of the Lord must not strive; but be gentle unto all men, apt to teach, patient."* I Timothy 3:3 says, *"Not given to wine, no striker, not greedy of filthy lucre; but patient..."* My, my, my! Sometimes it seems like the Lord asks us to do things that seem impossible, but He never asks us to do anything that He hasn't Himself done or is willing to do.

I love what John says in Revelation 1:9 *"and patience of Jesus Christ"* Jesus Christ was the most patient human being ever. He put up with His disciples, with the multitudes, with the Pharisees, with His family, His own brothers and sisters, and then He had to put up with the devil on top of all that! So, you and I, then, need to receive the Word of the Lord and be patient toward all men (I Thessalonians 5:14).

Ecclesiastes 7:8 says, *"Better is the end of a thing than the beginning thereof: and the patient in spirit is better than the proud in spirit."* Well, our minds and our souls are the things that always seem to cause us to lose our patience because we think way too much. We need to cast down imaginations (II Corinthians 10:5), and in our patience posses our souls (Luke 21:19). While we are going through it, know that tribulation works patience (Romans 5:3-4). The tribulation in our lives is working godly patience in us. May God grant you that today.

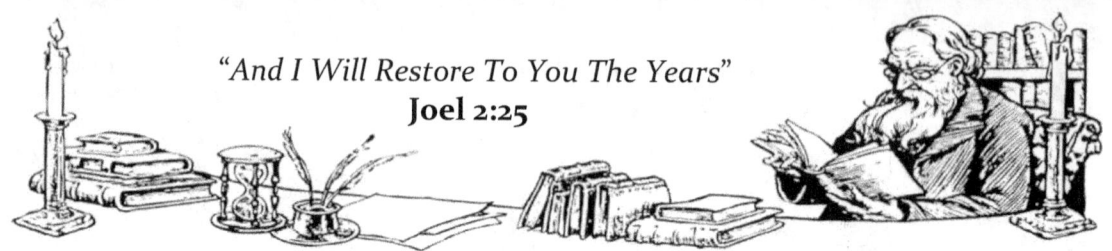

"And I Will Restore To You The Years"
Joel 2:25

This Scripture, *"And I will restore to you the years that the locust hath eaten, the cankerworm, and the caterpiller, and the palmerworm"* (Joel 2:25) is a very encouraging Scripture. It shows us God's plan for our lives – He will restore!

The Hebrew definition for the word *"restore"* means "to give back, to bring back to the first state or condition, to recover, to heal, to cure." This is God's great mercy in our lives, that He always looks to bring reconciliation, always wants to turn things around, and bring us back, to help and heal us.

David prayed in Psalms 51:12 *"Restore unto me the joy of thy salvation..."* So many of us have gone through hard situations or deep dark experiences and we feel lost, alone, and without help; almost as if we can never climb out of the hole that we are in. Yet the Word of God declares, *"And he shall be unto thee a restorer of thy life"* (Ruth 4:15). In Jeremiah 30:17 the Lord says, *"For I will restore health unto thee, and I will heal thee of thy wounds."*

This is our God. He will restore. This was His purpose when He came into our life; that which was lost could be gathered again. That which has happened to us can be turned around by the grace of God. Jesus said in John 16:33, *"In the world ye shall have tribulation: but be of good cheer; I have overcome the world."* David said in Psalms 138:7, *"Though I walk in the midst of trouble, thou wilt revive me: thou shalt stretch forth thine hand against the wrath of mine enemies, and thy right hand shall save me."* Bless His name! He shall be a restorer unto thy life.

All that we've lost; all that we've suffered; all that we've gone through has not been for a vain purpose. Somehow and someway, God will use everything in our lives for Isaiah declares, *"I form the light, and create darkness: I make peace, and create evil: I the Lord do all these things"* (Isaiah 45:7). Nothing happens to us that the sovereign God does not know and He is certainly watching out for us, ready to heal, ready to restore, and ready to come. And as you read this today, allow our precious and wonderful Savior Jesus and His manifest presence to surround you now. With Him He brings health and hope to bring you back to what you had before. All is not lost. He will restore the years the enemy has taken from you. The cankerworm, caterpillar, and palmerworm all speak of demon powers that have sought to steal the years of our lives.

As we look back over our lives we can see that many things have happened to us and many times it took years out of our lives. And it leaves us feeling empty and full of regret because we can't get those years back. But somehow, someway, God promises to restore that which the enemy has taken. Somehow and someway those precious years you lost, God will restore. This is God's Word and promise to you! *"He ever liveth to make intercession"* for us says (Hebrews 7:25). Likewise, I believe He ever liveth to bring reconciliation to our lives. There is nothing we've lost that God cannot bring back again. He will turn the curse into a blessing as the Scripture declares (Nehemiah

13:2). He will restore health, prosperity, but more importantly the years that were taken from us.

So many times in our lives we see that we lose relationships; we lose time; we lose money; we lose things and people and it can be devastating. Yet, out of the midst of all of this comes these words that are so powerful to our spirit, *"He restoreth my soul"* (Psalms 23:3). David of all people knew about the restoration of God. He can restore your soul today. Oh, let Him do it! He is waiting! His precious Holy Spirit is right here to help you, encourage you, and to bring you back to the first state or condition to cause you to recover. He wants to restore you. He wants to be a restorer of your life. Let Him do it. Rise up out of the ashes! Rise up out of the darkness because there is a light shining and His name is Jesus! Christ is our life the Bible says. His face is shining, leading us onward.

In all of the dark places He whispers, "I will be unto thee a restorer of your life and I will restore to you the years the enemy has taken from you." Look for it to happen today. Believe today for it to happen for with God nothing is impossible. Nothing is too hard for the Lord. He will restore. He will bring you back again. Amen!

"David's Three Anointings"
I Samuel 16:13

Here in I Samuel 16:13 we find David being anointed the first time. That David was anointed three times in Scripture is a type to us, that we will go through three stages of anointing in our own life. There are three different stages of light, revelation, glory, and the presence of God.

It all goes back to the three-fold principle. God told Moses to build the tabernacle after the pattern in the spirit. It was a three-fold building consisting of outer court, holy place, and most holy place.

As we receive these three anointings and enter into them, we are increased spiritually and we move to one level of glory, revelation, and light to the next level. We move from the outer court to the holy place. We stay there until we get to a place where we're in a complete flow in that realm, and then we move on to the most holy place. Now all of these three journeys take years, and perfection is at the end at a hundredfold. *"And these are they which are sown on good ground; such as hear the word, and receive it, and bring forth fruit, some thirtyfold, some sixty, and some an hundred"* (Mark 4:20). In the most holy place is a hundredfold, sixtyfold is the holy place, and thirtyfold is the outer court.

The Bible says II Corinthians 3:18 that we go *"from glory to glory, even as by the Spirit of the Lord."* Romans 1:17 says the just go *"from faith to faith."* Psalms 84:7 says we go *"from strength to strength."* Jeremiah 48:11 tells us we go *"from vessel to vessel."* Every one of these places is a rank and a revelation.

Three in the Scripture represents the Godhead and resurrection. So as we enter into the third anointing, what we do is we enter into a total resurrection and a true understanding of the Godhead. We experience resurrection at its completeness. We also have a complete understanding of the Father, the Son, and the Holy Spirit.

So we begin in the outer court with David's first anointing. Samuel took the horn and anointed him in the midst of His brethren. The Spirit of the Lord came upon him from that day forth. The Spirit of the Lord at our first anointing comes upon us from that day forward, and we're anointed in the midst of our brethren. Sometimes this can be very hard because our brethren resist the fact that we received an anointing.

So David goes on laboring under this anointing, fighting Saul, wrestling with all kinds of the dealings of God, until the second anointing. This one is found in II Samuel 2:4, *"And the men of Judah came, and there they anointed David king over the house of Judah."* Once Saul had died it was time to anoint David. The men of Judah, the praisers, came seeing that Saul was gone and anointed David king. Entering into the holy place means all the pieces of furniture in there are operative in our lives, just as in the outer court. Yet there is a calling, a drawing, and a pulling from the most holy place to a greater anointing and a greater revelation. David's third anointing was found in II Samuel 5:1-4. David entered into that most holy place anointing, where God was everything. David was now king over all Israel.

"Where Are The Nine?"
Luke 17:17

In this passage of Scripture in Luke 17 it says:

> "¹²And as he entered into a certain village, there met him ten men that were lepers, which stood afar off: ¹³And they lifted up their voices, and said, Jesus, Master, have mercy on us. ¹⁴And when he saw them, he said unto them, Go shew yourselves unto the priests. And it came to pass, that, as they went, they were cleansed. ¹⁵And one of them, when he saw that he was healed, turned back, and with a loud voice glorified God. ¹⁶And fell down on his face at his feet, giving him thanks: and he was a Samaritan. ¹⁷And Jesus answering said, Were there not ten cleansed? But where are the nine? ¹⁸There are not found that returned to give glory to God, save this stranger." (Luke 17:12-18)

DAY 353

Isn't it always the Samaritan, the stranger, who responds to God? The Samaritans were the half-breeds as far as the Jews were concerned, because of the Babylonyish captivity. They were taken and intermarried with other nations. So they were not considered full Jews. Isn't it always those not considered to be anything that seems to find the glory and grace of God? I remember reading this many years ago and as I read it, I kept hearing an echo going on and on again in my own mind saying, "*Where are the nine?*" The Lord said to me at that time, "I am still saying that today, where are the nine?"

If you look at it, Jesus told them to go to the priest. But that wasn't what He intended them to do, because He asks where the nine were. Many times the Lord will tell us to do something but He is really just testing us to see what our real response will be when He does something for us. He never expected them to go to the priest, but to give glory to God because they were healed.

But only one out of ten returned. That is why there is a remnant in the Scriptures. When one of them saw that he was healed, he turned back and with a loud voice glorified God, fell down on his face at Jesus' feet and gave Him thanks. But Jesus, though He was happy for that one man, said, "*Where are the nine?*"

And today, the Lord is still saying, "*Where is the nine?*" Where are the ninety percent of Christianity that does not come and give God glory, that are intent to go to an earthly priest, content to go to an earthly representative of God, but not to God himself? God help us that we not become one of the nine.

We should never mind being a Samaritan or a stranger. We must always have the heart that giving glory to God means more to us than the praise of men or doing what others might do. Like that Samaritan, let us turn back and fall at Jesus' feet today.

"Worthy Of Double Honor"
I Timothy 5:17

In this passage we find the great truth of how those that preach the Gospel shall live off the Gospel. There is a great deal of controversy about ministers being paid or taken care of with carnal (natural) things. However, it is the solemn duty of God's people to minister to Levites, those that God has called to the priesthood, to take care of them. Here the Apostle Paul says:

> "*¹⁷Let the elders that rule well be counted worthy of double honour, especially they who labour in the word and doctrine. ¹⁸For the scripture saith, Thou shalt not muzzle the ox that treadeth out the corn. And, The labourer is worthy of his reward.*" (Timothy 5:17-18)

Note it says "double honor" and not just honor. Those that labor doing the work of the ministry are to be rewarded with double honor, but also with natural things. In Romans 15:27, Paul wrote, "*if the Gentiles have been made partakers of their spiritual things, their duty is also to minister unto them in carnal things.*" If you have been ministered to of spiritual things, spiritual relations, or spiritual truths, then it is your duty to minister to those in carnal or natural things. This is simply the Word of God and should be obeyed. Paul writes to the Corinthians saying:

> "*¹¹If we have sown unto you spiritual things, is it a great thing if we shall reap your carnal things? ... ¹³Do ye not know that they which minister about holy things live of the things of the temple? and they which wait at the altar are partakers with the altar? ¹⁴Even so hath the Lord ordained that they which preach the gospel should live of the gospel*" (I Corinthians 9:11-14).

This is God's will that all His ministers be taken care of. The Lord has ordained this. They which preach the gospel should live of the gospel. In II Kings 22 it says:

> "*⁴Go up to Hilkiah the high priest, that he may sum the silver which is brought into the house of the LORD, which the keepers of the door have gathered of the people: ⁵And let them deliver it into the hand of the doers of the work, that have the oversight of the house of the LORD*"
> (II Kings 22:4-5)

The silver is to be delivered unto those that have oversight over the house of the Lord. Acts 4:37 says, the people "*brought the money, and laid it at the apostles' feet.*" We need to be giving a double honor to those that minister to us spiritual things. And we need to do it with a good and cheerful heart, as Paul says in II Corinthians 9:7, "*for God loveth a cheerful giver.*"

"Bound In The Bundle Of Life"
I Samuel 25:29

Here in I Samuel 25, David is angry at Nabal, Abigail's husband, for refusing his men food and provision. David is out to get some payback. Abigail, after hearing of his plan, goes to David to bring him food and ask for his forgiveness. She says to him, *"Yet a man is risen to pursue thee, and to seek thy soul: but the soul of my lord shall be bound in the bundle of life with the Lord thy God"* (I Samuel 25:29). In other words, his soul would be protected to live in the bundle of life with the Lord.

Likewise, you and I have been bound in the bundle of life with Jesus. The Hebrew word for *"bound"* here means "to cramp or to bind close together." God has brought us close together. He's protecting us so that we can live, and He's binding us in the bundle of life. The Bible says in Psalms 66:8-9, *"⁸O bless our God, ye people, and make the voice of his praise to be heard: ⁹Which holdeth our soul in life, and suffereth not our feet to be moved"*. What a tremendous word for you and me today.

Today, as we go about our activities, we can rest assured, not only does the *"angel of the Lord encampeth round about them that fear him"* (Psalms 34:7), but the Spirit of the living God and His grace has provided us a mighty shield of protection. We're bound in the bundle of life, in the Lord Jesus Himself. It says in Proverbs 8, *"Blessed is the man that heareth me, watching daily at my gates, waiting at the posts of my doors. For whoso findeth me findeth life, and shall obtain favour of the Lord"* (Proverbs 8:34-35). Have you found Him? If you have, you've found life and favor.

You're bound in the bundle of life today; you're protected to live. God is interested in your life. Jesus said in John 10, *"I am come that they might have life, and that they might have it more abundantly"* (John 10:10). The word for *"life"* used here is the Greek word *"zoe,"* which means "life as God is living it right now." I John 4 tells us, *"As he is, so are we in this world"* (I John 4:17). We are protected and bound in this great bundle of life. He keeps us from harm, devastation, and destruction as long as we trust in Him and walk holy before Him. In Psalms 16, David says, *"Thou wilt shew me the path of life: in thy presence is fulness of joy; at thy right hand there are pleasures for evermore"* (Psalms 16:11). He will show you the path of life. He will show you the narrow way, *"which leadeth unto life"* (Matthew 7:14). That life is the Lord Jesus.

Thank God today that you and I are in His *"everlasting arms"* (Deuteronomy 33:27) and that He carries us in His bosom (Isaiah 40:11). We're bound in the bundle of life. We are bound in Jesus.

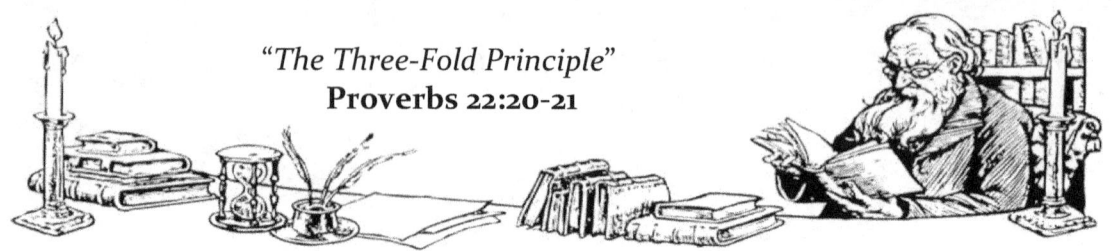

"The Three-Fold Principle"
Proverbs 22:20-21

DAY 356

If we are ever going to come to a full understanding of our God and what He is all about, and how this pertains to us in our walk with Him, we must understand this "three-fold principle." This principle summarizes God, His creation, His salvation, His baptisms, etc. in detail. Once this revelation dawns on us, so many loose ends of our theological thinking are going to be tied up. This principle is simple, but yet carries with it a mighty revelation. It helps us to see God in His workings and dealings with men. It defines and explains Him, the One True God, and His highest form of creation, man. It then shows us how He has given man a salvation to the uttermost, as well as, corresponding baptisms to enhance and to bless our lives.

The three-fold principle is simply defined as it follows. The three-fold God created a three-fold man who fell in the garden, desperately needing to be restored. Hence, God gave a three-fold salvation for every part of mankind, proceeding to give mankind a three-fold baptism to help and aid him to go back to everything He had originally planned. In short the three-fold God created a three-fold man, to whom, after he fell, gave him a three-fold salvation with a three-fold baptism to help him.

We can see this three-fold principle throughout the Scriptures. It is a remarkable revelation. It shows the completeness and thoroughness and compassion of our God. When you think about it, most of what God has done is in a three-fold manner. Today we will try to clearly demonstrate this principle and why it is so important. By allowing this truth access into our lives and minds we will have an overview of how our God works. To understand the three-fold principle Proverbs says:

> "*²⁰Have not I written to thee excellent things in counsels and knowledge, ²¹That I might make thee know the certainty of the words of truth; that thou mightest answer the words of truth to them that send unto thee?*" (Proverbs 22:20-21)

The word *"excellent"* in Hebrew means *"three-fold or weighty."* So God has written to us weighty, three-fold things in counsels and knowledge that He would make us know the certainty of the Scripture. In addition, by understanding the three-fold principle, we can then give an answer with words of truth to them that ask us (I Peter 3:15).

So, let's understand this principle. First of all, God is three-fold. I John 5:7 says, "*For there are three that bear record in heaven, the Father, the Word, and the Holy Ghost: and these three are one.*" The three-fold God, but one.

Since man was created in the image of God and God is three-fold, then man is three-fold, spirit, soul, and body. Genesis 2:7 says, "*And the LORD God formed man of the dust of the ground, and breathed into his nostrils the breath of life; and man became a living soul."* I Thessalonians 5:23 says, *"And the very God of peace sanctify you wholly; and I pray God your whole spirit and soul and body be preserved blameless unto the coming of our Lord Jesus Christ."* Man is threefold, (spirit, soul, and body), yet one.

After man fell, he needed salvation for every part of his being: spirit, soul and body. So God brought forth a three-fold salvation. Hebrews 7:25 says, *"Wherefore he is able also to save them to the uttermost."* This is called a great salvation (Hebrews 2:3). Isaiah 53:5 says, *"But he was wounded for our transgressions, he was bruised for our iniquities: the chastisement of our peace was upon him; and with his stripes we are healed."* We see this threefold principle here. Jesus was wounded and bruised for our sins in our spirit. He was chastised for our peace, which is in our soulish realm. And He took stripes for our healing, which is for our physical body. II Corinthians 1:10 says, *"Who delivered us from so great a death, and doth deliver: in whom we trust that he will yet deliver us."* This past deliverance of being born again was for our spirit. Our present deliverance is the sanctifying process of the Lord daily delivering our soul. And our future deliverance is when the Lord *"shall change our vile body, that it may be fashioned like unto his glorious body"* (Philippians 3:21).

To understand this completely, the three-fold salvation is called justification for our spirit, sanctification for our soul, and glorification for our body. This is a three-fold salvation which is actually one.

Finally, our baptism is three-fold as well. Hebrew 6:2 calls it the *"doctrine of baptisms."* Notice baptism is plural in Hebrew 6. The three baptisms are the baptism of blood, the baptism of the Spirit, and the baptism of water. I John 5:8 says, *"And there are three that bear witness in earth, the spirit, and the water, and the blood: and these three agree in one."* Once again we find three baptisms agreeing in one. The spirit of man is baptized, washed, or immersed in the blood of Jesus when we are born again. The soul of man is baptized or immersed in the Holy Ghost. And the body of man is baptized or immersed in water.

So, to summarize it again, the three-fold God created a three-fold man, to whom, after he fell, gave him a three-fold salvation with a three-fold baptism to help him. This is the three-fold principle.

"The Three-Fold Principle 2"
Hebrews 7:25

I want to continue with the three-fold principle. Here are more examples. Salvation is threefold: justification, sanctification, and glorification. Hebrews 7:25 describes it an *"uttermost salvation,"* one for each aspect of our being. Baptism is three-fold: blood, spirit, and water. God is three-fold: Father, Son, and Holy Ghost. Man is three-fold: spirit, soul, and body. This great three-fold principle is found all throughout the Scriptures. Moses' tabernacle had an outer court, a holy place, and a most holy place. It was called the "pattern after the spirit". Therefore everything revolves around this pattern. We were created in the image of God and just as God is three-fold but one, we are created three-fold but one.

Heaven is three-fold. The first heaven is the sky above us, the second heaven is the place of principalities and powers, and the Scripture speaks of the third heaven which is God's throne. The body of Christ is three-fold: thirty-fold Christians, sixty-fold Christians, and a hundred-fold Christians. The thirty-fold Christians are the backslidden Christians, the sixty-fold Christians are the ones we find represented in the *"woman"* found in Revelation 12, and the hundred-fold Christians are those who are the *"manchild"* or the *"bride."*

We see that the feasts of the Lord are three-fold as well. The feast of Passover (represents our salvation), the feast of Pentecost (represents the baptism in the Holy Ghost), and the feast of Tabernacles (represents the final harvest and the coming forth of the sons of God). There are three houses in the Scripture: the tabernacle of Moses, the tabernacle of David, and the temple of Solomon. The priestly ministry is three-fold: the outer court is where the priests ministered "to the people", the holy place is "before the Lord", and the most holy place is "to the Lord." Faith is three-fold: the measure of faith, the fruit of faith, and the gift of faith.

The ages of the church are three-fold: the law period (outer court), the church age (holy place), and the millennial age (the most holy place). There are levels of worship that are three-fold as well: thanksgiving (outer court), praise (holy place), and worship (most holy place). The three-fold principle continues with our precious Jesus: He is our Savior, He is our Lord, and He will ultimately become Jesus our Husband.

Noah's ark had three stories. God Himself is omnipotent, omniscient, and omnipresent. The Bible speaks of the sun, the moon, and the stars. This is the Father, the Son, and the Holy Ghost. It speaks of Him who was, and is, and is to come. Jesus said He was the Way, the Truth, and the Life. The Bible speaks of fathers, young men, and children.

There is so much to say about this three-fold principle that I have only scratched the surface, but I pray that you will get the study on the Doctrine of Baptisms so you can receive more about this. I pray that as you think on this three-fold principle today, that in understanding it, this will help tie up all the loose ends of your life.

"His Eye Seeth Every Precious Thing"
Job 28:10

DAY 358

There is nothing that happens, nothing that goes on in our life that God does not see or know about. The Bible says *"all things are naked and opened unto the eyes of him with whom we have to do"* (Hebrews 4:13). He sees everything. But more than that, so many times when we look at our own lives, we don't see very much that's precious and we don't think very much of ourselves. But hear the word of the Lord today, *"He cutteth out rivers among the rocks; and his eye seeth every precious thing"* (Job 28:10).

Being a pastor for as long as I have and ministering and counseling to thousands of people, I know that many people loathe themselves as we see with the woman thrown out in the street in Ezekiel 16. She loathed herself. This is so contrary to what God wants for His people. In spite of your weaknesses, in spite of all the foibles and flaws that you have in your life, God loves you anyway. He counted the cost before He came into your life. He knew full well who you were, who you are, and who you will be.

David saw this in his own life and said in Psalms 139:15, *"My substance was not hid from thee, when I was made in secret, and curiously wrought in the lowest parts of the earth."* God knows everything about us and if God would mark iniquities, who would stand (Psalms 130:3)? None of us would. God looks through all that we are and sees the real us.

For many of us, we were born into unfortunate circumstances to abusive parents, or to unloving parents, or to troubled households. And as such, we grow up inheriting these genes of all our relatives. All of us are born with proclivities to things that maybe are not really that good. We are the sum total of all that our mother and father were and their mothers and fathers were. We didn't ask for this. We were born with this and we must fight to be delivered from those things that are unclean or uncomely.

But when God looks at you, He doesn't see the worst in you. He sees the good in you. His eye sees every precious thing in you. God doesn't look on the outward appearance (I Samuel 16:7). God looks upon the heart. God looks upon the real you. God knows you. He knows everything about you. You can't hide anything from Him and yet He still loves you. Please believe that as I John 4:16 says, *"And we have known and believed the love that God hath to us."* It is not enough to know God loves you. You have to know and believe it in your heart so you never doubt it no matter the weaknesses that live inside of you.

One translation of Job 28:10 is, *"His eye sees everything of value."* You are valuable. There are things in your life that are of value to God and are of value to the human race. You are not without value. You are something beautiful and wonderfully created by God and you are full of value.

Two other translations read, "*He finds all kinds of beautiful gems*", "*He sees all the treasures there.*" Locked up hidden deep within all of us are beautiful gems and treasures that lie within us that are never brought out because we don't think it necessary or we don't think very much of ourselves. But we need to see ourselves as God sees us. His eye sees everything of value in us.

Another translation reads, "*He uncovers the precious stones in our lives.*" He will cut out the rocks in our lives to get those precious stones out of us. In time as we walk with the Lord faithfully and humbly serve Him, we will find that His preciousness will bring out the real, true us.

Please believe me when I say Proverbs 20:27, "*The spirit of man is the candle of the Lord, searching all the inward parts of the belly.*" Even today He is looking inside of you searching until He finds the hidden gems of value in you.

There are things in us that we don't even know exist right now that are beautiful and wonderful that the body of Christ needs and the world all around us needs. As Christians, we have the answer. We have what the world needs. But because of insecurities, inferiorities or unbelief, we don't allow these things to come forth and manifest themselves.

God sees those treasures within you. You must believe and see them for yourself. You are something of value. You are worth something. Jesus paid an awesome price for you. He was willing to die on a horrible cross, be beaten within an inch of His life, His body torn and flayed mercilessly, so that you can be free. I John 3:8 says, "*For this purpose the Son of God was manifested, that he might destroy the works of the devil.*" He came to destroy them and make you free.

His eye sees every precious thing. Don't believe the bad reports about yourself. You don't have to believe the unkind things people say about you. You don't have to believe the words that hurt and strike you deeply. Just know within you that there is treasure, value, gems, and precious stones inside of you that God placed there and He is going to bring them out. Never ever believe that He sees you any other way. When He looks upon you, He looks upon your heart and He sees every precious thing. And you are full of precious things today. Let the Lord bring them out of you. Share them with others and by doing so manifest His glory and His character in this earth!

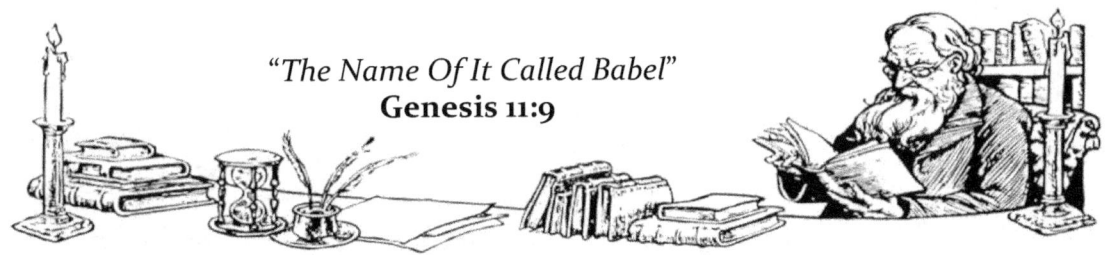

"The Name Of It Called Babel"
Genesis 11:9

DAY 359

Let's look today at the story of Nimrod in Genesis 11. It says in the previous chapter that he was a *"mighty hunter before the Lord,"* which in the actual Hebrew means a *"mighty hunter against the Lord"* (Genesis 10:9). Nimrod was the first type of the spirit of antichrist in the earth. As he journeyed with his people, they came to a place in the land of Shinar and dwelt there (Genesis 11:2). The Bible then says, *"⁴And they said, Go to, let us build us a city and a tower, whose top may reach unto heaven; and let us make us a name, lest we be scattered abroad upon the face of the whole earth...⁹Therefore is the name of it called Babel"* (Genesis 11:4, 9).

"Babel" in Hebrew means "confusion, mixture, and chaos." Paul tells us in I Corinthians, *"God is not the author of confusion, but of peace"* (I Corinthians 14:33). And in James, the Bible declares, *"For where envying and strife is, there is confusion and every evil work"* (James 3:16). Babylon, or Babel, is the manmade spirit of denominationalism or sectarianism. All over the world, men erect towers, churches and ministries in their own name. They desire to make a name for themselves and seek their own security and self-glorification independent of God. But they labor in vain, as it says in Psalms, *"Except the Lord build the house, they labour in vain that build it"* (Psalms 127:1). We live in a time when the body of Christ is glorying in men (I Corinthians 3:21) and elevating them to positions that they should never be placed. There is much confusion and mixture in the body of Christ, and it is not of God.

The people here in Genesis tried to build a house of God with brick, or dirt, for stone and slime for mortar, which speaks of human initiative apart from God. It speaks of the flesh and man, whereas the Lord should be the one building the house. We should not be saying, *"Let us build us a city and a tower...and let us make us a name."* The book of Hebrews is full of admonitions beginning with, "Let us," but they are admonitions of the Kingdom of God rather than Babylonish ones. Babylon is coming together in unity. Just as God is gathering *"together in one all things in Christ"* (Ephesians 1:10), Satan is gathering together all things in Babylon.

So, as Babylon comes into unity, what are it's goals? They want to build a tower, *"whose top may reach unto heaven."* They don't need God to do it; they're doing it themselves. This is, as Paul puts it in II Timothy, *"Having a form of godliness, but denying the power thereof"* (II Timothy 3:5). They also want to make a name for themselves. The book of John tells us, *"He that speaketh of himself seeketh his own glory"* (John 7:18). As it says in Psalms 147:10, God *"delighteth not in the strength of the horse: he taketh not pleasure in the legs of a man."* He is not interested in our strength or our own ideas and ambitions. We should *"let this mind be in"* us, *"which was also in Christ Jesus,"* a mind of humility and sacrifice (Philippians 2:5). We must seek to build up the body of Christ and the Kingdom of God, not our own ministries, churches, or reputations. If we do like the people did in this passage, we'll find that God will come down and scatter us abroad. We don't want to be scattered; we want to be joined together. And we don't want Babel; we just want the presence of God.

"The Word Of God Came Unto John In The Wilderness"
Luke 3:2

DAY 360

We find a tremendous irony here in Luke, how God calls and chooses His men and women. It says, *"Now in the fifteenth year of the reign of Tiberius Caesar, Pontius Pilate being governor of Judaea, and Herod being tetrarch of Galilee, and his brother Philip tetrarch of Ituraea and of the region of Trachonitis, and Lysanias the tetrarch of Abilene"* (Luke 3:1).

Luke is mentioning people in positions of governmental authority. He proceeds to mention the priesthood, the holy men. And then he says, *"the word of God came unto John the son of Zacharias in the wilderness."* (Luke 3:2) Did you know that John was born unto a priest? He was supposed to be spending his time in the temple preparing for the priesthood. Instead, he was in the deserts until his showing unto Israel.

God did not choose a normal priest. He didn't go to Annas and Caiaphas, the high priests, nor did He choose a political or governmental figure. In John 1:6, it says, *"There was a man sent from God, whose name was John."* He was just a regular man like you and me, but the Word of God came to him, because he was in the wilderness. You will find when God calls you and the Word of God is revealed to you, you may be in the wilderness. The wilderness is a type of the dealings of God to prepare us for ministry.

The Bible says when Samuel came to anoint one of Jesse's sons, that his youngest son David was keeping the sheep (I Samuel 16:11). His father didn't even believe in him or invite him to come. But Samuel said after seeing all the sons present, *"Are here all thy children?"* Jesse's response was, "Well, I have this young boy and he keeps the sheep." Although the youngest, David was ultimately a greater selection than all the other big and mighty specimens because he was doing the will of God. Jesus said:

> *"⁴²Who then is that faithful and wise steward, whom his lord shall make ruler over his household, to give them their portion of meat in due season? ⁴³Blessed is that servant, whom his lord when he cometh shall find so doing"* (Luke 12:42-43).

David was being faithful to do the simple thing: keep the sheep. God watches how we act in the natural and then rewards us spiritually. The calling of God did not come to his brothers, but to David, who was in the wilderness keeping the sheep. What a Word! God brings the Word to you in the wilderness. He doesn't choose the fancy folks. I Corinthians 1:26 tells us, *"For ye see your calling, brethren, how that not many wise men after the flesh, not many mighty, not many noble, are called."* It is the are-nots and the despised that God calls (I Corinthians 1:28). They are the ones willing to go to the wilderness. They're willing to go by themselves to keep sheep and kill a lion and a bear, when nobody is watching, but God. All the while, God is preparing them to carry a mighty anointing and to lead His people out of bondage.

The Word of God came unto John in the wilderness, not on a mountain. Are you in the wilderness? Then prepare to hear the Word of the Lord.

"For God Took Him"
Genesis 5:24

DAY 361

Enoch is only mentioned thrice in Genesis 5, Hebrews 11, and the book of Jude. Let's quickly look at these to see his story, how he was translated, and how God took him.

It says Enoch, *"lived sixty and five years, and begat Methuselah: ²²And Enoch walked with God after he begat Methuselah three hundred years, and begat sons and daughters"* (Genesis 5:21-22). It is important to realize Enoch lived sixty-five years before he begat Methuselah. After he begat Methuselah, for three hundred years he walked with God. Many times, having children will cause us to have a real walk with God. Three hundred is the number in Scripture for the faithful remnant.

It says, *"²³And all the days of Enoch were three hundred sixty and five years: ²⁴And Enoch walked with God: and he was not; for God took him"* (Genesis 5:23-24). It doesn't say that Enoch's wife or children were taken, or even that they walked with God. Enoch walked with God. The word *"walked"* here means "to rest comfortably with." In other words, Enoch had an intimate relationship with Him. He walked with God for three hundred years, rising to heavenly places in Him until, eventually, God took him. This earth could no longer hold him; he was too close to God.

In Hebrews 11:5 it says, *"By faith Enoch was translated that he should not see death; and was not found, because God had translated him: for before his translation he had this testimony, that he pleased God."* What caused God to take him, to translate him that he should not see death? Enoch had this testimony: that he pleased God. The next verse says, *"But without faith it is impossible to please him: for he that cometh to God must believe that he is, and that he is a rewarder of them that diligently seek him"* (Hebrews 11:6).

If you and I expect to be resurrected, translated, and caught up unto the Lord, then we cannot be concerned about our families. We have to be concerned with our own walk. II Corinthians 5:10 tells us, *"For we must all appear before the judgment seat of Christ"*. You can't walk with God for your spouse or children; you can only be an example to them. They must individually find their own way, and hopefully they too will rest comfortably with the Lord and have an intimate relationship with Him. We hope that they will *"grow in grace, and in the knowledge of our Lord and Saviour Jesus Christ"* (II Peter 3:18). We pray that they be prepared and approved for translation, or as it says in Hebrews 6:1-3, that God will *"permit"* them to *"go on unto perfection."*

Jude 14 says Enoch was the seventh from Adam. Seven in the Bible is the number for perfection and completion. So, Enoch is a type of the *"perfect man"* (Ephesians 4:13), the many-member son of God. It says he *"prophesied of these, saying, Behold, the Lord cometh with ten thousands of his saints."* My favorite translation of this verse reads, *"the Lord cometh in holy myriads of himself."* In other words, these people that He's coming back with are in His image. His saints can say, *"It is no longer I that liveth, but Christ that liveth in me"* (Galatians 2:20). Like Enoch, they were translated that they should not see death for God took them. I want God to take me. Do you? Let's let Enoch be the example to show us the way.

"The Lord Thundered From Heaven"
II Samuel 22:14

DAY 362

Today, we will see how our God answers us in our times of need. He comes mightily crashing with thunder and discomfits the enemy, separates them, and causes them to flee. Here in II Samuel 22, the Bible says:

> "*14The Lord thundered from heaven, and the most High uttered his voice. 15And he sent out arrows, and scattered them; lightning, and discomfited them. 16And the channels of the sea appeared, the foundations of the world were discovered, at the rebuking of the Lord, at the blast of the breath of his nostrils. 17He sent from above, he took me; he drew me out of many waters; 18He delivered me from my strong enemy, and from them that hated me: for they were too strong for me*" (II Samuel 22:14-18).

Is anything too strong for you today? Has your strong enemy that hates you got you in bondage? God is going to send from above, take you, and draw you out of those deep and many waters that you are in. He is going to do it by thundering. "*The Lord thundered from heaven, and the most High uttered his voice.*" When God utters His voice, it is like thunder. In Psalms 29:3, it says, "*The God of glory thundereth.*" It says in Revelation 4, talking about the throne of God, "*And out of the throne proceeded lightnings and thunderings and voices*" (Revelation 4:5).

The word "*thundered*" in the Hebrew means, "to violently agitate with anger, to war, to crash or bring trouble; to cause to tumble." When our enemies rise against us, God will come like mighty thunder and discomfit them. Job 26:14 says, "*The thunder of his power who can understand?*" Who can understand the thunder of His power? All we know is that this thunder is the voice of God. Psalms 77:18 states, "*The voice of thy thunder was in the heaven: the lightnings lightened the world: the earth trembled and shook.*" In Psalms 81:7, it says, "*Thou calledst in trouble, and I delivered thee; I answered thee in the secret place of thunder.*" God is going to answer you when you call from the secret place of thunder. That thunder is His marvelous voice that will discomfit and cause the enemy to go fleeing from you.

In Psalms 104:7, it says, "*At thy rebuke they fled; at the voice of thy thunder they hasted away.*" O how marvelous is our God. The God of glory thunders. When He thunders, it brings with it all of the resources of heaven, pounding out the enemy. It says in Psalms 18:13, "*The Lord also thundered in the heavens.*" The God of glory will thunder marvelously with His voice. Job 37:4 says, "*After it a voice roareth: he thundereth with the voice of his excellency.*" The God of glory thunders! When you are in need, surrounded by deep waters, surrounded by an enemy that hates you, believe God. Today, wait to hear as the God of glory will thunder, and His voice will cause the enemy to flee from you.

"The Race"
Ecclesiastes 9:11

Day 363

We want to look today at the principle of the race found in the Scriptures. Most people don't know it, but when we receive the Lord Jesus as our Savior, we enter into a divine race. This race is also called the "narrow way" (Matthew 7:14), "the highway of holiness" (Isaiah 35:8), and "the path of the just" (Proverbs 4:18). It is simply the way of the Lord and it's the way into the holiest place. It begins at salvation, and ends at the throne of God, the mercy seat. Here in Ecclesiastes 9:11 it says, *"I returned, and saw under the sun, that the race is not to the swift, nor the battle to the strong."*

First of all, many people don't know that we're in a race, but here Solomon calls it *"the race"*. Secondly, it says, *"that the race is not to the swift, nor the battle to the strong."* Also the Bible tells us in Psalms 147:10, *"he taketh not pleasure in the legs of a man."* He doesn't need our talent or our strength. For His strength is made perfect in our weaknesses. All He expects us to do is finish this race. As Hebrews 6:1 says, *"Let us go on unto perfection."*

He also says in Hebrews 10:38, *"If any man draw back, my soul has no pleasure in him."* How do we draw back? It is by not running the race anymore. Like the bride in Song of Solomon 5, who had taken off her shoes to get into bed and didn't respond when the Lord came to visit her. We can never settle down and quit. We must always be going onward and upward. We're pilgrims and sojourners looking for a city whose builder and maker is God.

In I Corinthians 9:24 it says, *"Know ye not that they which run in a race run all, but one receiveth the prize? So run, that ye may obtain."* Far too many believers don't know that they are to obtain something. There is a prize to be won. Philippians 3:14 says, *"I press toward the mark for the prize of the high calling of God in Christ Jesus."* The Amplified version reads, *"I strain to reach the end of the race."* Once again, the race begins at salvation and ends in the glory. Nonetheless, all throughout this race, which is our entire sanctification process and our walk with God, there are many exit signs on this narrow way. So many people take the exits and never get back on the path. It behooves us to realize that we're in a race and to run so that we can obtain the prize. We need to strain to reach the end of the race. Hebrews says:

> *"Wherefore seeing we also are compassed about with so great a cloud of witnesses, let us lay aside every weight, and the sin which doth so easily beset us, and let us run with patience the race that is set before us."* (Hebrews 12:1)

Today, let us all remember that there is a prize to be won and a race to be run. So, today, strain to reach the end of that race to receive the prize.

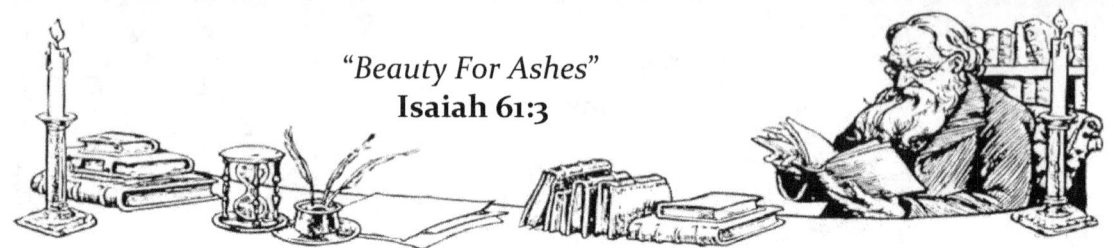

"Beauty For Ashes"
Isaiah 61:3

DAY 364

Oh what a marvelous truth this is, that in the ashes, in the degradation, and in the hard places in our life, God will bring beauty out of all of it. Here He says in Isaiah 61:3, *"To appoint unto them that mourn in Zion, to give unto them beauty for ashes."* Ashes are the remains of something that has been burned and destroyed. How can beauty ever be brought out of something burned or destroyed? It may seem impossible in the natural, but hear the word of the Lord today.

"Beauty" in the Hebrew means "to gleam, to beautify, an embellishment or something fancy." In other words, God is going to bring something gleaming, something fancy, and something embellished and beautiful out of the ashes out of our life. The word *"ashes"* in Hebrew means "to scatter or to cover over, to strew."

There are so many things that happen to us in this life, both good and bad. Many of them, however, have a great effect on our life. We, as the people of God, need to know that no matter what experiences we go through, God has a holy purpose. Romans 8:28 says, *"And we know that all things work together for good to them that love God, to them who are the called according to his purpose."* We really need to understand that all things are truly working together for our good and that God is going to bring a blessing out of it in all of our lives.

For example, consider the story of Joseph. In the end, Joseph said to his brothers in Genesis 50:20, *"But as for you, ye thought evil against me; but God meant it unto good, to bring to pass, as it is this day, to save much people alive."* From the ashes of Joseph's life that came from the hardships and the sufferings he went through, God was able to save the then-known world. God knew a famine was coming and he needed a man to use to save the people. Joseph experienced beauty for his ashes. He went in one moment from being dressed in prison garments in his prison cell, to being honored and made prime minister over the entire nation of Egypt.

In Judges 14, we find the story of Samson and the young lion, and it says *"Out of the eater came forth meat, and out of the strong came forth sweetness"* (Judges 14:14). He is saying here that out of the lion that came against him and attacked him (verse 5), which he killed and threw to the side of the road, was later found with honey in a honey comb in its carcass. In other words, out of the thing that was meant to destroy him, came forth meat; Meat represents something deep or something that he could eat and give life. Out of the strong, the thing that had come against him, came forth sweetness. Out of every bad situation, God can and will give beauty if we let Him. God will beautify and make to shine that which has been scattered over in our lives. Glory to God! Psalms 30:11 says, *"Thou hast turned for me my mourning into dancing: thou hast put off my sackcloth, and girded me with gladness."* It also says in verse five that *"weeping may endure for a night, but joy cometh in the morning."* As we go through this day, let's remind ourselves that God has a plan and that He is going to give us beauty for the ashes of our lives.

"One Another"
Romans 15:7

DAY 365

I am so grateful to the Lord that one of the glorious truths in the Scriptures is that God is making us one and that we are to love one another. It says here in Romans 15:7, *"Wherefore receive ye one another, as Christ also received us to the glory of God."* So many times we don't really receive our brothers but we judge them after the outward appearance. We need to begin (as God does) to look upon the heart of one another (I Samuel 16:7), because we are not only a body, but a family.

It says in Psalms 75:2, *"When I shall receive the congregation I will judge uprightly."* Its only when you are able to receive someone that you are able to judge them correctly. Have you received your brothers and sisters yet? Have you graced them and taken them as your own? One day, when Jesus' family tried to interrupt Him while He was preaching, He said *"Who is my mother? and who are my brethren?"* and goes on to say in Matthew 12:50 *"Whosoever shall do the will of my Father which is in heaven, the same is my brother, and sister, and mother."* You and I together form a family unit; we have a Father (God Himself) and you and I are brothers and sisters.

The Scriptures are full of admonitions about how we are to treat one another. It says in Colossians 3:13 that we are to be *"forbearing one another, and forgiving one another."* If we have the revelation of one another we can do this. Forbearing means *"putting up with"* even putting up with the things we don't really want to because we know it's the will of God to do it. There are things in all of us that aren't that great; weaknesses, foibles, and frailty; but God uses faulty men and we are still to be forbearing and forgiving with one another.

In John 15:12 Jesus said *"This is my commandment, That ye love one another"* and in Romans 12:10 it says *"Be kindly affectioned one to another with brotherly love; in honour preferring one another."* We are not to be ambitious, struggling, and striving with our brothers and sisters but we're actually to prefer one another. For example, let the other brother go first; let the other brother get the glory.

It reads in Galatians 5:13 *"...by love serve one another"* and in Hebrews 10:24 it says *"Let us consider one another to provoke unto love and to good works."* Today let's *"consider one another to provoke unto love and to good works."* Let's encourage each other or as Hebrews 3:13 tells us, let's *"exhort one another daily, while it is called Today."* We can do this. We can exhort and encourage one another! Ephesians 4:32 says *"be ye kind one to another, tenderhearted, forgiving one another, even as God for Christ's sake hath forgiven you."* If we get our eyes off of "I, me, mine" and the self-centered selfishness that radiates through the body of Christ, we can begin to receive one another and start exhorting one another. Then this one another principle will become a reality in our lives as we embrace one another as family, today and forever!

THE LITTLE BOOK
Index of Devotions
Sorted by Day

Foreword 3
Acknowledgements 4
DAY 1 - *Israel Doth Not Know, My People Doth Not Consider* 5
DAY 2 - *He Brought Me Up* 7
DAY 3 - *Take No Thought* 9
DAY 4 - *For His Name's Sake They Went Forth* 10
DAY 5 - *Delilah, Entice Him* 11
DAY 6 - *Good Things In Possession* 13
DAY 7 - *A Chosen Vessel* 14
DAY 8 - *Love Not The World* 15
DAY 9 - *Then Job Arose* 17
DAY 10 - *Not Living Unto Ourselves* 18
DAY 11 - *Judah Shall Plow* 19
DAY 12 - *As For Me* 20
DAY 13 - *Eat This Roll* 21
DAY 14 - *Let Him Glory In The Lord* 22
DAY 15 - *If I Perish, I Perish* 23
DAY 16 - *Have I Not Sent Thee* 25
DAY 17 - *In His Sanctuary* 26
DAY 18 - *Found Faithful* 27
DAY 19 - *Three Hundred Foxes* 28
DAY 20 - *Four Types Of Songs* 30
DAY 21 - *Knowing The Time* 31
DAY 22 - *Pride Goeth Before Destruction* 32
DAY 23 - *Thou Knowest Me* 34
DAY 24 - *His Father Called Him Benjamin* 36
DAY 25 - *Is Not My Help In Me* 37
DAY 26 - *Truth Is Fallen In The Streets* 38
DAY 27 - *He Is A Babe* 39
DAY 28 - *The Power Of The Highest Shall Overshadow Thee* 40
DAY 29 - *Therefore Michal Had No Child Unto The Day Of Her Death* ...41
DAY 30 - *Four Wonderful Things* 43
DAY 31 - *The God Of All Comfort* 44
DAY 32 - *When The Lord Shall Build Up Zion* 45
DAY 33 - *The Faithful God* 46
DAY 34 - *The Tongue Of The Learned* 48
DAY 35 - *Our God Turned The Curse Into A Blessing* 49
DAY 36 - *A Bundle Of Myrrh Is My Wellbeloved Unto Me* 50
DAY 37 - *He Satisfieth The Longing Soul* 52
DAY 38 - *Then David Arose* 53
DAY 39 - *My Heart Is Fixed* 55
DAY 40 - *Showers Of Rain* 56
DAY 41 - *The Soul Of The Wounded Crieth Out* 57
DAY 42 - *River Of Thy Pleasures* 58
DAY 43 - *If I Build Again The Things Which I Destroyed* 59
DAY 44 - *The Baptism Of The Holy Ghost* 61
DAY 45 - *Give Me Children, Or Else I Die* 63
DAY 46 - *Shepherd Kings* 65
DAY 47 - *What God Leaves* 66

DAY 48 - *I Will Not Go Out Free* 67
DAY 49 - *Give Me This Mountain* 68
DAY 50 - *And He Brought Forth His People With Joy* 69
DAY 51 - *To Make Thee* 71
DAY 52 - *That Holy Thing* 72
DAY 53 - *A Sound Of Abundance Of Rain* 73
DAY 54 - *Another Shall Gird Thee* 74
DAY 55 - *The Labor Of The Foolish* 75
DAY 56 - *Six Cities For Refuge* 76
DAY 57 - *The Lord Is Gracious* 77
DAY 58 - *Our God Shall Fight For Us* 79
DAY 59 - *Men As Trees Walking* 80
DAY 60 - *Full Of Power By The Spirit* 81
DAY 61 - *There Is Hope Of A Tree* 82
DAY 62 - *The Everlasting Arms* 83
DAY 63 - *Wandering From Our Place* 84
DAY 64 - *Which Hope We Have As An Anchor Of The Soul* 85
DAY 65 - *The Work Of God* 87
DAY 66 - *To Walk In All His Ways* 88
DAY 67 - *Altogether Lovely* 89
DAY 68 - *The Lord Shall Laugh* 90
DAY 69 - *Thou Turnest Man To Depression* 91
DAY 70 - *Confirmed Unto The End* 92
DAY 71 - *For The Battle Is The Lord's* 93
DAY 72 - *Set Me As A Seal* 95
DAY 73 - *What Is Man?* 96
DAY 74 - *Stir Up The Gift Of God* 97
DAY 75 - *Addicted To The Ministry Of The Saints* 98
DAY 76 - *He Was Zealous For His God* 99
DAY 77 - *My Dove, My Undefiled* 100
DAY 78 - *What Doth The Lord Require Of Thee* 101
DAY 79 - *I Knew It Not* 103
DAY 80 - *We Have This Treasure* 104
DAY 81 - *The Three Gates We Must Pass Through* 105
DAY 82 - *Put Away The Strange Gods* 107
DAY 83 - *The Gospel Of Christ Without Charge* 108
DAY 84 - *The Terror Of The Lord* 109
DAY 85 - *There Went With Him A Band Of Men Whose Hearts God Had Touched* 110
DAY 86 - *Handfuls Of Purpose* 112
DAY 87 - *Let Us Go Forth Into The Field* 113
DAY 88 - *Eagles' Wings* 114
DAY 89 - *A King To Reign Over Us* 115
DAY 90 - *And The Lord God Called* 116
DAY 91 - *His Eyes Behold The Nations* 117
DAY 92 - *I Will Surely Buy It Of Thee At A Price* 118
DAY 93 - *Masters Of Assemblies* 120
DAY 94 - *When He Was Come Near* 121
DAY 95 - *Where Is Mine Honor* 122
DAY 96 - *Passing Through The Valley* 123
DAY 97 - *Good For Me That I Have Been Afflicted* 124
DAY 98 - *The Goodness Of God Endureth* 125
DAY 99 - *How That By Revelation He Made Known Unto Me The Mysteries* 126
DAY 100 - *Thou Shalt Not Be For Another* 128
DAY 101 - *He Careth For You* 129

DAY 102 - *Answering A Fool*	130
DAY 103 - *Let Him Deny Himself, And Take Up The Cross Daily*	131
DAY 104 - *Let Her Alone*	133
DAY 105 - *God Hath Made Me To Laugh*	134
DAY 106 - *A Wise Man Will Hear*	135
DAY 107 - *If Ye Bite And Devour One Another*	137
DAY 108 - *Leaning On Jesus' Bosom*	138
DAY 109 - *Be Thou An Example Of The Believers*	139
DAY 110 - *Samuel Did Not Yet Know The Lord*	141
DAY 111 - *The Swelling Of The Jordan*	142
DAY 112 - *All Flesh Shall See*	144
DAY 113 - *Behold The Man*	146
DAY 114 - *Stewards Of The Mysteries*	148
DAY 115 - *I Set Before You Life And Death*	150
DAY 116 - *They Have Seen My Nakedness*	151
DAY 117 - *Not Slothful In Business*	152
DAY 118 - *The Glory In The Midst Of Her*	153
DAY 119 - *So Panteth My Soul*	154
DAY 120 - *When Ephraim Spake Trembling*	155
DAY 121 - *That We May Be Able To Comfort Them*	157
DAY 122 - *The Gift Of Grace*	158
DAY 123 - *Give Me, Make Me*	159
DAY 124 - *I Will Now Turn Aside And See*	160
DAY 125 - *The Heart Of The Fathers*	161
DAY 126 - *I Will Not Let You Go*	162
DAY 127 - *Who Shall Separate Us From The Love Of Christ*	163
DAY 128 - *Commit Thy Way Unto The Lord*	165
DAY 129 - *And The Lord Sent Nathan Unto David*	166
DAY 130 - *A Man Sent From God*	167
DAY 131 - *The Entrance Of Thy Words*	168
DAY 132 - *The Blessing Of The Lord*	169
DAY 133 - *My People Love To Have It So*	170
DAY 134 - *For Yielding Pacifieth Great Offences*	171
DAY 135 - *Walking In Integrity*	173
DAY 136 - *How Sweet Are Thy Words*	174
DAY 137 - *A Certain Damsel Possessed*	175
DAY 138 - *In Deep Waters*	176
DAY 139 - *Rise Up My Love*	178
DAY 140 - *When Lust Hath Conceived*	179
DAY 141 - *Thou Understandest My Thought Afar Off*	180
DAY 142 - *The Thoughts Of The Lord*	182
DAY 143 - *Men Ought Always To Pray*	183
DAY 144 - *In The Midst*	184
DAY 145 - *He That Hath Mercy On The Poor*	185
DAY 146 - *The Almighty, El Shaddai*	186
DAY 147 - *The Blessing Of The Lord Maketh Rich*	187
DAY 148 - *Let Us Consider One Another*	188
DAY 149 - *I Will Make You*	190
DAY 150 - *I Discerned*	192
DAY 151 - *Holding Our Peace*	193
DAY 152 - *Riches And Honor Come From Thee*	194
DAY 153 - *The Old Lion Perisheth*	196
DAY 154 - *God That Cannot Lie*	197
DAY 155 - *Whom The Lord Knew Face To Face*	199

DAY 156 - Let Them	201
DAY 157 - Ought Not Christ To Have Suffered	202
DAY 158 - God Is Preparing	203
DAY 159 - The Joyful Sound	204
DAY 160 - The Communication Of Our God	205
DAY 161 - I Will Trust Thee	206
DAY 162 - Who Shall Ascend Into The Hill Of The Lord	207
DAY 163 - Holding On To Your Vision	209
DAY 164 - Unto Us	211
DAY 165 - Being A Faithful Man Or A Virtuous Woman	212
DAY 166 - A Garden Enclosed	213
DAY 167 - The Fear Of Man Bringeth A Snare	214
DAY 168 - No Man, Lord	215
DAY 169 - Hath The Rain A Father	216
DAY 170 - The Manchild	218
DAY 171 - Lay Aside Every Weight	219
DAY 172 - The Bride Is The New Jerusalem	221
DAY 173 - Hope As An Anchor	222
DAY 174 - When Your Faith Is Increased	223
DAY 175 - Pride Hath Deceived Thee	224
DAY 176 - How Shall We Sing The Lord's Song In A Strange Land	226
DAY 177 - The Lord Sent A Word	228
DAY 178 - The Lord's Prayer	229
DAY 179 - All My Springs Are In Thee	230
DAY 180 - As A Bride Adorned	231
DAY 181 - She Judged Him Faithful	232
DAY 182 - My Heart Is Fixed 2	233
DAY 183 - He That Hardeneth His Heart	234
DAY 184 - When I Shall Recieve The Congregation	236
DAY 185 - Leaning Upon Her Beloved	237
DAY 186 - The Difference Between The Holy And Profane	238
DAY 187 - Five Wise, Five Foolish	239
DAY 188 - Am I My Brother's Keeper?	240
DAY 189 - Levels Of Growth	241
DAY 190 - Blessed Are The Pure In Heart	243
DAY 191 - The Elder Shall Serve The Younger	245
DAY 192 - Go Ye After It	246
DAY 193 - Be Of Good Cheer	247
DAY 194 - Wilt Thou Not Revive Us	248
DAY 195 - O Lord, Thou Hast Deceived Me	249
DAY 196 - Receive Not The Grace Of God In Vain	250
DAY 197 - And, Lo, They Were Very Dry	251
DAY 198 - Cease Ye From Man	253
DAY 199 - I Will Lift Up Mine Eyes Unto The Hills	254
DAY 200 - The Least Of All Saints	255
DAY 201 - Perfected Praise Is Ordained Strength	256
DAY 202 - Moses My Servant Is Dead	257
DAY 203 - Cease From Strife	258
DAY 204 - Let Us Run With Patience The Race	259
DAY 205 - To Him That Overcometh	261
DAY 206 - Not Be Offended	263
DAY 207 - Be Of Good Cheer 2	264
DAY 208 - The Lord's Message To His People	265
DAY 209 - Course Of Nature	266

DAY 210 - *Praising In The New Testament* ... 267
DAY 211 - *Get Thee Down To The Threshing Floor* ... 268
DAY 212 - *Casting Their Garments* ... 270
DAY 213 - *Clean Through The Word* ... 271
DAY 214 - *Jesus Beholding Him Loved Him* ... 272
DAY 215 - *Pattern Of The Early Church* ... 273
DAY 216 - *Pattern Of The Early Church 2* ... 275
DAY 217 - *For He Endured* ... 277
DAY 218 - *The Lord Hath Sought Him A Man* ... 278
DAY 219 - *A God At Hand, A God Afar Off* ... 280
DAY 220 - *I Am My Beloved's* ... 282
DAY 221 - *The Garden Of Nuts* ... 283
DAY 222 - *Every Man In His Own Order* ... 284
DAY 223 - *By Night* ... 286
DAY 224 - *Speaking Sound Doctrine* ... 287
DAY 225 - *Let Him Kiss Me With The Kisses Of His Mouth* ... 288
DAY 226 - *A Time To Dance* ... 290
DAY 227 - *The Fountain Opened* ... 291
DAY 228 - *Bind The Sacrifice With Cords* ... 292
DAY 230 - *I* ... 294
DAY 231 - *At Midnight* ... 295
DAY 232 - *I Will Heal Their Backsliding* ... 296
DAY 233 - *Thy Gentleness Hath Made Me Great* ... 298
DAY 234 - *His Compassions Fail Not* ... 299
DAY 235 - *His Hidden Ones* ... 300
DAY 236 - *Chiefest Among Ten Thousand* ... 302
DAY 237 - *Judah Is My Lawgiver* ... 303
DAY 238 - *When I Cry Unto Thee* ... 304
DAY 239 - *The Angel Of The Lord Encampeth* ... 305
DAY 240 - *Ready For The Marriage* ... 307
DAY 241 - *An Hundred Forty And Four Thousand* ... 308
DAY 242 - *Our Banners* ... 310
DAY 243 - *The Day Star Arise In Your Hearts* ... 311
DAY 244 - *Who Is A God Like Unto Thee* ... 312
DAY 245 - *Our Daysman* ... 313
DAY 246 - *He Hath Remembered His Covenant Forever* ... 314
DAY 247 - *The Face Of An Angel* ... 316
DAY 248 - *The Little Foxes* ... 317
DAY 249 - *The Little Chamber* ... 318
DAY 250 - *A Refining Fire* ... 319
DAY 251 - *Sowing Thy Seed* ... 320
DAY 252 - *The God Of Peace Shall Bruise Satan* ... 321
DAY 253 - *Gather Up The Fragments* ... 322
DAY 254 - *Ye Shall Find Rest Unto Your Souls* ... 324
DAY 255 - *Wisdom Is The Principal Thing* ... 325
DAY 256 - *How Long Wilt Thou Forget Me, O Lord?* ... 326
DAY 257 - *To Do Thee Good At Thy Latter End* ... 328
DAY 258 - *My Redeemer Liveth* ... 329
DAY 259 - *Betrayed By A Kiss* ... 330
DAY 260 - *Add To Your Faith* ... 331
DAY 261 - *The Sufferings Of Christ* ... 333
DAY 262 - *The Same Night In Which He Was Betrayed* ... 334
DAY 263 - *You Shall Be Free Indeed* ... 335
DAY 264 - *I Will Triumph* ... 336

DAY 265 - *More Understanding Than All My Teachers* 337
DAY 266 - *My Soul Is Weary Of My Life* 339
DAY 267 - *I Was Brought Low, And He Helped Me* 340
DAY 268 - *Launch Out Into The Deep* 342
DAY 269 - *Peter Went Up To Pray And Became Very Hungry* 343
DAY 270 - *The Firstfruits Unto God* 344
DAY 271 - *The Pearl Of Great Price* 345
DAY 272 - *I Am* 346
DAY 273 - *Where Would I Go* 348
DAY 274 - *If I Regard Iniquity In My Heart* 349
DAY 275 - *I Determined Not To Know Any Thing Among You* 351
DAY 276 - *My Strong Refuge* 352
DAY 277 - *I Will Speak, That I May Be Refreshed* 353
DAY 278 - *For My People Is Foolish* 354
DAY 279 - *Follow His Steps* 355
DAY 280 - *The Lord Calling As At Other Times* 356
DAY 281 - *Forget Not All Of His Benefits* 357
DAY 282 - *I Had Great Bitterness* 359
DAY 283 - *Thou Hast Been My Help* 360
DAY 284 - *A Lion In The Midst Of A Pit* 362
Day 285 - *How Dreadful Is This Place* 363
DAY 286 - *I Will Arise And Go To My Father* 364
DAY 287 - *Depression* 365
DAY 288 - *He Sent A Man Before Them, Even Joseph* 366
DAY 289 - *Moses Drew Near* 368
DAY 290 - *What You Do In The Dark* 369
DAY 291 - *God Is Not A Man* 370
DAY 292 - *My Word Like As A Fire* 371
DAY 293 - *The Way Of The Fool Is Right In His Own Eyes* 372
DAY 294 - *Thy Comforts Delight My Soul* 373
DAY 295 - *In Your Patience Possess Ye Your Souls* 374
DAY 296 – *A Lively Hope* 376
DAY 297 - *Make Excuse* 377
DAY 298 - *Perfect Through Sufferings* 378
DAY 299 - *Wash You, Make You Clean* 379
DAY 300 - *Brought Up The Ark Of The Lord With Shouting* 380
DAY 301 - *If Sinners Entice Thee* 382
DAY 302 - *If The Foundations Be Destroyed* 383
DAY 303 - *Delivered From The Power Of Darkness* 385
DAY 304 - *Willing To Justify Himself* 386
DAY 305 - *Ye Are Gods* 387
DAY 306 - *Turned Into Another Man* 388
DAY 307 - *To The Uttermost* 389
DAY 308 - *He Thanked God And Took Courage* 390
DAY 309 - *I Will Never Leave Thee Nor Forsake Thee* 391
DAY 310 - *The Heavens Declare His Glory* 393
DAY 311 - *Ask For The Old Paths* 394
DAY 312 - *Awake, O North Wind* 395
DAY 313 - *The Noise Of His Tabernacle* 396
DAY 314 - *God's Place For Us* 398
DAY 315 - *Who Is Worthy To Open The Book* 399
DAY 316 - *Honour All Men* 400
DAY 317 - *The Lord Turned The Captivity Of Job* 402
DAY 318 - *The Lord Thy God In The Midst* 403

DAY 319	A Stone's Throw	405
DAY 320	What Seek Ye?	406
DAY 321	Let The Dead Bury Their Dead	407
DAY 322	Cares Of This Life	408
DAY 323	I Flee From The Face Of My Mistress Sarai	409
DAY 324	Taken, Blessed, Broken, & Given	411
DAY 325	After Six Days	412
DAY 326	Jesus Wept	413
DAY 327	Dwelling Among The Tombs	414
DAY 328	The Mount Of Transfiguration	415
DAY 329	In His Favor Is Life	417
DAY 330	I Shall Not Want	418
DAY 331	A Zeal Not According To Knowledge	420
DAY 332	Ye Are My Friends	421
DAY 333	The Bones Of Elisha	422
DAY 334	I Love The Lord	424
DAY 335	Boast Not Of Thyself Of Tomorrow	425
DAY 336	Tasting That The Lord Is Gracious	426
DAY 337	Be Ye Angry, And Sin Not	427
DAY 338	God's Inner Pain	429
DAY 339	I Sought For A Man	430
DAY 340	Lord, Is It I?	431
DAY 341	Apes And Peacocks	432
DAY 342	A Very Small Remnant	433
DAY 343	A Man Shall Be As A Hiding Place	435
DAY 344	When The Philistines Heard	436
DAY 345	Not Destitute Of His Mercy And Truth	438
DAY 346	The Good Shepherd	439
DAY 347	He Hath Torn, He Will Heal	440
DAY 348	The Journey Is Too Great For Thee	441
DAY 349	Emmanuel	442
DAY 350	With Patience Wait	443
DAY 351	And I Will Restore To You The Years	444
DAY 352	David's Three Anointings	446
DAY 353	Where Are The Nine?	447
DAY 354	Worthy Of Double Honor	448
DAY 355	Bound In The Bundle Of Life	449
DAY 356	The Three-Fold Principle	450
DAY 357	The Three-Fold Principle 2	452
DAY 358	His Eye Seeth Every Precious Thing	453
DAY 359	The Name Of It Called Babel	455
DAY 360	The Word Of God Came Unto John In The Wilderness	456
DAY 361	For God Took Him	457
DAY 362	The Lord Thundered From Heaven	458
DAY 363	The Race	459
DAY 364	Beauty For Ashes	460
DAY 365	One Another	461

Glory Publishing, Inc.
Sound Doctrine For The Spirit Filled Church
www.GloryPublishingInc.com

About The Author

Samuel Greene, Ph. D.

One of the callings the Lord gave Brother Sam years ago was to help write sound doctrine for the Charismatic movement and Spirit-filled believers. Since 1976, Brother Sam has been teaching the Word of God daily out of which has come dozens of teaching manuals and books which are part of an eight year Bible College curriculum taught at churches and Bible Schools all over the world.

For more information about Brother Sam, his ministry, or if you would like to order any of his books, please visit us online at www.Brother-Sam.org.

On this website, you will find:

- Devotionals
- Sermons/Podcasts, Videos
- Study Manuals & Bookstore
- Downloadable eBooks
- Worship CDs

A Biblical Reference Dictionary Every Minister & Disciple Must Have!

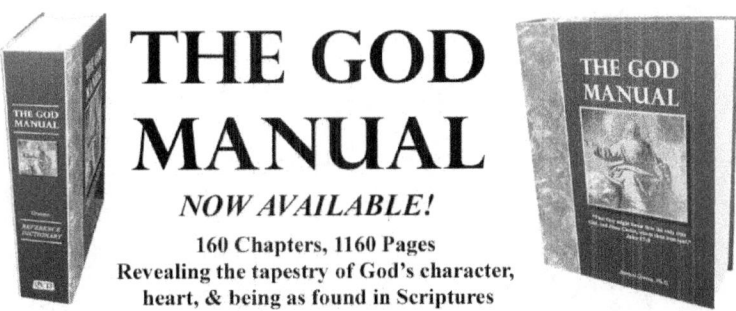

THE GOD MANUAL
NOW AVAILABLE!
160 Chapters, 1160 Pages
Revealing the tapestry of God's character, heart, & being as found in Scriptures

John 17:3 says, "...that they might know thee the only true God, and Jesus Christ, whom thou hast sent." The God Manual was written with hopes of seeking to reveal the correct Biblical image of who our precious Creator really is. With 160 lessons, it exhaustively teaches almost every aspect, characteristic, and attribute of God we can think of. In order to fulfill our calling to be conformed to Jesus' image, we must first know what that image is. Our prayer is that as you study these lessons your life will forever be changed, your worship increased, you realize that holiness is not an unattainable thing anymore, and most importantly you fall deeper in love with Jesus.
(ISBN 978-0-9831696-0-4)

www.ingramcontent.com/pod-product-compliance
Lightning Source LLC
Chambersburg PA
CBHW060228240426
43671CB00016B/2883